Strategic Sourcing Management

Strategic Sourcing Management
Structural and operational decision-making

Olivier Bruel

KoganPage

First published in French as *Management des achats* by Economica, Paris, in 2014
First published in Great Britain and the United States in 2017 by Kogan Page Limited

2nd Floor, 45 Gee Street	c/o Martin P Hill Consulting	4737/23 Ansari Road
London	122 W 27th Street, 10th Floor	Daryaganj
EC1V 3RS	New York, NY 10001	New Delhi 110002
United Kingdom	USA	India

© Olivier Bruel 2017

ISBN   978 0 7494 7669 1
E-ISBN 978 0 7494 7700 4

British Library Cataloguing-in-Publication Data

A CIP record for this book is available from the British Library.

Library of Congress Control Number

2016958922

Typeset by Graphicraft Limited, Hong Kong
Print production managed by Jellyfish
Printed and bound in Great Britain by CPI Group (UK) Ltd, Croydon CR0 4YY

CONTENTS

PREFACE

The strategic and operational management of procurement is a vast subject that can be tackled via strategic, managerial and organizational perspectives as well as through detailed descriptions of the major processes, tools and techniques used from a strictly operational point of view.

In addition, this domain is located at the fringes of paradigms traditionally dealt with in other management disciplines. Marketing and procurement issues are an integral part of B2B marketing approaches. The issues of outsourcing and the design of methods for collaborating with suppliers, or risk management, are traditionally developed by strategists. Competencies and human resources issues, as well as the problematics of performance management, classically fall within the responsibilities of HR or management control experts. Finally, purchasing information system issues are customarily the specialty of information system professionals.

In parallel, certain so-called 'basic' disciplines are necessary for the sound practice of procurement as 'fundamentals' to be mastered, including, for example, a minimal knowledge of aspects of international and contract law, as well as a good knowledge of methods in financial evaluation, investment decisions, financial protection from exchange risks, or the volatility of raw material prices.

Until now, these different areas of knowledge and expertise have not been assembled and made available in the form of a single all-inclusive publication. It therefore struck me as necessary for this second edition of *Strategic Sourcing Management* to preserve an analytical scope that was as far-reaching as possible: first, to provide company professionals with a permanent working tool that examines all major professional themes at all levels; and secondly, to offer a comprehensive reference work on methodology aimed not only at student specialization programmes, but above all at high-level continuous learning for executives and managers, that can be constantly referred to in the training context.

Finally, this work may be read as a whole, but also used by certain readers on an occasional basis when homing in on individual themes according to their specific needs. As a result, each chapter has been designed and written to be read independently without the need for too much cross-referencing with other chapters. For this reason, some slight repetitions have been deliberately included.

Olivier Bruel

Introduction

Procurement: a value-creator

Seeing procurement departments as value-creators rather than mere cost-killers or service-providers is, for today's market leaders, a reality that is fully acknowledged as an imperative. But a long road has been travelled to get to this point!

Around 25 years ago, apart from cases in the distribution sector and more rarely in industry and services, it was unknown for the executive managements of companies to pay more than a passing interest to their procurement departments. The latter were often attached to another role, whether operational or financial, and simply considered as a 'necessary evil', generally limited in effectiveness and only acting in the context of calls for tenders or negotiations. They were perceived as 'cost centres' and no one thought of considering them in terms of 'return on investment' let alone innovation. In addition, no medium-term vision or real strategic approach existed. All things considered, the activity of 'procurement' as it is currently understood was not carried out, but was rather that of 'supply' in reaction to short-term needs that had to be satisfied.

Then, in the world of business, consultancy and higher education, a few key figures became committed to advancing practices and to significantly raising the level of professionalism by backing the function's strategic contribution that, over time, has gained recognition. A few visionary executive managements launched and supported the first company projects entirely devoted to procurement.

A boom in concepts, methods and practices ensued, relying on innovations and research developed in the areas of general strategy, business-to-business (B2B) marketing, supply chain, finance and management control.

As a result, a body of procurement methodology was gradually constructed. We have gone through several phases in terms of strategic and operational objectives: starting from actions essentially geared towards minimizing purchasing costs, we have subsequently seen the development of upstream market approaches and the relationships of procurement departments with designers, purchasing stakeholders and internal customers. Gradually, the full perimeter of procurement was covered. Specialized training courses (ie dual vocational programmes such as those available at Master's level) have widely developed to place 'on the market' high-level young professionals. The best of these have been attracted by the function's different professions and career opportunities.

Strategic preoccupations have gradually offset purely operational aspects based on medium- and long-term visions. At the same time, technological innovations have emerged, namely in the design and deployment of internet tools devoted to the function, hence strengthening its reliability and operational efficiency.

Today, all business leaders in any market consider the procurement function as a 'natural' contributor to general strategy.

This attitude seems an obvious enough one to adopt when companies – whether in industry, distribution or the services sector – estimate that 40 to 80 per cent of costs (direct and indirect) noted in their company income statements stem from the purchasing of products or services.

Furthermore, for some 20 years now, many companies have shifted their focus back to their 'core business' via significant outsourcing following analysis of their value chain – a shift that has 'automatically' led to an increase in the scope of responsibility of purchasing departments as managers of the company's 'external resources'.

In a context of fierce competition and increased globalization, general managements expect purchasing departments to contribute to a company's competitiveness (through savings made on purchases, but also through the reduction of total acquisition costs including financial costs related to working capital and costs pertaining to various dysfunctions, ie quality-related). In parallel, with the development of supply-chain approaches, emphasis has been placed on a headlong search for flexibility and reactivity, as well as absolute control of the quality purchased.

But procurement departments should also play a part in a company's innovation processes, via their deep knowledge of supplier markets, via an ongoing process of technological and business intelligence aimed at finding new, innovative supply sources (ie in leading competitive countries) and detecting new or emerging technologies on the market, and also via their effective contribution to the design and development process for new products.

Finally, procurement departments contribute to identifying and mastering all risks facing the company upstream along the value chain: supply security, the longevity of supply sources, the protection of innovation jointly spearheaded by suppliers and of the confidentiality of information necessarily shared with the latter, legal and business traceability issues, along with ethical, social and environmental obligations. They therefore also need to be risk managers.

For all these reasons, the purchasing function wholly contributes to value creation today and has gone far beyond being a mere cost centre hingeing on short-term savings.

As a result, this book has been designed to cover this wide spectrum of current preoccupations in the triple dimension of competitiveness, effectiveness and efficiency. To cover these different areas, the work has been divided into four distinct parts dealing with the main components grouped as follows.

Strategic decisions and supplier policies

Part One first tackles the integration of procurement into a company's general strategy, then details the main strategic procurement decisions on the following themes: strategic segmentation and the implementation of a marketing-based approach to procurement; the contribution of procurement to innovation and product design, often qualified as 'upstream' procurement (the related notion of project procurement is also examined); design and deployment of a supplier policy and the management of associated supplier panels; as well as globalization and the deployment of an international procurement approach.

Also discussed are three major themes connected to a modern procurement department: the design of a generalized risk-prevention system; the implementation of specific policy and practices for ethical, sustainable and responsible purchasing; and procurement's contribution to decision-making and the management of outsourcing processes.

Operational procurement management

Operational management – sometimes called 'downstream' procurement – is more geared towards the short term. This is also the area where the procurement function interfaces with the company's supply chain, with the aim of integrating flow and master-scheduling management issues into its scope of preoccupation and responsibility.

Part Two therefore tackles the following points: quantitative forecasting and material requirements planning (MRP); issues relating to the economic optimization of replenishment systems; total cost of ownership (TCO) assessment and working capital requirements (WCR) management; analysis of a detailed call for tenders' procedure; the practice of international operations and specific legal reflexes for international purchases.

We have also decided to examine several issues pertaining to certain specific types of purchases: the purchase of services (including intellectual services), capital equipment (CapEx) purchases, the particularities of public-sector purchases in the European context, and financial issues and problematics relating to risk mitigation mechanisms for the purchase of foreign currencies and raw materials facing volatile markets and exchange rates.

The choice not to cover and devote a chapter to one particular operational dimension – procurement negotiation – is deliberate; we consider that this aspect has been widely developed elsewhere in an entirely satisfactory, detailed and coherent manner.

Organizational choices and resource management

Part Three is devoted to the management of all resources encompassed by the procurement function. In this way, the following topics are covered: organizational and structural decisions and choices for the positioning of procurement management in a company's organigram (particularly if it is made up of multiple business units); the analysis of the various procurement professions and the body of problematics concerning the management of procurement managers and purchasers; and the description, critical analysis and contextualization of different technical IT solutions and e-business electronic tools dedicated to procurement and short-term supply.

Performance and change management

The final part deals with more strategic considerations (thus linking up with Part One) for we turn our attention to procurement performance before going onto the monitoring of medium-term developments.

In this way, two main themes are covered in the area of performance management: the design and implementation of measurement and key performance indicator (KPI) systems as well as procurement-reporting systems including the issue of a company's intangible assets (or goodwill); and the issue of performance steering and the principles and practices of change management.

In addition, we will delve into the question of how a responsible procurement management, aiming to succeed in coordinating a collective project, can design and effectively carry out a structured internal and external communication plan.

We hope that readers will find that this work covers a great many of their concerns. This, in any case, has been the ongoing concern of the co-authors. Their greatest hope is for this work to truly contribute to the individual development of its readers, and also to more widely encourage deep reflection amongst company heads, thus helping to improve company performance and value creation.

Happy reading to all!

Olivier Bruel
Emeritus Professor HEC Paris

PART ONE
Strategic decisions and supplier policies

This part focuses exclusively on strategic procurement decisions – decisions that have the greatest structural effect on the function's performance.

In Chapter 1, we situate procurement within a company's general strategy by showing why and how it plays a key role and should be taken into account. After clearing up a few semantic matters, and going over the process in which a company develops its general strategy, we delve into issues relating to the procurement function, its missions and its economic contribution to corporate competitiveness as well as to innovation, development and value creation. A global presentation of the major decisions and key processes associated with the procurement function is provided.

Chapter 2 details the concepts and generic procedures involved in a marketing-based approach to procurement. We deal with the principles of strategic segmentation for procurement portfolios, then develop ways in which procurement strategies are defined by offering a detailed presentation of the main levers and best practices likely to be called upon. The major alternative strategies are also discussed in order to illustrate the necessity to differentiate approaches based on the logic and specificities of the main portfolio segments. Finally, a 'dynamic' short-term vision is examined by going over the key stages making up a typical procurement process.

In Chapter 3, the reader will find a thorough analysis of the company innovation process and its links with upstream procurement, with a focus on the ways in which the procurement function intervenes in product design and development, and also, more widely, in the definition of technical specifications. This entire area is examined via a detailed study of the different levers for specific actions.

Chapter 4 concentrates wholly on policies to be followed with suppliers, from various angles. Attention is paid, in particular, to the range of supplier profiles depending on the type of relationship that one wishes to establish (head-on confrontation or collaborative approaches), appropriate sourcing methods, as well as principles and methods to be employed for 'homologation' – in the UK, the process of qualifying suppliers – then the choice and management of a supplier panel. Practical and in-depth analysis of supplier relationship management (SRM) and collaborative supplier management is also provided.

Globalization is a crucial axis of procurement strategy, and Chapter 5 is exclusively devoted to this topic. Starting with an outline of arguments in favour of international deployment of purchasing, the chapter then details strategic and operational approaches for proceeding in this direction. A structured sequential approach for steering this type of evolution is put forward; the sequence of a project and its operational implementation are then discussed; the chapter concludes with a presentation of the main countertrade solutions in international sales strategies and the consequential impact on procurement activity.

Today, it is unthinkable to design a procurement strategy and to implement purchasing practices without taking into account and respecting ethical principles of social and environmental responsibility. Therefore, Chapter 6 is entirely dedicated to this topic, offering in-depth analysis of the issues at stake before explaining, in detail, the relevant approaches to be taken by a procurement department. Change management as well as the conditions for success are discussed in a practical and comprehensive manner.

Finally, it is undeniable that the general strategy of any mature company includes analysis of the value chain and refocusing on the 'core activity', very often leading to decisions of greater or lesser importance regarding outsourcing. Chapter 7 deals with these issues by showing how the procurement function is involved in these approaches and should take charge of their implementation. Decisions regarding complete or partial outsourcing of procurement activities themselves are also considered in depth from two viewpoints: why to outsource them and how to carry out such a project.

01
Procurement
Its integration in a company's general strategy

From a company's perspective, procurement is primarily a strategic function responsible for:

> sourcing (searching for) and acquiring capital equipment, goods and services requested (sometimes directly) by the final client and (always) by internal stakeholders in optimal conditions in terms of costs, quality and service, as well as contributing to value creation by innovation, all the while controlling the different short- and medium-term risks encountered when operating in this activity.

This function, located upstream in the global supply chain, should obviously today, and in practically all economic sectors, play a fundamental role in all companies (industrial, commercial or services, public or private) and in many organizations, even non-profit ones (such as associations and NGOs).

Before presenting the specific missions and contributions of procurement, and the way in which it is integrated into general strategy, it is fitting to position the function within the supply chain, and then to clarify the terminology that will be used throughout this book by its authors.

1/1 Definitions and introductory reminders: procurement, supply and supply chain

The terms used to designate the procurement function have long raised a fundamental problem relating to its perceived contribution. In addition, since the concept of the supply chain has emerged, many have wondered whether procurement is an integral upstream component of the chain, or whether it is an independent function. And where does the supply function stand in all this?

1/1.1 Supply chain and the procurement function

Let's go back to the generic definition of a company supply chain. As written by the author and certain of his colleagues from the Operations Management and Information Technology department of HEC Paris in their reference work, a company's supply chain, particularly in the case of an *extended* supply chain,[1] is made up by the combination of players, or entities, that together contribute to the satisfaction of end customers, thus representing, for the enterprise, its entire operational system for supplying its client markets (a global system hence organized into an industrial and logistical network from upstream to downstream).

Thus defined, any supply chain is *by nature mixed*, for it integrates both a company's *internal* resources and its *external* resources constituted by all of its suppliers and service-providers. All contribute jointly and collectively to global performance.

On this basis, in terms of organization, the supply chain department is in charge of the *design of this global logistical and operational system*, as well as *control of all of the company's flows, from the suppliers upstream to the final client downstream.* In this way, supply-chain management encompasses all management and flow-control activities, organized transversally throughout the company, and even beyond its own legal 'boundaries', in order to satisfy all aspects of end demand (cost, quality, delivery lead-times, flexibility, reactivity, additional specific services), all the while aiming to optimize, in economic terms, resource allocation and usage, and to eliminate any possible internal and external dysfunctions.

FIGURE 1.1 Structure of a supply chain

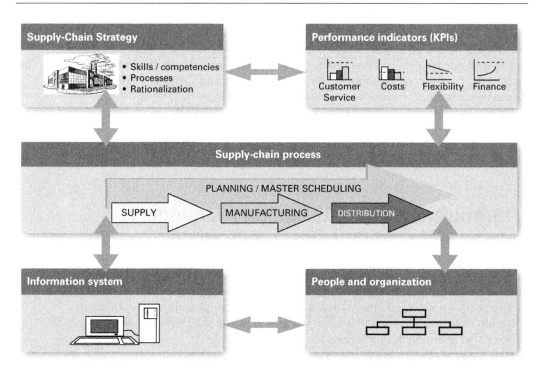

Indeed, referring to Figure 1.1, operational systems and flow control can only operate if:

- the company's general management has, in advance, made its structural outsourcing choices, thus defining the activities that need to be maintained internally and those that need to be outsourced, hence constituting the company's body of external resources;
- structural decisions have been made on a strategic level to design an adapted industrial and logistical system and to invest in plants, a storage network and physical distribution systems, and decisions made regarding innovation and product design processes etc;
- an integrated information system has been set up to follow up and steer all transactions on all levels of the system;
- an adapted organizational scheme has been clearly defined (structures, organigram and working groups of ad hoc project groups), whether it is centralized or not, with appropriate human resources recruited and ongoing training offered;
- a performance measurement system based on relevant indicators (KPIs) has been designed and is used periodically for reporting on operational performance.

Spotlight on downstream marketing: a vision focused on client markets

Still referring to Figure 1.1, in company downstream activities – in other words when dealing with clients – all supply chains integrate, under their responsibility, a physical distribution system which is an operational activity with a commercial nature. To set up such a system, it is necessary, at an earlier stage when more structural decisions are undertaken, to design a marketing strategy and also to define marketing action plans.

In this regard, marketing is an activity that consists in winning client markets. It is essentially strategic in nature and bears responsibility for a portfolio of products or services on offer, within a given competitive context, whilst distribution is part of the *implementation* of this strategy, with other elements in the marketing mix (including price policy, salesforce, communication and promotion activities) also playing a role.

Impact on procurement: a vision focused on external resources and supplier markets

A company's body of external resources is made up of companies (suppliers, subcontractors and various service-providers) that are all players within supplier markets. At the same time, the company has a portfolio of *needs* of all types (eg physical goods and various marketing services) to be satisfied.

It is thus possible to see a *symmetrybetween marketing and procurement*, and in this way consider procurement as *a strategic marketing function dedicated to a company's upstream activities*[2] whose main generic mission is to ensure, as well as possible, complete satisfaction of a company's current and future needs, with the objective and strategy of capturing supplier markets (most commonly in a competitive context alongside other 'procurement' rivals in these different markets). As in marketing, we refer to a *'proactive' approach*.

From this point of view, the supply function's responsibility is limited to taking charge of the operational execution of procurement contracts, and the control of physical flows between the company and its suppliers. Thus defined, supply is integrated into the supply chain as an activity dedicated to flows that interface with all suppliers.[3]

1/1.2 International semantics

The objective of this French-authored book is primarily to deal with general and 'global' procurement and supply-chain issues, on which many relevant publications, articles and works have been already written in English. In addition, as many companies have become international, English terms have spread to many organizations. For this reason, we wish to clarify three semantic points:

- *Sourcing* is systematically referred to in the English-speaking world, often to denote the upstream of any supply chain, as is the case in the supply chain operations reference (SCOR) model (APICS, 2016). It is commonly agreed that this term is a synonym of procurement as far as it covers the whole of the function from needs analysis and specifications up to purchase contracts. However, in this book, this term is generally restricted to the identification and qualification of new supply sources (see Chapter 4).

- Two other terms are commonly used: *procurement* and *purchasing*. These terms are synonyms, the first widespread in North America, the second in the UK[4] – even if, somewhat confusingly, in the United States, *purchases* denote what is bought by *procurement* departments. Readers seeking further semantic clarification are invited to refer to the glossary at the end of this work.

1/2 General strategic decisions: issues, guiding principles, strategic action plans

Our aim here is not to enter into a long, exhaustive discussion on strategic approaches, but to present the main issues, ways of thinking and major decisions that concern general management, in order to better grasp the way in which procurement should be inserted, in a coherent manner, into this overall system, and thus contribute effectively to global performance.

What, fundamentally, does 'general strategy' mean in the context of a company?[5]

First and foremost, let's remember that any strategy necessarily relies on *analysis of the context and the environment* of the company (in terms of competition, technology and economy) so as to define development opportunities. In parallel, whether the company operates in the industrial, distribution or services sector, strategic analysis consists in *defining the positioning* that it chooses to occupy on one or several markets, most often via the characteristics of its *business portfolio* (homogeneous groups of products or services) that are made up of specific areas of activity or strategic businesses (SBs, according to Michael Porter).

Bearing these two points in mind, general strategy aims to choose a given position in a competitive market context, with either all areas of activity coming from the same global market-conquest perspective, or else – more commonly – each segment or area of activity developing its own perspective. In doing so, general strategy singles out *different methods of 'attack'* (that make up its strategic plan) depending on the characteristics of the environment, and at the same time makes *choices on resource allocation* (financial, human, technological and so on) to which it commits on a medium- and long-term basis. These decisions, aiming to endow the company with a *sustainable competitive advantage*, target short-term profitability as much as medium-term development. The ultimate aim is obviously *value creation*, as well as the protection of future results by operating in businesses where the barriers to entry are huge.

These choices then need to be coherently developed within each of a company's major departments, in particular the procurement department. The expectation is that each department will bring its own contribution to global performance.

1/2.1 Internal and external strategic diagnosis (SWOT)

The main stages for determining a business strategy are illustrated by Figure 1.2.

Sectoral analysis: competitive context

The sector in which any company is active may be analysed in two ways by its top management: firstly, from the perspective of relationships between players and the competitive context; secondly, in terms of its structuring (segmentation) into business areas whose rationale or success factors vary according to each particular segment.

In general terms, whilst the objective is to end up with a SWOT-type[6] analysis, examination of the sector should help improve understanding of a market's prevailing rationale, the structure of the existing product or service offer, and risk factors.

Competitive environment: risks/opportunities

This analysis involves identifying a number of types of *threats* or *opportunities*. The configuration, hierarchy and dynamics of interactions between the players then enable the pinpointing of *key success factors*, in other words the strategic elements that need to be controlled in order to obtain a sustainable competitive advantage in the sector in question.

The first approach comprises the analysis and evaluation of the strong or weak positions of *suppliers* and *clients* via an examination of their concentration at every stage of the extended supply chain (distribution of market shares and production capacities, number of players at every stage, power relationships and real negotiation power, opportunities for upstream and downstream moves by certain players), the

FIGURE 1.2   The global strategic process

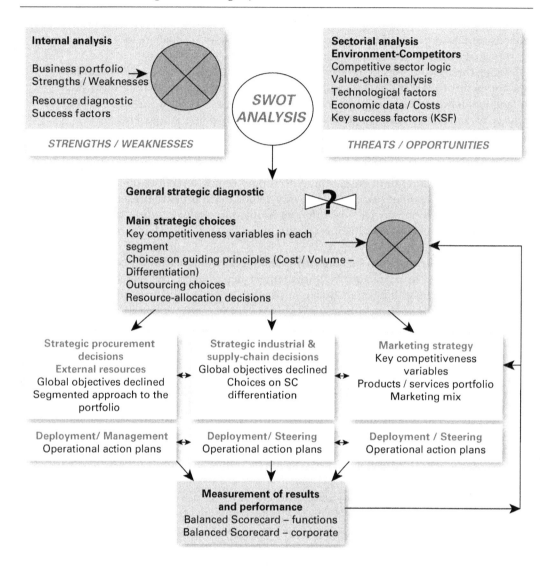

contribution of different players to the cost breakdown and to the performance of the finished products, the risks of product differentiation, the opportunities for upstream–downstream integration of certain players, and finally the distribution of added value throughout the value chain (corresponding to the company's extended supply chain).

The second approach focuses on external threats, such as the risk of *new entrants*, by examining: economic and technical barriers to entrance in the sector, ie by means of a possible 'entrance ticket' (eg costs relating to access to a certain research technology, or the purchase of licences and investments); the structure of production costs (fixed versus variable) and data on breakeven points, as well as the potential importance of economies of scale; required access to specific distribution circuits; the existence of strong contractual or collaborative supplier–client relationships between different 'links' and players in the supply chain; the existence of patents, norms and other restrictive technical standards or even protectionist measures or cultural barriers.

It is also necessary to focus on opportunities for developing *substitution activities (or alternative products)* that might constitute an external threat if their cost/value relationship were superior to that of the existing offer, as well as different response options (lowering sales prices; increasing the value of the product or service via the addition of functions; discontinuation of the current offer and switching to a substitution product if the company possesses the required resources and skills; or even a simple exit from the market).

These classic elements presented by Michael Porter's initial model can, today in 2016 be complemented by the expectations of various actors and associated risks in the area of *ethical, social and environmental responsibility,* known generally as corporate social responsibility (CSR). The risk associated with CSR can be seen as threats when approached as requirements for conformity to legislation or regula- tions (*compliance*). They can also be considered as new business or differentiation opportunities. In this universe, new actors (called *stakeholders*) have emerged, such as states, international organizations (including the UN, ILO or the European Commission), certain NGOs, consumer associations or even ethical funds managers.

Characteristics of a sector's products or services

This analysis involves characterizing the company's sector according to the 'profile' of the products that are designed, manufactured and commercialized. The objective then is to detect opportunities for the company to create or strengthen a significant *competitive advantage*, either via a head-on attack or via a differentiation approach. In this regard, the Boston Consulting Group (BCG) has long put forward an extremely useful matrix for sectoral classification, its Advantage Matrix in which it identifies four major types of competitive systems:

- First of all, so-called *volume* activity sectors in which cumulative production quantities define a major economic advantage whilst opportunities for differentiation remain limited, as illustrated by the industrial sectors of energy production, semi-finished steel or chemical products, standard electronic components or the production of many *standardized* general consumer goods.

- Next, sectors of activity distinguished by many opportunities for differentiation through *specialization*. In most cases, these result from client requests for products to be adapted for improved usage or else the adaptation of psychological characteristics inherent to the products. But differentiation can derive from many other types of actions, namely company-initiated *push*-type innovations.

- Thirdly, other *fragmented* sectors: neither volume nor differentiation seems to bring any decisive competitive advantage. There are many players and few technological entrance barriers; the price of the entrance ticket is low and size does not allow a competitive cost level to be reached. Sometimes these products have a short lifespan that also implies very great flexibility.

- Finally, sectors described as *stalemate*. Without any identifiable leadership, real technological barriers or know-how, a global overcapacity can be observed settling generally over the market. In this case, companies either seek to play by the rules of the game and (re)create viable niches or they decide to ignore them.

This matrix often needs to be adjusted or refined: whilst certain sectors can be associated with a dominant tendency, they may also tend to evolve (for example, the telecommunications sector, originally a 'volume' business, has largely taken on the characteristics of a 'differentiation' sector with the existence of new 'niches'). In addition, in the case of highly specialized companies, more often than not they are not 'single-product' companies but have within their ranges different products that can be positioned in markets or *competitive systems based on different principles*.

For example, a company producing office equipment could on the one hand offer a range of standard configurations, available on stock with very short delivery times, for a wide target market of non-specialist 'general public' clients, and on the other hand offer complex configurations, available exclusively on order, aimed at private or professional specialist clients with specific technical needs, particular demands in terms of performance, and for whom low prices and immediate availability are not their main purchasing criteria.

Internal analysis of the business portfolio (or product families)

Just like market analysis, strategic analysis requires a thorough internal diagnostic of the company's portfolio of activities or products, and in particular the detection of whether it corresponds to clear segmentation, which then logically implies a strategic action plan based on differentiation. Two types of analysis are useful for this purpose: first, the choice of a *segmentation logic* for the product portfolio that is clear and subsequently enables the selection of coherent key success factors (KSFs); and second, looking at the *lifecycle* of the products (or families of products), an assessment of whether the KSFs actually evolve (or should evolve) over their life in the market.

Segmentation of the product portfolio

Here again, BCG has put forward a widely used analysis model, the growth–market share matrix, essentially based on two segmentation criteria: the *globalgrowth rate* of the segment of activity in which the given product family falls; and the company's *relative* market share in this segment (defined as the ratio of its market share to that of its main competitor or else to that of all the competitors globally).

This approach is justified by reference to the theory of *experience-effect*. According to the theory, the greater a company's market share and the *cumulative* quantities that it produces, the more favourable its position in terms of production and procurement costs, and the greater the competitive advantage it accrues as it achieves the optimal profitability out of all the competitors on the market. In addition, this amplification mechanism is multiplied if the segment is growing globally; if this is not the case, the acquired positions stay frozen.

On this basis, the BCG matrix divides product families into four main categories:

- *Cash cows* are slow-growth products that have reached a 'mature' phase, thus requiring little in terms of development investment. On the other hand, their high market shares lead to strong profitability so these activities generate considerable cash flows as long as their cost structures are constantly overseen. They can contribute towards financing other activities.

- *Stars* are fast growers with dominant positions in terms of a company's profitability, thus enabling self-financing of the still considerable investment required by these products. These are nevertheless risk-bearing investments as the global market has not yet stabilized.

- *Question marks* correspond to high-growth activities with relatively weak market shares, as may be the case of products in an initial growth phase when first placed on the market. In this way, they require significant financing to maintain or develop their market shares, and are often in deficit at the outset in terms of profitability.

- *Dogs* are products that are low in profitability and have weak development potential. Generally needing little in terms of capital, they can nevertheless benefit from experience-effects. These activities should not be maintained in this undifferentiated high-risk state.

In terms of strategic actions to be undertaken, brief mention can be made of the following scenarios:

- abandoning dogs or maintaining them without specific investments (if a new design for these products can be undertaken at lower cost, it becomes possible to transform them into cash cows);

- making cash cows as profitable as possible to finance the development of new products;

- doing everything to maintain the leadership position for stars (commercial investments) whilst investing in experience-effect opportunities (productivity investments) – these are the future cash cows;

- repositioning, or even abandoning, question marks.

Development of KSFs at different stages of the product lifecycle

The other dimension to take into account concerns the way in which these KSFs can be expected to evolve over time according to the phases of a product's lifecycle and different customer expectations. Indeed, a company will not remain fixed (stabilized) in a given configuration in terms of its product range and competitive situation. It is necessary to have a *dynamic and variable vision according to the product under consideration*: key success factors will change and when this happens, require a shift in strategy on the basis of priorities that never stay the same for long. And these shifts may intervene differently on different products, that are never all at identical phases in their respective life curves. Table 1.1 illustrates this point by presenting a simplified reference schema.

TABLE 1.1   Success criteria along the lifecycle

Main phases	Introduction	Growth	Maturity	Decline
Main determining factors	Initial phase (innovative product)	Gain in market share (product leader)	Dominant position and mature technology	Finished product rivalled by new solutions
Main product feature	Innovative solution Adaptations Changes	Dominant solution (optimized in total cost)	Standard market solution (dominant)	Possible evolution into a 'commodity'
Global market volume	Slow growth	Strong growth	Stabilized sales	Quick or relative decline (apart from spare parts if applicable)
Clients	Innovators	Leaders with solutions whose reliability has been ensured	Market core (followers)	After-sales clients
Competitors	Few	Growing number (entrants)	Stability	Few (including spare-parts specialists)
Main success factors	Design / Innovation / Flexibility	Economic optimization / Flexibility / Reactivity / Quality	Low price / Reliability / Quality / Availability	Low price / Quality / Availability

Generally, a company shifts from a phase primarily characterized by innovation and adaptation to customers' specialized technological needs, to one focused on cost minimization for the dominant technical solution maintained and ensuring its availability on the market, before finally exploiting, in cash flow terms, a stable product with an optimal relationship between usage cost and advantages.

However, the end-of-life phase of products may diverge in the following ways: a) in certain cases, as the product does not face competition from any new solutions, it becomes a standard 'commodity' widely available on the market; b) in other situations, it is replaced by a new technology that is indisputably more interesting.

However, certain clients will continue to seek the initial product, for example, to supply their customers with spare parts in the context of after-sales obligations (this is the case of older-generation electronic components still required in complex systems, which customers do not wish to overhaul, and may also be the case in professional electronics, defence or aeronautics sectors). In this case, the product will survive in small volumes, with availability as an overriding priority, given the risk of its supply shortage.

The main conclusion to draw is that top managers need to divide their products commercially into segments or homogeneous groups, and to strive towards *organizing the whole of the supply chain including upstream processes (procurement) according to differentiated bases*.

1/2.2 Main strategic decisions

To sum up in a deliberately simplified way, the strategic plan defined by general management should always consist of clearly responding to (at least) the following issues:

- Globally, or more commonly from the perspective of families of products or services, what is the main approach that should be selected (cost/volume frontal approach or differentiation, and how)? Moreover, should the whole of the market be targeted or should a niche approach be chosen?
- In addition, how should development and further diversification – a condition for medium- and long-term value creation – be managed?
- As a consequence, what should be the priorities in terms of allocation of resources to the different activities and functions involved?
- What are the main transversal processes to be set up (eg budgeting or innovation), and how should the different functions contribute to them? More generally, how should different learning processes be deployed and controlled?
- Finally, what risks of all types might face the company and with the possibility of destroying value, and what prevention, mitigation and control systems should be set up?

Basic strategic alternatives

Here, the following two aspects need to be considered: the extent and nature of the chosen target(s) – eg client categories, specific needs, geographical territories – and as a result, the ways in which the company can 'respond' to market demand.

Looking at these two criteria together, we face the fundamental choice, already touched on in the external analysis of the sector, between two basic major strategies: the first that aims at primarily obtaining extremely low total costs in order to attack the market head-on with very attractive sales prices; and the second that involves seeking to stand out from the competition via more specialized products, possibly adapted to client niches, and accompanying them with additional services with a strong focus on specific needs.

Cost/volume strategy

For a given strategic segment, it is possible to choose to carry out a 'head-on attack' using, a priori, the same weapons as the competitors and offering similar products or services. This type of strategy is essentially based on an economic-type confrontation, with total cost being the sole discriminating criterion for the market (as the product offer is highly standardized). This kind of choice is primarily made by market leaders or else a few companies in an oligopoly. The markets for business-to-consumer (B2C) general consumer products or large retailers are perfect illustrations of this type of situation, especially in the superstore segment.

Such an approach aims above all at obtaining the lowest possible total costs, and is based on the *experience-effect* theory. When carried through to completion, as previously seen, this strategy enables the leader to be the 'master' of market prices, and hence tolerate smaller competitors by maintaining a better level of productivity and profitability. The leader may even practise price lowering (being the only one able to withstand this), forcing competitors to fall under its 'pricing umbrella,' with the aim of gradually eliminating some of them.

However, this strategy raises the following well-known risks: the emergence of technologically innovative substitution products (this risk disappears if barriers to entry into the market are great); or swift evolution in client expectations that must be met with flexibility and gradual product differentiation via sub-segmentation (eg via different quality standards or levels of complexity) no longer manageable by one type of equipment and know-how.

Differentiation strategy

Differentiation strategies are more common and can be expressed in the following two main ways.

The first aims at *sophisticating or enlarging the offer* extended to customers in a different way from competitors, relying on differentiation factors that are difficult, time-consuming or costly to obtain. This strategy backs the readiness of clients to pay for a new 'enriched' offer that makes up a new value proposition (eg a high-end car).

The second strategy has a *downward focus,* for example, *by simplifying the offer* to adapt to new market segments (in the marketing sense of the term). Illustrations include *low-cost* cars, or *low-cost* travel agents or some of the new airline companies.

In both cases, the aim is to create a positive differential between cost gap and price gap compared with the initial situation. This differentiation may essentially focus on the three traditional objectives of performance, that familiar trilogy of *cost, time* (responsiveness) and *quality*. But in most sectors, these traditional objectives are supplemented by factors such as the acceleration of events in all markets and recent changes in client expectations, as shown by Figure 1.3.

In terms of resource allocation and internal processes, these changes necessitate different types of improvements:

- Control of the order and delivery process (independent of the lead-time) requires the company to produce results in terms of reliability and reactivity.

- Capacity to innovate – internally or via collaborations with suppliers – whilst respecting increasingly short cycles for product (whether one or several)

FIGURE 1.3   Differentiation factors and performance criteria

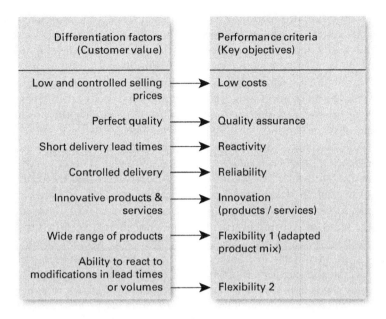

Differentiation factors (Customer value)	Performance criteria (Key objectives)
Low and controlled selling prices	→ Low costs
Perfect quality	→ Quality assurance
Short delivery lead times	→ Reactivity
Controlled delivery	→ Reliability
Innovative products & services	→ Innovation (products / services)
Wide range of products	→ Flexibility 1 (adapted product mix)
Ability to react to modifications in lead times or volumes	→ Flexibility 2

placement in the market, and continually offering more associated services, which requires another form of reactivity in terms of design and development (time to market).

- Capacity to offer a wide range of products, or to offer versions, options and adaptations to meet increasingly specialized needs, hence implying a capacity to innovate (adaptation of the product mix to client expectations).

- Capacity to respond quickly to modifications of all types in client demands, unexpected or erratic changes in sales volumes, which requires a company to be flexible. This capacity characterizes the company's ability to adapt to markets.

Ostensibly, the technical and organizational consequences of such improvements may entail higher costs than cost/volume strategies. Apart from the fact that certain markets are prepared to pay *premium prices*, experience proves that these actions often also boost productivity thanks to the implementation of just-in-time and total-quality approaches. They are also accompanied by a *simplification* of methods, management and organization processes (process re-engineering).

Focus (or niche) strategy

For medium-sized companies operating in large-volume strategic segments, a niche strategy is possible as a first step towards differentiation, on the assumption that the market is sufficiently small not to attract large-scale competitors and that the fairly specific investments necessitated will put off other players.

Development and value creation via diversification

Complementary to the above is the strategic issue of business development (even though differentiation strategy may be its first stage). The aim here is to make structuring choices for long-term business and turnover development. The following issues are thus tackled: principles in diversification through the development of new geographical markets; and the main directions in terms of innovation for new products.

Let's look at Figure 1.4 showing the development model designed by Igor Ansoff.[7] First of all, on the horizontal axis, the company may decide to increase sales by launching *new products in existing markets*. They may modify the product, create several versions of the product, or develop new models.

This diversification may come in two forms. Firstly, *derivative* (using a 'side-by-side' approach to develop products based on similar technologies in order to cover a whole range of uses targeting similar types of clients), as demonstrated by Apple, who has gradually succeeded in developing its entire range of iPods, iPhones and iPads. Secondly, *conglomerate* (describing multi-sector groups covering varied activities without there necessarily being any synergy between them), as shown in France by Bouygues, who operate in the construction, television and telecommunications industries, or groups such as Nestlé or Danone, whose activities include food processing, drinks and nutritional products, or even cosmetics companies.

This strategy sheds light on the necessary *innovation capacities*, whether these are to be found in-company or through co-development – even co-innovation – partnerships established with certain strategic suppliers.

Another path is possible: that of *disruptive innovation*, whereby the value perceived by the client is increased, or the price is lowered via simplification of the offer, as discussed earlier with regard to differentiation. Incidentally, Laurence Lehman-Ortega, Affiliate Professor at HEC Paris has developed the HEC Executive Columbus Lab, undertaking research into how value curves are affected by offer levels and

FIGURE 1.4   Igor Ansoff's Diversification Matrix

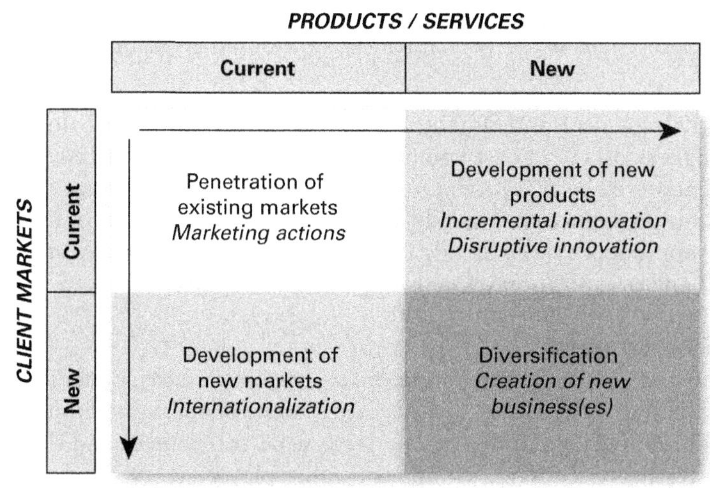

PRODUCTS / SERVICES

	Current	New
Current	Penetration of existing markets *Marketing actions*	Development of new products *Incremental innovation* *Disruptive innovation*
New	Development of new markets *Internationalization*	Diversification *Creation of new business(es)*

CLIENT MARKETS

value attributes. Indeed, this type of innovation (see Chapter 3) can potentially generate 'blue oceans', as referred to in the business strategy paradigm described by W Chan Kim and Renée Mauborgne.[8]

Notably, it is due to one of the recent major evolutions in business strategy that the procurement function has become involved with innovative partners that are so crucial to an enterprise. This development requires a new approach, even a new culture, for many companies have not yet latched onto the expansion of this approach whereby innovation is shared with suppliers, as an alternative to an internal innovation approach.

The other, vertical axis – that may be combined with the previous horizontal one – consists in increasing sales by introducing *products into new markets* (local, regional and global, via systematic international deployment). This approach can also draw new market segments via the development of different product versions (customization), the use of new distribution circuits (eg multi-channel B2C distribution), or the exploitation of new modes of communication (social networks on the internet).

Let us bear in mind that this diversification process and these development projects can be carried out in a number of ways: a company may act on its own, relying solely on its internal resources; it may set up partnerships with other companies ('vertical' partnerships with certain suppliers or focused 'horizontal' alliances with certain direct competitors via the organization of co-ventures); it may outsource all or part of one share of activity; it may even act by generating external growth (by taking over another company or business unit).

Resource allocation and economic performance

All these different actions can only be carried out if sufficient capital is raised, with demonstrable return on investment (ROI) and improved return on capital employed (ROCE). The ultimate aim, of course, is to achieve competitiveness, but it is also, and above all, to obtain value creation. This is also a way to ensure that *shareholder expectations* are satisfied (and that the debt ratio can be controlled).

In this way, these strategic scenarios should always, from an economic point of view, be simulated from different financial performance perspectives, as illustrated by Figure 1.5:

- Obtaining the lowest possible total costs (direct or indirect) to enable maximization of short-term *operational income* – an essential topic related to the value of total cost of ownership (TCO).

- Many companies will also seek gradual *'variabilization of costs'* that promotes flexibility by adapting to fluctuating markets, as well as an easier redeployment of activities – a topic related to certain outsourcing or subcontracting decisions.

- From a *cash flow* perspective, care is taken to measure and control *fixed assets as these affect cash flow and the working capital requirement* (WCR) – a particularly important point especially for procurement decisions and their impact on supply-chain networks associated with local or global sourcing decisions.

- *Investment decisions* can be considered in two ways:
  - ROI, assessed by calculation of net present value (NPV) or internal rate of return (IRR), but above all by ROCE – or return on average capital employed (ROACE) in the oil and gas industry, for example[9]– as a measurement of profitability;
  - but also *payback* (in other words the period of implementation or operational time required to cover initial investment by generated cash flows), a useful concept for assessing the capacity for rapid withdrawal if need be, also used complementarily when other financial criteria for investment profitability have been defined.
- If we focus on the minimization of risks (whose economic consequences related to likelihood of occurrence can be assessed – see the following section), attention should be paid to the *economic performance of all prevention measures* set up (*risk mitigation*).
- Finally, when considering longer-term value creation, we need to turn our attention to the *optimization of intangible capital (goodwill)* as the latter partially determines future development capacities, and hence medium-term results – an extremely important topic since goodwill largely intervenes as an element determining the security of future cash flow, as well as company value, and also since procurement and the supply chain contribute significantly to its constitution (see the analysis in Chapter 20).

Risk identification and mitigation

The risks to which any enterprise may be subject are extremely numerous and varied. These obviously affect all of the company's functions, and it is essential to control them as their occurrence is always ultimately *destructive of value*. In this work, only procurement and supply-chain risks interest us: readers can refer to these, analysed in detail, in Chapter 2.

In this overview stage, we simply wish to draw the reader's attention to regulatory changes in terms of traceability. Indeed, all companies are responsible for what they sell or resell. They must therefore ensure that materials and suppliers (including suppliers of suppliers) conform to national or even international regulations. Generally speaking, an increasing level of transparency is required to guarantee product traceability. This responsibility looks to be a major challenge for the future.[10]

1/2.3 Summarized vision of choices: the balanced scorecard company

An executive management can sum up its decisions in the form of a balanced scorecard (BSC) assessing the company as a whole – a step frequently undertaken, especially as it offers the huge advantage of clearly stating strategic choices and their impacts. Figure 1.6 presents the overall logic of this approach.[11]

FIGURE 1.5 Generic model for value creation

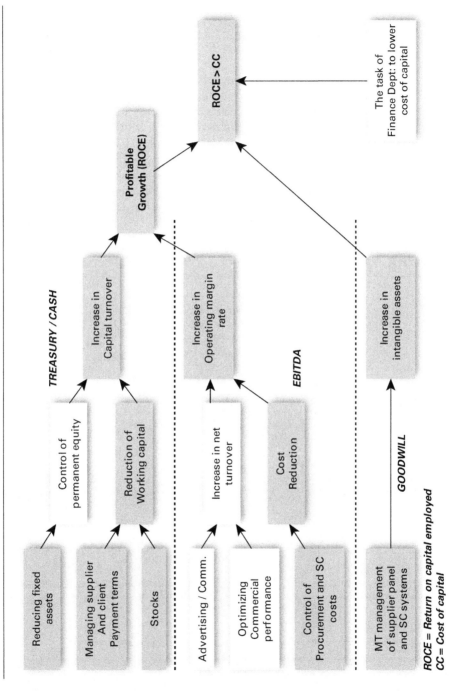

ROCE = Return on capital employed
CC = Cost of capital

Here, we will be looking at the underlying principles of the balanced scorecard before examining the features of the BSC in the procurement context. Regarding general strategic choices, the BSC is organized around the following main elements arranged into four different blocks. In each of the areas covered, appropriate indicators enable results to be followed and progress to be measured. Let's quickly examine these four areas:

1 *Commercial performance and value proposition for client markets*: looking far beyond objectives for growth in turnover, this point refers to improvement sought in the elements of client satisfaction already mentioned in Figure 1.3 (performance in terms of price positioning, respect of contractual lead-times and quality delivered, reliability, reactivity, flexibility, efficiency and demonstrated added value of the different services offered to clients, etc). If the company has a portfolio of products segmented into different families (eg standard products based on cost/volume versus specific tailor-made or customized products) then their commercial performance should be

FIGURE 1.6 General structure of a corporate balanced scorecard

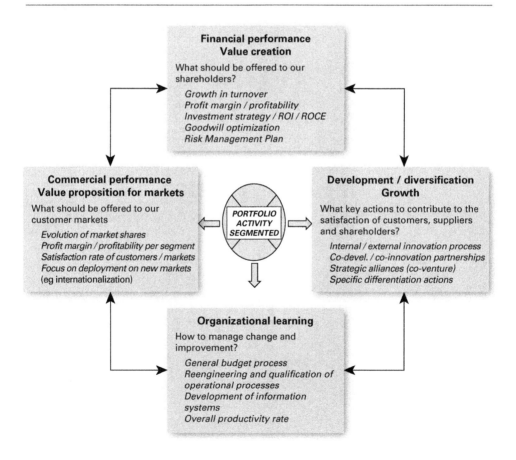

established on a 'differentiated' basis to enable them to measure the effectiveness of the segmented portfolio.

2 *Financial performance, resource allocation and value creation*: from the perspective of top management and according to the expectations of shareholders (and banks), the following points are generally specified, with 'target' objectives for results to be reached in the short and medium term:

- operational profit margin;
- global profitability;
- investment strategy;
- value creation via innovation; and, less commonly
- major elements of intangible capital (eg brand value, portfolio of patents, customer portfolio, and panel of recurring or strategic suppliers or even the upstream expanded supply chain).

Indicators of costs, profitability, investment and value creation are specified by major segment within the portfolio of activities. As well as examining value creation, *non-destruction of value* is closely scrutinized – an issue that draws us towards the clear identification of *risks* (of all types/internal and external) facing the company and also the follow-up of risk-control and mitigation plans implemented, accompanied by their economic balance sheet.

3 *Diversification, and development and growth processes*: the senior management essentially maintains an overview on improvements to the main internal operational processes directly related to their customer expectations concerning differentiated products or services. The day-to-day management handles and tracks the following elements (among others): action plans relating to the development of new customer markets (eg international deployment), as well as the efficiency and output of innovation processes, whether internal or via partnerships and collaborations.

4 *Improvement of internal operational processes and organizational learning*: this point affects all support functions as well as operational functions contributing to the management of a company's expanded supply chain. The formalization and simplification of processes are covered as well as the professionalization of staff and the efficiency of information and decision-making systems. Also within this scope is the follow-up of productivity, including the qualification of all processes in the ISO sense of the term.

1/3 Main missions and priority objectives of procurement (BSC)

Let's start off with a proposition: any company function should be *in line with the way of thinking and management decisions* outlined above if it wishes the general management to recognize it as contributing usefully. Otherwise, it will always be confined to an operational role, executing tasks without truly participating in strategic thinking. As a result, particularly where supply chains or procurement are concerned, functions that fail to fall in line with the schema are perceived as cost centres rather than investment or profit centres.

In this way, the four dimensions of a company's balanced scorecard (BSC) should be carefully set out at the level of each individual function if the desired effect is to demonstrate their true impact on value creation and development. Regarding procurement, beyond its fundamental mission reviewed in the introduction to this chapter (searching for and acquiring products and services for integration into the products manufactured and sold by the company or necessary for its operation), the indisputable conclusion stands out: its strategic priorities, followed by its ensuing operational objectives, should be expressed in a manner entirely coherent with the company BSC. With this basic principle thus defined, dialogue with the day-to-day management becomes possible and necessary. If any choices need to be made between alternatives, decisions can then be taken more easily, all the while striving towards coherence with and strategic contribution to the whole.

Only then, at a second stage, can appropriate action plans be designed, encompassing prioritized and targeted selections for procurement levers. The logic behind maturity models, aimed at defining the framework of operational procurement action plans and action plans for managing change, directly in line with this way of thinking, is examined in more detail in Chapter 21.

1/3.1 Strategic missions and operational objectives (procurement BSC)

Let's go over the four main areas of the BSC relevant to any general management and look at the impacts that these may generally have on procurement by referring to Table 1.2. Careful reading of the table offers a point-by-point illustration of the search for coherence with general strategy, to which we have already drawn attention. We can observe that the right column, listing procurement priorities, includes two types of data: a) operational objectives that are more *geared towards quantifiable and measurable results*, that can be directly integrated into the company's results (various costs, quality delivered, ROI of certain projects, etc); b) elements that are more defined as *procurement levers for action* (in other words, means of action) whose anticipated results, whether economic or qualitative, cannot be directly measured (eg development of a co-innovation partnership or development of international sourcing).

As regards procurement levers, appropriate representative indicators should then be found as a means to allow performance measurement (Chapter 20 provides greater detail on this issue).

To summarize this discussion of indicators, we can say that the system by which a procurement department reports to its top management should be structured according to the same BSC principle, or use a similar indicator 'dashboard'.

Another conclusion stands out: any procurement project or action plan integrating levers, actions and measures *that lack a strong and incontestable causal link* with one or several of the general management's objectives is a priori *aimless and hence useless*.

TABLE 1.2 BSC for procurement: link with company strategic decisions

Corporate strategic objectives	Procurement priorities and objectives
Financial performance / Resource allocation / Value creation	
Maximization of net profit margin	Minimization of the TCO (direct costs shared with the supply chain)
Minimization of the WCR	Actions to minimize inventories under its responsibility
	Generalized diminishing of cycles and lead times
Maximization of goodwill	Supplier homologation and structuring of the supplier panel and the network of N+1 suppliers
Minimization of risks (all types)	Setting up a system of upstream risk mitigation (preventative in nature) / Knowledge of supplier markets with anticipation of risks
Commercial performance / Market satisfaction (customers / suppliers)	
Competitive prices (with margins)	Control of TCO and acquisition costs
Respect of 'zero-fault' quality	'Upstream' quality in conformity and assured
Respected delivery lead times / Reactivity	Short and respected delivery lead times
Development of new markets (namely international)	Deployment of international sourcing (search for local suppliers according to a backing logic)
Flexibility with regard to market volume changes	Development of upstream just-in-time plans
	Constitution of 'targeted' ad hoc inventories
Development / Diversification / Innovation	
Search for significant drops in cost for current activities	Co-development partnerships based on 'design-to-cost' (incremental innovation)
	Deployment of global sourcing (low-cost logic)
	Search for outsourced solutions
Search for innovations in products / services	Co-innovation partnerships (disruptive innovation)
	Strategic alliances (co-venture)
	Development of new business models with strategic suppliers
	Deployment of an open-innovation system
International development	Deployment of international sourcing – cf. above (with ad hoc country coverage)

TABLE 1.2   *continued*

Corporate strategic objectives	Procurement priorities and objectives
Efficiency of processes / organizational learning mechanisms	
Ensuring the efficiency of the budget process	Effective integration of procurement in budgeting
Ensuring the efficiency of the innovation process	Effective contribution of procurement to the corporate innovation process
Development of a project-based approach	Integration of procurement in projects
Development of efficiency and effectiveness of all functions	Formalization and qualification of all procurement processes
	Optimization and qualification of all procurement information systems

Finally, commitment to procurement results should allow improvement and/or securing of the top management's position in the face of markets. For example, financial indicators should help boost the credibility of announced plans, and thus, strengthen the confidence of investors. In June 2012, during the 'procurement night' organized by the CDAF (*Compagnie des Dirigeants et Acheteurs de France*), a French procurement network, one investor requested that procurement departments keep to their savings commitments, as he had the impression that 50 per cent of them are phony. Not only this, he asked for the drafting of a roadmap setting out specific targets over time to enable commitments to be met (which, in his opinion, was not yet the case).

Anecdotes aside, suffice to say that procurement management should be able to commit to their results and participate in reassuring markets. This confidence will then lead to better goodwill, as shown in Figure 1.5.

1/3.2 Reconciliation of business portfolios and procurement portfolios

One important point still needs to be cleared up: that of the *apparent heterogeneity* between the basis of segmentation of a portfolio of strategic activities defined at a corporate level and that of a procurement portfolio. It is thus necessary to *reconcile both* before going into a definition of procurement strategies according to procurement categories.

Indeed, everything stems from the principle (logical, justified and already described above) that there can be no single supply-chain management method or procurement strategy for a company, and that, on the other hand, *the approach must be differentiated* according to the specificities of the different areas of activity or product families.[12]

On the other hand, traditionally – with regard to direct purchases in any case – a procurement portfolio is segmented into different categories (see Chapter 2 for details on this approach), defined according to principles that may be technically or needs-based, or else related to the characteristics of the supplier markets being considered. Most of the time, however, these procurement needs *are not directly linked* to the specific products or services to which they input, and even less to objectives for specific performances and/or expected differentiation, which may be entirely different depending on the particular finished-product family.

For example, a specific software application, embedded into a hi-tech system of which it is the core, may be a highly differentiating element in relation to competing product offers, and obligations relating to performance, reliability, innovation and traceability of updates will be of great importance; whereas a commonplace standard software application – purchasable on a very open, competitive market as a commodity – entails a very different procurement strategy, one that is more classic, whose strategic objectives are more geared towards cost for a guaranteed standard quality. And yet, in both cases, we are talking about the procurement of software services (a single category in a 'typical' procurement portfolio).

In this way, cross-analysis and the reconciliation of finished-product and procurement portfolios should be carried out systematically – formally and explicitly – before being translated upstream in the procurement BSC. There is direct impact on the 'commercial performance' and 'development/diversification' blocks (see Figure 1.6), as well as on investment issues within the 'financial performance' block.

1/4 Policies, strategies and tactical decisions

Relating to these objectives and adhering to the framework, the procurement department of a company should then define a general procurement policy; this should be divided into specific ranked principal dimensions, and subsequently into individual strategies with associated action plans. Figure 1.7 illustrates this approach.

1/4.1 Procurement policies and strategies: a typical marketing approach

To put things simply, in general terms, this approach borrows from the principles and stages of a 'reverse B2B marketing strategy'.[13] From their marketing colleagues, procurement can borrow two concepts – demand and supplier markets – to create the graph (top two blocks on the right of Figure 1.7), in other words the function's 'core activity': first, an understanding of all internal demand requirements as well as those of the potential supplier markets; secondly, a definition of action plans organized according to a prioritized 'mix' of levers – or action variables (in the way that we speak of marketing mix, we could also speak of 'procurement mix', even if the term does not exist!).

FIGURE 1.7 Strategic procurement planning process

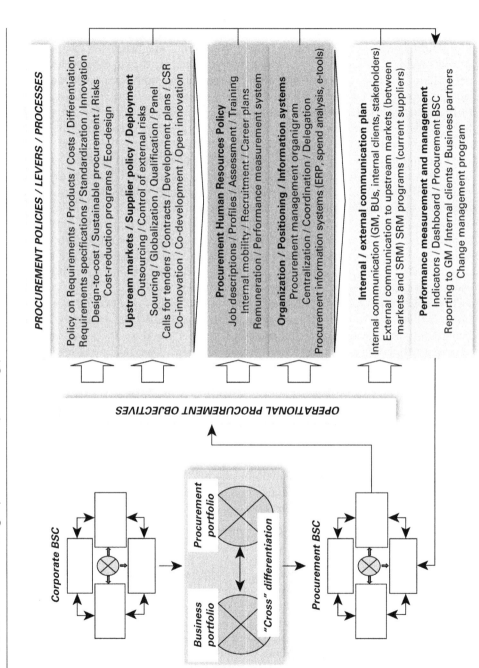

Parts One and Two of this book tackle these issues in detail.

Secondly (two central blocks on the right of Figure 1.7), it is necessary to make a coherent selection of all essential resource management elements enabling 'core activity' policies to be implemented: on the one hand, everything that concerns decisions on organization, the positioning of the procurement function, mechanisms for possible purchasing delegation, as well as the principles and methods for managing procurement human resources; and on the other hand, the complete system of information and decision-making systems, whether enterprise resource planning (ERP) modules or procurement-specific developments, such as tools for analysing external expenses or all internet applications (e-sourcing tools, supplier portals, procurement intranets and other dedicated collaborative systems).

Chapters 16, 17 and 18 of this work offer details on these issues relating to the management of human resources and information systems.

Thirdly (the last element of the mix – the fifth block on the right of Figure 1.7), an internal and an external communication policy is always necessary, for, beyond simple transactional relationships, a procurement department needs to transmit numerous pieces of information to its stakeholders, and also to offer them explanations, motivate and associate them in different processes, as well as in the design, then execution of its action plans.

Finally, (the bottom block of Figure 1.7), to qualify the network, in collaboration with management controllers and the finance department, an entire system for performance measurement and reporting to the top management and business partners needs to be designed. Apart from, first of all, enabling procurement results to be measured and compared with the objectives integrated in the BSC, this system allows medium-term change to be directed and managed. Deployed internally within the procurement management, the BSC (as part of the measurement tool for internal procurement activity) is also required for the management of purchasing teams.

Obviously, this already complex figure does not present a particularly dynamic vision of things. But the different choices of levers for action and operational action plans will *always need to take into account the maturity level* of the company, and of the procurement department, in terms of practices and professionalism. Whilst the overall logic should always be respected, the complexity of content will always need to be adapted to each situation including medium-term progressions. Similarly, successive action plans will need to evolve over time and become more complex (see Chapter 21).

All issues relating to communication, management of the procurement function and change management will be discussed in Chapters 19, 20 and 21.

Setting of operational procurement objectives

Ostensibly, these objectives need to be directly inferred from the objectives for corporate (and commercial) strategy. Their hierarchical order will above all depend on strategic priorities, and should be defined on the basis of the procurement BSC.

As can be seen above, certain objectives need to be ranked according to the different segments of the procurement portfolio (with all the procurement 'families' harmonized and grouped according to specific criteria – see Chapter 2 for details – and this will result in specific actions), each the result of sub-segmentation via a 'cross' analysis of the portfolio of activities. This is generally always the case for economic objectives and those relating to expected quality, service and innovation (level of quality, delivery lead-time, reactivity, flexibility, other services of all types including logistic and support services, search for new factors of differentiation via innovation, etc).

However, certain objectives may also be shared by procurement as a whole, whatever procurement segment we may be dealing with. Mention can be made of a few examples that illustrate this concept:

- deciding whether purchasers should get involved in the definition of requirements with users and contribute to the search for more innovative solutions (involvement in the setting of requirements specifications);
- deciding, for example, if supply should be dealt with by a single-source or multiple-source (at least two sources systematically) approach in order to manage certain operational supply risks;
- setting the maximum share of the supplier turnover to be accepted in order to avoid bilateral over-dependence (in relation to legal risks);
- binding the company (if applicable) to signing contracts on a yearly or multi-yearly basis in order to stabilize economic conditions and to allow time to define and follow performance improvement plans;
- defining company rules and standards in terms of social and environmental obligations, and translating these into procurement practices;
- specifying a compulsory level of requirements and professional ethics to be adhered to (such as commitments to suppliers), and more generally evoking shared values and principles of professional behaviour to respect (code of conduct).

Choice of procurement strategies and action plans

Strategic choices are made after undertaking a thorough analysis of the procurement portfolio, closely adhering to the principles of a SWOT-type strategic analysis (such as that used for product families in the development of corporate strategy). As will be seen in Chapter 2, these strategies should be defined by the simultaneous implementation of levers for action, aiming either to reinforce one's competitive buying position, often in a dominating manner via a 'head-on' attack on the market; or to seek differentiation and control of major risks, and to focus on internal or external actions aiming at value creation.

As for action plans, whether for procurement families or categories, these are structured according to an approach comprising several main aspects:

- actions aimed at acting on expressed requirements and terms of specification (level of quality, functional analyses, searches for alternative technical solutions, anticipation of more fundamental 'disruptive' innovations);
- actions directed towards supplier policies, from the establishment and make-up of the supplier panel, through to sourcing and qualifying, up to selection systems to be set up and subsequent methods for follow-up and performance improvement plans, including commitment to local content for international contracts that commercially require a share of local purchasing when projects are sold in other countries;

- actions that cross with the previous ones, but are exclusively geared towards the minimization of costs contributing to all elements of the TCO, from a value-creation perspective;
- finally, actions at all levels of procurement processes (and not solely focused on procurement contracts) aimed at analysing the different risks that may be encountered and setting up adapted systems for preventing them.

In parallel, resource management should also be subject to associated action plans that are to be carried out simultaneously, rigorously and stringently. *Two fundamental principles*, valid in all circumstances, are to be kept in mind:

Principle 1: progress can only be made in procurement performance, and complex and efficient action plans carried out, if the level of quality, skills and professionalization of human resources and information systems within the procurement function *allows it, and above all precedes action*.

Principle 2: progress always generates costs (fixed, or variable in the case of partial outsourcing of the procurement function). As a result, it is necessary to reason according to *principles based on short- or medium-term return*. However, if action plans are coherent with the BSC all the while following their own internal logic, if they are therefore rigorous and the promised results have a very high probability of being realized, then it is highly likely that the top management will approve them, due to their intrinsic profitability, and because they are in line with the management's way of thinking. A procurement management team needs to know how to sell itself as an investment and profit centre!

Main strategic, tactical and managerial decisions

In this way, from an operational point of view, the whole of the procurement function is organized, managed and structured around a set of processes and decisions that are strategic or tactical in nature, which constitute its scope of responsibility in the context of its 'performance commitments'.[14]

Table 1.3 at the end of this chapter sums up the main decisions to be taken by procurement management. We make no claims of exhaustive analysis here; the table is designed as a checklist of appropriate questions to ask on these key points. All these decisions and processes are covered in detail elsewhere in this book, along with the main methodologies necessary for setting up relevant solutions.

1/4/2 Participation of procurement departments in major internal processes

Alongside its own action plans, and because these represent precious opportunities to embark on *internal collaborative* approaches, it is important that the procurement department undertakes three major transversal processes.

Budgetary process

The necessity for the procurement department to get involved in the budgetary process does not seem, at first glance, obvious. But if we take indirect procurement

TABLE 1.3   Structural, tactical and managerial procurement decisions

Nature of the decision	Main questions
Structural decisions	
Vertical integration or outsourcing (procurement participation)	What is the company's value chain and what are the necessary and existing main competencies? Should it be broadly integrated or should outsourcing solutions be called upon? If yes, which ones and how? Is the supplier chain (1st to Nth position) controlled?
Differentiated procurement strategies	What strategic segmentation to set up for the procurement portfolio? What procurement levers and practices to deploy in priority, that will be adapted to the different identified segments of the procurement portfolio?
Quality policy	What quality management systems and practices to set up? What certification and quality-assurance system to implement?
Sustainable procurement policy (CSR)	What systems to set up in terms of ethics in procurement? What systems to set up in supplier policies regarding social and environmental responsibility (CSR)?
Sourcing policy	What strategies in terms of sourcing and supplier selection? What homologation / certification processes and practices to set up? What international deployment to carry out? Towards which countries or zones?
Supplier panel Supplier relationship management	How to structure the supplier panel? Which supplier profiles to favor? What management system to set up? Should improvement plans be followed with suppliers, and how? What types of relationships and modes of collaboration to set up with suppliers (partnership, cooperation or not)?

TABLE 1.3 *continued*

Nature of the decision	Main questions
Design and development of innovation products (procurement participation)	What transversal process of design and development to adopt?
	What management approach for product life cycle?
	How to put into figures and manage the TCO (total cost of ownership)?
	What contributions should buyers bring to the design and requirements-specification definition phase?
	What technological and business intelligence strategies to carry out on the supplier market?
	What types of innovation to develop (co-development, co-innovation, open innovation)?
Tactical decisions	
Inventory policy WCR management Flexibility management	What level of inventory in the upstream system and how to manage it?
	Should responsibility for this be entrusted to suppliers (VMI or vendor-managed inventory)?
	What alternative solutions to set up to ensure reactivity without supply risks?
Flow management	What supply planning system to choose?
	Should Internet tools be set up to manage flows with suppliers (EDI, dedicated portals, e-procurement)?
Transversal processes	What are the different processes to set up?
	How should functional entities (internal clients and all stakeholders) contribute to these?
Resources / Organization / Communication / Performance	
Procurement human resources	What specific competencies are necessary?
	How to acquire and develop these competencies?
	Which 'management by objectives' to implement and use?
	Which associated remuneration system?

TABLE 1.3   *continued*

Nature of the decision	Main questions
Organization of the procurement department	Is a dedicated procurement department necessary and how should it be positioned?
	How should it relate to the functional and operational departments?
	What to choose between centralization, coordination or decentralization of procurement (in the context of a multi-business unit group)?
	What purchases to decentralize and delegate? How? How to control relevance and respect of rules?
Information systems	What should be the architecture of procurement information systems?
	Should these be integrated, autonomous or outsourced? How?
	What connections with the integrated system (ERP)?
Knowledge management and change strategy	How to capitalize on knowledge and savoir-faire?
	How do lead change?
	How to associate the executives and business departments?
Performance measurement	Which performances to measure?
	Which measurement system to adopt and how to manage evolutions? Are evolutions in procurement maturity to be followed?
	Which reporting system to set up and to whom is it aimed?

(non-production spend) as our example, then a procurement action can have a nullifying financial impact globally if procurement budgets are not adapted accordingly. It is therefore important that the procurement management can, at constant volumes, correct future budgets as they are being produced by taking into account attained improvements in economic conditions.

To take another example: it is entirely deluded to think it is possible to maintain a certain level for a raw materials budget if market prices are rising due to a series of external causes. At best, one can try to contain the increase, or to set up a financial hedging mechanism for these purchases (see Chapter 12). Who is better placed than a procurement department to raise alerts on possible price hikes, and to assess the actual level of consequences to be taken into consideration in budgets?

Of course, there are still procurement departments that commit to yearly standard costs that become the annual objectives they attempt to achieve. But as market fluctuations occur more quickly, the yearly budgetary process is insufficient to allow these changes to be monitored: the objectives aim not so much at keeping to standard prices as to boosting improvement of profit margins. It is necessary therefore to be proactive in updating data on procurement costs and prices and to thus enable the company to secure its profit margins on its products. A 'short-loop' budgetary process based on purchase prices is therefore a key element for keeping profit margins under control.

It is also crucial to integrate into the budget the provisional results of certain procurement actions already undertaken (or that will be undertaken in the near future and that will produce an impact on the following budgetary period). Finally, during periods when costs are being drastically reduced, and after budgets have been defined in current economic decisions, proactive objectives may be put forward by procurement departments.

Investment process

For similar reasons, it is essential that procurement be represented on investment committees, for example, in industrial companies. In this way, topics may be brought to management's attention far upstream, enabling them to deploy necessary actions for studying the market and sourcing in ample time, and also to search for alternative solutions via a truly functional definition of requirements.

The essential lever implemented here is anticipation, enabling the procurement department to be informed early enough about important upcoming projects, and to adequately set to work in order to bring real added value in the long term. This intervention can also help promote standardization across procurement departments when they encounter different choices, now and in the future.

Finally, this is an opportunity for a company to commit itself, in advance, to a complete and uncompromising risk analysis (dealing with issues including dependence, guarantees, future availability of equipment, supplier sustainability, etc).

Innovation and development process for new products

In industrial companies, designers are most often focused on the characteristics of a product or the technical solution that needs to be acquired (technology, performance, robustness, etc). In addition, they may have preferences for certain regular suppliers based on a history of dealings with them, or based on their existing reputation on the market (brand-image effects, opinions of colleagues, etc). Finally, they may also be directly approached upstream by the suppliers themselves, or they may also, out of professional interest, undertake wide and systematic technological surveys that lead them to meet new suppliers.

If procurement departments are not involved very early on in this process of design and development, a number of problems may emerge, that will be difficult to correct subsequently:

- Certain specifiers may end up accepting 'over-quality' for a purchased product, as an easy solution thought to deal with certain future problems, without any evaluation of the resulting overall costs being rigorously carried out.

- Certain suppliers occupying dominant positions may be recommended whereas a purchasing department might choose to upset this power balance by introducing a duly qualified and motivated 'challenger' supplier.
- New suppliers may be highly recommended without any comprehensive and structured qualification process being implemented, hence bringing associated risks.
- In the context of a multi-entity group (covering several professional activities with separate income statements), the same request, more or less, may be sent to the same supplier or to several suppliers. Procurement information systems need to be able to establish correlations and to give specifiers the opportunity to confirm whether these requests can be dealt with together, offering them savings in time, procedures and results.
- Finally, it is possible that no serious assessment of risks may have been made with regard to an innovation from the point of view of its future 'buyability'.

In this way, when a procurement department gets involved upstream, it can correct potential flaws, or at least influence the choices made by design/development teams, by educating colleagues. Generally speaking, no directions or decisions should be taken without calling upon procurement or referring to a clearly defined procurement policy (eg in the context of delegation) long before any consultation or call for tenders is launched.

Notes

1 'Supply chain *étendue*' in French, see Baglin *et al* (2013) *Management Industriel et Logistique: Conception et pilotage de la supply chain*, 6th edn, Economica, Paris.

2 The term 'upstream,' when used to characterize procurement's scope of action, should be interpreted with caution, especially if it is used when referring to Figure 1.1. Indeed, certain suppliers may be organizations that intervene downstream in the distribution supply chain (such as transporters and storage companies), and that also fall within the definition and operation of a procurement strategy. It therefore seems preferable to speak of 'external resources' whatever the level in which suppliers intervene in the extended supply chain.

3 Beyond these semantic questions, the issue arises of how to translate these scopes of responsibility from an organizational (organigrammatic) perspective, and hence, how to position the different functions. This issue will be dealt with in detail in Chapter 16.

4 Paradoxically, however, the term *e-procurement* is used for electronic applications and internet tools dedicated to the electronic management of supplies (whilst the term *e-sourcing* refers to the use of collaborative tools for the full scope of procurement activities)!

5 See the following key reference for in-depth reflection on the issue: Lehmann-Ortega *et al* (2013) *STRATEGOR – Toute la Stratégie d'Entreprise*, 6th edn, Dunod, Paris.

6 Let's remember that SWOT (strengths, weaknesses, opportunities, threats) analysis enables internal assessment of a company's strengths and weaknesses, and at the

same time, external assessment of the sector. The aim is to identify non-exploited opportunities as well as potential threats that may limit the company's development and choices.

7 Professor of Strategy at the Graduate School of Industrial Administration within the Carnegie Institute of Technology, Igor Ansoff then became the founding dean of the Vanderbilt University's Graduate School of Management. His reference work *Corporate Strategy* was published in 1965.

8 The INSEAD researchers have published a well-known work that has already been around for some time: *Blue Ocean* (2005) Harvard Business School Press.

9 The NPV (net present value) and the IRR (internal rate of return) are two very well-known criteria used by financiers to evaluate profitability and to choose between different investment projects.

10 Revelations on dangerous products (1,800 measures taken against dangerous products in the EEC in 2011 according to the EEC's 2013 RAPEX report), food scandals (the horse-meat situation) and health crises (PIP breast implants) have eroded consumer confidence in producers, and raised awareness of the necessity to reinforce the transparency and quality assurance of supply chains. One example is the Dodd–Frank Conflict Minerals Act. Adopted on 8 August 2012, Section 1502 of the Dodd–Frank Act obliges companies subject to the SEC (Securities and Exchange Commission) to provide traceability for their use of materials (tantalum, tin, tungsten and gold) that may originate from conflict zones (cf www.sec.gov). Chapter 6 deals with all these new ethical and responsible issues.

11 This concept and the corresponding management tools were initially developed in a book whose main issues and principles are reviewed in Kaplan and Norton (1992).

12 On this topic, see Hofmann, Beck and Füger (2012).

13 Michiel Leenders, one of the pioneering professors in US research and publications in this area, used the term 'reverse marketing' in this context. See the (already dated!) work: Leenders and Blenkhorn (1988).

14 It is understood, we remind the reader, that the domain of *operational execution* of procurement decisions, in the strict sense of the term, is not the responsibility of the procurement function but that of the supply chain, even if in the course of these phases, the procurement management follows up the performance of suppliers and may intervene in handling certain rare types of disputes.

02
Procurement marketing
Segmentation and strategies

Strategic thinking on procurement corresponds, feature by feature, with a classic marketing approach geared towards a company's downstream markets. However, instead of having to position and sell a portfolio of products, procurement has a portfolio of requirements to satisfy. Instead of having to 'attack' a customer market (with choices on positioning vis-à-vis competitors), here a player 'attacks' a supplier market proactively, whilst seeking to position itself in relation to other buyers.

Both functions require an understanding of the supplier market and a segmentation of the product portfolio in question, before reaching strategies adapted to specific situations and meeting the company's objectives from a global perspective, but also from the perspective of individual procurement categories. As shown by Figure 2.1, the procurement marketing process encompasses several main stages.

First of all, the *portfolio of requirements must be segmented* into types, then supplemented by an analysis of the strategic characteristics of every procurement family. This analysis covers three different aspects: prioritizing purchases by size of financial significance; an analysis of all types of internal risks and opportunities; and finally, an analysis of the features of the respective supplier markets according to their constraints and opportunities.

The next stage involves *defining differentiated procurement strategies*. These are obtained by selecting the relevant combination of actions for tackling supplier markets. In this stage, we focus in particular on three elements of the purchase process: upstream phases related to the definition of requirements; downstream phases corresponding to the operational implementation of the purchase; and the so-called 'post-purchase' following the procurement.

The final stage involves the *implementation of operational action plans* including the deployment of procurement practices and actions such as internal and external communication on the defined strategies and procurement projects, the setting-up of systems to follow up performance and associated change management.

The following section will develop these points.

FIGURE 2.1   The global procurement marketing process

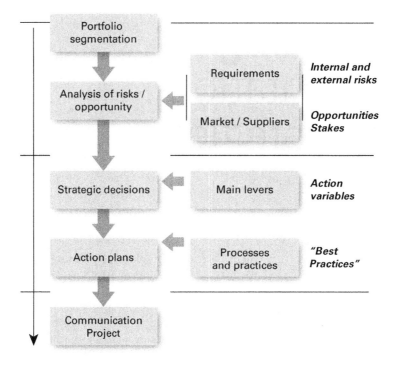

2/1 Strategic segmentation of the procurement portfolio

This stage involves grouping all products or services purchased by the company into homogeneous 'product families', also called 'purchasing categories'.

This type of classification can be undertaken from various perspectives, for no general rules exist. However, it always relies on the grouping together of suppliers, their activities and the segments of the market they serve.

2/1.1 Segmentation according to the nature of the products/ services purchased

The strategic importance of the goods or services being purchased is firstly determined by its technology, the quality requirements sought, or even the potential risks that the purchase brings to the company, as well as the recurrent or non-recurrent nature of the purchase.

Depending on the company's sector of activity and the importance of product categories in the procurement portfolio, we find segmentations that are based on function, others founded more on technology, and still others divided into families of purchases corresponding to three possible different levels.[1]

In this way, *functional classification* represents classification by area of activity, for example, raw materials, production components, subcontracting, general expenses. These purchases are all made in very different supplier markets and their characteristics, restrictions and needs all differ from one category to another.

Technological segmentation gathers purchases into product lines, corresponding to specific professional fields. For example, a 'raw materials' family may be composed of three product lines: light alloys, plastic materials and steel. This classification allows definition of, amongst others, the profiles of buyers and the organization of the procurement function.

Segmentation based on the *nature* of the purchase may vary from one company to another. However, the following divisions are proposed as a reference model:

- So-called *production* purchases, that are often extremely varied: diverse raw materials, components, complete subassemblies, consumable industrial products, whether these purchases are market *standard* (also called commodities) or products made to *specific* requirements.

- *Industrial subcontracting* services (from simple customization such as heat treatment to the supply of a complex component or function, whether in the context of a one-off or occasional need or manufacturing for a full subasssembly for the entire lifetime of a finished product).

- *Products for resale*, in other words finished products that the company supplies to widen its offer (eg a manufacturer of consumer hi-fi materials purchases products that it resells under its own brand; or a manufacturer of office products purchases full sets of equipment such as a copier paper feeding system to supplement its own offer).

- *Transport and logistics services*, to supply raw materials and components, if the supplier does not deliver goods delivered duty paid (DDP), and to deliver finished products to end-clients.

- Various *energy sources* and industrial fluids.

- *Technical services* (industrial maintenance works, spare parts, logistics services, etc).

- *Intellectual services* (studies, training, consultancy services, technical assistance, etc).

- *Telecommunications and software development* (specific or integrated (ERP) information systems, computer-operating systems, IT development).

- *Marketing and communications* (advertising space, market studies, graphic-chain production, promotional materials, etc).

- *Human resources services* (temporary employment agencies, labour services, recruitment).

- *Investment* purchases (eg buildings, production equipment, laboratory devices or computers).

- Purchases falling into *general expenses and other services* (equipment or vehicle rental, transport expenses of collaborators, services such as cleaning, security, office supplies, catering, reprography, consumables, facilities management).

In today's professional context, semantics have imposed a grouping of all these items into two macro-categories: *production* purchases and *non-production* purchases. The first describes all products and services that are integrated into the products or services designed, manufactured and sold by the company. The second includes all other purchases related to the company's internal operation (essentially, for the purposes of simplification, everything acquired from external suppliers of all types, except for capital).

These terms, being somewhat dated, have the disadvantage of being less relevant for service companies. We therefore prefer to use another pair of terms: *direct* purchases (in that they contribute to direct costs) and *indirect* purchases (following the same accounting process).

A second commonly used division also exists with links to the previous one: the distinction between *operational expenditure* (Opex) linked to the profit and loss statement, and *capital expenditure* (CapEx) that is project-based and follows different accounting rules.

2/1.2 Segmentation according to spend significance and o'risks/opportunities' analysis

Whilst the previous analysis, based on the nature of purchases, is useful for illustrating the variety of procurement situations and markets in question, and for identifying the nature of the procurement department's internal clients (functional and operational departments, business units, subsidiaries) interested in them, it is neither adequate nor relevant for arriving at a choice of procurement strategy that stems from managerial choices.

To decide on the most appropriate strategy, it is necessary, category by category, or even item by item within each procurement category, to deepen the analysis of the portfolio in three dimensions, as indicated by Figure 2.2.

The first objective is to rank the 'families' according to *their importance and financial significance* (amounts purchased) so as to prioritize efforts on those segments where potential savings are greatest (the same reasoning applies within each family for items to be prioritized and priority actions to be identified).

Secondly, analyses on *risks and opportunities, internal and external*, will need to be carried out, similar to the familiar SWOT analysis (see Figure 2.3).

Proceeding in this way, we can generally map out all procurement categories, enabling the identification of a variety of *procurement strategies differentiated* according to the specifics of each situation. It is clear that the decisive crossing point is to engage in an uncompromising in-depth scrutiny of both risk and opportunities, some of which have yet to be used or have been used ineffectively. Two axes need to be explored: requirements to satisfy (procured products or services), and supplier markets from which a company intends to make its purchases. We therefore speak of internal and external analysis that is to be carried out separately, then amalgamated.

FIGURE 2.2   Tri-dimensional segmentation principle of procurement portfolio

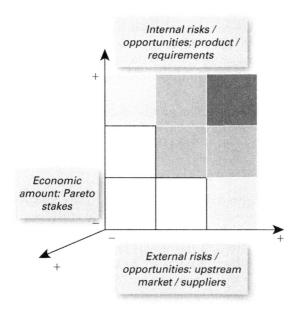

FIGURE 2.3   Risks/opportunities model for a procurement family

Strengths	Weaknesses
Characterizes dominant market position	Characterizes weak market position
Characterizes correct identification of procurement needs	Characterizes the specific nature of requirements or special-quality technical demands
Characterizes correct design of purchased products	Characterizes difficulties in identifying requirements specifications precisely
Characterizes a supplier market not being totally exploited	Characterizes supplier strategies evolving differently from expectations
Characterizes possible alternative-design scenarios	Characterizes market structures with dominant suppliers
	Characterizes restrictive rules, standards and legal constraints
Opportunities	**Threats**

General mapping of procurement risks

Table 2.1 presents the different categories of risks specific to procurement and customarily referred to. A careful reading of this table highlights the following points:

- Certain risks tend to be concentrated in *upstream phases* and as a result, need to be integrated into the definition of procurement strategies, whilst others relate more to the *downstream operational deployment* of strategies, so handling of them involves measures to be controlled in the implementation phases.

- From another perspective, certain risks focus more on the *definition of requirements (specifications)* and associated problematics, whilst others relate to *external issues*, in other words the general procurement environment, market issues on a domestic or global level, as well as the characteristics of suppliers (strengths and weaknesses).

One final crucial point remains to be made: talk of 'risks' means seeing the negative dimension of the issue in question, with the implication that these may entail – if they are manifested – loss in efficiency or a possible 'destruction of value'. The positive flipside of this analysis consists in also identifying 'opportunities' offered to purchasers, and which may be used advantageously. We are therefore dealing with a *dual analysis*.

For example, because we operate in a strictly *European* supplier market, whilst development potential exists through *global* sourcing (provided that targeted countries do not represent major geopolitical risks, and possess and master the technology in question), the identification of limits to competition also allows for the detection of a major opportunity that needs to be confirmed and put into figures in terms of total cost of ownership (TCO). The same goes for innovation.

Internal risks and opportunities (requirements to satisfy)

There are many different points to examine here. Let's single out the major ones, for experience shows that these usually make up the appropriate analysis grid.

Choice and appropriate definition of the scope of the purchase

Astonishing as it may seem, sometimes internal clients have not truly thought about what they are actually looking for! The purchaser's role, in this case, is to adopt a systematic and positive critical approach, one that creates value. To illustrate this point, we can take the example of reprography.

Classically, a first procurement approach may involve procuring items separately and successively: photocopiers (based on the availability of user service and the quantity of photocopies to be made); then equipment maintenance and after-sales service; finally, consumable supplies and paper. Three separate purchases with recurring problems of compatibility between contracts and responsibilities.

A second solution would be to procure on the basis of 'a photocopied page in a predetermined paper quality and at a target maximum cost of €x,' supplemented by 'service' performance objectives in terms of intervention deadlines in case of breakdown (service-level agreement or SLA). In this case, the solution is expressed in terms of a total service with a cost target. The two solutions refer to entirely different things, and the chosen service provider for the second approach, by nature a service integrator, will not have the same profile as one found by the first approach. However,

TABLE 2.1 Typology of risks specific to procurement

Risk categories	Main factors
Operational risks Requirements and Suppliers	Quality of the specifications and control of the quality delivered (conformity) Complexity and durability of the technology purchased Commodity versus Requirement with particular requirements specifications Control of delivery lead times and associated services Transport issues and interface for logistics service providers
Strategic and tactical market risks	Durability of supply sources (to confirm and follow up) Possible change in the structure of upstream markets (competition versus oligopolies, agreements between vendors, etc) Imposed suppliers / single sources (internal or external) Possible dependency situations (eg patents)
Price risks Speculative phenomena	Possible volatility of market prices Speculative mechanisms on raw-material and energy markets Supply difficulties stemming from possible associated shortages or quotas
Financial and monetary risks	Fluctuations in currency exchange rates Imposition of unfavorable payment conditions
Legal risks (judicial, regulatory, case law)	Intellectual and industrial property / Possible counterfeiting Royalties / Image rights Abuse of dominant position (percentage of the suppliers' turnover) Illegal subcontracting / undeclared employment / call for aid-assisted or disabled work Control of end destination Banned products and materials (REACH, RoHs)
Geostrategic risks Countries or zones	Factors characterizing countries in the case of global sourcing (Different types of risks: political, economic, logistical, industrial, legal, cultural, or managerial, social and environmental practices)

TABLE 2.1   *continued*

Risk categories	Main factors
Natural and climatic risks	Critical mapping of zones according to climatic accidents (floods, storms, hurricanes, typhoons, tsunamis, etc)
	Evaluation of the exposure of the main industrial clusters targeted in the main 'sourceable' countries
CSR (corporate social responsibility) risks	Social responsibility (Global Compact, ILO)
	Ethical and societal responsibility (respect of commitments, transparency, anti-corruption behaviour)
	Environmental responsibility (ISO 14000, national laws)
	Global responsibility for upstream supply-chain practices (suppliers)

global acquisition costs will have been controlled by 'variabilizing' them completely – in other words, by transforming them into variable costs.

Commonality or specificity of a need

Whether a requirements (or needs) specification is standard or specific is a crucial point. Obviously, a requirement that is standard (on the market) raises no problems, in theory, in terms of availability, and the supplier market is very often most likely to be competitive. On the other hand, a specific requirement (based on particular requirements specifications) sometimes limits the potential market, entailing fixed costs relating to the development of the technical solution, as well the design and manufacturing of tools that cannot be amortized on the volumes purchased (as well as potential problems relating to the level of delivered quality).

Nature of the requirements specifications and drive for innovation

The key issue is to work out how the requirements specifications are to be defined and on the basis of which principles. Typical requirements specifications generally include at least the following elements:

- *'Technical' specifications*:
  - a description of the product or service defining specific technical criteria and quality standards expected;
  - a choice between a best-efforts commitment and an expected performance outcome;
  - specific non-economic characteristics;
  - quantities and the provisional delivery plan (definition of timeframe);
  - specific arrangements for the order (including evaluation criteria for the supplier(s)).

- *Financial characteristics*:
  - the price level targeted if operation is based on an 'objective' acquisition-cost (target-cost) logic;
  - a possible plan for improving supplier productivity;
  - the invoicing currency;
  - the desired payment terms and the desired Incoterms®.
- *Scope, obligations and associated services*:
  - preliminary investment/tooling (non-recurrent fixed cost);
  - expected additional services (maintenance, training, technical documentation, help with the setting up of operational implementation);
  - transport and packaging conditions (impact in terms of cost);
  - conditions for delivery check on reception and tests (quality-control method);
  - guarantee terms (after-sales);
  - service performance commitments (SLA) or measurable criteria for the respect of delivery lead-times);
  - backup solutions in the event of *force majeure;*
  - obligations on safety (or buffer) stock to keep (service-level objective);
  - obligations to plan updates/upgrades (eg for software versions);
  - requirements in terms of confidentiality of information before, during and after the purchase;
  - finally, expectations in terms of responsible and environmental practices.

One key question remains to be addressed: for a set category or purchase, should requirements specifications be drafted *in detail* or should these be expressed in *functional* terms? In the first case, internal clients or specifiers predetermine a technical solution and the company looks for a supplier who can deliver it without questioning it (*logic of conformity*). In the second case, only the functions to be met (associated with environmental and/or interface restrictions) are defined; the supplier is given the freedom to choose a technical solution and in this way, innovation is promoted (with the solution tending subsequently to be assessed on the basis of the balance between perceived value and cost of acquisition).

Fast-evolving technology

Certain requirements relate to products (or services) whose technology is subject to very fast evolution, as is the case of electronic components for which the lifecycle of a generation is around three years. In this type of situation, if a company's requirements cover a 10-year supply period, the purchase of several successive generations needs to be managed, entailing possible problems in repeated qualifications and often a multiplication of development costs encountered throughout the component's full lifecycle. Integration of this diagnostic from the outset in the choice of components and suppliers helps improve a company's control over the issues of future availability, solution portability and perceived global cost.

Requirements for eco-design and compliance with legal obligations

In terms of the definition of requirements, sustainable development principles apply as of the product design stage when the management of the product's 'end-of-life' needs to be addressed and a solution found. Risk analysis should also include this issue, for solutions available on the market will need to be selected in relation to this criterion, and the detailed costing will also need to be integrated in a TCO-type approach.

Moreover, as far as purchased products are concerned, their compliance with various consumer protection and security obligations regarding dangerous or carcinogenic materials will need to be ensured – ie by specifying requirements and specifications in relation to European and international regulations (ie REACH and RoHs).

Quantities purchased and recurring supply needs

Procurement becomes easier when a requirement is associated with significant quantities that reach volumes attractive to potential suppliers. Being a 'key account' changes many things: not only can favourable financial terms be obtained regarding the company's procurement activities, but it can also develop 'interest' amongst the supply based creating a dialogue between the business and its suppliers regarding the benefits to be gained from innovation projects and production development.

Recurring demand is another important element for any business, but in a globalized market efficient forecast and planning systems are imperative. The risk lies in the inability to anticipate, hence commit to medium-term volumes and accordingly find the means to make a contract on, for example, an annual or multi-annual basis.

Possible patent protection

There are of course situations where the company is obliged to integrate an external patented solution into its products, which imposes restrictions on the economic power balance with the supplier (aside from the effects of volume and long-term commitment) and leads to the company depending entirely or partially on this solution's technological innovations (eg the Intel Inside effect in office equipment and Bosch Inside for electronic injection in the car industry).

Confidentiality and intellectual property rights

Finally, any discussion on the procurement of specific products (and particularly for strategic segments) necessarily raises the issue of protection of information (strategic and technical) shared with suppliers, namely in the co-development and industrialization phases of a new solution.

At the same time, when a company commits to a co-development process, questions are always raised about the intellectual property status of developments and innovations. Ignoring and failing to anticipate them in a collaborative approach may lead to conflicts and divergences in the relationship, and may even result in major risks relating to counterfeit.

External risks and opportunities (upstream markets, suppliers, business environment)

From another perspective, portfolio segmentation should take into account the specifics of supplier markets so as to adapt management systems to the different types of risks encountered. Risks are related, on the one hand, to the competitive structure of the market (monopoly, oligopoly or genuine competition), and on the other hand, to the characteristics of the technologies used by the suppliers (forecast life duration, technology stability, range of technical competencies existing in the market, capability of suppliers' equipment, etc).

Several points thus need to be covered in any minimal risk analysis of this dimension of segmentation.

Competitive structure of the market

From the outset, it is necessary to correctly identify the market structure with an emphasis on specifically diagnosing the competitive or non-competitive nature of the supplier market.

A point that often proves tricky relates to oligopolistic markets where the recurring question is to determine whether there exists a real or potential 'concealed' agreement in the supplier market. Let's not delude ourselves: such agreements exist in some industrial and economic sectors. And even if they are not organized formally, it may be a case of 'alignment of commercial practices' that amounts to the same thing. In this case, the purchaser will need to devise the best solutions for unlocking the market, alone or in collaboration with other industry colleagues.

A company may also find itself in a single-source situation, whether as a result of circumstances or the imposition of a predetermined solution: in this case, the situation should be managed from the perspective of optimal control of a situation where serious dependency exists.

Offer/demand balance

At any given moment, market balances may be upset: we can shift from favourable situations for buyers, for example, created from the existence of an overcapacity of supplier production matched by a general drop in global demand, to situations where market tension will automatically spark off price hikes, temporary or longer-lasting shortages, or quotas determined by suppliers in strong positions. In such situations, it is obviously preferable to be a 'key account' rather than a second-tier supplier.

Another recognized problem is that of having a single supply source, either because of the state of the market or because of a solution imposed by the client's specifications: how should this restriction be managed? A similar problem may arise in a group of multi-BUs whose general management imposes a subsidiary as an exclusive supplier.

Technical analysis of the market

In parallel with a commercial analysis of the market, it is appropriate to undertake a thorough technical analysis, typically covering the following questions:

- What is the forecast life of the technology of the product that we are purchasing today?
- How much does a shift from Generation I to the following Generation II technology cost (ie the concept of 'portability')? What would be the consequences vis-à-vis our clients?

- Are there alternative technologies that allow us to review our product design with realistic cost avoidance objectives that help improve value proposition?
- Is access to innovation blocked by the existence of essential patents? How should we free ourselves from such restrictions?

Specialization or wide-scope ability of suppliers

This point is essential for a B2B marketer. It is obvious that, from the point of view of their commercial offers, not all suppliers have the same profile. Some are generalists with a wide catalogue, whilst others opt for a niche strategy and specialize in certain market segments. Analysing and segmenting all suppliers systematically allows them to be targeted according to company requirements and the globalization possibilities thus offered.

Social responsibility or environmental risk

Sustainable development and its practices occupy an increasingly important role today (Chapter 6 delves into these issues later). This has an impact on procurement largely via social, societal and environmental responsibility issues that need to be integrated into the research and qualification of individual suppliers or even countries of source (perhaps even on a global scale). The issues also need to be incorporated into the practices of procurement management teams themselves, ensuring at the very minimum adherence to legal, regulatory and case law obligations, whether national or international. Management may also voluntarily choose to align their practices with international standards along the lines of ISO 14000 or ISO 26000, for example, or with the top-level assessment standards of recognized certification agencies (such as Vigéo in France).

Other regulatory or legal restrictions

Some industrial sectors are highly regulated, such as pharmaceuticals, chemicals or food processing. Buyers should be aware of this and understand the restrictions that will necessarily weigh down on them, ie in terms of traceability and the stretching out of lead-times that may result.

But many legal issues need to be studied carefully. These concern obligations under French, European or international laws, such as risks relating to industrial or intellectual property or else to positions judged as potentially abusive via 'dominating' suppliers. Certain social risks specific to service procurement situations also need to be anticipated (such as illegal subcontracting or undeclared employment, in other words the black labour market). Let's remember that illegal subcontracting, in the case of technical assistance or outsourced services, is a situation in which the service-provider's employees are placed at the disposal of the client, who treats these employees as members of its own staff without facing up to any of the obligations. Obviously these two illegal employment situations should be eradicated and explicitly referred to in contracts.

Finally, according to French law dating from 2005, companies are obliged to employ a certain minimum proportion of aid-assisted or disabled staff members. The threshold is set at a minimum of 6 per cent of staff for companies employing more than 20 employees. Details and ways to respond are developed in Chapter 6.

International procurement in low-cost countries

The last point for discussion here is one which has taken on major significance in recent years: the situation created by international procurement in LCCs (low-cost countries or leading competitive countries). Dealt with in detail in Chapter 5, this approach brings with it specific risks relating, first, to the countries or geographical zones with which cooperation is sought, namely on political, economic, social, logistical (infrastructure), monetary, fiscal, legal and cultural levels.

In addition to these country risks, the analysis of risks specific to the suppliers must itself be refined by notions relating to distance, but also to technical and technological capacities, as well as managerial and organizational practices in relation to foreign companies.

All these risk factors (internal and external, commercial or technical) may be covered in pre-formatted checklists used systematically by ratings teams coordinated by buyers, thus allowing the method to be practised more easily. Table 2.2 provides an example of such a checklist.

2/2 Choice of procurement levers or action variables

The second major stage of the global procurement marketing process consists in selecting the procurement strategies differentiated according to the specific procurement segments identified in the previous analyses. Any strategy is composed of a selection of actions or levers, which when implemented together dictates the way in which the company will 'attack' the supplier market, or improve its 'requirements profile' so as to be in a prime procurement position.

The key point relies first of all on understanding and identifying what are called 'procurement levers'. Before making a comprehensive list of these, let's define two basic concepts: upstream procurement and downstream procurement.

2/2.1 Upstream and downstream procurement

If we look at the way in which a product's total cost price develops throughout the process of design, development and manufacturing of a product or a complex industrial system, we see that the bulk of the cost is often predetermined in the design and development phase by technical decisions taken by various stakeholders, internal clients and specifiers (whereas procurement expenses actually incurred describe the symmetrically opposite curve over the same time scale). Figure 2.4 illustrates this idea.

Indeed, in many industrial sectors, empirical observation shows that significant potential savings can thus be made.

Let's take the case of a manufacturer of electronic remote-transmission systems for military purposes. The chosen example concerns the development and production of a shelter (to protect a set of electronic equipment as well as its users on the battlefield). The price quotation for this ensemble incorporated fixed costs for studies, basic equipment, various developments, an electromagnetic 'hardening' treatment (insulation) and the module's transportability by plane.

TABLE 2.2   Typical checklist for internal and external risk analysis

Internal risks / constraints of a technical nature
1/ Expected level of quality difficult to specify
2/ Requirements specifications not expressed in functional terms (or else draconian)
3/ Supplier imposed by the technical departments
4/ No pre-existing value analysis
5/ Quality requested uncommon on the market
6/ Frequent modifications of the expected specifications
7/ No drive for standardization
8/ New purchase (no past history)
9/ Confidentiality of data
10/ Slowness of the qualification process

Internal risks / constraints of a commercial nature
1/ Imposed supplier / single source
2/ Lack of forecast of requirements
3/ No consolidation of requirements
4/ Required lead time too short
5/ Relevance of the procurement file
6/ Limited buying power (on the market – *to specify*)
7/ Imposed purchase price
8/ Lack of existing rating for the supplier(s) multi EUS
9/ Presence of a supplier in the company itself
10/ Supplier(s) in contract with multiple contributors companies

External risks / constraints of a technical nature
1/ Single technological source
2/ Permanently evolving technology
3/ Possible choice between several technical solutions
4/ Lach of market standards
5/ Restrictive regulations
6/ Unequal supplier performance
7/ Short life duration of products
8/ Technical dependence vis-à-vis suppliers

External risks / constraints of a commercial nature
1/ Current supplier ill-adapted to the sector
2/ Product not "targeted" for the supplier
3/ No real competition (risk of "a concealed agreement")
4/ Monopoly or oligopoly
5/ Limited production capacity on the market
6/ Minimum volume imposed on purchase (quantities quantities)
7/ Rigid distribution system
8/ Necessary transit through distribution
9/ Restrictive heterogeneous legislations
10/ Brands / patents / licenses
11/ After-sales obligations

SOURCE: adapted from Roger Perrotin, "Le marketing achats," *Les Editions d'Organisation, 2005*

FIGURE 2.4 Economic issues in upstream procurement

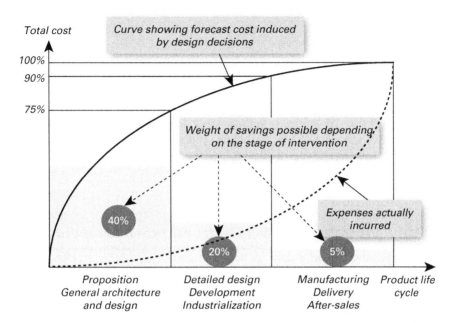

Taking all these budget items into account, the following were developed simultaneously: a so-called design-to-cost (DTC – analysed further in detail) approach including value analyses; client involvement in the approved adaptation of requirements specifications and hence automatically minimize the cost; and a co-development partnership with certain suppliers. In the end, compared with the preliminary quotation, the cost was finalized at 60 per cent of the initial 'unrevised' quotation.

Another example is found in an ensemble structured around a cathode-ray tube where final savings came to 38 per cent of the initial non-optimized quote. These real-life examples illustrate a significant potential for savings, also applicable in the procurement of services and performances. In all cases, if the procurement function intervenes in the early stages of the design process, savings 'via design and improvement of the requirements specifications' amounting to around 30 per cent of the cost can be made through its contribution. Otherwise, assuming that procurement only steps in downstream (in the classic approach, at the last phase of the process), its savings performance will only come to around 5 per cent, most often corresponding with the possible results of successful negotiation.

At the same time, it is crucial that the 'buyability' of an item, the component of a product for example, be assessed at the time of its technical selection. By 'buyability', we mean the minimization of a certain number of technical or market risks that the designer does not generally take into account. Indeed, the designer's motivation and own evaluation system almost exclusively direct him/her towards a drive for technical performance.

Which buyer has never found him- or herself in a single-source situation as a result of the selection of a non-standard component, whereas the designer should have been guided towards solutions that incorporated standard components? How many cases have arisen, where product choices are poorly steered through value-analysis processes due to technical ignorance of the supplier markets and their design or manufacturing capabilities?

In this way, in order for a company to be efficient, it needs to develop *upstream procurement that implies the effective participation of procurement departments in the design and development phases of products as well as in the definition of requirements specifications*, the objective being to develop a procurement portfolio that is optimized 'through design'. This approach guarantees that traditional procurement exercised downstream will then be carried out more easily and efficiently.

This approach entails a change in habits, and should be organized into a set of procedures with the use of specific procurement levers, given that the individuals in question (buyers, designers, design office engineers, internal clients) are not always accustomed to collaborating.

2/2.2 Main procurement levers and best purchasing practices

Once segmentation has been defined, the strategy for each procurement category consists in selecting a set of actions in order to reach the objectives set by general procurement policy (see Chapter 1). These actions correspond to levers that the buyer can and should play with, with a focus on those that seem to be priorities for the specific situation under analysis.

A generic list may be structured along two axes:

1 *Axis based on internal/external orientation*: it is possible to distinguish, on the one hand, levers for action relating to the requirement to satisfy and/or the procured product, and on the other hand levers relating to all possible actions directed at the upstream market as a whole or at potential suppliers in a targeted manner.

2 *Axis based on stages in the procurement process*: chronologically, certain levers are linked to upstream activities, and others are associated with downstream procurement practices. Then there are others that fall into the so-called 'post-procurement' phases that correspond to the stages of contract execution and operational implementation, under the responsibility of the supply chain, but during which the procurement function needs to set up reporting, database and knowledge management systems in order to prepare for the post-procurement implementation phase.

The levers that are the most used and practised in the professional world are presented in Table 2.3. Certain points are then reviewed in more in-depth commentaries. We have structured this presentation by combining the two axes.

Requirements-oriented internal levers

Levers relating to requirements or procured products and services include the following points:

- Regularly updating the *risks/opportunities analyses* to incorporate: 1) current and future requirements; 2) supplier markets and their evolutions.

- A 'procurement marketing' approach for each procurement family, to understand the issues and to identify the internal and external risks and opportunities with the aim of defining specific procurement strategies that are 'optimal' on economic and technical levels.

- In conjunction with internal clients and specifiers, setting up *technology intelligence* to identify requirements in information on future technologies (technologies, volumes, etc), and collect information on innovation forecasts and upcoming opportunities on upstream markets (with the identification of potential suppliers).

- Setting up a process for *defining requirements specifications* jointly with design and development services, or more generally with 'internal clients' (in the case of so-called 'non-production' or indirect purchases). This point refers to the necessity to specify a requirement in terms of the outcome to be reached, as long as these are expressed in a measurable manner (important for the procurement of services). In other cases, it aims towards standardized requirements specifications as guides to the expression of needs.

- Developing an *internal qualification* system to act as a screening process for new technological streams.

- Deploying a requirements *standardization approach* to avoid the multiplication of specific items procured by the company, with possible value-analysis or design-to-cost actions. The main aim is to 'comply better' with market standards and to give oneself the means to maximize procured volumes.

- From a quantitative point of view, implementing or improving a reliable *requirements forecast, globalization* and *planning* system. It is necessary to attempt to reach maximum quantities via consolidation to target the best possible power position for negotiation purposes. Globalizing also means seeking to group together complementary products or services procured from the same suppliers.

- Not hesitating to *outsource certain purchases* (an approach to develop in the context of risk analysis). The prime objective is to transfer a share of procurement (considered as non-strategic and/or standard and/or representing low value) to one or several external service-providers. The second is to free up buyers to focus on added-value tasks that represent their 'core activity'.

- Participating in *'make-or-buy' decisions*. Upstream in existing projects, or in design and development phases for new products, this involves assessing, from economic and strategic viewpoints, the possibility of outsourcing part of the company's own activities.

These points raise a few additional comments. Globalizing product requirements from a company's point of view means pooling the quantities that will potentially be procured independently by different units, in other words adding up the sums of purchases and also seeking – when relevant – to combine high-margin products and lower-margin products from the one supplier.

TABLE 2.3   The main procurement levers

	Knowledge of the market / Sourcing / Supplier relationships	Definition of requirements / Innovation / Internal client relationships
UPSTREAM PROCUREMENT (ANTICIPATION / DEVELOPMENTAL ISSUES) MID-TERM	Sourcing new suppliers Partially internationalizing the procurement portfolio (LCCs)	Technologically anticipating mid-term requirements (possible link with a mid-term technological plan)
	Constructing and managing the supplier panel Qualifying / homologating new suppliers	Specifying requirements in terms of required outcomes (functional specifications) it relevant Using a 'design-to-cost' approach
	Ensuring the sustainability of the sources	Promoting a simplification of requirements Seeking 'standard' market solution
	Setting up co-development partnerships	
	Contributing towards 'make-or-buy' choices	
	Outsourcing certain minor purchases (e.g. through global purchasing offices)	
	Analyzing / anticipating risks (markets / suppliers)	Analyzing / anticipating risks (procurement portfolio)
DOWNSTREAM PROCUREMENT (OPERATIONAL EXECUTION) SHORT-TERM	Segmented approach to the supplier panel	Segmented approach for the procurement portfolio
	Reduction of the supplier panel (if relevant)	Globalizing the requirements of business units / departments / divisions
	Setting up operational collaborations	Pooling (framework contracts)
	Making suppliers commit to results	Forecasting / planning needs over time
	Managing supplier performance (improvement plans co-defined with them)	Reasoning in terms of the global acquisition cost (or TCO)
		Convention (internal contractual approach)
	Setting up competition (call for tenders) / pre-selecting (if relevant)	
	Breaking down / Analyzing supplier costs (if relevant)	
	Negotiating (final phase often from a short list) / Deploying e-sourcing	
	Contracting (with a necessary focus on risk mitigation)	

TABLE 2.3   *continued*

	Knowledge of the market / Sourcing / Supplier relationships	Definition of requirements / Innovation / Internal client relationships
POST-PROCUREMENT	Setting up and managing a 'feedback' system	
	Rating supplier performance	Rating the satisfaction of internal clients and business partners
	Eliminating or putting 'under alert' defective suppliers	Deploying project summary reports (if relevant)
	Rating supplier satisfaction	

This is advantageous for suppliers in that they can amortize their fixed and/or developmental costs, benefit from a learning curve, and increase their market share with a given client.

This globalization should be supplemented by planning on requirements, which will allow the supplier(s) to guarantee supply, distribute workload more evenly over time, and better use their production capacity. Finally, quantitative globalization of requirements should, if possible, be accompanied by a reduction in the number of active suppliers having a consequential cumulative effect on the former.

External levers geared at the upstream market and suppliers

There are many levers relating to upstream markets and suppliers:

- Systematically carrying out *market studies* from a commercial or technological point of view.
- *Operating international sourcing.* Identifying potential suppliers for regenerating or expanding the supplier portfolio. A proactive approach for seeking new international sources, mainly for economic reasons (low-cost countries) or to take advantage of knowledge gained in certain global regions. Sometimes, this approach is carried out as a result of obligations regarding local suppliers imposed by the clients themselves (with or without countertrade obligations).
- *Qualifying new suppliers/constructing and managing the supplier panel.* A formal approach aiming to select potential suppliers on the basis of objective and verifiable criteria. The aim is to construct a panel of qualified suppliers that can, subsequently, be made to compete with one another via selective calls for tenders. When using this approach, the sustainability of supply deserves particular attention.

- Potentially *reducing the supplier panel*. The supplier base should be regularly optimized. In general, companies work with too many suppliers (as in the case of keeping on occasional suppliers, either due to a lack of any objective system for eliminating non-compliant suppliers, or quite simply to a classic resistance to change, fed by excuses of all types, that may ultimately be explained by an absence of courage or professionalism).

- Setting up *operational collaborative relationships*. A practice that consists in gradually directing suppliers towards an 'improvement plan' logic. This means looking for improvements over time in productivity or performance in the areas of quality assurance and logistics (supply chain). In doing so, apart from improving the satisfaction of internal clients, the buyer aims to reduce total cost (by reducing financial elements other than the sales price, ex-works in the strict sense of the term).

- Setting up *co-development partnerships*. Given, on the basis of the risks/opportunities analysis (see point above), that a company identifies different supplier profiles, this practice aims at looking for and setting up specific collaborative relationships (procurement of know-how and innovation from certain suppliers for co-development). Design-to-cost, supplier performance commitments on the basis of functional requirements specifications, and integration of suppliers to upstream projects, are the main elements of this approach.

- *Eliminating non-compliant suppliers*. If contractual corrective measures fail to result in a favourable outcome, non-compliant suppliers must be eliminated from the panel. This means banning them until they have successfully gone through the standard qualification procedure once again, following a recovery plan.

Final operational phase of the purchase (negotiation and contracting)

The main levers in this phase are the following:

- *Setting up competition via calls for tender* or any other classic consulting or electronic procedure (such as e-RFQs, possibly followed up by reverse auctions or e-auctions). As far as possible, proceeding via focused calls for tender, or even open ones (more rarely, except when compulsory as for public-sector markets). This approach requires comprehensive requirements specifications that include all elements that will then be referred to in the offer/selection rating process.

- *Cost breakdown analysis and management* of procured products. Necessitating, in the requirements specifications, that the price of a product or service be broken down into its constituent elements – the first objective being to check that the supplier understands the specifications, the second being to obtain the means to negotiate from a stronger position on the basis of 'identified batches,' or even to look for savings.

- *Negotiation on the basis of predefined tactical objectives*. A practice that expands the scope beyond commercial conditions alone. The buyer, with the help of the specifier and the user, must therefore define the sought-after objectives in advance.

- *Reasoning in terms of TCO*. This objective requires assessment of the economy of a purchase (product/service/equipment) by taking into account the global cumulative internal and external cost of the purchase up to its 'end-of-life', ie throughout its period of usage. This supposes evaluating risks, and anticipating and having access to an information system and an adequate TCO model.

- *Contracting on and controlling risks*. A practice justified by its making explicit the respective commitments of the two parties, this also allows definition in advance of all rules that will apply, beyond or during the delivery period, to corrective actions in the event of possible dysfunction. Optimization of the future logistics system should also be included in the contract, even if flow management is subsequently the operational responsibility of the supply-chain department.

A few additional comments can be made here. Setting up competition means consulting several suppliers in the market on the same basis (ie with the same requirements specifications), all potentially capable of supplying the sought-after product or service, from a technical (quality) and financial (minimum acquisition cost) viewpoint. In such an approach, the supplier's organization and their specialist knowledge may operate as a 'black box' for the company.

This is the type of relationship that a collaborative approach will seek to upset entirely, for in these conditions, the two players attempt to define improvement actions together, on the basis of transparency of information and a collaboration aiming to share risks and gains. In all partnerships, there is thus a notion of 'shared improvement'.

By 'cost analysis and management' as a lever for procurement, we understand the purchaser's capacity to break down (reconstitute) the production cost structure of a purchased product or service into its main components (cost breakdown). The objective is then to seek the most globally efficient supplier, or even collaborate with the supplier to diminish cost items, which may have a positive effect on lowering prices. The underlying aim of this approach is not primarily to find out the suppliers' margins in order to limit them in a dictatorial way, but rather to preserve them whilst diminishing the total cost of acquisition. This approach applies in particular to the case of procurement on the basis of particular requirements specifications, for example, industrial subcontracting operations.

In addition, the procurement function is often an efficient channel of information about competitors through the intermediary of suppliers. For example, if we learn that a competitor makes a particular choice on materials, this may mean that it has chosen one manufacturing process over another.

Execution of procurement contracts (supply)

The main levers of this phase no longer concern the procurement department directly but rather the supply or supply-chain divisions. Procurement may nonetheless be called upon in the event of disputes with suppliers, to contribute to their resolution.

Post-procurement phase

The main levers of this last phase are:

- Evaluating the *satisfaction of internal clients*. A key practice for objectively assessing user perceptions as a supplement to established 'technical' indicators. At the same time, this system becomes a communication tool for buyers.

- Measuring the *performance of suppliers*. A practice requiring the setting-up of a supplier performance measurement (vendor-rating) system, either periodically or ongoing in step with deliveries. A system aimed at taking all quick recovery measures, and also at updating the vendor-rating system. 'Field feedback' can be an interesting additional practice.

- Evaluating *supplier satisfaction* vis-à-vis the company. Symmetrical to the previous practice, and developed more recently (flowing on from sustainable procurement and reflecting the Industrial Relations Charter), this practice is in line with a collaborative-approach logic where joint satisfaction of the two partners is sought to enable simultaneous improvement of their efficiency. With certain so-called 'strategic' suppliers, the aim is to finish up with a shared business model. It is therefore useful to measure objectively how the suppliers perceive the company on a multi-criteria basis, not on the basis of promises made but on the basis of measureable results on all levels and commitments kept.

- Following up *commitments and inventories*. Although these partially flow on from decisions taken by logisticians and are followed up by financiers, buyers need to follow up all commitments and elements constituting the company's WCR in order to provide regular reporting on them (especially if they are responsible for a TCO, including actual financial costs for stocks and liabilities on all levels).

2/3 Definition of differentiated procurement strategies

Following in-depth analysis of the risks and opportunities, it is possible to analyse and model any procurement portfolio in the form of a matrix, as indicated by Figure 2.5, if we decide, for the sake of simplicity, to convert the initial problem expressed in a 3-dimensional space (see Figure 2.2) into a 2-dimensional representation (a single-risk scale synthesizing both internal and external risk values).[2]

2/3.1 Presentation of the generic matrix

For analysis purposes, we customarily break down the whole of a procurement portfolio into four macro-segments that group together all the procurement categories or families.

To simplify, the two lower groupings correspond to procurement categories associated with few risks, but that diverge in terms of the amounts purchased:

FIGURE 2.5   Matrix of alternative strategic issues

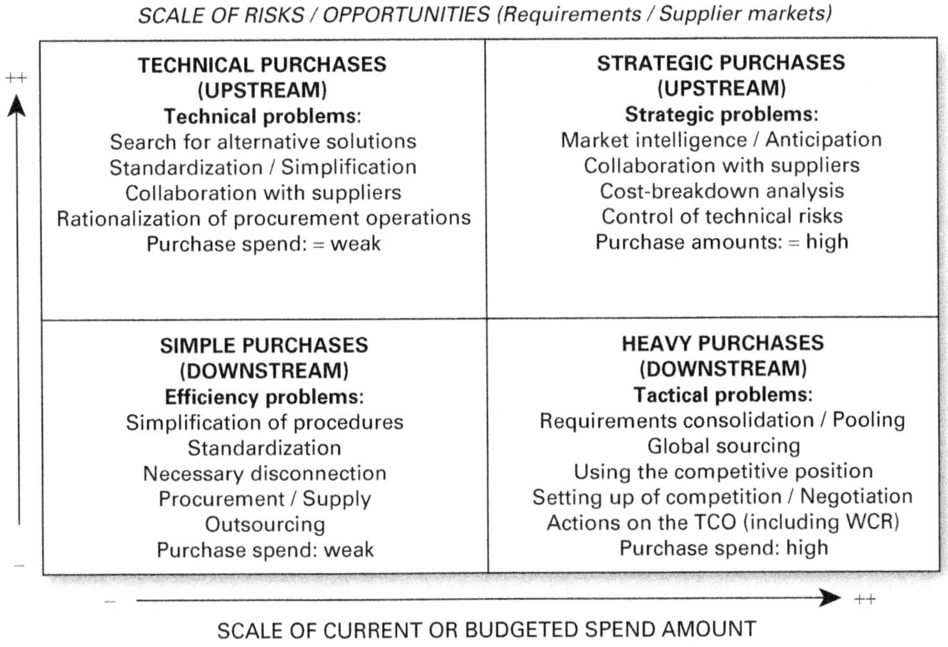

SCALE OF RISKS / OPPORTUNITIES (Requirements / Supplier markets)

TECHNICAL PURCHASES (UPSTREAM)	**STRATEGIC PURCHASES (UPSTREAM)**
Technical problems:	**Strategic problems:**
Search for alternative solutions	Market intelligence / Anticipation
Standardization / Simplification	Collaboration with suppliers
Collaboration with suppliers	Cost-breakdown analysis
Rationalization of procurement operations	Control of technical risks
Purchase spend: = weak	Purchase amounts: = high
SIMPLE PURCHASES (DOWNSTREAM)	**HEAVY PURCHASES (DOWNSTREAM)**
Efficiency problems:	**Tactical problems:**
Simplification of procedures	Requirements consolidation / Pooling
Standardization	Global sourcing
Necessary disconnection	Using the competitive position
Procurement / Supply	Setting up of competition / Negotiation
Outsourcing	Actions on the TCO (including WCR)
Purchase spend: weak	Purchase spend: high

SCALE OF CURRENT OR BUDGETED SPEND AMOUNT

- *'Complex' or critical purchases* are often standard direct purchases, situated very much at the 'core business'. They are characterized by the company occupying a strong position as a buyer in competitive upstream markets (player with a large 'purchasing volume'). The problem that arises does not lie in poorly oriented design or definition of requirements; it is reinforcement of the competitive position that is a priority, as well as minimization of the global cost of acquisition.

- *'Simple' purchases*, on the other hand, are made up of an extremely wide variety of purchases in low quantities, very often indirect in nature. The amounts in question are small, and the company is not in a dominant position in the supplier market. However, these purchases often consume a considerable amount of the buyer's time.

Most often, the solution lies in favouring the focused and efficient upstream intervention of the procurement department (targeting, for example, the definition of a product catalogue and a master service agreement following a call for tenders), then placing responsibility on users for allocated budgets, with supply being taken care of directly by them. The other solution involves entirely outsourcing the procurement of some of these non-critical families.

The two upper groupings (differentiated by their financial significance) are, on the other hand, made up of *highly technical or strategic* purchases operated on markets that are marginally (or not at all) competitive, but that are associated with very strong quality and technical demands:

- *'Strategic' purchases* may be composite categories, comprising specialized purchases with high development costs (technical parts or subassemblies, software development, etc) or standard purchases aimed at a narrow or highly volatile supplier market (eg raw materials). They are very often situated in the 'core business', and their handling mainly stems from the implementation of the most complex and sophisticated 'upstream' levers.

- *Technical purchases* are close to strategic purchases due to the existence of high technical risks, but differ from them as the financial risks for the company are lower. They do not contribute any differentiating added value to the company, and should therefore be rationalized.

Indeed, very often the same types of purchases are found here as previously, but the additional issue of resource management arises (the low value of these purchases does not allow, in theory, investment of as much time in extended and costly actions). A certain rationalization is therefore necessary, which may operate by a study of *standardization* options for all or part of the purchases in question.

Let's delve a little further into the analysis of strategies adapted to strategic and critical purchases, since the efficiency and competitiveness of the procurement function often depend on these.

2/3.2 The two basic procurement strategies

Let's examine in detail the principles behind the two strategies in question. Figure 2.6 is directly inspired by an approach developed years ago by AT Kearney, a reputed consultancy firm in the procurement field. The area on the left of the figure corresponds with so-called heavy purchases, the area on the right with so-called strategic purchases.

Heavy purchases

In this category, devoid of major risks but characterized by important economic stakes for the company, we generally find standard or 'customizable' purchases, commodities, or specific purchases for which supplier transferability is easy, not costly and relatively quick, as in the case of parts deriving from mature technologies with a broad and relatively competitive supplier market.

In addition, the company has a fairly dominant competitive position for procurement, and should seek to *reinforce this 'key account'-type position* via joint usage of the following levers:

- internal *globalization* (by a pooling of volumes to increase negotiating power), in conjunction with a reduction in the number of suppliers (to increase one's importance to each);
- *call for tenders* and the *setting-up of strong competition*, as well as detailed analysis of the structure of supplier cost breakdowns, are generally also important levers for creating conditions for adequate competition;
- *negotiation* (which must be vigorous) on prices and costs, contracts and agreements;
- *actions to reduce costs on all elements of the TCO*, namely the WCR (cost areas other than the strict ex-works procurement price);
- development of the supplier base (panel) to a wider scale, via international consultation and deployment to low-cost countries.

FIGURE 2.6 The essential procurement strategies

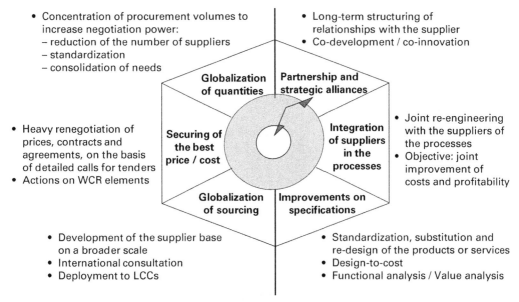

- Concentration of procurement volumes to increase negotiation power:
  - reduction of the number of suppliers
  - standardization
  - consolidation of needs

- Long-term structuring of relationships with the supplier
- Co-development / co-innovation

- Heavy renegotiation of prices, contracts and agreements, on the basis of detailed calls for tenders
- Actions on WCR elements

- Joint re-engineering with the suppliers of the processes
- Objective: joint improvement of costs and profitability

- Development of the supplier base on a broader scale
- International consultation
- Deployment to LCCs

- Standardization, substitution and re-design of the products or services
- Design-to-cost
- Functional analysis / Value analysis

Globalization of quantities

Partnership and strategic alliances

Securing of the best price / cost

Integration of suppliers in the processes

Globalization of sourcing

Improvements on specifications

Formalization driven methodology advocated by A.T. Kearney

In this way, levers customarily used in this procurement category tend to be in line with *'downstream' procurement* logic.

Strategic purchases

For strategic purchases or purchases associated with major risks or made from a very narrow and technical market, namely all those made on the basis of a company's specialized specifications, we seek to *promote differentiation* whilst *seeking cost control via design* with the following priority levers:

- *technology watch* that should feed the internal innovation process;
- *qualification* of suppliers who can be characterized as 'innovative' and the constitution of an *appropriate limited panel*;
- structuring of *medium- and long-term relationships* with suppliers according to *cost- and gain-sharing* mechanisms if possible, matched by *contracting* to guarantee the securing of the desired product and service performances (through payment terms, penalties, exit or reversibility clauses, etc), such as the long-term commitment to conditions, ie economic;
- frequent implementation of *co-development* processes with the possible application of *design-to-cost* approaches, also integrating *analysis of the costs of technical solutions* that are jointly developed according to a *shared business model*;
- clear and formalized handling of joint *intellectual property* and *innovation protection* should be carried out along with potential patent registration and remuneration mechanisms;

- in parallel, it is necessary to consider *standardization* or *product substitution* approaches via the redesign of products or services, or even the classic implementation of functional analysis and *value analysis*.

In the case of standard strategic purchases made in volatile markets, *market intelligence*, in other words the capacity to understand probable or possible evolutions of supplier markets, is generally decisive for the 'coverage' of short- or long-term purchases – either through mid-term supplier contracts (again), or the implementation of financial management (hedging) tools, mastered internally or with the help of financial partners (a topic tackled in Chapter 12).

This is therefore a case where 'upstream' levers are implemented, resulting in the simplification of the operational procurement phases, as well as the possibility of reducing ultimate costs.

2/4 The procurement process: a dynamic vision of procurement strategies

In the daily life of companies, the strategic and operational procurement approaches considered above are organized sequentially around a typical procurement process, as shown in Figure 2.7.

FIGURE 2.7 Main stages of the procurement process

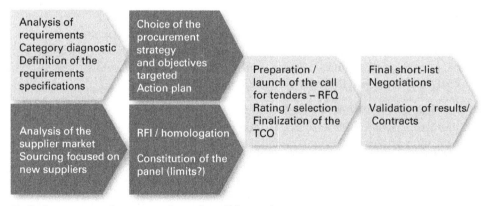

Preliminary approach upstream from the call for tenders

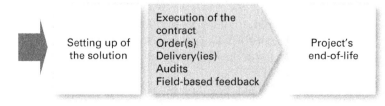

2/4.1 General presentation of the process

This section presents, in *chronological* and *dynamic* fashion, the major stages systematically covered for all purchases of significant size (ie during the renewal of a contract). The main stages are:

- upstream, we observe two parallel processes: an analysis of requirements resulting in a target procurement strategy; and market analysis resulting in the constitution of a supplier panel;
- next (in a timeframe programmed to satisfy the particular need, or to renew a contract coming to an end), preparation and launch of a call for tenders, followed by the rating of offers and selection of one or several suppliers if a final negotiation is desired (a shortlist situation);
- the negotiation phase, with the drafting and signing of the contract;
- implementation of the solution, possibly including, for a specific requirement, integration of all of the supplier's development and pilot-series stages;
- finally, the post-procurement phase, including deliveries and all on-the-ground feedback, with the settling of possible disputes, finishing with management of the product's end-of-life (recycling or recovery for destruction without environmental impact).

Two possible management levels (on two different horizons)

Certain stages (indicated in turquoise on the diagram) can be carried out independently of a particular call for tenders, for the simple reason that often they follow an unchangeable process: their implementation time – if it were necessary to wait for a call for tenders to follow its course – would be too long to allow for satisfactory performance.

Indeed, it is rare for a procurement manager to completely revise his/her segmentation simultaneously with a complete redefinition of procurement strategies.

This is why contract renewal and preparation for calls for tenders are ideal opportunities for partially adapting and updating procurement strategies tactically for all of the portfolio's families, without entirely challenging their basic logic choices (which are by their nature more long-lasting).

2/4.2 More detailed analysis of the key stages

Let's go back over some of these phases and describe their content.

Analysis of requirements

This phase is important, for a professionally managed purchase begins with a clear definition of requirements. The following actions should be undertaken and information gathered and analysed:

- understanding the structure of the activity (specificity of requirements);
- estimating the total amount of purchases and the amount's components;

- collecting detailed information on forecast volumes for the purchase to be made, as well as technical specifications and restrictions, the history of purchase prices, and the range of requirements;
- understanding and defining the main 'cost drivers'[3] from the known or reconstituted total cost structure;
- segmenting the family into sub-categories (in the case of procurement of a set of sub-families such as electronic components, themselves broken down into specific parts, etc);
- analysing internal risks and opportunities (technical and commercial);
- defining exploitation, legal and economic restrictions in such a way to ensure that they will be respected.

Selection of the procurement strategy

The aim here is to draw conclusions from the analysis of risks to select a procurement strategy as seen earlier in the chapter, taking into account the company's competitive position on the upstream market.

Sourcing and constitution of the supplier panel

This point will be covered in detail in Chapter 4.

Call for tenders and selection of the supplier(s)

This stage assumes that competitive suppliers have been professionally identified, with a multi-criteria evaluation and rating system for the offers. These principles will be developed in Chapter 10.

Negotiation and contract

Only at this point will the buyer's negotiation skills come into play, whilst many managers still reduce procurement to this type of activity alone (forgetting the whole procurement marketing upstream approach that is far more powerful and effective!)

Implementation of the solution

This stage raises no problems for a standard purchase as it consists in immediately executing the commercial terms specified in the contract. However, for procurement based on special specifications, the operation needs to be carried out over a number of deployment and implementation phases:

- implementation of the technical solution (with supplier quality assurance, FEMCA, product quality assurance- type approaches);
- a multi-stage process of product qualification and production: tooling, prototyping, production of industrial samples, pre-series and pilots, including the fine-tuning of quality assurance systems for the manufacturing process;
- once the production phase has started, systematic follow-up of supplier performance (delivery lead-times and quality as a minimum);

- various quality audits, as well as audits in relation to effective continued adherence to CSR rules (in relation to sustainable development);
- in case possible problems arise, implementation of short-term recovery plans and possible measures to 'alert' the contracted supplier if no significant recovery appears within a short timeframe;
- in the worst cases, a measure to 'permanently remove' the supplier from the supplier panel.

Notes

1 See Perrotin (2005), still a reference work.

2 This matrix is inspired directly by the already dated research by Kraljic (1983), the first portfolio purchasing model ever published.

3 We call *cost drivers* those elements that determine costs making up the cost prices of procured products or services. Familiarity with cost structures is helpful for then focusing attention on the means to achieve reductions in purchase prices. This is a key tool in the subsequent negotiation phase. It is one of the main motives that leads to using the procurement lever seen previously: *cost breakdown analysis and control.*

03
Definition of requirements and upstream procurement practices

As shown briefly in Chapter 2, we define 'upstream procurement' as the set of procurement actions and practices characterizing the direct intervention of the procurement department during the design and development phases of new products, and more generally its role in defining requirements specifications. This approach always involves buyers in the development and definition of requirements, during which they can defend their own viewpoint.

As far as the design of end-products is concerned, the focus is clearly on *direct procurement*, in other words all purchased materials, components, subassemblies and services that comprise the company's finished products.

However, all procurement, *even indirect*, also includes an upstream stage: that of the definition of requirements and the development of specifications. Here too, buyers may quite rightly be called on to intervene, by influencing decisions in favour of the company as well as all actors involved in the requirements definition process.

Who exactly are these different actors? They have a range of profiles depending on their role in the process:

- *internal clients*, in other words the beneficiaries of the purchase, who may be, for example, managers of functional or profit centres across all functions or divisions;
- if the process is managed within a project-based organization structure, the internal client is the *project manager* him/herself;
- a number of *specifiers* who may be involved in *technical and economic feasibility studies*, and then in development stages (design office, research and development department, finance department or management control).

In this way, from the outset we can see that upstream procurement (as opposed to downstream procurement) is not an area where procurement departments practice their profession independently of other actors; on the contrary, it is typically a *collective process* where each actor has a particular viewpoint to assert, and specific objectives or constraints to defend.[1]

This explains why it is appropriate to first analyse the organizational context in which the upstream procurement must or can occur.

3/1 Innovation, design and upstream procurement

]It is always possible to take an 'upstream' approach to procurement. However, this is greatly facilitated if the company has set up two systems: formal management of the product lifecycle and the process for new product design and development; and project-based organization to manage the whole of this process.

3/1.1 The stakes in new product design

The stakes associated with creating new products are considerable for companies. Managers have to make decisions when faced with several opposing factors (see Figure 3.1), and determine either: a) to take longer over development – the design department can then create higher-performing products, and it can also optimize product cost but development costs will be higher; or b) increase the resources allocated to a project and spend more on development – this allows higher-performing products to be created but these costs will have an impact on direct product costs.

FIGURE 3.1   Performance criteria in new product design

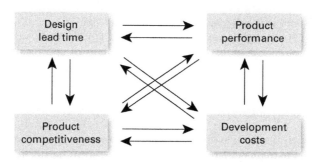

Development costs for new technologies and products are constantly on the rise (eg the creation of a new car model costs around €1 billion). Product design processes require the acquisition of new individual and collective skills, along with the mastery of new tools. These efforts should match efforts made right across the industry sector.

In this way, whenever competitors in an industrial sector make improvements in manufacturing performance, competition partially changes ground. A new challenge arises: that of being in a position to introduce innovations on the market as quickly as possible, making sure that products are developed effectively 'at the first strike' whilst keeping cost prices low and quality high.

Gradual constitution of total cost

It is long before manufacturing starts that purchase and production costs are determined by the selection of functionalities offered to the client, purchased materials and components, as well as the elected manufacturing methods. This predetermining of costs may be illustrated by Figure 3.2 (already seen as Figure 2.4 but replicated here).

FIGURE 3.2   Product design process from an economic viewpoint

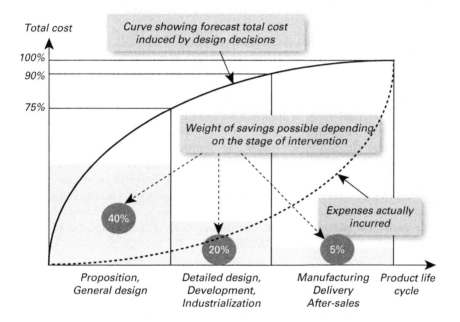

The three main stages of product development are shown on the horizontal axis of this diagram: design, development/industrialization and production. The vertical axis shows a cost scale expressed in cumulative percentages.

The upper curve depicts the evolution in the proportion of a product's total *anticipated* industrial cost, which is definitively 'fixed' by the decisions taken at each of the design and development stages. In this way, we can see that 75 per cent of a product's total future cost is determined by design decisions taken during the general design stage. This percentage rises to 90 per cent if such assessment is undertaken at the end of the industrialization stage.

The lower curve shows the corresponding evolution in the expenses *actually incurred* by the company over the same timescale. During the initial stages of development (in which 'everything is played out' with respect to the direct cost of the product 'in the long run'), the company spends little: human resources are highly skilled but limited in number; IT and simulation systems are used but there are few or no purchases, and no onerous industrial investment as yet.

There is therefore clear economic interest in focusing on product optimization research as early as possible in the process, the potential benefits being significant and the associated costs low. To illustrate this point, three percentages are specified in the diagram, showing for each main stage the magnitude of potential gains in the product's competitiveness.

Importance of short development cycles[2]

Developing products over a shorter lead-time expedites the rate of product renewal, thus better meeting client expectations. For example, when a company introduces a new product onto the market six to twelve months before its competitors, it can gain market share and generate *cash flow* earlier than the competition can. Steps to reduce cycles can also give rise to various competitive advantages depending on the company's competitive situation.

If the market – the company client (in B2B) or individual customer (in B2C) – agrees, and with no change to the date of the product's launch onto the market, the extra time set aside for the design stage can be put to good use to optimize the product by investigating a greater number of technical configurations in alternative designs. In this way, a company's capacity to develop optimized products within shorter cycles gives it the possibility of taking a technological lead in the sector, potentially establishing new standards.

By shortening development cycles, the company also secures the option of fast-tracking the launch date of a new product onto the market. Compared to the competition, the company naturally generates strong cash flow. It can also, after a certain number of successive product developments, be one 'technological generation' ahead, and as a result, gain a dominant market position. The automotive industry provides many examples along these lines (innovations in electronics, driver-assistance systems and safety equipment in particular).

Development costs

Development costs are to a large extent proportional to development cycles, owing to the predominant contribution of 'brain power' to the total cost – hence the importance of acting on lead-times, which enables, as a result, improvement in the return on investment into research and development.

3/1.2 Project-based organization and product lifecycle

The aim here is not to consider – in all its dimensions – project management and project-based management (splitting the project into sub-sections, organization of project teams, project planning, monitoring cycles and budgets, streamlining workloads and resources, information systems and management, etc).[3] However, the two following points should be emphasized: a) the course of any project should be broken down into 'macro-stages' which define a sequence to which the project's management should refer; and b) it is necessary to speed up the development process in such a way as to shorten design lead-times and expedite placement on the market of the product or service to be sold.

General sequencing of a project

The planning of every project should entail its organization into key stages. This process should be standardized in such a way that it is qualified (in the ISO sense of the term), and the following points understood and mastered:

- the nature of each stage, with a detailed list of decisions to be taken (necessitating the forecasting of the number of compulsory inter-stage project reviews throughout the process);
- a list of actors and contributors for each stage, specifying their contributions to decisions (information input, simulations, economic valuations, feasibility studies, tests, etc);
- the nature of accounting or other information systems used;
- the nature of the decision-making process and arbitration approach (respective roles of contributors and decision-making rights of the project manager).

To illustrate a multi-stage project process, we refer to Figure 3.3, based on a French systems supply company (designer and seller of complex civil and military equipment) that operates via calls for tenders on the international market.

A firm that designs and handles a *catalogue of finished products* will improve these products on the basis of either new client demands identified by the marketing department, or internal innovations that it offers to the market. Upstream of the product design stages themselves (the so-called 'upper upstream'), there is therefore a stage of pure innovation based on scoping and feasibility studies.

With regard to a company whose business is based on one-off complex projects, the scenario is similar. In this case, the company has no catalogue of finished goods, but its know-how is based on a portfolio of mastered technologies. If it is recognized as being technically competent, it can receive an invitation to tender for a specific undertaking. The so-called 'upper upstream' consists, in this case, in the company deciding whether or not it should respond to the invitation to tender in order to preserve its profitability, taking into account the assumptions and price forecasts likely to apply to this deal.

This diagram shows the various major existing project stages along with project reviews and necessary intermediate decisions. It does not show the detail of each stage, each of which comprises its own potentially iterative sub-processes.

Upstream of product manufacturing, the procurement management needs to be involved throughout the process, including the upper-upstream stage, to contribute to the response to the call for tenders. The specific contributions of the procurement department at all these stages will be discussed later on.

Acceleration of development processes and concurrent engineering

We have covered the traditional process that can be described as 'sequential', and thus determining the overall R&D lead-time. More often than not, this includes

FIGURE 3.3 Typical process in a call-for-tenders deal sequence

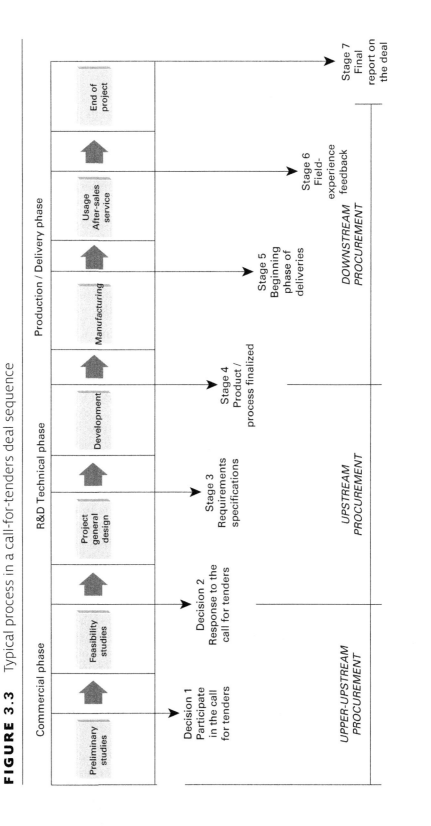

back-loops for internal or external negotiations, and for the development of viable solutions that represent compromises.

This process is often too long for the client's needs. We have shown the strategic importance of short development cycles; this is the reason why the traditional approach needs to be modified and accelerated. This will require successive overlapping phases, with one project stage commencing before the previous stage has finished, as shown in Figure 3.4.

Using this approach, we can carry out tasks concurrently to speed up the processes of each stage (without, however, contravening the principle of intermediate project reviews between stages themselves, the responsibility of the project manager). The term used to describe this is 'concurrent engineering', whereby we seek to organize a process so that the execution of research and development tasks overlaps instead of being sequential.

FIGURE 3.4　Concurrent engineering development process

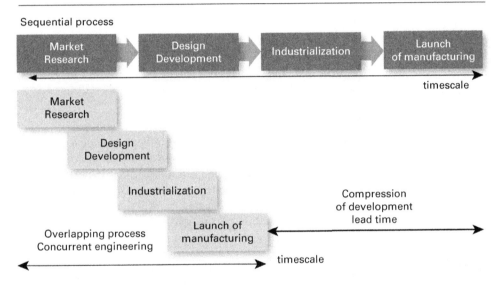

This approach to structuring development implies knocking down the traditional walls separating a company's various departments, in favour of teamwork and rapid identification of solutions acceptable to the whole company. Managing lead-times is also greatly facilitated by intelligent use of well-known planning methods such as project evaluation and review technique (PERT) or critical path method (CPM), and more generally, project management approaches directed by the project manager.

3/1.3 Disruptive or incremental innovation/open innovation

It is vital to understand the difference between disruptive and incremental innovation, as it is vital to company growth and has a major impact on the potential contribution that can be offered by the procurement function.

Disruptive innovation

This concept is based on the research of Clayton M Christensen.[4] Disruptive innovation can most often spur two types of developments:

1 Building on an existing market by introducing a *new technology* that fulfils functions and offers performance that traditional technology does not fulfil or that it delivers less successfully. This was the case with digital technology replacing film-based cameras.

2 Creating a *new market* through the use of *pre-existing or emerging technologies*, refocused to give birth to new products or applications that may or may not replace solutions already in place. This was the case with container ships that, to a significant extent, have replaced earlier forms of transport. It was also the case of tablets introduced by Apple, based on pre-existing technologies but combined for the first time to create a new product concept, and a new resulting market – which incidentally has not completely wiped out the market for traditional PCs.

Disruptive innovation is *essential*. It is a powerful means of differentiation from a competitive standpoint. It is very often *pushed* by the producer and not requested by the client: what client would have spontaneously expressed the need for a smartphone before inventors proposed and proclaimed them as a revolutionary and groundbreaking communications solution?

Incremental innovation

In contrast, incremental innovation is concerned with constantly *improving* a product, service or technical solution, by successive increments and in a (quasi)-*continuous* manner. This type of innovation is generally carried out not to directly develop new markets, but rather to improve product performance (with an impact on the company's relative market share), largely by lowering purchasing or production costs. In this way, the objective is more directly value creation to improve competitive standing, and (above all) to increase profit margins.

Open innovation

Another more recent term, *open innovation*, is based on the work of Henry Chesbrough.[5] It is based on the theory that value-creating ideas can come from outside as much as from inside a company, and that such ideas may be as useful for internal markets as external ones. The principles of open innovation are:

- developing multiple ways to identify new technologies (finding an idea within the company, enhancing it externally; seeking the idea externally, enhancing it internally and bringing it to the market; developing new markets by investing in start-ups);

- not simply investing in new technologies but also incorporating external know-how;

- finding help from innovative firms to explore the company's potential future interests;

- making research results (sales, purchases, licenses, etc) available to external parties rather than leaving them unused.

Thus defined, we can see *open innovation* as an approach that is typical of a disruptive innovation process which coordinates a mix of new ideas, largely supplements its system by calling on external service-providers or suppliers, and seeks above all to develop discoveries (whether they are directly used by the company or not).

To achieve this, it is important to adopt methodological tools for the generation of ideas, exchanges and the sharing of information (collaborative tools, dedicated platforms, etc). In addition, a company practising open innovation needs to be very open-minded and review its approach to the notion of 'boundaries', as well as structure itself in such a way as to be able to identify ideas originating from multiple sources. Regarding innovation service-providers or external suppliers, these may either be: existing suppliers already on the supplier panel but who have a strong 'innovator' profile (see Chapter 4 on this topic); primarily (indeed mostly) collaborations with entities (specialized research centres, universities with academic research centres, start-ups, public–private partnerships, links with competitiveness clusters/hubs etc) more in line with the company's approach. These collaborators may not become suppliers in the later exploitation stage, but their skills are well organized to target innovation.[6]

From an organizational point of view, most often a company developing this approach will do so by creating structures dedicated to this activity, and which may even be turned into subsidiaries, so as not to interfere with existing structures more suited to managing a main activity that is already well identified and stabilized, with clear-cut but formal processes.

The question that remains to be asked is whether a company's procurement management is in a position to bring true added value to this type of disruptive innovation process, eventually crossed with an open innovation-type approach. In reality, the answer is not entirely, or even not at all. In addition, academic research into this area is only at its early stages.

This explains why the procurement practices that are presented in the rest of this chapter correspond more with incremental-type internal innovation, or disruptive innovation in the form of highly controlled internal solutions, relying essentially on existing strategic suppliers.

3/2 Scope and specific practices of upstream procurement

In this innovative project context, upstream procurement should find its place by attempting to avoid a certain number of unfortunate situations that are all too frequent:

- designs managed exclusively by technicians (whose priority is to seek the 'beauty' of the technical solution, ie performance), that result in often large selections of *specific or rare components*, difficult to find on the market, raising *problems in the durability* of supply sources;

- choices of technologies that later raise problems in *transferability from one generation to another* on the supplier market, entailing *additional costs* – a problem that technicians sometimes fail to anticipate due to a lack of understanding about the possible evolution of supplier R&D policies;

- and finally, choices of products reaching *the end of their lifecycle on the market*, whose availability will quickly become a crucial problem, possibly necessitating *redesigns* that may have been avoided, and entailing new delays and additional development costs.

In this way, upstream procurement is always guided by two core objectives: guarantee of the future availability of purchases by controlling all supply risks, and at the same time, ensuring the competitiveness of purchases whose value can be enhanced in the long term (via decisions made today).

We will now turn to a detailed and systematic analysis of these different risks, already tackled more broadly in Chapter 2 of this work.

3/2.1 Procurement risks associated with product design

As Figure 3.5 shows, buyers should focus their attention on three different dimensions:

1 risks associated with the product or the service being purchased, and resulting from the precise definition of the requirement;

2 risks relating to the characteristics of the supplier market from a global perspective;

3 risks relating to the suppliers themselves, as well as their profiles and know-how, with regard to the policy on suppliers required by the company.

Definition of requirements

In this area, the following questions need to be raised:

- In the case of a particular purchase, is it appropriate to define our requirements in the form of detailed requirements specifications (an approach that necessarily assumes that we envisage a specific technical solution) or do we seek innovation from our suppliers (an approach that invites suppliers to meet functional requirements specifications by putting forward a new solution associated with an acquisition cost to be specified)? Also, if we set a target for the supplier to achieve, are we capable of describing the 'standard' for the performance commitment precisely?

    This question is particularly tricky to address when it comes to the procurement of services. For example, in the case of the purchase of cleaning services, this means specifying a 'standard of cleanliness' that we wish to obtain. But in the case of the purchase of continuing education services, what might be the relevant quality criteria if we speak of a performance commitment?

- Another very common risk is the following: has the internal client defined its requirements 'as tightly as possible', or does the company risk 'over-quality', often translated into high and unnecessary costs? This is for example the case

FIGURE 3.5 Main risks justifying upstream procurement

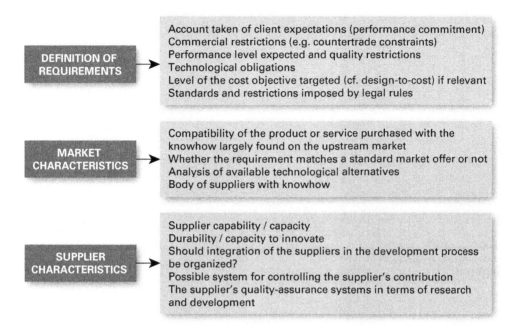

when draconian requirements are put forward in the interests of 'absolute security' (so-called 'zero defects') when few suppliers are able to fulfil them as special equipment is required.

- Has the scope of what we are buying truly been defined? Let's take the example of a CapEx purchase (a capital-investment item such as a piece of industrial equipment). Do we purchase a production line, and then buy spare parts and maintenance services separately? Or do we purchase a complete service from a single supplier over a long-term period to be defined, which would amount to purchasing one hour of an available machine at a global cost to be minimized, with SLA (including availability and service rates) conditions clearly defined from the outset and subsequently monitored? These are two very different approaches.

- Do companies whose business involves responding to international public calls for tenders automatically face countertrade-type obligations? This means that part of the system that they sell must, in exchange, be produced by *local companies* to which it is often necessary to transfer technology. In this case, it is necessary to look for competent local suppliers, and in many cases, tightly monitor their industrial and quality assurance systems.

- Some other key questions arise. Do we wish to set a target cost objective, and in what form? What decisive elements and vital points does this encompass?

FIGURE 3.6 Evolution of procurement risks according to a technology's position on its life curve

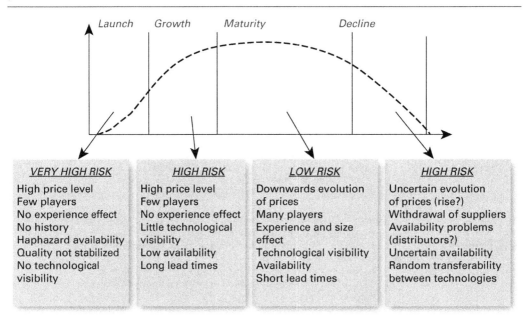

VERY HIGH RISK	*HIGH RISK*	*LOW RISK*	*HIGH RISK*
High price level	High price level	Downwards evolution	Uncertain evolution
Few players	Few players	of prices	of prices (rise?)
No experience effect	No experience effect	Many players	Withdrawal of suppliers
No history	Little technological	Experience and size	Availability problems
Haphazard availability	visibility	effect	(distributors?)
Quality not stabilized	Low availability	Technological visibility	Uncertain availability
No technological	Long lead times	Availability	Random transferability
visibility		Short lead times	between technologies

What real economic leeway exists? What possible *incentives* should be offered to suppliers?

- Is the technology that we envisage choosing positioned well on its life curve? Can a following generation be anticipated? To illustrate this important point, we refer to Figure 3.6 that illustrates the evolution of risks according to a technology's position on its life curve. The reader is invited to draw the main principles from the diagram without any additional commentary being made here.

Characteristics of suppliers

We will develop the issue of suppliers in more detail in Chapter 4. Here, however, we can raise the types of questions to ask ourselves (readers will find detailed justifications of these various questions further on):

- For all of our procurement categories, do we have a specific idea of the supplier profiles that we need? Do we wish for global or local suppliers (with the idea of using a pooling approach, but also benefiting from supplier proximity that offers greater responsiveness)? To illustrate this idea, let's take the example of an industrial cleaning, security or temporary staffing operation, or anything else that falls within the category of 'local services'. This purchase may be internationalized even if each of the company's subsidiaries wishes to individually use a service-provider located close to its site, hence benefiting from broad flexibility. Indeed, there are international suppliers that have numerous national subsidiaries and local agencies. In this case, we can benefit from the advantages of reactivity whilst guaranteeing the possibility of globalization of volumes along with homogeneity in the quality standards of services. We can also break down a global framework contract into local versions.

- Do we have reliable and verified information on current suppliers in terms of their technological and R&D capabilities? Can they operate according to co-development principles in conjunction with the company's teams?
- Are there any 'blacklisted' suppliers, and for what reasons? Can we help them – and in what way can we help them – develop in order for them to be approved?
- Do we really have good visibility of the innovative nature of suppliers' projects? Are we attractive enough to suppliers and considered by them as an ethical 'key account' client that respects commitments?
- Do we have real knowledge of how costs are broken down, and do we have an economic model for reference at our disposal?
- Are the company's suppliers (current or potential) capable of being organized according to the project management principles? Are they truly organized in this way?
- Do the company's suppliers (current or potential) offer guarantees in terms of durability and management quality?

3/2.2 The three basic principles of upstream procurement

Following on from the above, upstream procurement should be organized around three major basic principles summed up in Figure 3.7:

1 Carrying out systematic and in-depth analysis of the three categories of risk seen above.

2 On every possible occasion (at least for purchases said to be 'technical,' 'strategic' or 'standard major purchases'), systematically setting a target cost objective that serves as a guide in the search for solutions.

3 Finally, at least for all purchases meeting the company's specific requirements (ie excluding commodities), and even for services, always endeavouring to involve suppliers in the innovation and R&D approach in line with operational collaboration or co-development principles.

Two levels of intervention

For procurement management, there are *two main levels* of intervention in the innovation and product design approach: Level 1 concerns management of the technology portfolio, and/or management of the company's technical database and products; Level 2 relates to the design and development of a new finished product, considered individually, that needs to be optimized in a compromise between overall cost on the one hand, functionalities and performance on the other.

FIGURE 3.7   The three basic principles of upstream procurement

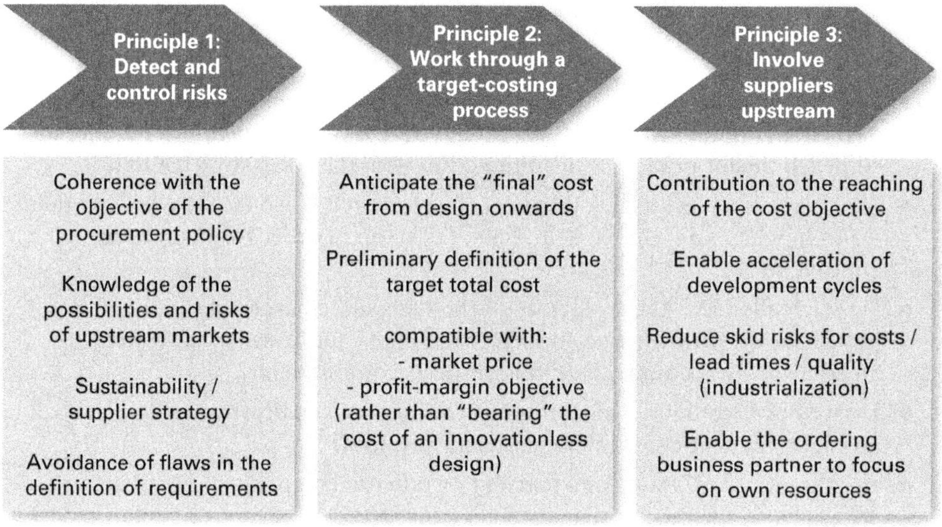

Principle 1: Detect and control risks	Principle 2: Work through a target-costing process	Principle 3: Involve suppliers upstream
Coherence with the objective of the procurement policy	Anticipate the "final" cost from design onwards	Contribution to the reaching of the cost objective
Knowledge of the possibilities and risks of upstream markets	Preliminary definition of the target total cost	Enable acceleration of development cycles
Sustainability / supplier strategy	compatible with: - market price - profit-margin objective (rather than "bearing" the cost of an innovationless design)	Reduce skid risks for costs / lead times / quality (industrialization)
Avoidance of flaws in the definition of requirements		Enable the ordering business partner to focus on own resources

The *first point* is a matter of carrying out ongoing research and development of the new technologies that will be necessary in the future, and that the company will need to purchase (if it has decided not to keep the skills in-house). It is also a matter of designing products on a modular basis, so that the design of modules (functions or subassemblies) can be optimized independently from the products in which they will later be integrated.

To take an example from the automotive industry, the development of new direct-injection or lighting systems (as well as the development of new energy-saving tyres, or LED headlights) has not been carried out in relation to a particular vehicle model, but in the framework of a medium-term technology plan, with close collaboration between equipment suppliers and vehicle manufacturers.

Similarly, development of standard platforms shared by the different models of a product line, or the constitution of a 'bank of equipment,' are not carried out with a particular product in mind, but with the idea of systematic reuse when successive vehicles are developed.

As far as the *second point* is concerned, everything is based on commercial and functional requirements specifications for the new model, including all functions and stylistic choices. Generally, a total cost objective is set (excluding commercial costs) that helps fix the target for a direct cost price to be reached for the product. The project team's goal is to optimize the new model whilst remaining within the cost objective. To achieve this aim, the team can, for example, borrow certain modules from the bank of pre-qualified systems in order to create the new vehicle.

The procurement department needs to be integrated into both of these procedures. To pick up on the terms mentioned in Section 3/1.2, Level 1 corresponds more with the so-called 'upper-upstream' phase whilst Level 2 is completely in line with 'upstream' procurement, *with the possibility of both levels being carried out in parallel and not necessarily sequentially.*

We can now investigate the techniques and practices that may be used by procurement departments for these two levels or processes. Note that *most of these practices are not specific to procurement departments* but must be mastered by them, *as well as by* all members of the design project teams.

3/2.3 Management of technologies and technical data

In this area, four key activities should be mastered: the use of technology intelligence; a qualification system for technical solutions; (possible) definition of upstream procurement policies; and finally, implementation of 'make-or-buy' decisions.

Technology intelligence and marketing

This activity is commonly shared at company level, but needs to be extremely well organized. As upstream markets are the subject of the activity, the procurement department should be at the heart of the process.

By 'technology watch' is meant a number of *structured information and research activities aimed at keeping the company permanently informed* about available or emerging technologies in its business, its sector of activity and its industrial network.

In large companies, a specific information system (database) is set up and fed by all actors whose activity naturally leads them to find out the latest news on technologies and their possible developments, such as design, R&D engineers, manufacturing engineers and buyers dealing with suppliers. But even salespeople, through their contact with customers, or even competitors, can contribute useful information via alternative paths!

There are two types of information sources: a) *formal* sources, the main ones being specialized trade press, scientific works and other media, specialized databases, patents filed worldwide, as well as consultancies or official bodies; b) *informal or less official* sources including competitors themselves, missions or study trips organized from time to time, trade fairs and expos, conferences, congresses and participation in professional clubs.

Technology watch should focus on the following points:

- *Scientific and technical knowledge,* usually resulting from fundamental and applied research.
- *Different manufacturing processes* available from suppliers, requiring knowledge of:
  - general principle involved;
  - manufacturing process;
  - expected performance (eg possible tolerances);
  - conditions required for optimum efficiency;
  - risks of failure or implementation difficulties;
  - corresponding financial models (typical structure of direct costs);
  - minimum volume required to validly amortize corresponding investments and enable breakeven point to be evaluated.

- Existing *materials*, used or usable (ie materials used by and known to the company, *substitutes* with corresponding manufacturing procedures and associated cost structures).

- *Products and components* that may be *technological alternatives* to those used by the company: we may therefore make future forecasts on the basis of comparative analyses and respective acquisition costs. Figure 3.8 illustrates this type of applied results, here using the already dated (and anonymous) example of a pump component likely to use three different technologies.

- *Potential suppliers, existing or emerging*, which requires implementation of a systematic sourcing policy in world zones where recent technical know-how exists (see Chapter 4).

FIGURE 3.8 Analysis of the estimated costs of three compared technologies

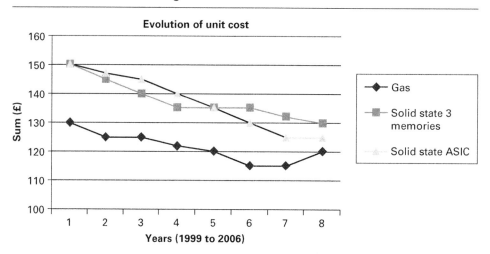

Referring to the two latter points, we sometimes speak of *technology marketing*. This type of systematic approach is typical of a large company. So what can be done by a small or medium-sized company? Two things: segmenting the procurement portfolio in order to target – by way of exception – categories that require more attentive intelligence; then calling on external experts (consultants) to carry out occasional studies aimed at resolving situations associated with major risks.

Standardization/portfolio of approved technologies

This procurement practice should be the buyer's second obsession. What needs to be remembered is that every time a designer settles on a specific solution when choosing a product's architecture, he or she brings the company up against the following risks:

- the need to select a new supplier, with all the required qualification stages;

- generation of fixed costs resulting from development of the new solution (specific studies, development cost and the manufacturing of new tools);

- the rationale for financial amortization for these fixed costs applies to the single volume (quantities) needed by the company and results in a mark-up of the unitary cost of acquisition.

As a result, every time it is possible to choose a product design that favours architecture scenarios incorporating standard market solutions, we should do so as long as the performance and functions in the requirements specifications are entirely fulfilled.

Certain companies have gone further by formalizing an *internal qualification process* for products, components or technologies so that they become internal standards, a process that feeds into a database on approved techniques. This approach follows an ISO-qualified and systematically applied process, as shown by Figure 3.9.

Managing the development of the supplier panel

The third procurement practice consists of sourcing and selecting new suppliers following clear definition (for each procurement family in question) of the supplier panel and supplier profiles.

This point is central to upstream procurement procedures and it will be developed in great detail in Chapter 4. For now, we will sum up the main points of this approach by setting out its guidelines.

Supplier panel and profiles

A 'panel', in relation to a procurement family, is the set of suppliers who are first targeted, then approved (thus preselected) in terms of their match with the purchasing company's needs. It is also necessary to decide on the profile(s) of suppliers who should be included in the panel.

Not all suppliers on a market are homogeneous: they are distinguished by their characteristics, skills and know-how. The company therefore needs to decide which profile(s) it finds interesting for the purpose of making a selection. Without going into the details developed later on, we briefly set out three possible profiles for a supplier:

- a *typical supplier* whom the company deals with in calls for tenders, possibly on a medium-term scheduled contract basis: a solution generally adapted to standard purchases, whether recurrent or not, carried out in a competitive market devoid of technical or security of supply risks;
- a supplier with whom *collaboration relationships are developed in order to improve its operational performance* in terms of lead-time and quality, without giving it responsibility for design of the product being purchased from it;
- a *strategic supplier* with whom so-called '*co-development*' *(or even co-innovation) partnership* relationships are developed, by involving the supplier in innovation, design and development of the company's products or services. In such a situation, the company expects collaboration to match specific needs, generally strategic in nature, where technological or technical skills are purchased rather than a product, in an area that the company has decided to relinquish its expertise.

FIGURE 3.9   Qualification process for a new technology or component

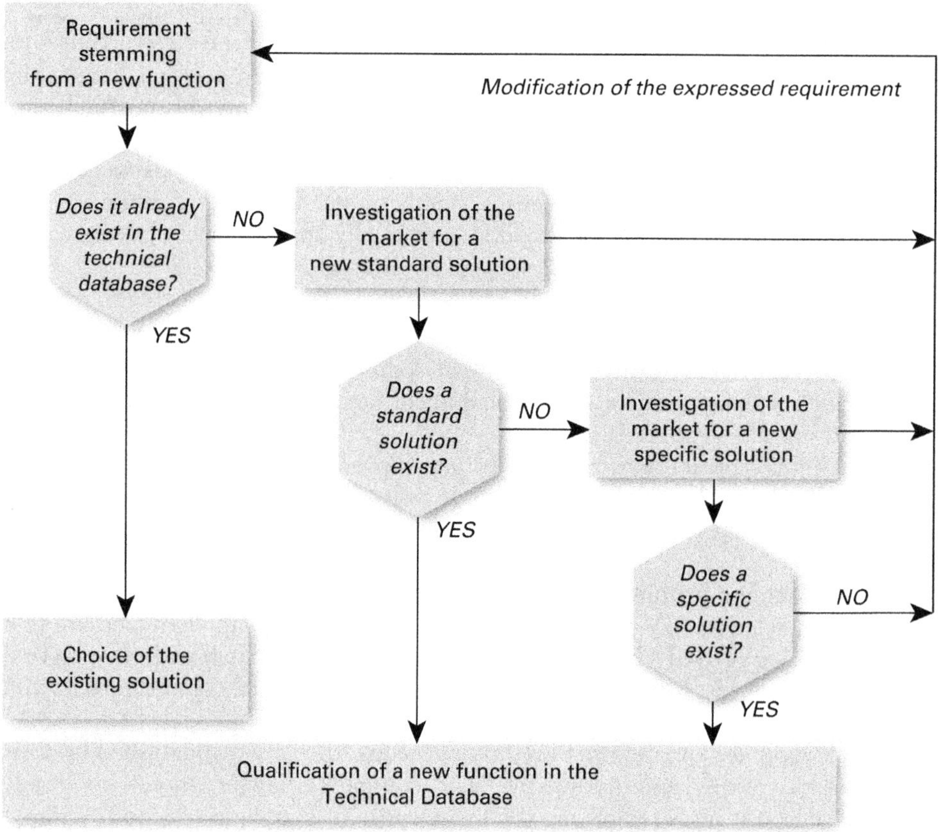

It is crucial that buyers coordinate the process of choosing the supplier profiles and that they ensure that the supplier panel provides the means to deal with all possible new product development needs.

To achieve this aim, apart from ongoing intelligence, buyers need to be familiar with the company's medium-term technology plan (if one exists) and to steer sourcing of new suppliers accordingly.

Management of the supplier panel

This entails implementing an *ongoing performance improvement process* in relation to the supplier panel (ie those from the second two categories mentioned above). This coordination should be permanently targeted at the following points:

- leading suppliers to adhere to quality assurance obligations via shared action plans;

- ensuring that they improve their industrial performance according to the classic quality–cost–lead-time triptych (maintenance of a high level of quality, minimization of direct costs, and adherence to delivery schedules);

- prompting development (technological, in particular) of the suppliers in the direction of the company's future needs;
- constantly monitoring active panel suppliers in relation to the global offer of the supplier market (in other words, keeping sight of real costs and market prices);
- for co-developer suppliers, defining and setting up methods aimed at integrating them into the product design and development process;
- finally, internally triggering developments to promote integration of suppliers and their improvement plans.

Upstream procurement policy

The term 'upstream procurement policy' (UPP) refers to the considered approach that, as a corollary to management of the company's technology portfolio, sums up *recommendations addressed by the procurement management to specifiers, internal clients and business partners for the purpose of steering product (or service) design choices and the drafting of requirements specifications*. This UPP also offers recommendations on the choice of suppliers and collaboration methods.

Defined in this way, a UPP corresponds to a synthesis of the three approaches seen above. This type of *formalized* thinking – that has scope for development – is a tool that may supplement (or replace) the presence of buyers upstream in project groups. The UPP enables specifiers and project managers to save time, to limit risks in their choices of technologies or components, all the whilst offering technological alternatives and advance checking of supplier adaptation to the company's current and future needs. This type of support is particularly important for the so-called 'strategic' procurement categories in a portfolio.

It should be noted that a UPP may also be useful for the purchase of services when internal and external risks seem significant.

A UPP contains, at the very least, a series of considerations and recommendations:

- a stringent inventory of internal and market risks, technological, industrial and financial, with an objective assessment of the company's competitive position;
- associated with these risks or recurring designer demands, the evaluation of additional costs incurred as a result of observations of the supplier market;
- advisory prevention measures and design recommendations generally geared towards:
  - preference for the most reliable and mature technologies for which the highest number of suppliers exists;
  - shedding light on options and possible variations by specifying the additional costs associated with complicating factors;
  - financial simulations for non-recurring fixed costs (linked to possible development of possible tooling);
  - indication of preferred suppliers if the company wishes to develop prototypes with a high level of demand for flexibility;

  – indication of the suppliers best able to supply the product in the series
    stage etc.
- possibly, design 'bans' relating to components or technologies at their end-of-life
  stages as they are associated with risky large-scale availability problems.

In this way, the UPP should be used as a guide to design, it should help save time, it should anticipate qualification for products and approval for suppliers. It should not set limits to innovation, but should signpost the design process whilst transmitting all knowledge about the supplier market.

In practical terms, the UPP cannot be defined by buyers alone, but in close collaboration with the design department and specifiers in order to meet their future requirements and expectations. This can sometimes be done via the intermediary of *buyer–engineer* teams, with both specialized in each important procurement category.

Make-or-buy decision

This last issue is characteristic of decisions that need to be made very far upstream, in relation to definition of a cost–benefit relationship and the relevance of a technical solution or product.

When the expression 'make-or-buy' is used, two different concepts are generally understood.

First, simple *subcontracting*, that consists in entrusting, to an external service-provider, all or part of a research, industrial-manufacturing, transport or storage activity. The subcontracting may take a variety of forms depending on the circumstances and the motivations of the ordering parties: this activity may be structural or purely cyclical (temporary but recurring use of additional production capacity).

In all cases, an 'ordering party' entrusts a subcontractor with completion of a task, according to specific guidelines. The subcontractor takes the place of the ordering party in the making of a product or the performance of a service. In this case, there is a hierarchical relationship between the ordering party and the subcontractor in that the former provides plans and requirements specifications, often specifies working methods, and imposes methods for the follow-up of quality (quality assurance).

On the other hand, *outsourcing* of an activity involves a company calling upon a supplier on a *permanent and long-term* basis because of the supplier's specific technical know-how when the company has decided to give up the activity internally as it is unable to operate it in a profitable manner.

The key point is the long-term transfer of activity, with the service-provider taking charge of the design and manufacturing of a finished product, or a service undertaken whilst assuming full responsibility. In this case, the ordering party purchases a finished product as a whole, instead of simply implementing a manufacturing order.

These extremely important decisions are dealt with comprehensively in Chapter 7 of this book.

3/2.4 Optimization of finished products (or systems in a project-based approach)

In this area, four techniques will be examined: value analysis, the definition of functional requirements specifications, design-to-cost, and co-development with suppliers 'at the heart of the panel.'

Value analysis

Value analysis (VA) is a method that sets out to reduce the cost of purchased products or components. Unlike the approaches previously referred to, since Frederick Taylor (1856–1915), the leading proponent of scientific management, VA has focused interest on the *costs of the functions* that the product intends to satisfy. Today, it is commonly applied in many companies. Initially used to reduce the costs of the *usage functions* of existing products, the method's field of application has widened to the design of new products, taking into account other so-called *symbolic statutory functions*. VA depends on three main concepts: functions, value and the cost of the product (or service).

Functions

The purchase of a product is related to the services that it will provide and the satisfaction that use of it will offer. To bring satisfaction, it must correspond to a client requirement and accomplish the functions expected by the customer. The first stage of the VA therefore involves defining these functions.

Functions are by nature diverse. For example, in the case of a pen, these include writing well, being easy to hold in one's hand, or being pleasing to the eye. One of these elements corresponds to the main function: a pen is made for writing in the way that a lighter is made for generating a flame. Any other functions are secondary.

We can also classify functions according to a product's usage (in this case we speak of *practical functions*) and other reasons that may motivate the purchase, such as beauty or fashion or social status (we then speak of *symbolic functions*).

Value

To fulfil a function, it is always possible to find several solutions whose respective costs can be determined. The lowest cost obtained corresponds to the value of this function. By proceeding in this way for each function, then adding up the values, we end up with the *functional value* of the finished product. The value is therefore equal to the sum of the costs of solutions included so that the product can fulfil all functions expected from it.

The objective of VA is therefore to provide the requested performance at the weakest possible cost. Another solution would consist in increasing value whilst maintaining the cost, but in this case, the product's characteristics would possibly exceed the client's actual requirement.[7]

Costs

The relevant costs correspond to the total acquisition cost (purchasing, transport, customs duties, other cost elements) in the case of purchased products, or the direct manufacturing cost (design, prototype, tests, tools, pre-production and industrialization) in the case of internal production.

The stages of a VA study

VA studies always require teamwork. A typical team is made up of representatives of the different departments that contribute to the design of the product (design department, R&D department, industrial methods, production, sales and procurement). Coordination of this group is handed over to a VA specialist.

This type of study requires seven main phases to be followed:

1 *Scoping*: this phase consists in specifying the characteristics of the product to be analysed: positioning, sales price, quantities, objective target cost price, etc. The group should be capable, at the end of this stage, of assessing the expected profitability of the study.

2 *Information search*: the team should gather all necessary documentation, whether technical, commercial or economic, about the product, its market, the competition, suppliers, etc.

3 *Analysis of functions and costs*: here, the different functions are identified which must be satisfied before pricing them. First, it is necessary to define the product's essential functions, then determine their costs. To do so, we can use checklists to review a very broad range of possible cases.

We can also follow a more intuitive form of reasoning by observing the product and its components as well as its relationship with the environment. In this case, a function is defined in terms of a relationship between the product and the environment in which it is used: the hand, the eye, the atmosphere, the paper, hence the functions of grip, aesthetics, ink drying. If the product is extremely technical, functional
requirements specifications will already have been drawn up by the client.

A calculation of costs should be made *for each function and not for each assembly, subassembly or component*: all parts that enable a function to operate are therefore included.

Next, these functions are ranked in decreasing order of importance. At this stage of the study, the rating of functions in decreasing order of importance and the rating of costs in decreasing order of amount often do not coincide: too much attention is given to functions of little importance and a great deal to secondary functions.

4 *Search for new solutions*: this stage corresponds to an intense period of creativity. It consists in finding new ideas or solutions that match the functions previously defined. Here again, different methods are possible: brainstorming use of lists that may put forward thousands of questions or open innovation.

5 *Study and evaluation*: the new solutions are subject to deeper studies and their costs are calculated via simulations.

6 *Proposals*: proposals can then be put forward on the basis of costs, but also the opinions of salespeople, or the way the solutions match customer specifications.

7 *Decision*: the group chooses a solution and decides to implement it.

Note that value analysis may also be used during a product's lifecycle. In this case, thanks to client feedback and experience with the quality, we can seek to optimize the product in order to maintain its commercial success and to strengthen its margins on direct costs.

The stages outlined here apply to a product as a whole. It is obvious, however, that this procedure can be used to optimize an individual elementary function, a subassembly or an elementary component.

In the same way, a service may be simplified via functional analysis that follows the same process.

Functional versus detailed technical requirements specifications

Very often, specifiers or internal clients define their needs in the form of extremely detailed requirements specifications. However, this approach is sometimes unproductive as it presupposes that we already have in mind a well-defined technical solution. If this is done in the context of a call for tenders, then we necessarily limit the innovation that suppliers can potentially contribute.

The opposite occurs when we define functional requirements specifications without suggesting a particular solution, thus leaving suppliers with a certain degree of freedom. This is not to say that all purchasing cases should be handled in this way: this approach is to be reserved for situations when we expect innovation and seek to challenge the established ways of doing things, as indicated by Table 3.1.

What are the main differences between functional requirements specifications (FRS) and technical requirements specifications (TRS)?

Functional requirements specifications (FRS)

The first answers the question: 'What?' or 'What is it meant to do?'. It describes a requirement or an expected result. An AFNOR (*Association Française de Normalisation*) standard defines FRS as 'a document in which the buyer expresses his or her needs (or those that he or she is given the responsibility of expressing) in terms of service functions or constraints. For each of them, assessment criteria and levels are defined, and each is given a certain degree of flexibility' (EN 1325-1 1996 standard).[8]

TABLE 3.1   Selection criteria for the type of requirements specifications

Types of situations encountered	FRS	TRS
Very strong internal standardization constraint		x
Strong confidentiality obligation		x
Technical obligation (use of patents)		x
Compulsory mastery of the technology		x
Strong pressure on costs	x	
Supplier's 'advanced' expertise	x	
Full commitment to buying with a 'performance commitment'	x	
Innovation as a high-priority requirement	x	
Compulsory switching of supplier	x	

The FRS therefore fundamentally relies on *functional analysis and description* of the product or the service being purchased. It includes a list of external functions and a possible presentation of constraints that may therefore be divided into three categories:

- *service functions*, in other words expected actions expressed in terms of a purpose to meet a given user's need (in this way, functional specifications translate the expected performance level of functions whilst conveying 'zones of freedom' or the flexibility that will be tolerated);

- *external functions* or product responses that translate its adaptation into the direct environment of use (description of the context of use);

- quite often, *design restrictions* that can partially limit the degree of freedom (adherence to certain internal technical rules, materials or components that is imposed for various reasons, patents to be used, respect of certain standards, etc).

If we consider the example of the purchase of a global reprographic service, a service function may correspond to compulsory service expectations (obligations) in terms of emergency repairs in the event of breakdowns (eg response time, maximum downtime). Adaptation to the environment may include the physical distribution of reprographic equipment in the company, hence taking into account the spread of offices and the volumes of copies that need to be produced. A physical restriction may be constituted by opening-hour limitations for scheduled maintenance operations so that the running of the company's services is not disturbed.

Technical requirements specifications (TRS)

This second type of specifications covers the 'How?' by describing the characteristics of a predefined solution. In this way, it defines exact specifications associated with maximum tolerances that must be respected. Whatever the form of the requirements specifications, the document should define detailed criteria according to which the responses of suppliers will be evaluated.

Main elements of a requirements specifications document

Readers are offered a few suggestions on how to draw up requirements specifications in Table 3.2. This table in no way sets out to be exhaustive: it aims only to provide a reference framework presenting the main points that are worth raising systematically.

Design-to-cost

Design-to-cost is a general approach that aims to steer product design economically. The idea involves setting a target cost in advance. Simulations are then carried out on all technical solutions that are tested according to the criterion of the total direct cost price, and solutions are chosen or eliminated on this basis.

We talk about a cost 'objective' as it is evaluated according to a sales price and gross profit objective, then broken down into the product's subassemblies. This cost becomes an imperative target for all actors, including the procurement department (and the suppliers who may be involved in this strategy). It often takes on contractual value between internal departments and with external partners.

TABLE 3.2   Main elements in a requirements specification document

Main outline of the requirement	Functional or detailed description? (functions to fulfill or detailed specifications)
	Outcome or best-efforts obligation?
	Specific technical criteria (risks and quality requirements)
	Environmental constraints to match / CSR expectations
Other characteristics of the requirement	Quantities / volumes
	Specific order conditions (delivery conditions, desired contractual procurement horizon, etc.)
	Transport and packaging conditions
	Control-on-receipt conditions and tests
	Outline of offer-evaluation criteria
Economic characteristics and expected information	Cost target (possibly) with bolus-malus
	Transparent cost breakdown (possibly)
	Payment and invoicing conditions
	Price-revision conditions (if relevant)
	Invoicing currency
	Productivity-improvement plan
	Fixed development cost (NRC or non-recurring cost)
	Tooling cost (if relevant)
Procurement scope (related additional expectations)	Associated services (e.g. maintenance, training, technical documentation)
	Warranty terms and after-sales conditions
	Stock obligations and supply-security conditions
	Obligations to update the solution (e.g. upgrading of software)
	Obligations to manage the product's end-of-life (e.g. recycling methods)

The concept of cost raised here is the *product's (or service's) anticipated cost price, in stabilized industrial conditions, or even the client's end-use conditions.* To allow decision-making on the level of each subassembly or each product function, the global target cost must be broken down, *via a functional breakdown of bills of materials* (BOM) of the product or total system, into target unit costs.

This approach offers the advantage of reassuring the end-client. As far as the company's internal functioning is concerned, it also allows all actors to get involved in a formal system of client–supplier relationships. In addition, it enables co-development approaches with partners to be steered for the 'purchased part' of the product. There is therefore clear affirmation of the notion of a *collective contract*.

Thanks to the cost objective, deviations from plan and subsequent budget overspending can be avoided; the approach curbs attempts to stretch performance that ultimately lead to cost increases unmatched by relative value increases in the eyes of the client.

General approach for determining the target cost

The principle behind determination of the cost objective is summed up by Figure 3.10 as follows. The setting of the cost objective is a crucial and delicate issue as the approach is implemented in the *initial design* stages. Margins of error can be significant. That said, the major interest of the approach lies in deciding on the product's configuration and its ultimate cost whilst *few actual expenses have been incurred*.

The process necessarily starts with strict functional analysis of the product or system, with the aim of optimizing (simplifying) it. Traditional methods such as value analysis (presented above) should be used for this purpose. It is necessary for the functional requirements specifications to be well defined in advance in such a way as to be totally in sync with the client's requirements, without any omission of expected functions but also without over-specifying the quality standard required. Next, the cost objective can be evaluated according to two main approaches, as the figure shows.

The so-called 'marketing' approach is fairly simple as it involves identifying a market price from which an initial total-cost value is deduced depending on the contribution sought, according to the following basic equation:

$$\textit{Direct target cost} = \text{Sales price} - \text{margin on expected direct cost}$$

This information will then be used as a reference to offset the analytical evaluation that is carried out in parallel. The latter approach consists of reconstituting the different cost elements using simulations including 'purchasing and production standards' developed from the analysis of supplier markets or solutions already qualified in the technical database).

Internal database and simulation tools

There are no specific rules for compiling reliable, high-quality internal and external databases. These depend on: well-structured product nomenclature or service classification, according to a functional breakdown that corresponds exactly with the technologies and the panel of potential suppliers; the quality of the available background history enabling calculations to be made (standards such as hourly rates, labour operating times, realistic machine rates, standard supply costs).

This method also implies the use of software packages very similar to quote-preparation software (such as PRICE, used by system-providers in the electronics, avionics, aeronautics equipment and space industries).

For this technique, the quality of analytic accounting and budgetary information is critical. This quality can be examined along two dimensions:

- *space*: all useful data about the purchase (ie from suppliers, production and supply-chain departments) should be gathered into a single coherent base; above all, this data should be made accessible to all decision-makers (even if it remains decentralized in information systems belonging to the different departments);

- *time*: these standards and elementary costs should be projected to a sufficiently distant horizon and updated.

The logical end of design-to-cost is economic optimization of the product. This being the case, in the worst possible scenario, it should also enable decisions on *abandoning continuation of a product's design in sufficient time* if its technical and economic feasibility is not demonstrated, hence avoiding the build-up of pointless development and launch costs.

An oft-cited major disadvantage of the design-to-cost approach is that suppliers are not motivated to seek to improve the product *beyond* the threshold defined when the cost objective is set. In the face of this valid argument, it is important to find *motivating factors* to ensure that all ulterior improvements are incorporated into the project: for example, definition of improvement plans formally developed with suppliers, envisaging for example *partial refund of the savings obtained* (an example followed by the *Centre National des Études Spatiales* with its contractually specified system of bonuses and penalties used with different collaborators involved in the Ariane project).[9]

Co-development with 'partner' suppliers

This point will be reconsidered in Chapter 4. For the sake of thoroughness, bear in mind that co-development implies that suppliers (co-developers) are physically associated with the project groups, or with development platforms. In this case, we can genuinely speak of mixed teams within the design group.

Usually, the product is developed by functions: in this way, there will be as many design teams as there are identified functions, with the teams operating in parallel according to the principles of concurrent engineering, explained earlier.

This topic is therefore related to that of project-organization methods, which the purchasing company should already have set up internally.

3/3 Organizational consequences of upstream procurement

An entire chapter of this work (Chapter 16) deals with the organizational and human aspects of the procurement function. This is why we will here limit ourselves to the specific aspects of upstream procurement. Let's remember how upstream procurement imposes change in the organization of a procurement management (see Figure 3.11).

FIGURE 3.10   Methods for determining the cost target

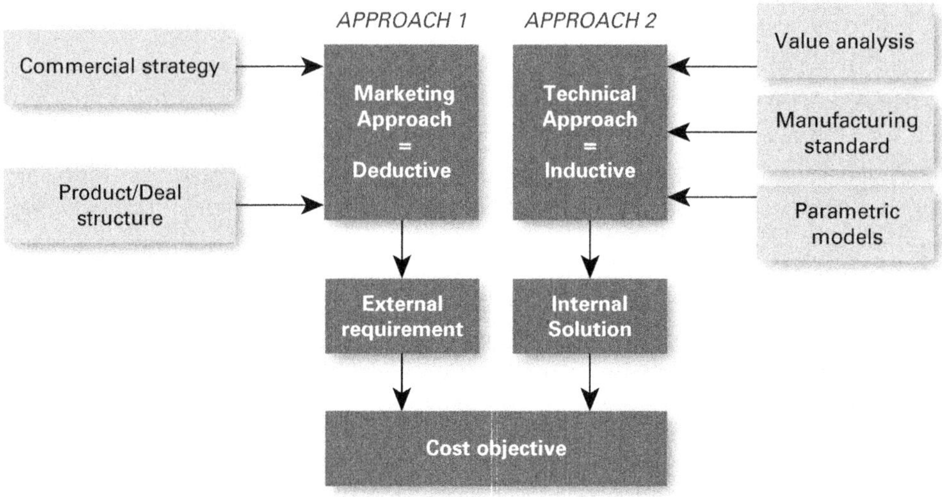

The essential points to note are as follows:

- Apart from the 'category' buyers (found at the bottom of the diagram) who are supplier market specialists, most often organized according to the main segmentation of the procurement portfolio, we see two new specialized jobs: *project buyers* (or programme buyers) who are integrated into product development teams, on a full-time basis if possible; and *upstream buyers* who are real technologists with close links to design department engineers, who work on technology portfolios and upper-upstream activities.

- For upper-upstream activities, it is possible to set up *buyer-designer* teams so that upstream procurement policies may be jointly defined; in addition, this strategy offers the essentially psychological advantage of legitimizing procurement, and above all requires companies to think in terms of the 'buyability' of products or services in their daily decisions.

- The professional profiles and training levels of project and upstream buyers should be very close to those of engineers in the R&D departments so that they are conferred with legitimacy, enabling them to be listened to as value-added contributors.

FIGURE 3.11 Organization of a procurement department for upstream procurement

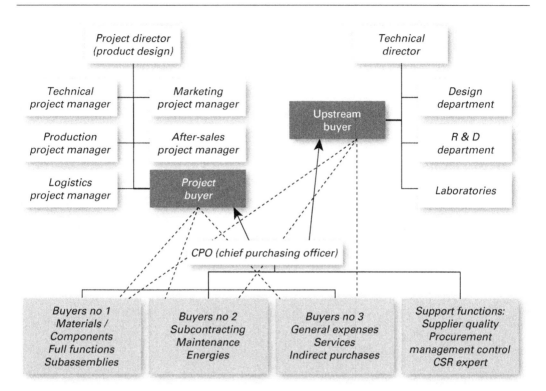

Notes

1 People also often speak of 'project procurement'. The term is not exactly interchangeable because in a project management context, procurement is carried out from the upstream to the downstream stages of the project's course. However, the upstream stages are the ones which are simultaneously the least understood and the least mastered, hence the similarity between the two terms and situations.

2 The concept of shortening design and development cycles, that reflects a company's ability to place products on the market quickly, is called 'time to market'.

3 Readers wishing to delve into this subject in detail are invited to consult Baglin *et al* (2013) Chapter 24. Obviously many other books in the literature do exist!

4 Christensen, CM (1997) *The Innovator's Dilemma*, Harvard Business School Press.

5 Henry Chesbrough is faculty director of the Berkley Center for Open Innovation and author of the reference work *Open Innovation* (2003).

6   No doubt in order to ensure better protection of future innovations, and to remain owners of potential discoveries, certain large groups have organized such innovation systems *internally* by relying on entities with adapted profiles. This development is often achieved by external growth and the takeover of small dedicated start-ups (open innovation solution through *insourcing*). The company Genzyme, a subsidiary of Sanofi, a biotechnology specialist, is a perfect example of this development model.

7   This is nevertheless what is expected by certain company departments that have at their disposal a negotiated budget and that wish to obtain maximum value for this available budget. This is for example the case of many marketing category purchases.

8   On this topic, readers may wish to refer to Pinçon (2004).PricewaterhouseCoopers

9   To examine this topic more closely, the reader can consult the (already dated) article by Bruel (1994).

04
Supplier policy
Sourcing, supplier panel and supplier relationship management (SRM)

Supplier policy is a core element of procurement policy, that, as we have seen, contributes directly to a company's corporate strategy. A procurement manager confronts a number of issues and types of decisions in this area:

- Should a number of different supplier profiles be defined, and how should the suppliers be qualified and selected as a result?
- Should new suppliers be sourced on an ongoing basis, and what methods should be employed for this?[1]
- How should new suppliers be approved and on which criteria?
- Should a supplier panel be formally established? And based on which segmentation principles? How can its development be guided?
- Which processes and tools should be set up to develop supplier relationship management (SRM), in other words, the set of collaborative systems enabling optimal joint steering of the upstream supply chain?

We will deal with these questions in order.

4/1 Types of supplier profiles

In a modern procurement approach, a company's suppliers are not – and nor should they be – homogeneous. At the same time, there is no room for working with a list of suppliers that is compiled piecemeal and 'randomly' on the basis of choices made in past calls for tenders.

A coherent approach consists in *defining supplier profiles* required for the performance objectives set by the procurement department and taking into account the procurement portfolio segmentation. This type of classification is therefore closely linked to the *structure of the desired supplier panel.*

A number of supplier–portfolio segmentations are possible depending on the chosen 'angle of attack' and the procurement department's prime objective. The main segmentation methods are presented below in terms of their operational character, from which it will be seen that the segmentations converge in a multi-dimensional global approach.

4/1.1 Segmentation by suppliers' strategic contribution

The first typology, following the rationale of strategic objectives for procurement performance, consists in defining the target supplier profiles to look for. Two major lines of enquiry are examined: the extent of the desired strategic contribution from the suppliers (are we looking for a purely tactical contribution or participation towards value creation?); and the extent of the expected economic contribution from the suppliers (are we interested in an approach aiming at minimizing the purchasing cost alone, or systematic analysis of the total cost of ownership, as well as innovation actions in line with a cost avoidance-type principle as seen in Chapter 2?).[2]

Although there may be a continuum in how relationships with suppliers evolve, professional practice has a tendency to develop four *alternative relationships* that may co-exist as they correspond to different needs. We will examine each of these in turn:

- a traditional, so-called 'power-relationship' approach;
- a classic planned procurement approach aimed at minimizing the purchasing cost;
- an operational collaboration mode seeking to optimize the upstream supply chain and targeting minimization of the TCO;
- a so-called co-development partnership geared towards innovation and value creation.

This classification is illustrated by the model in Figure 4.1. (© Philippart M.)

Traditional 'power-relationship' approach

This first approach is familiar to traditional buyers: head-on confrontation, power struggles, aggressive negotiation, the setting up of competition with possible divisions, challenges and reversals, imposed price cuts that are unaccompanied by a search for sustainable solutions but matched with a focus on payment terms, and no particular loyalty in relationships.

This type of approach is still practised. Admittedly, it may be justified in certain one-off purchase operations in contexts outside the company's core business. This approach may also be determined by the sales attitude adopted by a supplier not wishing to engage in a collaborative relationship. We will not probe further into this topic, but instead concentrate on the three other main approaches.

FIGURE 4.1   Supplier strategic operational contribution matrix

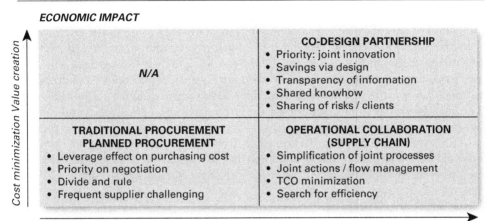

ECONOMIC IMPACT

		CO-DESIGN PARTNERSHIP
	N/A	• Priority: joint innovation • Savings via design • Transparency of information • Shared knowhow • Sharing of risks / clients
TRADITIONAL PROCUREMENT PLANNED PROCUREMENT • Leverage effect on purchasing cost • Priority on negotiation • Divide and rule • Frequent supplier challenging		**OPERATIONAL COLLABORATION (SUPPLY CHAIN)** • Simplification of joint processes • Joint actions / flow management • TCO minimization • Search for efficiency

Cost minimization   Value creation

Tactical objective   *Strategic contribution*

DOMINANT STRATEGIC FIELD

Classic planned procurement approach

This approach corresponds with a first level of maturity. Still traditional in spirit, its implementation nevertheless comprises the following points:

- a search for minimization of the *purchasing cost* and not merely the supplier's sales price;
- forecasting total requirements so that it is possible to commit to medium-term volumes, and thus prioritize the advantages of volume purchases;
- framework contracts or open orders rather than counting exclusively on one-off spot purchase practices.

Using this approach, the buyer does not always actually enter into a collaboration strategy with the supplier. The supplier's internal operations remain a 'closed book' to the buyer. In particular, there is no transparency on costs, nor is there any collaboration to look for systematic cost reduction via joint analysis and planning. In order for a planned procurement strategy to exist, demand must be continuous.

Operational collaboration

This is the first type of approach that can be described as 'collaborative' in relation to suppliers. In this case, the company does not expect innovation from its suppliers: it maintains full responsibility for the purchased product or service. However, there exists an intention to jointly seek *minimization of the total cost of ownership*. In this way, the notion of a purchasing cost or price, in a strict sense, is overridden: all other variables of the purchase and cost drivers wielding an economic impact are analysed, and operational solutions effectively set up.

As a result, this approach leads to a drive for optimization of the whole operational system at the company–supplier interface, in other words the area covered by the upstream supply chain. It also encompasses the two main elements characterizing the supply chain: improvement in quality and delivery of a quality assurance system, and minimization of the working capital requirement (WCR) via actions on cycles and delivery lead-times, and gradual minimization of stock levels at the interface.

In this kind of relationship, the first imperative condition is *transparency of information* between the two partners, not just analytic accounting data, but also non-accounting data such as information on quality. The second condition is *sustainability of the relationship*, entailing long-term agreements (multi-annual contracts) as well as joint definition of a reporting system (performance indicators) and *shared* improvement plans.

In this type of relationship, the company itself may contribute to the action plan, by compiling a database accessible by suppliers and adapting its requirements forecast and upstream flow-planning systems to meet the expectations of the supplier.

Co-design partnership

This approach does not exclude the previous one, but it places a primary focus on the *contribution to innovation* expected from suppliers. From the viewpoint of the purchasing company's corporate strategy, following an analysis of how it can refocus on its 'core business' matched with an analysis of its technology portfolio, here we are concerned with technologies or activities that it has decided to outsource. The company no longer merely purchases products or services, but looks to gain access to product and/or process technologies, or even specific know-how.

As a result, it seeks suppliers that need to take responsibility, in a *significant and balanced* manner, for innovation and the development of new solutions within the cost restrictions or targets. This situation is described as 'co-development'. In certain cases, the collaboration involves joint innovation further upstream (see Chapter 3). In this approach, the following points characterize relationships with suppliers:

- crucial transparency of information, including medium-term strategic data and confidential technical data;
- critical setting up of joint organizational systems (integrated project teams) and new processes dedicated to implementing co-development mechanisms;
- a research and development approach based on target costs (design-to-cost) entailing shared design savings;
- maintenance of shared ongoing improvement plan principles based on objective reporting systems using quantified indicators;
- alignment and harmonization of the two partners' development strategies.

Mutual competitive advantages and genuine 'business growth' should be generated by this collaboration. In certain cases, the term 'shared business model' is no exaggeration.

4/1.2 Segmentation by suppliers' operational risks and responsibilities

This typology is related to the preceding one, but is even more explicit about the desired supplier profiles, specifying the share of responsibility that the company seeks to hand over to the supplier and the associated business risk. This typology provides details on the resources and means required by suppliers, physically and operationally. Figure 4.2 illustrates these points, and is drawn from the example of an equipment manufacturer in the automotive industry aiming to clearly classify its suppliers of spare parts, subassemblies and complete functions. Three main categories emerge from this (with risk increasing from the bottom upwards): subcontractor, manufacturer and co-developer.

Subcontractor profile

A *subcontractor* is almost exclusively a toll manufacturer, whose single responsibility is to execute one or more processes in relation to detailed specifications given by the ordering party. The only obligation is that of conformity. The subcontractor's sole responsibility is to undertake the design, production and maintenance of tools, and (possibly) suggest a more efficient production process. Otherwise, the subcontractor is expected to provide the requested industrial performance and to control manufacturing of the product. Only these elements are audited by the ordering party.

Manufacturer profile

A *manufacturer* is given full responsibility over the development as well as the production of a finished product. Only product design remains the responsibility of

FIGURE 4.2   Typology of operational supplier profiles

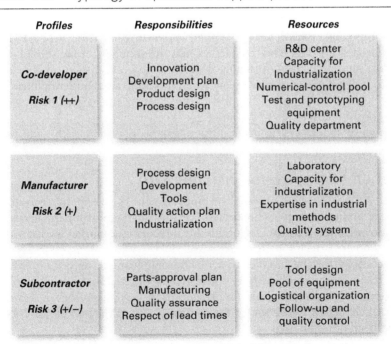

Profiles	Responsibilities	Resources
Co-developer **Risk 1 (++)**	Innovation Development plan Product design Process design	R&D center Capacity for Industrialization Numerical-control pool Test and prototyping equipment Quality department
Manufacturer **Risk 2 (+)**	Process design Development Tools Quality action plan Industrialization	Laboratory Capacity for industrialization Expertise in industrial methods Quality system
Subcontractor **Risk 3 (+/−)**	Parts-approval plan Manufacturing Quality assurance Respect of lead times	Tool design Pool of equipment Logistical organization Follow-up and quality control

The scale of risk ranges from 1 (very high risk) to 3 (minor risk).

the ordering party. In this case, the buyer looks for a supplier with industrialization, production and logistical capabilities. The supplier is also in charge of the procurement, supply and quality control of raw materials and necessary components (even if specifications may be imposed by the client).

Once the product and process have been approved by the ordering party, the manufacturer must take full responsibility for the delivered product. For example, the manufacturer is responsible if vehicles are recalled as a result of flaws identified by customers. The real risk for the buyer lies in the supplier and product approval stages. After that, risks are partially transferred to the supplier.

Co-developer profile

A *co-developer* has a partner status that also applies in the upstream stage of the lifecycle of the subassembly or function with which it is entrusted, and its involvement in the design and R&D stages is expected. The risk related to selection is very great because of the strong impact of choices on the buyer's 'core business' purchases, and the effect on critical features in terms of the product's performance and quality.

There is also a financial risk that should be planned for – namely that of financing the research and development stages as these are likely to spread out over several months or even years. However, the transfer of after-sales responsibility to the supplier is complete, in exchange for a necessarily long-term relationship. In the case of the automotive industry, the relationship lasts for at least as long as the sales lifetime of the vehicle model, plus the (after-sales) warranty period for spare parts.

4/1.3 Segmentation by product lifecycle

The third approach involves linking 'supplier' policy to phases in a product's lifecycle. In this approach, the company recognizes that the supplier profile should evolve as the product matures and performance objectives progress. If one supplier does not manage to 'follow' the company by evolving, it is valid to change suppliers to meet the new priorities. This approach applies to direct procurement (product components, material goods or software applications).

As shown by Figure 4.3, four main stages can be identified, each with distinctive features and consequences for supplier policy.

Innovation (disruptive or incremental)

The upstream phase is characterized by innovation of the company's products from the vantage point of future technologies. For this stage, the company needs to look for an innovative service-provider, preferably a recognized market leader, for the key contribution here is technological expertise.

It is necessary for the supplier to set aside significant resources for the project, but as a result, they should gain a competitive advantage through its involvement. In addition, the innovation should represent, in the supplier's eyes, a strategic and commercial challenge, as it does for the company, even if the two parties look at the challenge from different angles.

FIGURE 4.3 Supplier profiles and product lifecycle

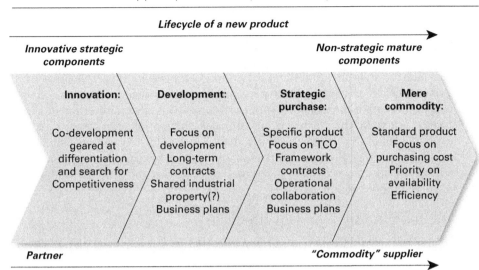

Lifecycle of a new product

Innovative strategic components   *Non-strategic mature components*

Innovation:	**Development:**	**Strategic purchase:**	**Mere commodity:**
Co-development geared at differentiation and search for Competitiveness	Focus on development Long-term contracts Shared industrial property(?) Business plans	Specific product Focus on TCO Framework contracts Operational collaboration Business plans	Standard product Focus on purchasing cost Priority on availability Efficiency

Partner   *"Commodity" supplier*

Expectations with regard to suppliers

Let's look at the example of a European aviation equipment manufacturer that, several years ago, set up a co-development partnership with a global electronics leader from the United States. The supplier placed considerable research means at the client's disposal, and even spearheaded the development of a new application to be integrated into the embedded security systems of latest-generation planes produced by one of world's two co-leaders. On top of this, the supplier helped its client to market this new system to US airlines for the retrofitting of aircraft fleets already in use.

However, development costs largely exceeded the target cost restrictions that would allow the operation to be commercially successful. The supplier nonetheless took up the challenge as the new application could be widely exploited in other civilian markets outside of the aeronautics sector and generate significant cash flow. In agreeing to this collaboration, the supplier managed to self-finance development of this new technology through the partnership with its client. For innovation strategies located far upstream, it is therefore necessary for the business plans of the two partners to be in sync, and for there to be a win–win situation. In this case, industrial performance is not seen as a major element for value creation.

Development (product and process)

The development phase follows on from the innovation phase. The technology is known, and it is now a matter of adapting it to a new product by developing a specific application requirement. A typical example is the case of automobile equipment manufacturers when they develop functions aimed at new models from existing product technology.

In this case, the supplier's profile is that of a co-developer as seen above in 4/1.2.

Strategic purchase in a mature phase

At this stage of the product's life, its components have been stabilized and optimized. Even if they are specific to the buyer company, their quality level and the industrial process by which they are manufactured have been established. The priority aim is to generate cash flow. The buyer's role is to look for a supplier capable of offering a minimum global cost, hence a skilled manufacturer equipped with efficient supply-chain management. This may be the same type of supplier as for the 'development' stage, although in this case a different set of objectives are to be met, and different skills implemented. Alternatively, a complete new supplier whose profile features operational excellence may take over the role. Often, a dual-source solution is implemented: the first supplier maintains a relative market share in order for development phases to be amortized, whilst the second is given the larger production volume, enabling a controlled TCO to be obtained.

'Simple' commodity (end-of-lifecycle)

This last phase in the lifecycle of a product or component is characterized by maintenance of reasonable sales prices via the securing of low cost levels whilst retaining flexibility and responsiveness as a priority, along with quality control. Sometimes, availability becomes the main problem for a product at the end of its life. Technical support should be minimal. This stage may be the responsibility of the supplier involved in the 'strategic purchase' stage, or it may sometimes also be transferred to suppliers with specialist profiles.

In the case of components reaching the end of their lifecycles, for example, in the electronic components sector, the transfer may be made to focused distributors.

This outline should make it clear to readers that it is necessary to cross over several supplier portfolio segmentation analyses, and to define the desired profiles distinctly, in order to manage the qualification process rather than to merely pay lip-service to them, operating blindly and at the whim of the tender process. Management of the supplier panel, a topic we will address below, consists – among other tasks – in making sure that appropriate suppliers are available for the company and its strategic procurement priorities.

4/1.4 Internal and external success conditions for partnership

If we focus on partner relationships, certain success conditions are recognized by practitioners. These are presented in Figure 4.4 and can be read without any need for systematic or detailed commentary. However, three of the points listed in the figure merit special attention.

Commitment of the top management and the organizational structure

A company's top management needs to be heavily involved in order for these techniques to be deployed effectively. Here, we are dealing with the strategic component of the procurement function and the value-creation process, complementary to segmentation of the procurement portfolio. In comparison, the call-for-tenders process and negotiation are dealt with at a shorter-term operational level (that can for practical purposes be delegated to on-the-ground teams using modern e-sourcing-type tools).

This commitment should be supplemented by effective implementation of a project-based organization aimed at steering the product lifecycle (PLC) lifecycle – organization that necessitates another major managerial decision.

Finally, these techniques require a shift in relationships. Trust should be established between the protagonists, associated with genuine transparency of information. There is no way for this result to be reached if, objectively speaking, there is no strategic business convergence or medium-term horizon enabling measurable results to be obtained.[3]

This is why top executives who echo the demands of some shareholders today by targeting short-term cost-saving or even cost-killing results encounter difficulties in justifying and deploying partner-based approaches.

And yet, a study carried out in the automotive industry in 2005 showed that the most profitable makes (BMW, Audi, Toyota, Honda) were the ones that made partnership work the best (according not just to the suppliers themselves, but also to the buyers who considered this relationship as offering the best opportunity for maximizing return on investment).

Let's note finally that partnership does not match, structurally, with a buyer's dependence on its supplier. It is indeed possible, and necessary, to continue comparing suppliers with competitors, or in any case *match* the supplier's results with *market* cost levels. But this implies keeping an ongoing watch.

FIGURE 4.4 Success conditions for partnership relationships

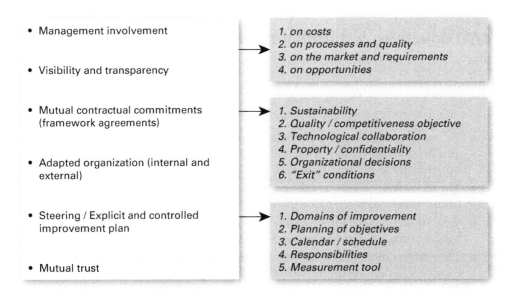

Contractual commitment

Some consider partnership contracts to be useless, as partnerships essentially depend on humans, their values and their states of mind.

We, however, believe that a global contractual framework should be defined, with mention of the aim, the terms, the rules on transparency, information protection and risk prevention, aspects relating to intellectual and industrial property for innovation, performance measurement criteria, change management methods and possible exit conditions.

On another level, a specific, focused *'implementation' contract* can be signed for each product, describing obligations relating to a set purchase, in terms of quality, cost and lead-time (QCL), whilst still referring to the main contract for the terms of the relationship.

Improvement plans and a system of indicators

One thing needs to be remembered: we cannot speak of a partnership if no defined performance improvement plan and joint follow-up exists. In addition, a system of indicators should be set up to clearly demonstrate progress and results obtained, internally and externally.

4/2 Principles and methods in detecting new sources (sourcing)

Too few companies have a systematic sourcing policy that consists in *permanently* looking for new suppliers, rather than merely for a particular requirement when a new call for tenders is launched.

4/2.1 Objectives, justifications and costs of sourcing

Why and in what circumstances should sourcing be carried out?

Objectives of sourcing

The main reasons for sourcing are the following:

- We wish to 'regenerate' the supplier panel: this is the most usual reason, the idea being to open up or to maintain competitiveness between suppliers, or occasionally to remove dependency on a supply source.
- The technology needed for the requirement is new for the company: in this case, it is necessary to search the market for a suitable supplier.
- We wish to take advantage of innovation in the proposed solutions: the idea here is to issue functional requirements specifications for a new application.
- The performances of the current supplier panel are not satisfactory: we may consider eliminating certain non-compliant suppliers that need to be replaced.
- We decide to internationalize the supplier panel in order to meet one of two major objectives: identifying countries with local or 'regional' know-how, or looking for suppliers in low-cost countries.

Financial stakes

Companies very often hesitate to source for two main reasons: first, they think that they lack sourcing know-how, imagining that it is a highly specialized skill that is difficult to develop; next, they often believe that these approaches are extremely costly, and that the cost of obtaining information will be far too high compared with the advantages that it may reap.

Both these views are erroneous. First of all, it is possible to implement a simple and efficient sourcing method using one's own means, before eventually calling upon sourcing specialists.

In addition, there is a wealth of *free information sources* that offer many tips. These are useful as long as they are applied systematically, using a research design template that, with a little experience in this type of research, can be followed easily.

Table 4.1 presents a summary of the main research methods and information sources, indicating whether they are available free of charge or not. This and the Table 4.2 present techniques that allow: a) gathering information on countries which the buyer envisages investigating in an international sourcing approach; and b) obtaining information on existing potential suppliers in these targeted countries.

The reader is invited to go through the tables; below are a few comments on the main approaches recommended.

4/2.2 Sourcing methods

When sourcing, we need to proceed in several stages, especially when research is a priori international.

First, it is necessary to collect macro-economic and technical data on various countries, and to select the countries on which to focus in the next stage.

Next, for these countries, analysis should be conducted and the results cross-referenced in the following two areas: an investigation of the products or services existing in each country, and the identification of potential suppliers in each country. This second analysis should allow a wide range of information to be gathered, that will subsequently facilitate the rating, selection and qualification of product–supplier teams.

Country information and ratings

A selection of the main tools for information on countries is presented in Table 4.1. An abundance of information is available free of charge and can be obtained from public services or government bodies. The opinions and experience of colleagues with similar procurement portfolios, facing similar search concerns, are another rich source of information. In addition, specialist websites gathering the input of international experts are packed with macro-economic, political and social information. Such websites also offer general information on the markets and economic sectors existing in all countries. The website referred to has been abundantly used by the author and his students, with great success.

This information will then open the way for proceeding to a country-risk analysis, to be developed in Chapter 5.

TABLE 4.1   Summary of sourcing and country-rating methods

Descriptions	Payable / Free (P/F)	Methods / Bodies	Comments / Internet addresses (examples)
Initial identification of countries to target	F	Overseas embassies and economic missions representing one's own country	
		Foreign embassies in one's own country	
		Specialized trade press	**www.purchasing.com**
	P	Customs authorities	Information on import flows with mentions of origins (countries and categories)
Rating of countries on a multi-criteria basis	F	Overseas embassies and economic missions representing one's own country	
		Foreign embassies in one's own country	
		COFACE	
		Opinions and experiences of colleagues	Targeting similar or comparable industries
		Other professionals Benchmarking clubs	Network to build
	P	Expert trips	Internal or 'delegates' (specialized service-providers)
		Specialist web sites	IHS Global Insight

Search for information on products

A two-pronged approach is generally used for these two types of searches. As far as products or technologies existing in different regions of the world go, it is necessary to map out their geographical locations, which can be an extremely long and delicate procedure. There are websites that can help users get started.

However, this is often inadequate. Here again, information gleaned from colleagues can be valuable in helping to get an international expansion process off the ground. There are clubs for procurement executives and managers that act as forums for exchange of information, extremely useful for this kind of approach. Obviously, such information is only very general in nature, and no confidential or 'sensitive' information is exchanged at this point for ethical reasons.

4/3 Qualification of suppliers

When potential suppliers are targeted, it is appropriate to define a system for 'qualifying' them. This system constitutes the upper level of a 'two-storey' supplier selection process, as shown by Figure 4.5.

FIGURE 4.5   Two-stage homologation/selection process

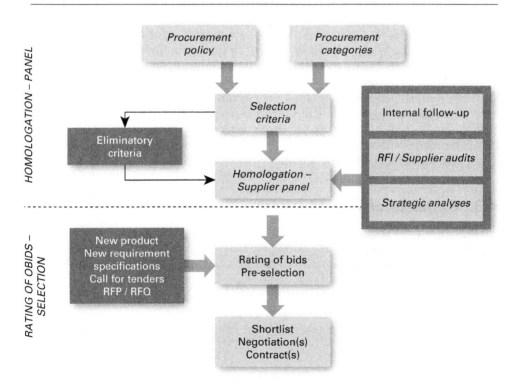

Search for information on potential suppliers

This search is essential as it involves obtaining reliable and detailed information that will allow new suppliers to be qualified before entering into discussion with them after their participation in calls for tenders.

The methods, some of which are free of charge and others paid-for, can be grouped into several major categories:

- the use of official or public sources, relying as far as possible on those with prior experience in these matters;
- systematic use of generalist or sectoral web tools;
- use of websites specializing in suppliers and financial or quality rating specialist websites;
- the implementation of in-depth analyses and audits carried out locally.

Table 4.2 provides details on the different yet complementary approaches. The reader is invited to review the table carefully and to test out some of the methods to become more familiar with them.

SOURCING SERVICE-PROVIDERS

It is always possible to outsource a sourcing strategy. But the problem with doing that, apart from the cost of the service, lies in an absence of learning experience for the company. For this reason, this solution is only valid for starting off a strategy, or to meet non-recurring requirements or else requirements not related to the core activity.

The process implies the prior gathering of necessary information on identified potential suppliers, as seen above, by making enquiries via traditional means or via internet applications known as e-RFI (requests for information).

Next, suppliers are assessed according to a series of criteria that determine their eligibility for qualification. If the criteria are met, they will join the panel and on this basis alone, they are likely to be called upon to participate in future calls for tenders.

In this way, qualification is a *crucial passage* before a supplier is invited to participate in calls for tenders. In certain companies, buyers known as 'panel managers' or SRMs may be wholly dedicated to this activity.

4/3.1 Formal qualification criteria

Qualification criteria may be very broad, and will depend on each procurement category and its particularities. However, the only criteria that should be considered are those that *assess a supplier as an organization*, in other words without any link to a particular product (which would require a specific call for tenders).

Table 4.3 provides a list of approval or qualification criteria that could be used as a reference guide for this type of analysis.

TABLE 4.2   Summary of supplier-search methods

Descriptions	Payable / Free (P/F)	Methods / Bodies	Commentaries / Web sites (examples)
Identification and gathering of detailed information	F	Search motors (without 'intelligence')	www.google.com
		Search motors (thematic)	www.yahoo.com
		Specialist trade press	www.usinenouvelle.com
			www.purchasing.com
		Trade exhibitions (lists)	www.salons-online.com
			www.tscentral.com
		Overseas embassies of one's country	Economic missions
		Foreign embassies in one's country	See addresses according to targeted countries
		Opinions of colleagues	Focusing on similar products or technologies
	P	Generalist online directories	www.pagesjaunes.com
			www.kompass.com
			www.europages.com
			www.thomasregister.com
			www.tipcoeurope.com
		Community web sites	www.globalsources.com
			www.dnb.com/purchase/psourcing.htm
		Web sites specializing in product types or activities or regions	www.european-sourcing.com
			www.asiansource.com
			www.jimtrade.com
			www.supplierbusiness.com
			www.surfingparts.com
			Miller Freemans Directories
			www.trgnet.com

TABLE 4.2   *continued*

Descriptions	Payable / Free (P/F)	Methods / Bodies	Commentaries / Web sites (examples)
Rating (other aids for this phase)	F/P	As above	See all items
	F	Supplier web sites	See addresses directly
		Requests for information made directly to suppliers	'Classic' method e-RFI
	P	Specialist trips (audits, either internally or with delegates)	Industrial, logistical, quality, managerial audits
		Financial-rating bodies	**www.dnb.com** **www.scrl.com**
		Quality-certification bodies	**WWW.AFAQ.FR** Other overseas bodies
		Service-providers with added value (sourcing specialists) – selection	**www.synertrade.com** **www.sourcingparts.com** **www.buyingpack.com** **www.k-buy.com**

TABLE 4.3   Supplier qualification criteria

Skills required	Supporting evidence
Quality skills and procedures	• existence of an operational quality assurance system • existing certification (ISO 9000, V2000) • past statistics on 'delivered' quality • existence of a quality action plan underway
Demonstrable R&D skills	• capacity for innovation proved by number of patents filed, or design-related savings generated by previous developments • high-quality R&D-specific tools functioning effectively • equipment to run tests and create prototypes • ability to reduce development cycles
Industrial skills	• capacity, capability of the equipment and efficiency of manufacturing technologies in place • average qualification level of the labour force • capacity to develop own tools (or take direct responsibility for their design and external production)

TABLE 4.3 *continued*

Skills required	Supporting evidence
Flexibility/ logistical organization	<ul><li>organization of physical flows within the company</li><li>demonstrated ability for just-in-time deliveries (or fast series changeovers)</li><li>demonstrated respect for contractual delivery lead times (based on past history)</li><li>average manufacturing cycles</li><li>planning system in place (guaranteeing flexibility and responsiveness)</li><li>genuine capacities for handling load fluctuations</li></ul>
Responsiveness	<ul><li>on call for swift intervention (response to quality incidents)</li><li>capacity to offer additional services (adapted packaging, logistical links with the client's different production units)</li><li>capacity to take charge of the logistical interface or to manage stocks (VMI)[4]</li></ul>
Competitiveness	<ul><li>actual productivity measured (or overall equipment effectiveness)[5]</li><li>capacity to provide a breakdown of direct costs</li><li>existence of a productivity improvement plan underway</li></ul>
Compliance with sustainable development obligations	<ul><li>actual compliance with the company's social obligations (international, local)</li><li>actual compliance with social and ethical obligations (international, local)</li><li>actual practice of environmental protection in the production process and the eco-design of products (ISO 14000)</li></ul>
Sustainability/ management skills	<ul><li>financial stability demonstrated by a few profitability indicators and monitoring of the debt ratio</li><li>belonging to a group/position and reputation on the market</li><li>variety of client portfolio and commercial risk mitigation</li><li>existence of a business plan proving control over company development</li><li>quality of the management (executives) and adaptation of structures (project teams and key account management)</li></ul>

4/3.2 Suitability for the procurement strategy

These criteria amount to judging a potential supplier *as an organization*. They presuppose that the buyer has a specific idea about the *'target' company* best suited to the procurement strategy of the specific category for which one is making up the supplier panel.

In this way, *cut-off thresholds* need to be established for certain criteria, translating the levels of acceptance below which a given supplier is deemed not to reach the minimum expected performance and therefore cannot be approved.

In addition, it is obvious that, depending on the procurement family, not all criteria can (or should) carry the same weight, and their distribution necessarily depends on the respective strategies. Referring back to the variety of supplier profiles seen in 4/1, it is necessary to have at least three target profiles (co-developers, manufacturers, subcontractors) crossed-matched with as many procurement categories.

This strategy is therefore crucial as it sets the choices that will predetermine procurement performance for every category or segment.

4/3.3 Qualification team and process

There is an obvious risk of subjectivity and empiricism intruding into the criteria-listing, weighting and supplier-rating operations. It is an especial risk taken by the buyer whose practice consists in choosing a supplier 'intuitively'. This is essentially due to the *subjectivity* of assessments (mainly for non-quantitative criteria), the *incompetency* of certain buyers in certain areas, and the *heterogeneity* of individuals (if certain suppliers are rated or certain criteria analysed and weighted by different people).

For these reasons, it is useful to form a *qualification team* made up of competent *stakeholders* for the supplier panel in question – specifiers and designers, end-users or internal clients, 'qualiticians' (qualification audit specialists), supply-chain members, buyers etc – and to call on other experts (eg from the finance department) if the need arises. There is therefore greater scope for the chosen criteria to cover all important points, for ratings on each point to be as relevant and objective as possible, and for the overall appraisal of each supplier to best sum up the entire set of criteria. In addition, a rating system of this type is collective, and thus creates *co-responsibility* between the different players vis-à-vis top managers.

In this team, the procurement department is a de facto stakeholder, and it is even preferable for the department to be the *coordinator* of the process. Procurement is moreover best positioned for weighting certain criteria and rating the suppliers.

4/4 Management of the supplier panel

By this point, it is clear that a supplier panel is made up of a set of suppliers who are constantly approved and managed, and who meet the buying company's requirements. As a result, management of the panel consists of three main points:

- upstream sourcing aimed at feeding the panel with new suppliers;
- constitution of the panel in relation to the company's requirements, and by procurement category (with the important additional question being the number of suppliers needed to make up this panel);
- directing the panel, involving the effective follow-up of the suppliers, generating improvement action plans, or even the elimination of certain under-performing suppliers.

4/1.1 Structure and steering of the supplier panel

The supplier panel cannot remain constant, and new suppliers should enter it regularly. Some suppliers will therefore be beta-tested before their inclusion on the panel is confirmed. It is crucial to find suppliers that the company needs today or will need tomorrow. Figure 4.6 illustrates a typical panel structure.

The 'core panel' will consist of the profile categories seen in Section 4/1. For reasons of convenience, there is no mention of subcontractors or one-off spot supplier categories generally needed for secondary purchase segments.

Suppliers 'on warning' are those whose measured performance has dropped below the quality threshold. In this case, a recovery plan is established between the buyer and the supplier, generally accompanied by a timed schedule and list of highly detailed corrective measures. A supplier who does not bring performance levels up to the minimum expected standard may be removed from the panel according to the terms specified in the contracts. This may even entail an end to a supplier's collaboration whilst a contract is underway.

As a result, a supplier in this position who wishes to collaborate once again with the company will need to go through the approvals procedure again and demonstrate that the required performance level has been re-established.

This is why another category of suppliers needs to be identified: those 'on probation,' to whom a formal performance improvement plan has been submitted. This procedure may also eventually be accompanied by the buyer company placing qualiticians and technicians at the supplier's disposal to offer help and to transfer certain know-how and methodologies. In this situation, the investment into the procedure should be costed as it will need to be amortized by future collaborations.

Through this process, we show that procurement is not just about the balance of power: it is also in the company's interests to have efficient and profitable suppliers, and it is entirely possible for it to contribute towards this goal through joint work on shared improvements.

Supplier panel size

A classic question then arises: how many suppliers should there be on a panel? This question is posed as if an answer can always be produced by applying a prescriptive model. Obviously, this is not the case, and common sense should prevail. Let's remember that the answer depends mainly on two factors that must be weighed up: on the one hand, a certain minimum number of suppliers is necessary in order to guarantee that real competition exists when a call for tenders is launched to the panel suppliers;[6] and on the other hand, there should not be so many that focus is

FIGURE 4.6   Structure of the supplier panel

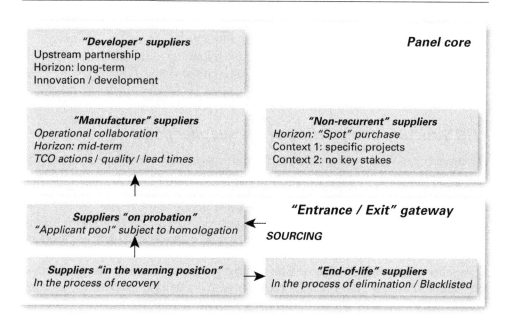

lost. Let's not forget that in any procurement category, the greater the number of suppliers, the more the total volume of purchases will be spread out between them (thus diminishing the relative importance of the company vis-à-vis each of them, and its ability to position itself advantageously as an adequately sized 'key account'). In addition, having to follow (and manage) too many suppliers always means doing little or nothing at all due to a lack of the human resources needed to invest time in the task!

It is therefore vital that the buyer continually bears in mind the way in which he or she wishes to manage the panel's development, as illustrated by Figure 4.7.

This is a process of ongoing improvement, with the fundamental purpose of establishing direct relationships with the company's main suppliers.

4/4.2 Measurement and follow-up of supplier performance

This activity requires the operational performance of suppliers to be measured *objectively*. There are two main procedures that should be carried out regularly: a) *audits* of all types (the same as those carried out during the qualification stage) to ensure that the systems in place continue to operate (ie quality assurance plans, sustainable development practices, improvement of logistics, measurable results for productivity action plans); b) implementation of a *performance measurement system in relation to deliveries* that consists in monitoring the supplier on the basis of observable results.

The reader will find below a simplified example of follow-up implemented by a European aeronautics company for its so-called 'panel core' suppliers (Figure 4.8).

FIGURE 4.7 Dynamic steering of the supplier panel

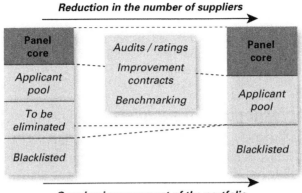

Reduction in the number of suppliers

Panel core	Audits / ratings	Panel core
Applicant pool	Improvement contracts	Applicant pool
To be eliminated	Benchmarking	
Blacklisted		Blacklisted

Ongoing improvement of the portfolio

FIGURE 4.8 Follow-up of the operational performance of suppliers

Measuring rods:				
Each order line of every delivery is rated out of 100 points, broken down into the				
4 following criteria:				
	Respect of the delivery date		35	points
	Conformity with quality standard		30	points
	Conformity with the quantities ordered		20	points
	Conformity with administrative requirements		15	points
		TOTAL	100	
General principle applied: demerit, in other words, a point-loss system				
Domains	**Indicator**	**Principle and measuring rods**	**Total**	**Frequency**
Date	cf. Order form	2 points per day late 1/2 point per day early		Real time
Quality	cf. Respect of the requirements specifications	Every line that does not respect all requirements earns a score of "0"		Real time
Quantities	cf. Order form	In the event of a gap, whatever the quantity in question, every incomplete line will be penalized as follows:		Real time
		2 points if the missing quantity equals or exceeds 5 %		
		No points lost if the missing quantity is less than 5 %		
		2 points if the quantity exceeds the quantity ordered		
Administration	Accompanying documents	Missing or erroneous information on the delivery note Absence of certain documents		Real time
		If a piece of information is missing, the order will earn a score of "0"		
		TOTAL	out of 100	
		Frequency of communication, analysis and meetings	semester	
		Performance objective for "Operational Collaboration" -class supplier	> 90 points	

The strictness of the system applied here is apparent. But this should not be surprising, for the company is only echoing the strict standards imposed by its aeronautical manufacturing clients: the whole of the supply chain should share risk vis-à-vis the end-client in this way. It also needs to be remembered that suppliers are perfectly familiar with the system and accept it as a driver of improvement; in addition, they have all acknowledged their acceptance of this system, given that these rules are systematically annexed to contracts.

4/4.3 Development plans of suppliers

Management of a panel also means seeking the ongoing improvement of suppliers, and defining performance improvement plans. To do this, two main stances can be adopted: either allowing suppliers to define improvement plans themselves, and 'restricting' the company to approving them, then overseeing their implementation; or becoming involved, as the ordering party, in diagnosing performance and defining jointly designed improvement plans with suppliers.

In the second scenario, it is necessary to develop an extremely robust diagnostic methodology. The major aspects of one such methodology are present below, developed by several members of the Department of Operations Management and Information Systems (MOSI) of HEC Paris and published in 1996 (for use, at the time, in relation to second-tier suppliers in the automotive supply sector), then largely reproduced by Baglin and Capraro in their 2002 work, which remains entirely relevant today.[7]

The methodology relies on the principles of *lean production*, an approach initially developed in the 1990s that involves seeking optimization of a company's operational system and improvement of its industrial and logistical performance.

Scope of the diagnostic

Whilst the trilogy of cost–quality–lead-time remains unchanged as goals for industrial companies, the way that these are attained has changed tremendously.

Yesterday, in order to obtain low manufacturing costs, we sought to increase the speed of direct production labour. To obtain good quality, we multiplied monitoring processes at every stage of the process. To deliver quickly, we maintained abundant stocks of finished products.

Today, we know that a high level of quality can only be reached and maintained by seeking to do things 'right first time' (preventative approach) and by involving all players, from the engineer in the design department to the operator, in the search for perfect quality. For fast delivery, we know that it is necessary to increase the flexibility of the production equipment, and thus its ability to react to enable flows to be accelerated.

As for low costs, we no longer seek to obtain these by focusing solely on direct production costs but by analysing the relevance of all types of costs, with no exceptions, and by systematically seeking more economical means, bringing these to the level of the 'strictly necessary' in order to reach the same production result.

In the context of mass production, we once placed importance on minimizing the consequences of dysfunction: we would protect ourselves from delays by building up stocks, from defects by multiplying checks, from breakdowns by organizing repair teams and by backing up crucial equipment. In this way, we increased fixed assets and staff that proved useless if no problems arose.

Lean production endeavours to optimize how we meet objectives in quality control, cost minimization, cycle reductions, flexibility and responsiveness, by operating in five different areas:

- suppression of all unnecessary safety devices that generate cost overruns;
- detection and elimination of all operations with no added value, which often amounts to simplifying flows and internal processes;
- reduction then suppression of all internal dysfunctions of all types (organization of flows, planning systems, non-quality, etc);
- combatting wastage of all types;
- streamlining and decompartmentalization of the company.

These goals for improvement are generally met via action plans organized according to the themes presented in Table 4.4. Here, we recognize the elements that characterize deployment of a joint just-in-time and total-quality approach, including a new managerial dimension.

Implementation rules

In order to meet the objectives, it is important to have, at one's disposal, necessary tools and a diagnostic strategy that enables helpful signposting of the process to

TABLE 4.4   Different focuses for a supplier improvement plan

1. Design and development of new products
2. Procurement strategy and professional practices
3. Flexibility and just-in-time
4. Use and saturation of bottleneck equipment
5. Controlled quality: 'zero-fault' organization
6. Elimination of operations with no added value
7. Streamlining and decompartmentalization of the supply chain
8. 'Power' to the workshops: accountability
9. Teamwork (primacy of the 'collective')
10. Ongoing improvement process

follow. What makes the two suggested references particularly interesting (French Ministry of Industry, 1996; Capraro and Baglin, 2006) is that they provide practical details on such tools. Readers are encouraged to consult these sources: the co-authors' recommendations are grounded on long experience as consultants, and their effectiveness has been well proven.

4/4.4 Restructuring of the upstream supply chain

Management of the supplier panel can also be greatly impacted by a desire to significantly influence the restructuring of the upstream industrial network of supplier sectors. As an example, let's look at the automotive supply industry of some 30 years ago.

As Figure 4.9 shows, car manufacturers at that time dealt 'directly' with a large number of first-tier suppliers, often small-scale, alongside bigger equipment suppliers. This was accompanied by often complex procedures for monitoring suppliers, as well as numerous subassemblies of a large number of basic components coming from these different suppliers. Added to this were disparities in the quality level of the delivered products or components, giving rise to problems of reliability.

As a result, car manufacturers came to seek a cut in the number of their first-tier suppliers, by gradually entrusting them with overall responsibility for subassemblies or complete functions of a vehicle. In this way, they made it a priority to create links between companies, even mergers, by selecting certain leading suppliers and encouraging repositioning of the smallest (or even the most fragile) ones in new, larger-scale conglomerates. The lower part of the figure illustrates this repositioning.

FIGURE 4.9   Supply chain restructuration mechanism

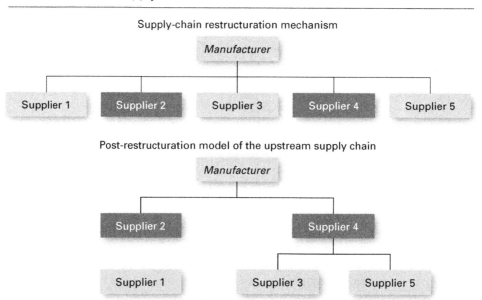

By proceeding in this way, car leaders counted on gaining several advantages:

- paring down their supplier panel whilst dealing with more financially solid 'integrator' companies made accountable for the overall quality of more complex subassemblies;
- due to their increased financial standing, these new suppliers were able to self-finance industrial investments as well as their own R&D services, and gradually become co-development partners (thus evolving into mature equipment suppliers);
- the continuity of working with former small-scale suppliers, which would otherwise have vanished, was ensured by their integration into larger groups;
- finally, car manufacturers found this process to be an important source of internal value creation through the drastic reduction of intermediary subassemblies.

4/5 SRM: collaborative steering of the upstream supply chain

As we have already seen, a company can maintain its competitiveness by improving its relationships with suppliers. This observation has spawned the concept of supplier relationship management (SRM). Supplementing customer relationship management, which aims to improve relationships with clients, and supply-chain management, which focuses on integration of the global logistical chain, SRM constitutes the final vital link in a chain running between the end-client (downstream) and the supplier (upstream).

Through creation of a collaborative environment with suppliers, SRM sets itself the goal of nurturing innovation, improving the flexibility of supplies, ensuring a better service, and controlling product quality whilst cutting procurement costs.

To shed light on this point, we will draw from the extremely interesting and relatively recent research of Jean Potage; whilst simplifying its content, we will remain loyal to the spirit and richness of these original reflections.[8]

4/5.1 Different levels in relationships and communication

The model highlights several (possible and desirable) levels in relationships, and hence, in communication linking a company and its suppliers. A simplified version of the model is shown in Figure 4.10. Our commentary below outlines our own vision based on, but paring down, the original model. This approach should be considered as a baseline. The schema should subsequently be adapted to every supplier according to its degree of importance and status in the eyes of the company; it also needs to be adapted to each company, according to its size and the resources that it can mobilize in this process.

The first level of relationships is purely *transactional*. There is no interactive communication here, but the stage is devoted to the execution of contracts, and the management of interfaces between planning systems and order/delivery handling systems, with corresponding physical supply flows and their associated accounting chain.

FIGURE 4.10   Different levels in supplier relationships

			MAIN CONTENT	MAIN FEATURES
5 levels of supplier relationships	VALUES	5	Ethics Respect of commitments Social responsibility Environmental responsibility	One-to-one relations Management / KSM meetings Project teams Confidentiality agreements
	POLICIES	4	Innovation Technological perspective Product/market developments	Restricted supplier conventions / KSM Joint supervision / project teams Non-disclosure agreements / SRM
	PANEL IMPROVEMENT PROCESS	3	Qualification principles / RFI Expected performance criteria Improvement plans Enlarged performance indicators	Supplier conventions Assessment meetings Information on intranet portal / SRM
	CONTRACTS	2	RFP – RFQ calls for tenders Selection criteria Negotiation	Technical communication on contractual expectations
	TRANSACTIONS	1	Contract execution Management of physical flows Accounting chain	No communication

Main features (except for 1 and 2) ──────▶   3 and 5 | 3, 4 and 5 | 3, 4 and 5

Competitive S-C supplier | **Innovative supplier** | **Co-business partner**

PRIME Model simplified. © 2010 Jean Potage

The second level is *contractual*. Covering the scope of operational procurement, this type of relationship is directly linked with the call for tenders organized for the product/service to be purchased. It incorporates the search for commercial-type compromises and the negotiation stage. Communication does not really play a role here; instead, this is a transaction of a commercial nature.

The third level targets the medium term, and corresponds to *supplier qualification* and *panel steering* with the aim of improving the panel by structuring it and overseeing risks. At this stage, real communication should be established on requirements in terms of qualification, different supplier profiles that the company is looking for and wishes to have on the panel, thresholds for requirements and expected performance for a certain number of criteria, as well as control of a certain number of risks (regulatory and legal conformity, operational risks, etc). Once suppliers have joined the panel, the procurement department will address suppliers on *improvement plans* and this process will rely on periodical assessments, jointly analysed on the basis of recognized and shared indicators.

The fourth level is described as *policy-based*. At least for 'core panel' or strategic suppliers, this level consists of exchanges (confidential in nature) on medium- or long-term policy visions, including disclosures on future projects or more strategic developments. This is a collaborative partnership: the company openly discusses its development projects and diversification wishes whilst suppliers present their own projects on technology or product developments. Technology intelligence is shared; co-development, or even co-innovation, is developed. In certain cases, the parties may jointly develop new activities with a shared business plan (sharing of risks and profits, co-investment in the development stage). Both parties approach one another as 'key accounts,' and communication is regular and in depth. In addition, various project teams often sustain communication on a practical level.

The fifth and final level is that of *values*, if parties wish for these to be shared, which is increasingly the case, in terms of the deployment of sustainable, responsible and ethical procurement. Here, it is necessary to look for a shared vision, to confirm it and to make it known, as it will influence behaviour on all levels.

A priori, for each relationship level, the persons *assuming responsibility for the relationship* in the company are not the same (even if there may be a number of actors) whenever the company's size allows for it. Management of the first level is the domain of the supply chain. The second and third levels are usually managed by the buyer or the procurement manager, with the chief procurement officer (CPO) only involved for arbitration decisions in relation to panel management and supplier profiles. The fourth level should fall under the responsibility of the procurement department manager, with the collaboration of other operational managements involved and the supervision of top managers. The last remains under the operational management of the CPO, but implies the co-leadership and direct intervention of the top executives.

4/5.2 Differentiation of relationships depending on supplier profiles

Apart from the case of one-off suppliers, or secondary suppliers with regard to the volume of business handled, we have seen above that three types of profiles commonly exist in a supplier panel:

- Suppliers whose expected performance is mainly defined in terms of *competitiveness* (conformity to quality, short lead-times respected, flexibility, and low and controlled costs); there may be a few hundred or even a few thousand of these.

- Suppliers whose relationship is based on *operational collaboration* and joint improvement of performance on a broad spectrum: Jean Potage describes this type, characterized by the requirement of the 'trust' value, as 'co-performance' suppliers; there may be a few hundred of these.

- Finally, partners contributing to value creation by *innovation*, in relationships described by Jean Potage as 'co-business'; there may be a few dozen of these.

The last two categories are called strategic as they contribute to value creation. Whilst the first categories relate to short-term costs, the second ones relate to the derivation of innovation that generates diversification and medium-term development and profitability.

It is clear that communication and relationship content cannot be the same from case to case. The indicators used, the frequency and means of communication, and the nature of the actors involved obviously vary. The dominant features of relationship and communication choices appear on the right column in Figure 4.10. At the bottom of the figure, we identify the collaboration indices that reflect their dependency against each supplier profile.

4/5.3 The role of key supplier managers (KSMs)

In some large (or very large) companies, the issue of management and follow-up of the system of communication with each of the suppliers is raised, given the complexity of the task (at least for suppliers from the two categories said to be 'strategic'). This concern has given birth to a new *integrator* function known as a key supplier manager (KSM), whose role encompasses the overseeing of one or several suppliers.

Usually, a KSM does not undertake this mission full-time; nor does he or she necessarily belong to the procurement department. In fact, certain top managers outside of the procurement department, including day-to-day managers, are perfectly capable of taking on this responsibility.

Notes

1 Here, the term 'source' is used in its restrictive sense. 'Sourcing' in English-speaking (particularly US) literature generally covers the whole of the procurement process from the detection of new suppliers up to the final selection of a supplier following a call for tenders, right up to the signing of a procurement contract. In addition, the SCOR (supply-chain operations reference model) interprets 'sourcing' as the whole of the procurement function. In this book, we limit the term to the detection of new supply sources, thus its strictest meaning.

2 On these issues, the reader is invited to consult Philippart, Verstraete and Wynen (2005) that continues to be applicable today.

3 On this key topic of trust in relationships with suppliers that should spread to all levels of the company, read Poissonnier, Philippart and Kourim (2012).

4 The VMI system is analysed in Chapter 9.

5 A supplier's overall equipment effectiveness (OEE) denotes the rate of use of industrial equipment. This indicator is commonly referred to in industrial management, and consists in measuring the relationship between the machine hours actually dedicated to manufacturing – based on a level of normal effectiveness – and the equipment's nominal operation hours. Details on calculations and the main elements can be found in the following work: Baglin, G, Bruel, O, Garreau, G, Greif, M, Kerbache, L and van Delft, C (2013).

6 Indeed, the rationale of forming a panel following a qualification procedure implies that we steer clear from launching calls for tenders open to all suppliers on the market (unless we wish to test certain new suppliers by calibrating them against approved suppliers). This approach should therefore be followed with care if a company is subject to legal obligations applying to public markets – a point that will be discussed further on.

7 On this topic, see French Ministry of Industry (1996) and Capraro and Baglin (2002).

8 Jean Potage, former global chief procurement officer of Thales, is currently a consultant and expert lecturer at the Polytechnique and HEC Paris. We refer the reader to his article published in French (Potage, 2010) where he puts forward and describes his original model.

05
Globalization and international procurement

One of the fundamental elements in procurement today – at least in large and/or market-leading companies – is the international redeployment of supply-chain activities. This is a basic shift that has characterized procurement strategy in the last 15 years or so, in step with well-considered strategic analysis, and is also a consequence of permanent structural developments in the global economic environment.

5/1 Developments in the global economic context and new strategic issues

What, then, are these new developments? Closed markets have long ceased to exist. Global exchanges have been completely freed up and are organized by the World Trade Organization (WTO). The competitiveness stakes in markets are now global. Protected markets no longer exist, or are rare (only protection via patents remains solid without altogether protecting against the risks of illegal counterfeit or copies that are more difficult to contest). With the exception of certain countries or regions, and largely for economic reasons, customs duties have dropped to extremely low levels. What's more, certain regions of the world are now legally organized to be entirely duty-free (eg Europe or South America).

At the same time, there are great disparities (set to linger for quite a while, even if more recent developments are gradually moving the boundaries) in existing standards of living, economic policies and thus production costs. This situation prompts transfers in industrial activity, all the more so as international transport costs (potentially making industrial solutions and international supply chains more expensive) remain at fairly low price levels and thus still have a relatively minimal impact on the acquisition costs of products (so long as pollution factors are not included in the equation).

Finally, following technology transfer between developed countries and less developed ones, the world now encompasses zones of technological skills that make up a new global distribution of know-how. In particular, Western Europe has lost a number of technology leadership titles, and this evolution has been backed up by significant delocalization of the industrial and research centres of its countries' companies. Without mentioning the quasi-complete elimination of the industrial network in many economic sectors of technical or, even more significantly, of consumer goods. Even certain service activities have been exported to a wide number of emerging countries (eg software services to India).

In this liberated global economic context, companies have seen their 'degree of freedom' grow and their economic 'playground' turn global. At the same time, their shareholders demand yet more value creation: this pressure is translated into an ongoing search for minimization of total costs, but also by the development of trade in new countries with local suppliers. It therefore comes as no surprise that procurement departments have tended to approach international reorganization of their procurement portfolios in a well-thought-out and proactive manner.

5/1.1 Objectives of international procurement

In concrete terms, the main objectives to date are concentrated around three major themes:

- support of the company's international development in different global markets;
- the search for the most groundbreaking know-how, now often found amongst suppliers on any continent, depending on the technological area in question;
- finally, the search for the lowest possible acquisition costs, with the aim of maximizing profit margins.

International development of business and optimization of the global supply chain

The first factor prompting expansion of the company's procurement horizons is a need for coherence that a procurement department will seek to maintain when the company's entire supply chain is subject to international reorganization – a shift that may be prompted by commercial reasons in particular.

Let's take the example of a company producing consumer goods that supplies a major mass-retail brand. When this organization sets up in a wide range of Asian countries, quick economic calculations indicate that there is no question that it should import certain products (with a heavy pressure on prices) from Western Europe. The company will therefore need to redefine its supplier panel in such a way as to include a significant number of new 'local' suppliers in order to act effectively on the cost function of the new international supply chain.

To a certain extent, this is exactly the same process that has historically been followed by many industrial companies such as automotive suppliers who have striven, in their choice of new industrial sites, for geographical proximity with the assembly plants of their car-manufacturer clients.

Local content obligations

Another argument of a commercial nature, familiar to companies selling turnkey projects internationally, whether in the construction, aeronautics, rail, petrol or energy supply industries, is that all projects commissioned by states, regional authorities or semi-public companies will require the development of local suppliers when they grant access to local markets. Procurement departments must therefore anticipate bids by approving potential, sometimes mandatory, suppliers.

Countertrade obligations

Broadening this argument, many business development situations are characterized by different types of industrial countertrade obligations (see Section 5/6 in this chapter), including offsets, that apply to many companies responding to international calls for tenders launched by overseas countries. This is a variation of the preceding obligation that has been widely practised but that is now losing popularity in favour of the 'local content' approach that aims at longer-term development.

Access to new know-how

In many cases, know-how and R&D leaderships have shifted territories across the world. For example, Europe as a whole has completely given up certain technological fields. This is a logical follow-on from low-cost-country sourcing, where the LCC initially acted as the world's factory. Things have now moved on requiring innovative approaches to the use of resources to finance these developments (in the so-called leading competitive countries).

In this way, today it is possible to map the world according to major product or process technologies, and to direct collaboration choices according to the actual skills existing in a growing number of countries.

Reductions in direct costs (total acquisition costs)

One common objective is of course economic in nature: the goal is to improve the competitiveness of procurement via a search for reduced direct costs. Indeed, after a reduction in acquisition costs has been secured through traditional procurement methods (negotiation, actions on all factors making up the global acquisition cost, the volume effect, globalization paired with shrinkage of the supplier panel, and more generally all upstream procurement practices), procurement managers still have the solution available of widening sourcing on an international scale.

Around 15 years ago, Christophe Horvat[1] highlighted this argument when making a comparative analysis of major procurement levers in terms of economic efficiency, based on his own experience (see Figure 5.1, where figures on the horizontal axis are expressed in (indicative) percentages of respective cost reductions). Only product redesign initiatives, using the upstream procurement approaches seen in Chapter 3, seem more effective or to work on the same scale as international deployment of procurement.

Obviously, and especially when we speak of international procurement *aimed at repatriation* to satisfy a demand from traditional developed markets (as is the case for many European companies), the right economic criterion to take into consideration should not be mere purchasing cost (ex-works starting cost) but the *global acquisition cost with delivery* (as in a DDP Incoterm).

FIGURE 5.1   Comparative analysis of the efficiency of international sourcing

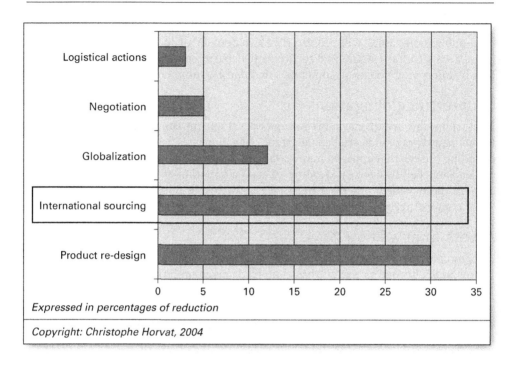

Expressed in percentages of reduction

Copyright: Christophe Horvat, 2004

Neutralization of exchange rate differentials

In this case, the motivation is essentially financial, or to be precise, monetary. It mainly affects all companies that sell products sold all over the world in a key international currency, ie the US dollar (aeronautics, all turnkey engineering professions, etc), and that seek to neutralize the negative impact of exchange rate differences. This is a matter of ensuring that sales in dollars are maximally offset by purchases also carried out in the 'dollar' zone or the equivalent, so as to avoid *inherent risks in unfavourable exchange rate variations*, or even worse, risks of unforecast fluctuations. Here again, the procurement department can play a major role in its company's financial balance and cash flow.

Re-energizing the competition (cumulative impact)

The ultimate purpose of international sourcing is to put pressure on the company's usual suppliers. There are two common motivations for this: first, the desire to bring down average purchasing costs (it is understood that this is not necessarily a matter of shifting all purchases in a category to one or several sources in a low-cost country); secondly, and this is sometimes stated quite explicitly, the aim to put pressure on suppliers so that they themselves internationalize their industrial bases (or at least partially). This allows the buyer to keep the same suppliers whilst taking advantage of economic results, without directly bearing the operational or image-related consequences. The existence of this practice is a fact; we can obviously take a more or less severe view on the ethics of such an approach.

5/1.2 Current practices of European companies

What can be said about the situation in 2015, at the time this book was written? Practically all major economic sectors, including services, have been internationally restructured, whether via procurement or new operational bases. Moreover, those companies that are not part of this wave are largely struggling (the European automotive industry is an excellent example). While economic reasons continue to contribute significantly to this phenomenon, other strategic objectives also play a role, and some of these take priority, namely coherence with commercial development and the conquest of new markets. The acquisition of new skills is another important motivation.

Taking the example of France, it can be seen how its trade balance – for the last five years at least – also reflects the extent of the phenomenon, as well as the continuing closures of industrial sites, their downsizing in terms of size or staff numbers, or even their delocalization.

Of course, it is possible to recite a few ritualistic comments or to set out arguments on the necessity for 'outrageous' development of innovation and 'top-range' policies for goods, that would be the solution to all the difficulties that we face. Honesty forces us to note that companies operate on an open global market and that the necessary maintenance of their competitiveness compels them to deploy their business internationally (in terms of sales, but also their purchases) – notably in order to ensure their continuity in their historic national local markets.

In addition, for 20 years now, international redeployment and the spread of know-how have been organized on a global scale. In many cases, in certain sectors or for certain technologies, it has become practically impossible to find competitive suppliers in certain economic regions of the world. In this way, buyers are – and, increasingly, will continue to be – called upon to keep on developing purchases on an international scale.

Yet many obstacles exist, preventing this task from being accomplished in a professional manner. Many companies – in certain European countries for example – lack sufficiently competent human resources trained for international practice, starting with problems relating to *real mastery of the English language*. Buyers should be capable of negotiating in English, but so also should the whole of the 'logistical chain', including technical specifiers, logisticians and qualiticians. All technical sets and plans should be available in English. The solution of using interpreters is only a last resort.

There is also an *internal reluctance*, based on preconceptions that are sometimes, even often, entirely incorrect, but that are well-rooted in mentalities:

- buyers are frightened of not being able to easily source new competitive, and above all *reliable* suppliers;

- supply-chain staff and salespeople are reluctant to supply sufficiently reliable forecasts – often a crucial condition for making an international supply chain run economically – associated with constraints for scheduling and responsiveness that sometimes leaves much to be desired;
- the financier focuses on a quasi-automatic rise in cyclical stocks and work-in-process inventories as well as necessary safety stocks, without taking into account the global acquisition cost;
- the qualitician is faced with having to carry out audits and monitor the quality of remote suppliers, whose language no one speaks;
- the R&D department would prefer to deal with nearby suppliers with whom co-development could be carried out more easily;
- in certain cases, industrial leaders fear that a movement that starts off with redeployment of procurement to countries deemed low-cost may then spread to industrial delocalization as a consequence of 'make-or-buy' and outsourcing decisions;
- finally, there is a general fear that protection of know-how is impossible (in the case of non-standard purchases) and that gradually, copies and eventually new competitors will emerge;
- ideologies circulate based on fears of local job losses indirectly related to these choices.

Externally, amongst a company's existing suppliers, there are also deep – and completely understandable – fears. The suppliers face the risk of losing large production runs and only keeping short-run projects that are incompatible with a high level of productivity. They may also fear new competition in terms of costs, hence purchasing prices, that gradually leads to the compression of their margins to an unbearable point.

It is therefore necessary to be equipped with a robust methodology that allows sound development of international procurement solutions, whilst objectively controlling the various possible risks.

5/2 Internationalization of the procurement portfolio: a coherent strategic approach

We cannot validly speak of internationalizing procurement strategy without situating it in the wider context of general company strategy and its scope for international deployment.

5/2.1 International company strategies

This issue relates to medium-sized or large companies with international activities. In this case, the basic questions that they need to resolve are the following:

- Regarding industrial facilities, how many industrial units must be designed, and with what degree of specialization (multi-product or specialized)?
- What factors should be taken into account when setting up these units (proximity to markets, proximity to the geographical zones producing raw materials, countries offering low-cost labour, etc)?
- As a complement, how should the international storage network be decided on?
- What organization should be adopted for the transport system (multi-modal)?
- What procurement strategy should be deployed (sourcing, localization and supplier profile, qualification system)?

Choices will be steered by three main criteria:

- The first objective is to achieve a minimized global total supply-chain cost (in particular, production costs will depend on the direct cost structures of the countries where industrial units are set up as well as purchasing costs, the second cost item being logistical storage/transportation costs).
- The second objective is always to seek to stay close to client markets: in this way, the company can be more flexible, shorten delivery lead-times, or even envisage 'local' adaptations to provide specific products or services for clients; this is also a way to better 'counteract' the weight of local competition.
- Finally, to the extent that the issue of localization is jointly tackled with possible outsourcing, the third objective is to be able to benefit from 'regional' know-how that pre-exists amongst local suppliers.

Analysis of current practice reveals that companies can be categorized according to four types of different strategies as shown by the model in Figure 5.2.[2]

International strategy with a domestic base (starting point): Type 1

Offering a first solution in terms of evolution, this strategy is simple: the company has a fundamental national base. All industrial activities (design, development, production) are carried out in the country of origin. Certain purchases may be made internationally, but only on a limited and occasional basis.

Sales in global regional markets are carried out through sales representation services or independent importers. When local manufacturing is considered, it is often reserved for rare local markets, in the form of a licence transfer to local manufacturers. Products are therefore not specifically adapted in any way. The economic advantage of this strategy is weak. However, it may boost a dominant competitive position in the various countries and does not truly target growth (only a marginal turnover).

As far as the supply chain goes, however, this solution remains simple as we are talking exclusively of exports from the predominantly domestic industrial base.

Multi-domestic strategy with regional autonomy: Type 2

Taking a completely opposite approach, a company involved in international activity may choose to accord greater autonomy to regional entities situated in the various countries where the company decides to operate in the market. Each entity fulfils all

FIGURE 5.2   Four dominant international strategies

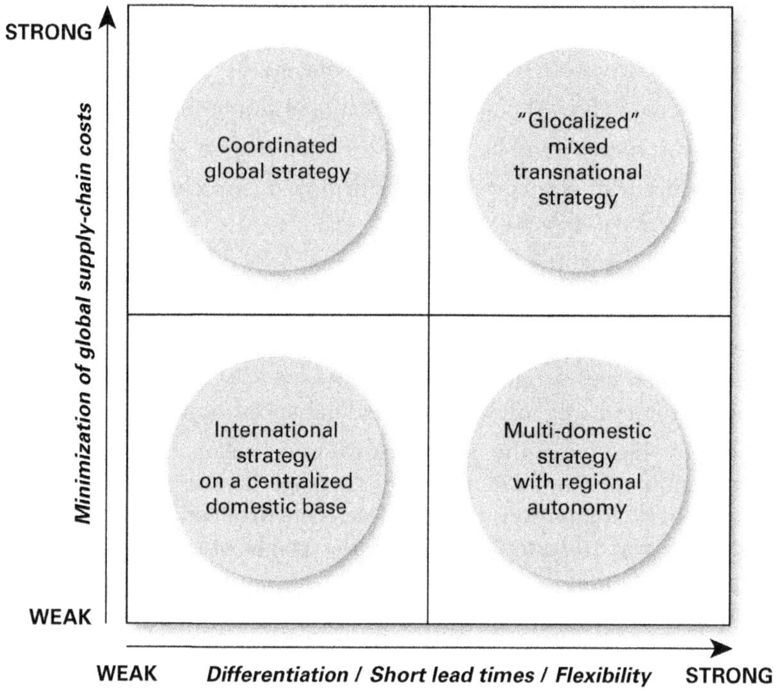

supply-chain functions. These entities may also be business units that are entirely independent, legally and economically.

Absolute priority is given to flexibility and adaptation to specific local characteristics. However, cost reductions remain limited and synergies are weak. In this case, performance of a function may then eventually be pooled: in this way, for procurement, responsibilities would be spread between worldwide subsidiaries and cross-supply flows would be possible. Procurement of certain raw materials or joint components could even be globalized.

For example, in the service sector, McDonald's demonstrates this type of strategy. If we compare a McDonald's restaurant in one country to its equivalent in another, Coca-Cola bottles may stay the same, but purchases are largely and predominantly from local or regional sources (even if certain dishes or recipes are standard).

Coordinated global strategy: Type 3

In this case, the management of international operations is very heavily centralized. However, the global network will be organized, managed and operated according to the economic and know-how advantages existing in the main regions where the company is set up. In addition, advantage is taken of the existence of levels in product structure (ie one level corresponding to the manufacturing of components and subassemblies, then a second level for the final assembly of finished products).

In this way, manufacturing units in charge of components can be set up (and specialized) in those countries that are the most interesting in terms of availability of raw materials, the existence of competent local suppliers and the minimization of production costs (low-cost countries).

Meanwhile, assembly units can be set up in consumer zones, in different markets and close to end-clients, in order to boost reactivity and flexibility. However, the dominating basic principle remains repatriation of constituents to the main domestic markets.

The existence of a central 'steering entity' (supply-chain and R&D managements) allows standardization procedures to be carried out for products and components, and facilitates the circulation of knowledge and skills throughout the group's units.

Upstream, there is one function that benefits greatly from this centralized approach: procurement, that naturally operates on a global level, and for sourcing in particular, notably by relying on existing installations in different regions. For example, Western companies in the sectors of household appliances, hi-fi or video products, as well as office goods, clearly represent this strategic approach.

Mixed transnational strategy ('glocalization'): Type 4

This type of strategy is a cross between the two previous ones. Business units are, a priori, organized to operate fairly independently; in particular, they may be completely in charge of the design of their products, the objective being to focus entirely on their respective local or regional markets.

In terms of production, the assembly phase is still based in regional markets 'close to the end-client' and to the distribution network, local in nature. However, synergies are highly organized for procurement and *intermediary* production entities. Purchases are 'globalized,' and intermediary plants are specialized in order to attain strong economic performance. These plants feed the various markets according to cross-movements managed by high-performance global logistics. Finally, the mission of this type of group is to repatriate cash flow to countries considered suitable from a taxation point of view.

This supply-chain strategy is therefore based on the search for a permanent compromise between three elements:

- 'downstream' responsiveness and flexibility with a priority on proximity to client markets;
- 'upstream' standardization and globalization with a systematic search for competitiveness in purchases and industrial productivity;
- complexity resulting from the international logistics system thus created, that should nevertheless be entirely controlled in terms of lead-times and global costs.

The typical economic sector that illustrates such a strategy is the automotive one, that manages to take advantage of global and local optimization simultaneously – hence the coining of the name 'glocalization'.

Resulting industrial and distribution choices

If we refer to the matrix model in Figure 5.2, the choices of supply-chain structures for industrial and distribution networks are closely linked to international strategy.

Figure 5.3 sums up the predominant characteristics of the network structures observed according to the four types of international deployment strategy. In this figure, the term 'regional' refers to geographical zones or continents on the global scale ('local' being reserved for specific national markets).

FIGURE 5.3   Global industrial network structures

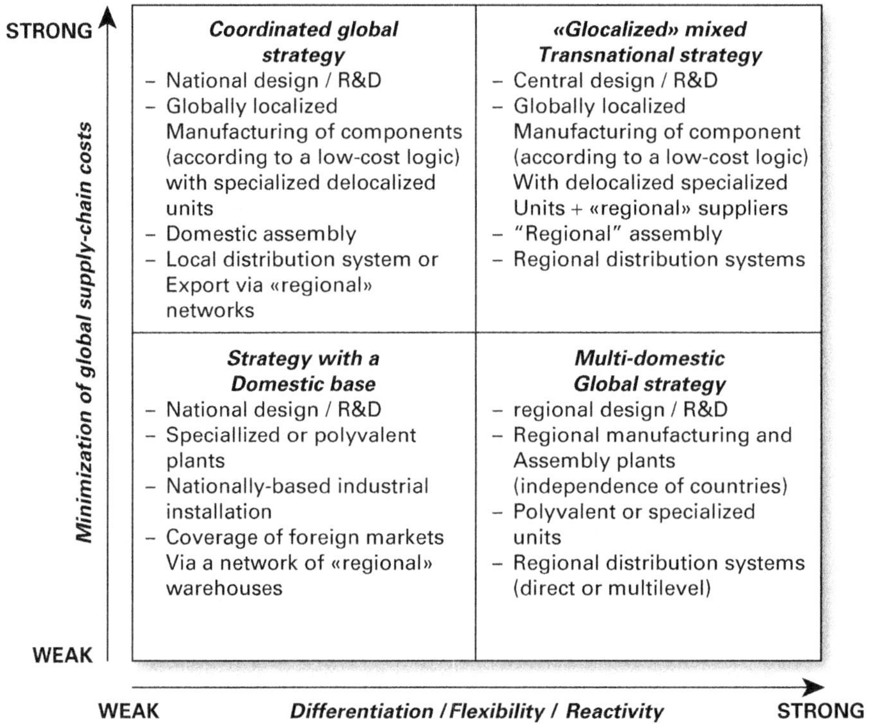

	STRONG	*Coordinated global strategy*	*«Glocalized» mixed Transnational strategy*
Minimization of global supply-chain costs		– National design / R&D – Globally localized Manufacturing of components (according to a low-cost logic) with specialized delocalized units – Domestic assembly – Local distribution system or Export via «regional» networks	– Central design / R&D – Globally localized Manufacturing of component (according to a low-cost logic) With delocalized specialized Units + «regional» suppliers – "Regional" assembly – Regional distribution systems
		Strategy with a Domestic base	*Multi-domestic Global strategy*
		– National design / R&D – Speciallized or polyvalent plants – Nationally-based industrial installation – Coverage of foreign markets Via a network of «regional» warehouses	– regional design / R&D – Regional manufacturing and Assembly plants (independence of countries) – Polyvalent or specialized units – Regional distribution systems (direct or multilevel)
	WEAK		

WEAK   *Differentiation / Flexibility / Reactivity*   STRONG

5/2.2 Procurement internationalization strategies

International procurement strategy cannot be defined independently from the framework that we have just presented. From a methodological point of view, attention should therefore be paid to the overall coherence of the approach. Examination reveals three different situations that a procurement management may find itself facing (Figure 5.4):

- *occasional* international procurement actions, or imposed by clients, tending to characterize Types 1 or 2 companies;
- companies following a Type 3 strategy will, on the other hand, carry out a *global approach for their procurement portfolio*, developing a well-thought-through strategy that is implemented systematically;

- finally, companies following a Type 4 approach will also carry out a systematic approach, but one that is *largely reliant on their international establishments via business units* or subsidiaries spread out geographically.

FIGURE 5.4   Alternative international procurement strategies

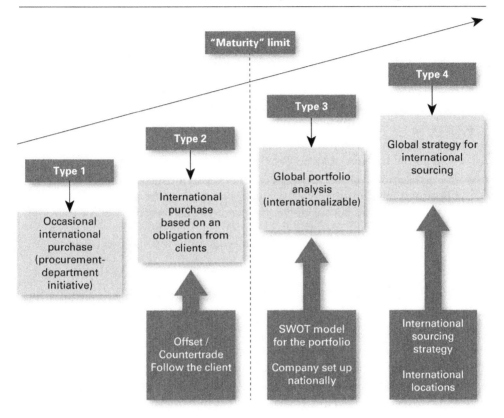

Type 1 does not merit any particular discussion; however, we will quickly discuss international procurement imposed by the client.

Procurement based on commitment from a client

Situations justifying this approach may differ in nature, but three classic cases exist:

- the client company that obliges its supplier to follow its *international commercial expansion*, in the way that a distributor can oblige its suppliers to do if they wish to continue to be referenced when it opens up new retail spaces;
- the client (in this case a state) that imposes an *offset obligation* on its supplier and/or an obligation to use a *local supplier* for part of the system or product being purchased;

- the client company that imposes a place of origin, sometimes even a specific supplier, for a *component of the system* that it intends to purchase (eg when the client wishes for the process control systems of automated equipment being purchased to come from such and such a brand or to be produced by a particular Asian supplier).

In this kind of situation, the company cannot avoid making a purchase in a country with which it is not necessarily familiar, from suppliers that it has to search out and approve, and then audit, direct and monitor, for it will be legally responsible with regard to the end-client. The main problems that it may encounter in this case are the following:

- implementation of a specific sourcing process dedicated to the operation;
- compilation of a specific database on the markets;
- qualification audits, then development and deployment of a quality-assurance system, and finally implementation of an industrial and logistical solution, with partial transfer of technology and know-how;
- in organizational terms, it is not generally ready for such distant international operations: not always having the means to delegate the task, it will therefore need to form an ad hoc taskforce that may rely on external expertise. However, its fundamental procurement organization is not modified (unless it has a permanent international sourcing expert who can be mobilized as needs arise).

Systematic global analysis of the procurement portfolio

In this type of approach, as activities are sustainable, we can commit to the following actions after strong support has been secured from the top management for the procedure to begin (possibly in the form of a company project presented as such):

- definition and systematic application of a global methodology for analysing the procurement portfolio in view of identifying 'internationalizable' categories;
- global and permanent approach to international supplier markets in the technologies identified in advance;
- analysis and rating of risks in a certain number of pre-targeted countries on a global scale;
- systematic sourcing followed by the formal approval of suppliers in the chosen countries in view of feeding a panel of pre-qualified 'international' suppliers (pre-qualified by in-house experts or by calling on external local or multi-country consultants on the basis of recurring collaborations);
- international calls for tenders (when possible, for it may prove essential to develop local networks via the development of suppliers, and even, in the long term, by training institutes to teach the skills of tomorrow) with subsequent deployment of a global information and management system;
- from an organizational viewpoint, restructuring of the procurement department accompanied by the development of employee professional qualifications and skills (the underlying principle no longer being a small dedicated team but an entire department reconfigured to offer the right skills to replace the former ones).

Generalized international sourcing

This approach largely reproduces the features of the previous approach. The major difference relates to the nature of the global procurement organization set up. In this case, we will be able to *take advantage of the entities* in different foreign countries: the procurement management itself will become *globally distributed*, multicultural and multi-skilled.

5/3 Formal process for the international deployment of procurement

The following observations are made from the perspective of a continuous, systematic approach. The general methodology that should be followed is summarized by Figure 5.5.

Let's tackle the main stages of this process that address basic common-sense questions requiring answers, and in this order:

- What? Which products or services to internationalize and for what reasons?
- Where? In which country(ies) and with which supplier(s)?
- How? How to deploy procurement and which operational solutions to implement on the ground to guarantee the system's operation?

Note that prior acquisition of all types of information on products, countries and suppliers was discussed in Chapter 4, which presented a list of all main sourcing methods practised.

5/3.1 Selection criteria for an appropriate procurement portfolio

The first step is to go back to the strategic analysis of the procurement portfolio, but from an internationalization perspective.

Size of the purchase and appropriate cost structure

Let's start off with an obvious point: we only decide to delocalize a purchase when the yearly sum of purchases guarantees very significant genuine savings in terms of absolute value, or value creation through the development of new markets. For manufacturers,[3] efforts required are generally so great that time devoted to the process should largely be amortized. The main stage consists in embarking on a cost structure analysis for all procurement categories. Two cost items should always be examined attentively:

1 The 'raw materials' part, namely in relation to savings that may result from obtaining supplies from the country of origin, benefiting from more interesting – or less fluctuating – regional prices (a supplier's offer pegged to local costs rather than a global rate), or gaining freedom from supply restrictions linked to export quotas.

FIGURE 5.5   General process for the internationalization of procurement

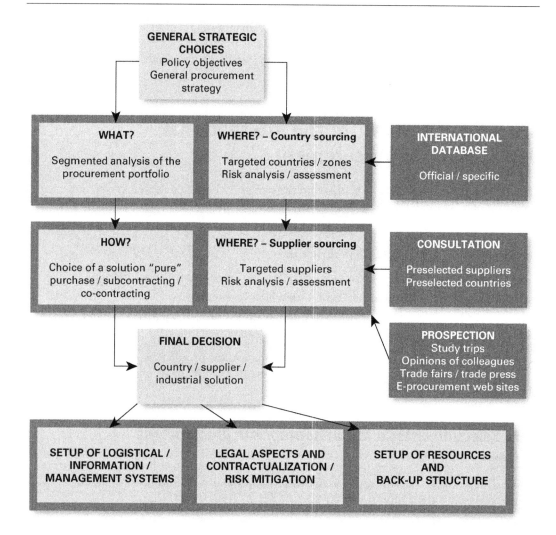

2 The 'transformation cost' (itself split into the cost of labour, machine amortization and the cost of tooling). Regarding labour, this is an element that naturally makes deployment to low-cost countries interesting. However, for purchases of specific parts made according to subcontractors' plans, the cost of tooling is sometimes decisive, notably if competent and competitive toolmakers are present in certain developing countries.

Indeed, labour–cost differentials are very significant depending on which countries we are looking at, and in certain cases may offer opportunities to make savings of around 40 per cent on direct costs. But more recently, we have seen these gaps shrink for certain countries such as eastern China, whilst others, such as the United States, are becoming more competitive once again as a result of exchange rates (to be followed on a medium-term basis).

It is obvious, nonetheless, that the utmost prudence should prevail during the analysis. Indeed, the cost differential should be substantial, for practice shows that many other costs (beyond direct variable costs) always end up bringing down the differential and trimming the supposed margins. In fact, we should reason in terms of TCO, in the sense of global cost of acquisition and ownership (that is, including the WCR figure of any solution).

Access to raw materials and technological mastery

Other motives spurring the internationalization of certain purchases are of two types.

Regarding raw materials, beyond the cost (in the narrowest sense), we can aim for direct access from a producer rather than going through a distributor, thus deleting a level of margins (that may represent 20–30 per cent of the cost), and allowing greater visibility of any shortage or availability risks.

In addition, certain countries sometimes have quota practices, that might be avoided. We can sometimes also benefit from tax advantages from the exporter country.

Regarding technologies, we have already discussed the expertise that has developed in certain countries. But sometimes this argument is strengthened by the *quality of the production technologies set up*. Indeed, due to the gradual effect of delocalization, investment has stopped in certain European countries, whilst on the contrary, new investment has been made in emerging countries, resulting in a more up-to-date industrial equipment fleet corresponding to the latest manufacturing technologies with a better level of productivity.

However, one crucial criterion should always be examined in detail: the degree of technical criticality of the products (crucial quality of key elements, high level of technology produced) and lead-times (in the case of complex large projects, we may proceed by avoiding delocalization of parts situated along the project's critical path). We are therefore still operating within a cross-analysis framework.

Another phenomenon that has consequences for costs is the significant arrival of shale gas in the United States, that has lowered energy costs by 15–30 per cent depending on sources. For industries that are heavy energy consumers, this is a major competitiveness factor.

Dollarization of purchases

For Europeans, due to the euro settling in the long term at a higher level than the dollar, and for European companies mainly selling their products in US dollars, delocalization of procurement has greatly increased recently in order to neutralize the effects of exchange rate differentials. In addition, companies today situated downstream along supply chains all pass these factors on to their first-tier suppliers. In particular, this concerns hi-tech industries (aeronautics, avionics, civilian and defence electronics, and automotive in particular).

Caution about knee-jerk reactions

It is necessary to keep an open mind in this type of portfolio analysis. For example, it may well be that certain services, local in nature, can nonetheless be considered as internationalizable. This may even extend to signing a contract with a global supplier whose head office is overseas in a low-cost country even if the service can be carried out in each country where the company is physically established.

The European exception concerns the second version of the Bolkenstein Directive, which requires employees of a supplier in any European member state, operating in another EU country, to be remunerated according to the laws of the country where the activity is operated.

5/3.2 Criteria for choosing target countries

The second stage of the methodology relates to the choice of countries on which to focus. This choice essentially relies on the following steps:

- *an initial delimitation of a relevant geographical perimeter* taking into account the characteristics of purchased parts, entailing for example restrictions in terms of transport options and costs (this may lead to choosing between central Europe and South East Asia);
- next, systematic rating of the different identified countries according to a *multi-risk analysis* discussed in Section 5/4;
- finally, a choice of the targeted country(ies) with a definition of the systems to set up in order to *prevent risks* that are real but whose degree of seriousness is considered as non-prohibitory.

Without prejudging the results of such an approach, it can generally be said that today's 'target' procurement regions for Europe remain central and eastern Europe, Japan, South Korea, China and its satellites, even if for certain purchases India is developing quickly (we can cite the case of development of offshore IT services in the Bangalore region), the United States as well as certain Latin American countries.

Regarding India, this country's attractiveness remains inferior to that of China as it offers less dynamism and openness to the rest of the world for the same salary levels. It also has more restrictive legislation, its logistical systems and infrastructures are lower in quality, and its diaspora less active (not to mention its caste system that continues to impose partial social restrictions).

5/3.3 Criteria for choosing suppliers

In each of the chosen countries, suppliers need to be sourced using the techniques already covered in Chapter 4. As for any purchase, criteria must be defined and met before proceeding to the approval of appropriate suppliers. At the end of this two-level procedure (countries/suppliers), the company therefore has at its disposal a set of pre-qualified solutions, available for future calls for tenders.

As far as supplier choice and qualification criteria go, some of these are particularly crucial for international procurement carried out in low-cost countries. The following is a non-exhaustive list that singles out the key themes:

- *Sustainability/management/shareholders*: particular attention is required when examining the supplier's sustainability in relation to the probable duration of the operation. When looking at the nature of shareholders, it is necessary to take care to avoid the intervention of 'mafias' or shareholders deemed unreliable. The supplier's organization needs to be scrutinized for its capacity to manage a long-distance relationship according to a 'key account' principle.

- *Quality and CSR organization and performance*: this is generally still a delicate matter in many countries. It is therefore necessary to audit the quality system in place and the processes customarily used by the suppliers, bearing in mind the notion of operational quality assurance. In terms of social and environmental responsibility, minimum adherence to national (local) rules or international standards (such as ISO 14000 or 26000-type, or strict Global Compact or ILO-type rules, or even regulations such as REACH and RoHs) should be assessed with the greatest possible objectivity.

- *Technical know-how and mastery of tools*: a key point in the case of subcontracted works, the design, manufacturing and maintenance of tooling equipment should be examined and assessed carefully.

- *Control of cycles and lead-times*: this point is always crucial, and consistently generates cost overruns or rescheduling of operations. Apart from a country's infrastructure and logistics service-providers, audit the supplier's flow-planning and flow-management system should be thoroughly audited to make sure that it guarantees optimal adherence to manufacturing lead-times.

- *Information system*: during operational phases, the company and its supplier will be connected by the delivery-call and requirement-planning system. Without necessarily requiring a sophisticated ERP or EDI-type electronic data exchange system, it is necessary to check that the supplier has (or can) set up a system that can interface with that of the company, at a reduced cost.

- *Intellectual property (or risks of counterfeit)*: one should not hesitate to look closely into steps that need to be taken in order to avoid this risk, very real in certain countries, and taking into account the country's habits and usual contractual practices.

These criteria are essential. There are many examples of buyers who have not followed these recommendations scrupulously (either to speed up the process or to quickly take advantage of a seemingly competitive supplier who in fact does not adhere to all the criteria) and who then find themselves facing serious, even illegal situations, with dramatic business or economic consequences.

5/4 Analysis of country risks

To make a final choice of one or several 'target' countries, it is essential to rate all risks (but also opportunities!) characterizing each country in a formal and systematic manner.

5/4.1 Risks to consider

This presupposes having a reference grid applicable in all circumstances and for all purchases. Below, we present a simplified list, based on practical experience, of the main classes of risks that need to be analysed, divided into major areas. Figure 5.6

FIGURE 5.6   Risk factors in the analysis of target countries

Political, economic and monetary factors:

- Political stability
- GDP (evolution)
- Inflation / exchange rates
- Foreign investments (foreign direct investment)
- Research expenses
- Average interest rates
- Countertrade practices

Sustainable development:

- Environmental protection (regulations and practices)
- Social laws (obligations)

Labor and social policy:

- Average cost (evolution)
- Welfare costs
- Working hours
- Absenteeism
- Average productivity
- Training system
- Unemployment rate

Environmental factors:

- Customs procedures
- Customs duties
- Import / export quotas
- Energy (availability / cost)

Raw materials and equipment:

- Availability of raw materials
- Accessibility cost / quality
- Technical capability
- Competent toolmakers
- Local maintenance offer

Cultural and legal factors:

- Usual languages spoken
- Negotiation habits
- Industrial-property law
- Innovation protection
- Corruption

Financial factors:

- Incoterms practiced
- Usual payment conditions

Logistics and operational systems:

- Local transport (cost, available capacities, network)
- Transit procedures
- "Local" third-party certifier

clearly points out which points need to be examined and rated. Details on these various criteria are available from the various sources already listed in Chapter 4. We will not go over each item in detail here, but will limit ourselves to a few comments on certain points.

Political, economic and monetary factors

This point does not call for any particular comment. The factors characterize a country's economic dynamism, its attractiveness and its vision for future development. Aim to avoid countries that show signs of genuine political risks.

Business environment factors

Apart from the resulting economic effects, this point should be assessed in terms of the ethics of various practices and the ensuing effects on control of timeframes.

Logistical and operational factors

It is obvious that logistics are a matter of concern. By 'third-party certifier' we mean the organizations permanently established in the country, to whom it is possible to delegate the ongoing quality and CSR audits and follow-up exercises that are very often necessary (under the management of and according to rules defined by the departments responsible for quality and for sustainable and ethical procurement). A word of warning: in this case, the cost and efficiency of such a service should be meticulously investigated.

Labour and social policy

The costs of labour, their likely fluctuations, as well as those of welfare contributions, need to be measured. Average productivity should be analysed by a comparison with appropriate domestic equivalents. Good-quality training systems are a guarantee that a country's suppliers have qualified and competent labour at their disposal, and that the future is under control.

Finally, there are some who believe that a fairly high unemployment rate guarantees ongoing pressure on salaries; this assumption logically should hold true, but this type of reasoning may collide with ethical considerations.

Raw materials and equipment

These points have already been discussed in this chapter.

Cultural and legal factors

One comment can be made: language problems consistently arise in these types of operations. The solution does not simply lie in having an interpreter; we must bear in mind that many contacts, even beyond the suppliers' personnel, will be involved (customs, freight brokers, logistics service-providers in particular).

It is also necessary to remember that we are not merely speaking about oral communication: a great many written documents, plans and technical reports will be exchanged with suppliers. In this way, mastery of a *common language* should be confirmed as genuine. The same diagnostic should also be carried out within the buyer company itself.

Legal points have already been raised and deal mainly with the protection of intellectual (tooling and product) property.

Financial factors

Beyond exchange rate issues, these relate to Incoterms® and property transfer rules (see Chapter 14). As a complement, certain countries ordinarily impose payment terms that are hard to get around, such as letters of credit, whose mechanisms may generate risks and significant delays. More explicitly, this refers to payment of goods upon their being loaded onto a ship, even if the goods are only received in Western Europe five to seven weeks later, and when the container is opened some extremely unpleasant surprises are revealed in terms of quality or conformity to specification.

Beyond direct financial factors, other financial criteria are to be taken into account, such as tax, customs duties, leasing (in its various forms) rather than purchasing, or else buyback systems (according to the country's rules and practised financial rates). These techniques will be discussed later.

Adherence to sustainable development rules

The last key point is discussed in detail in Chapter 6. On top of international rules and references commonly acknowledged by the global community, it is necessary to draw up a detailed inventory of local laws and regulations on environmental protection, as well as legal obligations in the area of social matters or corrupt practices.

Indeed, it is important to check that potential suppliers adhere to the legal obligations in force in their country, or which are applicable worldwide, before eventually insisting that they adhere to more rigorous standards defined by the buyer company itself. In any case, an audit on how suppliers handle social and environmental aspects should verify this matter. *This is a matter of legality just as much as it is a matter of a company's own ethical demands.*

5/4.2 Risk management systems

The risks identified should be rated, for a very explicit reason: it is a way to ascertain *whether to eliminate certain countries* if the limit of risks defined by the company is overstepped. If this is not the case, actionable *risk-prevention or mitigation systems* should be set up so that the procurement department can demonstrate to the general management that all aspects have been analysed and that the system is 'under control and quality assessed'.

As a supplement – one that is essential – these prevention measures should be quantified and *their cost integrated into the total acquisition cost* of the procurement solution so that evaluation of the return on investment is reliable and realistic. It could be said that *this body of 'prevention costs' constitutes the 'insurance premium' of international procurement.*

In the following section, our general commentary is combined with details of risks relating to the purchased product, country risks, market risks and supplier risks.

Evaluation methodology: gravity, incidence, criticality

From a methodological point of view, here we are situated on familiar ground for practitioners of quality management methods, namely FMECA (failure mode, effects and criticality analysis). Three main attributes characterize a risk.

The *gravity* of a risk relates to the impact that its occurrence will (or may) have on performance or the expected result. In this way, we can put forward a rating scale from 'very low' to 'very high' gravity which may mean blocking a project, including a complete stop on compliant deliveries. It is in this regard that one can (and should) also quantify the associated costs.

The *incidence* of a risk characterizes its probability of taking place.

The *criticality* is the combination of the two preceding concepts. In this way, it can be expressed succinctly in the following manner:

$$\text{Criticality index} = \text{Gravity} \times \text{Incidence}$$

The choice of rating scales is extremely important. These scales should be discriminatory. In all circumstances, this type of analysis, undertaken uncompromisingly, will enable a project manager – or a procurement committee – to make a choice if, in addition, it sets *rejection thresholds* (as a supplement to the presentation of associated prevention methods).

At the same time, it is essential to evaluate the *economic consequences* resulting from risk-generating events: indeed, *any prevention measure will therefore be envisaged from the angle of reducing the probability of economic risk*.

For the sake of clarity the reader will find a series of rating tables directly drawn from a real-life situation (from the automotive industry) presented at the end of the chapter. Their realism and their operational character thus illustrate the procedure of identification, risk rating and comparison, and can be used as a point of departure that lends itself to adaptation. In these tables, probability is not visually represented.[4]

Risk reduction and prevention/mitigation

After an assessment of the probable risk has been made, it is necessary to define which decisions and concrete measures need to be implemented in order to prevent, ie reduce or eliminate, the major identified risks. These can be grouped into themes, already covered in the list above, in the following manner:

- definition and technicality of the requirement;
- environment (country) and characteristics of the upstream market;
- selection system according to the policy on suppliers;
- sustainability of the supplier relationship;
- configuration of the supply chain and management system in place;
- and finally, intercultural communication systems.

Let's go over these points by looking at the prevention dimensions that we need to think about and that must be *costed*, in the form of a checklist of important questions (see Table 5.1).

Let's note that one final class of risks has not been discussed here: that of *natural or climatic risks*, commonly known as *force majeure* risks. And yet they are increasingly common (floods, tsunamis, tornadoes, typhoons, etc). Their probability can now be quantified, and nowadays it is possible to cover these risks with insurance. Indeed, we cannot ignore them and their consequences: just think of how climatic phenomena (floods) have affected central Europe, namely the Czech Republic, in recent years, or more recently Thailand, interrupting the activity of many local companies in the main industrial clusters. Not to mention the Japanese tsunami that stopped operations at many businesses dependent on exclusive suppliers for a certain length of time, and more recently, devastation related to the typhoon in Malaysia.

TABLE 5.1   Checklist of risk questions

Theme	Questions
Definition and technicality of the requirement	• Have we thoroughly analysed (objectively and uncompromisingly) the procurement solution's complete conformity with technical specifications? • Are we certain that we really control the innovation and industrial protection? • Are we sure that the requirements specifications are well expressed according to international standards, and that the latter have been fully understood?
Country environment and market	• Have we rated the country or market risks carefully, and defined very strict tolerance thresholds? And in every aspect? • Are information sources reliable, and validated by cross-checking? • Has this analysis been carried out for a horizon at least equal to the project's lifetime (in relation therefore with a provisional ROI)?
Supplier policy and selection	• Has sourcing been carried out according to a reliable procedure, with uncompromising 'on-the-ground' audits? • Have all conditions guaranteeing the supplier's longevity and sustainability been well assessed? • If a local representative (IPO) proves to be the only secure solution, have we inventoried the possibilities for setting one up? Have we taken due consideration of the necessary training procedures? Are we sure about the local representative's impartiality and resistance to possible attempts at corruption? Have we made a thorough assessment of the provisional cost?
Sustainability of the supplier relationship	• As the relationship with a supplier in a distant developing country is by implication long-term, are we certain that we have only qualified suppliers with a 'long-term' partner profile? • Have we objectively analysed the necessity or not to implement safety stock, justified by anticipation of operational problems relating to quality or fluctuations in supply lead-times (including interfacing transport)? • Have figures on risks been integrated into the global cost? • Have we factored in the possibility of third-party certifiers (possible link with IPO)? Do they exist in the targeted country? Are there any possible delegation problems? • Have we set up an internal management and system control structure? Is it permanent or available on demand? • Aren't we obliged to set up double sourcing?

TABLE 5.1   *continued*

Theme	Questions
Supply-chain management	• In the event of risk relating to the solution's supply chain, have we considered a partnership with a local freight forwarder? Is this possible? What would be the cost (commissioning)?
Communication system	• Are the information and planning systems truly compatible? If there are any doubts, what measure(s) do we set up to mitigate risks?
	• Have the various actors mastery of the chosen language of communication at a professional level? If not, what has been decided?

5/5 Course of the project and operational implementation

A deployment project should be carried out in a structured fashion according to a sequence of stages. Figure 5.7 illustrates the launch of such a systematic procedure.

5/5.1 Planning of deployment to a developing country

From experience, it takes at least one year for this process to unfold before the first production deliveries are made. The figure is sufficiently explicit about the content of each of the major stages. Let's remember that the security solutions examined in the previous section should be implemented and validated *before any operational start* of the chosen solution.

The figure raises the concept of a *project team dedicated* to these operations. When we begin a process, it makes sense to set up such a group, which meets the need for a special 'commando' team. However, it is also necessary to think quickly about sustainable changes to the procurement management depending on the chosen strategy.

5/5.2 Possible structures for the procurement department

From this perspective, three main modes of organization are possible, from the simplest (Types 1 and 2 strategies) to the most complex (Type 3 strategy).

International buyer

In this case, depending on the situation and prior to any international project, the company may already be structured in an acceptable manner or it may not. The basic

FIGURE 5.7   Deployment in four main stages

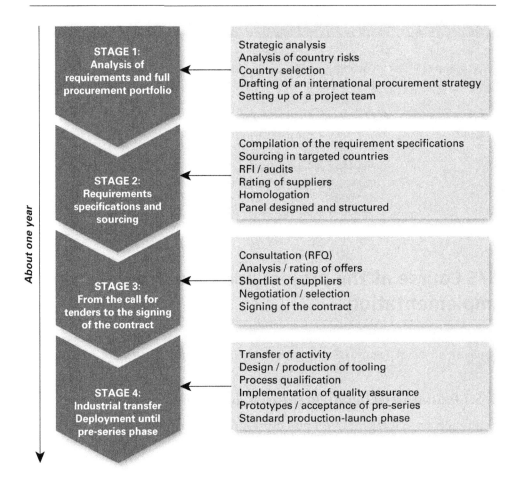

idea is to have a buyer role entirely dedicated to the design and management of a *supplier panel*, and thus freed from short-term call for tender processes.

In terms of internationalization, this buyer's mission is to widen sourcing operations to other countries and other suppliers. All steps to look for new sources, rate new countries and analyse risks will be entrusted to the buyer. He or she may often (using specific budgets released for this purpose) rely on external expert advice.

However, in the short term, once this upstream work is accomplished, it will be the existing buyers, specializing in major procurement families or categories, who will need to take over the launch of calls for tenders, the selection process and the deployment of new procurement solutions. And this without always being specifically trained for international procedures, hence entailing certain risks of errors, or at the very least, time wastage – thus the necessity for appropriate internal or external training.

To follow up operations, ie on a technical and quality level, it is necessary to plan to have company experts travel regularly to carry out the required audits and monitoring procedures.

Whenever it is possible and within a country's resources, we can rely on *local third-party certifiers*, already established and commissioned for this purpose, though obviously not on an exclusive basis. The advantage of this solution is to purchase expertise whilst keeping the costs of the quality assurance solution variable. In this way, the option of backtracking, in the event of unforeseen problems, remains, economically at least, possible.

International purchasing office (IPO)[5]

In this case, the nature of the procurement organization is transformed by the establishment of remote long-term local structures. An IPO may be a single person, if possible exclusive to the company if volumes allow costs to be amortized. What is necessary is for the person to be a national or native of the country (or zone), someone therefore very familiar with the local mindset, and also with any possible peculiarities or cultural issues, so as to anticipate all types of 'risk-bearing situations'.

This individual must also have a perfect awareness of the company's objectives, constraints and main methodologies, in order to partially take on delegated responsibility. Finally, this system[6] offers an advantage: all the IPOs (that may therefore each consist of one person) make up an *exclusive network* that is competent, multicultural and mobile, intervening in the upstream procurement process, then downstream in the follow-up and flow management phases.

These buyers can (and should) also carry out fairly lengthy visits to the central management team in order to communicate, to understand specific requirements, as well as to get to know all actors and stakeholders in the procurement process, namely specifiers and internal clients. This is therefore a true structure, entirely devoted to international activity, that 'doubles up' and supports the existing procurement department.

International procurement department

In this type of organization, a global worldwide procurement department is formed, relying tangibly on (or even integrating) the procurement services of business units or subsidiaries set up in the different regions. The network thus constituted is permanent, multicultural, and understands the company's specific needs. Each local buyer plays the role of a local purchaser that benefits the global collectivity. Audits and follow-ups of local suppliers are thus facilitated and optimized in terms of cost.

The procurement and supplier database is obviously regional or global. The standard of quality of the panel suppliers is homogeneous whatever the region. The qualification procedure is universal, favouring a uniformity of requirements. This does not prevent the strategy from also relying on local suppliers depending on needs. We therefore have the possibility of deploying a global strategy based on three pillars in terms of supplier policy:

- As far as possible, and for all purchases that lend themselves to it, *worldwide globalization* of requirements, bringing the advantages that we already know of:

- standardization of product or service offers;
- reduction in costs (volume effect);
- reduction in development periods;
- increased control of quality;
- reduction of transfer risks;
- and economies of scale through the amortization of total fixed costs.
● When cost minimization becomes decisive, a search for *suppliers in low-cost or developing countries* for the benefit of all entities.
● Whilst ensuring the development of reactive *local suppliers* (closer proximity with sources of consumption, neutralization of monetary risks due to exchange rate variations, facilitated countertrade systems, and use of a distinctive 'regional' competency).

In order for deployment to proceed more smoothly, we recommend always having a *reverse implementation* plan. Indeed, in the event of changes in company strategy or priorities, it is necessary to preserve a certain agility and to prepare backtracking scenarios and costs, if necessary, in order to have them validated at the outset of the project.

5/6 International procurement and countertrade[7]

Why talk about countertrade here? Basically because international procurement, if geared towards certain suitable countries, may largely and directly contribute towards (or accompany) the commercial development of certain companies. And thus be a key variable in commercial strategy and value creation.

The United Nations Commission on International Trade Law offers the following definition of the practice:

> those transactions in which one party supplies goods, services, technology or other economic value to the second party, and, in return, the first party purchases from the second party an agreed amount of goods, services, technology or other economic value.

Meanwhile, the OECD puts forward the following definition:

> an international commercial operation in the framework of which the seller has to accept in partial or total settlement of his deliveries, the supply of products (or more rarely services) coming from the purchasing country. The main difference with respect to a normal commercial deal is the link created between an export deal and an inverse commercial transaction not necessarily directly related to the export deal.

Historically, 'buying in order to be able to sell' has progressively become an obligation in international transactions – an element without which many markets are no longer accessible. This purchasing obligation was long perceived as a restriction that companies would try to reduce as far as possible, or would even not respect their commitments at all, preferring to pay the contractually determined penalties. These 'forced' purchases were, at the time, a supplement to credit, a new financing mode, enabling countries with non-convertible currencies to continue their purchases without generating cash themselves – hence a measure tolerated by companies.

Today, in order to export to numerous countries, it no longer suffices to have the right products or avant-garde technologies while relying on a solid international network. It is also necessary to import and commercialize the products of one's clients, or even to accept to partially share technologies.

5/6.1 Origins of the valuing of procurement

As of 1986/1987, French public authorities started to see the 'glorification of procurement' as an effective solution for the development of foreign trade – a solution that it was then necessary to 'sell' to state administrations and businesses. The aim was to make all public or private purchases serve to obtain a counterpart in the form of a sale of goods or services.[8] From the recommendations formulated at the time to achieve this end, let's consider the ones that are still applicable today:

- re-evaluating of the buyer's function: as export did not fall within the buyer's scope, it was necessary to take into account the company's general interests; profit-sharing in the form of productivity bonuses; systematic bridges to be built between the procurement and sales functions;
- training of buyers in international trade techniques (countertrade transactions);
- coordination of the procurement stream (advisory committees made up of exporters and buyers under the aegis of economic development offices based in each country);
- creation of procurement–sales consultation cells with internal trade-off procedures within the company;
- reinforcement and rationalization of intercompany information networks to anticipate the needs of the global market;
- reorganization of the countertrade office of the French Directorate General for External Economic Relations (DREE) with an inventory of flows of purchases per country of origin in conjunction with the Directorate General for Customs and available import credit;
- for the public sector, systematic demand for trade-offs in the military sector;
- encouragement of debt-swap operations whether in the form of capital (acquisition of a stake) or exports from the debtor country including discounts, taking into consideration the provisions made by banks;
- priority support, via adapted tax conditions, for international trade companies in order to facilitate their establishment overseas.

Many of these proposals were implemented, first reluctantly, then out of necessity. Companies quickly realized that it was necessary, in a 'seller'-slanted universe, to use the procurement lever in order to obtain export contracts. In this way, operations were no longer solely a means to secure the payment of sales, but increasingly became 'a highly effective sales argument', or even a competitive advantage that it was necessary to employ in order to succeed internationally, in all countries on the planet. In this context, it seems useful to specify the different techniques available to international trade protagonists, especially buyers.

5/6.2 Different types of international countertrade operations

As variations on a specific type of financing that may be used in combination with classic financing, these trade-off methods share in common a capacity to mitigate a lack of means of payment affecting private or public companies in all countries, including those with convertible currencies. We have selected the main methods.

Barter (swap) operations

This is the oldest-known type of countertrade transaction, and is sometimes still used today. *Theoretically, it involves a simultaneous flow of products of equivalent value without any transfer of funds.* According to this same theoretical vision, this operation is the object of a single contract matched with a transferability right.

In practice, the exporter only proceeds to send goods after receiving those of the client, in order to check their quality and thus ensure that resale of the received products can guarantee payment of those to be exported. This amounts to establishing two reciprocal contracts, on the understanding that the party who delivers first benefits from a bank guarantee, for example in the form of a standby letter of credit.

Such agreements can also be formalized on a national level. Each country establishes a list of products needed by the other country or that it agrees to receive (without impacting its own industry). By referring to market prices, each product is valued in terms of units of account in the so-called 'clearing-currency' account'; the aim is to play on quantities so that the total valued for each country is equal (eg $100 million clearing).

We will not go into detail about these mechanisms as this type of trade-off remains less practised than the following ones.

Countertrade procurement

This is a transaction in which the seller commits to make purchases of goods or services in the client's country in return for a sale that is only granted on this condition. It is the object of two separate contracts, one for the forward flow, one for the reverse flow, both linked by an umbrella agreement.[9]

Detailed characteristics
The purchase of products by either party may be staggered over a relatively long period. Purchases are invoiced and paid in currencies in both directions.

The value of the reverse flow is the object of a *coverage rate*, a percentage of the value of the forward flow. The rate is fixed by authorities depending on the crucial nature of the imported product to the country's development, and may be higher than 100 per cent: for example, to sell $100 worth of perfume, it may be necessary to locally purchase $125 worth of products, whereas to sell medicines, the rate remains very low. Meanwhile, the sum is determined by the competition; in terms of commercial strategy, the company that can generate the maximum reverse flow is favourably positioned to obtain the contract.

Records are made of purchases in evidence accounts held by banks approved by the parties. If the coverage rate is not respected, two sanctions are possible: payment of a contractually fixed penalty, payable pro rata of the value of counterpart purchases not carried out; cancellation of the forward-flow import licenses.

If it proves impossible to find a 'straight' importer to meet all the import requirements, it is then necessary to approach the target country demanding counter-purchases and to look for products that are available, and above all, *eligible*. If the company manages to find products that it can buy itself, the problem of the reverse flow is resolved. Otherwise, it is necessary to find a trading company that commits to subrogate the counterpart procurement obligations.

Often, the design, packaging and characteristics of the products on offer may not correspond with the standards applicable in Western countries. This is not the case for raw materials, such as petrol products, which are not always eligible or are only eligible at an extra cost.

Delocalized outsourcing of production

Before renouncing a sale, why not *outsource production*, in the country in question, of a product meeting 'Western' standards that already has secured trade opportunities? Indeed, another solution adopted by many companies consists in subcontracting, by delocalizing part of their annex production to a target country, thus also benefiting from savings on labour costs. By choosing to buy rather than to produce, they generate *purchase consideration* that may be deemed goodwill purchases which will facilitate the obtaining of import licences for *future* sales contracts on condition that they are classified as such by local authorities.

Countertrade procurement is justified for all countries that have a trade balance deficit in a foreign currency, on the understanding that funding of their external debt absorbs a significant share of their currency exports. Being unable to ensure the unrestricted convertibility of their own currency, the solution for finding the cash that they lack is to demand that all their suppliers purchase locally for a sum in proportion with their sales, in order to contribute to offsetting their balance of payments.

Additional countertrade should therefore be used as an argument in negotiation, to facilitate sales flows and to tackle the competition. Let's not forget that all such purchases need to be recorded before and not after the fact, not only in order to obtain a certificate discharging the party of its commitments, but above all, in order to generate extra cash to favour their obtaining future contracts.

Repurchase and buyback agreements

This is a system thanks to which an exporter *sells technology from one of their products or a turnkey production unit* to a partner–client, who pays largely with products based on the technology sold.

This partial recovery of production of the new capacity set up may stretch out over several years until the contracted amount is settled and bridge loans reimbursed. The products may be commercialized by the licensor or by third parties such as trading companies.

Motivations of the technology licensor

As the technological advantage of a product lasts for shorter and shorter periods, companies are condemned to continually look for more innovative products corresponding to the requirements of an ever more demanding market.

Many companies may be reticent to cede a manufacturing licence, especially when this request is issued by an emerging or developing country. Indeed, they fear that products manufactured in more advantageous conditions will quickly make their way to their own market, and are loath to feed their own competition in this way. These fears are understandable, but unjustified, for a technology buyer will always end up finding another licensor of a more or less similar product. It therefore becomes illusory to try to protect one's traditional market, especially in the context of globalized transactions.

A positive strategy – for meeting such a demand – possibly consists in replying favourably, especially if production capacity for the product in question is close to saturation and the market is still buoyant.

Setting up a repurchase operation is therefore a solution that avoids having to increase capacity because the licensed products are received in payment, this time manufactured by the partner: it may well be that the investment saved can be devoted to innovation. The ceded technology should not be obsolete; improvements to the industrial process should be regularly provided; quality control should be ongoing: this is in the interests of both parties.

Motivations of the licence holder

Emerging or developing countries do not always have up-to-date know-how for bringing value to their resources downstream, and are constantly on the lookout for new technologies. Buyback agreements are therefore welcome as they enable them to obtain such technologies without paying for them in currency, all the while creating export flows, even if they are not, at least initially, the object of a transfer of cash.

It is also possible that the supplied equipment may be the object of a leaseback sale, with delivery of the products constituting a guarantee for payment of instalments to the bank looking after the lease-purchase.

This partnership over several years secures, and even allows increase of the number of jobs provided by the licence holder. It also opens up to the latter new markets in bordering countries, thanks to the superior quality of its new production meeting Western standards and thanks to very competitive prices.

Such agreements have multiplied all over the world as they are the basis of any imposed or voluntary subcontracting strategies: getting things made rather than making them oneself, buying rather than producing. The notion of a supplier–client is replaced by that of collaborative contracting.

This partnership relationship may be considered as the first stage of a cooperation that may ultimately turn financial if the partnership proves effective. Before investing, in the context of partial outsourcing, it is better to engage in a buyback operation to test the relevance of a partial disinvestment project and to test the chosen partner, with whom it is possible to end cooperation at the end of the contract if the licensor's expectations are not met.

Direct and indirect offsets

An offset is an industrial and commercial cooperation that takes a more elaborate form than the buyback. It was originally initiated by countries with convertible currencies (eg Australia, Norway, Spain) as a means to develop their key industries, and also to reduce the value of imported goods. The offset therefore sets out to be a vector of development, technologically speaking, for the buyer's country while promoting job creation.

Indeed, in an offset operation, in order to reduce the sum of the purchase, the buyer asks the supplier to participate locally in the manufacturing process; the former therefore offers to partially replace the latter. This implies a technology transfer that the supplier can either accept or refuse, on the understanding that this is a *sine qua non* condition for obtaining the contract. There are two major categories of offsets: direct or indirect.

Direct offset

This offset implies the buyer's participation in the manufacturing of the sold good, and is translated by two features: local production of part of the purchased good, which reduces the cost, on condition that the buyer has the necessary skills; and a technology transfer including a transfer of patents and licences, staff training, or even the supply of certain specific equipment.

The supplier is therefore obliged to take on a new subcontractor, knowing that the buyer will subsequently continue this production for its own purposes. This is a type of forced delocalization, which may prove positive either in terms of economic gains, or in terms of markets. In this way, such a sale comprising offset obligations compels the seller to rethink its production strategy especially if sales of the good in question are carried out in different countries demanding offsets.

The buyer's role is essential, for it is this party that sets the requirements specifications of products handed over and oversees checks on them before the end-product is assembled.

When the buyer's country lacks the industrial infrastructure and adequate technological level to enter into co-production agreements, or when the seller refuses to cede the key technology to avoid creating a new competitor, there may be recourse to indirect offsets.

Indirect offset

This term covers a technology transfer that bears no relationship with the purchased good, requested when a direct offset is not possible. This arrangement may be made in the form of a buyback and/or a simple counter-purchase of goods and/or services.

Once again, the requester country wishes to put a value on purchases by asking the supplier to contribute know-how in order to accelerate development of the former's industrial network using high-performance technology, to enhance natural resources by investing upstream to create a maximum level of added value, and above all, to create jobs.

Offsets are one of the keys to opening up a country's market. The buyer, now a partner, can market the products stemming from the co-production to other companies engaging in offset obligations, doing so in the form of buybacks. Sales to countries with which duty-free cooperation agreements exist may also be facilitated.

In this context, exporting also means delocalizing know-how and production, strengthening commercialization networks in order to sell one's own products, as well as those manufactured by these partners, for in the event of default, foreseen penalties risk whittling away margins.

This is also a path to follow when a company wishes to save on customs duties, to avoid quota systems resulting from anti-dumping measures, and therefore to position itself better for sales and purchases.

The BOT: build–operate–transfer

The term corresponds to the following triad:

- building or making a planned investment;
- operating the completed installation;
- transferring ownership of the installation to the licensor.

From the viewpoint of a government or local authority, this is a way to get a priority investment made by a consortium – the concessionaire – that will benefit from a long-term operating concession allowing the latter to make a profit from the investment. Once again, a search for savings in cash is the trigger for this mechanism which enables heavy investments to be made without spending liquid assets that may be unavailable.

Many areas of application exist, in industrialized as well as emerging countries: roads, highways, public transport, irrigation and electricity production dams, water treatment, household and industrial waste treatment, telephone lines, ports, airports, hotels, shopping malls, hospitals, mining and agricultural operations, tunnels (such as the Channel Tunnel or the Hong Kong Cross-Harbour Tunnel), and so on.

Thousands of projects are filed with the World Bank by emerging or developing countries looking for foreign investments as their local companies do not adequately master the technologies necessary for the construction or operation associated with the planned investments, not forgetting political risks that make investors nervous.

The structure of a BOT implies two categories of protagonists:

1 The *granting power*: the authority of the country that plans the investment, sets the time period of the concession, defines the requirements specifications, and specifies the guarantees granted in order to offset any possible political and economic instability that may be detrimental to the project's profitability.

2 The *concessionaire*: a consortium of local and foreign private companies that, in the context of a joint venture to be created, commits to an industrial or public infrastructure investment that needs to be made profitable during the lifespan of the concession.

The project should benefit from the support of local authorities, namely for the coverage of risk and the transfer into foreign currency generated by the project in local currency, bearing in mind that assets are granted as guarantees to the lenders who commit solely on the basis of the project's capacity to be self-financed in the foreign currency. There is no first-degree sovereign guarantee for the project's completion.

One of the specific characteristics of the BOT is the major and uncustomary involvement of banks in this type of project. Banks can in fact negotiate privileged conditions with international credit organizations whilst asking for coverage from private or public insurers. They are often shareholders in the joint venture, along with suppliers of equipment and raw materials, design offices, on top of the prime contractor and the operator.

Profitability depends on the buyer–clients (offtakers) – either end-users (telephone, transport) or public buyers (electricity or water distribution), with whom a binding long-term contract to take the production must be settled. Invoicing in the local currency raises the problem of its convertibility and its inflation rate. Recourse to related operations may be an appropriate response. Several variations exist:

- BOOT (build–own–operate–transfer): the concessionaire becomes the owner during the duration of the concession for legal and tax reasons;
- BOO (build–own–operate): the concessionaire becomes the owner without having to restore the infrastructure as the local authority does not consider itself to have the means to take care of its operation;
- BO (build–operate): used to develop a natural resource, with operation concluding when the resource is used up.

Methods for implementing related operations

The financial and legal arrangements of these operations represent one of the keys to the success of countertrade. Indeed, even if there is a 'cascade' or 'drawer' system requiring the intervention of several companies from several countries, it is necessary – in the event that the operation is interrupted due to a case of *force majeure* – for there to be the means for all operators who meet their commitments to be paid or to have access to deliveries. It is therefore necessary, at each stage of the operation, to set up security in the form of transferable credit, back-to-back swap contracts, guarantees in the vein of the standby letter of credit. Many banks have a specialized unit for carrying out this type of financial engineering.

On the legal front, a certain number of clauses are specific to these operations and need to appear, following negotiation, in the contracts binding the parties: clauses on non-exclusivity, the freedom to select third parties, the freedom to choose destinations, exoneration, a penalty clause, the keeping of proper accounts, and their release to the other party (see the specialized bibliography).

All these techniques, that may be used in combination, aim on the one hand to enable cash to be generated, and on the other to allow public or private buyers to value their purchases thanks to a bonus, or to enable the sale of the products or services of companies. All these arrangements contribute to improving the flow of international trade and to reducing imbalance in transactions between all countries.

5/6.3 Valuation and involvement of the procurement function

How procurement can contribute, in a countertrade context, is firstly to *redirect purchases to new countries where sales potential for the company has been detected*, in order to facilitate and enable future sales.

Valuation of procurement also means asking regular suppliers, domestic or overseas, to contribute, through their own networks, towards selling off part of the 'commodity money' (goods received in payment for an export, whose sale generates cash), when these countertrade goods are not raw materials for the company.

Endeavouring to find a trade-off, for all of a company's purchases of goods and/or services, is not often part of a buyer's job requirements. And yet, this *counter-export* is a powerful catalyst for developing the sales of a company's products, technologies or services.

In other words, a renewable 'straight' purchase, that is one without any exportable compensation, carried out in a country with non-convertible currency, can be sold as a 'sweetener', proportional to the service rendered, in the form of purchase consideration, enabling the beneficiary to sell in the latter country and to be paid in a strong currency.

This approach *therefore consists, for the buyer, in anticipating a valuation system for the company in the context of sourcing*, particularly outside of traditionally known markets.

Taking the initiative to counter-export, spontaneously offering to help a potential client directly or indirectly to find new opportunities, greatly facilitates negotiations and can open the door to possible subsequent partnerships. The notion of 'seller' and 'client' is increasingly substituted by that of commercial and/or industrial partner.

For example, in the *sogo-shoshas* (general trading companies) integrated to most Japanese industrial companies, the functions of the buyer and the seller are closely linked, a situation that facilitates cross-purchases. Thanks to their highly elaborate information transmission networks, these trade companies can optimize buyer and seller flows, and efficiently value the purchases of those on behalf of whom they act.

In this way, by tapping into existing flows, agreeing to divert certain flows, or generating new procurement trends, the company opens up to new markets on condition that it takes into account the point of view of the buyer who must watch over the price's equilibrium, quality and supply security.

Alerted by the valuation of purchases, the buyer benefits from an opportunity to improve on costs: if the buyer approaches its traditional suppliers to contribute to this system, greater transparency and control of the TCO can be obtained. The procurement department's participation in delocalization operations, in securing them, therefore represents a major contribution that it can make to the company's strategy.

When a company succeeds in generating 'forward and reverse' flows that are profitable, it is clear that the systems set up will not be placed in the public arena as they may well also serve the competition. This is why great discretion should surround these operations that, over time, evolve and often become increasingly complex. Trading one's purchasing power, by directing it to those destinations to which one wishes to export, *engages a company's strategic drive and implies the setting up of a specialized interface* with the skills for coordinating all internal and external operators.

As stated in Section 5/4.2, the reader will find, in the four sections of Table 5.2, a comprehensive example of risk rating in the following areas:[10]

- risks relating to the definition of requirements;
- risks relating to the economic environment of the purchase;
- risks relating to sourcing and the choice of supplier;
- risks stemming from the operational management of flows and the relationship with the selected supplier.

TABLE 5.2 Examples of risk assessment

Requirement risk assessment

Code	Risk category	Risk factor	Range	Part 1	Part 2
Product specification					
1	Expertise requirement	20 – Expert 10 – Developer 1 – Manufacturer 0 – Subcontractor	0–20	10	1
2	Product maturity	10 – New design that requires product & process development and validation. Untested design 1 – Product to develop from an existing product or product mainly defined. Tested design to adapt 0 – Existing product and tooling. Drawing and specification defined	0–10	10	1
3	Product design complexity	10 – New complex product design 1 – Moderate complexity of design 0 – Simple product to design. Few functions. Simple specification.	0–10	10	0
4	Safety concerns	10 – Safety characteristics concerned (airbag-related…) 0 – No safety impact	0–10	0	0
5	Process / technology complexity	20 – New to industry 10 – New to company 0 – Existing technology	0–20	1	0
6	Tooling / control gauges complexity	10 – New complex tooling 1 – New tooling without particular difficulty or modification of existing tooling 0 – Existing tooling	0–10	0	1
7	Transfer of technology	20 – Valuable knowhow / exclusivity 0 – Standard technology	0–20	1	0

TABLE 5.2   *continued*

Code	Risk category	Risk factor	Range	Part 1	Part 2
Delivery					
8	Programme timing (time-to-market)	20 – Critical 10 – Compressed 1 – Adequate 0 – Ample	0–20	1	1
9	Volume and ramp-up	10 – High & fast 1 – Low & fast or high & slow 0 – Low & slow	0–10	1	1
10	Demand volatility	20 – Significant in volume and critical in diversity 10 – Low in volume and critical in diversity 1 – Low in volume and significant in diversity 0 – Low in volume and low in diversity	0–20	1	1
Quality objectives					
11	Quality objective	10 – Demanding (<15 PPM) with reliability commitments 1 – Standard (50 PPM) 0 – Large (100 PPM)	0–10	10	1
12	End-user expectations	10 – critical: functional and aspect parts 1 – aspect parts 0 – low (hidden parts)	0–10	10	1
Cost					
13	Design-to-cost, VA / VE	10 – to perform 0 – not necessary	0–10	10	0
		High risk ≥ 20	**Results**	**64**	**8**

TABLE 5.2 *continued*

Economical environment risk assessment

Code	Risk category	Risk factor	Range	Part 1	Part 2
Country					
1	Political stability	10 – Unstable political regime 1 – Democratic system or a stable authoritarian system 0 – Mature political system & effective democracy	0–10	0	1
2	Economy	20 – Country's economy faces crisis 10 – Emerging market 1 – Macroeconomic fundamentals generally strong 0 – Mature market economy	0–20	1	1
3	Legal system	10 – Country's legal structure will be contradictory, incoherent and unpredictable 1 – Likely to be rather unwieldy and contradictory 0 – Reasonably effective corporate and civil law systems, clear and mature	0–10	1	10
4	Tax	10 – Country's tax system will be murky and incoherent 1 – Rather unclear, incoherent and sometimes contradictory 0 – Reliable and relatively clear tax system	0–10	0	1
5	Operational: - Infrastructure - Labour - Administration	20 – Severe operational obstacles and poor business environment 10 – Significant operational obstacles but adequate business environment 1 – Few operational obstacles and the overall business environment is good 0 – Excellent business environment	0–20	1	1

TABLE 5.2   *continued*

Code	Risk category	Risk factor	Range	Part 1	Part 2
6	Security	20 – Violent crime will be common, organized crime entrenched 10 – Relatively serious crime problem. Organized crime likely to be significant 1 – Violent crime will be relatively unusual 0 – Very low level of crime	0–10	0	0
Supply market					
7	Market risk	10 – Undeveloped or unknown local market. Purchasing strategy not possible 1 – Supply market place identified but leverage points not identified 0 – Supply market place identified. Leverage points identified. Able to influence the market	0–10	1	10
8	Subcontractor's availability	10 – Hardly no tooling maintenance and subcontractor availability 1 – Poor maintenance and subcontractor availability 0 – Tooling maintenance and subcontractors in related technology widely available	0–10	1	1
9	Availability of raw material	10 – Risk of penury 1 – Raw material to be imported or local-standard raw material 0 – International-standard raw material available locally	0–10	0	1
10	Cost of material and energy	10 – High material or energy cost volatility 1 – Cost of material or energy subject to local increase due to stability of procurement 0 – Cost of material or energy not subject to local increase	0–10	0	1

TABLE 5.2 *continued*

Code	Risk category	Risk factor	Range	Part 1	Part 2
11	Market standards / norms	10 – Hardly no standards and norms, or not applied 1 – Lack of standards and norms 0 – International standards recognized and applied	0–10	0	1
Exchange rate					
12	Exchange-rate volatility	10 – High exchange-rate volatility 1 – Medium exchange-rate volatility 0 – Low or negligible exchange-rate volatility	0–10	1	1
Transportation					
13	Transportation type and cost	10 – Poor country transportation facilities, long-distance freight (sea) 1 – Good country transportation facilities, long-distance freight (sea) 0 – Good country transportation facilities, small-distance freight (truck)	0–10	0	1
14	Cross-border taxes, tariffs and duty costs	10 – High cost, customs clearance complex and unpredictable 1 – Standard cost but subject to change. Standard customs clearance 0 – Stable cost and simplified customs clearance. In WTO	0–10	0	0
		High risk ≥ 10		**Results 6**	**30**

TABLE 5.2 *continued*

Supplier risk assessment

Code	Risk category	Risk factor	Range	Supplier A	Supplier B
Profile and management					
1	History in automotive industry	20 – New to industry 10 – New to our company and automotive industry 1 – New to our company but supplying automotive industry (≥50 %) 0 – Existing to our company	0–20	0	1
2	Shareholding profile	20 – Unknown shareholders 10 – Public company linked to local government 1 – Private company or joint venture 0 – International shareholders	0–20	0	1
3	Financial criteria	20 – Unknown financial results 10 – Low D&B, high net debt / equity, very low EBITDA, high penetration rate 1 – One of financial criteria is NOK but not critical 0 – All financial ratios OK	0–20	1	0
4	Workforce and management	10 – Need to recruit expert on a technology or senior management position 1 – Need to recruit qualified operators or middle-management position 0 – Few or no recruitments	0–10	0	1
5	Supplier manufacturing facility	20 – New facilities, not built 10 – New facilities, building already / already built but not in operation 1 – Expanding 0 – Existing	0–20	0	1
Technical expertise					
6	Expertise in the product technology	20 – New technology for the supplier (e.g. from injection to extrusion) 10 – New process within similar technology (e.g. new mechanism) 1 – Similar process to existing products 0 – Existing and same products	0–20	0	1

TABLE 5.2 *continued*

Code	Risk category	Risk factor	Range	Supplier A	Supplier B
7	Knowledge of specifications and customer standards	10 – New OEM to the supplier. Need assistance 1 – New OEM to the supplier but familiar with similar APQP 0 – Has already developed a product for the OEM	0–10	1	10
8	R&D capability	20 – Unsuitable R&D capacity for the required expertise. No program management 10 – The supplier lacks some R&D equipment or expertise. Will have to subcontract some activities. Poor program management 1 – The supplier has all R&D capacity for the new project. Program management has to be improved 0 – The supplier has all R&D capacity for the new project. The effectiveness of its program management has been proven	0–20	1	0
Quality					
9	Certification	10 – No ISO 9000:2000 certification 1 – ISO 9000:2000 certified and in process to ISO TS 0 – ISO TS or QS 9000 certified	0–10	0	1
10	Company assessment	10 – C 1 – B 0 – A	0–10	1	1
11	Quality performance in programme	10 – Poor or no experience in quality-development tool 1 – No experience in APQP with our company but shows competencies in quality-development tool (FMEA, special characteristic, etc.) 0 – Experience in APQP with our company	0–10	0	10
12	Quality performance in series	10 – External rejection rate (PPM) results much higher than quality objective 1 – External rejection rate (PPM) results to improve 0 – External rejection rate (PPM) results in line with quality objectives	0–10	1	1

TABLE 5.2 *continued*

Code	Risk category	Risk factor	Range	Supplier A	Supplier B
Cost					
13	Competitiveness	10 – No accurate cost breakdown 1 – Some doubt in the cost breakdowns 0 – proven competitiveness	0–10	0	0
Logistic performance					
14	Production planning and capacity	10 – Issues in production planning and inventory management leading to high misdelivery rate 1 – Existing production planning and inventory management to be improved. Some misdeliveries 0 – Efficient production planning and inventory management leading to low misdelivery rate	0–10	1	1
15	International logistic experience	10 – No experience in international logistics (customs clearance, freight, insurance…) 1 – Limited experience in international logistics (0 % – 30 % export DDU or DDP) 0 – Experienced in international logistics ($\geq$ 30 % export DDU or DDP)	0–20	1	10
Sustainable development					
16	Respect of human rights, labor and environment standards	20 – Infringement of human rights. Children employed. Harmful to environment 10 – No respect of labor and environment international standards 1 – Some minor health & safety or environment issues 0 – Committed to the United Nations Global Compact	0–20	1	1
	High risk $\geq$ 10		**Results**	**8**	**40**

TABLE 5.2 *continued*

Relationship risk assessment

Code	Risk category	Risk factor	Range	Supplier A	Supplier B
Willingness to pursue the relationship					
1	Supplier point of view	20 – Nuisance 10 – Exploitable 1 – Development 0 – Core	0–20	0	1
2	Internal LCC image	10 – Significant LCC image 1 – Little LCC image 0 – No internal LCC image	0–10	1	1
Cross-cultural communication					
3	Inter-cultural communication	10 – High difference in values, norms, attitudes and behaviour 1 – A few differences in cultural aspects but common values and norms 0 – Common values, norms, attitudes and behaviour	0–10	1	10
4	Distance	10 – Long distance between two parties 1 – Medium distance 0 – Small distance	0–10	0	10
5	Language	10 – Some key actors of the relationship do not speak English 1 – English is mainly understood but some documentation needs to be translated 0 – Both parties fully master English and documentation is in English	0–10	1	1
6	Business practices	10 – Business practices are very different 1 – Major differences in business practices 0 – Few differences in business practices	0–10	0	1

TABLE 5.2 *continued*

Code	Risk category	Risk factor	Range	Supplier A	Supplier B
Contracting					
7	Contract coverage	20 – Terms and conditions of the collaboration are not covered by contract 10 – Terms and conditions of the collaboration are insufficiently covered by contract 1 – Terms and conditions of the collaboration are partially covered by contract 0 – Terms and conditions of the collaboration are properly covered by contract	0–20	0	0
8	Industrial and intellectual rights	10 – Intellectual-property rights, non-competition and confidentiality not covered by contract 0 – Intellectual-property rights, non-competition and confidentiality covered by contract	0–10	0	0
9	Product liability	10 – Product liability not covered by sufficient insurance subscribed by the supplier 0 – Product liability covered by sufficient insurance subscribed by the supplier	0–10	0	10
Supply chain					
10	Incoterms	10 – EXW 1 – FCA, FOB, CFR, CIF, CPT, CIP 0 – DES, DEQ, DAF, DDU, DDP	0–10	0	0
11	Safety stock	10 – No safety stock 1 – Contracted safety stock located in LCC 0 – Contracted safety stock located nearby customer	0–10	0	0
Payment					
12	Payment instrument	10 – Payment by letter of credit 1 – Payment by SWIFT	0–10	0	0
		High risk ≥ 10	**Results**	3	34
		Range	0-20	0-10	
		Relation A	0	1	
		Relation B	10	1	0
		High risk ≥ 10	**Results**	3	34

Notes

1 See, on this topic, Horvat (2001).

2 These developments are inspired by the research of Hitt, Ireland and Hoskisson (2003).

3 Unlike discount distributors dealing mainly with one-off promotional operations, and purchasing significant batches of standard products or the equivalent.

4 These documents have been reproduced from the professional thesis by Canonne (2005).

5 Certain French companies have set up a comparable solution: use of specialized importers for certain countries (ie Asian, including China) and for certain types of products. In this case, we operate an outsourcing of product- and supplier-sourcing activities, then procurement follow-up, as a replacement for permanent in-house local representation.

6 The author's former seminar participants include the CPO of a major brand in specialized distribution, who set up an IPO in this way. The structure, meeting the description of 'virtual', is made up of five exclusive correspondents based in the major world zones of interest in terms of sought-after products, which are then included in the range if they are qualified.

7 In the previous French edition of this book, a detailed chapter entirely devoted to this theme was written by Guy Azambre who has since passed away. In homage, we have decided to maintain this theme and to reintegrate it into the section on international procurement issues, in a more concise form. The reader is invited to also consult, as a supplement, the specialized bibliography at the end of the work.

8 'The objective of valorizing procurement is set to become one of the main elements of our foreign-trade policy that will foster sustainable recovery of our foreign transactions. Public and private companies should, alone and under their own responsibility, negotiate terms on countertrade without however compromising our supply security' (Prouteau report, drafted at the request of Michel Noir, French Minister of Foreign Trade, 27 March 1987).

9 Under French law, these commitments are null for the object comprises too great a margin of uncertainty (French Court of Cassation). This is why many contracts of this type are not made under French law.

10 These tables, taken from the professional thesis of Stéphane Canonne, HEC GSSC Master graduate (2005), are here reproduced with his consent.

06
Sustainable procurement
Risks and implementation

OLIVIER MENUET[1]

Whilst some still consider sustainable development and procurement as contra-dictory, feedback on the evolution of procurement in recent years – research work and academic studies as well as international initiatives – prove the opposite. On the contrary, their combined action acts as a true lever for innovation and for long-term value creation.

Organizations, large and small, private and public, have much to gain by following this path: the construction of mutually beneficial long-term relationships with suppliers, anticipation of risks, reduction of costs and development of new markets. Responsible procurement helps to generate performance that is global, sustainable and shared. Today, it represents an opportunity for the procurement function to be renewed, and its expertise and its strategic input to be further established vis-à-vis general management and other internal functions.

Contributing to transforming the traditional company model, increasing global performance via the securing of the supply chain, creating long-term partnerships with suppliers, being a player in the raising of social standards on a global scale, or increasing the value of ethics and deontological conduct in client–supplier relationships... these are the complex stakes that procurement will need to respond to in coming years. Beyond mere adjustments translated by a few actions on the side-lines of classic activities, it is a matter of committing to an in-depth transformation of the procurement profession and those who practise it: the ambitious objective targeted is for the new 'sustainable procurement' dimension to be both a means and an end.

6/1 How CSR is renewing procurement approaches

The concept of sustainable development emerged in the report *Our Common Future* submitted to the United Nations in 1987 by the committee chaired by Gro Harlem Brundtland (European deputy and former Norwegian prime minister). This report underlined the economic, environmental and social limits of the way in which industrialized countries had been developing since the middle of the 19th century. An alternative was put forward: a more 'sustainable' ('viable, habitable and equitable') mode of development, born from a rebalancing between economic efficiency, respect for the environment and social advancement, seeking 'to meet the needs and aspirations of the present without compromising the ability to meet those of the future'.

6/1.1 The importance of sustainable development

Two ideas are inherent to this concept: that of 'needs,' including those of the least privileged, for whom answers need to be offered, and that of the limits of the 'finite' world in which we live. It took 200,000 years for the human population on Earth to reach 1 billion, then 150 years for it to climb to 7.35 billion individuals (November, 2015). Most forecasts announce figures of around 9–10 billion inhabitants in around 2050, 80 per cent of whom will inhabit developing countries, and 60 per cent of whom will live in cities.

The production of goods and services increased twice as quickly as demographics did over the 20th century. Most consumption indicators are on the rise (energy, raw materials, water, paper, etc), raising the question of the continuity of our model in a world where resources are not inexhaustible.

A number of elements reflect the stakes of a model that is approaching its limits and is in the midst of a critical stage today:

- financial deviation – an over-financialized economy; short-term market pressures; present corruption in many countries capable of reaching 25 per cent of GDP in certain developing countries; serial financial scandals; neglect of negative externalities (such as waste and pollution);

- social inequalities (in developing as well as developed countries) – difficult access to basic necessities (drinking water, food, health, etc), violation of basic rights (including schooling, child labour, human rights), persistence of discrimination;

- degradation of the environment – depletion of resources, degradation of biodiversity and ecosystems, climate change.

Our lifestyles are no longer sustainable:

> People used the equivalent of 1.5 planets in 2007 to support their activities [...] If everyone in the world lived like an average resident of the United States or the United Arab Emirates, then a biocapacity equivalent to more than 4–5 Earths would be required to keep up with humanity's consumption and CO_2 emissions.

In the face of these risks, all players, including economic ones, are called to act.

The concepts of impact, externality and extended responsibility

A company's decisions and activities produce impacts (changes undergone) on shared heritage: the environment, social fabric, economic balances and society in general. These impacts may be positive (eg job creation) or negative. They may be direct (related to its object) or indirect (repercussion on its activity).

Impacts are measured over the whole of the value chain (the lifecycle of the activity, products and services), but they overstep the walls of the company and extend to its entire sphere of influence: both in its domain (geographical or functional) and its relationships (political, contractual or economic) in the context of which the organization has the capacity to influence the decisions or activities of other organizations.

Responsibility hence extends to externalities. Economists call an externality 'the external effect that an agent's production activity produces on the well-being of another without either of the two receiving or paying a compensation for this effect'. In this way, it relates to secondary effect of the activity when interaction between the emitter and the receiver is not accompanied by any trading counterpart.

An externality may also be positive (benefit) or negative (cost) depending on whether its consequence is favourable or unfavourable. Pollution in its sundry forms is a typical example of a negative externality: when a factory disposes of its waste in the environment, it inflicts, without offering any counterpart, a nuisance on the region's inhabitants.

Companies are called into question for their externalities, for example, for the practices of their suppliers. (In 1997, Nike was accused of having its products manufactured by subcontractors employing children; in 2004, Accord's image was associated with the working conditions practised by its hotel-cleaning subcontractor.)

They may be asked to be 'accountable' for these externalities (in other words, to integrate the costs associated with compensation) that may have repercussions on a region's public health or economic impoverishment (cf delocalization, retrenchments, illiteracy due to child labour).

CSR: corporate contribution to sustainability

CSR (corporate social responsibility) is defined by ISO, in the context of the ISO 26000 norm, as the 'responsibility of an organization for the impacts of its decisions and activities on society and the environment.' Committing to a CSR approach implies voluntarily choosing and accounting for transparent and ethical behaviour that contributes to sustainable development including the health and welfare of society, takes into account the expectations of stakeholders, and is integrated throughout the organization and implemented in its relationships. It relies on the following basic practices:

- identification of the social, environmental and economic impacts of the organization's decisions and activities;
- identification of the stakeholders and dialogue with the latter;
- definition of the relevant and priority spheres of action organized around seven core themes: the organization's governance, good business practices, the environment, working conditions, human rights, contribution to local development and consumer-related issues.

Amongst the reasons urging companies to include CSR stakes in their strategies, we can cite: pressure from stakeholders, the identification of new risks (industrial, image-related, commercial, energy- or development-related), and an awareness of opportunities (cost reduction, product innovation, the value of good practice in terms of image, internal mobilization).

Pressure from stakeholders

Stakeholders (any group or individual who affects or is affected by the accomplishment of the organization's objectives) – in other words civilian society, institutions, consumers, employees and their representatives, and suppliers – are placing more and more pressure (eg in the form of product boycotting, protest campaigns, circulation of articles and petitions, court cases) on economic players to speed up their integration of CSR principles (see Figure 6.1).

FIGURE 6.1 Main stakeholders and their expectations

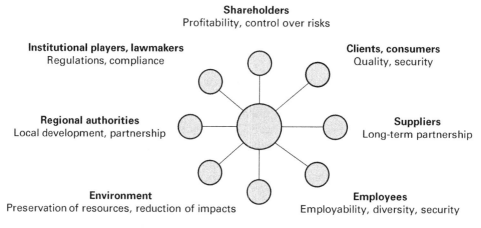

Shareholders
Profitability, control over risks

Institutional players, lawmakers
Regulations, compliance

Clients, consumers
Quality, security

Regional authorities
Local development, partnership

Suppliers
Long-term partnership

Environment
Preservation of resources, reduction of impacts

Employees
Employability, diversity, security

Civilian society, NGOs
Consultation, transparency

SOURCE: © Des Enjeux & des Hommes.

Institutional players

These offer frameworks for promoting good practices.

Whilst, at the start of the 1970s, scientists and humanists were the only ones to pay attention to sustainable development, since the middle of the 1980s, the leaders of international organizations and nations have gradually taken its stakes into account. States act through international agreements, such as the Kyoto Protocol, followed by 21 Conferences of the Parties (COP 21: Paris, November–December 2015). The most important international initiatives are the following:

● The Conventions of the International Labour Organization (ILO), the United Nations agency overseeing international labour norms.

- The Global Compact, launched in 2000 by Kofi Annan, Secretary-General of the United Nations, that invites companies of all sizes, on a voluntary basis, to commit to and to give a yearly account of their progress with 10 principles relating to human rights, the environment, labour and corruption:

  > Governments cannot do it alone. Civil society groups have a critical role, as partners, advocates and watchdogs. So do commercial enterprises. [...] We are not asking corporations to do something different from their normal business; we are asking them to do their normal business differently'.
  > Source World Summit, Johannesburg, 2002

- The *Global Reporting Initiative* (GRI), a set of guidelines and recommendations on CSR indicators, aimed at companies wishing to implement initiatives and measure their progress. Today the world's most widely used frame of reference, it includes all topics relating to suppliers and the supply chain (environment, employment, human rights, products). Coming into force in May 2013, the GRI G4 places an even greater emphasis on the role of procurement in CSR.

- The ISO 26000 norm that defines, on an international scale, the notion of corporate responsibility for public and private organizations.

Lawmakers

These harden the laws that protect the environment. Laws and regulations increasingly frame practices in order to encourage sustainable production and consumption modes. In this way, the following are in force in Europe (non-exhaustive list): EMAS (Eco-management and Audit Scheme) regulations; REACH (Regulation on Registration, Evaluation, Authorization and Restriction of Chemicals) legislation; the French Environmental Code; the EuP (Energy-using Products) directive; the RoHS (Restriction of Hazardous Substances) directive; the WEEE (Waste Electronic and Electrical Equipment) directive; and the European Ecolabel.

Looking at France in particular, the Grenelle Bill 2, promulgated in July 2010, lists, theme by theme, the objectives entrenched by the Grenelle Bill 1 of the *Grenelle de l'Environnement* (Grenelle Environmental Roundtable). This is a bylaw that implements measures in six major areas: construction and urbanism, transport, energy, biodiversity, risks and governance.

NGOS and representatives of civilian society

These trigger changes in mindsets. They challenge the model of overconsumption in Western countries, and attack, head-on, companies whose practices and offers they would like to see progress. Whilst NGOs have always been active in relation to certain sectors such as chemicals, energy, automobiles or forestry, they have more recently slanted their action towards the banking and insurance, luxury or information technology sectors.

Beyond their stance of opposition or denunciation (recent campaigns include Greenpeace's protests, widely circulated by the internet, against the use of palm oil in products marketed by Unilever/Dove or Nestlé/Kit Kat), NGOs are equipped with specific skills for 'carrying the torch' to legal and financial ground. Some of these bodies are increasingly positioning themselves as 'expert partners' that accompany companies in their evolutions (cf the WWF/Lafuma partnership to reduce the impacts of textiles, the FIDH/Carrefour partnership for human rights at work).

Financial sphere

This takes into account the sustainable involvement of companies. In France, the decree implementing the *Nouvelles Régulations Economiques* (New Economic Regulations) bill has, since 2002, forced listed companies to give an account of their social and environmental impacts in their yearly management's discussion and analysis. Through the bill on 'national commitment to the environment', also known as Grenelle 2, this requirement for transparency and extra-financial reporting has been extended to non-listed companies, whilst also stipulating verification of the reliability of data by an external third-party body.

The financial community has also turned its attention to the topic through the development of socially responsible investment (SRI) funds and extra-financial ratings agencies. Certain stock exchange indices have created a sustainable development category (such as the Dow Jones Sustainability Index or the FTSE4Good) presenting companies recording the best performances in this area. At the same time, financial investors, aware that implementation of the Kyoto Protocol (and the carbon market) would necessarily have repercussions on the value of shares, launched the Carbon Disclosure Project (CDP) in 2000.

Consumers

These are progressing in their awareness of sustainable development, but remain wary. Whilst consumers are increasingly responsive to the stakes of sustainable development, they are also increasingly suspicious of offers 'stamped' as green. A 2011 survey into French consumer attitudes, carried out by Ethicity, TNS Media Intelligence and Aegis Media Expert, in partnership with the ADEME (French Environment and Energy Management Agency), confirmed this trend. It identified eight groups of individuals and three major families:

> ... the hard core (in favour of SD and extremely keen on information) has remained constant for three years at around 40 per cent of the population, but is weakening, compared to 2010, in favour of a more sensitive group (25 per cent) hindered by financial difficulties. At the same time, the rupture is accentuated with over a third of the population that seems to be in denial.

Whilst there is still a significant gap between purchasing intentions and consumption acts, the trend is visible (eg worldwide sales of products with fair-trade origins today represent a market of over €6 billion compared with €1 billion in 2003). Consumers explain this disparity by the lack of appeal and the cost of sustainable products, the profusion of environmental and label-related allegations, and the lack of transparency of companies (concrete proof and information, for example on manufacturing conditions).

These figures and tendencies clearly point out the risks to which companies are subjected: risks of mistrust of the brand and risks of degrowth ('consuming better means consuming less'). They are informative about the challenges for marketers who need to integrate, in their offers, answers to meet these new expectations:

more quality and less quantity, usage and not necessarily ownership, greater (price) accessibility to products, processes for answering questions about the traceability of production conditions, inclusion of impacts produced throughout the products' lifecycles.

All these challenges will necessarily transit between the marketing and the procurement departments, as the latter is in charge of bringing into the company those products and services that it does not produce itself. There is therefore a very strong community of thought surrounding the issue of sustainable development in general, and CSR in particular, amongst buyers and marketers.

Risks relating to stakeholders

More globally, it is responding to the expectations and pressures of stakeholders that constitutes a challenge for companies. To assess the dimensions of this challenge, companies need to map out their stakeholders and set up dialogue and consultation initiatives in a context nourished by a combination of several factors:

- the publication of the Stern Review, which demonstrated that it would be less expensive to fight climate change than to undergo its consequences;
- the effect on the general public of films by figures such as Al Gore, French photographer Yann Arthus Bertrand and French ecologist Nicolas Hulot;
- the growing visibility of these topics in the press;
- the multiplication of headlines on 'green growth';
- the emergence of 'alternative consumers' with high purchasing power, whose choices take into account social or environmental criteria, now representing 15–25 per cent of the population in most major developed countries (France, Japan, United States etc).

Analysis of the critical stakes represented by CSR enables us to identify some latent risks of not responding adequately: degradation of image and reputation, degrowth or a strong decline in certain sectors of activity, financial sanctions in the event of non-respect of laws/the regulatory framework, loss of market share in the face of more CSR-active competitors, and risks of boycott (cf fall of Mattel's stock prices during the scandal on dangerous toys), and so on. Indeed, stakeholders can sanction those practices that they deem to be irresponsible:

- NGOs do not hesitate to 'name and shame', a practice that also includes social aspects (cf NGO initiatives for the Clean Clothes Campaign);
- investors (in particular retirement funds or long-term sovereign-wealth funds) may exclude companies from their funds on the basis of social and environmental criteria;
- clients may 'give the cold shoulder' to products and services whose manufacturing conditions seem unworthy to them;
- suppliers can denounce, via the media, the practices of certain buyers and the consequences that these may have (eg the race towards cost-killing may draw less attention to the quality of the products manufactured, to factory working conditions, to the respect of environmental norms etc);

- employees and their representatives may become a brand's main critics, using the internet and social networks as new sounding boxes for their recriminations.

As shown by Figure 6.2, the need to respond to stakeholder expectations brings companies up against new challenges: at the very least compliance with their expectations, and ideally, anticipation of them, innovation, seizing value-creation opportunities, and setting themselves apart by improving their 'global performance' (economic, environmental, social/corporate).

In this way, sustainable development stands out as a solution for economic players, bringing them a new vision that is expressed on every level:

- on an economic level, through awareness-raising on the rarity of natural resources, through improved management of business with suppliers and subcontractors;

- in supply methods, through the analysis and integration of environmental and social criteria in choices (on products, services, suppliers, manufacturing countries);

- in production methods, through the reduction of negative externalities throughout their cycle;

- in decision-making methods, through integration of the long-term, a broadened vision of the world including 'future generations', rediscovery of the local dimension, and an evolution in relation to 'richness creation'.

FIGURE 6.2   Risks and opportunities: different company strategies

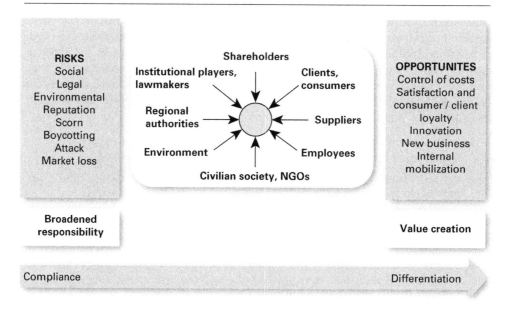

SOURCE: Des Enjeux & des Hommes.

6/1.2 Key role of procurement in introducing CSR into a company

As the overseer of sustainable procurement policies, the procurement department is directly affected by these issues. In this capacity, it will be prompted to review its practices and to acquire new tools. CSR considerations may also bring opportunities to create new synergies (with the sustainable development, marketing, R&D and human resources teams) in order to deal with questions that may require partnered approaches. Finally, the procurement function can also see the raising of these issues as a chance to reposition itself as a source of strategic advice vis-à-vis management bodies.

CSR has gradually worked its way into companies. From production to logistics, via marketing, communications, human resources, procurement or finance, all of a company's functions are concerned with sustainable development today. It is in more recent years that procurement departments have begun to seek support on CSR matters. Could this relative 'lag' be due to the fact that procurement's main mission has been considered to be purchasing in such a way as to generate short-term savings, and therefore contradictory by nature with the principles of sustainable development? This attitude would imply a reductive vision of the function.

Today, almost all companies believe that they should steer their decisions and offers by listening to and dialoguing with their consumers or clients. Marketing is *the* function inside the company that ensures this dialogue. This is the function that helps with the design and positioning of the offer in order to boost it on the market. We therefore consider it to be a key function in the implementation of CSR strategy, by nature geared towards listening to the company's stakeholders.

In order for a company's CSR strategy to be diffused to the whole of the company's upstream and downstream chain, procurement is *the* function that can translate, implement and manage these commitments (Figure 6.3).

In this way, marketing and procurement are two key and complementary functions that enable the company to commit long-term to a CSR strategy with its main stakeholders.

6/2 Concept, definitions and risks of sustainable procurement

More and more, the procurement function is viewed as a creator of value for the company. Unless the company has the resources to carry out production internally, procurement is also the function that manages the company's suppliers, ultimately considered as external resources and no longer as mere *sub*contractors.

According to the 2011 HEC Alumni/Agile Buyer survey on the priorities of procurement departments, despite the importance of managing procurement costs, cost-killing buyers are rarely recompensed for their savings on procurement (42 per cent of those surveyed receive no performance bonus on procurement savings). On the other hand, supplier risk management is an essential objective for 66 per cent of

FIGURE 6.3   The key role of procurement in CSR

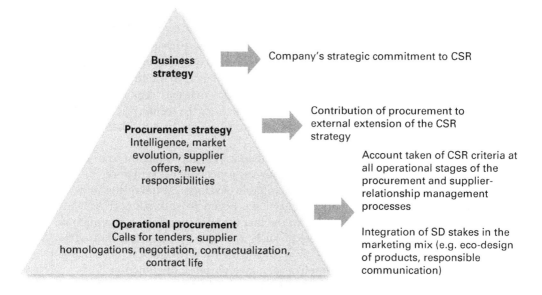

the procurement departments surveyed, as well as the increase of procurement in low-cost countries (44 per cent of respondents) and the professionalization of buyers.

In spite of the intentions declared loud and clear, one is forced to admit that cost-saving (short-term, most of the time) remains the prime priority in procurement departments of a majority of companies.

All this may seem extremely contradictory in view of the global stakes surrounding us, but also in the light of the historical evolution of the procurement function in the last three decades or so. And yet, at the same time, sustainable development has not fallen by the wayside in spite of the recent economic crisis. In addition, responsible approaches initiated by the highest levels of companies cannot be coherent without the active participation of the whole of the value chain and all functions, including procurement.

All therefore points to us being situated at a turning point and procurement preparing to emerge on new foundations. These weak signals, increasingly repeated and ordered, may well be the precursor of a future transformation of 'classic' procurement into 'sustainable' procurement.

6/2.1 Upsurge of sustainable procurement

Company buyers have a key role to play in applying more sustainable principles in their companies, namely by expressing sustainable development policy in various contexts: in the operational processes of procurement, in relationships with suppliers, in the method for calculating global and long-term performance. Their influence over the choice of the company's marketable and non-marketable goods should steer the latter towards compliance with social and environmental principles.

The upsurge of concerns about responsibility amongst procurement heads has uncontestably grown regularly in the last few years. As shown by Figure 6.4, according to the 6th edition of the biannual HEC/EcoVadis Barometer published in November 2013,[2] sustainable procurement occupies third place amongst the strategic priorities of procurement heads. Cost reduction (direct and indirect) is at the top of the list (100 per cent), followed by risk reduction (95 per cent) and compliance (93 per cent), on a par with sustainable procurement (93 per cent).

FIGURE 6.4   Priority level of sustainable procurement for procurement heads (global)

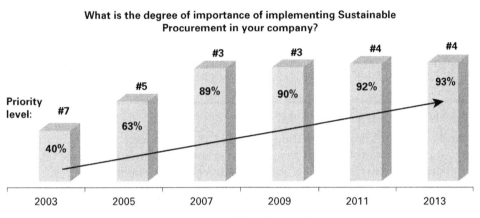

What is the degree of importance of implementing Sustainable Procurement in your company?

SOURCE: 6th HEC Sustainable Procurement Barometer (November 2013).

This upsurge and its inclusion amongst the top five concerns for a period of eight years, at a time when restrictions relating to the economic crisis at the end of the 2000s could have ousted CSR, are due as much to new risks in terms of corporate image, mirroring an evolution in public opinion, hence that of clients and society in general, as to the pressure of new regulations.

6/2.2 Definition of sustainable procurement

CSR is, according to official terminology, corporate social responsibility. The concept can also be designated by the term 'social and environmental responsibility', which spells out the two dimensions that have most often been the great oversights of capitalistic development. One example illustrates this attitude: if you ask any procurement manager 'who is your no. 1 supplier?' he or she will give you the name of the company from which the company derives its highest business volume in terms of the sum purchased. Whereas for a great majority of companies, the number 1 supplier is in fact nature and biodiversity! We have a tendency to forget this as it is an invisible resource, 'free of charge', hence absent from indicators.

AFNOR (the French Association for Normalization) defines sustainable procurement in the following manner:

It is the procurement of goods or services that, throughout the supply process, integrate social, environmental and economic responsibility, based on the sustainable development principles stated during the Earth Summit in Rio de Janeiro in 1992, as well as the different international conventions or texts in force in the domains of sustainable development (environment, human rights, labour rights...), as well as internationally recognized good practices, namely in the context of the fight against corruption. Whether it is public or private, this procurement therefore gives priority to goods or services that respect the environment or integrate a certain level of social responsibility by promoting the equity of exchanges and supporting optimal transparency.

When we speak of sustainable procurement, we therefore refer not only to the products and services that are purchased, but also the procurement practices of companies, internally in their processes and externally in the way that they relate to suppliers, as well as notions of ethics and global performance, shared and sustainable.

According to the United Nations Development Programme (UNDP):

> sustainable procurement is all about taking social and environmental factors into consideration alongside financial factors in making purchasing decisions. It involves looking beyond the traditional economic parameters and making decisions based on the whole life cost, the associated risks, measures of success and implications for society and the environment.

Sustainable procurement may cover several aspects:

- *Ethical procurement*: ensuring that suppliers respect international norms such as human rights, preservation of the environment, basic labour rights, the rules of hygiene and security, the fight against corruption.

- *'Green' procurement*: favouring the purchase of products that are more respectful of the environment: eco-procurement, eco-responsible purchases, fight against pollution, reduction of the ecological footprint, recycling and management of the end-of-life of purchased products.

- *Solidarity sourcing*: (in France) making purchases from specially protected and adapted work environments (companies employing disabled persons) and from sectors promoting social inclusion (professional inclusion of those removed from the sphere of employment).

- *Fair-trade procurement*: supporting trade between developed and developing countries and paying producers in less wealthy countries equitably.

- *Efficient procurement*: integration of lifecycle analysis (LCA), in other words a TCO approach in a broad sense, as well as evaluation of a product's environmental impacts on the whole of the lifecycle.

Procurement, as a transversal function within the company, as a function interfacing between the company's internal and external dimensions, is at the heart of sustainable development issues. This positioning permits it to propel change in the company, but also in supplier markets. In the same way as for other areas such as quality, certain requirements that the company sets for itself are applicable to its suppliers, and sometimes mandatorily, as is the case with ethical aspects. A company that develops these values cannot afford to have suppliers that tarnish its image. This is an extra risk, and a new aspect to take into account when assessing suppliers.

6/2.3 Sustainable procurement: major principles and the concept of responsibility

Sustainable procurement demands a more systemic and dynamic vision of relationships with internal clients and external suppliers.

A more systemic vision because it is a global one, taking into account the individual at the heart of an increasingly globalized society. We have already witnessed the debut of a movement in which procurement pays less interest to short-term profit at all costs, and more to mutually beneficial relationships with players in the supply chain. It is a matter of continuing this movement whilst also integrating into it corporate and environmental dimensions. In other words, such an approach leads us directly to a more acute awareness of all stakeholders in an organization: suppliers, other internal departments, as well as representatives of civilian society, politics, associations supporting environmental protection and so on.

Next, a more dynamic vision as it targets the long term. It is common to see organizations restricted by short-term visions, and procurement is no exception. Construction of a long-term vision ensures greater sustainability for the company, facilitates the coordination and reactivation of innovation, as well as the shedding of old models. This is the type of vision that enables procurement to fully participate in the company's strategy.

Whilst major French groups, whether constrained by the law or else voluntarily, have progressively committed to CSR tactics for more than 10 years, it is only in the last few years that these organizations have translated their sustainability approaches on the ground, in the procurement function.

Amongst the many tasks carried out to bring responsibility to procurement, a survey carried out amongst CAC 40 companies and published by the ORSE (French CSR observatory) in 2010 notes an 'upsurge' of sustainable procurement policies as of 2008. In the same year, one company out of two formalized or intensified its CSR approach. The survey also highlights three start-up phases to 'the integration of CSR in procurement': the 2000–04 phase involving 30 per cent of CAC 40 companies, mainly in the consumer goods sector; the 2004–06 phase including 40 per cent of companies, namely in the banking and insurance sector; and finally the 2006–08 phase comprising the remaining third.

The survey also lists the reasons behind these strategies. Whilst over 75 per cent of respondents communicate, in their sustainable development reports, on the management of CSR risks relating to supply and reduction of environmental impact, many other motivations are noted (a total of 12, including improvement of social conditions and health/security amongst suppliers and subcontractors, support for SMEs, support for the employment of disabled persons, the development of green products, the improvement and perpetuation of relationships with suppliers, etc). This range of answers reveals the element of vagueness that lies in the notion of responsibility when applied to procurement.

Another survey carried out by Ernst & Young also points to a heterogeneous level of maturity amongst companies questioned on their sustainable procurement strategies. From the collection of environmental data (70 per cent) to recourse to 'fair-trade' labelled suppliers (22 per cent) via the purchase of waste-recycling services (67 per cent) or developmental support for certain suppliers (39 per cent), the diversity of operational initiatives set up shows the extremely wide field that is covered by the notion of sustainable procurement.

One last survey, undertaken by KPMG on the procurement profession in 2008, also brings out the difficulties that buyers have in finding the meaning that CSR may take on in their domain. Carried out amongst 600 senior executives from all regions of the world, results show that whilst 42 per cent of respondents review the performance of their suppliers in environmental and human rights aspects, whilst 43 per cent integrate social and ethical factors into their procurement decisions, and whilst 33 per cent are committed to strategies for reducing environmental impact, only one-third of companies consider sustainable development to be a moderately important criterion in the choice of a supplier. These results speak loudly about *the gap between discourse and reality*. KPMG also emphasizes the fact that these issues are regarded more as a type of checklist, an initial filter for committing to a supplier; their stakes are not truly appropriated and concretely translated into the profession.

Figure 6.5 indicates the main motivations driving companies according the last HEC survey in 2013.

This research, in the same way as many other studies carried out on the topic (ie the HEC/EcoVadis Barometers established biannually for 10 years), teaches us that general management and procurement departments no longer ask themselves 'why commit to such an approach?' but rather 'how?' – and that the answer to the latter question is not obvious to many.

6/2.4 Issues in sustainable procurement

Control of image risks

The first motivation driving the implementation of a sustainable procurement policy is the management of risks relating to the company's image, which translates an evolution in public opinion, and therefore the opinions of clients.

A procurement department, due to its role in linking the company to outside markets, is subject to more risks than other functions within the organization. It enters into relationships with other organizations and suppliers, and cannot always oversee all of their processes or behaviour on upstream markets.

A company's image and its reputation are two distinct notions. Image is an integral part of a company's identity, for it refers to the perception and the objective representation that the public has of the entity. Corporate image results from a set of signals that the company sends out internally and externally (its logo, the positioning of its products, etc) and is largely influenced by its communication tactics.

The notion of corporate reputation emerged later, in the 1990s. Originally, the concept was largely tied up with a company's financial situation, its capacity to convince financial experts and investors, and its stock value. Today, reputation is based on the subjective perceptions (value judgements) of stakeholders and on the more global idea of the company's business performance. Whilst image and reputation may both be positive or negative, a company's image is set to evolve quickly depending on stimuli and occasional hazards; reputation, on the other hand, is constructed and evolves over time through the continuity of the company's performance.

FIGURE 6.5 What is the motivation for establishing a policy of responsible buying in your association?

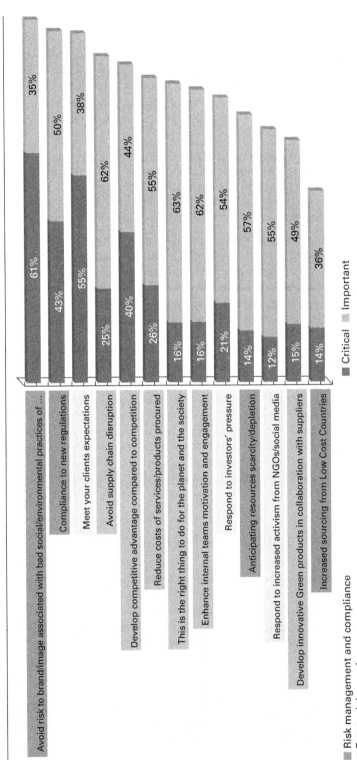

Avoid risk to brand/image associated with bad social/environmental practices of ... — 61% / 35%
Compliance to new regulations — 43% / 50%
Meet your clients expectations — 55% / 38%
Avoid supply chain disruption — 25% / 62%
Develop competitive advantage compared to competition — 40% / 44%
Reduce costs of services/products procured — 26% / 55%
This is the right thing to do for the planet and the society — 16% / 63%
Enhance internal teams motivation and engagement — 16% / 62%
Respond to investors' pressure — 21% / 54%
Anticipating resources scarcity/depletion — 14% / 57%
Respond to increased activism from NGOs/social media — 12% / 55%
Develop innovative Green products in collaboration with suppliers — 15% / 49%
Increased sourcing from Low Cost Countries — 14% / 36%

■ Critical ■ Important

■ Risk management and compliance
■ External demands
■ Internal drivers

SOURCE: 6ème Baromètre HEC / EcoVadis Achats Responsables 2013.

We can draw on two examples to illustrate these concepts: that of Greenpeace's attack on Kit Kat, and the Barbie doll affair afflicting Mattel. Whilst Nestlé's image was stained by Greenpeace's denunciation campaign, it suffered few consequences outside of a restricted circle of 'ecologists,' mainly because its core activity is not to save the planet. However, the Mattel affair seriously wounded the toy company's reputation which, in the eyes of the general public, no longer had the means to carry out its activity and to guarantee the security of its products (as, indeed, attested by various internet sites consulted:

> The company Mattel was sentenced to a heavy fine of $2.3 million for marketing children's toys presenting health risks, namely under the Fisher Price brand and Barbie doll accessories. The lead content of paint used on toys by the manufacturer Mattel was higher than the authorized threshold (lead is considered extremely dangerous for children's development, and can cause lead poisoning, colic, anaemia, etc).

After distinguishing between the concepts of image and reputation, it is interesting to look at the vision of professionals and the impact that sustainable procurement strategies may have. According to the HEC/EcoVadis 2013 Barometer, image protection constitutes, for 96 per cent of respondents, the main objective targeted by the implementation of a sustainable procurement approach. 'Compliance with new regulations' and 'response to client expectations' tie for second place in objectives (93 per cent of responses).

In an applied research project published in 2010 entitled *Value of Sustainable Procurement Practices*, PWC, EcoVadis and INSEAD demonstrated – for the first time – the financial added value that a sustainable procurement policy can generate. This profitability can notably be observed in the area of the reduction of CSR risks. Indeed, an environmental, social or corporate scandal relating to a supplier's deviant practice may lead to the recall of many products, fines, a cut in market share, boycotting from consumers, and so on. Accused of non-compliance or even abusive practices in low-cost countries, companies have hastened to act in such a way as to demonstrate their good faith and their taking of 'co-responsibility' in the supply chain. According to the survey, a company's stock value could fall by around 12 per cent due to a recognized CSR risk on the market.

Compliance and regulatory anticipation

Another important motivation relates to the respect of new regulations being enforced. On the international and European level, reflections on environmental and social matters have been led, in the last few decades, by organizations such as the United Nations Global Pact, the International Labour Organization (ILO) or the Organization for Economic Cooperation and Development (OECD) via their Guiding Principles for multinational companies.

There are also many regulatory texts relating to sustainable development. This global regulatory framework is translated into recommendations or else into standards and laws.

The European Union treats sustainable development and CSR as priority subjects that are the basis of its long-term strategy, targeting the following objectives: limiting climate change and its effects, limiting the negative effects of transport, promoting more sustainable production and consumption modes, encouraging the sustainable management of natural resources, limiting public-health risks, fighting social exclusion and poverty, and ensuring global sustainable development. This strategy ('a catalyst for policy-makers and public opinion, to change society's behaviour') and this ambition position Europe as a leader in relation to other regions of the world, also obliged to comply with the rules that the EU imposes upon its member states.

Here are a few regulatory texts relating to sustainable development and CSR:

- The European REACH Regulation on the registration, evaluation and authorization of chemicals, as well as the restrictions applicable to these substances, offers a regulatory framework for the use of chemicals in Europe. Adopted at the end of 2006, REACH applies in all EU countries and aims to eliminate the most toxic chemicals from the EU in order to protect the health of employees, consumers, the population, and to improve the quality of the environment. In this way, since 2008, any chemical, manufactured or imported, must be recorded with the European Chemicals Agency (ECHA). Permission is granted to substances whose risks are controlled. It is said that implementation of this regulation has allowed between 2,000 and 4,000 cancers per year to be avoided. In France, the regulation applies to some 4,000 companies in different sectors: chemicals, metallurgy, surface treatment, mass distribution, microelectronics, paint, maintenance etc. In all, 30,000 substances are concerned, and no non-recorded product can be commercialized.

- The European directive on Waste Electrical and Electronic Equipment, known as the WEEE, promotes the recycling of WEEE by requiring manufacturers and importers of such equipment to take charge of the costs of collecting and handling their waste.

- The European directive RoHS (2002/95/EC), coming into force in July 2006, limits the usage of six dangerous substances (lead, mercury, cadmium, hexavalent chromium, polybrominated biphenyls, polybrominated diphenyl ethers) in electrical and electronic equipment (EEE) commercialized in Europe. The RoHS directive applies to the following equipment: large and small household appliances, computing and telecommunications equipment, electrical and electronic tools, toys etc.

Two French laws are particularly important in the field of sustainable development: the *Loi sur le Handicap* (bill on disability) and the *Loi du Grenelle de l'Environnement* (Grenelle Environmental Roundtable Bill).

- As seen in Chapter 2, the bill on disability passed on 11 February 2005 requires all companies with over 20 employees to employ a minimum of 6 per cent of disabled people within their ranks. Half of this 6 per cent may be reached by indirect employment via procurement from specially protected and adapted work environments employing disabled persons. Companies that fail to meet this obligation are subject to payment of the AGEFIPH tax (from 400 to 600 times the minimum hourly wage since 2006, which can represent thousands or millions of euros). Detailed analysis of solidarity sourcing of this type is offered in Section 6/3.

- The bill on national commitment in favour of the environment, known as the Grenelle Bill 2, affects company procurement in the following areas: energy efficiency of buildings, change in types of transport, reduction of energy consumption and carbon content in production, preservation of biodiversity, waste treatment and preservation of health, new governance, publication of CSR information and certification by an external third party (eg an auditor).

Control of operational and financial risks

The exhaustion of resources has been the object of many scientific studies for several decades. Primarily accusing meteorological phenomena, climate change and the over-exploitation of resources, experts point out the inadequacy of harvests and the low levels of stock, sometimes seriously endangered (eg fish and the impact of over-fishing). For a number of years, international institutions such as the United Nations, the OECD, the Food and Agriculture Organization and the World Bank have also been in agreement that the phenomenon of resource depletion, accentuated by the excesses of speculation and the continuing financial crisis, has largely weakened markets and led to a surge in prices and their increased volatility. Throughout the world, agricultural products have gone up in price, and the same goes for energy costs and animal feed, therefore bringing repercussions on production costs.

These observations raise the question of food security and more specifically, that of the security of supplies for buyers. Whether they are already obliged to, or are spontaneously doing so out of anticipation, companies have committed to deep reflection on the operational and financial risks associated with diminishing resources; some have even reviewed their strategies if not their business models.

Cost reduction

The stakes of a sustainable procurement approach do not merely come down to what we stand to lose, but can also be presented as *opportunities to reduce costs and create value*. Cost reduction may come in several forms:

- reduction of internal costs (by buying more energy-efficient products and consuming less);
- reduction of demand (internal clients looking for weaker purchasing costs request products with fewer specificities);
- cost reduction imposed by compliance with environmental and social regulations (with the possible reduction of the sum of environmental-type taxes to be paid by the company).

The TCO approach emerged as a response to the desire to maximally cut production costs. By integrating factors other than price into the assessment of an offer, this method seeks to eliminate all superfluous elements and to optimize the entire value chain. As such, it joins up with the objective followed by a sustainable procurement approach to meet needs exactly whilst also minimizing environmental and social impacts. The simplest example is that of the new-generation light bulbs whose acquisition costs are higher than those of classic light bulbs, but whose reduced energy consumption and longer lifespan generate economic gains during their usage phase.

Analysis of a product's overall cost, encompassing *all phases of its lifecycle* and notably its usage phase, also helps steer teams towards designing high-quality products with boosted sustainability. The PWC/EcoVadis/INSEAD study (2010) already cited shows that on average, cost reduction engendered by a sustainable procurement project represents 0.05 per cent of its turnover.

New business models

A sustainable procurement policy may create growth opportunities for the company's turnover through the creation of new business models. Indeed, sustainable development has spawned new markets and new companies whose business models are structured around this notion.

To anticipate the opening up of their markets to competition, companies in the water, energy, transport and postal service sectors are developing more responsible offers and products in order to stand out from their European rivals. This tendency has a strong impact on procurement, increasingly considered as a function that brings added value through its control of the supplier market (market maturity, innovations, tendencies) and its faculty to be attentive to the expectations of its internal clients.

In 2005, General Electric launched its Ecomagination initiative to place eco-designed offers on the market. Its ambitious objectives have been well and truly reached ever since, with dozens of products and services commercialized, representing a turnover of several tens of billions of dollars. Although the initial investments were considerable, these offers confirm the group's capacity to innovate, and undeniably carves out its place as a pioneer in its markets.

6/3 Implementation: different categories of actions

6/3.1 Different aspects of sustainable procurement

Let's go over the various aspects already mentioned in Section 6/2.2, and develop them more fully, looking at different avenues of reflection and action.

Green procurement

This consists of the procurement of products that are more respectful of the environment (or that cause less impact). Integrating only a few environmental criteria at its outset, today such purchases are selected via increasingly detailed procedures as eco-design develops in organizations.

The legislative environment

Since the start of the 2000s, the international institutional and legislative context has accelerated the consideration and the implementation of initiatives on a European level. It is thus that France, looking to extend European sustainable development strategy, has committed to initiatives following this direction, namely through the

Grenelle Environmental Roundtable that is still an international reference today. The Grenelle produced a formal legislative framework structured around three elements:

- the planning law on implementation of the *Grenelle Environnement*, known as the Grenelle Bill 1, adopted definitively on 23 July 2009 and promulgated on 3 August 2009;
- the draft bill on 'national commitment to the environment', known as the Grenelle Bill 2, adopted by the French Council of Ministers on 7 January 2009;
- the bundle of greening tax measures in the 2009 Finance Bill, known as Grenelle 3, adopted on 9 December 2008.

The Grenelle Bill 1, via 57 articles and 13 themes, set environmental objectives such as the cutting of emissions of gases with greenhouse effects by a factor of 4 by 2050 ('factor 4'), the development of organic agriculture (target of 6 per cent of the country's usable farming land devoted to organic agriculture in 2012, and 20 per cent in 2020), and a 7 per cent reduction in the production of household waste per inhabitant every year for the next five years.

The Grenelle Bill 2 is made up of almost 200 decrees and defines the rules for implementing the commitments of Grenelle 1. It constitutes a type of roadmap for France in terms of sustainable development, built around six major themes: energy efficiency for buildings; organization of transport that is more respectful of the environment; the reduction of energy consumption; the preservation of biodiversity; the control of risks, waste treatment and the preservation of health; and the implementation of a new ecological governance and the foundation of more sustainable consumption and production.

Corporate obligation to report on CSR

Following Article 116 of the NRE bill dating from 15 May 2001 requiring the accountability of French listed companies regarding the way in which they take 'social and environmental consequences' into consideration in their activities, Article 225 of the Grenelle Bill 2 sets out to be more specific and demanding about RSE reporting. It thus widens the reporting obligation to non-listed companies and requires certification of the published indicators by an external third party.

Environmental labelling

Amongst the leading measures of the Grenelle Bill 2, experimentation with environmental labelling commenced as of 2010 and was officially launched on 1 July 2011. On an international scale, this was the first-ever national initiative to go beyond carbon-content display and to be based on multiple criteria. Several objectives are followed including: integration of sustainable development in the criteria for choice of products, and raising consumer awareness on environmental issues (emissions of gases with greenhouse effects, consumption of natural resources, impacts on biodiversity, etc); evaluation of the efforts of companies having undertaken to reduce the environmental impacts of their products.

Eco-design

The ADEME (French Environment and Energy Management Agency) defines eco-design as an approach that 'consists in integrating environmental aspects as of the product-design phase, whether for goods or for services'. Indeed, up to 70 per cent of a product's costs and 80 per cent of its environmental and social impacts are determined during its design. 'This integration relies on a global and multi-criteria approach to the environment, and is based on consideration of all stages of the lifecycles of products.' The lifecycle refers to all of a product's stages, from the extraction of raw materials to the end of its life, passing through production, distribution and use.

A global and multi-criteria approach leads to account being taken of all environmental impacts generated by the product or service. This includes resource consumption, waste production, gases with greenhouse effects, water, air and soil pollution, and so on.

An eco-design approach should also preserve the quality of a product's usage and image. It not only allows the product's environmental impacts to be diminished, but also encourages and promotes more responsible consumption modes in society. Indeed, 52 per cent of household emissions of greenhouse gases are related to products consumed (manufacturing, provision and end-of-life treatment of products and services). An eco-design approach helps cut the level of emissions, notably through several actions: choice of materials with lesser impact (recycled, renewable, etc), recourse to cleaner manufacturing procedures and technologies, optimization of logistics and transport flows, end-of-life recycling (materials, components, product, etc).

Eco-design also helps to reduce requirements in natural resources by seeking volume/mass optimization, as well as fostering the recycling of products and their sustainability (reliability, repairs, modularity, etc). In France, household waste totals 390 kg per year per inhabitant, with almost 90 kg comprising packaging waste. Eco-design approaches, through their anticipation of end-of-life procedures, assist in diminishing the quantities of waste produced, via their preference for separable materials, the optimization of waste collection, and product recycling.

Consumers are expecting more responsibility from companies, namely in relation to the products that they commercialize.

Lifecycle analysis (LCA)

Developed in the 1970s, LCA is an environmental assessment method for products (goods or services). It should not be confused with 'single-criterion' methods such as the French Bilan Carbone®, a method trademarked by the ADEME for measuring greenhouse-gas emissions on the scale of an organization (company, administration, local or regional authority).

Not merely limited to greenhouse gases, LCA inventories and quantifies inflows and outflows of energy and materials throughout the stages of the lifecycle: production of raw materials, manufacturing of the product, transport (intervening upstream and downstream of the manufacturing process), product use, and its end-of-life. The result is translated into environmental impacts, whether in terms of the greenhouse effect, depletion of natural resources, acidification, eutrophication, and so on.

As the object of normalization (ISO 14040 and 14044), LCA is the most sophisticated tool today in terms of global and multi-criteria environmental assessment. It enables a product's environmental stakes to be identified whilst emphasizing the relative weights of the different stages of the lifecycle; it classifies impacts in order of priority and it singles out the inflows and outflows on which action is required.

Unlike single-criterion tools, this method allows avoidance of pollution transfers (improvement of one stage in the cycle may deteriorate another stage: the reduction of emissions of gases with greenhouse effects may engender increased consumption of natural resources). It also permits definition of a coherent eco-design approach adapted to these impacts.

The advantages of such an approach stem from its rigorous and exhaustive nature (an inventory of all impacts). However, it requires a long and costly process. In practice, simplified approaches are possible:

- partial LCAs (eg focusing on measurement of greenhouse-gas effects), whose great flaw is that pollution transfers are poorly assessed, and also that impacts on which external stakeholders may position themselves in the future are excluded (eg measuring CO_2 in the automobile industry amounts to hiding the impacts of particle emissions on human health, likely to become a major social issue in the future);

- simplified protocols: the ADEME suggests such approaches on its website (eg the *Passeport Éco-produit* (eco-product passport);

- customized simplified protocols undertaken by companies that have already carried out LCAs on their leading products.

These strategies would benefit from being carried out in partnership with the different entities in question, internally (marketing department, sustainable development department, R&D) and externally (suppliers, distributors), from the perspective of a learning organization.

Downstream communication with consumers is more difficult to undertake, for reasons to do with the technical complexity of the subject, the obligation – via the ISO norm – to make explicit details on the LCA whenever it is referred to rather than merely communicating on aggregate impacts, and the difficulty for the consumer, focused on the usage stage, to grasp the product's lifecycle.

Since 2008, reflections on the *Social* Lifecycle Analysis (SLCA) of products have been initiated, namely by the United Nations. In conformity with the ISO 14040 and 14044 norms, the SLCA supplements the LCA by including the social and socio-economic impacts generated during the lifecycle (human rights, working conditions, health and security, governance, socio-economic repercussions and so on). The new, complex and unfinished nature of this methodology, based on quantitative but also qualitative data, makes its application difficult today.

New varied approaches: industrial ecology, cradle-to-cradle, biomimetics, functional economy

Other eco-design approaches have found concrete applications in the last decades. Whilst industrial ecology and 'cradle-to-cradle' draw inspiration from LCA, biomimetics follows the example of nature to set up eco-design strategies, and the functional economy transforms the economic model by focusing on a product's usage value.

Industrial ecology advocates a systemic approach that is inspired from ecosystems and nature, where the waste of some becomes the raw materials of others. In this way, industrial ecology goes further than LCA in that, rather than aiming to limit the flows of materials and energies, it targets a closed-circuit operation. This is translated by the reduction or pooling of these flows, and the creation of streams for product recycling, conversion or reuse, with companies, plants and cities forming an ecosystem.

Belonging to the industrial ecology family, the concept of *cradle-to-cradle* (C2C) emerged at the end of the 1980s and began to find concrete application at the start of the 2000s thanks to the research of German chemist Michael Braungart and US architect William McDonough. The approach changes paradigms as it consists in thinking, as of the product's design, of ways to disassemble the materials that compose it, to recycle them and reintroduce them into the production cycle, thus placing value on the waste. Ultimately, it is an approach whereby industrial processes are reinvented so as to create an economy with a 'positive ecological footprint'.

The methodology necessarily implies recourse to non-toxic, biodegradable or compost-friendly materials/components so that they can be reused. As such, it goes beyond the mere concept of recycling (recycled products are not necessarily non-toxic) and reduces the negative impact on man and nature. The C2C approach is the object of certification delivered by the MBDC (McDonough Braungart Design Chemistry) firm.

Biomimetics is another approach that, inspired by the observation of nature, aims to copy living models for a sustainable industrial application. This concept was perfected in 1997 in the United States by biologist Janine Benyus, and from the outset, aroused the interest of some top companies such as Nike, Procter & Gamble and Levi Strauss. A source of unlimited innovations, biomimetics has applications in many fields today. For example, lotus leaves with self-cleaning properties when in contact with water inspired a German firm to design an outdoor paint that cleans itself with rainwater. This product has been used in over 300,000 buildings in the country. Numerous other applications have been born, such as snow tyres with extra grip that mimic gecko foot pads, passive cooling systems inspired by termite mounds, or the *shinkanzen* (Japanese high-speed train) copying the beak of the kingfisher.

The *functional economy* is a different approach from those that we have just seen, for it is not based on an environmental strategy but a change in economic model. Its aim is to designate value to a product's usage function, rather than to the number of units it sells. Xerox, the US manufacturer and seller of photocopiers, was amongst the first to launch this type of approach. After producing some ultra-sophisticated equipment, the firm decided to rent out devices rather than selling them at a prohibitive price. Another example is that of the Michelin Fleet Solutions, whereby Michelin sells mobility services instead of tyres (the tyres are billed on the basis of the distance they cover). The success of the offer notably lies in an eco-design approach to the tyre itself, whose grip and endurance are enhanced. This offer enables clients to diminish their impacts and their costs, namely in terms of fuel consumption and maintenance, all the while generating profits for Michelin.

The circular economy
The circular economy is an economic concept in line with sustainable development, whose objective is to produce goods and services whilst limiting the consumption and wastage of raw materials, water and energy sources. This is a matter of deploying a new economy, circular rather than linear, based on the principle of 'closing up the lifecycle' of products, services, waste, materials, water and energy. According to this system, the waste of some becomes the resources of others.

In its second report *Towards a Circular Economy*, published in January 2013 during the Davos Forum, the Ellen MacArthur Foundation, in conjunction with McKinsey & Co, indicates that the value of circular opportunities for consumer goods could be as much as $700 billion, in other words 1.1 per cent of the global annual GDP in 2010, not to mention 'secondary' benefits in terms of innovation, preservation of agricultural land, or the creation of local jobs.

Solidarity sourcing

In France 'solidarity sourcing' describes – according to AFNOR – purchases made 'from structures employing persons in difficulty: a public removed from employment (professional insertion through economic activity) and disabled persons'.

Disability
Following the principle of France's Bill no. 2005-102 of 11 February 2005 on the equality of rights and opportunities, and notably given the high taxes payable in the event of non-compliance with this law, procurement of this kind is increasingly widespread. It should also be noted, at the same time, that the intrinsic value of this approach accounts for its growth in the professional world.

Solidarity sourcing may be made from what the French call *entreprises adaptées* (EAs or 'adapted companies') or *établissements et services d'aide par le travail* (ESATs or 'establishments and services providing assistance through employment'). These inclusive structures have the same objective: to enable disabled persons to pursue a remunerated professional activity. Their difference stems mainly from their status. The ESATs (protected work sector) are medico-social bodies that welcome heavily disabled persons who cannot work in any other environment. Workers here are provided with flexible working conditions. They do not have the status of employee and cannot be dismissed. They are however subject to certain rules of the French Employment Code such as security, hygiene, occupational health and paid leave. The EAs (adapted work sector) are managed as 'classic' structures, but disabled workers hold at least 80 per cent of production positions. These companies work as subcontractors or else place staff at the disposal of companies from the so-called 'conventional' sector. Disabled workers in EAs have an employee status and benefit indiscriminately from the same rights and duties as any other employee.

Today, the protected and adapted work sector is made up of approximately 2,000 structures in France, and constitutes a job generator for up to 150,000 disabled persons who cannot, temporarily or long-term, find their place on the ordinary employment circuit.

These structures offer a whole range of services, in the form of subcontracting or worker postings; they cover many sectors and activities: eg laundry services, printing and reprography, office and garden maintenance, catering, logistics and handling. Around 1,000 professions are involved. The structures are often as competitive as so-called 'classic' companies, but a real disparity exists in the maturity of companies in the protected and adapted sector.

The EAs and ESATs are grouped into networks or associations, the best-known being the *Union Nationale des Entreprises Adaptées*, the *Groupement des Etablissements et Services d'Aide par le Travail*, and *l'Association des Paralysés de France*. The aim of these associations is to provide support and promotion of the protected and adapted work sector by drawing them to the economic milieu as far as possible. This takes place through the creation of partnerships with so-called 'classic' companies that offer training on know-how and professionalism.

The French IAE ('integration through economic activity') sector

Solidarity sourcing can also be undertaken from a number of specialized French IAE structures: the ETTI (temporary-work integration companies), the EI (integration companies), the AI (intermediary associations), the ACI (integration workshops and construction sites), neighbourhood associations and finally the GEIQ (groupings of employers for integration and qualification). All these structures are contracted by French departmental directorates of employment and training.

Fair-trade procurement

Fair-trade procurement refers to the purchase of products stemming from fair-trade. Although fair-trade has only really taken off in the last 20 years, its origins can be traced back to the 1950s and 1960s when organizations in developing countries wished to put forward an alternative form of trade, and a form of philanthropy to finance development emerged. Supported by alternative globalization (alter-globalization or the global justice movement) activists, this 'trade for development' gradually took form between developed and developing countries (first through the sale of craft products, and today through consumer products such as coffee), challenging international trade systems that are unfavourable to developing countries. Indeed, 'trade, not aid!' was the demand of these countries during the first United Nations Conference on Trade and Development (UNCTAD) held in Geneva in 1964.

Fair-trade was originally inspired by an age-old tradition: cooperation, supplemented by fair pricing, democratic organization of work, the elimination of intermediaries, long-term commitment, protection of the environment, and local community development. The notion of 'fair pricing' implies a stable price established through an agreement between the chain's protagonists, covering the fundamental needs of producers and their production costs, including social and environmental costs, thus enabling a sufficient margin to be made for investments.

Fair-trade responds to challenges facing society regarding populations in developing countries via ongoing economic support for workers, but also via their training or even the provision of education for their children, community development, or improvement of the status of women. According to Fairtrade International (FLO) Labelling over 1.2 million producers and workers present in 58 developing countries took advantage of fair-trade in 2011.

Today, fair-trade operates through two sales channels:

1 The *integrated channel* represented by the IFAT (International Federation for Alternative Trade), characterized by its own distribution network. Today, it assembles almost 500 organizations committed to fair-trade strategies in over 70 countries.

2 The *certified channel*, following the example of the Max Havellar, Transfair or Fairtrade labels certifying products that satisfy a body of fair-trade criteria. The FLO gathers all national certification initiatives (19 in 2011, covering 23 countries) in the one organization.

The two streams united in 1998 to become part of the same network, and agreed, in 2001, on a common definition of fair-trade:

> a trading partnership, based on dialogue, transparency and respect, that seeks greater equity in international trade. It contributes to sustainable development by offering better trading conditions to, and securing the rights of, marginalized producers and workers – especially in the South.

At the start of the 1990s, the proportion of sales of craft products compared to agricultural products was 80 per cent to 20 per cent. Ten years later, the ratio was inverted (26 per cent compared to 74 per cent), and agricultural products are gradually gaining ground thanks to the commitment of major distribution brands.

Ethical procurement

Consideration of ethics in procurement relates to both the content of the procurement process but also the ways in which it is implemented. Ethical procurement, according to AFNOR, involves 'taking into account social or moral preoccupations; the approach refers to the social and corporate responsibility of buyers, namely in terms of human rights'. In other words, ethical procurement follows a goal of social progress, and aims for products that are manufactured in conditions respectful of basic social rights, as defined by the conventions of the ILO, namely the banning of forced labour, non-discrimination, or compliance with health and safety rules for workers.

The topic of ethics is fundamental, for in a world where the race towards growth appears essential for survival, pressure placed by buyers on their suppliers, wherever they may be, may have repercussions, sometimes fatal, on the supplier's employees, and by extension on the employees of their suppliers' own suppliers.

Responsibility must therefore be shared. It falls upon business leaders (clients and suppliers) to ensure decent working conditions and responsible practices vis-à-vis their employees. Indeed, it is not enough to simply demand one's suppliers to respect norms; the ordering-party company has a duty to act as a role model. The social accountability norm SA 8000 may complement the work of the ILO and help any organization wishing to commit to such an approach.

Deontology: translation of ethics into professional conduct

Whilst ethics lays down values, principles and rules of conduct, deontology is its concrete application in the business world. It aims to find practical solutions on the behaviour to adopt in certain situations where ethics may play a role.

Usually, a deontology code deals with the following issues: respect of individuals, protection of a company's tangible and intangible assets, employee conduct, the company's relationship with its clients, relationships with suppliers and partners, respect of confidentiality, gifts and other perks, conflicts of interest, the duty of vigilance and prevention.

Today, organizations may equip themselves with ethics or deontology codes/charters, or even both. An ethics charter is specific to an individual company as it depends on its culture, its history, its stakes etc. Meanwhile, a deontology charter may be specific to a company just as it may be shared by the one profession or sector of activity.

It should also be noted that ethics and deontology are notions that evolve over time, and continually progress, enhanced by dialogue, transparency, and feedback from real-life experience.

Efficient procurement

This consists of applying the approach to the third aspect of sustainable development, namely the economic aspect, using the total cost of ownership (TCO) approach. The TCO is a notion developed in detail elsewhere in this work, particularly in Chapter 9. A 'responsible' buyer should take the TCO into account in order to make enlightened choices and to offer sound advice to ordering parties.

This concept is best demonstrated by calculations on the financial performance of energy-saving light bulbs compared with classic incandescent light bulbs (minus 36 per cent, according to the ADEME).

Reference to the TCO enables measurement of cost avoidance, indirect costs (the price to pay for non-compliance with an environmental law), indirect gains (eg solidarity sourcing that may exempt the company from having to pay the French AGEFIPH tax), the sum of aids or subsidies that the company can claim in the event of sound management of externalities, and so on. Looking at the TCO also sometimes leads to questioning of the needs expressed by users thanks to a more global approach.

6/3.2 Sustainable procurement labels

A set of labels has developed to attest to and bring value to corporate compliance with environmental and social demands in the eyes of the public. They have become an indispensable tool in procurement strategy. Buyers must nonetheless remain prudent, faced with the jungle of labels, and ensure that their suppliers meet the criteria for the granting of certification. ISO has identified three types of environmental labelling; ecolabels, self-declarations and eco-profiles.

Official ecolabels

An ecolabel certifies the environmental and/or social qualities of a product (good or service) or a process. It is characterized by a double guarantee (attesting to its quality of use and to its ecological quality), a multi-criteria approach based on the product's lifecycle, its dynamic and progressive nature (the label is granted for a set period), a voluntary approach (it is granted as a result of a company's initiative to seek it), and selectiveness.

There are some 50 ecolabelled categories of products and services, thus enabling responsible buyers to include sustainable development criteria in the technical aspects of their requirements specifications before launching calls for tenders.

The reference norm is the ISO 14024. Many countries have an official label, and the Global Ecolabelling Network (GEN) keeps an updated list of national systems.

Thanks to the objective and reliable information that they present, ecolabels help guide consumer choices. They also encourage industrial leaders to improve the ecological quality of products.

Environmental self-declarations

Defined through the norm ISO 14021, these are environmental claims advanced under the sole responsibility of the manufacturer, untested by the opinion of a third party. Most of the time, they only refer to one environmental characteristic of a product, or a single stage in its lifecycle.

Eco-profiles

Addressed by the norm ISO 14025, eco-profiles may be defined as the granting of access to quantitative data, a photograph at a moment t of a product's environmental impacts. This is a voluntary step taken by industrial leaders who develop, through a multi-criteria and multi-stage approach (LCA), their own evaluation reference system. The quality and utility of this category of labelling vary from one product to another. Moreover, it does not always facilitate the comparison of products, which is the main purpose of these labels.

6/3.3 Translation of principles into internal processes

Translating sustainable development into procurement operations may seem like a long and complex exercise. But this is not the case, for *existing processes are not called into question*. Indeed, for the sake of an approach's relevance, coherency and longevity, sustainable procurement cannot and should not involve specific operational systems (procurement processes and tools). It is really a matter of supplementing existing processes, not with any extra stage or phase, but by adding new criteria or dimensions to them. Integration of CSR into existing processes also contributes to better appropriation of the strategy, and facilitates its deployment amongst a company's teams.

Sustainable procurement approaches are based on a triple responsibility: that of the products, the suppliers and the buyers. The integration of CSR into existing procurement processes means bringing this triple dimension to all stages of the procurement process, from upstream to downstream (Figure 6.6), as follows:

- expression of the requirement: conditions placed on environmental, social and corporate costs and impacts;
- development of the procurement strategy: in the course of which CSR criteria on admissibility and offer-rating will be defined and weighted;
- sourcing and selection of suppliers: integrating CSR into the choice criteria;

FIGURE 6.6   Motivations for sustainable procurement

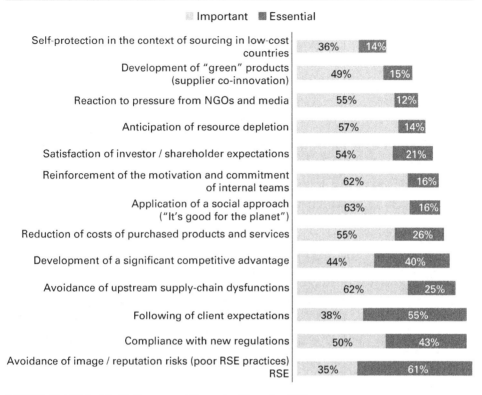

SOURCE: 6th HEC Sustainable Procurement Barometer (November 2013).

- selection and contractualization of offers: insertion of CSR clauses to supplement other classic quality control team (QCT) clauses;
- contract execution: during which recourse to evaluations and audits helps ensure that suppliers respect the commitments that they have undertaken.

Sustainable procurement also implies an evolution in the management of supplier relationships (see Section 6/3.4) and a change in the buyers' stance vis-à-vis their stakeholders (Figure 6.7).

This change in stance occurs in the following dimensions: openness, letting-go, questioning, transversality, partnership and dialogue between multiple players (including stakeholders), long-term vision, global approach (TCO).

6/3.4 Support of suppliers and new relationships

The implementation of a sustainable procurement approach would be neither sincere nor efficient without the support and establishment of mutually beneficial relationships with suppliers. Indeed, a socially responsible procedure (cf ISO 26000)

FIGURE 6.7 CSR in the phases of the procurement process

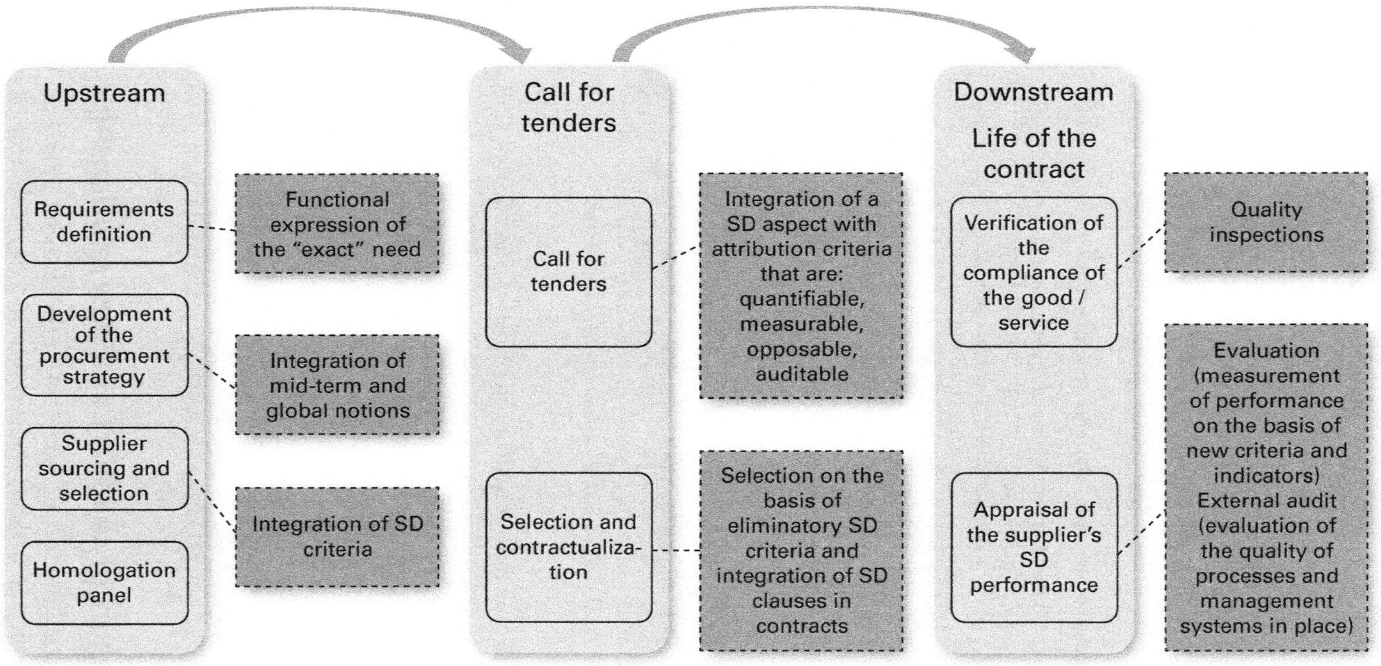

commits the company with regard to its sphere of influence, and therefore implies dialogue with its stakeholders. In addition, as far as sustainable procurement goes, relationships with suppliers are characterized by a dual risk–opportunity approach that, in both cases, commits to helping the relationship evolve towards a partnership. At the heart of global performance lies the notion of 'shared responsibility' between the buyer and the supplier. The ISO 9000 standard on quality management already referred to the principle of 'mutually beneficial relationships' as a lever for value creation, for both the client and the supplier. The establishment of mutually beneficial relationships furthermore allows companies to develop more flexibility and responsiveness in the face of market developments or of client requirements and expectations. It also participates in optimizing costs and resources. According to the AFNOR management tool FD X50-193, mutually beneficial relationships involve:

- establishing relationships that balance short-term gains and long-term considerations;
- a pooling of acquisitions and resources with partners;
- identification and choice of key suppliers;
- implementation of clear and open communication;
- organization of the sharing of information and future plans;
- setting up joint development and improvement activities;
- inspiring, encouraging and recognizing suppliers' production improvements.

AFNOR also refers to mutually beneficial relationships in its documentation, as follows:

> The principle of mutually beneficial relationships is culturally the most difficult principle to promote but the most promising for the future. When all of a market's players understand that their common interest lies in cooperation rather than confrontation, it will be possible to advance our current negative- or zero-sum game strategies towards win–win strategies. Considerable economic progress can be envisaged.

6/4 Performance indicators and ROI

6/4.1 Management via indicators[3]

In an analysis of the communication of 125 companies from the Global 500, the ORSE (French CSR observatory) and EcoVadis found that almost 60 per cent of the panel of respondents published 'performance indicators of their sustainable procurement policy'. Similarly, the 2013 HEC/EcoVadis Barometer indicated that an increasing number of companies are using indicators to manage their sustainable procurement approach (indeed, the percentage of companies having no such indicators has fallen from 24 per cent in 2009, to 15 per cent in 2011, to only 11 per cent to date).

Activity indicators or result indicators

When committing to the path of sustainable procurement, it is no longer possible to steer a procurement department on the basis of a single indicator that globalizes all other indicators. It is necessary to shift from a steering system based solely on economic performance (the 'bottom line') to a 'triple bottom line'-type governance, where three dimensions – economic, ecological and social – are taken into account on the same level in the performance assessment process. Generally speaking, KPIs can be divided into two categories (see Chapter 20): *activity indicators* that measure the degree to which actions are implemented (eg percentage of suppliers evaluated/audited on their CSR performance; percentage of buyers trained in CSR and sustainable procurement); *result (or impact) indicators* that indicate the degree of performance attained thanks to allocated means and resources (eg percentage of expenses contracted with suppliers committed to a CSR approach, emissions of greenhouse gases generated in the supply chain).

Whilst a combination of the two types of indicators is indispensable for managing change, it is often easier, when initiating a strategy aiming at sustainable development, to use activity indicators, which can then quickly be supplemented by result indicators, without which it is impossible to assess the relevance and efficiency of the approach, and thus be credible.

Main sustainable procurement indicators used

Without being exhaustive, the list below supplements the recommendations of the Global Reporting Initiative (GRI) and offers a panorama of the sustainable procurement KPIs most commonly used today. These are mainly activity KPIs, demonstrating that practices are still heading towards maturity:

- percentage of buyers with sustainable development (SD) objectives, a variable component in the salary indexed on CSR elements;
- percentage of procurement-family strategies including SD criteria, based on LCA;
- percentage of requirements specifications integrating SD criteria;
- percentage of calls for tenders including an SD rating;
- percentage of contracts signed with SD clauses;
- percentage of suppliers who have signed the CSR Charter and/or the Global Compact;
- percentage of suppliers who have filled in an SD questionnaire;
- percentage of suppliers with a strategy for attaining SD norms;
- percentage of suppliers assessed on CSR;
- percentage of CSR audits carried out;
- number of CSR improvement plans with suppliers;
- rate of accident-rate reduction amongst suppliers;
- rate of reduction of CO_2 emissions in the supply chain;
- percentage of eco-designed products;
- percentage of referenced 'green' products (ecolabels etc);
- percentage of products that are recyclable, recycled, transformed at their end-of-life;
- percentage of 'green' energy purchased;

- total purchases obtained from fair-trade sources;
- volume of solidarity sourcing purchases (disabled workers and professional integration) sources;
- total purchases procured from SME/VSEs;
- total purchases procured from local suppliers;
- rate of compliance with supplier payment deadlines.

6/4.2 Measuring the value creation of sustainable procurement

As sustainable procurement is amongst a company's priorities, procurement heads look for ways in which to measure its economic benefits and thus demonstrate the added value in committing long-term to this approach. Already certain tangible benefits can be measured, as shown by responses gleaned internationally in the 2013 6th HEC/EcoVadis Barometer (Figure 6.8). The main points to draw from this are as follows:

- 48 per cent measure cost reductions (eg reduction in packaging or energy consumption);
- 41 per cent measure minimization of their supply chain-related risks (eg image, compliance);

FIGURE 6.8   Benefits measured by the implementation of sustainable procurement

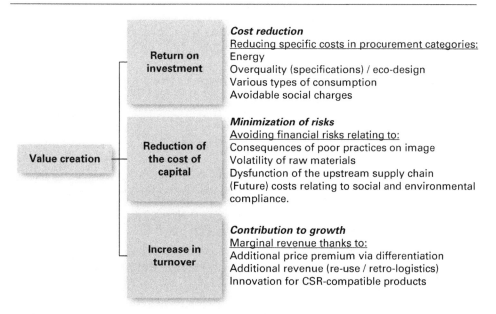

SOURCE: 6th HEC Sustainable Procurement Barometer (November 2013).

- 35 per cent measure environmental benefits (eg reduction in CO_2, water consumption or waste production).

However, these measures are by no means universally implemented. Indeed, 30 per cent of respondents to the survey admit to only carrying out their evaluations on a few sustainable procurement cases and – even worse – 45 per cent indicate measuring nothing at all, or even considering it to be unnecessary (25 per cent). Let's remember that sustainable procurement is amongst their priorities. Finally, we need to point out that (only) 7 per cent measure benefits in financial terms. It is probably here that it is necessary to go further and show companies how ROI can be measured for sustainable procurement.

Lining up sustainable procurement with financial levers to measure value creation

Even if there are limits in showing the value creation of every individual action in sustainable procurement, it is possible to have an overall vision stretching in three major directions as described in the 2010 PWC/EcoVadis/INSEAD survey: cost reduction, risk reduction, and increase of turnover accompanying business development. Figure 6.9 illustrates this 3-dimensional approach.

FIGURE 6.9

Improving the ROI of sustainable procurement via cost reduction

There are several ways in which to measure cost reduction relating to sustainable procurement: the diminishment of internal costs through the eco-purchase of more energy-efficient products and technologies; the lowering of external costs through the redefinition of requirements based on 'exact requirements' and technical specifications including criteria on sustainability, recyclability, etc (eg new packaging, new upstream logistics); and the reduction of new environmental taxes (CO_2, waste) or social taxes (disabled employment) (Table 6.1).

Improving the value of capital via the reduction of CSR risks

This element is the major motivation for procurement heads to embark on implementing a sustainable procurement policy. Risk reduction is not simple as it implies knowing how to apprehend and anticipate several dimensions: scandals from the supply chain, supply interruptions, fines, rarity of resources, costs for current and future measures to meet compliance requirements, etc. Table 6.2 shows examples of the impacts of CSR risks in procurement.

Increase in turnover through new 'sustainable' offers

The third macro-lever for measuring the benefits of a sustainable procurement policy lies in taking account of new business models that can generate an increase of turnover. This new (indirect) way of seeing positive impacts requires a change in approach to global measurement.

In the 6th HEC/EcoVadis Barometer of 2013, 19 per cent of managers measured an increase in the value of their brand and 18 per cent claimed to gain value from their sustainable products through premium prices. Indeed, whilst a response to CSR stakes is a starting point allowing a company to keep its licence to operate, the development of products to a high level of CSR represents taking a further step that may act as a positive factor for the brand's differentiation. A recent Nielsen survey carried out amongst 6,224 consumers worldwide showed that 43 per cent of buyers would be prepared to pay higher for a product with better CSR standards (see Table 6.3).

6/5 Managing change towards sustainable procurement

An organization's alignment with the company's strategy is a condition for the latter to be implemented. This shift is often complex as habits will be overturned, prompting the classic obstacles to evolution: change cannot be merely decreed, but must be accompanied by a whole series of measures and provisions, namely a thorough initiative targeting people and the internal communication processes.

TABLE 6.1   Sustainable procurement and cost reduction

Levers for cost reduction	Results
Reduction of packaging. **LEGO** reduced its packaging purchases by reducing the quantity of wrappers used.	The 'Green Box Initiative' reduced the volume of boxes by 18% and the CO_2 impact due to packaging by 10% (2012).
Efficiency of the resources used. **PEPSICO UK** invested in tools and processes in order to cut by 50%, over a 5-year horizon, its water consumption and CO_2 emissions in the cultivation of potatoes, oats and apples necessary for the production of its products.	Agriculturalists reduced their CO_2 emissions by 7% and their water consumption by 10% as of the project's first year. The fields required 18% less fertilizer and the company launched growth of a new potato variety whose yield is said to be 17% higher and whose water consumption is 33% less (2012).
Eco-efficient innovation. **ADIDAS**, in collaboration with one of its suppliers, developed a new dry-dyeing process for its clothing, leading to the elimination of water consumption and cutting by 50% the energy and products necessary for the process.	Two years after the implementation of this new process, the company saved the consumption of 25 million liters of water compared to the old dyeing method.
Tax reduction. **SNCF**, through its solidarity-sourcing program, promotes purchases from the protected and adapted work sector encompassing companies employing disabled persons and enabling clients to benefit from a reduction in the AGEFIPH tax that they need to pay.	In 2012, SNCF managed to save an equivalent of 2.4 million euros (the equivalent of 453 disabled-worker jobs amongst its suppliers).
Efficiency of the resources used. **SAINSBURY** undertook research with its suppliers to reduce water consumption in its stores. The company set up water-reducing taps, water-saving toilets and a system for recuperating rainwater.	The company reduced its water consumption by 50% in its stores, and cut its water bill by 2.4 million dollars (2012).

SOURCE: 6th HEC Sustainable Procurement Barometer (November 2013).

TABLE 6.2   Sustainable procurement and cost reduction

Levers for cost reduction	Results
Environmental scandal. The oil spill from BP (British Petroleum) installations in April 2010 polluted a large roportion of marine life in the Gulf of Mexico and was the biggest oil slick on the history of the United States.	BP shares fell from $59.50 (10 Aril 2010) to $28.90 at the end of June 2010. The pension funds affected lost around 39 million dollars (2010).
Product content. Because of a poor assessment of the lead-content rate in the products of a tier-two supplier, MATTEL was forced to withdraw from the market around one million children's toys in the United States (2007).	The company spent 110 million dollars on withdrawing its toys from the market and on a communication campaign. MATTEL's shares fell by 18% between August and December 2007.
Scandal in the supply chain. In 2006 **WAL-MART** had to face accusations regarding its corporate responsibility vis-à-vis its suppliers, on non-compliant working conditions, namely the use of child labor in low-cost countries.	In response to the scandal, a Norwegian fund sold 414 million dollars' worth of WAL-MART shares. This exclusion from the Norwegian sovereign fund led to an 11% fall in the company's share values between June and July 2006. Moreover, between 2 and 8% of the store's customers stopped buying from the chain in reaction to the controversy (2006).
Supply security. **OLAM** purchased raw materials from 3.5 million small farmers. The Cashew Initiative in the Côte d'Ivoire supported 40,000 farmers (in other words 10% of the national production of cashew nuts): an increase in the performance of their harvests from 300 to 500 kg per hectare in 2015.	Creation of 4,000 jobs; the cashews no longer had to be sent to India or Vietnam as they could be processed locally, thus helping to develop the local economy and to cut CO_2 emissions by 80%.
Cost of social compliance. **IMPACTT** is a project to the value of 880.000 pounds supported by eight major retailing brands including MARKS & SPENCER, SAINSBURYS, TESCO and MOTHERCARE. The project concerned 665 clothing factorie s in Bangladesh and India employing over 100,000 persons. An innovative training program was set up to improve efficiency, quality and working conditions.	Employee turnover fell by 65% and absenteeism by almost one-third, thus demonstrating greater professional satisfaction. At the same time, the efficiency of factories increased by 30%. On average, the monthly salary went up by 12.5% (in yearly terms: a total of 4.8 million pounds) in 2013.

SOURCE: 6th HEC Sustainable Procurement Barometer (November 2013).

TABLE 6.3   Sustainable procurement and increase in turnover

Levers for turnover increase	Results
Brand value. **SAM'S CLUB** became the leading distributor of fair-trade bananas in the United States in October 2007.	In 2011, 1.6 million boxes of certified bananas were sold, generating the sum of 1.6 million dollars to finance development projects in Colombia and Ecuador.
Client loyalty. **Patagonia** recovers used clothing to recycle and manufacture new clothing.	Between 2005 and 2012, the company recycled 34 tons of clothes into new clothes.
Price positioning. **KRAFT** has committed to buying SD-certified coffees for 100% of its European brands.	The Rainforest Alliance label granted to coffee from the KENCO brand led to two-figured growth in sales in Great Britain. In Sweden, coffee sales for products with the same certification doubled (2012).
Brand value. **THE SUSTAINABLE DINER** purchases local and seasonal products exclusively. All meat is organic and fish is certified MSC.	The turnover of Fish & Grill Brasseries increased by 12% (2012).
Supply security. **CRED** has become a market leader for fair-trade gold. Since 2005, the company only buys gold from a gold mine operated according to SD criteria where working conditions are good and prices guaranteed. CRED uses 40 times fewer minerals to extract gold.	CRED sold 65% of fair-trade gold in Great Britain, and its turnover is constantly evolving.

SOURCE: 6th HEC Sustainable Procurement Barometer (November 2013).

6/5.1 Humans at the heart of change

The success of a sustainable procurement approach relies on the men and women who will implement the new processes and tools. It is therefore essential, first and foremost, to share information on sustainable development with these actors, so that they can grasp the overall stakes (global level), and the impact on the company and their professional practices (local level).

Communication to impart meaning

This is about imparting meaning to the expected change and ensuring that all individuals feel involved and motivated about becoming an agent of change themselves.

As in the implementation of all transformation processes, this communication phase helps to give visibility and coherence to the choices made, to make the approach credible (commitment to SD may be risible if it is not considered as a 'genuine' project), to raise awareness of good practices, to encourage goodwill, to promote collaborative work and the pooling of knowledge, to recognize the efforts of actors, to demonstrate the good intentions behind the strategy, and to lift a priori resistance. To do so, it is necessary to:

- inform people, from an early, upstream stage, about the reasoning behind the new strategy, in order to legitimize it;
- present the potential gains but also the future repercussions and likely difficulties to be faced;
- keep leaders and managers well informed so that they support the project *politically* and bring it to life;
- offer information throughout the project, thus avoiding a 'communication blow' effect;
- quantify the results obtained, including small victories.

Raising awareness to trigger change

The practice of sustainable procurement requires overstepping the traditional intervention boundaries, too often limited to product acquisition, in order to execute a call for tenders according to requirements specifications defined by an internal client. In this way, the buyer is led to venture upstream and positioned to intervene in *project engineering assistance* (upstream procurement), questioning the requirements specifications from the viewpoint of functionality, enabling the internal client to benefit from solutions identified amongst the suppliers, and co-constructing innovative solutions with the internal client.

Communication is insufficient for obtaining this change in stance. It is necessary to set up *awareness-raising initiatives*, to encourage dialogue and exchange between actors on the ground so that they can express their possible reservations, and – above all – the reality of the situations that they encounter in the front line, in their dealings with stakeholders (internal clients, local management, suppliers, etc). These initiatives will lead buyers to reflect on and challenge ways of proceeding:

- to transition from a stance of reproducing practices and a priori reticence (usual attitude: 'it can't work') to a stance of openness ('why not?') and agreeing to let go in the face of uncertainty and risk-taking;
- to commit to a strategy of ongoing progress (or *Kaizen*, consisting in small improvements made gradually);
- to operate in a mode of permanent questioning, opening up to transversality and collaboration with new actors;
- thinking outside of the box and exploring different perspectives in order to slowly integrate the 'CSR thinking mode' (global, long-term and partner-based) into the heart of decisions (organization, products, competences, management modes, relationships with stakeholders, etc).

The instigators or leaders of this type of project and approach need to focus on the following points:

- listening to others: allowing them to express their fears and desires, giving them the opportunity to speak, detecting 'weak signals' from the field;
- promoting transversal communication;
- setting up a network of relays close to the field to ensure that there is fluid two-way communication (from the top down and above all, from the bottom up);
- offering systems that allow for dialogue, such as seminars, information meetings, working groups, etc.

Training to equip for action

Any change that potentially modifies roles, responsibilities, methods or tools questions existing skills and requires the acquisition of new knowledge, both *savoir-faire* (knowing how to do) and *savoir-être* (knowing how to act). It is important to give players the means to upgrade their skills for these new aspects of their profession. Training plays a double role: it gives players the means to act and also reassures them about their capacities in the face of new circumstances. It is all the more useful in the sustainable procurement domain where there is a strong element of novelty and changes are complex.

Without needing buyers to become specialists in sustainable development, training should bring them an indispensable level of knowledge about basic concepts and the associated vocabulary. It should deal with the main stakes in procurement (risks and opportunities) and promote general comprehension of the legal framework of sustainable procurement, references, standards and legislative changes, and the whole technical corps. At the same time, it should remain extremely concrete, allowing buyers to train up on methods and tools that they will need to use to implement the approach, for the goal is to get them to practise their profession *differently*, and this, as autonomously as possible.

Apart from the acquisition of new bearings and know-how, training should also urge buyers to question themselves on their *savoir-être*, ie in their relationships with ordering parties (from the taking of the brief to advice), or else on transversality, translated subsequently by their ease with collaborative work.

6/5.2 Key elements to remember for leading change towards sustainable procurement

In summary, there are two dimensions to bear in mind.

First, a sustainable procurement policy that:

- carries out a diagnostic on the current impacts of the whole of procurement (products or services) on corporate, social and environmental levels;
- defines a framework that integrates corporate, social and environmental criteria on short-, medium- and long-term bases;
- includes the procurement department in the strategic decision-making process;

- sets up codes of good conduct integrating CSR criteria and communicates them to suppliers in their local language;
- sets up a process guaranteeing control of responsibility over the whole chain of its suppliers;
- participates in the work of national and international authorities on introducing environmental and social criteria into the conditions for regulating trade rules;
- reflects on the difficulties of applying certain clauses in certain countries;
- trains buyers in the handling of corporate, social and environmental responsibility.

Secondly, a procurement management that sets out to be responsible, and that:

- bases requirements specifications and rules for calls for tenders on positive contributions to sustainable development by range of products and services;
- selects supplies whose negative impacts are the slightest possible on the ecological, human, social and cultural environment;
- regularly follows up and supports suppliers on the working conditions that they offer and their compliance with international obligations in this area;
- practises positive discrimination with regard to local suppliers who are the most committed to CSR, all the while guaranteeing equity in the processes of call for tenders and procurement;
- chooses between the rule of the 'best global cost of ownership offer' and that of the 'lowest-price offer';
- monitors the compliance of supplier practices with the implemented codes of responsibility;
- includes suppliers in the strategy to increase the company's legitimacy, ie through an education and support programme helping them to integrate CSR criteria;
- contractualizes its relationships with the suppliers on a multi-annual basis (adherence to payment deadlines, fast resolution of conflicts, taking local context into account, etc);
- includes local stakeholders in the local modifications of contracts;
- recognizes that suppliers have a right to make mistakes and to improve on an ongoing basis without sanctioning them the first time that they default (support with diagnostics, initial training or continuing education, availability of experts, etc);
- guarantees the property, including genetic and intellectual, of the resources of so-called 'weak' stakeholders;
- obtains the listing of the company amongst ordering parties and investors integrating or demanding corporate, social and environmental responsibility;
- and also – and above all? – introduces sustainable procurement criteria in the yearly objectives of buyers and procurement managers.

6/5.3 Current assessment and prospects

As a general conclusion, if we refer back to the content of the HEC/EcoVadis survey already cited, certain key points and teachings shed light on the standing of the practice today.

Sustainable procurement is amongst the top four priorities of procurement managers, 93 per cent of whom rank it as one of the critical or important elements of their strategy. Their motivations are of three main types: risk and compliance, external demand (clients and investors) and value creation. These motivations vary, however, depending on the country.

For example, in North America, the top motivation is related to compliance, probably due to new CSR regulations that have emerged on corruption, human rights and conflict minerals. Meanwhile, in Europe, motivations are related to CSR risk management, naturally, but also emerging – and increasingly strong – demands from clients (who themselves are developing their own sustainable procurement policies!).

CSR risk management nonetheless remains the main trigger, with 80 per cent of companies getting suppliers to sign codes of conduct and 58 per cent focusing their efforts on the most at-risk suppliers. However, a growing number of procurement managers consider that sustainable procurement is also a lever for global performance, and they integrate CSR criteria in their calls for tenders (79 per cent) and in the way that they manage their strategic suppliers (72 per cent).

In addition, 91 per cent of companies take CSR elements into account in their choice of suppliers (compared with 76 per cent in 2009), even if only one-third of them have defined a minimum weight for these criteria in the overall assessment score (on average 10 per cent of the score).

In spite of everything, the greatest stumbling block is related to *contradictory objectives between short-term profit* (direct savings on purchasing prices) and implementation of a genuine sustainable procurement policy that necessitates *a longer-term approach*: 80 per cent of companies face this dilemma. For example, the integration of CSR in the individual objectives of buyers is developing steadily (40 per cent of companies in 2013, compared with 16 per cent in 2009), but at the same time, TCO approaches that could enable a better integration of sustainable development stakes in procurement processes are used by only 20 per cent of companies (12 per cent in 2009).

Finally, measurement of value creation generated by sustainable procurement policies is still in its infant stages. Even if 55 per cent of companies indicate that they measure specific benefits (eg cost reduction for 48 per cent, risk reduction for 41 per cent, positive impacts on the environment for 35 per cent), only 7 per cent specify that benefits are translated into their financial accounts. More astonishingly or alarmingly yet, given the actual inclusion of CSR criteria in procurement, 45 per cent of companies declare that they measure no benefits and 25 per cent admit that they do not see the necessity.

In short, even if sustainable procurement is gaining a reputation in companies all over the world, globally it is still in its early stages of maturity, and a more pronounced systemic and holistic approach is required in order for it to progress. The HEC Barometer demonstrates that companies that have undertaken to value their sustainable procurement policies are the ones that are the most advanced in the area; more global progress thus depends on others setting themselves on the same track!

It was at the start of the 21st century that sustainable procurement was born in the most visionary companies. One decade later, its principles have been solidly integrated into the priorities of procurement managers. Gradually, processes, tools and organizations are maturing. However, despite this swift rise in its importance, there remain some significant difficulties that may prevent greater diffusion of sustainable procurement in all companies. The following issues may be points of hindrance in the coming years:

- A necessity for true change management at the heart of the company's decision-making processes that largely exceed the strict frame of the procurement function (measurement of value creation rather than cost reduction: in other words, more 'value in' versus less 'costing out').

- A lack of CSR maturity within supplier markets: the heterogeneity of the CSR levels of suppliers requires considerable investment from the CSR or quality teams of large ordering parties to support them in their improvement and ongoing amelioration plans.

- The limits of CSR audits for social criteria in particular: auditing missions generally lead to short-term improvements but more rarely to significant changes in the practices of suppliers on the ground.

- The lack of financial valuation of sustainable procurement policies: the financial sphere has not always seized hold of the value-creation levers outlined in this chapter, which limits the deployment of CSR in procurement.

- Issues relating to suppliers in the N+X tier: the longer the supply chain, the higher the CSR risks, but the lack of visibility or traceability of the social and environmental practices of remote suppliers may generate major risks for a company that commits to a sustainable procurement approach, sometimes to the detriment of its reputation for honesty.

- The management of CSR databases is complex: how, for example, does one simply and reliably measure the environmental footprint of the upstream supply chain?

- Sustainable procurement heads can be their own enemies: by committing energetically to new issues requiring a change in paradigm and a new business approach, they risk isolating themselves, wearing themselves out, or losing sight of their CSR strategic objectives in favour of shorter-term requirements (eg collecting CSR data for the annual report).

- The isolation of teams working internally on sustainable procurement: the fact that within a procurement department, a specific team and team leader are dedicated to sustainability, the rest of the department may consider CSR issues as specific to that particular team, which may result in less transformation of their own practices or even strategic decisions and choices between the short and long term.

- The lack of international standards on sustainable procurement and CSR evaluation of suppliers: such standards could facilitate the deployment of sustainable procurement policies, namely by providing a means to compare companies (and their suppliers).

All these elements send sufficiently strong messages indicating that the progress of sustainable procurement will rapidly reach an asymptote if it is not handled via an in-depth transformative approach to the procurement function. It is therefore the responsibility of procurement heads or of emerging new leaders to understand the stakes in order to incorporate them in their long-term vision. And then to have the intelligence and courage to manage the change that is required and that will create value: added value (through global performance), ethical value (the hows and whys of sustainable procurement), and human value (finding meaning in and giving meaning to procurement).

Notes

1 This chapter benefits from joint research carried out, since 2003, with Agnès Rambaud-Paquin, founder and director of the firm Des Enjeux et des Hommes.

2 Bruel, EcoVadis *et al* (2013) This survey, the most comprehensive and the most recent one, presents the responses of 133 international leaders from 24 European and North American countries.

3 Readers should bear in mind that the whole of Chapter 20 is dedicated to procurement performance measurement, globally and in all of the function's dimensions. The text includes the general methodological procedure to follow.

07
Outsourcing, 'make-or-buy' decisions and simple subcontracting

Why is the theme of outsourcing, subcontracting and delocalization raised in a book on procurement?

What are the main differences between outsourcing (defined as 'make-or-buy' decisions), subcontracting and delocalization? What are the practical methods and problems relating to their implementation? These are the questions that will be addressed here.

Outsourcing, subcontracting and delocalization are three topics tackled here because these types of decisions are, for many, strategic or tactical in nature; they lead to the gradual widening of the scope of responsibility of procurement through the transfer of activities, previously internal, to suppliers or external service-providers, and they often involve buyers in decision-making about, and then the operational management of, suppliers.[1]

7/1 Preliminary definitions: outsource, subcontract, delocalize

To 'outsource' is to:

> permanently transfer, to an external service-provider (through long-term contracts) an activity previously undertaken internally, with a full transfer of responsibility to the latter, generally entailing the takeover of the company's personnel in question, or even certain assets (premises, materials and equipment) by the service-providing supplier.

This decision is usually definitive, for the company voluntarily abandons, in this way, an activity that it previously mastered internally.[2]

To 'subcontract' is to merely:

> entrust to another company on a temporary basis, whether in a recurrent manner or not, an activity for which internal competency is nonetheless maintained, without any transfer

of staff or equipment, and keeping a hierarchical relationship between the service-providing supplier and the company.

In this context, the company does not lose the corresponding know-how; it simply calls upon an external solution to supplement its own activity.

To 'delocalize' is to:

internationally (re)deploy industrial activities or services, partially or fully. In this process, there is usually a cessation of activity in the original country of operation for new activity to be re-established in new countries.

Initially, this term was mainly used to describe industrial activities. These days, many other service activities are concerned, for example, the transfer (offshoring) of software production activities to India or call centres to leading competitive countries.

Delocalization is not necessarily synonymous with outsourcing: the new entities created may be fully under the responsibility of a service-provider, but the financial and operational arrangements imply the involvement of the company. In certain cases, the company sets up by itself in another country and finances the whole of the investment. We will examine these alternative approaches in Section 7/4.

Whilst the principles of outsourcing and delocalization are easy to grasp, subcontracting may come in different forms. The professional terminology commonly used comprises different terms whose distinctions are worth specifying here.

Occasional capacity subcontracting

Capacity subcontracting may be defined as the temporary allocation of work overload to one or several companies by a specifier.

This overload may be occasional, in which case the subcontracting becomes a capacity adjustment variable in the event of rapid and unforeseen changes in the company's orders.

It may also be a solution when faced with momentary insufficiencies or dysfunctions in internal production tools (eg serious breakdowns on specialized work stations or long preventive or scheduled maintenance operations).

Regular capacity subcontracting

Regular subcontracting results from a tactical decision made by the prescriber.

In some cases, the company may wish to postpone investments to increase capacity (the quantities concerned do not justify it). For a certain period, as long as quantities do not make it profitable to set up an integrated industrial base, the corresponding workload is given to an external subcontractor.

Another possible situation is where the specifier's activity inherently fluctuates (notably on a seasonal basis, as is common in the toy, clothing or leisure industries). Rather than setting up production capacity that can handle the maximum load, the company 'clips off" some of its load at peak moments and systematically calls upon subcontractors. In this case, the phenomenon may recur.

These two types of subcontracting convey a hierarchical order: the subcontractor executes a task according to the prescriber's requirements specifications. Sometimes, even the production process is partially defined and the subcontractor merely accomplishes the task according to demand.

Specialty subcontracting

In this situation, suppliers are no longer subcontractors in charge of merely executing a task: they are given a direct role in the design and development of the production process, or even in the adaptation of the resulting products. Such suppliers are free to choose their own working methods, and they take full responsibility for the manufacturing undertaken. The hierarchical relationship mentioned previously is less (or even no longer) pronounced and the two partners are in fact on a relative equal footing with reciprocal obligations. This situation is close to the outsourcing of a production activity.

Total subcontracting

In certain industrial sectors, we sometimes speak of *total subcontracting* to designate the former status. However, the specifier generally keeps the technical capacity within the company.

7/2 Current outsourcing motivations and practices

From a strategy standpoint, outsourcing stems from consideration of the company's value chain, detection of its 'core business,' and analysis of its distinctive competencies and know-how, according to the meaning defined by the works of Michael Porter.[3]

Activities characterizing the 'core business' may themselves be divided into two categories: those that determine the company's economic or qualitative performance (*without being distinctive competencies*) and those – more specific to the company – that create a competitive advantage in relation to competitors.

The first describe key support functions such as the management of information systems or logistical activities, for example, for an industrial company, but they are common to all companies in any one economic sector.

The second correspond more to a search for differentiation compared with the competitors (eg marketing, R&D, or manufacturing technology).

Outsourcing may nonetheless be carried out for both these types of activities. By choosing certain activities to maintain internally, the company can therefore 'focus' and take advantage of a high level of specialization, all the while optimizing resource allocation.

In parallel, by relying on external service-providers who themselves are specialized, the company takes advantage of their specialization, usually at a more advantageous cost price (on the hypothesis that often service-providers, cumulating several clients, benefit from *economies of scale* resulting from a volume effect via globalization, and can more easily amortize the fixed cost of acquisition of highly specialized competencies).

Not just an economic logic

For a company, the logic of gradually deploying outsourcing corresponds to the progressive creation of a network of interlinked partners, constituting a *supply-chain network* that is co-responsible for the performance vis-à-vis the end-client. The growing complexity of outsourcing operations thus highlights several fundamental issues:

- top executives are necessarily involved and the number of protagonists participating in the decision-making process is growing (including the procurement management);
- there will be multiple selection and decision-making criteria: in any case, these will largely exceed mere economic considerations (analysis of the respective costs of internal and external solutions);
- reciprocal contractual obligations will become more complex;
- follow-up, management and performance-monitoring constraints will impose in-depth reflection on the notion of particularly complex 'service obligations' (formerly referred to as 'service-level agreements');
- in this way, the selection criteria for a service-provider will go beyond those for a 'mere' non-strategic purchase. Clearly, the true challenge is not to select a supplier on the basis of short-term considerations, but to establish lasting partner relationships associated with the finding of a balance between competencies, cost and quality of service.

Panorama of activities frequently outsourced today

In their article, Quélin and Duhamel (2003) present the results of a survey carried out about a decade ago amongst 180 European industrial companies (notably French, German, Belgian and Italian). Eighteen activities stood out, during the pre-survey and validation stage, as the object of considerable outsourcing, and their practices were therefore analysed. As shown by Figure 7.1, the levels of outsourcing of these activities were extremely variable. The figure shows that four responses were possible:

- no outsourcing for the function in question, in light grey;
- outsourcing for less than 85 per cent of the activity, in medium grey;
- outsourcing for over 85 per cent, in dark grey;
- no response ('don't know').

This ranking clearly indicates that six activities are the most affected by outsourcing:

- office systems and IT management including network management (67 per cent);
- industrial maintenance (67 per cent);
- waste treatment (67 per cent);
- logistics and all associated services (namely transport) (65per cent);
- telecommunications (64 per cent).

These are all support functions that cannot be described as the 'core business' of the industrial companies surveyed. At the time of the survey, the three activities cited as having the greatest development potential for the next two years were IT management, logistics and payroll services.[4]

FIGURE 7.1 Ranking of outsourced activities

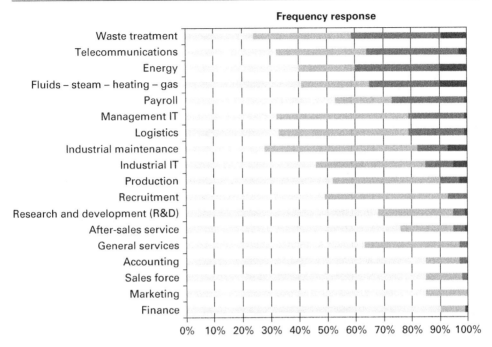

SOURCE: © Quélin / Duhamel, *European Management Journal*, October 2003.

Motivations for outsourcing

Plain managerial common sense, as well as academic and professional literature, point to six main reasons pushing decision-makers to outsource:

- reduction of direct or indirect costs, but related to operations;
- *variabilization* of costs allowing greater flexibility without economic risks (eg handing over transport activities, billed according to the number of kilometres and tonnes transported rather than financially taking responsibility for an internal transport department largely made up of fixed costs) as well as facilitation of understanding precisely how costs are actually incurred;
- focus of internal resources on operations considered as having added value;
- reduction of capital tied up in operations;
- access to external know-how and competencies.

Aside from the 'cost variabilization' argument, Figure 7.2 illustrates, for the 18 activities analysed, the relative weight of the different motivations behind such decisions. Three main reasons were analysed per interview: economic motivation (lowering of direct costs), indicated in light grey; refocusing on the core business, medium grey; the search for an external competency, dark grey.

FIGURE 7.2 Main motivations for outsourcing

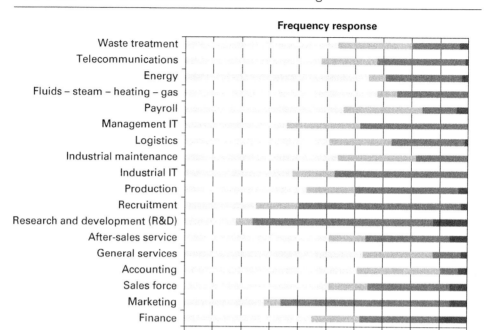

Obstacles to outsourcing

In a symmetrical manner, the survey referred to also analysed the main risks for the outsourcing process. These were assessed in terms of negative consequences resulting from the implementation of such systems. The main risks were listed as the following:

- risks of dependency on the supplier or service-provider are real and may be of two types:
  - if we choose a single source, we may no longer have clear visibility of the market price;
  - we risk not keeping up with knowledge on new technologies likely to appear on the market (this risk exists even if the relationship has been placed into a contractual framework).
- the possibility of costs, initially unforeseen and difficult to forecast without prior experience, always exists, namely costs relating to the management of the external solution and performance measurement;
- the loss of internal know-how is obviously the immediate consequence (some believe that it is nevertheless necessary to keep, within the company, a *lead expert* in the sector with the capacity to judge or even to set up searches for external expertise on a periodical basis);
- we can also cite possible difficulties relating to the supplier's 'production' capacity, hence variations in the quality of the supplier's performance (application of a contractual penalty fails to cancel out the various operational consequences when a service-provider defaults);

- finally, in France, when an outsourcing process is deployed, the company always runs a considerable labour risk: that of job action directly related to a particular operation, or more generally the onset of long-term tension in the company climate. Following the operation, relationships between the different staff categories thus created are not so simple to manage either (in the event of the activity being undertaken on the company's premises).

The main motivations and risks associated with outsourcing, seen above, are taken directly from the study by Quélin and Duhamel (2013). It seems important to now offer a summary of the decision-making criteria when outsourcing is considered.

7/3 Decision-making criteria for a make-or-buy decision

The criteria for choice are numerous, and should be weighed up carefully. Table 7.1 illustrates a dual analysis, presented symmetrically, that should govern choices.

This table sets out to be generic, in other words certain criteria are specific to outsourcing whilst others are shared with subcontracting. Let's now analyse and comment on some of these criteria in detail.

7/3.1 Main reasons for 'buying'

Access to know-how or a specific competency

The specifer who aims to refocus on a core business expects an external partner to have better expertise in a particular specialty and to take full responsibility for the quality of the supplied service. The prescriber keeps within the company those technical processes that it best understands and masters, including those that determine the product's *distinctive* performance or its production lead-time. Incidentally, this is also a way to delegate risky or difficult-to-perform technical operations to others.

At the same time, the company 'refocuses', that is, it concentrates its financial resources and its human and material means on activities that contribute most directly to competitive advantage. In addition, in doing so, it directly keeps under control the elements on which it has decided to base its differentiation in relation to its competitors.

Create a competitive situation for a group's entities

In certain cases, namely industrial groups in which certain divisions supply others with various components, semi-finished products or services, corporate top managers often wish to maintain at least one exterior supply source in order to promote a climate of competition and put pressure on transfer prices with regard to internal business units. In this way, calls for tenders are systematically organized and subsidiaries live in a permanently competitive context: their need to demonstrate their competitiveness and their competency is ongoing.

TABLE 7.1   Overview of a make-or-buy decision

Criteria in favor of buying	Criteria in favor of making
1. Strategic	
Focus on 'core-activity' activities Access to external knowhow Creation of competition between business units (pressure on transfer prices)	Focus on 'core-activity' activities Protection of a specific knowhow (namely innovation) Protection of industrial property (fight against counterfeit or prevent the emergence of future competitors)
2. Economic	
Obtain lower direct costs Cost variabilization Shift of cash-flow efforts to the service-provider Shift of investment efforts	Obtain lower direct costs (depending on the break-even point and profitability threshold) Amortization of fixed and structural costs (economies of scale) Cost of managing the outsourced solution
3. Operational	
Better management of fluctuations in load (acquisition of a certain flexibility) Better reactivity	Shortening of operational cycles Better control of the security of supply flows
4. Risk mitigation / minimization	
Shift of technical risk	Control of country and / or supplier risks (of all types, with figuring of prevention measures)

Minimization of internal investment risk

The second tactical reason sometimes amounts to choosing to put off an investment until quantities to be produced reach a set level, thus ensuring minimum profitability (for instance, a period of growth on a new product's life curve). At the same time, this allows the inherent risks of a dicey forecast to be diminished and offers an opportunity (if need be) to improve one's know-how during fine-tuning stages in collaboration with a subcontractor specializing in the area.

Subcontracting also gives the company the option to stop, without any great financial risk, an activity whose development seemed possible, but whose performance finally does not match up with forecasts.

Response to regular fluctuations of loads

Let's take the case of a company that produces seasonal articles, such as gardening accessories or swing-sets. Deliveries to distributors are concentrated within a limited period: from 15 January to 15 June.

In these conditions, the factory cannot have its manufacturing match the same fluctuations as end demand even if it may endeavour to follow it roughly. It therefore makes a compromise between:

- accumulation of stock during quiet months (from September to December);
- adaptation of the production capacity via the employment of temporary staff and variations in working hours and via the adapted scheduling of paid leave on the calendar;
- calling upon several subcontractors to handle part of the load (20 per cent) over the two or three critical months – these are selected according to the types of articles that they know how to produce competently (manufacturing technology) and their production capacity.

Obtaining lower direct costs

One key motivation for companies remains the securing of more competitive cost prices. These may come from lower processing costs (if the service-provider is based in a region or country where salaries and social charges are advantageous).

Savings may also result from better productivity that is obtainable from a supplier with a greater level of specialization, and, in the case of an industrial supplier, for example, with a machine fleet that is less costly and/or amortized on larger quantities, or else a supplier with a better mastery of the technology. Alternatively, they may come from lower R&D costs and overhead expenses.

Ordering parties must nonetheless remain prudent. If direct cost is the sole criterion, mere economic logic may lead to outsourcing more and more. Yet when the company's own activity is reduced, its fixed costs are gradually spread out over lower quantities and its apparent hourly rate may gradually increase as a result. This may lead to flawed decisions.

At the same time, a comparison limited to direct variable costs is often inadequate, especially in the case where the subcontracting option entails financing or the provision of costly tooling, or when initial fine-tuning studies suggest a high non-recurring cost (NRC) at the onset of the collaboration. In this case, it is appropriate to carry out a study on the breakeven point to evaluate the threshold from which subcontracting proves worthwhile (see Section 7/3.3 for an illustration of this point).

Better cash flow management

Another economic motivation relates to the possible alleviation of cash flow efforts. Indeed, instead of paying regular salaries and their associated social charges, labour costs are borne by the subcontractor whilst the specifier always pays with a certain delay depending on the negotiated payment conditions. This observation also applies to material procurement costs when the subcontractor operates with materials purchased by him- or herself.

7/3.2 Main reasons for maintaining an activity

On the other hand, other extremely valid arguments support integration of an activity already undertaken by a company.

Protection of know-how and industrial property

Outsourcing or subcontracting often means transferring part of one's know-how and innovation projects. Whilst products can be protected by patents, industrial protection of a manufacturing process or specific know-how is tricky. In these conditions, subcontracting – almost necessarily translated by a transfer of technology or knowledge – may raise some drawbacks.

As a result, it is important to examine the means (contractual or otherwise) to help prevent competitors from having access to know-how developed in the context of external collaborations of this type. For many, this aspect is a cogent reason for choosing to maintain the integration of hi-tech manufacturing, considered 'sensitive' or highly confidential, within the company's internal services.

In certain foreign countries, local habits, culture and practices are conducive to piracy or counterfeiting. Certain industrial or service processes are copied very quickly (whatever the regulations in place, even if these are strict and based directly on international regulatory standards), and it is possible to find competitor products on the market in very short periods. In addition, a design may be 'lifted' by companies other than the one contracted; those familiar with such regions will recognize this capacity to digest innovations and to replicate them with sometimes surprising levels of quality.

Better security of supply

Transport resulting from general subcontracting may introduce extra cycles. This argument carries less and less weight in that it is now possible to set up 'just-in-time' systems with suppliers. Meanwhile, the security of external supplies depends on the confidence of the specifier in its partner who must ensure the security of its own supplies. The prescriber may well be involved in negotiations with certain second-tier suppliers of the direct suppliers. In this way, the procurement department should pay attention to managing an entire economic chain of supply and no longer simply its first-tier suppliers.

Economies of scale and an ensuing cut in costs

This argument primarily applies to industrial activities. Any company may look to improve its competitiveness by implementing the concept of the *learning curve*, using an approach such as the one put forward by the Boston Consulting Group. In order to reach the lowest unitary costs, a company needs to try to group together all of its manufacturing in order to obtain high cumulative production volumes, and thus benefit from accumulated experience. This observation leads it to set up larger production units that allow it to take advantage of economies of scale.

However, this reasoning often leads to contradictory results, even if an economic advantage appears to be obvious 'on paper'. Indeed, the implicit hypothesis when following this reasoning is that the level of activity and the level of average productivity will not be altered by the simultaneous manufacturing of products of different types.

However, a company's range of products is made up of categories of articles that meet the demands of different strategic segments, with equally different 'marketing'-type characteristics (quality, service, differentiation), for the markets or client segments to which they are aimed presumably have different expectations. The one production unit cannot generally (or only with difficulty) satisfy several levels of quality when differences between them are too pronounced.

In addition, once organized, the production unit will either be extremely productive (high productivity) or extremely flexible, but will have trouble meeting the two objectives perfectly and simultaneously.[5, 6]

7/3.3 Analysis of the breakeven point of outsourcing

Comparative financial examination of direct costs or discounted cash flows is not enough. It is also necessary to compare the solutions linked to subcontracting options, taking into account two basic items of data: the distribution between fixed and variable costs in the direct costs of the two solutions, and the forecast volumes (or quantities) over the time period of the decision.

To illustrate this point, let's take the example of a manufacturing activity for which long-term outsourcing or subcontracting is envisaged. The type of solution selected is never independent of the structure of production costs, which can be estimated as a set of fixed and variable costs.

Fixed costs are made up of capital depreciation costs and management/staff salaries, as well as industrialization and quality monitoring costs. Variable costs include raw materials, naturally, but also the costs of staff directly involved in manufacturing. The meeting point of the line tracing income (turnover) and the curve indicating total costs sets the position of the breakeven point, which is the level of activity at which income balances overall costs.

In an industry that relies little on automation, fixed costs are low and variable costs are high. On the contrary, when we invest in automated processes, capital costs rise while variable costs diminish.

Let's take the example (using fictional but realistic data) of a manufacturing company producing shirts in Europe (Figure 7.3). Annual volumes sold may vary a great deal, depending on whether they are upper-end items in small series or standard models in large series aimed at the mass-retailing sector. For every item in the new collection, there is always a choice between several alternative industrial solutions, and it is necessary weigh up the choices systematically.

Here is how the problem is expressed, taking the example of a shirt:

- **Traditional process:** European manufacturing ('artisanal' system, skilled labour, inexpensive multi-purpose equipment). Fixed costs come to €20,000 whilst the variable direct cost per unit is €12.

- **Delocalized traditional process:** manufacturing by an Asian subcontractor (lower variable cost, in other words €8, but higher fixed costs due to logistical costs relating to distance and quality assurance costs, in other words €40,000).

- **Automated process:** manufacturing in Europe but on a largely automated assembly line using robots and a computer-operated handling system (fixed costs: €100.000 and direct cost per unit: €5).

FIGURE 7.3   Outsourcing decisions: comparison of production-cost structures

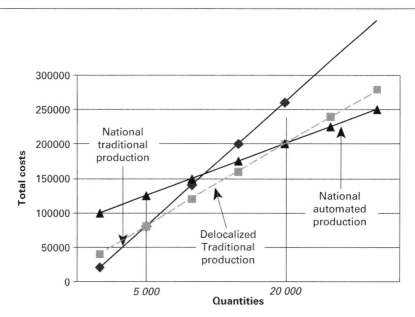

If we compare these three solutions by mapping them out on a graph in a breakeven analysis (equivalent profitability thresholds), we can see that the choice will essentially depend on the quantitative forecast of sales: for small volumes under 5,000 units, the 'traditional' solution is appropriate, far more than it would be in Asia, for it largely offsets the fixed costs resulting from delocalization; however, beyond 20,000 units in the one season, automation of the 'domestic' solution would become economically profitable and far more flexible!

This type of forecasting naturally impacts on risks, that the company will need to accept and bear. Indeed, if activity levels fall as a result of an over-optimistic forecast, in the first scenario the risk is low for we can lower the variable loads. In the third scenario, the risk is high for disinvestment is rarely possible, and we can quickly find ourselves below the breakeven point. In this way, investment in highly productive but costly equipment implies that we are bound to overburden production capacity. From this vantage point, the delocalization solution proves to be not too risky, but entails a fairly high implementation cost and much longer cycles.

This illustration, based on the example of the manufacturing of a product over one given season, may be *generalized for application in long-term situations*. It indicates clearly that the decision is not binary: it depends on a comparison of cost structures, the volumes in question over the time period under study, and the management of risks relating to the location of service-providers. Finally, let's remember that we often tend to underestimate the ongoing fixed costs of subcontracting, especially if it is delocalized (backup and quality assurance structure).

7/4 Organizational choices for delocalization: direct control, subcontracting or outsourcing

When setting up overseas, supply-chain managers are often faced with the following choice (Table 7.2), with systems that can be divided into two main categories.

The first two solutions rely on external industrial competencies in collaboration with local industrial companies.

Let's remember that specialty subcontracting involves looking for demonstrated local technical know-how. In this case we benefit from a capacity to innovate and knowledge of the local market, as well as of its needs and expectations. However, in proceeding this way, the prescriber cannot really follow a differentiation approach, and does not have control over the development of the products.

TABLE 7.2   Industrial alternatives for international delocalization

	Advantages	Disadvantages
Knowhow subcontracting	'Turnkey' system Innovative professionals Optimization of flows	No industrial differentiation (same as competitors) Control of the standard of quality
Capacity subcontracting	Quick deployment (depending on the country) Easier flexibility Process expertise	No product innovation Control of the standard of quality Management of upstream and downstream flows
Joint-contracting (JV)	Sharing of risks and competencies Proximity of clients	Deployment lead time Cost of deployment Rigidity of the solution
Industrial delocalization	Depends on the formula (integration, JV, subcontractor) Actions on the costs Proximity of markets	Costly in terms of resources (monitoring) No contribution of external expertise

Capacity subcontracting (theoretically) allows the specifier to control the development of products, but it comes up against the problem of the subcontractor's compliance with a specific standard of quality.

In both cases, a local backup structure will very often be necessary to manage these two solutions (production follow-up, quality and CSR audits), representing significant fixed costs.

The two other solutions imply investment decisions and capital contributions. These are therefore decisions that imply a long-term perspective (for a satisfactory IRR – or NPV) and, as a result, are less flexible.

Certain countries also practically impose *joint-contracting* (*joint ventures*), as was the case in China at a certain time. In other cases, the company delocalizes its own manufacturing units or invests marginally (without the joint closure of units on its domestic territory).

In all cases, to decide on which country in which to set up activity, aside from the case of assembly plants that we wish to locate close to client markets, it is necessary to have a decision-making method primarily based on an analysis of country and supplier risks. This point is related to decisions on international procurement analysed in detail in Chapter 5.

7/5 Implementation of outsourcing

The outsourcing process should follow a certain number of stages in order to avoid randomness and the omission of key objectives, hence criteria for evaluating the anticipated performance. Let's examine the main phases.

7/5.1 Managing the process over time

Study phase

This phase involves members of the top management, or at least not simply and directly the procurement department (even if the latter may contribute, upon request, by providing information on facts or market opportunities). This analysis is an opportunity/feasibility study whose aim is to define, clearly and uncompromisingly, a certain number of points, namely by replying to questions such as:

- What are the exact limits of the function or activity to be eventually outsourced?
- What real benefits do we expect?
- What risks are taken? Have these been rated objectively with a forecast *degree of criticality*? Are we absolutely clear on the unacceptable risk thresholds? Have we planned on the a priori feasibility of risk-mitigation measures?

Preparation phase

This is a matter of clearly defining the scope of the activity to be outsourced, and the associated performance commitments. Here, we follow the logic of defining requirements specifications. In addition, it is necessary to anticipate the transfer process and to prepare the social arrangements for the subsequent deployment.

Finally, the procurement management should intervene in the targeting of potential service-providers and their pre-homologation, in view of the following operational phase. The following questions need to be raised:

- What are the *functional* requirements specifications (discussed elsewhere in this book) that we envisage for this activity? What are the *performance* requirements?
- What, in particular, apart from the 'activity' content and functions to transfer, are the service obligations (service-level agreement) that we define for this operation? This is related to the standards of quality expected.
- Related to this, what performance measurement and follow-up system is expected (which criteria are measurable and quantifiable in particular)?
- Last major point: have we considered and put into cost figures an exit solution (if outsourcing should become problematic)?

Decision-making and partner-choice phase

This is the stage at which the procurement department intervenes the most frequently: the process of calls for tenders, selection and final-round procedures during negotiations. One point needs to be emphasized: during this phase, and especially if the requirements specifications have been well defined in functional terms, we should expect *service-providers to enhance the company's initial demand*. This should be a proof of their competency and illustrate their willingness to collaborate.

It is therefore necessary to be extremely reactive and to use this opportunity systematically. For example, several stages may be envisaged for responses to the call for tenders in order for the initial need to be gradually adjusted, guaranteeing genuine competition between the potential service-providers up to the end of the selection process.

Effective activity transfer phase

The transfer phase is wholly focused on operational deployment. A few questions classically come up:

- How can activity be transferred in practical terms without any break in continuity?
- Is it plausible for a double system to co-exist during a break-in period? For how long? When and according to which criteria should the switch be made definitively?
- What type of organization should be set up to monitor and manage the deployment? A project team or an internal expert? Who does this team report to? What level of delegation?

- How should the measurement and follow-up system designed in the previous stage be launched?
- Who is actively in charge of managing corrective actions to be undertaken by the service-provider?

Follow-up and renegotiation phase

This phase, an important one, is by definition continuous. It aims to gradually raise performance levels, and also to ensure that *both parties* (the company itself and the service-providers) are satisfied and that their respective competitiveness is boosted. Indeed, this is a condition for the system's sustainability.

In this way, the company will progressively evolve towards a *network organization* (we also refer to a *company operating in an extended supply chain*) with distinct characteristics: interdependency of the players with a relative loss of autonomy, redeployment of assets between them, and real transfers and risk-sharing (labour risks, as well as commercial and financial ones). Above all, let's not forget that synchronization of the whole system will always come at quite a high cost... and will have to be integrated into the TCO!

7/5.2 Transfer and management of staff: a delicate point to oversee

In such operations, the human factor is naturally crucial in the setting up of the operation itself, but also insofar as (and whether) the different personnel groups continue to physically have contact with one another.

This point alludes to well-known concerns: evaluation of and absolute compliance with legal obligations regarding staff that is the object of the transfer, namely in terms of the maintenance of benefits and work contracts; contractual adherence (obviously verified) to the hierarchy between the company and its service-provider; and periodical verification that there is no gradual drift towards illegal subleasing of employees and that the company does not find itself involved in illegal subcontracting.

This last risk is particularly delicate and common for outsourced activities that the service-provider executes in the context and within the walls of the client company. What does it consist of exactly? To answer this question, let's go over the legal provisions in French and European legislation.

Sublease of employees and illegal subcontracting

If the form and spirit of the contract covering the service or technical assistance are not respected, this may lead to the company head being criminally sentenced for the illegal sublease of employees, the subcontracting or assistance contract eventually being nullified, and the subcontracting contract being reclassified as an employment contract. This risk lies in the ambiguity that may exist between the contribution of skill and expertise, and the provision of staff, inseparable from the service.

In France, several legal references apply in this context:

- temporary work, regulated by Article L.124-1 of the *Code du Travail* (Employment Code);

- illegal sublease of employees, regulated by L.125-al. 1 of the *Code du Travail*, stipulating explicitly that 'any profit-making operation having the sublease of employees as its object is banned…, when it is not undertaken in the framework of provisions relating to temporary work';

- illegal subcontracting, regulated by L.125-1-al.1 that stipulates that 'any profit-making labour-supply operation that results in causing harm to the employee or avoiding the application of the provisions of any laws, regulations or labour conventions or collective agreements, is banned'.

Good legal practices

To simplify, and to ensure the absolute compliance of a service-provision operation in the case of outsourcing or subcontracting, it is appropriate to define the service's object as an *activity or task with added value*, and not as a staff-supply operation. To do so, and according to the criteria commonly analysed by law courts, the following points should be examined scrupulously:

- the object of the service should be defined in terms of activity;
- the choice of the subcontractor or service-provider should necessarily be based on their technical expertise, bringing added value, and not enter within the company's area of competency (or subject to the acquisition of specific competencies);
- the result-oriented performance commitment should be clearly defined;
- the deliverables should be precisely identified.

It follows that remuneration should be in the form of a set fee for an activity (and not be calculated on the basis of the number of participants multiplied by the number of hours worked), and payment should only be made upon delivery of the finished work (or other deliverables). In this regard, it is always necessary to favour fixed-price contracts and to remain extremely prudent on invoicing according to the time spent on the task.

From another perspective, the service-provider is the sole employer of the staff that it takes on, and is entirely responsible for them, with all ensuing obligations. In particular – and on a more anecdotal note – the client company must take care that the environment of the supplier's staff is distinct from that of its own staff, even if the service-provider's staff performs its activity within the company's walls. To give an example, free access for the supplier's staff to the company cafeteria or their sharing of other advantages specific to company staff becomes, before the law courts, a criterion for non-adherence to the law.

In the same way, material and equipment necessary for the execution of tasks that are the object of the contract should be supplied by the service-provider to its staff, except in certain obvious cases, such as facilities management, where the service-provider fulfils the mission using the client's equipment.

These considerations illustrate the extreme care that procurement departments need to take when issuing initial requirements specifications, then when the contract is signed. In all cases, it is appropriate to carry out a detailed diagnostic of the outsourced activities (for those performed internally) by looking at the exact nature of the service, the way in which the service-provider's employees are managed, the mode of payment and the conditions in which the activity is carried out.

7/6 Outsourcing of the procurement function

Amongst the activities that can be outsourced within the company's core business along its value chain, is procurement itself (even if the study by Quélin and Duhamel mentioned previously did not identify it as such).

Outsourcing of the procurement function means the:

transfer, full or partial, of procurement activities, whether initially integrated or new, to external service-providers offering added value. This outsourcing may occur: within a procurement scope to be defined, or for activities within the procurement function, or a combination of both.

To illustrate this approach, let's start by observing the levels of current practices in this domain.[7]

7/6.1 Assessment of observed practices

The Aberdeen Group conducted an extremely wide survey in the United States, gathering replies from qualified senior value-chain executives representing 750 companies. Several points are worthy of particular note:

- the main motivations for outsourcing procurement, fully or partially;
- the main procurement segments outsourced;
- the main procurement activities actually outsourced.

Motivations for outsourcing procurement

Let's take a detailed look at Figure 7.4: we observe that motivations are generally very close in their range and order of priority. First of all, we outsource what others, more specialized, are capable of buying better and hence less expensively than ourselves (ie due to their know-how and the greater volume that they represent on supplier markets). But we also expect a reduction in transaction costs as well as improved use of human resources by the procurement function with a refocusing on the 'core business' of the function, and hence the company.

Main procurement segments outsourced

Figure 7.5 focuses on the procurement segments that are the most outsourced. Caution is required when referring to the figure: it represents the aggregate result of practices, averaged between a wide number of companies, and should in no case be taken as a reference norm. But it is interesting in highlighting that in terms of priority, the procurement categories that are outsourced do not constitute the 'core business' for many companies, and practically all concern *indirect purchases*, many of which relate to general expenses. These observations very clearly translate an application of the main motivations observed in the preceding figure with: staff transport and travels (ie other than logistics or the transport of goods) for 46 per cent of interviewees; and reprography and temporary work services for around 35 per cent.

FIGURE 7.4   Motivations for outsourcing the procurement function

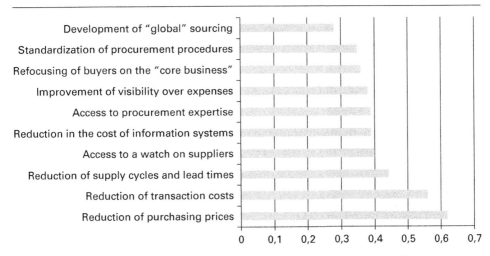

Only the purchases of software, marketing services and maintenance correspond more with 'core business' activities, which are outsourced in accordance with objectives for acquiring external skills and know-how.

FIGURE 7.5   Main procurement categories outsourced

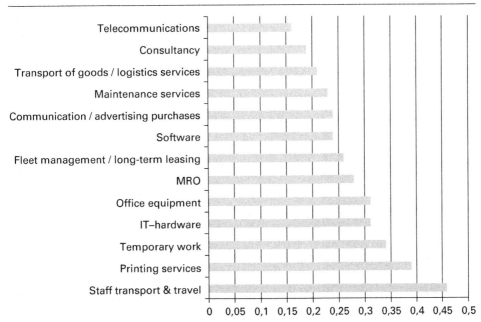

Main procurement activities outsourced

This point is different. We have already seen that the procurement function is structured around upstream and downstream phases, the first being prior to any purchasing act, the second relating to calls for tenders and post-purchase phases. It is possible to envisage handing over some of these activities to service-providers in order to focus internally on certain other priority activities.

In the same survey, the following results emerge, as illustrated by Figure 7.6:

- the two most outsourced activities (drawing around 35–40 per cent of responses) relate to purely transactional tasks and the management of supplier databases (concerning e-procurement automation solutions) – these are downstream tasks in the procurement process;

- then, 31 per cent of interviewees outsource support in finding new suppliers (for lesser-known or less well-controlled markets or procurement categories), by nature an upstream task;

- thirdly, around 25 per cent of replies concerned activities supporting sourcing and the qualification of new suppliers, supplementing the previous external contributions, also upstream tasks.

FIGURE 7.6   Main procurement activities outsourced

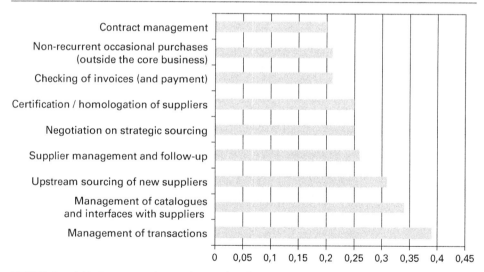

SOURCE: Copyright: Procurement Outsourcing Benchmark Report, Aberdeen Group, March 2004.

These responses illustrate the great heterogeneity of specific situations, but they clearly highlight the fundamental duality underlining recourse to outsourcing in procurement processes. If we compare this US study with a benchmarking survey carried out by the author in the context of the French ACA (a leading French professional association whose members are top executives and managers specialized in sourcing, procurement and supply-chain management), we can see that French companies are globally more reticent to outsource procurement.

Reservations of procurement top managers vis-à-vis outsourcing

Why do European procurement managements harbour greater reservations about taking recourse to outsourcing? Objective scientifically measured data is unavailable for France, but the US survey offers clues on the reasons, that can certainly be extrapolated. As shown by Figure 7.7, we fundamentally run up against a 'loss of control' over operations.

This argument seems to translate an apparently objective risk, intrinsically related to recourse to an external service-provider. But in fact, as confirmed by in-depth interviews carried out in parallel by the author with the procurement managements of large companies, this risk relates more to a feeling of *loss of power*. It seems that the technical risks of outsourcing procurement are sometimes used as alibis for what is experienced as a diminishing of responsibilities, or sometimes even proof of a certain 'internal incompetency'.

FIGURE 7.7   Main causes for the reticence of procurement top managers

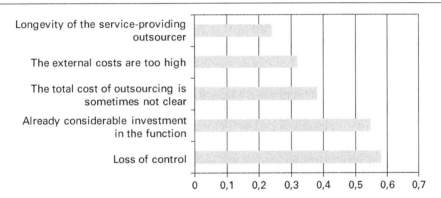

SOURCE: Copyright: Procurement Outsourcing Benchmark Report, Aberdeen Group, March 2004.

It is also true that the outsourcing process is quite often directly triggered by a decision of the top management – initially directly contacted by consultancy firms or service-providers promising significant short-term procurement savings – that then imposes the solution on the procurement head. The latter therefore sees this threatening procedure thrust upon him or her in a poor light.

The second argument is also worth remarking upon (with humour and a dose of astonishment): it is not because investments have been made in intangible capital (mainly to be understood as human resources) that one should deprive oneself of other means and new solutions enabling even greater improvement of the function's performance. And yet, procurement departments often lock themselves up in a 'negative-loop' logic based on the amortization of past investment.

Meanwhile, the third argument is altogether surprising: that total costs might be high or not may constitute an acceptable argument; reservations about their lack of clarity are more unexpected. The merit of outsourcing is that the company is presented with an invoice, and one at least knows what the service in question costs, incidentally most often coming in the form of variable costs. However, it is also true that many fail to compute the cost of managing the external solution in their decisions, and as a result, can afterwards easily claim its apparent high cost without ever really being able or willing to relate these costs back to financial results following an ROI and value-creation rationale.

7/6.2 Decision-making model: three main aspects

As a result, it is important to have a clear strategic vision of the outsourcing possibilities for procurement before getting started on such a process. To do so, it is necessary to continuously go back to the main issues that will be structured around three aspects:

- reference to the segmentation of procurement portfolios to point to potentially outsourceable procurement categories;
- detailed analysis of the different phases of the procurement process, from upstream to downstream, with a stringent identification of distinctive competencies or activities with no direct added value;
- a general diagnostic of the company's *maturity level* in terms of procurement practices in order to better adjust its priorities in relation to a change management schedule.

Portfolio segmentation

We have seen earlier that definition of procurement strategies depends on a preliminary segmentation of the portfolio, as recalled and illustrated by Figure 7.8 (following the logic of the matrix model developed in Chapter 2).

In general, procurement said to be 'strategic' is made up of categories that the procurement department should control directly; historically, the presence of critical factors gives priority to these categories (eg know-how, volume, dominant position in the upstream market). In this case, outsourcing is practically never appropriate. It would be logical for the same to apply to 'strategic' or 'technical' purchases.

That said, it may happen that some procurement categories are based on highly specific technologies for which there is no internal expertise (for example).

In other situations, for example, big projects involving *very technical purchases* that by definition are *one-off*, the procurement management may genuinely need backup and decide to rely on external expertise.

These are grounded justifications for outsourcing certain procurement segments, or calling upon (via subcontracting) occasional expertise services.

However, the category that is uncontestably the most easily outsourced is that of 'simple purchases'. In this group, we find all purchases representing low volumes and expense, as well as *many indirect purchases with no identified major risks*, whether technical or quality-related (such as many general-expense items, consumables or office supplies, or sundry other non-core business purchases in low volumes).

In this case, the procurement function's priority objective is not so much to reduce purchasing costs themselves, but to increase internal productivity and to reduce transaction costs. Additionally, many service-providers have the required level of

FIGURE 7.8 Outsourceable categories of the procurement portfolio

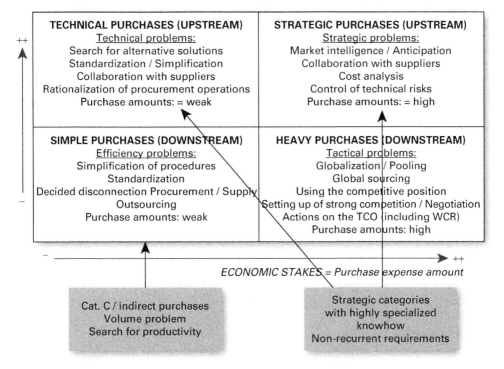

SCALE OF RISKS / OPPORTUNITIES (Requirements / Supplier markets)

TECHNICAL PURCHASES (UPSTREAM) Technical problems: Search for alternative solutions Standardization / Simplification Collaboration with suppliers Rationalization of procurement operations Purchase amounts: = weak	**STRATEGIC PURCHASES (UPSTREAM)** Strategic problems: Market intelligence / Anticipation Collaboration with suppliers Cost analysis Control of technical risks Purchase amounts: = high
SIMPLE PURCHASES (DOWNSTREAM) Efficiency problems: Simplification of procedures Standardization Decided disconnection Procurement / Supply Outsourcing Purchase amounts: weak	**HEAVY PURCHASES (DOWNSTREAM)** Tactical problems: Globalization / Pooling Global sourcing Using the competitive position Setting up of strong competition / Negotiation Actions on the TCO (including WCR) Purchase amounts: high

ECONOMIC STAKES = Purchase expense amount

Cat. C / indirect purchases
Volume problem
Search for productivity

Strategic categories
with highly specialized
knowhow
Non-recurrent requirements

staffing competency, some being central purchasing organization, others rely on e-solutions and catalogues offering multiple forms of reporting to their clients. These circumstances often allow risk-free outsourcing, implicitly enabling buyers, thus freed up, to refocus on their core business, if their experience and professional abilities so allow.

Detailed analysis of the phases of a purchase process

One question that must be answered (for pre-identified procurement categories) is the following: which activities should eventually be outsourced? Several observations may be made, as illustrated by Figure 7.9.

Support for sourcing and panel management

Upstream along the process, procurement managements often have limited tools for managing their supplier panel and for detecting new supply sources, namely in the context of international deployment, and the qualification of new suppliers. In this case, outsourcing consists of:

- permanently handing over procedures for sourcing and broadening the supplier panel;

FIGURE 7.9 Outsourceable activities of the procurement process

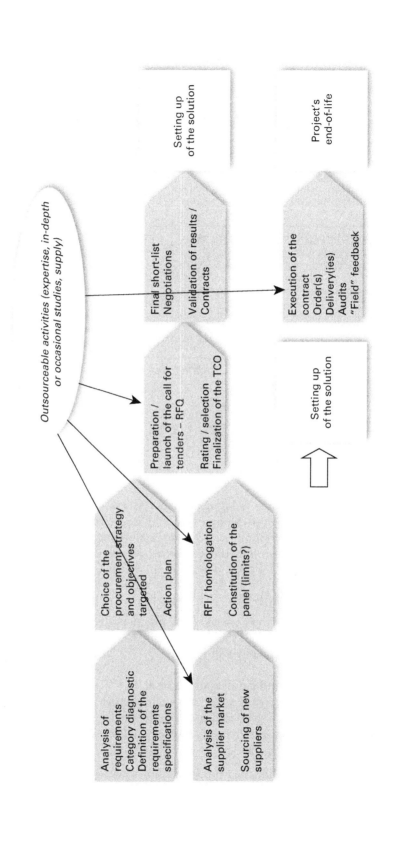

- or looking for support from service-providers mastering the area of competency in certain identified procurement categories;
- or finally, outsourcing approaches in the supplier-selection process based on reverse auctions.

It is at this level that service-providers with added value, ie relying on a set of internet tools, may be called upon to cover the field known as e-sourcing and e-RFQ.

Outsourcing of the operational supply chain
Downstream, the procurement department has the possibility of automating the whole supply chain (management of flows and downstream transactions), from order placements or delivery calls, up to reception and sometimes even the payment of invoices, rather than developing a specific internal application. It is on this level that we speak of *e-procurement*, a service that may be carried out by a specialized service-provider offering tools integrating these functions (see Chapter 18).

Consideration of the level of maturity

The last aspect of the diagnostic consists in overall observation of the *stage of maturity* of the company's procurement practices. We will return to the notion of the company's stages of maturity in terms of procurement performance in depth in Chapter 21.

To keep things simple at this stage, let's limit ourselves here to saying that it is possible to define several levels of development in a company, and to express these different stages according to a progress model that can then serve as a reference in two ways: a) first of all, positioning, through a global diagnostic of the function, the level of professionalism of the procurement processes and practices mastered in the company; b) then, defining priorities in terms of short-term evolution, expressing them in the form of an action plan broken down into action variables, main processes, tools and information and performance measurement systems, management of human resources and communication policy.

Outsourcing of the function is naturally one of the action variables, amongst others, to which recourse can be taken, depending on the company's stage of the maturity in terms of procurement. Table 7.3 demonstrates this idea in a simplified manner by offering three main levels of evolution, its objective being only to illustrate the principle behind this approach. The table reads from 1 ('immature') to 3 ('very professional practice').

It seems clear that different drivers and usage of outsourcing solutions will disrupt the evolution of a company's procurement department's maturity, depending of course on its management priorities. There is a dual focus on simultaneously improving efficiency and productivity, and the acceleration of the impact and competitiveness of the procurement department via the acquisition of external competencies.

7/6.3 External service-provider or group purchasing organization (out- or insourcing)?

This point is directly related to the organizational issues also addressed in Chapter 16. More specifically, a choice exists between an entirely externalized solution calling

TABLE 7.3   Levels of maturity and outsourcing methods

Levels	Principles / Context	Objectives	Priority focuses of outsourcing
1	Immature procurement function Partial deployment of practices Resources with limited competency	Setting up the procurement department Making savings visible quickly Acquiring expertise Refocusing	Global outsourcing (activities) in a scope outside of the 'core business' Mainly directed at 'indirect procurement' Appropriate for SMEs / SMIs
2	Procurement function deploying internal and external levers Implementation of centralization / pooling Existing segmentation of the portfolio	Spreading professionalism throughout the portfolio Working on all TCO (total cost of ownership) components	Search for focused category-related expertise Sourcing focused on new markets Automation of transactions (e-procurement)
3	Mature and recognized procurement function Controlled downstream approach Upstream approach deployed Generalized TCO approach	Improving the value creation of procurement Reducing transaction costs Improving efficiency	Continuing the automation of transactions Supporting suppliers in the deployment of e-procurement / e-sourcing solutions 'Focused' expertise on demand

upon an external service-provider or participation in a group purchasing organization that hands over a proportion of the procurement responsibilities to a suprastructure in which the company participates.

External service-providers 'with added value' (outsourcing procurement)

A service-provider to whom procurement is outsourced may have one of two main profiles: 1) a company specialized in certain types of categories, with recognized procurement expertise, as may be the case of a central purchasing organization, or a specialized service-provider (eg focusing on temp work, office supplies and various consumables, long-term leasing of vehicles); 2) a company essentially created around an internet tool platform offering global services (eg quite often sourcing-type procurement expertise but above all offering clients availability and use of a set of computing functions making up a continuous chain covering all or part of the process).

The latter services most often comprise two main dimensions that correspond to two types of identified needs: specialization covering all e-sourcing stages, or specialization dedicated to the process of ordering with e-procurement-type tools. Sometimes service-providers include both dimensions in their offers. Finally, some offer collaborative tools to manage interfaces with suppliers.

Many CPOs consider that the choice of the service-provider is a major risk of outsourcing. Here, the company will seek to establish long-term relationships based on collaboration and constructed along the principles of a partnership. The main criteria for the selection of the service-provider will flow from this goal. Below is a non-exhaustive list placing an emphasis on certain criteria considered essential:

- relevance and robustness of the company's business model and its price policy in terms of positioning on its market, and in terms of internal rationale;
- level of commitment accepted by the service-provider to operate effectively with a performance commitment (previous experience);
- quality and richness of the service-provider's second-tier suppliers (important point for service-providers offering internet solutions, supposed to have a list of useful suppliers in the case of sourcing);
- recognized sourcing competencies demonstrated in operations of a similar nature;
- proven capacity to support suppliers (eg for the deployment and updating of electronic catalogues);
- existence of a system for keeping a watch on and following up suppliers;
- proven 'category-related' purchasing expertise (with references for past purchases); on this topic, business cases are highly recommended for assessing effectiveness on the basis of past experience; in addition, real-life cases may be put forward during the selection phase to demonstrate the know-how of potential service-providers;
- capacity to train and support company staff in the event of a scheduled withdrawal;
- finally, quality of the reporting system suggested by the service-provider.

Voluntary purchasing groups (so-called central purchasing offices)

This second formula relies on both the concept of *globalization external to the company*, and the principle of *partial outsourcing* of a proportion of its procurement activities. We will not go into a long legal commentary on the topic,[8] but instead present the principles and mechanisms of such solutions.[9]

A group purchasing organization is a purchasing supra-structure (at a higher level), which companies can join for part or all of their purchases. As a structure that deals with negotiation and contractualization, its activity targets the signing of global master service agreements as well as support for its members' procurement departments and qualified suppliers.

Agreements signed by such a structure may be of two types: 1) *substitutive*, in other words they completely substitute local agreements; or 2) *additional*, in other words they are added to local agreements that may continue to apply in parallel.

Most often, these agreements concern use of a listing mechanism (with the technical means for the group members to access the shared databases); they assume commitment to the volumes of activity announced, and they incorporate a certain number of benefits in terms of services offered to suppliers (supply of regular delivery schedules, access to the market following various audits, potential for tests and experimentation, development of reputation internally, etc). In this way, the structure is both a globalized buyer and an internal 'seller' of duly qualified and managed suppliers.

If the structure is substitutive, it is the only 'entrance gate' allowing suppliers access to member companies; it commits all members to the quantities they have stated and negotiated, and it commits to supply the services promised to the suppliers directly (or via the direct action of the members' procurement departments).

If it is additional, suppliers will have two listing levels to cover; it favours growth of the purchasing volumes already committed to on a local level, and it supplies services to suppliers only by differential in relation to those already offered by each of the members.

The conditions for the success of such a supra-structure are quite logical and easy to list:

- definition of clear game rules between members, for the business situation creates cross obligations;
- respect of strict equity amongst members in a context of absolute transparency;
- ensuring that members have the capacity to align themselves with joint proposals (namely in terms of requirements specifications, but also validation by all the company steering committees and the principle of unanimous decisions, absolute respect of all commitments undertaken with suppliers and the purchasing organization, commitment to apply all contractual terms in the field scrupulously and faithfully, uninterrupted supply of the 'feedback' system);
- respect of commitments to procurement resource allocations during the 'action' phase (additional or in the form of shared-time assignment).

Thus presented, group purchasing organizations manifest a type of outsourcing of procurement to an entity in which each member company is a stakeholder (the solution is possibly subsidiarized). As a result, this solution may be entirely appropriate for indirect purchases in multi-BU or multi-branch industrial groups, or even service companies or organizations operating as networks (eg hotels, care or hospital establishments) – the application of the insourcing principle.

However, volume should be substantial in order for a significant ROI to be attained. This volume requirement also implies that all companies involved have a similar maturity level in terms of procurement practices (see Chapter 21).

Service-providers with specific expertise

Alongside the previous outsourcing solutions (independent or pooled) taking charge of the whole of the purchasing process for one or several categories, there are service-providers who can bring specialized expertise or a specific service, at a given moment in the process. In this case, the priorities are recognized competency (above all) and the economic business model (subsequently). Two well-known French examples will illustrate this idea: the company EcoVadis, a centre of expertise on sustainable procurement with worldwide coverage, namely for carrying out CSR audits on products or suppliers; and the company Asian Inspection specialized in quality audits on suppliers, namely Chinese.

Notes

1 This chapter largely benefits from research and publications on outsourcing by Professor Bertrand Quélin, a member of the strategy department of the HEC Group, and the author of the two following articles: Quélin B (2003) Externalisation stratégique et partenariat: de la firme patrimoniale à la firme contractuelle?, *Revue Française de Gestion*, no. 144 (June); and Quélin, B and Duhame,l F (2003) Bringing together strategic outsourcing and corporate strategy: outsourcing motives and risks, *European Management Journal*, vol 21, no. 5 (October). Despite these works being published some time ago, we refer to them here as their content remains entirely topical today and enables us to deepen issues of continuing relevance.

2 In a related manner, the professional world also speaks of *insourcing* in relation to large groups consisting of multiple profit centres. The term means that one or more activities are outsourced to a specialized entity that remains part of the group (eg a subsidiary that operates according to the logic of an *'internalized external' service-provider*).

3 For deeper discussion on these issues, the reader is invited to consult the following well-known work: Porter ME (1985) *The Competitive Advantage: Creating and sustaining superior performance*, Free Press, New York.

4 Procurement does not feature as an activity in the functions put forward to interviewees. However, procurement is increasingly the object of full or partial outsourcing. This decision will be analysed in detail in Section 7/6.

5 There are nevertheless approaches that allow this compromise to be made in a satisfying manner. To illustrate this point, readers may consult the following work: Bruel, O and Kerbache, L (2004) 'Les enjeux stratégiques de la supply chain,' in *Les Echos – L'Art du management* (October).

6 In the case of outsourcing, economic reasoning often implies a comparative analysis using financial methods customarily used for investment decisions (ie NPV and IRR). As in all resource allocation situations, we need to compare discounted cash flows and the respective rates of return. For further explanations, apart from the financial literature listed in the References, the reader is invited to refer to the more detailed text in Section 11/2 of this work dealing with investment purchases.

7 The observations made below draw from a study that was published some time ago: Minahan, TA (March 2003) The procurement outsourcing benchmark report: Accelerating and sustaining cost savings, Aberdeen Group, sponsored by Prosero & ICG Commerce. The continuing relevance of the conclusions prompts us to retain this reference.

8 On the legal front, this type of structure may be established with the characteristics of a French SA (*société anonyme* or limited company) or GIE (*groupement d'intérêt general* or EIG (economic interest group)). See the specialized bibliography. One important point: competition law is a key factor to take into account (cf European Directive of 10 January 2011 according to which all criteria that may hinder free competition on the market – in relation to illegal horizontal and vertical agreements – should be identified). Sanctions may be significant. The concept of agreement should be distinguished from that of a threshold for dependency and abuse of a dominant position. In practical terms, a critical threshold should be adhered to, from the perspective of both suppliers and ordering parties: not representing more than 30 per cent on the market (market segment).

9 Reading of this section should be supplemented by the discussion in Chapter 16 (Section 16/2) on the issues raised by the organization of procurement departments.

PART TWO
Operational management of procurement

Once a strategic framework has been clearly defined, it is up to operational management to take over and ensure that implementation takes place efficiently and effectively. The aim of Part Two is to delve into some of the most important aspects of this stage. For certain topics, it is also an opportunity to show how procurement and supply chain (as functions) should collaborate closely.

First of all, it is essential for the procurement department to have as exact an idea as possible of the forecasts of demand in terms of quantities, as well as their scheduled planning over time. Chapter 8 deals in detail with this issue, and presents tools for forecasting and planning methods. Particular attention is paid to the case of recurrent and one-off purchases with differentiated treatment as appropriate. Procurement on the basis of inventory levels or requirements planning is also the object of specific analysis.

Chapter 9 is devoted to the economic optimization of procurement from different perspectives: the minimization of acquisition costs and TCO, boosting the reliability of service rates using safety (or buffer) stock, and the management of cash flow at the interface with suppliers. The chapter tackles the economic optimization of supplies, notably in certain practical situations commonly encountered in procurement (consolidated supplies, discount systems offered by suppliers), presented with examples. The reasoning behind safety stock and, more generally, client service is specifically discussed. Minimization of TCO in the context of 'remote' international purchases is analysed as an element shared between procurement and supply chain. Finally, in-depth explanations are provided on collaborative management of cash with suppliers and reverse factoring techniques.

Chapter 10 is set aside for the procedure of calls for tenders. We go over the basic sequence of the process, then focus, with the help of an example, on the core issue of the rating of offers and the multi-criteria selection of suppliers.

Often, this work draws its examples from direct procurement families involving physical products or tangible goods. Yet today, the procurement of services makes up a significant part of the procurement portfolio of many companies, even industrial ones. As a result, it seemed necessary to deepen examination of the specific aspects of such purchases. In addition, capital purchases (CapEx) are associated with specific issues inherent to the investment process: these are also examined in detail in Chapter 11.

For Western European companies, the internationalization of procurement port-folios – outside of operation in the Eurozone – always raises problems of financial protection against exchange rate risks (many such companies incidentally seek to 'dollarize' their procurement today). In addition, the energy and raw-material markets are characterized by recurring problems of speculation and price volatility against which companies should protect themselves. Chapter 12 details the nature of the risks incurred, and presents the customary trade-off and hedging techniques.

This work is first of all aimed at buyers in private companies and organizations (with a clear profit-making objective). However, public companies, organizations and services represent a significant proportion of the GDP in many countries, and their cumulative amounts of spend are considerable. Moreover, many other organ-izations, such as NGOs, are also subject to the obligations associated with public procurement, namely if they rely on national or international public donors that impose upon them 'public-type' conditions for calls for tenders and contractualization. For this reason, Chapter 13 presents all purchasing and contractualization rules for the public sector, both in France and in Europe. We also look at how and why the practices of public-sector buyers are nonetheless called to increasingly evolve in such a way as to integrate 'private practices'.

In Chapter 14, the reader will find discussion of certain operational aspects relating to the international practice of procurement, in a reference framework already mentioned earlier in the work. Here, all major international procurement operations are analysed in detail, the most important being the Incoterms® and the appropriate way to use them, logistical aspects of international trade (ie transport and customs), as well as methods of payment and different financial guarantees.

Similarly regarding internationalization, buyers should be well equipped on the legal front. Chapter 15 sums up the specific legal considerations to take into account and to integrate in approaches. Emphasis is placed – with a strong practical focus – on the key levers to use in global sourcing, then in the contract-drafting stages.

08
Quantitative forecasting and requirements planning

Amongst the first downstream levers in which a procurement department should seek to excel, even at a relatively early level of maturity, *quantitative forecasting* and the *planning of requirements over time* stand out. There are many reasons for this:

- having information that is as reliable as possible over the medium term enables suppliers to:
  - get organized;
  - plan their own production resources;
  - consequently obtain attractive pricing conditions in exchange for amortization of their fixed costs#
  - sign global contracts.
- in the short term, these elements are helpful for the management of supply flows, and for the appropriate placing of orders or scheduling of deliveries.

Buyers should be familiar with a set of methodologies, as they may be called upon to participate in selecting and setting them up, even if this is fundamentally a management responsibility that falls upon the supply chain department.

8/1 Segmentation of methods for quantitative forecasting and for supply and procurement planning

Procurement departments encounter different supply situations depending on the nature of the procurement and certain characteristics of the requirements to satisfy.

8/1.1 Segmentation into procurement categories

As shown by Figure 8.1, for the purposes of requirements forecasting, several categories of procurement can be identified (following a different segmentation than that previously described in this book for strictly strategic procurement decisions):

- on the one hand, the company undertakes direct procurement of physical goods of all types (commodities, products, subassemblies and components), for which requirements *recur and depend directly on a downstream delivery and production plan*;

- on the other hand, there is procurement, direct or indirect, that is *managed by inventory systems*, when a choice has been made for a product to be managed on the basis of its inventory monitoring, hence *independently* by disconnecting its replenishment from the sequencing of a downstream consumption plan;

- finally, any company purchases a large number of items or services on a non-permanent basis (described as non-recurrent or spot-purchases), for which a specific forecasting and decision-making method proves necessary.

FIGURE 8.1   Different procurement planning methods

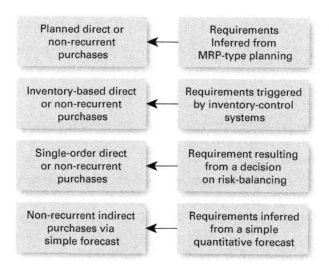

Planned recurrent direct purchases (items linked to a plan)

In this case, the whole procedure stems from the supply chain's planning system, upstream from the procurement process, that calculates requirements according to a top-down reasoning going from manufacturing plans to end-products. This approach to the calculation of requirements, based on MRP logic, will be analysed in detail in Section 8/3.

Other purchases, such as those of spare parts whose actual requirements are based on a scheduled preventative maintenance plan, can be assimilated to this situation.

Inventory-controlled recurrent direct purchases

For these articles, short-term orders (or delivery calls) are based on the setting up of inventory- and supply-control systems that will be presented briefly and summed up in Section 8/4. These are usually reorder-point or periodic-replenishment systems (or a combination of both) with which inventory managers are familiar. Rules covering, for example, order-release mechanisms and the calculation of economic quantities will help determine the forecast requirements.

Non-recurrent direct and indirect procurement ('single orders')

These purchases, non-recurrent by nature and not permanently stocked, imply a method that involves weighing up different risks, on the understanding that very often, it is impossible to place a second order to attempt to correct the first one. These purchases may concern direct or indirect procurement.

Their number has considerably increased, notably ever since industrial companies began to delocalize their manufacturing, or to undertake long-cycle purchases in remote countries. Indeed, in this case, local habits and customs, but also restrictions relating to the manufacturing process and to long distance, compel minimization of the number of orders, or even necessitate single orders. Especially if the purchased products have a 'short lifecycle' on the market: this is precisely the situation facing buyers of fashion products or products that are the object of limited sales promotions.

In all cases, a forecasting system is necessary 'from the outset'. As for the calculation of requirements and quantities to supply, this will depend on specific situations (see Sections 8/3, 8/4 or 8/5).

8/1.2 Segmentation according to the time horizon of supplier requirements

The other approach to forecasting and planning on requirements relates to the time horizon for which these are expressed. For the purposes of analysis and simplification, we can distinguish two time horizons for supplier requirements.

Long- and medium-term forecasting

The first horizon (medium-term) remains to be defined in each situation. Its main objective, once the supplier is selected, is for the company to inform the supplier about its global requirements so that the supplier can manage production resources *in advance*, eventually make decisions on adjusting loads/capacities, even smooth the workload curve and anticipate manufacturing whilst limiting risks, all the while being sure of amortizing fixed production and set-up costs.

Very often as well, this 'global' forecast is the basis of negotiation on purchasing prices calculated from anticipated cumulative global quantities for the purposes of the signing of a master agreement.

The possibility of uncertainty in forecasting may be translated into an open order specifying a *minimum* quantity, with the contract including clauses on incremental price reductions for ranges of order quantities beyond the contractual minimum depending on the overruns possible with predetermined threshold effects. This may sometimes simply take the form of a year-end remittance mechanism applicable to the total turnover purchased.

Short-term forecasting

Short-term forecasting complements the preceding type: it should enable the definition of firm quantities to be ordered over a shorter horizon, or even steer forecast delivery calls in the context of a global yearly contract.

On this horizon, suppliers have resources in place; the aim is to set up production and manage short-term flows. Whilst the first type of forecast was an action variable for procurement, this one is useful for supply.

In Section 8/2, we will refer back to this double aspect of the forecasting system to be set up.

8/2 The company forecasting process

The basic objective of a forecasting process is to meet the need for information via anticipation: it is a matter of providing, at the right time, quantitative forecasts that are as close as possible to future consumption, and evaluating potential deviations as accurately as possible.

The forecasting process is a global procedure comprising six stages. It requires, on an occasional or (most commonly) ongoing basis, the participation of many people representing a number of the company's functions (Figure 8.2).[1]

8/2.1 Identification of forecasting requirements

Initially, it is necessary to begin by understanding the need for information and by identifying the global forecasting structure to implement. It is therefore necessary to identify the following elements: the forecast's required time horizon, its basic unit of time and its degree of aggregation.

Required forecasting horizon

The supply chain manager should in fact have simultaneous access to forecasts for different time horizons, corresponding to specific types of decisions pertaining to upstream supply choices. In short, three main forecasting and planning horizons co-exist.

Long-term forecasts (from several months to several years) are used to adjust a company's global capacity (production and storage) to future demand. These forecasts are typically associated with *structural decisions* on investment (or disinvestment) in production, transport and storage resources, or are the basis of strategic industrial decisions (diversification or launch of new products).

As far as procurement is concerned, the main task is to continue identifying candidates for the supplier-selection process, at least for recurrent suppliers in charge of large or strategic purchases, hence those related to the core business.

Medium-term forecasts (from several weeks to several months) are necessary for defining a supply, production and distribution planning. Over this horizon, major structural factors determining logistical or industrial capacity are often not very flexible, but it is possible to take recourse to *intermediary adjustments of a tactical nature* (flexibility in working hours, overtime, subcontracting, temp work, etc). This is true for the company itself, but also, by implication, for its suppliers and subcontractors.

FIGURE 8.2   The global forecasting process

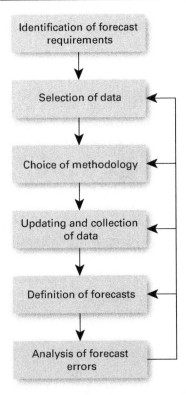

Short-term forecasts (from several hours to several weeks) tend to determine *operational activity*: supply of direct purchases, preparation of orders, scheduling of logistical and industrial resource etc. These may lead to minor capacity adjustments, but are basically used for the placing of firm orders.

It is important to realize that, all things being equal, the greater the forecasting time horizon, the greater margin for forecasting error. Intuitively, this mechanism corresponds to the fact that the greater the time horizon, the greater the number of potential hazards or external events likely to widen the gap between the forecast made at the start of the period and the actual request at the end.

Figure 8.3 illustrates these different horizons with a summary of the types of decisions raised for each in the three stages of any supply chain. We also see a *very short-term* horizon (that does not operate on the basis of forecasts, but of firm client orders) on which the processing of orders and deliveries is carried out.

Basic forecasting period (horizon breakdown)

A second characteristic to identify is the basic forecasting period, in other words the unit of time into which the forecasting horizon is divided. Depending on the situation, forecasting may be on an hourly basis (as for the frequentation of a company cafeteria), weekly (eg for the design of a production programme for household electrical products) or monthly or quarterly (for planning for adjustments to major resources). Ostensibly, there is a certain relationship between the forecasting horizon and the elementary period. Generally, over short horizons, we need forecasts for short elementary periods, and vice versa.

FIGURE 8.3   Different forecasting and planning horizons

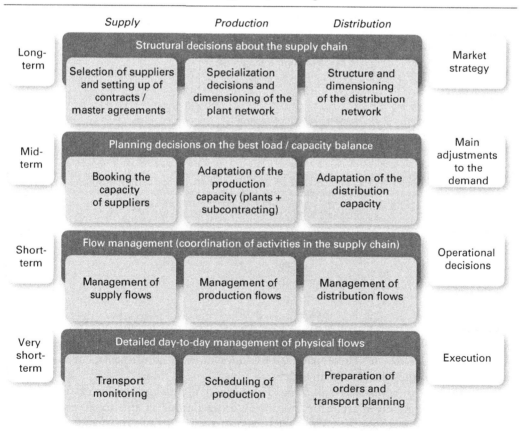

Degree of data aggregation (consolidation level)

This is the *degree of detail or precision* of the forecast. For example, for a manufacturer of clothes and fashion products, a very detailed (or disaggregated) forecast specifies the number of items in each fabric, combined with each of the colours in the collection, and every size. A more aggregated forecast will merely express the total number of items of all types.

The choice of the degree of aggregation depends on the use of these forecasts for decision-making: do we need a forecast by category of items (eg to plan the use of an industrial resource or to book production capacity from a supplier), or on the contrary, by a simple reference method (to configure the inventory-control process for the article or to operationalize replenishment orders)?

Note that often, the aggregation of elementary demands is likely to simultaneously lead to *reduction in the error of the aggregated forecast*, through a risk-compensation phenomenon, provided that consumption follows a comparable development path (this is common sense, but also statistically proven).

8/2.2 Choice of the forecasting methodology

Once we have identified and recorded the data to be used to estimate future consumption or demand, the next step is to choose the way in which to calculate forecasts from this data, in other words the forecasting methodology. Two main families of methods co-exist: *qualitative* and *quantitative* approaches.

Qualitative forecasting methods

Qualitative or subjective approaches are essentially based on *intuitive expert opinions* that informally synthesize a complex and varied set of information to construe an opinion that is referred to as a forecast. Mentioned here for the record, such approaches are used very little for the planning of production and/or supply.

They are commonly used, for example, by marketing specialists seeking to antici-pate demand deductively by future analysis of its decisive elements (Delphi method)[2] or experimentally, on the basis of market studies, test markets, customer-panel sur-veys or order-book developments. These subjective methods are nonetheless associ-ated with a few disadvantages that cannot be ignored.

First of all, in a supply-chain-type environment, demands to be forecast are generally extremely numerous (typically, several hundreds or thousands of pieces of data per month), and the workload involved in evaluating all these forecasts, even 'intui-tively', is enormous. Moreover, the inconsistency of the subjective approach, related to the numerous irrational factors likely to disturb the forecaster, is restrictive. We have reason to fear that forecasts change depending on whether the forecaster is in a good or bad mood, or whether the sky is blue or overcast!

Quantitative forecasting methods[3]

Quantitative forecasting methods are based on developing *explicit mathematical models*, calculating forecasts from historical data. These methods present the advantage of being implemented automatically with the help of software. In addition, as these methods are explicit, it is easier to analyse and to improve on them.

Statistical extrapolation of requirements

When these mathematical models assess future demands directly from historical demand, we speak of *statistical extrapolation methods* based on past demand. In this case, the approach involves identifying the changing dynamics of historical demand (such as growth or decline) and extrapolating these dynamics into the future (assuming that markets will keep their past 'rationale'). Amongst these techniques, we can cite the following approaches:

- simple or weighted moving averages;
- decomposition of time series with a calculation of trend and seasonal coefficients for medium-term forecasting;
- exponential smoothing, simple or with corrections for trends and/or seasonality;
- more sophisticated methods integrating self-adaptation mechanisms such as the Winters model;
- finally, specific extrapolation models for forecasting items whose sale is concentrated within a short, limited period ('single-period' models).

Simple or multiple regression methods

Another forecasting strategy consists in establishing, on the basis of historical data, a relationship between demand or consumption to forecast and one or several other so-called 'explanatory' variables. In this case we speak of a *causal method* or *statistical regression*. Explanatory variables may either be internal to a company, or external and related to the economy or to the competitive situation.

For example, it is known that consumption of mineral water depends on air temperature: knowledge of the daily temperature (or even temperature forecasts for coming days) enables the producer to hone sales forecasts. The methods for calculating requirements (cf the explanation later in Section 8/3) also follow an associative logic.

We can note, amongst these techniques, the following approaches: a) simple or multiple regression models; and b) complex econometric models such as the Box–Jenkins method.

8/2.3 Calculation and elaboration of forecasts

Apart from the choice of the method to be used, the internal process to be followed is extremely important, namely from an organizational point of view.

Forecasting group or committee

The first idea that comes to mind is making the person in the field (seller, producer, distributor) responsible for sales forecasts for the data concerning him or her. This approach seems ideal: the forecaster has relevant information at disposal and is personally affected by the quality of the forecasts. However, experience indicates that such forecasts risk being biased, namely because they interfere with sales objectives and/or remuneration methods.

The other option involves entrusting forecasting to specialists, experts in statistical methods, disconnected from the field in order to avoid any potential bias. Unfortunately, this approach generally proves inefficient because it leads to a separation between 'specialist' forecasters and the forecast users, for whom the methods used lack transparency. At the slightest forecasting error, this lack of understanding can trigger, amongst users, mistrust of the forecasting unit.

An efficient solution should combine the strengths of the two alternatives described above. The forecasting process should use well-adapted formal models, and at the same time, involve users in the data collection and processing stage as well as the stage when the forecasts themselves are exploited.

In this light, an efficient forecasting evaluation approach would potentially correspond to the following schema (Figure 8.4). The idea is to set up a forecasting committee composed of representatives of those functions with access to critical information (typically the sales and marketing functions) and the person in charge of statistical forecasting. Meanwhile, buyers and suppliers are positioned as 'internal clients' of such groups; they may nevertheless participate in them in order to better grasp future trends.

FIGURE 8.4   Forecasting committee's synthesis

Calculation of forecasts: priority and processing of exceptions

One of the problems facing companies when setting up a forecasting system is the number of demands to forecast, typically numbering several hundred (or even several thousand in certain cases). To maximize the amount of time available during the forecast calculation stage, the use of computerized mathematical models helps lighten the workload considerably. However, these forecasts still need to be validated, or even revised, if necessary, by the forecasting committee.

In order to effectively steer the activity of the forecasting committee, we evaluate the criticality of demands via an *ABC-type analysis* (also known as *Pareto's law*) of products purchased, manufactured or sold according to criteria that are usually the turnover produced or the quantities sold.[4]

Forecasting efforts can then focus on A-category items to deal with 80 per cent of the forecasting problem, with less effort spent on B- and C-category items (or by accepting in advance greater protection levels for them – through safety stock – to cover forecasting errors that are intuitively more significant). It is appropriate to represent ABC analysis by a curve (Figure 8.5). This type of analysis has many other applications, namely in inventory management, as we will see in Chapter 9.

FIGURE 8.5   ABC or Pareto analysis

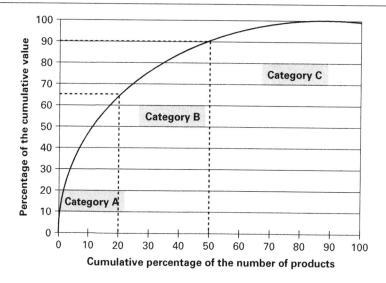

Initially, the forecasting committee will quickly validate the majority of forecasts associated with low-criticality situations – this can generally be achieved through a purely statistical approach. It will then spend more time on improving forecasts for products or components that represent the bulk of the company's activity or turnover.

8/2.4 Forecasts and requirements for planning

Generally, we have seen that three main time horizons co-exist for forecasting and planning. The corresponding forecasting approaches were summed up in Figure 8.2. To summarize, the forecasts for requirements on these three main horizons are:

- *long-term*: forecasts for each *macro-category* of products (demand depends on economic, social, political, technological evolutions, and on competition);
- *medium-term*: forecasts for each *homogeneous category* of products (analysis of different manufacturing and associated supply programmes);
- *short-term*: *article-by-article* forecasts (efforts to simplify data collection and application as their usage is frequent).

To operate soundly, the whole of the forecasting process should follow a formal procedure and be explained to those concerned. Indeed, when an approach is clearly defined and understood by all, the various actors or users of the forecasts can participate in discussions on the subject, and it can also be rigorously validated by statistical means. This pairing of procedural clarity and statistical validation constitutes the best way to avoid forecasting bias. Forecasting is thus carried out in a climate of coherence and trust, more conducive to communication, especially when various functions within the company are stakeholders of the process. In this way, forecasting becomes a joint challenge shared by all.

8/3 Calculation of supply requirements using MRP (recurrent direct procurement)

Buyers are not in charge of monitoring this system. However, as users of the information that it produces, they need to have a full understanding of the calculation mechanisms.

The starting point is a sales and operations plan (S&OP), subsequently broken down (for an industrial company) into a production and distribution plan (PDP) that generally covers a time period ranging from several weeks to several months. The procedure for establishing the PDP aims to set the globally achievable production plan, taking into account the forecast demand and the available production capacity. At the end of this procedure, the company thus has programmes that it will need to implement in order to prepare specific manufacturing and supply orders.

Whilst the PDP concerns families of products, requirements calculation works on a shorter horizon, around several weeks in length, and for the clearly specified basic references of bill of materials (BOM) products. On this timescale, output consists of firm orders or forecasts of requirements that are highly accurate in terms of quantities and items to be manufactured.

To calculate the requirements of components and raw materials, it is necessary to have specific knowledge of the *structure* or composition of the products to manufacture (ie the BOM), normally indexed in a technical database (a specialist subject that we will not elaborate on here).

8/3.1 MRP and calculation of net requirements

The method for calculating requirements is known as material requirements planning (MRP). All ERP-type integrated information systems include an MRP module.

The principle of calculating net requirements

The calculation principle can be described as a succession of BOM-explosion operations, clustering requirements for the same parts generated by different product-assembly programmes, then integrating a retro-planning mechanism to take into account production and supply lead-times. To understand this procedure better, we will now break it down into several stages.

Phase 1: calculation of quantities

Here, we will refer to the example of a model based on three levels: the end-products are composed of subassemblies, themselves assembled from component parts manufactured using purchased raw materials (Figure 8.6). Let's look at the different stages.

1 We start off with the demand for end-products (firm orders or sales forecasts). This constitutes the gross requirements at level zero.

FIGURE 8.6   Definition of manufacturing and purchasing orders

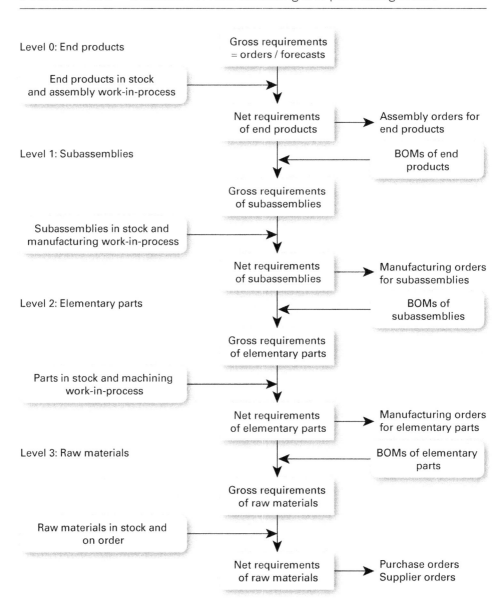

2 We subtract the stock (and work-in-process) of end-products eventually available. This provides us with the net requirements of end-products, resulting in the assembly orders for the plant.

3 We break down these net requirements of end-products, using their BOMs to determine the quantities (gross requirements) of subassemblies needed in order to be able to proceed to assembly.

4 We subtract the stock (and work-in-process) of subassemblies to obtain the Level 1 net requirements that generate the subassembly manufacturing orders.

5 We break down the subassembly manufacturing orders, using their BOMs to determine the quantities (gross requirements) of component parts needed for the manufacturing of the subassemblies.

6 We subtract the stock (and work-in-process) of component parts to obtain the Level 2 net requirements. These generate the machining orders for elementary parts.

7 We break down the machining orders for component parts, using their BOMs to determine the quantities (gross requirements) of raw materials needed in order to proceed to the machining of parts.

We subtract the stock (and work-in-process) of raw materials, using their BOMs to obtain the Level 3 net requirements. These net requirements correspond with the orders for raw materials that must be placed with suppliers.

We can observe that certain subassemblies and spare parts are purchased: in this case, their net requirements directly generate purchase orders.

We also see that this procedure, in which eventually available inventory is subtracted for every level, results in their resorption according to a planned forecasting methodology. Applied strictly, the procedure leads to eliminating all stock in the different BOM levels. We will see later that combination of certain stocks is nonetheless necessary.

Phase 2: definition of the order schedule

This procedure, as described above, does not take into account the lead-time needed for preparing or supplying the products at each level. It is now appropriate to introduce a *lead-time offset* between the date on which we wish to make end-products available and the date on which we set up manufacturing (ie on which the components need to be at our disposal). This offset is therefore at least equal to the lead-time needed to meet the corresponding manufacturing orders (or the delivery of orders from suppliers in the case of purchased products).

Thus, generally speaking, the procedure for calculating net requirements between one level and a level below is the following:

1 We position the requirement for a composite item in the manufacturing cycle of an order, at the launch date of this cycle.

2 We break down the needs for the composite item to obtain the gross requirements of each component, using the composite's BOM.

3 For every component, we subtract the stock and the possible work-in-process inventory to obtain the net requirements. We eventually add external requirements (eg requirements for spare parts).

4 The net requirements of each component become the gross requirements of the next level down; the procedure is recommenced from the first point until we reach the lowest level of the BOM.

We can point out that in the case of a component that is common to several composite items, we should logically add up the gross requirements that appear on the same date before calculating net requirements.

Starting with the schedule of requirements for end-products, we apply the procedure described above for each of the time periods. In this way, we obtain a full schedule of requirements for every level, that is translated by manufacturing orders (runs to set up) and purchase orders (orders to place with suppliers).

Justified inventories in MRP systems

The principle of the MRP method is to 'absorb' stock that may already exist at each level. This therefore aims to make the production process operate without stock, by creating, if carried out to the extreme, a complete interdependency between the levels of the supply-chain system. However, four reasons may lead to the accumulation of stock: 1) the manufacturing of quantities higher than net requirements; 2) the introduction of safety margins in time; 3) the necessity to smooth the workload; and 4) the consolidation of orders for economic reasons.

Justification 1: Guaranteed availability of quantities

The coefficients that appear on BOM assignments are *technical* coefficients. But during the manufacturing of parts or products, we often notice that actual consumption is higher than theoretical consumption: disparities may be due to defective and rejected parts, components of dubious quality or a poorly executed manufacturing process.

To avoid obtaining, at the end of production, lower quantities than those determined by the calculation of requirements, we need to take into account this probable over-consumption by increasing the quantities whose production we set up. For example, if, to knit a sweater, we need 1.3 kg of wool, plus or minus 5 per cent, then to make 1,000 sweaters (and to avoid the risk of shortage), we will order a weight of wool equalling 1,300 × 1.05, in other words 1,365 kg. On average, 65 kg in stock will be left over. We will subtract this residual stock when making the next calculation of net requirements.

In addition, forecasting errors and variations in demand may prompt a greater volume of materials to be ordered or safety stock to be maintained (not aiming for a complete depletion of available stock), so as to keep the option of increasing, on a short-term basis, production quantities, thus avoiding shortages.

Justification 2: Introduction of safety margins in lead-times

The duration of time necessary for the processing of a batch depends on factors specific to the operations of the route sheet (set-up time, unit time for machining or assembly, and series size) but also numerous elements exterior to the manufactured batch: if a machine breaks down, the batches that it must process will be delayed; if a purchased component is not delivered on time, the launch of production will be delayed, etc.

The actual duration is also closely related to the workshop's workload during the period when the batch must be manufactured, as well as the order of priority of other batches. The load on a piece of industrial equipment may engender unforeseen waiting periods due to the creation of queues at workstations.

As these waiting periods vary in length, the planner should include a *safety margin* in the offset in order to avoid any risk of delay in the availability of products, which would result in a shortage at the next level of the BOM. Offsets included in calculations are thus increased in relation to technical lead-times, in such a way that they can be respected most of the time.

In many cases, the offset is specified by the introduction of a waiting period before each route-sheet operation. The manufacturing cycle is thus increased, but the associated load is spread out over a longer period. This allows those in charge of manufacturing a certain flexibility for organizing their work and catching up possible delays.

Justification 3: Workload smoothing

The calculation of requirements generates a schedule of demands, stemming from the different BOM explosions carried out for higher levels. Next, it is necessary to transform the calculation into a production and supply programme capable of satisfying this succession of requirements to ensure a certain smoothing of the workshop's workload.

Indeed, the load resulting from manufacturing orders stemming from the requirement-calculation procedure may, for certain workstations and at certain periods, exceed the available capacity. If no intervening action is taken, then certain orders will not be able to be met within the given lead-times. What this then triggers are knock-on delays for manufacturing orders. We can modify production capacity (eg by deciding to include overtime), but we can also endeavour to smooth the work-load if capacities are available upstream.

To smooth the workload, we attempt to bring forward certain orders (to the extent that this is possible): in this way, the load at one period will diminish and the load at the preceding period will increase. Waiting stock will be created (as the products manufactured will not be consumed immediately). But this approach also results in modifying the calculation of requirements for lower levels as the need for components making up the products whose manufacturing is put forward will arise earlier.

Justification 4: Consolidation (pooling) of production or supply orders

Calculation of requirements from a manufacturing schedule engenders, for each item, a succession of manufacturing or purchasing orders that may be staggered over a long period. For example, for item x, we will need to manufacture 50 units for Week 15, 125 for Week 17 and 25 for Week 18. In workshops, it may be more advantageous to set up production of the 200 units needed in one batch (a single set-up operation to be made for each of the machines specified in the item's route sheet, allowing time to be saved, and thus, useful capacity to be increased). More generally, in this way, for every item, depending on its characteristics and the set-up time involved, we can define rules for consolidating orders.

Apart from economic reasons, technical restrictions relating to manufacturing (or transport) may also lead to the consolidating of orders.

If we consolidate several successive orders, it is necessary to run production of the total requirements on the date of the first order: in our example, the 200 units will be needed for Week 15. The parts that are not immediately consumed will remain in stock: here, 125 units will be stocked for 2 weeks and 25 units for 3 weeks. Consolidation rules should therefore be applied level by level, for the requirements of lower levels can only be determined after manufacturing orders have been grouped.

Consolidation *can also take place for commodities or components purchased to benefit from discounts on quantities or to make savings on transport costs.*

Customary consolidation (or batching) rules

There are many possible approaches to consolidation (or batching). For each item, the best rule must be determined. Let's cite the main rules used and suggested as possible options by standard software:

- *Lot by lot*: this rule is about not consolidating: every net requirement gives rise to a manufacturing or supply order. We use this rule in particular to process specific orders.

- *Economic order quantity*: we establish a consistent set order size by applying a formula based on average demand. This rule is only applicable if demand for the component in question is relatively regular. Calculation methods will be examined in Chapter 9.

- *Fixed period coverage*: requirements are consolidated over a predetermined period (eg monthly). For items managed according to this rule, there will be at least one batch set up per month.

- *Average cost per period or average cost per unit*: this rule consists in calculating the total management cost (set-up cost plus storage cost) of successive consolidations over 1, 2, 3 etc periods per simulation. We stop consolidating successive orders as soon as the average management cost per period or per unit increases compared with that of the previous consolidation.

There are also algorithms to optimize consolidation: we will not go into these here but recommend that readers consult specialized works.

8/4 Supply based on inventory systems (recurrent purchases)

For certain purchases, supply is *directly managed by an inventory-control system*, for a decision has been made to *disconnect calculation of these requirements from complex MRP planning*. Often, this is because these items are common to a wide number of products or subassemblies, and we can observe that their consumption is fairly regular. As a result, consumption is likely to be able to be *forecast directly* using one of the quantitative forecasting methods mentioned earlier, rather than by *deduction*.

In this case, supply of the item depends on the implementation of an inventory-control and resupply system: it is appropriate, here, to explain which are the main systems commonly used in the professional context.

Two basic decision-making rules exist for defining an inventory-control system, expressed in the form of two questions: 'ordering when?' and 'ordering how much?' Then, in the course of everyday management, we need only set up inventory monitoring, and procurement decisions will automatically result.

Ordering when? Answering this question amounts to determining the event that triggers the placing of the order. Two main systems are used: either we place an order according to a set frequency, for example, once a week or once a month; alternatively, we place an order when the actual inventory reduces and falls below a minimum level, called an inventory-reorder order point.

Ordering how much? The reply to this question partially depends on the reply to the preceding question. Indeed, if we place orders at set dates for a set quantity, we can never adapt to demand fluctuations. Therefore, it is necessary for the time factor or the quantity factor to be variable. In this way, we deduce the principles of the two main inventory-control systems as follows:

1 If the order comes up when a minimum inventory level is reached, we *always supply the same quantity that must be predetermined* (an 'order-point' system). In this system, the date at which the order is placed is therefore variable: if consumption accelerates, the order point will be reached earlier; if it slows down, the order point will be reached later (Figure 8.7).

2 If, however, the placing of the order takes place at a *set frequency that must be predetermined*, we supply different quantities from one order to the next to bring the inventory level back to a reference level, the 'replenishment' level (in a 'periodic-replenishment' system). The basic principle is the following: at a set frequency (eg every month, every semester etc), we evaluate the available stock and we bring it back up to the set *replenishment level* via a replenishment order. This order is therefore usually equal to the demand from the preceding period. (Figure 8.8).[5]

FIGURE 8.7 Logic of the re-order point inventory system

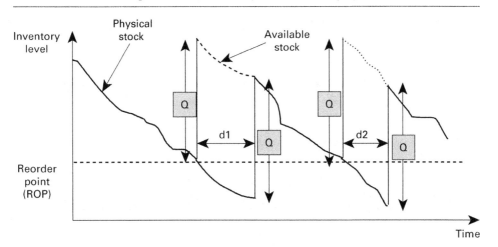

FIGURE 8.8   Logic of the periodic replenishment inventory system

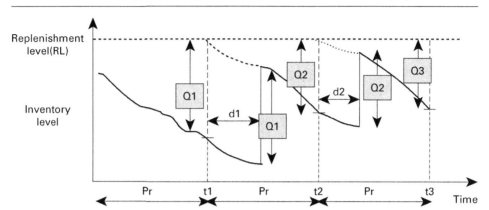

8/4.1 Commentaries on the reorder order-point system

The selected hypotheses, corresponding to the most common cases, are based on the fact that demand and lead-time fluctuate respectively around an average. In this case, the order point is equal to the average consumption level during the average lead-time increased by a quantity aimed at covering the risks related to the demand and to the lead-time that we call safety stock:

Level of the order point = *average* consumption during
the *average* lead-time + safety stock

If the order point is set too high, the average stock increases as well as the inventory-holding cost. If, on the other hand, the order point is set too low, the average stock diminishes, but the risk of shortage rises. When consumption grows, the order point is reached more quickly and resupply is ordered earlier. As long as safety stock can absorb the swell in demand during the lead-time, there is no shortage.

Let's also note that here, the notion of 'replenishment lead-time' exceeds that of the supplier's delivery lead-time: this in fact refers to the *total inventory replenishment cycle, ie including transport time, as well as internal waiting time and administrative processing time that are added onto the supplier's strict delivery lead-time.*

The system requires us to be able to place an order *as soon as* the reorder-point is reached. This can sometimes raise genuine difficulties:

- Numerous items can come from the one supplier. As different items probably reach the order point at different dates, it is not easy to consolidate such orders.

- The organization of production amongst suppliers is often such that an order will only be taken into consideration when the next manufacturing programme is established (eg weekly or monthly). As a result, the lead-time risks being extended. As the registering of an order is periodic, the system no longer operates as an order-point system. It is necessary, in this case, for it to be associated with a flexible production organization or the existence of a stock of end-products held by the supplier.

● Knowledge of the level of available stock at any moment, thus in *real time*, is necessary in order to keep informed as soon as an article reaches its order point – a necessity which may entail significant management costs.

When inventories are monitored by an integrated information system, there is ongoing knowledge of the inventory levels. It is even possible to set up a link between systems with the supplier's ERP planning module.

To sum up, the reorder-point system is better suited when one or several of the following elements are present: strong variability in demand; items that, due to their prices or their importance for the company, require strong protection against stock shortages; the supplier has a flexible production system and/or access to a permanently available supplier inventory.

8/4.2 Comments on the periodic replenishment system

The principle of this system consists in examining the inventory level at regular intervals and placing an order equal to the quantity consumed (or demand) during the last interval between two orders. The quantity ordered at the end of each set period is therefore equal to the difference between the available stock and the reference replenishment level.

When the lead-time is greater than the length of an interval between two orders, there may be several simultaneous orders. This does not present any difficulties if the system allows the tracking of *available* stock (which is the sum of the physical stock and placed orders not yet delivered).

The maximum stock corresponding to the replenishment level should cover the demand not only during the lead-time, but also during an interval between two successive orders. As in the previous system, we should take into account variability of demand and of the lead-time to decide on a possible safety stock level. In this way, the replenishment level is met by the following formula:

Replenishment level = *average* consumption during the interval between two orders increased by an *average* supplier lead-time + safety stock

When the replenishment level is set too high, average stock is high and the inventory-holding cost increases. However, when the level is too low, while we may gain on the average stock and the cost of ownership, we increase the risk of shortage.

Often, production programmes are set up by suppliers at regular intervals. By coinciding replenishment frequencies with multiple set-up frequencies (on the supplier's side), orders can be taken into account without any disturbance.

The advantage of a periodic system is that it allows the possibility of consolidating orders for different items placed with the one supplier, which can cut administrative expenses and generate savings in relation to order preparation and transport.

However, the system operates 'blindly' within a period of time: in this way, any instantaneous unexpected variation in demand will leave the system impervious (unlike the reordering-point system). To protect oneself in this situation, we are generally led to increase the safety stock.

To sum up, the periodic replenishment system is preferable when one or more of the following elements is present: a) low variability in consumption and lead-time; b) impossibility of taking orders continuously due to production organization on the supplier's side; c) items whose low consumption value – through the combination of the unit cost and the quantity – mean that a significant average stock does not lead to overly high holding costs.

The determination of quantities in the order-point system, and that of set schedules for orders in the periodic system, result from the economic rationale based on minimizing the total cost of ownership. This will be discussed at length in Chapter 9.

8/5 Single-period supply (non-recurrent procurement)

A fairly frequent situation concerns *items with set periods of use or (very) short life-cycles* for which total cumulative consumption should be covered by a single order. This is the case of fashion items, all products and objects relating to promotional campaigns of limited duration, as well as many other sales operations – especially when these products are also ordered from suppliers in distant countries (entailing long transport times).

The issue involves taking into account a range of characteristics and obvious habitual risks:

- the sales forecast is often very difficult to define and associated with significant uncertainty (due to the promotional context or fashion phenomena);
- the manufacturing time is sometimes long and the single order must be issued well in advance to build up a stock of products available in time for sale;
- ordering too small a quantity brings the risk of losing sales and having costs relating to stock shortage, or even damage to the company's image;
- ordering too large a quantity may lead to unsold lots and incur costs for selling them off via parallel channels (or getting rid of them via discounts or at a loss).

Formulation of the basic problem

In this case, the right decision does not consist in ordering the quantity corresponding to the average requirements forecast, but in looking for *the quantity that minimizes the anticipated total cost by taking into account the respective risk probability.*

One of the possible model solutions to the problem relies on the *marginal* principle: calculating the quantity threshold from which the order of an *extra (or marginal) unit* leads to *equal* hopes for marginal gain and marginal loss. In this way, we discover, according to the *marginalist principle of balance* (largely used by economists), the optimal solution. Figure 8.9 illustrates this problem (if we assume that the final demand may be situated on either side of the initial requirements forecast symmetrically and according to a normal distribution).

Consider the following elements: C is the item's direct purchasing or production cost; Pv, the item's normal sales price; Ps, the resale price of the surplus item; and R, the unit cost of shortage.

Let p^* be the probability of shortage corresponding to the optimal order (when we have the risk–balance situation). We therefore have:

Hope of gain = margin + saving on shortage = p (Pv – C) + p R
Hope of loss = cost of the surplus = $(1 - p)$ (C – Ps)

At best (optimal decision), the hopes of gain and loss should be equal, in other words:

$$p^* (Pv - C) + p^* R = (1 - p^*) (C - Ps)$$

and therefore:

$$p^* = (C - Ps) / (Pv - Ps + R)$$

When we know the probability distribution of the demand, it is then possible to calculate the size of the lot that corresponds to the probability of shortage p^*.

FIGURE 8.9   Single-period order problematic

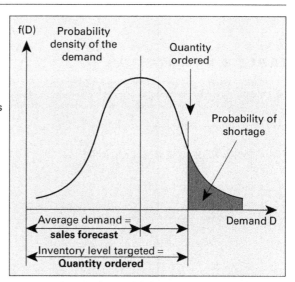

Pv = unit sales price
C = direct manufacturing cost
R = unit cost of shortage or sales loss
(non-satisfied demand)
Ps = resale price of surplus item
(second-choice discount or sell-off
network)

In this case:

Pv – C = expected margin per unit
C – Ps = net cost of a surplus (*)

f(D)   Probability density of the demand
Quantity ordered
Probability of shortage
Average demand = sales forecast
Inventory level targeted = Quantity ordered
Demand D

(*) In this case, we make the hypothesis that there is not IN ADDITION any extra fixed cost for handling the discount sales. Otherwise, it would be necessary to increase (C – Ps) with an extra cost.

A real-life example

XYZ is a European clothes manufacturer, specializing in the design, manufacturing and sale of items for underwear, homewear and sportswear for men and women but especially for children and teenagers. This specific case concerns two children's sportswear items: NEMO and VADOR. Both are aimed for sale specifically in the 'back-to-school' campaign run by a major French retail brand in all of its national stores. This campaign is to last three weeks only in the stores; any unsold items are then to be withdrawn from sale and sold off in parallel sales channels later (along with other products in the same situation, at heavily discounted prices).

The retailer includes these items in its promotional brochure for the back-to-school season, and sets aside shelf space for the anticipated products, but it is the manufacturing company XYZ that takes responsibility for risks, either of missed sales opportunities or of being left with unsold items at the end of the promotional period.

Given the low level of their prices, as for all 'simple' items in such situations, their manufacturing needs to be carried out in an Asian country, by a supplier known for its quality, but who has imposes a crucial condition: the absolute necessity for a *single order to be placed three months in advance* for the total quantity of each item to be manufactured. In addition, these items will be *delivered in one go* by sea container to Le Havre, and available only two weeks prior to the start of the campaign. It will no longer be possible to 'put things right' by replenishing during the campaign given the extremely long lead-time and the short sales period.

In Tables 8.1, 8.2 and 8.3 we find a series of details on these products. With regard to the forecast, for a large quantity of products sold of a similar nature we have observed, *in the past*, that actual sales are distributed according to a normal law on average value equal to the sales forecast with an identical standard deviation (cf Table 8.1 and Figure 8.9).

TABLE 8.1   Forecast sales

	NEMO	VADOR
Forecast on average sales	32,000	65,000
Forecasting error (standard deviation)	2,600	15,000
Distributor's sales price (€)	3	6
Resale price (€)	2	4

In the event of stock shortage (due to not having ordered enough), there is an administrative shortage cost, as well as loss of turnover (Table 8.2). However, if XYZ has ordered too many items, at the end of the 'back-to-school' operation, unsold items will be left over, giving rise to a second promotion in which prices are lowered.

TABLE 8.2   Cost of shortages

	NEMO	VADOR
Administrative cost of shortage (€)	1	10
Cost of handling surplus / unit (€)	0.75	1.5
Discount sales price (€)	1.5	3

In addition, this sales operation will entail its own cost relating to the handling and management of sales in stores. The corresponding figures are supplied in Table 8.2.

In these conditions, what should be the quantities ordered for the two products? By applying the reasoning seen above, the reader will see that we arrive at the following choice of quantities (Table 8.3). We observe a significant difference with the average sales forecasts.

TABLE 8.3   Choice of quantities ordered

	NEMO	VADOR
p^*	0.3846	0.1724
$1 - p^*$	0.6154	0.8276
Value of x (cf. normal law curve)	0.2934	0.9447
BATCH = Quantity to order	32,762	79,170

Alternative risk management approach: the option of delayed differentiation

Fairly often, the BOM of these products comprises an intermediary stage for product manufacturing (eg materials or subassemblies with long lead-times, but with relatively moderate direct costs per unit compared with that of the end-product).

Extending the example of the case of manufactured textile items described above, we can illustrate this typical situation clearly, using fabrics that entail a manufacturing cycle of 1.5 months in length. However, the cycle for the manufacturing of end-products (and possibly for transport if airfreight is chosen) is short (around two weeks) and, in any case, may often be shorter than the duration of the product's sales life: we can therefore decide to partially postpone the final assembly and proceed to *successive replenishment* operations.

In such conditions, the *single-run* method presented above will apply *on the level of subassemblies* (we will order the fabrics in one go, taking all risks of end-of-season sales or lost sales opportunities *on this level*). However, we will manufacture end-products in successive batches by closely following the gradual evolution of *actual sales* as the sales period unfolds and error in the forecasting of final cumulative sales diminishes.

In the event of fabric surpluses at the end of the season, these may eventually be used in the manufacturing of other *specific* end-products using patterns already designed in the context of other promotional operations, thus generating extra cash flow.

At worst, this fabric can be sold off by a parallel network of discounters, minimizing surplus costs as the unit cost in any case remains far less than the direct cost of the end-products.

Notes

1   Many elements of Section 8/2 borrow from Chapter 9 of the work: Baglin *et al* (2013) *Management Industriel et Logistique: Conception et pilotage de la supply chain*, 6th edn, Economica, Paris.

2   This consists in asking a group of experts, through successive questionnaires, to indicate their opinions on questions asked (the questionnaires are filled out separately to avoid any bias induced by cross-influence). The first responses, anonymously, are sent to other experts along with statistical elements (median, first and last quartile). Informed of the opinions of other experts, the second group are asked to make a new forecast and to justify it, especially if it diverges from the average opinion. In this way, we arrive at a general consensus with a tight range of forecasts, or an almost universal opinion with a few divergences justified by strong arguments, or two diverging groups of expert opinions.

3   No forecasting method or technique will be detailed here. The reader is invited to consult, on this topic, two bibliographical references: *Management Industriel et Logistique: Conception et pilotage de la supply chain*, as well as Bourdonnais, R and Usunier, JC (2013) *Prévision des Ventes: Théorie et pratique*, 5th edn, Economica, Paris.

4   Such a classification consists in sorting items on the basis of decreasing values to single out a main sub-category from others whose relative importance is less. By cumulating the turnovers produced, we often see that around 20 per cent of items make up 80 per cent of the turnover: these are the A-category items. The following 30 per cent share around 15 per cent of the turnover between them: these are the B-category items. Finally, the last 50 per cent, called the C-category items, make up the remaining 5 per cent of the turnover.

5   There are variations on these two basic systems that we will not examine here: the periodic order-point system and the periodic-replenishment system with a threshold.

09
Economic optimization of procurement

TCO minimization, service levels for internal clients and shared cash management

As a basic principle, we tend to make a distinction between procurement and supply-chain management. On this basis, buyers should focus solely on purchasing costs (nonetheless, usually including the procurement of transport interfacing with suppliers), whilst supply-chain specialists are responsible for, and have complete freedom to decide independently on, logistical and storage aspects, being accountable for supply costs exclusively.

Meanwhile, financiers observe – sometimes with dread – the severe financial consequences resulting from decisions on the company's cash and working capital requirement (WCR), without really having the means to influence them.

In addition, certain buyers have a tendency to forget that they are not procuring 'for themselves', but for internal (or external) clients, and that this mission requires – on top of appropriate acquisition costs – maintenance of high service levels depending on the clients' legitimate requirements and expectations.

Hence, a context rife with conflicts and power struggles, most often explained by a poor level of economic trade-offs and the choice of incorrect performance criteria.

This chapter presents some of these key issues, for we believe that mature procurement departments are obliged to play a privileged central role – and at the highest level – in all decisions of this type (given that they are in charge of managing the company's external resources in optimal conditions for competitiveness and value creation): a role that is to be played not as 'dictators', but as coordinators of an internal multi-function process, using an approach that is collaborative as possible, involving suppliers to the maximum level.

9/1 Economic optimization of upstream inventories[1]

When direct purchases are managed on the basis of inventory levels, before tackling the possibilities for reducing purchasing costs, or even before acting upon the total cost of ownership (TCO), it is first of all appropriate to weigh up the *internal* costs involved and to choose the best supply policy that minimizes inventory costs. These costs are the sum of three elements: the delivered duty paid (DDP) purchasing cost itself, the holding cost of carrying stock, and finally the ordering or replenishment cost. One last cost element may be included, concerning the definition of safety stock: the cost of shortages.

As far as the *purchasing cost* is concerned, let's recall that this is the *direct cost of the purchased product when it is added to the inventory*, made up of the sum of a certain minimum number of basic costs: purchase price per unit, payment terms and any possible exchange rate effects, amortization in the unit cost of certain non-recurrent fixed costs (development costs or costs for specific tooling), and transport costs if this is not included in the quotation. This amounts to the direct cost price of the product upon its reception, prior to quantitative and qualitative incoming inspection.

The *holding cost* is made up, on the one hand, of storage expenses, and on the other hand, of the creation of a financial asset that engenders financial costs. Storage costs are made up of the cost of managing the warehouse and storage equipment, warehouse staff costs, insurance premiums and various expenses such as lighting, heating and insurance. These storage expenses may vary or not depending on the nature and the quantity of the products stored. In addition, ownership of these products generates a financial asset which entails a cost that can be estimated in two main ways: through the average cost of the company's permanent resources (so-called 'cost of capital'), or through the expected rate of return on invested capital.

The TCO (inventory management plus financial asset) is expressed by a percentage (generally on a yearly basis), defined by finance management, which is applied to any average inventory value in order to calculate the actual storage cost. In total, the TCO of stock may represent between 15 per cent and 40 per cent of the value of this stock. In this way, stock to the value of €1 million, if the cost of ownership is 30 per cent, costs €300,000 per year.

For certain specific products, it is necessary to add the cost of obsolescence, of non-quality or possible deterioration. The greater the volume of stock, the higher the risk of obsolescence (dead or unused stock), and so the higher this cost. This cost is generally taken into account by an additional percentage combined with the previous one.[2]

As for the *ordering or replenishment cost*, this corresponds to all of the following internal operations: monitoring of inventory levels, issuing then following up the order, delivery reception operations, quantitative and qualitative inspections, then reception followed by checking and payment of the invoice. All these costs are largely independent from the size of the order, and they arise for every new order/delivery (except in the case of payments made periodically for cumulative delivered quantities).

9/1.1 Reminders on the main inventory-control systems

As already seen in Chapter 8, Section 8/4, two inventory-control principles prevail in the professional world: 1) 'reorder-point' systems, characterized – for a given reference – by two management parameters: the alert threshold and a fixed order quantity to be determined; and 2) 'periodic-replenishment' systems, characterized by two management parameters: the level of replenishment, and a fixed time interval between two orders to be determined.

The ways in which to determine the two parameters have already been presented. It is now time to show how the economic order quantity (EOQ) or economic order interval (EOI) is to be calculated (depending on the type of system chosen).

9/1.2 Calculation of the economic order quantity Q* (reorder-point system)

The economic quantity is the order quantity that minimizes the sum of acquisition costs and storage costs. If we only consider ownership and ordering costs, we see that this economic quantity results from a balancing of choices: ownership costs increase with the value, and therefore, with the quantity inventoried: to reduce them, small orders should be multiplied; on the other hand, supply costs increase with the number of orders placed and deliveries received: to reduce them, only large orders should be placed.

First of all, using simple hypotheses we will present the methodology for calculating the order quantity that minimizes the total cost of inventory and replenishment control for a single reference with a simple basic model. Our hypotheses are as follows:

- consumption is linear (basically constant per unit of time) and foreseeable with little scope for uncertainty;
- the delivery is received in one lot for every order placed;
- the purchasing cost is fixed whatever the quantity ordered (no discount on quantities – a hypothesis that we will explore later);
- the delivery lead-time is known and generally respected;
- we do not allow stock shortages.

These hypotheses are represented in Figure 9.1, where Q is the quantity ordered, and D the demand (here shown constant).

FIGURE 9.1   Simple economic quantity model (Wilson's model)

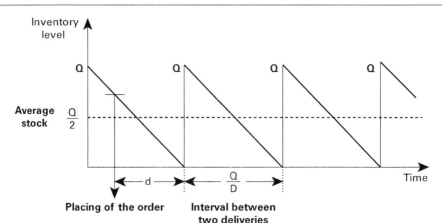

We note that the actual inventory level varies in a quasi-linear fashion between Q and 0. The average stock owned is Q/2. Let C be the unit cost of ownership, and let us initially assume that C does not depend on the quantity ordered. We therefore need to seek, if it exists, the minimum sum of the below costs depending on the quantity ordered:

Total ordering cost + total holding cost

These costs must be defined over one discrete time period, often a year, in such a way as to be easily reconstituted by the accounting system.

Calculation of the reordering cost

This is equal to the multiplication of the unit ordering cost (called L) and the number of orders placed. To satisfy a demand D during the period by resupplying Q quantities, it is necessary to place D/Q orders. Using our notations, the ordering cost over the period is therefore:

$$D/Q \times L$$

The evolution of this cost as a function of Q is represented in Figure 9.2. For example, if yearly consumption of an item is D = 100, and if we order Q = 25 units every time, we will place D/Q = 100/25: in other words, 4 orders on average over the year. If every order entails an ordering cost of L = €10, the ordering cost for the period considered (the year in our example) will be: D/Q × L = 100/25 × 10 = €40.

We see that this cost diminishes when Q increases: when Q = 100, it is equal to €10 (a single order over the year). On the other hand, when Q = 10, it is equal to €100 (10 orders over the year).

FIGURE 9.2   Total variable cost curve (Wilson's model)

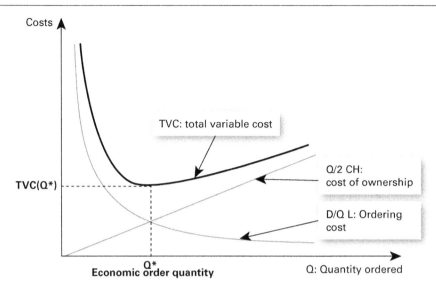

Calculation of the inventory holding cost

The average quantity in stock is Q/2; the average value of the stock carried is therefore Q/2 × C (C being the value per unit of the item). Let us designate as H the yearly rate of holding stock expressed as a percentage. The yearly total holding cost is expressed as:

Average quantity in stock × unit cost × holding cost, in other words Q/2 × C × H

For example, if we carry Q = 25, supposing that C is €100 and H is 25 per cent per year, then we find Q/2 × C × H = €312.50. The evolution of this cost depending on the value of Q is represented in Figure 9.2. It is linear and grows when Q increases: when Q = 100, the ownership cost is €1250, and when Q = 10, the ownership cost is €125.

Calculation of the total variable cost of supply (TVC)

Let's call the total variable cost of inventory management and replenishment the TVC: this is the sum of ordering and stock-holding costs (without discounts on the unit purchasing price; the yearly sum purchased on the other hand does not vary and therefore does not enter into the formula). Its analytical expression is therefore:

TVC = D/Q × L + Q/2 × C × H (here 40 + 312.50 = €452.50)

The total variable cost TVC is also represented by Figure 9.2. Let's note that it is essential for D and H to be defined coherently, in other words, for their values to be expressed *over the same unit of time*. In addition, the formula giving the TVC clearly shows the sum of two *competing* costs, the cost of ownership being proportional to Q whereas the launch cost varies in the opposite direction according to hyperbolic systems logic.

Determination of the economic order quantity Q*

The *economic quantity* is therefore the quantity of units ordered (at every delivery call or order) that leads to the minimum TVC. Expressed mathematically, we find Q* by deriving the TVC in relation to the variable Q:

$$(TVC) = CH/2 - (D/Q^2)L$$

Optimally, as the derivative is nil (the second derivative being positive, it is definitely a minimum), we determine the following formula following simplification:

$$Q^* = \sqrt{2DL/CH}$$

Optimally, the expression of the total variable cost is: $TVC^* = \sqrt{2DLCH}$.

Let's note that the minimum TVC is obtained when the holding cost is equal to the ordering cost. This is what stands out graphically in Figure 9.2. The formula giving Q* is universally known under the name of the *Wilson Model*. This economic quantity is therefore the quantity that should be ordered for this item in the case of a reorder-point system to minimize the total cost of inventory management.

9/1.3 Determination of the economic order interval N* (periodic-replenishment system)

In the case of a periodic-replenishment system, we look for an *economic periodicity* (or fixed interval between two orders). This may be inferred directly from the economic quantity, for the optimal number N* of orders to place corresponds to N* = D/Q*. It would also be possible to directly seek the optimal number of orders by expressing the total variable cost TVC as a function of N and deriving it:

$$TVC = N \times L + (D / 2.N) \times C \times H$$

The optimal number of orders thus corresponds to the formula:

$$N^* = \sqrt{DCH/2L}$$

This formula is important, for it indicates that the optimal frequency of supply (and of associated delivery) is proportional to the square root of the annual sum value of purchases (DC), with ordering and holding costs being the same whatever the product considered.

We have only considered the simplest inventory control model that (theoretically) allows us to evaluate the economic quantity, or economic interval, for a basic item, depending on whether its supply is steered by an order-point system or a periodic-replenishment system.

This economic parameter truly minimizes the item's *total* management costs. However, in a real-life situation, if forecast consumption is not constant, or if the inventory-replenishment lead-time is not perfectly respected, we have seen in Section 8/4 in the previous chapter that it is appropriate to budget for a safety stock at the same time. In this way, this *safety stock* generates an *additional storage cost* that should be added to the total cost determined above, for both types of inventory systems, to determine the total acquisition cost. We will see how to proceed later.

9/2 Minimization of acquisition costs via trade-offs with suppliers

For purchased items, given the reality of the professional world, several classic situations arise. Two of them can be justified via economic approaches that rely on collaborative strategies with suppliers or be intelligently integrated into the negotiation process: first of all, the potential existence of categories of items purchased from the same single supplier, opening up access to advantages from a possible grouping of orders in a single order and a single delivery; next, the possibility that the supplier offers discounts, reductions and rebates on the ex-works purchasing cost per unit depending on the quantities ordered (here, it is a matter of the order playing on a 'volume effect').

9/2.1 Pooling supplies from multi-item suppliers

It is common to reduce administrative or transport costs by pooling orders of several items from the one supplier on the same dates (and therefore, same delivery). We will now demonstrate, using calculations, how to determine the optimal number of pooled orders to place with a supplier. To pool the orders of n items, let's use the following notations:

- C_i, the unit cost of the item i (with i ranging from 1 to n articles);
- H, the joint holding cost (as a percentage);
- D_i, the demand for each item i;
- L, the cost of launching the *pooled order* (by definition lower than the sum of the unit costs of the orders if these were placed independently according to a separate management system for each reference);
- N, the number of pooled orders for the category of items considered;
- n, the number of different component parts pooled together.

The cost of a pooled order brings savings for two reasons: possible pooling – often less costly – of transport (on top of a better carbon print via the likely reduction of trips required),[3] and lower order management costs. As a matter of fact, all orders imply two sub-categories of costs: a) a *fixed cost*, whatever the number of items ordered or order lines, that corresponds to the administrative processing of the order, possible follow-up of the order, and processing of the post-delivery invoice; b) a *variable cost* (that depends on the number of items ordered and delivered at the same time) that includes the proportional costs of reception and storage-handling operations.

In this way, the cost of a pooled order (by convention always L) can generally be expressed in the following way:

$$L = Lf \text{ (fixed proportion)} + n\ Lv \text{ (variable proportion of the cost)}$$

where n is the number of item references ordered simultaneously.

If, in our model, our rationale is *transport neutral*, with the notations seen above, the total variable cost TVC can be expressed thus:

$$TVC = NL + \frac{H}{2N}\sum_{i=1}^{i=n}D_iC_i$$

and the optimal number N* of orders is then equal to:

$$N^* = \sqrt{\left(H\sum_{i=1}^{i=n}D_iC_i\right)2L}$$

In this item-grouping hypothesis, it is necessary to manage supply of all references by a *synchronized periodic-replenishment system*, guaranteeing the simultaneity of orders, according to this basic periodicity. In addition, it is necessary to determine, in parallel, the respective replenishment levels for all references in the group. Next, for each separate reference, the quantities to order during the pooled order are identified directly (at the order date) by calculation of the difference between the actual level of available stock and the relevant pre-calculated replenishment level.

For example, let's take the case of a company that supplies a series of seven spare parts (differently-sized valves) presented in Table 9.1 and purchased from one manufacturer. The table lists, for every reference, its unit value and its annual consumption forecast. The cumulative yearly value of consumption comes to €2,607,500.

TABLE 9.1   List of spare parts: consumption and value

Elementary references	Annual consumption (units)	Unit value (€)	Annual consumption value (€)
AO518	358	3,500	1,225,000
AO525	200	5,000	1,000,000
XT623	75	2,500	187,500
XT454	350	100	35,000
XT578	25	2,000	50,000
PV211	100	170	17,000
PV212	62	1,500	93,000

In this case, the ordering cost per unit is €150 and the cost of holding stock is 20 per cent per year of the purchasing cost. We have also calculated that fixed ordering costs represent around €100 whereas the marginal cost per order line is around €0.50 (this cost mainly corresponds to the reception inspection depending on the order lines).

If we calculate, using the simple Wilson Model, for each of the references, *considered independently of the others*, its economic order periodicity with its corresponding total management cost (taking €150 as the unit cost of an order), we come up with the results shown in Table 9.2, which would entail a total management cost for the category of €26,227 per year.

TABLE 9.2 Total cost of spare parts

References	Optimal number of orders per year (N*)	Total variable cost (€/year)
AO518	28.58	8,573.21
AO525	25.82	7,745.97
XT623	11.18	3,354.10
XT454	4.83	1,449.14
XT578	5.77	1,732.05
PV211	3.37	1,009.95
PV212	7.87	2,362.20
Total		26,227.00

We observe, without any great surprise, that the economic periodicities (column 2) do not guarantee the simultaneity of orders, and that they are higher when consumption values are higher.

If we decide to pool their supply by applying the pooling model seen above, we find that the joint periodicity should be N* = 24.07, in other words around one order every two weeks worked, with a yearly TVC = €21,664 (in other words savings of 18 per cent) according to the formula:

$$TVC = N \times (100 + 7 \times 50) + (20\% / 2 \times 7) \times 2,607,500$$

This cost does not include the cumulative yearly total purchasing cost of the references (€2,607,500), which, if taken into account, would give the yearly *total acquisition cost*. Another important point to observe is that this joint periodicity is very close to those of the references whose consumption values are the highest (in the independent management scenario seen above). Hence the following idea: it would be possible to further improve on this result by operating in the following manner:

- defining a sub-category of n leading references, for example, in this case the first two references AO518 and AO525, representing around 85 per cent of the total consumption value between themselves (new application of Pareto's Law!);

- calculating the joint periodicity of these two references (here, N* = 33.35), with these two references generating a *basic order*;

- then calculating for the other references, taken in *decreasing* order of consumption value, whether it is worthwhile ordering them with every basic order, or else once out of every two orders, or else once out of every three orders, etc, depending on the costs engendered (*on condition, therefore, that their own periodicities are all fractions of the basic periodicity*).

According to this reasoning, we find that it would be necessary to order the following (the reader is invited to check the calculation):

- XT623 and PV212 every *two* basic orders;
- XT578 every *three* basic orders;
- and XT454 and PV211 every *four* basic orders.

The total cost for the category would then be €19,154.41, in other words allowing savings of 37 per cent compared with independent management (*an additional marginal gain of 12 per cent* compared with total pooling with imposition of a single joint period). In this last scenario, the supplier would receive, around every two weeks worked, one pooled order, which would not include seven order lines every time, but at least two.

The economic stakes may therefore be considerable. But this approach can only be generalized if buyers have operated intelligently upstream, by reducing the number of suppliers, and sourcing generalist suppliers (offering multiple items) enabling a concentration of volumes, that allows for the consolidation of orders, a consequential increase in the volume of turnover carried out with each supplier, and hence improvement of the company's negotiation position. The additional savings calculated above result almost entirely from the action of a buyer who sets up the appropriate conditions: in this case, the supply planner merely takes advantage of the situation created, outside of his or her strict scope of responsibility which is more geared towards implementing the decision.

9/2.2 Taking advantage of large orders via supplier proposals

In order to increase their sales and cut their inventory management costs (ie the costs of setting up manufacturing or preparing client orders), it is possible for suppliers to grant discounts when orders received exceed a certain quantity threshold. They may even offer reductions that increase when the order size grows. In fact, three types of offers commonly exist:

- the supplier offers a *yearly rebate* on the basis of a *cumulative* total turnover carried out with the client, in the form of an end-of-year rebate;[4]
- the supplier offers an *unvarying discount for each order*, that is, a reduction in the sales unit price when the quantities ordered exceed a certain threshold, and that applies to *all the quantities* delivered;
- the supplier offers a *discount exclusively on the marginal quantity* above a predetermined quantity threshold, ie the first n units are always paid at the basic rate, and *only those that exceed* the threshold quantity are eligible for the discount. In this case they are termed *incremental discounts*.

This last commercial proposal is more complex to break down into calculations; we have chosen not to go into this in this book, and will focus instead on the issue of uniform discounts.

The question that the buyer must answer is the following: is the sum of inventory management and supply costs (that we refer to as TVC) *and* purchasing costs reduced if the supplier's offer is accepted? The answer is obvious in the two following cases: 1) the economic order quantity calculated by the Wilson Model with the basic price exceeds the threshold set for the discount: as the new economic quantity is higher (Q* varies in the opposite direction to C), it will exceed the threshold even more, and we will come out as winners both in terms of the TVC (as C diminishes) and the product's purchasing cost (equal to the cost multiplied by the demand – in other words DC); 2) the new economic quantity brings us over the discount threshold, and here we are also winners in terms of the total variable cost and the purchasing cost of items.

However, if the new economic quantity *does not reach* the discount threshold, it is necessary to compare the total minimum costs obtained, on the one hand, with the old price (without a discount), and on the other hand, with the new purchasing cost per unit (including the discount). Figure 9.3, in which we have called C_1 and C_2 the unit costs with and without discounts, TVC_1 and TVC_2 the corresponding total variable costs, and R the discount threshold, indicates that the minimum TVC_2 compatible with the discount is obtained when Q = R.

It should be understood that the TVC_1 curve corresponding to the unit cost C_1 is only valid for the interval of quantities '0 – R' and that, on the other hand, the TVC_2 curve corresponding to C_2 is valid for the interval 'R – ∞'. We see that the minimum of the TVC cost for curve 1 corresponds to $Q_1{}^*$, while the minimum for curve 2 is necessarily reached for an order quantity equal to the discount threshold R (TVC-type curves necessarily having only a single minimum).

We should therefore compare the respective values of TVC_1 and TVC_2, in other words, using the same notation as before, giving:

$$TVC_1 = (Q_1{}^* / 2) \, C_1 H + (D / Q_1{}^*) \, L + C_1 \, D$$

$$TVC_2 = (R / 2) \, C_2 H + (D / R) \, L + C_2 \, D$$

FIGURE 9.3 Determination of the economic quantity with a discount threshold

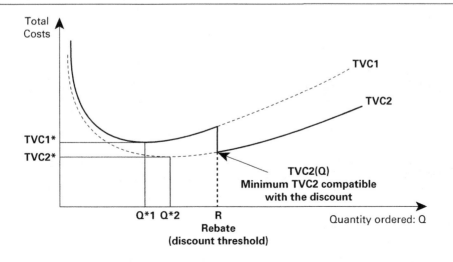

It is necessary for us to choose the lowest value. Naturally, if $TVC_2 (Q = R)$ were lower than TVC_1*, it would not have been useful to consider purchasing costs to make the decision. In short, in a situation with a discount on quantity, reduction of the product's unit cost has three consequences for the total cost:

- the purchasing cost DC diminishes as the unit purchasing cost C is lower;
- the ordering cost $(D / Q) \times L$ also diminishes as the economic quantity increases, bringing down the number of orders;
- finally, the holding cost $(Q / 2) \times C \times H$ is modified without us being able to tell in which direction: indeed, the diminishing of the unit cost C tends to bring it down, but increase of the economic quantity tends to increase it.

The problem would not be changed in any way if we were dealing with several discount thresholds: in this case, several total costs in the form of TVCs would need to be compared in order to validly decide between them.

For example: let's consider Sound Import, a buyer of Chinese electronic equipment purchased from a European importer. These devices are used as loyalty bonuses for the company's main sales activity. Let's focus on a small camcorder model, for which yearly purchases total 1,000 units, evenly spread out over 250 working days. To simplify, let's hypothesize that consumption of the camcorders is more or less constant. The basic price of the importer is €100. The pre-calculated yearly cost of ownership of a camcorder in stock, notated as CH, is €18 (for the holding rate is 18 per cent per year). The management cost of an order (notated L) is €100.

However, in order to encourage buyers to buy less frequently but in larger quantities, the importer offers the volume-discount rate in Table 9.3 (price delivered to the store, excluding VAT). It is necessary to determine the optimal order quantity and the minimum ordering and storage costs.

TABLE 9.3   Spare parts: volume discount prices

Quantity ordered	Unit price (€)
from 1 to 99	100
from 100 to 249	90
250 and over	75

Without any discount, for a unit cost C_1 of €100, the economic order quantity is $Q_1* = 105$ to the closest round figure, for a total cost including the purchase turnover of $TVC_1 = €101,897$. Let's now evaluate the total costs of each of the other two solutions, after first calculating the respective economic quantities for the other two costs C_2 (€90) and C_3 (€75). This calculation gives the following (closest round figures): $Q_2* = 111$ and $Q_3* = 122$.

As the quantities are both lower than the discount thresholds, it is relevant to compare, with the initial solution, only the respective total costs for the two ordering quantities 150 and 250. The respective results are evaluated by applying the generic reference model already seen:

$$TVC_i = (R / 2) C_iH + (D / R) L + C_i D$$

which, here, gives $TVC_2 = €91,882$, and $TVC_3 = €77,087.50$: the new economic order quantity is therefore 250 units.

In general cases, one specific point nevertheless merits attention: it is possible that the calculation may call up a new economic quantity that is *very high compared to forecast consumption*, covering, for example, several months of activity (here, 250 items ordered represents average consumption over three months). This may create risk if users have reason to change their items without necessarily being able to anti-cipate changes, namely for sales reasons. We then risk finding ourselves with unsold and unusable camcorders (whereas orders in batches of 100 would allow a low coverage rate and an extremely minimized risk of overstock). Therefore, in all cases, the buyer should present this alternative explicitly to the internal client when making a decision with a three-dimensional assessment of costs/advantages/risks.

A general lesson can be drawn by buyers: usually, gains of this type may be extremely significant, and the key condition for leading a supplier to make offers in this direction is to have a firm grasp of the latter's internal processes, by having a good idea of the supplier's cost structures, as well as fixed manufacturing set-up and delivery-preparation costs. Such gains are not obtained via 'aggressive' negotiation with the supplier (targeting directly to diminish the latter's gross margin) but thanks to an approach enabling the latter to lower costs that are then carried over to the client (partially at least): this is the basis of a 'win–win' relationship.

9/2.3 Improving the responsiveness of suppliers

Improving reactivity is a matter of aiming to reduce lead-times. Two objectives are thus usually sought: *client-service level*: enabling the internal client to have a *more flexible* management (following consumption more efficiently, having the means to forecast needs over a shorter horizon, etc); *investment in stock*: via the shortening of the cycle, it is also possible to globally lower the level of cyclical or safety stock through an auto-induced effect (indeed, the average inventory level is quasi-proportional to the supplier's lead-time, and any safety stock will be reduced in volume, the shorter the average period and standard deviation).

As a result, it is crucial to look to minimize these lead-times and to secure them. The supplier, if sufficiently mature, can be entrusted with responsibility over up-stream inventory management, or even be led to deploy a genuine 'just-in-time'-type approach. If, on the other hand, the supplier's capability level is low, we can envisage having the latter organize stock and being in charge of replenishing it, according to contractual obligations.

Constitution of contractual stock by suppliers

In the event that the supplier is not ready to deploy a plan to improve lead-times (often the case with small or medium-sized companies), we must accept the composi-tion of stocks and of end-products from the supplier's perspective; and determine them accordingly, taking into account the supplier's limitations regarding flexibility, with stocks maintained at a jointly decided predetermined 'target' level. Proceeding in this way protects the client company from the supplier's operational constraints, while guaranteeing short lead-times. It is appropriate to verify whether, overall, the company comes out a winner financially (by weighing up savings on the cost of managing the inventory internally, against any increases in the prices of the supplier who potentially marks up prices as a result of extra financial costs). At the same time, three actions can be undertaken:

- providing the supplier with a forecast of planned requirements (delivery schedule over a horizon to be decided on jointly), offering the supplier a certain visibility;
- defining in parallel with the supplier a gradual stock-reduction plan, resulting from actions aimed at improving responsiveness structurally and sustainably (collaborative logic that involves supporting this supplier in the improvement of methods);
- placing even more responsibility on the supplier via the performance commitment, endeavouring to deploy a vendor-managed inventory (VMI).

Possible deployment of the vendor-managed inventory (VMI)

In this solution, suppliers are called to *take over direct responsibility* for replenishing stocks of end-products situated physically on their own premises or on their clients' premises. This is a matter of supplying warehouses whilst following management rules defined in advance in the purchase contract: in doing so, we create an *operational collaboration* relationship with suppliers by adding a logistical dimension to contracts. The VMI is thus the basis for continuing replenishment of the warehouses and stores of major retailers, but it may also apply upstream along the supply chain for industrial companies.

The system unfolds in five main phases (see Figure 9.4):

- Phase 1: the company's IT system delivers to its internal clients.
- Phase 2: the platform sends information to the supplier daily on products (accumulation of quantities delivered for each item).
- Phase 3: with knowledge about the platform's inventory as well as its outflows, the supplier can determine an optimal replenishment (before carrying this out, the supplier asks for the client's confirmation by addressing a 'delivery proposal' to the latter).
- Phase 4: most of the time the client confirms the delivery.
- Phase 5: the supplier delivers the proposed quantities.

The aim of the system is to supply warehouses and/or stores according to management rules defined in a collaboration contract between the company and its supplier. The VMI has the following objectives and results: anticipation of the clients' requirements through monitoring of their consumption; reduction of stock shortages to improve the service rate; lowering inventory levels in warehouses (of both the company and the supplier) to cut costs over the whole of the upstream supply chain;

FIGURE 9.4 The operational principle of the VMI

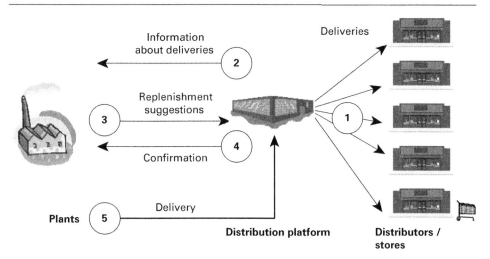

optimizing truckloads or reaching delivery minimums; and improving management of the upstream supply chain by integrating an approach where flow is 'pulled' by real consumption.

In this system, stock may be physically located on the supplier's premises, or on the client's (even if it is on consignment and remains the supplier's property until outflows of stock establish the transfer of property and trigger invoicing).

Improvement of the logistical interface between suppliers and the company

The logistical interface and the issue of transport constitute the last points to be analysed. There is no use for a supplier to manufacture product quickly if the delivery then has to sit for several days (or even far longer) in some form of transport vehicle, then in a depot or sub-depot system, prior to being delivered to the client. The transport and physical distribution system should also be transformed in order to contribute to the acceleration of cycles and the reduction of in-process delivery and stock.

Today, there are various trends in company upstream and downstream transport and distribution: the restructuring of storage systems (reduction of the number of levels, setting up platforms rather than warehouses); for road transport, the restructuring of vehicle fleets that sometimes become unsuitable (due to a change in the quantities transported and the frequency of deliveries); and finally, partial subcontracting or full outsourcing of this function to service-provider companies that have widened their range of services (transport, storage, order preparation, inventory management, even minor pre-manufacturing operations).

Regarding upstream supply, three approaches are possible.

If the supplier approves of the measure in the context of its own strategic analysis, with the client's agreement, the supplier may decide to set up its plant or an *offsite workshop in the immediate vicinity* of that of its client, or as a cluster within the client's plant. Such a development should be economically justified by the volume of activity and the duration of the collaboration, and enable a return on investment (ROI to be assessed).

The second solution relies on the principle of a warehouse or *platform* that interfaces with the client company. From the company's perspective, this platform physically concentrates flows coming from various suppliers (eg with large deliveries carried out by full trucks), combining them at a delivery point (cross-docking principle) and then redistributing them to production or distribution units via a transport terminal. This structure, as a concentration point, allows optimization of preparation costs incurred from the various suppliers in question.

The third possibility consists in *playing on the 'transport' variable*. In this way, by grouping suppliers 'regionally', the company can take charge of organizing and managing the upstream transport system (whether it does this by itself, or much more commonly by outsourcing responsibility to external service-providers). By proceeding thus, the company can opt for a more efficient and economic organizational mode.

One technique consists in the setting up of joint solutions such as the organization of *collection rounds* to various suppliers (often called the 'milk run'). In this case, the company purchases products from suppliers at ex-works prices, and at the same time, it purchases the logistics service separately. This service purchase is often preferable to an integrated transport service: the company can take advantage of specialist skills, and from an economic standpoint, variabilize transport costs, which offers flexibility and minimizes financial risks without locking up long-term capital.

In conclusion, buyers and logisticians are, here, necessarily joint decision-makers on the main options. The role of buyers in particular is to play an active role in finding outsourcing solutions and in the actual purchase of transport and/or storage services.

9/3 Minimization of the TCO (total cost of ownership) in global sourcing choices

In Chapter 5, we elaborated on the utility and strategic importance of international deployment of procurement. If we source internationally by choosing a supplier established in a given country, we in fact choose (or effectively 'predetermine') an upstream supply chain, with its main characteristics and associated cost structure.

Chapter 2 was an opportunity for us to provide an exhaustive list of the numerous risks encountered in procurement strategies, justifying the setting up of prevention or mitigation measures. Such measures engender costs (most often fixed and recurrent), according to an 'insurance premium' logic in relation to the sourcing solution implemented, which must be taken into account objectively when costing any procurement decision.

Finally, the gradual deployment of sustainable procurement, mentioned in Chapter 6, ie on the environmental front, entails certain savings (eg control over certain types of consumption), but also costs relating to management of the end-of-life of products and purchased materials.

All this implies that a major decision is to be made by procurement departments: choosing, as the single (and only relevant) economic criterion in decisions, the TCO. This decision-making criterion is all the more relevant for 'critical' or 'strategic' procurement if carried out 'long distance', for example, in a new developing country – a situation where strict ex-works purchasing costs do not make much sense. Table 9.4 presents the major elements.

Utilization of this concept of cost is the only way to give the top management a clear overview of the actual economic impacts of any acquisition process, namely by highlighting the impact on short- and medium-term cash flow as well as 'true' financial value creation. Finally, the breakdown of this global cost helps to underline the major cost determinants, with the different responsibility centres that have an impact on global performance. This is therefore an excellent management tool.

Referring to Table 9.4, let's go back to international sourcing, most often 'long-distance' procurement from a remote developing country (eg Asia, including Japan, the Indian subcontinent, Eastern Europe, Central and South America) – a situation that gives rise to the following main characteristics:

- The choice of a country, with its logistical and transport infrastructures, its customs and regulatory procedures, entailing costs and risks relating to fluctuating lead-times (independent of the supplier's processing times in the strict sense).

- The choice of a country integrated in a given monetary zone, entailing risks on exchange rates when we no longer work in the Eurozone (in the case of a European buyer).

- Payment conditions most often specific to certain countries (or certain suppliers) that may be unfavourable for the buyer (eg cash settlement, or payment with a cost-generating letter of credit).

- A geographical location that entails choice of an intercontinental mode of transport (air versus sea) within a long or short lead-time, for which respective logistical costs must be compared whilst taking into account the effect made on in-process deliveries and stocks structurally linked to the situation.[5]

- The choice of a supplier who may present risks in terms of quality and fluctuating lead-times (added to possible variations in cycles strictly linked to the return transport seen above), often entailing the setting up of generally greater safety stocks than in the case of a domestic or local solution, or even the necessary intervention of quality-audit service companies set up locally and operating on the client's behalf.

- Customary supplier practices in terms of production planning, that themselves may generate higher volumes of manufacturing in-process than a domestic solution: for example, by only accepting considerable volumes with deliveries at low frequencies, the purchasing company needs to launch orders on the basis of forecasts over long time periods (rather than in 'pull' mode allowing great reactivity).

TABLE 9.4 Breakdown of the total cost of ownership (TCO)

Determinants	Cost items (detailed description)
Purchasing cost (in the strict sense)	Supplier's sales price (ex-works price)
	Upstream administrative cost of the purchase (sourcing, qualification audits, RFI, RFP, RFQ) *Cost to amortize on procured volumes*
	Non-recurrent fixed cost (studies, tooling, industrialization, setup) *Cost to amortize on procured volumes*
	Costs induced by the main purchase (licenses, contract amendments, developments, services, etc.) *Depending on the type of purchase*
	Spare parts (outside of guarantee – CAPEX purchases)
	Supplier's payment conditions
Logistical cost of supply	Logistical delivery cost (transport, handling, external warehousing)
	Payment of forwarding agents & service providers (all protagonists)
	Insurance and payment guarantees
	Cost of storage (cyclical stock & in-progress deliveries with impact on WCR)
	Cost of management of supplies / deliveries (delivery schedules and calls, reminders, cost of the information system)
	Cost of reception (handling, quality inspection)
Risk coverage	Protection from exchange rates (depending on the currency in the contract)
	Storage cost (safety stock for coverage of fluctuating lead times / non-quality)
	Local specific technical support (e.g. quality-assurance in the case of sourcing LCCs)
	Processing of non-quality operations (client returns, supplier returns, disputes, repairs, replacements)
	Cost of production shutdowns or rescheduling (following delivery delays, supply-chain dysfunctions)
End-of-life costs	Recycling of end-of-life products (cost of reverse logistics)
	Reprocessing of products
	Administrative cost of end-of-life management
	Cost of environmental rehabilitation
	Resale or re-use value (cost offset by associated saving)

All these characteristics typical of situations where sourcing takes place in remote emerging countries are themselves generators of additional costs beyond strict ex-works purchasing costs, including the following main elements:

- the cost of transport (depending on the selected mode), including pre-carriage, the main form of transport and post-carriage; as well as remuneration of forwarding agents to whom all customs and regulatory procedures can be delegated (a solution favoured by Western buyers);
- financial impact on the WCR due to in-process deliveries and average cyclical stocks (directly proportional to the different replenishment cycles);
- similarly, financial impact of safety stock set up (to cost according to the service-level rate chosen to face the various hazards affecting lead-times and the non-conformity of certain deliveries);
- remuneration of auditing, supplier qualification or quality-control companies, or even other local backup structures operating on the company's behalf;
- protection against exchange rate differentials (if relevant) depending on the monetary zone and the transaction currency, and the securing of payment procedures;
- finally, sometimes customs fees upon reception, or all other types of import or export taxes depending on the country of origin.

To illustrate the economic impact of such a situation, let's take a real-life example, which we simplify here, and which is interesting on a methodological level as it is entirely costed. The e-commerce company ToolExpert is physically located in the suburbs of Paris (its storage site, in any case): it is specialized in the sale of large-scale tools and electrical equipment for home repairs and gardening.

Many pieces of equipment featured in its catalogue are produced in China, representing yearly traffic of around 50 tons, with ex-works purchasing prices totalling €1,200,000 (in our example we neutralize all questions relating to the currency by transposing all data into euros).

Upon the arrival of a new head at the helm of the procurement and supply chain department (and his participation in an HEC Paris executive-training course), the top management agreed to make a comprehensive diagnostic of the logistics of importing products from China, to reconstitute a TCO over one year that is as realistic as possible, in order to tackle the key question of the system's continuity and responsiveness. A final detail to note is that the quality produced by the suppliers fluctuates, which entails management costs, and sometimes upsets relationships with certain final customers (giving rise to returns and exchanges).

9/3.1 Transport alternative: sea or air

For such sourcing schemes, the trade-off is simple: should we favour maritime transport (sea container) or is it preferable to use air transport (air freight)? In the case of ToolExpert, the practice used at the time of the analysis was maritime transport.[6] Figure 9.5 depicts the upstream supply chain in a simplified form.

Sea (container ship)

This solution involves ordering and receiving around 10 deliveries per year by standard 5-tonne sea containers according to the following arrangements: pre-carriage by truck between the plant in central China and the port of Shanghai (cost of around €485), then main transport by ship (billed €0.40 per kilo), finally arrival at the port of Le Havre with post-carriage via the A13 highway to a warehouse in the suburbs of Paris (cost of around €560). In addition, in a container, products need to be packaged into 52-kg parcels (costing €25 per parcel). The cost of insurance comes to €0.25 per kilo.

The total cumulative time period from the Chinese plant up to the warehouse in France represents an average of 60 days (ie the total supply cycle, objectively measured).

FIGURE 9.5 The logistical system from China to France

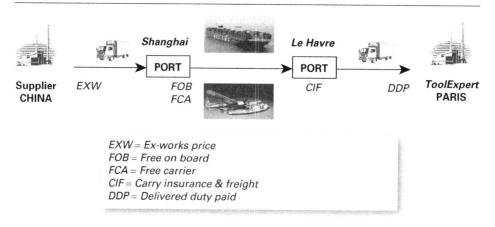

EXW = Ex-works price
FOB = Free on board
FCA = Free carrier
CIF = Carry insurance & freight
DDP = Delivered duty paid

Air (cargo plane)

The air option would enable the frequency of deliveries to be increased whilst reducing the size of orders (30 air containers of only 1,660 kg) and the average total lead-time would drop to 8 days on the basis of comparisons obtained from colleagues in the industry. For these dispatches, air freight would be billed at €1.70 per kilo, to which would be added transport upstream (€200) and downstream (€150) per container, packaging (€0.50 per 10-kg package) and transport insurance (€350 per container).

Obviously, whatever the transport mode, supply cycles vary in non-negligible ways. Analysis shows that we can make the hypothesis of a normal distribution-type variation with standard deviations of respectively 10 days and 3 days by ship and by plane.

Apart from the VAT to pay upon entrance in France (not relevant to this example as it is fiscal in nature), duties imposed by the customs administration for this type of product coming from China are 5 per cent and calculated on the CIF (cost, insurance and freight) value.

In addition, internal analysis ascertained the following points: the fixed cost of ordering and administrative management for a delivery is estimated at €60. When required for costing, the company applies a stock ownership rate of 25 per cent per year, broken down into financial holding costs (14 per cent per year) and handling and management expenses (11 per cent per year). At the time of the analysis (use of the shipping method), an average stock was held by the Chinese supplier for 20 days.

As for the problem of the supplier's fairly frequent non-compliance, to deal definitively with this issue and upon the advice of a colleague, at the time the problem arose, a decision was made to call upon a local audit and quality-control company, guaranteeing quality at the departure point before the loading of goods onto the container. This company's services are invoiced in the form of a commission of 4.5 per cent of the purchased amount on the basis of the ex-works price.

In these conditions, what is the true comparative TCO of the two transport modes for ToolExpert, and which more qualitative criteria can (should) be integrated in this decision?

9/3.2 Comparative costing of the TCO by boat and plane

Let's consider the real-life context with the help of Figure 9.5. It follows the same logic for each mode of transport, and the three main segments are shown with the four main Incoterms® that apply here, useful 'transit points' in the costing of the two solutions, for certain costs are assessed on the basis of products' value that varies depending on their *physical positions* in the export, then import flows.

Moreover, in this case we have three cost subassemblies: those directly related to expediting and transport, those relating to the financial impact of work-in-process stock and orders on the WCR, and those relating to the securing of the upstream supply chain.

Expediting cost

To the costing data at our disposal, we add customs expenses and all costs relating to transport. Note that (for the purposes of simplification) we have not introduced into the example any costs relating to the remuneration of possible forwarding agents. Given the frequency of dispatch for the two modes, the relevant costs are uniform over the year, totalling €130,050 by ship and €173,600 by plane.

The total annual dispatch cost does not include the number of products purchased and invoiced itself, in other words €1.2 million.

Cost of inventories and impact on the WCR

The second calculation relates to the assessment of ex-works stock, in-progress orders in the process of transport and arrival, with the costing of annual costs for the two solutions, which merits a few comments.

First of all, all stock can be assessed in terms of days and then translated into quantities by the use of a parameter that is the 'average daily flow transported' equal to 140 kg per day (obtained by dividing the 50 yearly tons by the number of days in the year).

The ex-works stock at the Chinese supplier is made up of an average cyclical stock, to which is added a small safety margin. Taking the example of the ship, as a container has a 5-ton capacity, the maximum stock at departure is 5,000 kg, and the average stock is 2,500 kg – in other words 18 days – increased to 20 days, thus including 2 days to secure its manufacturing process. Meanwhile, the average stock of the air freight option is equal to 6 + 2 days (the security margin is in theory identical, as it is independent of the mode of transport selected).

Calculation of orders in the process of transport does not require any particular comment: account is taken of the duration of transport multiplied by the average flow per day.

Upon arrival in France, average cyclical stocks in the ToolExpert warehouses are the same (depending on the respective size of containers). However, safety stock should be calculated to ensure the expected service rate of 95 per cent, taking into account fluctuations in the possible respective transport times.

We recall that the number of flights is triple the number of ship passages, and that as a result, a service rate by plane of 98.5 per cent is necessary to have the equivalent protection by ship, set at 95 per cent at the time (3 flights needing to be combined successively for a single ship passage, for $0.985^3 = 0.95$). The term 'safety coefficient' corresponds to the number of standard deviations to be taken into account in each option.

TABLE 9.5   Calculation of cost of inventory

Start stock	20 days 2,800 kg	8 days 1,120 kg
Stock in transit	60 days 8,400 kg	8 days 1,120 kg
Arrival cyclical stock	2,500 kg	833 kg
Service-level target	95%	98.3%
Safety coefficient	1.64	2.12
Safety stock	2,310 kg	900 kg
Arrival stock	4,810 kg	1,733 kg
Total stock	16,080 kg	3,990 kg
Value start stock (EXW)	€67,200	€26,880
Value stock in transit (FOB)	€206,470	€27,070
Value arrival stock (DDP)	€127,950	€47,610
Value stock in warehouse (subtotal)	€195,150	€74,490
Total stock value	**€401,620**	**€101,560**
Cost of stock in warehouse (25%)	€48,788	€18,623
Cost of stock in transit (14%)	€28,906	€3,790
Total annual stock cost	**€77,693**	**€22,412**
/kg	€1.55	€0.45

Next, the costing of different stocks is easily achieved, taking note of just one important point: start and arrival stocks are valued at 25 per cent (for they are managed inside a warehouse) with alignment of the Chinese supplier's stock costs with ToolExpert (in the absence of reliable data, which would need to be validated and which would also probably be false), whereas 'in-process' stock along the transport phase should only be valued at 14 per cent (the figure is in relation to the financial asset only, as 'on board' storage on the means of transport does not engender any marginal management cost, but is included in the transporter's price).

Management and securing costs

We are left with all other costs including all cost items already mentioned, administrative in nature (order management) or related to protection against quality risks (remuneration of the local backup quality-assurance structure). So-called 'commercial' safety stock (set at one month at the request of the sales department) was considered as additional stock, placed at the disposal of the sales department, without any further calculations and on an internal 'contractual'-type basis.

If we calculate total acquisition and ownership costs compared over the year (taking into account the €1,200,000 ex-works value as well), we arrive at the following figures: container ship: €1,491,353/cargo plane: €1,480,768 – in other words, a respective unit cost of €29.83 and €29.62 per kilo.

To put it another way, air and sea freight cost exactly the same! There is a difference of around €10,585 on a yearly basis. In addition, we see that in both cases, if we evaluate the DDP unit costs with delivery to the Paris suburbs, they are respectively €29.83 and €29.62 for the sea and air alternatives.

This means that the two methods are of equal cost, and that the supply chain and risk protection represent a surplus of around €5.70 per kilo on average for an ex-works purchasing cost of €24 per kilo. Taken independently, these options undoubtedly remain competitive compared with sourcing in Europe, from a strictly economic point of view. However, two other factors should be taken into account, no doubt very significant for senior management and the marketing department.

9/3.3 Marketing insights and carbon footprint

As the demand for electric tooling on the European market fluctuates, and therefore is quite difficult to anticipate in terms of *itemized units*, salespeople (the buyer's clients) would no doubt appreciate a highly reactive solution, capable of reconstituting a good *mix of products* in stock within a tight deadline. More precisely, an estimated 10 per cent or so of sales opportunities lost over a year is due to *incomplete* stock. Given an average unit sales price within the network of €55, the resulting loss in gross margin is around €140,445 per year, according to the following calculation: $(55 - 29.72) \times 50,000 / 9$.

In addition, as the supplier cycle already lasts four weeks (in other words, around 30 days), if 60 cycle days are added for the shipping option, we must accept and endure a total cycle of at least three months. This is not compatible with the response times required by an extremely volatile, and relatively unpredictable, market. From this perspective, for salespeople, the air freight option is by far *preferable for its responsiveness and flexibility.*

That said, if we calculate the carbon footprint of both solutions on the basis of the number of yearly trips (all things being equal in other respects), given the average distances of both trips, with emission rates for the boat and the plane being 10 g CO_2/ton and 500 g CO_2/ton per kilometre respectively, *the plane pollutes 34 times more* for the China–France trip, emitting a total of 238 tons per year compared with only 7 tons in the case of the ship (figures calculated from to the emission standards available from ADEME, the French Environment and Energy Management Agency).

9/3.4 Summary assessment: final decision

So what recommendation should be made to top managers by supplier chain managers and buyers thinking 'corporate strategy'? In our opinion, it is up to the buyer to lead reflection on this matter, as the manager of external resources (the supply chain manager here being only the operational executor of the decision). And the choice seems quite limited, in the form of two solutions:

1 Endeavouring to find or develop a *geographically closer source* (why not Western or Eastern Europe, or a country such as Turkey, or in the Maghreb region?), undoubtedly more costly in terms of the ex-works price, but likely to be able to offer just-in-time operation, with weekly deliveries, largely reducing the WCR as a result, with better tracking of actual sales and an acceptable carbon print.

2 Keeping the *Chinese supplier*, but using a *mixed transport approach*, more favourable in terms of flexibility and from an environmental point of view (a hypothesis to test amongst others):

   – for *products with a high sales volume* from the range whose sales forecast is the most reliable, operating by anticipation on the basis of the forecast and using the cleaner shipping option;

   – and for *products with more erratic sales* (or even for hand peaks in demand for other products), operating in reaction to 'urgent' demands (with tight deadlines) by using the air freight option.

This implies that the supplier should have the ability to handle this *differentiated management* of its production. An opportunity to test sustainable partnership?

In all cases, making generalizations from this example, environmental performance can always be highlighted, and become a marketing-type argument if the market is likely to be sensitive to this factor. This can then become a differentiation element compared to competitors.

The buyer should be capable of studying this type of feasibility directly with marketers and senior management, without losing sight, every time, of the overall cost, supplemented in this example by impacts on sales. The true criterion for the decision thus becomes *maximization of the operational margin and value creation* (apart from structural costs).

9/4 Keeping a high service level via safety stock

Safety stock is stock that should be kept permanently in order to cover any consumption higher than the forecast quantity for a given period according to a preliminarily defined service level. This deviation in consumption is common as forecasts are rarely accurate. Indeed, all inventory-control systems have to face risks of different types: actual consumption differing from the forecasted demand; the supplier's delivery lead-time turning out to be longer than expected; a lower quantity delivered than ordered (partial delivery or problems of non-conformity). The existence of one or several of these risks means that the product's availability over a given horizon may be problematic. If we wish to limit interruptions to delivery, we should foresee the holding of *safety* stock (abbreviated hereafter as *Ss*).

If the level of the safety stock is high, the product's availability increases to meet the demand. But increasing the safety-stock level amounts to increasing the total holding costs. These costs may be particularly significant in the case of products with short lifecycles, often associated with volatile demand (and hence a necessity for a higher safety stock!). In addition, safety stock can also suddenly become obsolete if a new and more attractive or higher-performance substitution product arrives on the market.

The safety-stock level is determined by the use of different methods, but it is mainly based on the two following elements: the nature and importance of the risks characterizing demand and/or the replenishment lead-time, as well as the level of service that we wish to offer the client. In addition, the size of the necessary safety stock also depends on the inventory-control system (reorder-point or periodic-replenishment) that is adopted.

9/4.1 Service level, shortage costs and safety stock

To present this problematic clearly, we first need to mention the possible different approaches to determining safety stock.

In the event that calculation of the safety stock is carried out on the basis of the risks affecting demand and/or the replenishment lead-time, it is important to characterize the probability distribution of the random variable (demand and/or replenishment lead-time). In the event that calculation of the safety stock is carried out on the basis of the level of client service, we then undertake economic analysis of the costs of storage, ordering and *shortage* (Figure 9.6).

Two major types of approaches co-exist and the basic question remains: which one should be chosen?

Shortage-cost approach

If a *unit shortage cost* can be defined fairly accurately, then it is possible to rely on an economic reasoning (similar to those seen above) that includes in the total cost of acquisition a formulation of the *mathematical expectation of the total cost of shortage* over the calculation period. However, it is often still very difficult to

FIGURE 9.6   Alternative method for determining safety stock

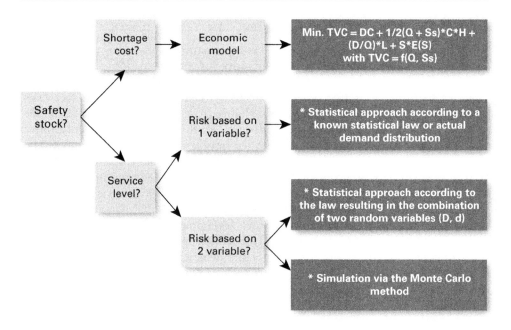

evaluate the cost of shortage if we list the elements making up the consequences of the shortage:

- cost of possible rescheduling, or even stoppage (in the worst-case scenario) of the manufacturing units (the case of a product's components and subassemblies);
- cost of the implementation of troubleshooting solutions entailing a significant marginal cost;
- cost of late penalties or – worse – possible creation of a 'value-destruction chain' through a knock-on effect (eg the case for example of spare parts for after-sales contexts).

Target service-level approach

This is the reason why buyers and/or supply planners often prefer to base their calculation on a service level defined with their internal clients. The level of client service can be expressed, depending on the case (and the needs or preferences of users), as:

- the probability that a shortage appears between two successive orders, whether partial or complete;
- the relationship between the number of units (or orders) delivered immediately without shortage and the total number of units (or orders) to deliver;
- the number of days (or periods) without shortage out of the total number of days (or periods) under consideration, that can be interpreted as the average probability of shortage over time.

9/4.2 Differentiated inventory system and consumption curve situations

Two other elements should be analysed carefully: the issue of the safety of the supply system is raised differently depending on the inventory-control system, for the *interval of risk, and hence of protection* to cover, is not the same, and methods for determining safety stock obviously depend on the types of demand from the viewpoint of their statistical logic.

Inventory-control systems and protection interval

For a basic risk-free model in a reorder-point system, we have seen that the safety stock is set as nil, and the average stock is Q/2. If safety stock is added, the results can be generalized as shown in Figure 9.7.

Let AD_d be the average demand during a delivery lead-time. When the safety stock Ss is set up, the order point OP is easily calculated as follows:

$$OP = AD_d + Ss$$

and the average stock thus becomes:

$$(Q/2) + Ss$$

Looking at this figure, we can already notice that the higher the quantity Q ordered, the lower the average shortage cost as we find ourselves less frequently with low stock, and thus in a risk shortage position.

We observe that in such a system, the inventory manager runs a risk of shortage only during an interval of time equal to the supplier's replenishment cycle (and at every new order/delivery). Outside of these periods, there is no risk as the available stock is higher than the order point. In this way, the *protection interval is equal to the supplier's total delivery cycle.*

FIGURE 9.7   Safety stock and reorder point

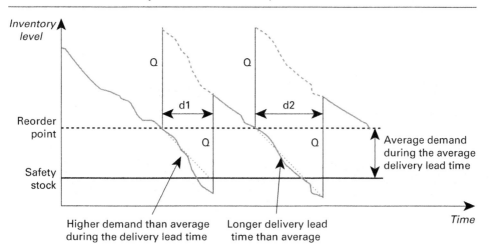

If the item is managed by a periodic-replenishment system, the situation is different as the risk is faced over a longer period, as shown by Figure 9.8.

FIGURE 9.8   Safety stock and periodic replenishment

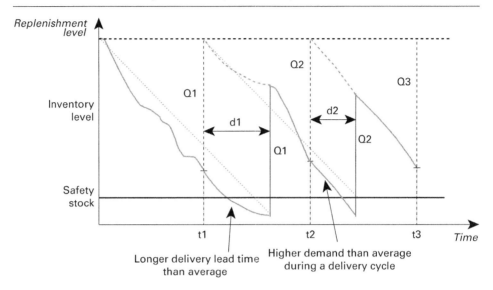

Indeed, in this case, let's imagine that the manager makes a bad ordering decision at the date t1: the error can only be rectified by a second decision at t2, but this is effectively dealt with by a postponed delivery with a delivery lead-time 'd' that will enable satisfactory levels of stock to be available.

Therefore, in this case, the protection interval to take into account is equal to an *interval between two successive orders (T) plus the supplier's delivery cycle d*. The period of risk is therefore longer than in the previous system: logically, for the one item analysed, this system will bring higher safety-stock costs (a statement that is true before any validation calculation is performed).

Different statistical types of consumption curves

Not all purchased items have the same types of demand. In certain situations, demand has a high average level and their risks are distributed symmetrically to those for average demand; in other cases, we deal with quite erratic consumption, so the distribution of forecasting error is less logical or easy to describe.

Items with high consumption and inventory-turnover levels

These are items whose consumption is relatively regular over time, such as a company's standard components or commodities. Such demands are generally represented by a normal law of probability (also called Gauss's Law). This type of law, apart from its general formulation, is characterized by two parameters: the average value of the demand, notated as AD, and the dispersion of this demand evaluated by the standard deviation, notated as σ_D.

References with low turnover and consumption levels

These are often more atypical products whose consumption is intermittent or erratic (long periods of non-consumption may alternate with minor periods of consumption). Consumption, moreover, concerns small quantities and fluctuations around the average level may represent several times this figure. Typical examples are markets for spare parts or products characterized by great variety such as customized products (or integrating a very high number of options or variations).

Such demands are modelled with the use of Poisson distribution. Apart from its general formulation, this type of distribution law is characterized by a single parameter: the average value of demand per unit of time, notated here as AD. We can then easily evaluate the associated probabilities.

9/4.3 Statistical determination of safety stock

To determine safety stock using a statistical method, we need to have the *distribution of demand or consumption over units of time equal to the protection interval*. This may therefore sometimes lead to reconstituting this probability distribution in such a way as to have the right data to start the calculation process.

Calculation using a statistical approach

Let's consider Figure 9.9. We have reproduced the case of an item (managed as a reorder-point system) with a high turnover level, with an illustration of its histogram (using the principles developed above). On the figure, *Dpi* is the demand during the protection interval, *ADpi*, its average, f(Dpi), its probability density, S_{op}, the level of stock reached when an order is issued, and Ss, the safety stock equal to $S_{op} - ADpi$.

FIGURE 9.9 Weekly distribution of consumption

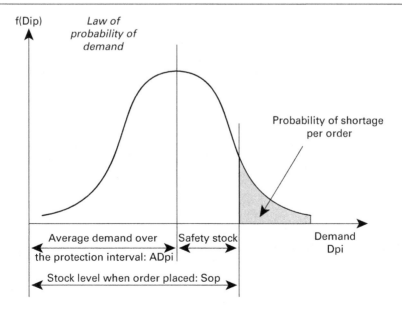

Numerical example for an order-point system

Let's suppose that distribution of demand follows a normal law. The average demand, the *weekly Dpi*, is 100 with a standard deviation σ_{Dpi} of 20; the supplier lead-time is five weeks (period respected by the supplier). We wish for the probability of shortage to be less than 5 per cent, in other words, for service levels to be 95 per cent.

The standard deviation of demand during the lead-time (successive weekly demand being independent) is $20\sqrt{5}$. Indeed, the variance of demand over five weeks is the sum of the variances of demand for each of the weeks. In order for 95 per cent of the area under the curve f(Dpi) to be at the left of S_L, it is necessary to have a standard deviation of 1.645 times the average (figure to check in a normal-law distribution table). The safety stock is therefore equal to:

$$20\sqrt{5} \times 1.645 = 74 \text{ units}$$

As a result, the order point OP is:

$$OP = S_{op} = 500 + 74 = 574 \text{ units}$$

as 500 is the average demand during the supply lead-time.

Numerical example for a periodic-replenishment system

Let's take the same parameters and suppose that the order periodicity is a week (in other words, one weekly order issued to the supplier). The standard deviation becomes $20\sqrt{10+5}$, and the safety stock is $1.645 \times 20\sqrt{15} = 128$ units.

Here we can make an important observation: for an equal level of protection and for a given identical shortage probability, safety stock is always higher in a periodic-replenishment system according to the following relationship (where d is the supplier's delivery period and T an interval between two orders in a periodic system):

$$\sqrt{(d+T) / d}$$

Calculation using an economic approach

If we seek to set the level of the safety stock *from a cost of shortage*, we will be led to formulate a function of total variable cost (TVC) integrating safety stock as an additional variable of the problem. For example:

$$TVC = (D/Q) L + (Q/2 + Ss) C H + DC + S E(S)$$

In this generic formulation, we see that the safety stock Ss is logically integrated into the costing of an additional storage cost. In addition, we see evaluation of the total cost of shortage emerging as the multiplication of the unit cost of shortage S and a *mathematical expectation* of shortage E(S), itself a function of the safety stock.

By *mathematical expectation*, we should understand the necessity to determine, over the reference calculation period (generally a year), a weighted cumulative quantity of supply shortages: this quantity results from probable shortages associated with probabilities that actual consumption will exceed the safety-stock level set up.

Calculations are not of an exceeding mathematical complexity; however, we will not go into them here, and refer the reader to more specialized works.

9/4.4 Alternative approaches to safety stock

Other different measures may allow companies to rationalize their supply and provide alternatives to the systematic constitution of high levels of safety stocks. Amongst these, we can mention the following approaches depending on the professional situations encountered: the centralization of stocks in a single warehouse, the coordination of stocks by a centralized information system, the segmentation of products associated with a focused location of storage sites, the substitution of products, and an appropriate supplier policy (double-sourcing).

Centralization of the distribution system and of stocks

In a regional multi-depot storage network, there is generally one safety stock per site, whose level is defined by the service rate desired by the local clients. It may be economically worthwhile to centralize these different stocks in a single central safety stock.

If regional demands are statistically independent, the total safety stock to keep in the central warehouse is equal to the sum of the various regional safety stocks divided by the square root of the number of depots. To illustrate this point, let's take the example of a company with five regional depots, with safety stock of 100 units per centre. Let's suppose that this level of safety stock corresponds to a level of service of 95 per cent, and that the company decides to replace the five regional depots by a central warehouse. In this case, the centralized safety stock should be $500/\sqrt{5} = 225$ units. These 225 units constitute the level of the single centralized safety stock required for a global service rate of 95 per cent. The saving of 275 units is substantial and indicates the extent to which physical centralization of stock is an extremely valuable measure if real-life conditions allow it.

Coordination of inventories by a centralized information system

A company with a multi-site warehousing network can also avoid having a significant safety-stock level in each depot, provided that it sets up an integrated system centralizing information that can thus be shared.

Real-time knowledge of the available stock *at each site* helps avoid shortages by drawing on other sites to fulfil orders. This is a means to centralize and aggregate the offer *virtually*. This virtual centralization may be translated by a reduction in safety stock at all the sites without penalizing the service level to clients.

Segmentation of products and focused locations for storage sites

In many activities, the number of products to oversee amounts to several thousand. It is therefore appropriate to try to constitute *homogeneous categories* to apply the same management policy to all items in each of these categories. This classification method is most often based on ABC analysis or Pareto's Law. In this specific case, segmentation may be carried out in relation to the turnover rates of products in stock.

Category A components – not very numerous but benefiting from a very high turnover rate – must be stocked in local regional depots *near* clients. We will preferably use an inventory control system that offers great flexibility, resulting in a restricted safety-stock level.

On the other hand, *Category C references* – very numerous and with a low stock-turnover rate – must be stocked in a *central warehouse*. This centralization, as seen above, will allow maintaining a far lower safety stock than if the products were all physically available in the regional warehouses.

This segmentation suggests a possible focusing of storage depots and enables rationalization of the configuration of the upstream supply-chain network.

Segmentation according to categories of service levels

In a company stocking a wide range of different components (eg distribution companies), the finance manager is concerned with total investment in safety stocks for *all component categories*.

Common sense could lead to a sales policy based on differentiation of service levels depending on sales imperatives and risks. Let's take a concrete example. A car dealer analyses his categories of parts in this way (see Table 9.6). We see that all wearing parts and consumables corresponding to 'quick service' and 'flat-price operations' need to be available with a service rate of 100 per cent. However, for bodywork parts, safety stocks may be low because longer repair lead-times are acceptable to customers.

Indeed, in the event of an accident, it is necessary to wait for an insurance expert's assessment before proceeding to repair, which leaves – given normal intervention times – the time to resupply the parts urgently before the vehicle enters the workshop. Strictly speaking, it is even not necessary to carry safety stock if the manufacturer's

TABLE 9.6   Service-level requirements depending on product characteristics

Categories	Urgency requirement	Service level	Number ref.
Mechanical parts (wearing parts)	High	95%	2,500
Quick service / flat rates (spark plugs, brake pads, etc.)	Absolute	99.99%	500
Oils, tires	Absolute	99.99%	200
Bodywork parts	Within 1 day	60%	1,200
Sundry equipment and accessories	Within 1 day	50%	960

supply lead-time allows for reception of the parts within the available 'time window' before the car is returned to the client.

Substitution of parts in the case of shortages

In spite of the good intentions of companies to maintain high service vis-à-vis clients, the multiplication of products increases the risk of stock shortage. When a shortage arises, the company keen to keep its clients may offer a replacement product, even if it is more expensive. This apparently costly sales proposal may be not so costly if we consider the risk of losing the client and the cost of extra safety stock that it would have been necessary to carry in order to avoid the shortage.

To extrapolate on this idea, the company may consider, on the one hand, a larger safety-stock policy for a limited number of products qualified as replacement products, and on the other hand, reduction of the level of safety stock for a range of 'substitutable' products whose demand is extremely volatile.

A appropriate supplier policy: double-sourcing

It is rare that a company has to limit itself to a single supply source, except for extremely specific hi-tech products. In the case of standard products whose demand is fairly volatile, thus requiring high safety stocks, we can imagine a double-sourcing system: a first (main) supplier in charge of delivering stable quantities to meet that proportion of the demand that tends not to vary; and a second ('troubleshooting') supplier to whom we attribute coverage of the variable demand.

As the second supplier handles demand risks, its safety stock needs to be high, whereas that held by the first supplier should be practically non-existent. In addition, the first supplier generally practises a significantly lower price than that of the second supplier (who in fact invoices a 'safety' service, but with a variabilized cost, whereas a permanent safety stock engenders a fixed cost). In other words, this is a solution that is popular with finance departments etc.

The result of this double-sourcing is close to an upstream supply chain in which one part (first supplier) focuses on efficiency whilst the other part (second supplier) enables great responsiveness and flexibility. This policy allows the total safety-stock level to be reduced, and as a result, to minimize total costs.

9/5 Collaborative cash management and reverse factoring[7]

Reverse factoring is a financing solution for suppliers of goods or services. However, instead of being initiated by the supplier who wishes to finance client receivables (as in classic factoring), this method is *initiated by the client*, who thus allows the suppliers to easily finance the amounts due to them with the help of a factoring company (factor). This flexible debt-collection programme, underpinned by the buyer's firm and irrevocable commitment to pay the invoice at its maturity date, offers the supplier the option, via the approval of the invoice, to get financed in exchange for a trade discount in the context of a true win–win partnership.

It has only been recently that the realization has dawned in France that financing of the upstream supply chain is crucial. The securing of supply is starting to become a serious matter for consideration in these times of economic instability, and at the same time, the solidity of supplier cash flow is not very reassuring for industrial or distribution companies. This is why reverse factoring is seducing more and more specifiers and end-users.

9/5.1 Description of the economic, financial and regulatory context

Since 2008, the succession of financial crises (sub-primes, the collapse of banks, the sovereign-debt crisis in the Eurozone) has profoundly changed the banking environment in which companies operate, resulting in a toughening of access to credit. Added to these crises, an increased volatility of financial markets (currencies, raw materials, rates) has generated difficulties for decision-makers who need to deal with unstable and unpredictable markets. In addition, the tsunami in Japan in 2011, a major natural catastrophe, resulting in major consequences for buyers (ie stock shortages amongst Japanese suppliers), has accelerated the raising of awareness.

More difficult conditions for company access to credit

In the fourth quarter of 2011, 35 per cent of banks recognized that they had tightened their conditions for access to credit, either by raising their margins, or more simply on the level of granting loans. Bank scoring became stricter and credit quality (or credit standards) took on a fundamental importance. While major companies do not suffer too much from this tightening of credit when they maintain sound financial performance, they quickly see credit conditions deteriorate when their financial health changes. As for SMEs, banks know how to distinguish between 'good and bad' risks.

There is nothing astonishing about all this when we know that the Basel III agreements have required banks, since 2013, to improve their ratio of loans granted to equity. The fear of systemic risk (the 'domino' effect, with the collapse of one bank entailing the collapse of the whole banking system) has given rise to new prudential regulations that oblige banks to reinforce their financial structure. They can increase their equity, which they have done by increasing capital and/or reducing their credit commitments.

Company bankruptcy on the rise

Fear of bankruptcy freezes all bank loans. And this fear reinforces the role of credit managers in companies: in charge of recovering client debts, these managers are capable of assessing the risk profiles of clients, their financial quality, and measuring the probability of bankruptcy in the case of some.

Company fragility is all the greater when a company is young and small in size. A fall in turnover accompanied by an increase in trade debt often leads a company to file for bankruptcy. Causes are many, but we can cite non-payment or delay in payment of clients (21 per cent of cases) as the main cause for business failure. Figure 9.10 illustrates this strong correlation.

FIGURE 9.10   Correlation between business failure and payment delays

COMPARATIVE EVOLUTION OF THE NUMBER OF FAILURES AND PAYMENT DELAYS

(quarterly data over 12 months / 15-year period)

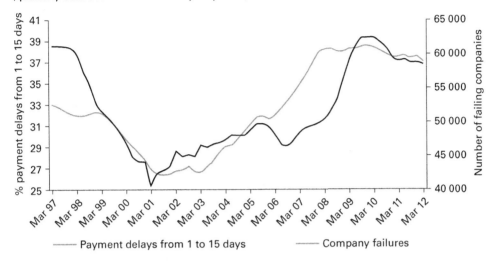

——— Payment delays from 1 to 15 days   ——— Company failures

Lengthening payment periods

Intercompany credit is the first means of financing used in business transactions. The signing of a trade agreement between a supplier and a client foresees different mandatory clauses such as the price, possible discounts, payment periods and applicable late-penalty rates.

A comparison of payment terms in Europe indicates that northern countries such as the Scandinavian countries or Germany have shorter payment periods, whilst southern countries, namely Spain and Portugal, have payment periods three times longer on average than Germany. It is also proven that the longer the payment period, the more payment delays lengthen.

The Altares firm shows in a study that only 41.5 per cent of European companies pay their bills at the deadline agreed upon with the supplier. It also observes that companies that postpone their supplier payments by over 30 days present a failure probability multiplied by six. Delay in payment has in some way become a barometer of company solidity.

One first regulatory response (the NRE)

The French bill titled *Nouvelles Réglementations Economiques* (NRE, New Economic Regulations), aimed at fighting late payments in business transactions, is a response to the European Late Payment Directive 200/35/EC of June 2000. The bill constrains companies to demand mandatory late penalties beyond a supplementary period of 30 days. The NRE law targets the diminishing of client risk by eliminating late payment and cleansing client–supplier relationships. According to Article 53-2 of the bill, penalties are payable without any reminder being necessary: as a consequence, non-respect of payment deadlines gives birth to a debt. The creditor therefore has an obligation, when a payment is late, to determine the sum of the penalty due, to record and invoice it.

In spite of the NRE law, the outcome has been mediocre. Only 28 per cent of companies demand late penalties. From a commercial point of view, very few companies dare to ask for them, for cultural reasons, nor is it common practice to bill interest on late payments. Similarly, a demand for penalties causes relationships between the two parties to worsen, and transactions and exchanges to become more tense in the future.

If a debt has not been paid at the close of the fiscal year, the creditor must temporarily stop the sum of late penalties at this date. Penalties are payable on the day after the payment date mentioned on the invoice. The rate applied is that of the European Central Bank plus 7 points, with the minimum rate being 1.5 times the legal interest rate.

The toughening of the NRE Bill: the LME in 2008

An extra step was taken by the French bill *Modernisation Economique* (LME, Economic Modernization). Its main objective was to help increase the cash of VSEs and SMEs supplying large groups or industrial companies. Reducing payment periods amounts to lightening the WCR of companies, small or large, and placing the burden on that of distribution companies which have few supplier debts to honour.

Regarding mass distribution, the payment period practised is around 120 days; in other words, these companies do not pay for their stock. Major industrial companies have seen reductions in their stock financing. In other words, what is oxygen for some may be asphyxia for others, unless the bank loans no longer needed by some are

FIGURE 9.11   Late penalties and their application

Late penalties and their actual application (2004–2011)
(in % of companies surveyed)

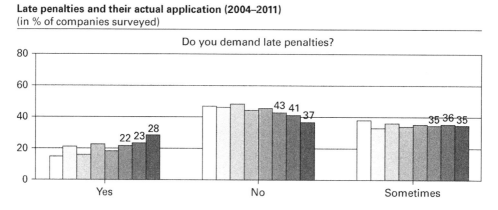

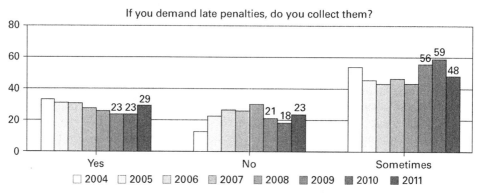

SOURCE: AFDCC, 2011 survey.

transferred to others with the help of appropriate measures – an unlikely scenario in the current circumstances.

Indeed, it was necessary to reduce payment periods and be harmonized with European countries to make France more attractive. Payment periods were previously longer in France than in other European Union countries. The fact that a law sets a limit on client payment periods helps boost competition, namely on prices. In addition, this law reduces the risk associated with intercompany credit as the billing account over 'x' months diminishes.

The LME has applied since 1 January 2009, and overturned the French payment period landscape: the objective was to shorten payment periods to 45 days from the end of the month, or 60 days (net and calendar) from the issue date of the invoice. In spite of dissuasive sanctions envisaged, there are strategies that can be used to get around them, hence avoiding impact on a company's WCR. Here is a non-exhaustive list of existing techniques:

- at the supplier's initiative, the issuing of an invoice can be deferred for up to one month in order to grant extra credit to clients;
- at the debtor's initiative, payment of supplier invoices can be globalized at the end of the month, whatever their chosen computation mode; the client may also make abundant use of self-invoicing;
- invoices may be processed externally by overseas payment centres to justify the application of longer deadlines; or else the client abusively excludes the LME by way of a foreign element: a subsidiary, a delivery place;
- calling on an alternative in the mode of calculation and simulation of every transaction, in order to retain, case by case, the most advantageous option (60 net days, 45 days from the end of the month);
- an application of derogatory payment periods for suppliers whose activity does not stem from the agreements in question;
- delaying usage of certain payment instruments, with a late transfer of cheques or bills of exchange that defer the payment of the debt;
- the client may invoke false disputes;
- the abuse of stock on consignment (this practice, already mentioned above, consists in leaving financial responsibility of stock for as long as possible to the supplier).

From the supply chain to supply-chain finance

In this financial crisis context, companies are seeking to optimize their cash flow relating to supply-chain activities. However, supply-chain management has remained largely focused on physical and information flows, and does not include financial management or financial flows. Companies have also stayed limited to the steering of these flows without paying heed to impacts on the management of cash and the WCR. And yet the supply chain has become a concern and a focus of attention for various reasons.

In the face of the economic crisis and volatility in recent years, companies have become more concerned with the financial situations of their suppliers: the supply chain has thus turned into one of their core preoccupations. Indeed, as discussed previously, suppliers have seen a lengthening in their payment periods, pressure on prices, and a growing difficulty in finding financing. The relationship between clients and suppliers needs to become more collaborative.

To respond to the current situation, the supply chain must be reactive to deal with market hazards. As a result, the ambition is to integrate financial risks and issues at the heart of management. Indeed, until now, as financing and cash flow issues have not been taken into account, they have been a 'weak link' and an unexploited source of income. Yet these elements have a considerable impact on income, cash flow and operating costs, as well as profits.

In addition, this understanding of the extended supply chain is directly linked to globalization; in other words, if a supplier defaults, risk spreads to other links of the chain and has an impact on the whole of the company. Companies have become aware that absence of a collaborative approach between cash management and financing needs related to operations has a very negative impact. In this way, they have become interested in creating long-lasting and trustworthy relationships with their suppliers.

9/5.2 Reverse factoring mechanism

The reverse factoring mechanism, still very rare, is analogous to classic factoring in that it involves three players: the client, the supplier and the factoring company. As with classic factoring, the aim is to finance receivables owed by a client to a supplier via a financing third party (a factoring company), enabling the supplier to immediately receive cash for the goods or services sold to the client (minus interest withheld by the financier).

But unlike classic factoring, the strategy is not instigated by the supplier, who, in this case, would present client receivables to the factoring company in order to be paid in advance: it is in fact *initiated by the client* – generally a fairly large company – who establishes a list of invoices eligible for reverse factoring. The supplier chooses from this list those invoices for which it wishes to be paid immediately by the factoring company. This is therefore a real collaboration between the supplier, the client and the factoring company. In this way, the supplier takes advantage of an enhanced financing rate, the client benefits from a return on the profit produced by the financier, and the latter makes a profit by financing the supplier.

History and evolution of the concept

The concept is not, in itself, recent. The process was developed by automobile manufacturers Fiat, who used this kind of financing in the 1980s to improve their margins when dealing with suppliers. The principle then spread to the mass-distribution sector – a sector where payment periods are at the heart of negotiations.

In the 1990s, due to a rise in current rates, the margins made were too low to guarantee the system's continuity, and it fell somewhat by the wayside. Similarly, at the start of the 2000s, even if current rates diminished, discount rates also diminished, giving suppliers other financing solutions, so reverse factoring did not especially interest them.

Today, we have reached a balance that allows guaranteeing benefits in reverse factoring for all its actors, and this is why its development and expansion have ensued. This evolution is also due to technological progress (ie dematerialization) and information systems that allow a certain automation of the process as well as accelerated management of invoice processing.

Since the 2008 financial crisis, banks have been seeking more solid financing, thus leading them to finance debts of sound quality. In proceeding in this way, they ensure a better ROI and thus improve their activity. As far as prescribers are concerned, the key stakes consist in consolidating the financing of their suppliers in order to ensure that the latter have a long-lasting activity, and that they are privileged in the delivery of goods or services. Finally, the obvious interest for suppliers is to have a financing solution at more advantageous rates, without harming their clients' WCR.

Comparison of the concept with other financing solutions

Let's look at a few figures. In 2011, the reverse factoring market was still very weak, representing 3 per cent of the global factoring market valued at approximately €153 billion of receivables covered. The growth of classic factoring was around 13 per cent in 2011 compared with its 2010 figure; reverse factoring represented 10 per cent of classic factoring in France, while it represented 25 per cent of factoring in Italy or 30 per cent in Spain. Almost 90 per cent of companies interested in this technique have a turnover of €5 billion or over.

For a company, different options can be considered for successful management of its WCR:

- recourse to bank overdrafts or current-account overdrafts;
- the management of debt via securitization and factoring;
- reverse factoring for a company's debts owed to its suppliers.

To understand the process of reverse factoring, it is necessary to be familiar with factoring and invoice discounting. Indeed, we can consider that reverse factoring takes advantage of these two solutions, and distributes profits to the three players. To clarify this mechanism, we now present in Figure 9.12 seven key points for each of these solutions.

FIGURE 9.12   Comparison of the three methods

	Invoice discounting	Factoring	Reverse factoring
Eligibility	All invoices	All invoices	Payment-approved invoices
Financing	At the client's initiative	At the supplier's initiative	At the client's initiative
Financed sum	100% of the invoice (minus discount)	Partial sum	100% of the invoice
Interest rate	According to the supplier's situation	According to the supplier's situation	According to the client's situation
Payment	Immediate	At maturity	At maturity
Impact on the WCR	Negative	None	None
Financial gains	Sum of the discount (but implies an immediate cash outflow)	None	Part of the margin

Operation of reverse factoring

As shown by Figure 9.13, reverse factoring encompasses three players: one or several financial establishment(s), the party placing the order and the supplier(s).

First of all, the individual placing the order is a buyer with an excellent reputation, like a distribution or industrial company, hence associated with reduced risk. Before the conclusion of a business contract, the buyer offers the supplier early payment of payment-approved invoices via the factor who intervenes as a third-party payer. The buyer attributes the supplier with a financial partner in the context of possible financing by the latter. Indeed, if the supplier needs to assign any client receivables, financing of invoices can be unblocked by the factor. The financing rate is extremely attractive as it is perfectly correlated with the buyer's sound rating. Differences in rates can mainly be explained by the prescriber's rating.

The buyer negotiates remuneration in the form of a discount with every supplier, and offers the factor's simplified factoring contract. Once an agreement is reached, the supplier addresses the invoice to the buyer ie the individual who requisitioned the item. The latter receives and validates these invoices. Next, the prescriber chooses which invoices to finance.

The supplier chooses amongst the financeable invoices, visible on the portal, then addresses a file of invoices to which he or she grants 'payment approval' to the factor. The bank accesses the correctly submitted invoices and offers financing to the supplier. Validated invoices are viewable by the suppliers who can ask for early payment of them.

The factor makes a cash advance without recovery, paying the invoice(s) immediately, minus the discount. Finally, the factor returns the discount to the company after deducting financial expenses. The ordering-party buyer commits firmly and

FIGURE 9.13   Operating cycle of reverse factoring

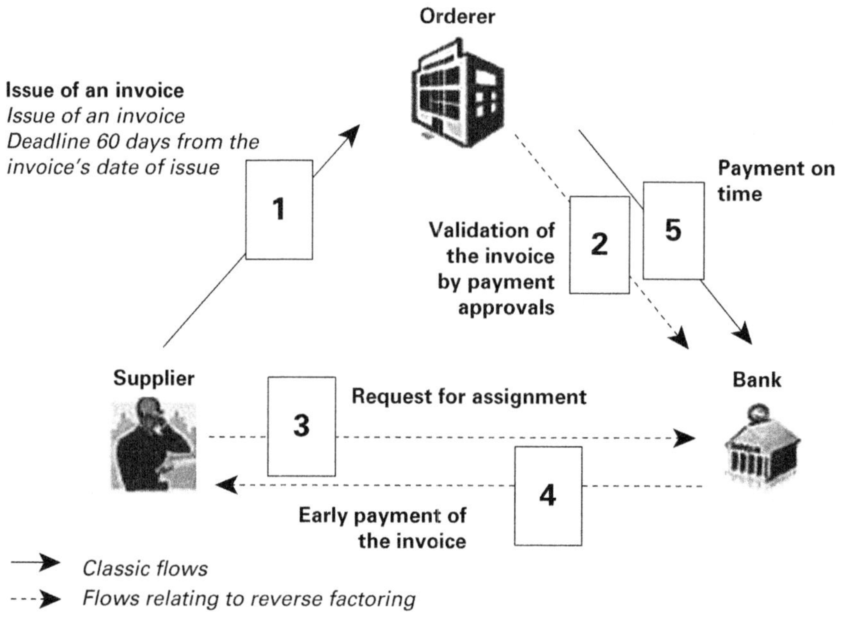

SOURCE: © Mazars, 2011.

irrevocably to reimburse the factor for the submitted supplier debts at the maturity date in reverse factoring. However, there is also the option of long-term factoring, designed to postpone payment of an invoice (Figure 9.14).

FIGURE 9.14   Payment/delivery schedule

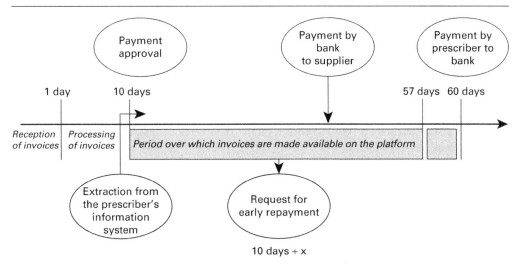

9/5.3 Advantages of reverse factoring

In the case of classic invoicing or classic factoring, invoices carry several risks: a fraudulent invoice (illegal, incorrect calculation or input error); poor estimation on the part of one of the parties regarding the invoice's object (eg a badly accomplished service); poor estimation of payment periods etc. By taking recourse to reverse factoring, these risks are heavily reduced.

Increasingly, we realize in the business arena that the success of one party leads to the success of another. As a result, allowing your partner to benefit from preferential rates has a more or less long-term beneficial effect on your own activity.

The advantages of reverse factoring

Reverse factoring programmes can support, qualitatively and quantitatively, the WCR, and more generally, the operation of any company. They meet a number of objectives that are not necessarily mutually exclusive: capturing a proportion of income from advanced payments made by suppliers, supporting the practice of invoice discounting without altering cash flow, and reinforcing the WCR, within certain limits.

Other objectives, not directly financial, motivate companies to adopt such programmes: for example, strengthening the links with supplier partners (which may prove an excellent long-term strategy), gathering different company functions together in a global unifying project without any real geographical limits, and deepening understanding of the micro-processes inherent to purchase and payment flows.

Reverse factoring techniques can therefore draw music from two strings that are sensitive in any business: increasing profitability and reducing capital employed.

In this respect, they are a powerful tool for optimizing capital employed (ROCE), usable by finance and procurement departments.

Capturing a proportion of income from advanced payments

In its collaborative format, reverse factoring leaves complete flexibility to the supplier to advance its invoice or not. If the supplier opts for an early payment, the cost that is then paid to the other stakeholders (the financial establishment and eventually an electronic third-party platform) should legitimately be shared with the prescriber. Indeed, it is the party who originates this financial transaction thanks to the transmission of information on his or her irrevocable intention to pay such and such an invoice at such and such a date. It is also the prescriber who, thanks to the business relationship established with the supplier, enables production of the income inherent to early payment. This so-called collaborative approach can therefore:

- offer suppliers an option for financing their receivables at an a priori attractive rate;

- bring suppliers an easy solution for deconsolidating their receivables that satisfies their own interests, for example, the choice of periods coinciding with their interim or annual statements (and not on set dates);

- for prescribers, capture part of the expenses paid by suppliers for their early payments, and hence supplement their income.

The reader is invited to consult Figure 9.15.

FIGURE 9.15

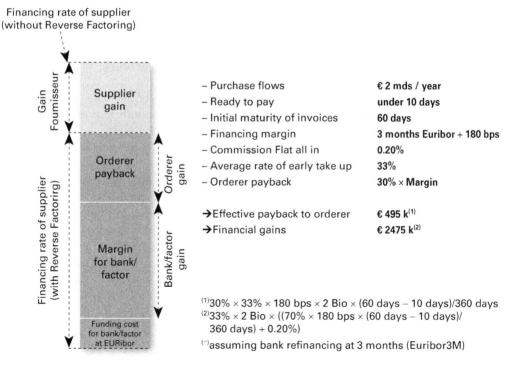

Financing rate of supplier (without Reverse Factoring)

Gain Foumisseur

Supplier gain

Orderer payback

Margin for bank/ factor

Funding cost for bank/factor at EURibor

Financing rate of supplier (with Reverse Factoring)

Orderer gain

Bank/factor gain

- Purchase flows   € 2 mds / year
- Ready to pay   under 10 days
- Initial maturity of invoices   60 days
- Financing margin   3 months Euribor + 180 bps
- Commission Flat all in   0.20%
- Average rate of early take up   33%
- Orderer payback   30% × Margin

→ Effective payback to orderer   € 495 k[1]
→ Financial gains   € 2475 k[2]

[1] 30% × 33% × 180 bps × 2 Bio × (60 days – 10 days)/360 days
[2] 33% × 2 Bio × ((70% × 180 bps × (60 days – 10 days)/ 360 days) + 0.20%)
[–] assuming bank refinancing at 3 months (Euribor3M)

SOURCE: Bfinance.

Supporting the practice of invoice discounting

Another approach of reverse factoring is based on systematic advance billing, pre-negotiated between the ordering party's procurement managers and some of its suppliers. This negotiation leads to the obtaining of an invoice discount in exchange for quick payment ('quality payment'). In doing so, the prescriber takes charge of the interest and expenses inherent to this type of reverse factoring, which are far less than the advantage extracted from the obtained discount.

This form of reverse factoring does not degrade cash flow in any way, and hence the WCR of the buyer who finally pays at the exact maturity date of the invoice. This approach therefore enables companies, who already practise invoice discounting, to restore their cash flow situation (these quick payments are ensured by the intervening bank rather than them dipping into their treasuries or short-term loans). Companies that until now have had recourse to discounts in exchange for quick payment can now achieve the same result without altering their cash flow.

In short, this approach allows: benefit from advantageous purchasing conditions through the granted invoice discount, far more favourable than taking on the engendered financial expenses; and leaving the company's cash flow and WCR in the same situation as they would be in if payments were executed on the maturity date.

'Financial' improvement of the WCR

Reverse factoring can also, subject to certain restrictions, support the WCR beyond the legal contractual payment period (maximum of 60 days in France). Like non-recourse assignment – that should nonetheless be restricted to a 'reasonable' limit of 25 per cent of client receivables or 5 per cent of the total balance sheet – it is also a 'treasury-generating' tool. In this way, certain groups with no tangible client items (typically the B2C distribution sector), or that either cannot or refuse on principle to assign debt, see reverse factoring programmes as a means to 'vary' the supplier resource, the very one placed under pressure by the standardization of payment terms in recent years. This approach is based on an in-depth reading of the legal framework and rests on at least three main principles:

- the negotiation of terms beyond the 60-day rule (eg 90 days) should be accompanied by a financing offer for a more attractive 'cash' payment than that otherwise extended to the supplier;
- the supplier should have total freedom in the choice of whether to bill in advance or not;
- the underlying collaboration of the banks involved is breakable at any moment.

The approach thus allows, for the buyer, the variation of a resource on the balance sheet that is not characterized as a financial debt and that, as a result, supports the WCR; meanwhile, participating suppliers benefit from more generous quick payment conditions in exchange for the acceptance of the terms' special allowances, but that in reality never apply.

A solution in which everyone wins

Advantages for the supplier

By having invoices paid earlier, the supplier can manage cash flow needs more easily, and at the same time reduce expenses related to management of their client account.

In addition, given that it is the client who commits to pay, the invoice's financing rate is more advantageous than if it were subject to the traditional factoring technique (see Figure 9.16).

FIGURE 9.16

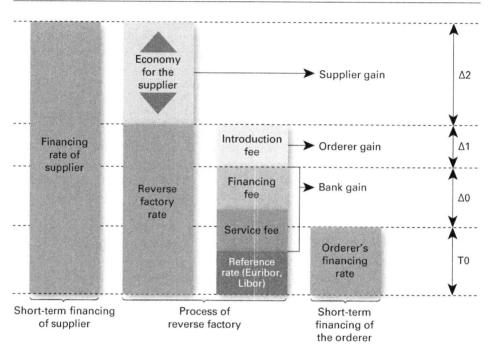

SOURCE: Mazars, 2012.

Reverse factoring proves useful for SMEs whose clients are large companies, for the technique is in line with a sustainable relationship whereby a client allows a small supplier to benefit from its large size.

In a classic factoring system set up by the supplier, if ever a problem arises in the payment of an invoice (whether due to poor service, a client's financial problem or otherwise), the financier recover the money advanced from the supplier that cannot be recovered from the client. However, in the case of reverse factoring, as we deal with invoices whose payment has been approved, once the financier pays the supplier, the financier can only obtain payment from the (large) client. The supplier is therefore protected as soon as the payment is received, unlike in the case of simple factoring.

Finally, in an invoice discounting model, suppliers are 'condemned' to being paid in cash systematically (or depending on the deadlines agreed upon), whatever their cash flow situation. The advantage presented by reverse factoring is that the supplier has a choice on whether to factor an invoice or not, depending on needs.

Advantages for the client (ordering party)

Reverse factoring means that the client no longer has to pay each supplier independently; instead, all invoices can be submitted to a third-party financier, the factoring company, that then facilitates management of invoice payment, which can incidentally be further simplified by the use of a specialized reverse factoring platform.

The relationship with the suppliers is improved, for suppliers benefit from better rates thanks to the client, generally a large firm, and payment times are reduced; meanwhile, the client only pays invoices on the date initially agreed upon.

Use of this solution also helps to sustain the suppliers' activity. Indeed, by ensuring that they have a preferential financing means, certain suppliers can continue their activity and face their possible cash flow problems more easily. Allowing suppliers to take advantage of this improved financing rate is also a substantial advantage in a negotiation, and can thus ensure a better result and/or a more sustainable relationship.

Finally, depending on the conditions negotiated with the factoring company, the client can benefit from the passed-on profit made by the factoring company. The buyer is remunerated in the capacity as purchasing adviser in relation to the factor, for the prescriber opens their address book up to their financial partners. The client thus achieves extra income without impacting WCR.

Advantages for the factoring company (the financier)
By intervening in invoice payment, the factoring company makes a profit by making its money available and taking charge of the payment of invoices in time. However, unlike the case in simple factoring, this time the factoring company is placed at the heart of a more sustainable business relationship.

Another advantage for the factor is to work with large clients directly rather than going out to look for each supplier. Indeed, in a factoring system as in a reverse factoring system, the factoring company can deal with all the suppliers of one client. However, in the first case, the risk of each invoice corresponds to the risk of each supplier whereas in the second case, the risk concerns a bigger client (whose risk is thus reduced).

9/5.4 Obstacles to the deployment of a reverse factoring programme

Despite its virtues, reverse factoring remains the province of a few rare companies (no more than 20 or so programmes truly operate in France), for it comes up against numerous obstacles that many organizations struggle to overcome.

Unifying departmental teams with different objectives

Few financial activities encompass all functions with an organization as does reverse factoring. Indeed, the setting up of a reverse factoring programme, whatever its ambition and geographic extent, requires the active participation of many professions and partners inside a company (finance, cash flow, accounting, procurement, IT) as well as others external to it (suppliers, financial partners, possible technological partner, auditors, possible credit insurer).

The association of all these teams, whose cultures, restrictions and targets are different or even divergent, is undoubtedly the main reason for the meagre success with which it has met to date. The principles and financial mechanisms behind it need to be explained and re-explained clearly, namely using examples.

It is also crucial that these different functions are unified at the highest level, by senior management, defining a leading global objective for all players involved.

Raising the support of an adequate population of suppliers

The second hindrance most often noted is the incredible difficulty in enrolling suppliers into a given programme. In this way, numerous programmes underway have very few participating suppliers and are thus largely under-utilized. Indeed, it is an extremely tricky matter to obtain a supplier's adherence to a programme when obstacles are inherent in their own organization: receivables may already mobilized in a factoring or securitization programme; the supplier may have committed to not assigning debt, including in a non-recourse format (following the drafting of negative-pledge clauses); and internal regulations, strict or even dogmatic, may forbid the assignment of any client receivables.

But many suppliers fail to subscribe as a result of what proves at times to be poor communication. In this way, there may be failure to perceive the 'derecognizing' effect of the financing offered, poor calibration of the financial conditions offered, an inappropriate and thus disadvantageous accounting classification, or an over-hasty assessment of the obstacles inherent to assignment.

It is therefore essential for heads of finance departments, representing both buyers and suppliers, to be involved in this communication. It is also crucial that the scaling of the conditions offered to the suppliers respond to two main principles: first, *finer initial segmentation of the supplier base* than one based on mere size. This fine segmentation aims to identify the level that will raise the supplier's maximum adhesion by referring to indicators that reflect conditions of access to liquidity and sensitivity to 'derecognition' (rating – commitments depending on a financial ratio – sensitivity to business or country risk – existence and quality of possible credit insurance); second, *regular dynamic repositioning of the conditions on offer*: indeed, the suppliers' situations tend to evolve (degradation of supplier risk and of supplier markets, uncovered increased need, desire to not call on the usual financial partners, increased awareness of deconsolidation, etc). A regular review of conditions is therefore necessary, whether to boost the conditions of suppliers systematically using financing, or to encourage its use by suppliers who rarely or never do so.

Not restricting reverse factoring to being an extra means to dress up the balance sheet

Several industries face a toughening of their WCR. This toughening is already well entrenched for B2C distribution companies that, in the absence of client receivables, have witnessed practically no advantage in the standardization of payment terms. On the contrary, these distributors have had to absorb a considerable loss in 'supplier resources' as they have gradually conformed to the requirements of the LME.

This future toughening of the WCR is also anticipated by many groups whose epicentre of activity has shifted and is continuing to shift to emerging countries. Indeed, their new local clients in these dynamic regions comply with unfavourable payment terms. Most often, these same groups cannot protect themselves by applying payment terms equivalent to their suppliers whose agreements are on a global rather than a local scale (and therefore closer to the payment terms that prevail in Europe).

B2B service companies, for whom the weight of supplier accounts payable is relatively restricted, but who are associated with genuine client accounts payable, are fully affected. And in their case, this recent deterioration cannot, more or less naturally, be transferred to suppliers.

All these phenomena prompt the setting up of preventative measures capable of absorbing the reductions in working capital. Reverse factoring, in its capacity to recreate the supplier resource, is one of the defensive means available. However, pursuing this objective exclusively brings a risk with its execution, or at the very least, constitutes a hindrance to the implementation of such reverse factoring projects.

Validation of an invoice has a largely underestimated value

The fundamental basis of a reverse factoring programme relies on a company's capacity to generate payment approvals within a relatively short lead-time. This information is not easy to produce, all the more when the deadline is tight. Any player has a 'natural tendency' to put off validation of payable invoices for as long as possible. Yet information on the validity of a given invoice has a certain value.

It reassures the supplier in question regarding the absence of a dispute or error, and also regarding the client's intention to pay. For the financial establishment issuing this invoice, information on the intention to pay is crucial: it eliminates the risk of dilution inherent to all debt mobilization and fully reinforces the self-liquidating character of the financing.

The more quickly this information is transmitted, the greater the number of suppliers who will thus be informed. It is no doubt by repositioning this concept at the centre of the debate and by recalling the value that it represents that protagonists gathered around a reverse factoring project will be more efficient.

Avoiding reclassification of the operating debt into a financial debt

The major issue relating to this type of programme is the reclassification of the debt. We understand 'debt reclassification' as the transition from an operational debt to a financial debt when recourse is taken to a discount. Several reasons exist that may lead to such a reclassification, and this will be the view taken by the auditor.

As soon as the procedure resembles a financial product, it will be reclassified as a financial debt, and this is what the prescriber will seek to avoid at all costs. If the mechanism instrumentalizes the supplier debt, it may become a financial product and therefore have an impact on debt ratio. The buyer wishes, by postponing payment, to keep a trade debt and for it not to be transformed into a financial debt. As we have explained, the supplier will invoice the client according to the conditions provided in the contract, and it is the banker who finances the cash flow requirement. The bank therefore captures the discount as it is the party that makes the payment. Many factors could be the object of reclassification, and the auditor will keep a vigilant watch on these. On the prescriber's balance sheet, there will be no change: there will still be a debt to pay at the end of 60 days, for example, and the banker will be reimbursed.

In order for the debt not to be reclassified, there must be no tripartite link, for each party plays a dissociated role. There is also a bilateral agreement between the bank and the prescriber (and an agreement between the buyer and the supplier). In fact, the prescriber's involvement in this operation should be calculated and well thought-out because if this party is overly involved in the process, risks of reclassification will arise.

9/5.5 The challenges, stakes and future of reverse factoring

The success of a reverse factoring programme relies on a platform's functions. The platform is the communication link between all the chain's actors, allowing information to circulate fluidly, as illustrated by Figure 9.17. There are several types of platforms.

Platform choice and operation

Bank platforms
As forerunners on the reverse factoring market, banks offer platforms with the most basic functions. The operating cost is included in the package offered to suppliers following their assignment. However, a prescriber wishing to modulate or change suppliers or financial partners must take responsibility for financial costs and manage such changes. Banks are aware that they need to have multi-bank platforms, and are gradually in the process of changing their software programs.

FIGURE 9.17 The workspaces of each party

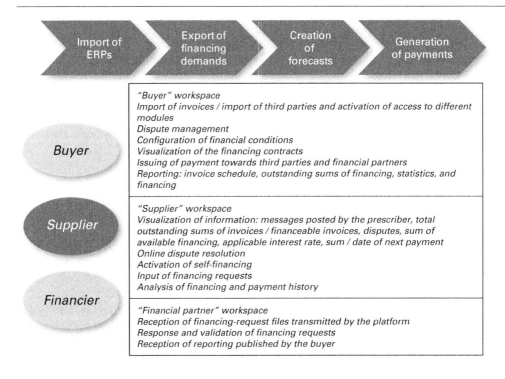

| Import of ERPs | Export of financing demands | Creation of forecasts | Generation of payments |

Buyer

"Buyer" workspace
Import of invoices / import of third parties and activation of access to different modules
Dispute management
Configuration of financial conditions
Visualization of the financing contracts
Issuing of payment towards third parties and financial partners
Reporting: invoice schedule, outstanding sums of financing, statistics, and financing

Supplier

"Supplier" workspace
Visualization of information: messages posted by the prescriber, total outstanding sums of invoices / financeable invoices, disputes, sum of available financing, applicable interest rate, sum / date of next payment
Online dispute resolution
Activation of self-financing
Input of financing requests
Analysis of financing and payment history

Financier

"Financial partner" workspace
Reception of financing-request files transmitted by the platform
Response and validation of financing requests
Reception of reporting published by the buyer

Multi-bank platforms

There are a growing number of multi-bank packages that share deployment between several banks, with risk and financial gains spread between them. The advantage for the prescriber is to have a more consolidated vision of its position. In addition, the prescriber has the freedom to manage its financial parties and to play on competition.

For the financier, the multi-bank platform is a means to replace a fairly expensive hub model. A single connection suffices for the bank to communicate with its clients, themselves connected to the hub. The disadvantage of these platforms is that their prices are often very high. They sometimes seek positioning between the banker and the prescriber with the aim of taking their remuneration.

'Purchase-to-pay' platforms

'Purchase-to-pay' platforms (P2P) are multi-bank third-party platforms that offer a set of functions geared at the dematerialization and automation of certain operations such as the order, reception, invoicing and validation of the invoice.

The subscription of suppliers to a prescriber's request is already carried out by certain P2P functions. Upon the issuing of invoices, the supplier can visualize financing proposals and associated financial expenses. This, in a way, is a marketing tool to promote reverse factoring.

A core issue: dematerialization

For companies, paper invoices often represent a loss of workspace and productivity, not to mention a waste of paper. For example, it is estimated that an office worker consumes an average of 75 kg of paper per year!

Dematerialization stands out as a solution to this problem, and is a genuine challenge in reverse factoring. Paper flows are cut by around 60 per cent, but it should be remembered that virtual invoices necessitate energy. Dematerialization is a technique stemming from 2001/115/EC adopted by the European Commission, authorizing the dematerialization of invoices for tax purposes. It was carried into French law in 2003, and enables French companies to dematerialize their invoices and eliminate the circulation of paper invoices. Growing in European companies since 2005, this technique uses and exploits electronic means to make paperless operations. As a result, an invoice is deemed 'dematerialized' when the different processing and invoicing methods of companies take place electronically.

Once dematerialized, the processing of an invoice that once took 12 days falls to only 3 days. While an employee processing supplier accounts could deal with 15,000 invoices manually per year, an automated solution allows 80.,000 invoices to be processed. The financial gain is not negligible, for the invoice processing cost of around €19 by manual means is cut by 50 per cent following automation.

The obstacle to e-invoicing remains the multiplicity of document formats (tiff, PDF, xml, EDI, CSV, etc) and distribution channels (letter, fax, e-mail, web, etc). Companies therefore need to have a system capable of dealing with different types of documents and formats, and to set up accessible archiving.

An advanced stage of reverse factoring: collaborative management of the WCR

Classic reverse factoring is tending to wane in favour of collaborative reverse factoring. The main objective here is not to make maximum profits on the discounts granted. In a collaborative version, the prescriber approaches the relationship with suppliers in a completely different way: here, the buyer offers to help the supplier deal with financially turbulent periods. In this way, collaborative reverse factoring helps to secure the positions of both via collaboration. This is a win–win relationship that guarantees the securing of suppliers for the buyer and liquidity for the supplier. Each wishes for their respective businesses to endure by leveraging risks of all types (market, clients, suppliers, prices, etc).

The problem tackled from a collaborative perspective can be expressed in the following manner: the prescriber does not want, in any circumstances, deterioration of its WCR. It wishes to lengthen payment periods, which amounts to increasing the supplier's risk of failure. Given that risk rises, the financing cost increases. The prescriber's responsibility is called into question. The prescriber should support the supplier and work in the same direction by paying when the invoice is due. Risk-sharing should be bilateral. For this to happen, the 'zero payment extension' approach creates added value on four levels: global reduction of the burden of interest and therefore the product's price; global reduction of the WCR; reduction of the risk of shortage and thus late penalties or loss in income; and streamlining of production.

With this aim of working together, a collaborative reverse factoring programme is more attractive to suppliers. The supplier has a certain freedom to decide on whether to get financing or not, depending on cash needs. This is a real operational lever resting on the equitable distribution of financial gains between the different players. The use of technological platforms ensures its rapid deployment. Collaboration can commence very quickly.

Collaborative WCR highlights the need to pool and optimize the cash needs of different players in the chain, and to innovate in terms of financing. This facilitates the liquidity of stock via adapted asset valuation and 'collateralization' solutions.

The future of supply-chain finance: business pools using auction systems?

One prospect for the future of supply-chain finance lies in a vertical grouping of businesses. Companies with an identical 'solvency quality' can gather (eg three companies rated BBB+) in order to amass a greater volume of outstanding bills and to be able to negotiate with banks more aggressively.

In this context, supply-chain finance will become more democratic, for an auction system between offerors of outstanding bills will be set up. The auctions will enable suppliers to benefit from the best offer each day. The supplier will call on the 'best bidder' on a financial market, allowing considerable masses of money to be drained. The opening of this market to auctions is liable to increase the market share of foreign banks, already quite active, to the detriment of Eurozone banks.

Notes

1 For deeper discussion of the issues raised in Sections 9.1, 9.2 and 9.4, the reader is invited to refer to the following work: Baglin *et al* (2013), Chapters 13 and 14.

2 Taking into account a single stocking rate – expressed as a percentage – to represent all costs means that we consider all these costs as being *variable*, which is false (certain cost items relating to storage are fixed and independent of the quantity stocked). This said, it is possible to demonstrate that this approach does not taint the relevance of results (or very little).

3 Concerning transport costs, if it is suitable to take into account this type of saving in a pooling situation, and as we decided earlier to habitually integrate this unit cost in the direct purchasing cost DDP, it would be appropriate to *break down the purchasing cost to separately show transport apart from the ex-works purchasing cost in a pooling model.*

4 This first situation of a discount on quantity does not call for any particular remarks and does not justify any complex model, in that the buyer meets a cumulative need over the contract's horizon – and no more! However, the interest is obvious in the case of *double-sourcing*: in such a situation, the spread of volumes ordered between two suppliers should integrate this element – amongst other decision-making criteria – when choosing the master scheme for *shared supply*.

5 Not to mention the comparison of energy assessments, respectively carbon and gas with greenhouse effects, between the two long-distance transport modes, or even between a global (distant) source and a local supplier (eg in Western Europe for a French company), which may be decisive for final clients and for business!

6 All quantified data in the case has been modified. However, the situation described remains fully relevant from an educational and professional point of view (our thanks to Professor Gérard Baglin).

7 This section was written by Gilles Huart, co-author of Chapter 12 of this work.

10
Calls for tenders
Major stages, selection process and post-procurement follow-up

The opening up of competition via a call for tenders procedure *is not the sole universal means* of procurement. Indeed, depending on the strategic segmentation of the procurement portfolio, we have seen that the choice and combined use of appropriate levers will vary. However, the introduction of competition in this way is recommended and used in many situations, and for this reason, we dedicate an entire chapter to the subject.

We can further note that some characteristics of calls for tenders seem to be well known and mastered. However, many errors on the *basics* of the practice can still be observed, and we believe that it is useful to go over the fundamental operational elements, if only for the benefit of professionals who have recently taken on positions of responsibility. Finally, small and medium-sized enterprises (SMEs) or very small enterprises (VSEs) will find here the basis for a procurement practice that represents the first level of professionalization of the procurement function.

We will begin by examining the structure of a call for tenders process, then look at the characteristics of each step, before focusing on decision-making on the selection of suppliers.[1]

10/1 Structure and process of a call for tenders

Figure 10.1 presents the classic major stages of a call for tenders process. These must be scrupulously respected in a traditional 'manual' approach to guarantee the full efficiency of the procedure. But they also structure the main offers of e-sourcing tools proposed by specialized service-providers, which will be examined in Chapter 18.

We will go over the main points before detailing each of the main stages. As seen in the central body of the figure, the procedure is composed of seven main stages.

At the top of the figure, dotted lines frame those operations that have bearing on the procedure, but that should normally be carried out *earlier* and over a *medium-term horizon.*

FIGURE 10.1   General process of a call for tenders

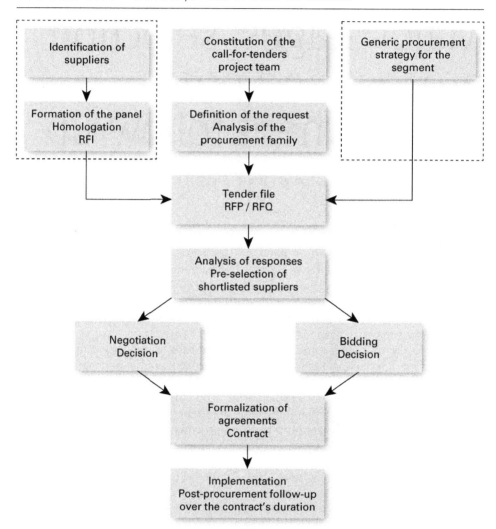

Indeed, for companies that lack maturity in procurement, the establishment of a procurement strategy for a category, as well as the formation of the supplier panel, are operations that are very often carried out and updated with every new call for tenders. We therefore run through the whole of the process at every contract renewal, and unfortunately under time pressure. This does not allow for an efficient updating of the panel, which in fact relies on an ongoing process, namely of sourcing and 'supplier qualification'.

10/1.1 Preliminary medium-term operations

This is the reason why, in terms of supplier policy, we recommend proceeding according to two *sequential* processes: sourcing and the formation of the supplier panel, including the selection and approval process, whose principles and details were dealt with in Chapter 4; then the preparation and execution of the whole call for tenders procedure, taking place over a short-term horizon, most often punctuated by the renewal of contracts approaching maturity for recurrent purchases.

For other purchases, namely non-recurrent ones, this procedure is initiated for every new procurement requirement in step with the launch of new projects.

In particular, in terms of tools and information systems, the company already has – for suppliers on the panel – all technical, industrial, financial and managerial information, namely thanks to the sourcing undertaken, information supplied in response to RFIs (requests for information), and visits and supplementary audits that may have been carried out.

Concerning the *generic* procurement strategy for a procurement category or segment, this should similarly be designed and decided upon independently of the launches of short-term calls for tenders, for two major reasons: a) it is necessary for there to be a certain continuity in the approach over time; and b) in the context of segmentation of the procurement portfolio, a procurement segment includes a number of items or sub-categories of products or services that are often based on the *same generic strategy* although these may give rise to many separate calls for tenders. Taking a segmented approach would most often prevent the formation of a global vision and risk resulting in inconsistencies.

However, what may differ from one call for tenders to another relates more to *tactical decisions specific* to the market conditions of the moment, or else to the security requirements and to the particular specifications of the purchase under consideration.

There is one important *exception* to this anticipatory, separate and systematic handling of the supplier panel and the procurement strategy: the case of companies that operate on the basis of *deals* (such as system suppliers), or that may have to handle *systematic requirements for new purchases* for *never previously purchased* functions, subassemblies or services, and for whom it is recommended that the procurement strategy and the supply panel are dealt with in a single process.

10/1.2 Major stages of the short-term process

Let's now look in detail at the major stages of the central process, on the assumption that we have a panel of pre-qualified suppliers and a reference strategy.

Formation of the project team

A call for tenders should be managed by a team endowed with actual responsibility to carry out the process. Depending on the situation, this team and its leadership will be defined differently:

- in the case of a centralized procurement department with specialized buyers for product/market pairs, the buyer in question (the category or commodity manager) assumes effective responsibility, in association with the main users in question;

- in the case of multiple, closely coordinated business units within a group (see Chapter 16), coordination is undertaken by the lead buyer and the call for tenders managed by and under the joint responsibility of all of the buyers making up the procurement category committee, representing all users from the various profit centres concerned;
- in (less frequent) cases of non-strategic procurement *delegated* to users, the procedure can remain under the responsibility of the users as long as a *qualified reference process* is identified, available, used and all its principles and terms respected.

This project team will have several missions before the actual launch of the process:

- communicating the new call for tenders (ie to all current or potential users);
- gathering all data, quantitative (volumes, prices in particular) and qualitative, for requirements – a task whose duration or complexity depends on whether an integrated (ERP-type) information system exists or not;
- developing the work plan and *ex-ante* scheduling of the call for tenders operation.

There is no divergence in the sequential process of these operations when e-sourcing electronic tools are used.

Definition of the request and the requirements specifications

The analysis of requirements is a key stage that includes:

- detailed understanding of the activity in question and the nature of the specific requirements to satisfy;
- in particular, it is necessary to decide at this stage whether the company is looking for innovation in the technical solution or not: this will have an immediate consequence on the nature of the requirements specifications to be drafted (technical or functional), as described in Chapter 3, Section 3/2;
- analysis of the cost structure of products or services to be purchased and their cost drivers;
- definition of technical, legal and economic restrictions to operation;
- definition of the main technical, quality and sales risks, and analysis of methods for responding to them.

Thanks to this analysis, the requirements specifications can be drawn up. Table 10.1 reviews the main elements (already seen in Chapter 3). This document should be defined jointly with users. In parallel, different aspects of preparation for the later stages of the process should be undertaken.

Possible adjustment of the generic procurement strategy for the segment

This may be necessary depending on the call for tenders in question (in particular, specific security requirements may lead to reconsidering policy on the distribution of supply sources, eg mono-sourcing or double-sourcing).

The first solution, mono-sourcing, may be imposed by supplier exclusivity, if specifically requested by the end-client, or if there is only one service-provider who can guarantee the level of quality sought, or if the product is protected by a patent.

TABLE 10.1   Main elements in a requirements specifications document

Main outline of the requirement	Functional or detailed description? (functions to fulfill or detailed specifications)
	Performance or best-efforts commitment?
	Specific technical criteria (risks and quality demands)
	Environmental restrictions
Other characteristics of the requirement	Quantities / volumes
	Specific order conditions (delivery conditions, desired contractual lead time, etc.)
	Transport and packaging conditions
	Receipt conditions and tests
	Outline of offer-evaluation criteria
Economic characteristics and expected information	Cost objective (if relevant, depending on the purchase)
	Transparent cost breakdown (if relevant, depending on the purchase)
	Payment and invoicing conditions
	Price-revision conditions (if relevant)
	Invoicing currency
	Productivity-improvement plan (depending on the contract horizon targeted)
	Fixed development cost
	Tooling cost (if relevant)
Scope (related additional expectations)	Associated services (eg maintenance, training, technical documentation)
	Guarantee conditions and after-sales conditions
	(Possible) obligation to constitute safety stocks and possible supply-security conditions
	Obligation for scheduled updating of the purchased solution (eg upgrading of software)
	Obligation to manage the product's end-of-life (eg recycling or re-use methods)

It may be followed deliberately to take advantage of a company's purchasing power, to reach a volume effect and thus enable securing a low acquisition cost, or even to guarantee consistency of quality.

The second solution, double-sourcing, aims at supply safety for items for which a substitute is difficult or expensive to develop, as well as greater flexibility when it is necessary to adapt to requirements that fluctuate in quantity, in the absence of the possibility of adequately forecasting their development in advance. This solution may be an alternative to the holding of stock if a company wishes to operate with 'zero stock,' following a just-in-time approach.

In this case, we generally choose a main supply source for the bulk of the purchase volume, for which we negotiate tight prices, and a secondary source to ensure flexibility and security. But to be credible, it is necessary to reserve for the second source a minimum forecast volume so that that it effectively ensures the desired security whilst investing in the business relationship as it offers an acceptable profit margin.

This adaptation of the procurement strategy should *mandatorily ultimately be submitted to internal clients and specifiers* in order to establish clear foundations for the procurement department's commitment in terms of results expected. It is at this stage that decisions should be made on any *possible trade-offs*.

Possible estimation of target costing and simulation of targeted potential gains
This task should take into account the specific situation under consideration. Do we expect to benefit from purchases in the context of recurrent procurement of commodities or standard products? Do we instead seek innovation from suppliers in terms of a solution, and if so, are we following a target-costing logic? Or is it a case of an indirect purchase accompanied by strict budgetary restrictions, where we aim rather for the solution's 'richness' and originality at a set fixed budget?

RFP or RFQ?
Contrary to what is said by some, these two terms describing a supplier consultation are not identical. Referring back to the differences in the situations mentioned above, let's present their main divergences.

An RFP is a *request for proposal* in the case of a specific purchase for which we expect suppliers to put forward proposals on new or adapted solutions (even if the buyer company refers to the technical solution currently in use). The price and economic conditions are therefore not the only variables in the purchase selection process.

It is logical, when operating via the RFP, for calls to tender to take place over several stages (at least two) as the technical solution is fine-tuned, with all suppliers being 'recalibrated' to the normal amendments in the request expressed by the buyer. Given the broader range of information that may then be requested from suppliers, an RFP may constitute a preliminary stage prior to the launch of an RFQ.

An RFQ is a *request for quotation* where the technical requirement is perfectly defined (or even other logistical-type requirements), and where we expect suppliers to *solely* submit a price. As price is the only competition variable, selection is consequently a single-criterion process.

An RFQ is appropriate for perfectly standardized purchases, or for the second phase of specific purchases after we have ensured that all suppliers are 'in line with' a definitive requirement that has been perfectly defined by the client.[2] At this stage, we should carry out a formal preparation of the *principles for analysing offers and choices on evaluation criteria* that will enable the subsequent selection of suppliers (cf see Section 10/2); we also need to form the offer-rating team.

Tender file and call for tenders

This stage, essentially administrative in nature, is presented in Table 10.2 that sets out its main elements.[3]

TABLE 10.2 Content of a call for tenders

Content elements	Description
Letter of introduction	Introduction to the objectives and general description of the procurement request
Confirmation of receipt	Predefined document that the suppliers must return
Information for suppliers	The company's objectives and field of application Company context
Guide to the call for tenders (specific principles governing the process)	Schedule and programme Time restrictions Confidentiality (issue of) Evaluation process (phases, main criteria) Instructions on responding
Requests and specifications (statement of the requirements specifications)	Quantities Specifications for the products or services purchased
Terms and conditions	Terms and conditions of the offer and the establishment of business relationships
Supplier questionnaire	General information on the supplier (organization, financial structure, client references, quality assurance...)
Answer guide	Instructions on how to respond (medium, form, deadline...) Standard form to be filled in
Annexes	Attached documents (eg order form, invoice...)

Analysis of responses and selection of a shortlist

Once responses have been received and validated (for completeness of their content and the absence of interpretation errors as well as errors that use of electronic tools may promote), the rating team undertakes a multi-criteria analysis of the tenders received in order to choose a shortlist. The whole of Section 10/2 is devoted to this procedure, clarified by a detailed example.

At the end of this phase, the following activities need to be carried out:

- rejecting non-competitive or blatantly incomplete offers, or those in which suppliers have not satisfied certain *eliminatory thresholds* for certain criteria (quality, price or other) that have been preliminarily announced;
- informing these suppliers with an explanation on the reasons and causes of their disqualification (the idea is to give them the means to compete subsequently in future calls for tenders with adjusted service levels);[4]
- informing the suppliers still in the running, possibly with final clarifications on the requirement so as to embark on the final selection phase;
- preparation of a virtual internal document on the decision, enabling *ex post* communication to all internal actors on the reasons and justifications for the choices (even if the main actors have been represented on the rating team that dealt with the process).

Such explanation is particularly important for rejected suppliers with supporters within the company who may contest decisions. This is the reason why the rating team should include relevant users and specifiers, as well as quality managers (in most cases).

Final negotiation or auction

Two alternative procedures are possible: 1) either via *electronic auctions* when appropriate for the situation and type of procurement; or 2) traditionally via *parallel and/or adversarial negotiation* between the preselected suppliers.[5]

Here, we will recall a few key (even basic!) points on the negotiation stage in the general context of presenting the global process:

- The success of the negotiation will depend on the quality of its preparation.
- The point is to consistently exploit and refer to the clearly defined procurement strategy and tactical requirements that have been pre-identified. The 'crucial' (non-negotiable) points will obviously also necessarily have been identified.
- We will be better armed (especially with regard to economic conditions) if, on the one hand, we have access to a systematic comparison of the suppliers in the running based on the responses received, and on the other hand, if we have first established a reference economic model for the purchase under consideration.
- At the same time, we will anticipate 'contractualization' effectively by evaluating all risks, to envisage all expected *prevention measures* that will need to be defined explicitly.

This stage thus concerns the *negotiation tactic*. The lead buyer decides if it is appropriate to carry out negotiation alone or in a group, and defines the respective roles. For important negotiations, a type of 'dress rehearsal,' in the form of a 'role play' for example, is advisable, to anticipate the various counter-arguments.

Formalization of agreements (contractualization)

This stage essentially focuses on contractualization – a topic dealt with thoroughly in Chapter 15. However, we here insist upon a few key points concerning practice that should be 'reflex' queries on the part of buyers:

- Concerning the contract, it is necessary to remember to carefully *distinguish between a purchase contract* (for the acquisition of a product) and *a service or outsourcing contract* (that does not generate the same types of risks and should be addressed differently).

- If the purchase takes place *internationally*, it is necessary to make clear which laws and location will apply for reference, and therefore to guarantee that the respective interpretations of the two parties are well aligned. Attention must also be paid to having the logistical and financial terms, as well as the responsibility mechanisms relating to the Incoterms® optimally serve the buyer's interests and being fully defined.

- In the event of transactions carried out with *emerging countries*, whose cultural context and customs patently differ from those of the buyer company, there must be vigilance on a true convergence of interpretations, with particular prudence with regard to countries where the 'written contract' does not hold the same meaning as for Western countries, namely those applying Napoleonic law versus Anglo-Saxon law.

- Outside of the object of a contract and the reciprocal obligations that it creates, let's bear in mind that a contract should also include the *operational solutions anticipatorily offered to mitigate all risks* of the purchase (in particular, as far as possible, all defaults and all disturbances likely to arise, variations in raw material and component prices subject to speculation, and quality-related difficulties unforeseen by both parties, etc, will be analysed and clear operational and economic responses provided).[6]

Obviously, buyers are not lawyers, but they should understand (and apply) legal 'pressure points' and as a result, optimally guide the lawyer whose role remains essential to the written concretization of the commitments taken on either side.

This agreement finalization stage should also lead to *definition of the system for monitoring supplier performance* (see Chapter 4), as well as the terms (if relevant) of relationships, monitoring and periodical meetings aimed at managing the collaboration.

Operational implementation of the procurement and post-procurement monitoring

In the case of procurement of a 'market' product (or a standard commodity), the situation is simple. When the scheduled delivery(ies) take place, the delivered quality and compliance with lead-times, the accuracy of invoiced prices and administrative obligations should be verified before the invoices are paid. A simple monitoring system is set up to issue advance reminders especially if a lean production approach has been decided upon.

The procedure is completely different for procurement based on particular specifications, for we begin with a key phase in which the industrial solution is deployed by the supplier before entering a stabilized operational phase until the end of the contract (eg automobile manufacturers producing new sub-systems aimed at a manufacturer's new model).

In this case, a schedule for the 'step-up' and development of the solution will need to be established according to the stages presented in Figure 10.2.

We assume that the product has been designed in its definitive version, that it is perfectly defined according to target costing (which implies that we have also defined the major technological choices for the production process).

Development and finalization of the process

This stage has the following aims and characteristics:

- Definitive fine-tuning of the production process, with a very clear (FMECA-type)[7] analysis of the risks associated with the selected process, and appropriate capacity studies.

- Finalization and set-up of the product and process quality-assurance system,[8] and more broadly, definition of all indictors that make up the supplier's dashboard in the monitoring phase (quality and lead-time indicators; no price indicators as price is fixed contractually, but indicators to monitor additional costs associated with the management of the supplier and with the handling of failures and disputes arising in the course of collaboration that can be described as the cost of non-quality).

- Definitive specification of packaging and transport methods (even storage if this option has been chosen).

- Detailed definition of the whole of the product launch plan.

FIGURE 10.2   Development stages of a new technical solution

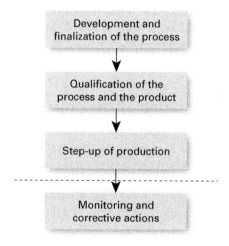

- Design and production of possible specific tooling, including their qualification by the client.

Qualification of the process and the product

This crucial stage consists in qualifying the product/process pair in real industrial conditions, as well as all associated services envisaged in the requirements specifications. It mainly comprises:

- prototyping and the approval of delivered parts or products;
- definitive approval of the associated industrial and logistical process;
- approval of the quality system in place and the system's traceability enabling a guarantee of responsiveness in the event of future defects;
- validation of the supplier's supply system for all raw materials and all necessary procurement for the manufacturing of the product, with an associated security plan.

Step-up of production

Production can finally begin. This stage most often includes pre-series and enables final checks to take place.

Follow-up and corrective actions

Here, we are in the operational phase throughout the contract's lifespan. All quality-assurance systems should logically operate and the management of foreseen development plans is implemented.[9] In particular, breakdown solutions in the event of delivery default (delays) are activated, as well as claims in the case of major quality problems.

Some cost drivers should possibly be shifted to the failing supplier (obviously provisions for this should be included in the contract beforehand):

- costs of defective parts;
- penalties resulting from additional administrative costs;
- specific costs corresponding to particular corrective actions (systematic inspections and checks of batches, sorting operations, etc);
- partial cost impact stemming from the consequences of failures in the client's industrial process. In the automotive industry, for example, this may consist in asking the supplier to take charge (fully or partially) of the economic consequences of vehicle recalls from car distributors, corresponding to changes in parts following serious quality incidents relating to components. There is no contradiction in penalizing a supplier and simultaneously implementing a development plan with the same supplier.

10/2 Multi-criteria selection of suppliers

To rate suppliers professionally, it is necessary to define a process and an explicit offer evaluation and selection system. This system, already mentioned earlier in this work, should be formally organized into successive phases presented by Figure 10.3. Our aim here is to analyse in detail the phase of the process visible at the bottom of the figure (*it is assumed that the supplier panel receiving the call for tenders pre-exists*).

10/2.1 Selection process and criteria

Rating and selection on the basis of a call for tenders generally takes place in two stages.

Rating principles

An initial preselection stage is carried out, based on criteria designed to eliminate those offers which do not comply with certain thresholds (eg a specific technical skill, specific industrial equipment, a price lower than a benchmark level, an adapted geographical location, etc).

Some of these criteria are *the same as those used for the sourcing and homologation phase*, examined in detailed in Chapter 4. We nevertheless will go over them here as it is highly possible that their respective weights will not be the same depending on the specific situations and the specific requirements of various purchases (nevertheless belonging to the same category or segment).

FIGURE 10.3   Reminder of the multi-level selection system

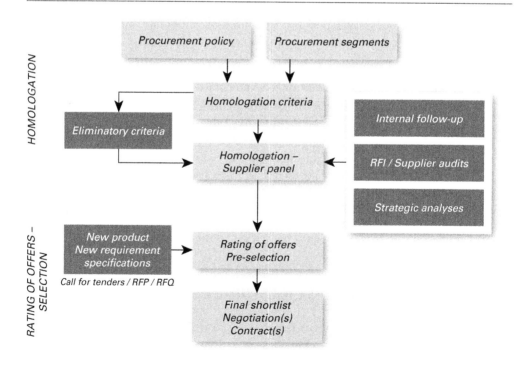

A second stage consists in *rating* the suppliers still in the running according to a scale to be defined for each of the criteria. Ultimately, a single supplier is selected if the call for tenders explicitly points to one. But most often, we will proceed to the selection of a shortlist prior to a final negotiation phase.

Database (reminder)

The formal offer-rating system implies the compilation and use of a database, relying on internal and external information. Indeed, the rating procedure supposes that the company has gathered and makes use of specific information on the suppliers. *We should not pass judgements on the basis of intuitions, image or subjective information.*

Some information is internal in origin (eg transactional data managed by the ERP or quality-management system). Other information should be obtained by responses to the call for tenders that, effectively, should include other elements on top of mere translation of the requirements specifications. Finally, some of the information can only be collected outside the company (financial or professional bodies, plant visits and audits, quality and logistical audits, test series, etc).

Multi-criteria analysis and nature of relevant criteria

This evaluation should rely on the use of *formal and explicit analysis* guaranteeing the objectivity of the procedure, and also enabling clear communication on the decision taken (internally but also vis-à-vis non-selected suppliers, giving reasons for rejection, so that they may be more competitive in future calls).

It is thus necessary to define a list of selection criteria *along with the relative weight* for each in a particular purchase. This task is often entrusted to a multi-functional team as the procurement department rarely has all information and skills at its disposal.

What is most important at the outset is to determine a detailed list of decisive criteria in such a way as to make the decision objective. This list should translate the procurement policy and tactical approach adopted for the call for tenders. Table 10.3 presents a non-limitative list of criteria generally used (some of which logically carry on from those used in the qualification phase seen earlier).[10]

10/2.2 Implementation of the system: a detailed example

To present the supplier-selection procedure in action, here is a simple example of a European aeronautics company that we will call Aero Equipments.[11]

Background to the situation

This company is an equipment supplier in the aeronautics sector, producing a number of systems related to aircraft motorization and integrated into the engines of major international manufacturers. Our exercise focuses on the case of the PX303 injection pump, perfectly defined by requirements specifications and purchased from two suppliers in parallel, Pearle and Airpro, a double-sourcing strategy chosen so as to avoid delivery failure.

TABLE 10.3 Sample list of supplier selection criteria

Activity area	Selection criteria
Technical, research and development competency	• workforce and proven competency of research teams • ability to provide technical information and to offer training (for technical purchases as well as equipment goods) • ability to manage and/or undertake the design and production of specific tooling • quality of development and monitoring equipment.
Manufacturing competency	• availability of an adequate manufacturing capacity (with the possibility of flexibility of equipment and load fluctuations) • technical level of machines and equipment (adaptation of the technology used) • an effectively practised maintenance policy • in the event of specialty subcontracting, availability or not of own necessary tooling • qualification(s) and motivation of the workforce (quality of the work environment).
Product and process quality	• understanding of and compliance with the company's requirements specifications (if relevant, in the case of functional requirements specifications, efficiency of the specific technical solution proposed) • proposed product (or material) qualified by technical services • satisfactory or easily adaptable quality-assurance and traceability system in place • conforms to level of quality expected in practice (rejection rate) • satisfactory after-sales service and repair guarantee.
Lead-time/flexibility	• proposed lead-time conforms to requirement, and under control • complies with stated lead-times, demonstrated by business history • supplier's logistical system a priori enables lean production and/or delivery • efficiency of the flow-planning system (production and logistical system) • storage capacity if necessary (stock on consignment) • supplier's capacity to manage stock under its responsibility according to a VMI (vendor-managed inventory) • supplier's demonstrated capacity to manage transport directly.

TABLE 10.3 *continued*

Activity area	Selection criteria
Global cost of acquisition/economic conditions	• price and/or competitive costs breakdown (depending on a reference to be defined) • payment conditions/incoterms/possible exchange-rate risks • economic conditions for responsibility for transport (depending on the geographic location) • other costs implied by the purchase (constitution of stocks, financial impact of in-process production in relation to supply cycles, impact of delivery conditions) • competitive global cost of acquisition (or ownership).
Delivery conditions and service	• ability to deliver the totality of the ordered quantities (on a historical basis) • execution of the deliveries in order (thus facilitating the monitoring of receptions) • quality, transparency and anticipation of information • quality of the packaging (offer of specific packaging) • error-free compliance with the routing instructions (ability to deliver to one or several predefined sites).
Ability to adapt/ reactivity	• quick to react when difficulties arise (eg by sending technicians) • capacity to integrate short-term modifications in deliveries • capacity to adapt manufacturing plans.
Financial security/ sustainability of the company/management	• financial health (cash flow, debt rate, etc) • sustainability of the management • client relationship system in place (key-account approach).

This procurement category is made up of specific complex assemblies, produced from detailed technical requirements specifications in the context of a subcontracting relationship (the supplier being responsible for the quality of the product delivered). Clearly, the requirements for quality and complete reliability are of foremost importance; but the economic imperatives of engine manufacturers, the ordering parties of Aero Equipments, impose great cost control. This category represents around 25 per cent of direct (production-related) procurement. In addition, this type of product is the object of aeronautical certification as is the case for all components of devices equipping motors.

To set the context, the procurement policy is based on the following main elements:

• a desire to operate in stringent conditions of utmost professional ethics (respect of commitments to suppliers);

- a desire to place a priority on quality and on seeking the competitiveness of purchases, translated by the obtaining of a minimum global purchase cost;
- a necessity to watch over the security of suppliers (this objective should be achieved, when possible, by the maintenance of two suppliers in parallel for the one subassembly even if distribution is managed in an uneven manner);
- if possible (in the event of a subcontracting relationship), subject to the verification of technical competency, endeavour to promote regional employment by maintaining one batch of work for local service-providers;
- commitment (in the case of a subcontracted segment) to sign yearly markets to stabilize economic conditions and to give oneself the time to define and follow performance improvement plans;
- only working with partners mastering aeronautical technologies and enjoying a good reputation in this sector on an international scale.

The current distribution of the market for the PX303 pump is: Pearle (60 per cent) and Airpro (40 per cent).

For all subsequent economic costing, we specify the following three cost elements: the company has evaluated its unit cost for delivery calls and reception handling at £150; its cost of capital comes to 10 per cent per year; and its management, inventory monitoring and storage costs are costed at 5 per cent per year.

It is September 2013 and we are anticipating annual demand for 2014.

The subassembly: the object of the call for tenders

Situated at the end of the power-supply circuit, this pump is located upstream from the fuel injector. A high-pressure and high-flow pump, the PX303 was initially designed by Aero Equipments for this specific application. The annual requirement for 2014 is estimated at 660 units, whose forecast consumption is roughly regularly distributed over time (as it is directly related to the rhythm of engine assembly on the assembly line).

This type of component systematically gives rise to qualification of the supplier prior to any collaboration. This qualification is carried out in reference to requirements specifications, morpho-dimensional characteristics to be complied with (insertion of the subassembly in the end-product), operational characteristics (such as flow) and reliability and 'maintainability' characteristics.

In spite of quality-assurance systems, the company maintains systematic monitoring of the products received. This monitoring also applies to the transmission of supplier documents attesting to compliance, necessarily accompanying batches and without which a batch cannot be declared 'available' for assembly (aeronautical traceability). In the event of non-compliance, the defective pump is returned to the supplier who must replace it as quickly as possible.

Following the launch of the call for tenders, five suppliers respond, the two current ones as well as three other companies: Hightec, Flytop and Motor Werke.[12] Here follows, for each supplier, information on each supplier and extracts from their responses.

Pearle

Pearle is a recognized storage management initiative (SMI) in the world of aeronautics, a current subcontractor of the company on which it relies for 70 per cent of its *total* workload as it is entrusted with the manufacturing of several mechanical components for Aero Equipments. For the pump, Pearle carries out 60 per cent of deliveries. The pump alone represents 25 per cent of Pearle's workload.

Pearle is a small business employing 150 people. Created five years earlier by a former Aero Equipments technician, its premises are found 50 km from the company's plant in Coventry. Pearle's financial results have been deteriorating for the past three years, with the last year recording an operating loss (3.5 per cent of turnover).

Pearle manufactures this product according to plans supplied to it by the design department of Aero Equipments. The supplier has no prototyping facilities or sophisticated methods department. Pearle uses the manufacturing tooling also provided by the buyer five years earlier, with a forecast lifespan of another three years.

Quality: over the past year, the percentage of parts rejected at the reception inspection has come to 1 per cent of deliveries. No real quality assurance exists for the manufacturing process. No improvement plan is underway.

Production: at the present time, Pearle's production capacity is saturated by the manufacturing of PX303 pumps. However, the production equipment and staff seem to be adapted and competent.

Sales conditions: the ex-works price comes to £605 (excluding tax) with a 30-day deadline for payment. Taking into account the amortization of equipment belonging to Aero Equipments, the total cost comes to £641 (excluding tax) for the company.

If the company wishes for a price including delivery, Pearle can take charge of transport and will invoice it at £30 per pump delivered under its responsibility.

Scheduling of requirements/deliveries: Aero Equipments places its orders for deliveries according to its manufacturing programme (on the basis of weekly deliveries). It provides an anticipated order schedule for a 6-month duration, rectified every month.

Pearle makes available its entire storage depot from which Aero Equipments can be delivered depending on slight fluctuations in its requirements. Indeed, the current contract stipulates that the company must maintain safety stock of 30 devices.

Airpro

Situated 150 km from its customer, this company supplies 40 per cent of Aero Equipments' pump supplies. Four years ago, Airpro satisfied almost its entire demand, but wished to partially withdraw from this level of commitment. Aero Equipment now represents a total of 5 per cent of the company's overall supply of hi-tech mechanical components.

Airpro has around 700 employees. It belongs to a large group that has developed thanks to the automobile and aviation markets (a deliberate diversification strategy), thus sheltering it from the risks of under-activity. Airpro is the subsidiary positioned in the aviation niche, and has sales relationships with most national and even international manufacturers.

Quality: the company has a reputation for the quality and technicality of its products, the conscientiousness of its sales organization, and the efficiency of its after-sales service (in the event of operations on client premises). For the PX303 pump, manufactured according to requirements specifications, the rejection rate upon reception is no more than 0.1 per cent.

Production: with highly professional production methods, Airpro has developed its own tooling for manufacturing (whose cost is included in the unit price below). A high level of equipment and labour are available.

Sales conditions: the current sales price is £709 (excluding tax), *delivered free of charge*. Airpro would keep the same price for the coming year. A payment deadline of 60 net days.

Order/delivery conditions: Airpro has no specific order conditions but it only delivers in batches of 60 items (probable counterpart to the free delivery). It uses its own means for deliveries. The normal delivery lead-time of three weeks (no stock held) is generally respected right down to the day.

Finally, it has adapted to the requirements of Aero Equipments by developing specific packaging.

Hightec (new supplier)

Located 500 km from the company, Hightec formerly supplied the pump to Aero Equipments as a subcontractor using Aero Equipments' tooling (today used by Pearle). It is now an independent company that achieves a limited turnover with Aero Equipments.

Today, Hightec has the reputation as a company at the cutting edge of technology. Following directives issued by its CEO, it devotes 5 per cent of its turnover to research. Its design department, composed of three engineers, is recognized in the aeronautics milieu. In terms of methods, Hightec is extremely professional and has set up a quality-assurance system for its manufacturing.

New proposal: six months ago, Hightec offered the company a new type of pump. This pump relies on a new technology that, according to Hightec, would enable improvement of both manufacturing and operation, but it necessitates the use of new parts and alloys.

Until now, the product offered by Hightec has not been approved by Aero Equipments: indeed, tests carried out give reason to foresee a rejection rate of around 0.3 per cent given the more elaborate technology. However, other clients of the company have confirmed a high level of quality upon reception (with a rapid exchange of parts if problems arise).

Sales conditions: these are summed up below in detail:

- market conditions: annual addressable market of 100 to 700 pumps;
- sales price: from 100 to 199 units: £1,000 (excluding tax), ex-works price from 200 to 399 units: £850 (excluding tax), ex-works price; 400 and over: £700 (excluding tax), ex-works price;
- delivery conditions: delivery lead-time of one month;
- payment conditions: 30 net days;
- cost of external transport (independent company): around £50 per device.

Sectoral situation: three months ago, Hightec entered into a firm 2-year contract for this type of pump with a competitor of Aero Equipments. Aeronautical 'qualification' was obtained for the new pump without any problems.

Flytop (new supplier)

Flytop is a medium-sized company with 350 personnel located 150 km from Coventry. It is recognized in the aeronautics sector for the quality of its manufacturing.

Aero Equipments has never engaged in a sales relationship with Flytop, which was the preferred supplier of Mac Douglas, a major competitor of Aero Equipments on the civil aviation market.

Following the partial failure of the launch of a new range of Mac Douglas aircrafts, Flytop finds itself in a difficult situation (its production capacity is under-utilized and partially available in the short term). In this way, the company has made contact with Aero Equipments to offer its services. As the conditions on offer are interesting, the company envisages using this new supplier.

Quality/manufacturing: Flytop is known for the rigour of its quality control during manufacturing, demonstrated by an almost non-existent rejection rate (0.1 per cent) of deliveries according to industry sources. In addition, Flytop agrees to 100 per cent quality control prior to dispatch on the basis of a monitoring plan for its customers.

The machine fleet is a priori adapted to machining for the PX303 pump.

Tooling: however, to take charge of the manufacturing of the pump (a system that it did not manufacture for MAC DOUGLAS), Flytop must use production tooling that it does not possess. Given its just-balanced financial situation, the specific set of tooling should be provided to it by Aero Equipments.

This equipment may either be purchased directly by Aero Equipments (at a cost of £50,000) or transferred from Pearle to Flytop (transfer of Aero Equipments' equipment *at a transfer cost that we will estimate at nil for the purposes of simplification*). In this case, amortization should be linear over five years.

Sales conditions: these are summed up below in detail:

- order: annual addressable market of 250 pumps (maximum);
- initial price: £580 (excluding tax) ex-works (not including amortization of the Aero Equipments tooling set);
- payment: 30 days at the end of the month;
- transport cost: £50 (excluding tax) per device.

Delivery: Flytop does not wish for any particular conditions for the order per unit (minimum: 25 pumps per delivery for packaging reasons). The company commits to a delivery lead-time of 15 working days following the placing of a delivery order. Storage would be possible in the plant of Flytop, made available to AERO EQUIPMENT but in consignment.

Motor Werke (new supplier)

Aero Equipments has never obtained supplies from Motor Werke, and is unfamiliar with this company. The subsidiary of a German group, it employs 1,500 people and is very well established throughout Europe. It has specialized in the market for products and supplies aimed at public-works equipment and automobiles. In a plant in the Midlands, it carries out production and assembly activities. It imports a certain number of products from Germany, which it distributes on the British market.

The German company, with its various subsidiaries, occupies the No. 2 rank on the international supply market for automobiles and public-works equipment. It has a reputation for aggressiveness and sales reliability, as well as its flexibility in adapting to its clients' technical problems.

Just recently, the company made contact with Aero Equipments. Taking account of its leading position (30 per cent of the British pump market for automobiles and public-works equipment), Aero Equipments invited the company to submit proposals for the PX303.

Quality: fine reputation, but not in the aeronautics sector.

Technical proposal: product (pump) largely meeting the performance demanded by Aero Equipments, but using a system based on a different technology. To date, it has not received aeronautical qualification. In addition, this pump does not altogether conform to the dimensional specifications expected by Aero Equipments, consequently entailing slight assembly modifications (estimated cost of a new design: £60,000). However, Motor Werke offers to assign a 2-engineer team to take part in adaptation of its equipment to the specificities of the Aero Equipments engine. The company demonstrates a genuine desire for collaboration over a number of years rather than simply 'pulling off a deal'.

Sales conditions: these are summed up below in detail:

- price: £665 (excluding tax), delivered free of charge;
- annual market: minimum of 300 pumps;
- deliveries: in batches of at least 50 items;
- payment: 60 days at the end of the month.

Delivery: the announced delivery lead-time is three weeks, with Motor Werke holding no stock of this adapted version of its standard pump model.

Comparative rating of the offers

In this type of selection situation, a plausible and simplified rating table may take the form as shown in Table 10.4. We can make a few explanatory comments on the different dimensions of the tool.

First, as these potential new suppliers had been added to the supplier panel, the group *pre-validated* the companies against certain structural criteria, as part of the approvals process. Certain of these criteria are not examined here; we will focus on the detailed selection stage on the basis of the rating of offers.

We see that the rating group has selected six main 'macro-criteria' with figures on their respective weights in bold (see the second column). Next, each criterion is subdivided into 'detailed' criteria with their own weight distributions for the corresponding 'macro-criterion'. It is clear that technical and industrial aspects come first in the selection, for the economic aspect only weighs a total of 15 per cent.

Regarding weighting, it is generally highly advisable to express the problem of respective coefficients as the distribution of a total weight necessarily equal to 100 per cent. Indeed, in this case, as the total is 'imposed', we *naturally find ourselves in the situation of having to rank in order of importance* and therefore define priorities! Otherwise, 'non-decisions' may flourish.

The choice of criteria is also essential; this choice should be in sync with the situation, but it is *base-building* as well. Indeed, a rating should not be undertaken if the team does not have reliable and validated information on all the suppliers beforehand. Hence the necessity to have established the criteria before the call for tenders and the definition of the content of the RFP.

TABLE 10.4 Multi-criteria rating table

Criteria	Weight	Pearle		Airpro		Hightec		Flytop		Motor	
Technical competency / R&D renown	**10%**										
Supplier's knowledge of the sector	5%	5	0.25	5	0.25	5	0.25	5	0.25	0	0
Design office / Understanding of the functional requirements specifications	5%	2	0.1	5	0.25	5	0.25	5	0.25	3	0.15
Manufacturing competency	**20%**										
Availability of an adequate capacity	10%	4	0.4	3	0.3	5	0.5	2	0.2	5	0.5
Technical level of equipment	5%	5	0.25	5	0.25	3	0.15	4	0.2	3	0.15
Availability of tooling	5%	5	0.25	5	0.25	5	0.25	0	0	3	0.15
Quality	**25%**										
Qualified product	10%	5	0.5	5	0.5	0	0	5	0.5	3	0.3
Qualification related to quality assurance	5%	0	0	2	0.1	3	0.15	5	0.25	3	0.15
Rejection rate	10%	0	0	5	0.5	2	0.2	5	0.5	1	0.1

TABLE 10.4 continued

Criteria	Weight	Pearle		Airpro		Hightec		Flytop		Motor	
Lead time / flexibility	**20%**										
Length of lead time	7%	5	0.35	3	0.21	2	0.14	5	0.35	3	0.21
Reactivity for defective parts	3%	3	0.09	5	0.15	4	0.12	5	0.15	1	0.03
Storage capacity (supplier stock)	3%	5	0.15	0	0	0	0	5	0.15	0	0
Respect of lead times	7%	5	0.35	5	0.35	3	0.21	4	0.28	3	0.21
Economic conditions	**15%**										
Price	10%	3	0.3	3	0.3	2	0.2	5	0.5	3	0.3
Payment conditions	2.50%	5	0.125	4	0.1	3	0.075	3	0.075	5	0.125
Coverage of transport	2.50%	4	0.1	5	0.125	0	0	0	0	5	0.125
Sustainability / financial health	**10%**										
Financial health	5%	2	0.1	5	0.25	5	0.25	3	0.15	5	0.25
Management quality	5%	4	0.2	5	0.25	4	0.2	5	0.25	2	0.1
TOTAL	**100%**	**3.665**		**4.135**		**2.945**		**4.205**		**2.85**	
RANKING		**3**		**1**		**4**		**2**		**5**	

Finally, the rating scale is not neutral: it should avoid ratings being too scattered, but nevertheless allow offers and suppliers to be adequately differentiated. In addition, unlike in Table 10.4, we recommend that the scale be set to even numbers: any odd-numbered scale offers those who hesitate about a rating to 'chicken out' or 'take the easy way out' by choosing the 'average' score (a 'decisive' scale of 1 to 4 is often the most suitable).

For any given supplier, their respective score for each criterion appears in the first column whilst the second column provides the corresponding weighted score. The sum of these weighted scores makes up the supplier's global score, enabling a comparison with the other tenderers. In this way, all comparisons are possible and usable.

We can see on Table 10.4 that Motor Werke and Hightec received 'zero' scores for two basic criteria: their overall scores are still calculated, but the operational decision is rejection in this operation in the absence of pre-existing qualification (per criterion and globally). We therefore arrive at a shortlist comprising three suppliers that remain in the running.

This formalized process is interesting for three main reasons:

- it allows introducing rationality into an evaluation which could otherwise easily become intuitive;
- it offers output that is easily communicable internally and externally;
- it involves specifiers and internal clients in active participation in decision-making that, by nature and by choice, is collective. As a result, the buyer does not have to re-explain a decision as would be required if proceeding in two stages.

Simulation of the global purchasing cost

Generally, the new supply solution should be compared to the current situation in terms of global cost, if the buyer does not have an objective *target* cost. In any case, the anticipated costing of the global cost should be undertaken in all circumstances. Finally, let's remember that here, we are obliged to retain two suppliers in order to respect the strategic objective of double-sourcing aimed at securing supply.

Current market (present situation)

Table 10.5 illustrates the method for calculating the simplified global cost for the *current 2013 market* with the suppliers Pearle (60 per cent) and Airpro (40 per cent of the global volume). Certain costs in the table are mere sample figures, introduced for illustrative reasons, for which corresponding information was not available for the real-life example. For the rest, we see that the calculation (as a whole) includes the following elements:

- the unit price of the supplier (increased by the transport cost, depending on the case);
- the amortization of tooling;
- the cost of deliveries and storage (working capital requirement);
- the cost of non-quality;
- the cost of monitoring and managing the supplier;
- the saving resulting from payment conditions.

TABLE 10.5   Calculation of the current global cost of acquisition

Hypotheses:

AERO EQUIPMENT cost of capital	10%	
Cost of inventory management	5%	15%
Unit cost of delivery	150	
Working weeks / year	48	

	Pearle	Airpro	Total
Market distribution	60%	40%	
Consumption / year	660	660	
Market / year	396	264	660
Unit starting cost	605	709	
Unit amortization	36	0	
Carriage	30	0	
Unit cost incl. delivery to AERO	**671**	**709**	**686.2**
Unit cost storage / year	100.65	106.35	
Deliveries (units / delivery)	8.25	60	
Cost of delivery / year	7 200	660	**7 860**
Cost of storage / year	415	3 190	**3 605**
Cost of non-quality	0	0	**0**
Cost of development	0	0	**0**
Cost of supplier monitoring	0	0	**0**
Cost of acquisition / year	265 716	187 176	452 892
Subtotal	273 331	191 026	464 357
Unit total price	690.23	723.58	703.57
Payment conditions (days)	30	60	
Resulting saving	−2 066.80	−3 076.90	**−5143.70**
Cumulative total COST	**271 264.20**	**187 949.10**	**459 213.30**
Unit total COST	**685.01**	**711.93**	**695.78**

It thus appears that in 2013, the average weighted unit cost of the pump is £695.78. This is the cost price DDP including delivery to the user (in other words, the client's plant). We note that inventory costs are calculated by taking into account an inventory management rate of 15 per cent per year, whilst savings related to payment conditions apply only to the cost of capital of 10 per cent per year.

New solution chosen

After examination of Table 10.5, the rating committee could objectively observe that the 'double-sourcing' solution that would be both the most economical and logical for 2014 would be to retain the pair consisting of Flytop (38 per cent of the global volume corresponding to the 250 pumps that the company can manufacture) and Airpro (62 per cent to make up the 660 yearly pumps). These two suppliers would be retained as they occupied the top two rankings for the rating (scores above 4). Table 10.6 illustrates the corresponding costing.

The new unit global cost would be equal to £692.02, in other words a reduction of (only) −0.54 per cent compared to the pricing in the current year. However, technical and quality concerns would be eminently better satisfied, at an 'approximately' equivalent cost. However, this solution heavily penalizes Pearle and amounts to removing 25 per cent of its global load – a move which risks placing it in great short-term difficulties, or even forcing it to cease operations! However, if this were to happen, the other manufacturing requirements that Aero Equipments currently entrusts to this supplier would suddenly have to be redeployed to other sources.

Reading between the lines, we are facing a common situation in which a medium-sized company, set up to deal with a spinoff operation, now finds that this one customer represents 70 per cent of its total turnover.[13]

Nonetheless, Pearle is technically competent and reputable, and is penalized mainly because of its quality problems.

Possible alternative

In this way, a second 'school of thought' within the rating committee suggests, whilst redirecting the bulk of volume towards Airpro and Flytop, maintaining Pearle for lower quantities in 2014, with the aim of helping it to deal with its quality problems, thus following a conciliatory collaborative approach.

As shown by Table 10.7, the market for 2014 would then have a 'transitory' character, with three suppliers according to the following distribution: Flytop (38 per cent, in other words 250 units), Airpro (40 per cent, in other words about 260 units), and Pearle (22 per cent, in other words about 150 units). This lower figure would enable the latter to focus on quality (with the support of the client's quality experts).

This third solution is the economical equivalent of the others (even more economical than the previous one) as it represents a diminishing of the unit global cost by 0.7 per cent to a cost of £690.69.

It is a solution that assures the future, for it would avoid placing one supplier in an unbearable position that would bring the risk of its disappearance in the long run. By proceeding to deal with an undeniably tricky short-term problem in this way, Aero Equipments would contribute to retaining a good level of competition in what is already a restricted market.

TABLE 10.6   Calculation of the new global cost (logical solution)

Hypotheses:

AERO EQUIPMENT cost of capital	10%	
Cost of inventory management	5%	15%
Unit cost of delivery	150	
Working weeks / year	48	
Flytop delivery (units)	25	
Flytop carriage (hypothesis)	60	

	Flytop	Airpro	Total
Market distribution	38%	62%	
Consumption / year	660	660	
Market / year	250	409	660
Unit starting cost	580	709	
Unit amortization	36	0	
Carriage	50	0	
Unit cost incl. delivery to AERO	**666**	**709**	**691.64**
Unit cost storage / year	99.90	106.35	
Deliveries (units / delivery)	25	60	
Cost of delivery / year	1 500	1 022	**2 522**
Cost storage / year	1 248	3 190	**4 438**
Cost of non-quality	0	0	**0**
Cost of development	0	0	**0**
Cost of supplier monitoring	0	0	**0**
Cost of acquisition / year	166 500	289 981	456 481
Subtotal	169 248	294 193	463 441
Unit total price	676.99	719.3	702.18
Payment conditions (days)	45	60	
Resulting saving	−1 941.80	−4 766.80	**−6 708.60**
Cumulative total COST	**167 306.20**	**289 426.20**	**456 732.40**
Unit total COST	**669.22**	**707.64**	**692.02**

TABLE 10.7   Calculation of the global cost (transitory solution)

Hypotheses:

AERO EQUIPMENT cost of capital	10%	
Cost of inventory management	5%	15%
Unit cost of delivery	150	
Working weeks / year	48	
Flytop delivery (units)	25	
Flytop carriage (hypothesis)	60	
New tooling set	10 000	Linear over 5 years

	Flytop	Airpro	Pearle	Total
Market distribution	38%	40%	22%	100%
Consumption / year	660	660	660	
Market / year	250	264	145	660
Unit starting cost	580	709	605	
Unit amortization	40	0	36	
Carriage	50	0	30	
Unit cost incl. delivery to AERO	**670**	**709**	**671**	**684.80**
Unit cost storage / year	100.50	106.35	100.65	
Deliveries (units / delivery)	25	60	8.25	
Cost of delivery / year	1 500	660	2 636	**4 796**
Cost storage / year	1 256	3 190	415	**4 861**
Cost of non-quality	0	0	0	**0**
Cost of development	0	0	0	**0**
Cost of supplier monitoring	0	0	0	**0**
Cost of acquisition / year	167 500	187 176	97 295	451 971
Subtotal	170 256	191 026	100 346	461 628
Unit cost price	681.02	723.58	692.04	699.44
Payment conditions (days)	45	60	**30**	
Resulting saving	−1 941.80	−3 076.90	**−756.80**	**−5 775.50**
Cumulative GLOBAL COST	**168 314.20**	**187 949.10**	**99 589.20**	**455 852.50**
Unit GLOBAL COST	**673.26**	**711.93**	**686.82**	**690.69**

The final decision

The final decision for this (generally applicable) example *can only be 'political'*, and not purely technical and economical.

In this case, the operational players have fulfilled their mission and the end decision does not fall upon them. A purchasing committee composed of leaders ultimately had to make the call by integrating medium-term interests or even commitments (ie ethical ones) created by the past imprudence of buyers who allowed Pearle to occupy too great a volume of the procurement portfolio.

There is a strong likelihood that the procurement policy will be reviewed and strengthened in a direction characterized by less dependency on suppliers, and/or – in an opposing or complementary manner – the absolute necessity of setting up a systematic collaborative approach with them. This point should be examined in relation to the development of suppliers dealt with in Chapter 4.

Notes

1 The other well-known process is short-term supply, triggered by the purchase request or delivery call and ending with the payment of the invoice. This process will not be developed here as it does not engage the responsibility of the procurement department, but that of managers of upstream flows and/or supply planners.

2 This is precisely the core problem of procurement undertaken via electronic auction tools when suppliers consider that the 'dice are loaded' (the levels of comprehension of the requirement not being the same among them) and that the auction is not ethical from this viewpoint.

3 The call for tenders can only be sent to qualified suppliers on the panel (called, in this case, a 'closed' call for tenders). This is not the common and legal rule for public procurement. However, when the idea is to calibrate a new supplier against those on the panel, it is conceivable to include the latter in the competition. This way of proceeding is also an effective and motivating method for specifying the company's level of requirement in view of the new supplier's subsequent qualification (on condition that the supplier is then informed on its positioning and the exact nature of improvements to be made).

4 It is also possible (if automation of the rating system allows it) to transmit graphics to the rejected suppliers enabling them to position themselves in relation to *all the suppliers* (whilst preserving the anonymity of individual cases for deontological reasons)!

5 We have decided not to tackle the principles, rules, tactics and techniques of negotiation in detail in this book. The combinations of situations would be too numerous to describe, and this subject would necessitate an entire work. Excellent books on the topic already exist. We therefore recommend that the reader consult a specialized bibliography.

6 This approach crosses over with the rules involved in sustainable development approaches vis-à-vis suppliers. It also offers the merit of pacifying relationships, and largely decreasing all possible resulting disturbances.

7 The FMECA is a method well-known to quality managers for analysing and prioritizing industrial risks. It is described in all specialist works dealing with quality. The reader can find an introductory description of this tool in Baglin *et al* (2013), Chapter 20.

8 Same reference as above, encompassing the reference chapter as a whole.

9 The reader is invited to refer to Chapter 4 that provides details on what is to be understood by a 'supplier development plan' in a collaborative approach.

10 An important reminder: if the purchase in question concerns a category *for which there is no supplier panel* (the prior object of qualification for certain structural criteria), it is extremely important to reintegrate these criteria in this level of the call for tenders procedure, namely in relation to obligations and practices in terms of ethics, and social and environmental responsibility.

11 This example drawn from a real-life case has been disguised and simplified while nonetheless preserving the realism and relevance of the original professional situation, the objective here being essentially educational.

12 In the real-life example, a higher number of suppliers responded. However, this number has been deliberately reduced in this text to simplify the presentation of the example. All names have obviously been invented.

13 Let's remember that in such a solution, if the supplier is led to file for bankruptcy following the withdrawal of an important client, and other creditors bring the case to justice, European case law has defined a threshold beyond which the client company may be sued for 'abuse of a dominant situation'. The figure below which it is appropriate to remain is 25 per cent of the supplier's total output. As a result, we understand that this 'dependency' limit is reproduced by the procurement policies of many large companies, and to be mandatorily respected (beyond simple common sense).

11
Procurement of services
CapEx purchasing decisions

Why devote a whole chapter to the procurement of services and CapEx?[1] Regarding the first, because the bulk of procurement concepts and methods was historically developed for the direct procurement of tangible products or goods, and it seems important to emphasize the *main differences and specificities* offered by services, including intellectual services. This applies in all companies even if they are industrial in nature, and even if this so-called *indirect* procurement does not represent, for a certain number of them, their core business.

Regarding the second, because the stakes involved are considerable, and because, from an entirely different angle, they concern balance sheet items unlike other purchases classified as operating expenses on a profit & loss statement, commonly known on the other hand as OpEx.[2]

Also, because these operate according to a complex logic based on individual projects, often non-recurrent, involving multiple protagonists belonging to various departments or functions within the company.

All the same, this brief chapter makes no claims for exhaustiveness via in-depth examination of each category. Specialized readings will be necessary for readers seeking particular expertise.

11/1 Procurement of services

11/1.1 Different procurement categories

What are the main procurement categories making up this 'macro-category' of services? Let's examine a fairly widespread method of segmentation.

Reference segmentation

We can refer to the list of categories below representing the purchasing items most often encountered by a majority of companies. In this way, we find, in order, the portfolio made up of the following main categories:

- *information technology (IT) and telecommunications*, including software development and the purchase of software from IT services companies;
- *industrial services*, including subcontracting operations, maintenance, security, the cleaning of industrial plants and premises, cash transport for banks;
- *transport and logistics*, including storage, goods transport, vehicle leasing and rental, or corporate fleet management;
- *marketing and communications*, including market surveys, commercial events, lobbying, promotional objects, advertising, printing and the whole graphics-creation chain;
- *labour services*, including temporary staff and recruitment;
- *R&D and engineering*, including the purchase of technical studies, services for the development of new processes or equipment, etc;
- *other general services*, a broad category in which we find business travel, company catering, the cleaning of administrative premises;
- *various intellectual services*, which includes training, legal or tax advice, auditing and accounting companies, technical assistance in projects, etc;
- *rental and construction of offices and buildings*;
- *purchase of information* comprising elements such as financial information, economic studies and analyses, technical documentation, etc;
- *financial services* such as cash flow management or factoring.

It should also be noted that these purchases are carried out variably under the direct responsibility of the procurement department.

Difficulty of defining services

The following unique characteristics distinguish service procurement from other procurement types: the content and relative 'tangibility', their original nature of the service compared with material goods, the legal framework to which these purchases refer, and finally the relationship established with suppliers.

Relative tangibility

Even if services include a material element (eg a poster in an advertising purchase, a vehicle in a car rental, or a computing program on a server in a software service), this tangible object is only an element of the content and of a more integrated service.

In general, the core of the service usually involves an *original intellectual design* whose result may certainly be measured, but with more difficulty than for a physical product whose combined technical and functional characteristics facilitate the definition of the requirement and the *ex post* monitoring of its conformity.[3] Tangibility is not, however, the absolute criterion for indicating if we are dealing with a service or not.

This being the case, some purchases are purely material and do not differ from the purchases of products or components: for example, promotional objects distributed as bonuses by mail-order companies, e-commerce websites or publishers to subscribers (although categorized as 'marketing' purchases, there is nothing intellectual about them).

Originality and deferred production of a service

Even if certain services, namely intellectual ones, are truly customized creations (eg a company's new application software on the basis of specific requirements specifications), there are others that become standard 'products' similar to tangible goods.

However, many intellectual services practically always derive from an *original creation* raising legal intellectual-property issues (even if the services become 'standardized' and are subsequently the object of recurrent consumption).

Other services, on the other hand, are non-original in nature, and a priori, we do not purchase a creation, but a product according to professional or sectoral reference norms in the context of missions that can be specified fairly easily in terms of content (eg purchase of interim services).

Another characteristic then becomes essential in services: in this type of purchase, we often acquire the *subsequent production* of a good or service or event. *The production of the service follows the purchase and does not precede it* as in the case of a physical product. Hence the difficulties in defining the requirement in advance, then having all guarantees and assurances regarding the compliance of the 'future' service.

Sometimes, in addition, the requirement is fine-tuned during the production delivery period in a manner that is practically unforeseeable at the outset (eg a public-works construction site may be partially disturbed by the discovery of objectively unforeseeable difficulties due to underground geological characteristics discovered during the course of works). At other times, the content of the second phase of a service will be based on conclusions and works from the first phase, and this, depending on the client: for example, the design and development of new original software applications.

Specific legal standards

Here again, standards will often differ.[4]

The purchase of a product is classically based on a *sales contract* whilst the purchase of a service relies on a different legal framework. Most often, it will be a *business contract* or *service contract* when the buyer delegates to the service-provider the ulterior production of a product or service on a specific basis. This type of contract raises the question of the *specificity* of what the latter is asked to carry out in terms of accomplishment, and the latter's *degree of autonomy* in the execution of the operation.

Here, we have a choice between an *outcomeperformance commitment or a best-efforts commitment* or else a complex combination of the two since an obvious choice does not always stand out. For example, a subcontracting operation for toll manufacturing may entail a mere best-efforts commitment but the situation can change completely if the buyer wishes to entrust the supplier with responsibility for the delivered 'product', leaving the supplier the freedom to decide on the means used. Most of the time, incidentally, the buyer will seek to control both by qualifying the expected and measurable outcome, as well as first of all qualifying the resources and process to be implemented put forward by the supplier for achieving the task (see below).

Close client–supplier relationship

More than for industrial goods, everything here hinges on the notion of *intuitu personae* (importance of the identity of the parties). Upstream and partly during the accomplishment of the service, many buyers (and internal specifiers) may refer to the 'unique and irreplaceable' nature of a service-provider. This argument is often well founded, bar the extreme belief that a company should be condemned in the long term to no longer changing sources.

Downstream, however, during and after the service delivery (eg during the guarantee or after-sales period), the notion of *intuitu personae* is relevant. Internal and service-provider teams often develop very close relationships, largely exceeding the formal limits and technical clauses of a contract, where the one-to-one relationship quality, conditions of trust and certain jointly developed know-how make it extremely difficult to change service-provider (not to mention the considerable lengthening of lead-times in order to go through the learning phases once again).

Another specificity of services is that very often (ie for intellectual services) design and production largely rely on (for the 'value-added' component) the competency and intervention of several of the supplier's high-level experts. But collaborators move around, and good ones risk being 'headhunted' and leaving the company.

This implies a risk relating to the sustainability of the relationship in the 'post-procurement' phases (take the example of software upgrading or interfacing with other future developments deliberately postponed after an initial development). Without a doubt, everything can be anticipated and introduced at the initial contract, in terms of mitigation of future risks: notwithstanding such measures, changes in human resources with expertise and 'memory' of the past make the solution extremely difficult.

This notion of duration clearly illustrates the specific risk of procurement of a service resulting from a decision to outsource definitively as in those situations studied in Chapter 7 of this book. This is why some buyers attempt to follow the professional developments in the individual careers of certain experts (the concept of *traceability of competencies*).

11/1.2 Main drivers for the procurement of services

The absolute and intrinsic specificity of the procurement of services is most often based on an illusion, sustained by suppliers in particular. Regarding the principles, ways of thinking and processes for choosing procurement levers, what has been said about the procurement of tangible goods and products globally applies to services. It is nonetheless true that certain specific issues pertaining to services will need to be kept in mind to direct analyses and approaches.

Definition of requirements specifications and commitments

Amongst these, the definition of requirements specifications is fundamental as it is a matter – as for any purchase – of saying *what one wants* and *describing one's requirement*.

Under no circumstances should the buyer yield to the following arguments, too often heard in companies (occasionally amongst buyers, and most of the time amongst users):

- *Why should we describe our requirement in detail because it's up to the supplier to help us to formulate it in detail during the design stage?* This confuses the concept of expected result (outcome requirements specifications) with that of expertise or competency to find the 'optimal' technical solution capable of solving the problem raised.

- *Why should we invest a considerable amount of time in defining our expectations in detail when this operation concerns a non-recurrent one-off requirement?* Apart from the fact that it precludes learning anything which would benefit any future procurement beyond the one-off service, the attitude underlying this remark demonstrates a failure to understand that control over production and subsequent compliance is possible only in relation to a precise initial standard, and that any savings in terms of time risk being largely outweighed by cost overruns resulting from service-provider initiatives, whose relevance we will not be in a position to evaluate.

For these reasons, it is necessary to adhere to a few fundamental principles, the main one being: *the requirement to be satisfied should be precisely defined in the form of functional requirements specifications.*

Following the principles and methods largely defined in Chapter 3, such requirements specifications offer the advantage of characterizing the requirement in terms of *functions to fulfil and measurable results to attain* (which the buyer should obviously be aware of!). However, no detailed characteristics of the solution or process for achieving these should be provided, so as not to influence the technical solution that will be put forward and then selected. It is precisely up to the service-provider (a supposed expert in the field) to come up with an *innovative solution* that meets requirements specifications, is reliable, and offers the best cost/results relationship.

However, in order to help the service-provider to offer an adapted solution, we may provide a supplementary document describing the standards used by the company: eg for an IT development, it may be useful to specify that company *X* uses Java language or Framework Dotnet.

For example, for a non-strategic but sometimes costly purchase, such as the cleaning of building premises, apart from data setting out the scope of the service and certain constraints regarding its execution (ie time slots and periods, or physical limits), the buyer's role comes down to determining *the standard of cleanliness* that he or she wishes to obtain, and which should be measurable. However, it is up to the service-provider to offer the set of the most suitable technical and human resources (staff, frequency of intervention, type of equipment or techniques, etc). The prescriber will then weigh up the associated cost to decide whether to accept the offer or not.

This approach prevails when it is not a question of the company's 'core business' or the company does not possess any internal expertise. However, even in the latter case, the principle remains that of entrusting suppliers with the responsibility to innovate: as a result, competition will first of all play on the comparative content of offers, then on the comparative total acquisition cost.

Outcome performance or best-efforts commitment?

In his book, Xavier Leclercq replies to this question with: 'Both, Captain!' And he's right. So what logic operates here? Everything starts off with functional requirements specifications, defined in terms of the performance(s) or functions to accomplish: it is therefore important that *quantifiable and verifiable indicators* are defined in order to allow both:

- At the time of 'delivery' or validation of the service (reception of a worksite or a new management software), to assess the compliance of the supplier's service, and eventually to enable implementation of a penalty system in the event of default.

- Later, during the operation phase, to ensure maintenance of performance in operational conditions. For example, for a facilities management service, this performance commitment will be checked and measured regularly in terms of compliance with service conditions defined from the outset in the service-level agreement (SLA), and all engaged actions, according to objectively measured observations with predefined indicators (telephone waiting time when calling the hotline, average waiting time before onsite repairs, etc).

But the supplier must, if possible, also be evaluated on the basis of *a best-efforts commitment that the buyer will have taken care to define simultaneously*. At the start of an operation, the buyer does not have (or only very rarely) an absolute guarantee that the result will actually be reached, even if the company has usually incurred expenses, or even made a series of staggered payments before the final performance of the service.

In this way, a wise buyer will make sure to qualify the resources (or partners) that the supplier intends to set up or use to carry out the operation, and then ensure compliance with this commitment throughout the operation (taking care, for example, that payments are made according to observations on progress and the production of intermediary 'deliverables').[5]

Additional key elements of requirements specifications

Certain key elements characterize services specifically:

- We mentioned earlier that the company's requirement should be defined, but also its *scope* (if only by clearly expressing exclusions) as well as *imposed constraints* (eg the continued use of certain existing software systems with which interfacing is required, the necessary 'step-up' of a solution, methods for spreading geographical deployment, anticipation of future updates for the solution, etc).

- It is essential to state (and therefore impose) the production of *intermediary deliverables* that are measurable and verifiable, and can be made the object of reports; at the same time, intermediary decision-making methods will be defined.

- The *allotment* of an intellectual service is often compulsory for subsequent analysis of the cost breakdown (see below), and to facilitate reporting.

- The operation's *schedule* should mandatorily be formalized (in conjunction with the obligations pertaining to deliverables).

- In anticipation of the service-provider selection phase, it is necessary to ask for (human) *resource profiles* of those who will be assigned to the project (demonstrated skills and experience), as well as to check guarantees on their 100 per cent availability as of the start of the project (beware of shared resources!).

- In no circumstances should it be forgotten that the company's *internal resources* will be mobilized: it is necessary to identify precisely which resources and to quantify their volume. Indeed, the project's TCO should include this cost for the purposes of top management (even if there are no external expenses, and so no generation of cash-out), and contributors (ie specifiers) should be informed in advance so as to be available.

- Regarding the *project's cash flow*, payment methods and the invoicing schedule are not neutral subjects (ie for large projects), for they touch not only on the issue of coverage of expenses *actually* incurred by the chosen service-provider, but also the sharing of financial costs due to the staggering of production (service-providers will be all the more motivated to respect the lead-time as they bear part of this financial risk).

- Regarding pricing conditions, from the point of view of the service-provider's motivation, it may be prudent to envisage *compensation for attainment of the result* or adherence to the lead-time as part of the total invoicing (the concept of 'success fees' in the world of consultancy, commonly practised by certain firms).

- Finally, all risks relating to *confidentiality* should be analysed (including the service-providers' operation methods) and an explicit request be made for concrete prevention measures.

Procedures for call for tenders

A few points specific to the purchase of services can be mentioned here:

- There should be clear definition of the supplier *panel* to which the call for tenders is to be sent (ie taking care to introduce competition between long-time partners – if they exist – and 'outsiders' in order to drive innovation).

- Prior to the call for tenders, it is important to *pre-qualify* a sufficiently high number of service-providers (an RFI may thus be necessary before the actual call for tenders (RFP) – see on this point the notion of the supplier panel to be formed).

- According to certain service-providers, it is advisable to *give sufficient notice to the service-providers focused upon* about the upcoming launch of a call for tenders so that they may organize in advance an adequate response system. (Let's not forget that in this profession, sales roles are often undertaken by the producers themselves, and that their availability must be scheduled ahead of time, particularly in well-known high-level companies with an extremely heavy planned workload).

- Above all in terms of services, it is necessary to estimate *realistic response times* according to the usual standards of the professions in question.

- Particular attention is to be paid to the choice of the company's players who are to participate in the *rating of offers* and the selection of the service-provider, namely technical and financial specifiers, and including lawyers in the final negotiation of the contract (particularly for a purchase of specific intellectual services with a complex subdivision and by nature involving multiple actors).

- Finally, it is necessary to be extremely clear on the *breakdown on the financial offer* and the system of late penalties.

Single or multiple service-provider(s)

For many large-scale intellectual services, eg the development of complex software systems that have a strong influence on a company's operation and value creation, it is a perfectly common situation for the services themselves to require strong management, undertaken by a large firm, but for their application to necessitate the intervention of other specific competencies (not necessarily represented by the firm's collaborators). The project owner thus immediately is faced with a straightforward dilemma: *should a single service-provider who will act as an integrator be selected or is it better to operate with multiple service-providers acting according to a prior subdivision of duties?*

Several considerations should be taken into account (some of which are just common sense!).

Requirement definition phase and call for tenders' strategy

The multiple service-provider approach often enables better coverage of requirements via an enrichment of the proposal compared with the initial requirements specifications (the sum of the 'best in every business').

However, it is equally obvious that the buyer company subsequently faces a complex problem of coordinating, interfacing with and totally controlling the project management. In this case, the contracting should be undertaken by a full-time internal team (engendering an often considerable additional cost, which is nonetheless frequently overlooked). If disputes arise between actors, possibly seeking to cast responsibility for interfacing on others, their management should also fall solely upon the company.

This setback vanishes when the solution chosen is that of a single integrator service-provider and the contracting is outsourced. It is nonetheless necessary to have the means to clearly identify the specific cost (marginal cost) of coordination, and therefore to request the relevant costing in the offer.

Most of the time, however, it is advisable for the contractor–buyer to qualify other companies that will intervene in the project along the upstream phase of the contract. Subcontracting cannot take place without having all actors identified, then qualified separately. That said, during the production phase, legal responsibility will fall solely upon the selected project leader.

Project management, allotment and commitment

This phase is always greatly facilitated if the following points are addressed:

- request for a *single contact* to represent the service-provider, endowed with full responsibility for delivery (even if there is a subcontracting chain to manage);

- definition of and request for *strict reporting methods* for the project management, along with, at the end of the delivery of each batch, the handover of tangible and verifiable deliverables by the service-providers, clearly defined from the outset, as well as intermediary validation reports (enabling timely corrective actions rather than a discovery, at the conclusion of the service delivery, of a possible major level 1 or level 2 defect);

- in the event of necessary changes to the project when it is already underway, the *management of possible amendments* must be perfectly controlled. In particular, it is necessary to be sure about who takes responsibility for changes: only amendments resulting from explicit requests of the buyer (supplements to the initial requirements specifications) are receivable and costed as such, and not supplementary works resulting from shortcomings of the service-provider(s) or non-approved initiatives etc.

Maintaining a clear distinction between the buyer and the internal client

Regarding service-providers, it is necessary for the roles of the buyer and the internal client to be clear, for the nature of the contributions of the two players are not the same.

The internal client (or requester) should remain in the role of specifier: this party is the supplier's end-client and the recipient of the purchase. The cost is attributed to this party's budget. The buyer may offer the internal client support in the formal expression of the requirement, suggest possibilities for extending the content of the service at a low marginal or no cost, offer information on market possibilities that the internal client may be unaware of. But the internal client remains the sole technical decision-maker as the holder of the budget. In short, the internal client (sometimes assisted by a specifier) bears responsibility for the technical part of the requirements specifications, and the technical validation of offers.

However, in order to operate more freely, the internal client should not take on the role of the buyer, mainly geared at economic and risk-mitigation issues. Both jointly contribute to the selection.

11/1.3 Fragmented supplier markets

Their specificity results from the fact that the markets for many services are generally *fragmented*: in other words, the network of local service-providers is dense (depending on the situation, 'local' can be taken to mean the national or even regional establishment of suppliers). This observation remains true even for global service-providers of significant size, possessing agencies or local representative offices close to the client (eg car rental companies, cleaning companies, IT service firms, consultancy firms).

In terms of services, proximity often plays an important role. Many services entail relationships based on direct and frequent contact, as well as responsiveness, which seems to be at odds with concepts such as global mono-sourcing, the consolidation of volumes or the financial advantage resulting from economies of scale.

The only relevant question for the buyer is to find out if there really is a *size effect* for the purchase of the service, and if one can consequently gain an advantage by working with a large-scale national or global supplier via the latter's local entity. This means examining two main questions: 1) What are the objective competitive advantages that a global supplier can bring? and 2) Can we gain an economic advantage by calling upon such a supplier?

Distinctive advantages of a global supplier

We can mention some of these without being exhaustive:

- large-scale service-providers can more easily develop their *own original methodologies* as they more often have the means to finance R&D activities with their own funds;

- at the same time and for the same reasons, these suppliers may have an efficient economic *watch or intelligence system* (eventually operating on an international scale if the supplier is established worldwide);

- large-scale service-providers generally have a *wide client base*, enabling them to gradually dispose of a large database, gain experience in implementing solutions in different contexts, and thus allowing what is (improperly) referred to as a *benchmarking of practices*;

- size enables the mobilization of *larger teams*, which permits a service-provider to follow the company in big projects, and which also allows the follow-up of implementation in different entities spread out geographically or even located in different countries;

- finally, a large-scale service-provider can finance and amortize *cutting-edge expertise*, which would not be the case for a smaller structure (unless operation is carried out in constituted networks that must then be qualified).

Economic advantage and size of the service-provider

On the economic scale (cost structure and price of the purchased service), size is not necessarily decisive. It can even be noted in certain cases that the service-provider's size and renown go hand in hand, and we then risk coming across a price policy based far more on brand image than on the intrinsic quality of implemented resources.

The only valid argument should therefore be based on an objective analysis of the cost structure, and thorough analysis of its breakdown.

11/1.4 A specific pricing issue

As for an industrial purchase, the issue of a service's pricing may be addressed from two main perspectives: knowledge of the market price if this notion is relevant for the company and if such a reference price exists; and analysis of the cost breakdown of a set service that enables grasping the cost drivers in order to better assess justification of the specified price. The calling for competition will then do the rest.[6]

Limits to realism and relevance of market prices

One piece of common sense to bear in mind is the following: everything depends on the specific character of the service, if we recognize that the concept of market price is contradictory to the specificity and non-recurrence of a service. Indeed, it is generally understood as being in the supplier's interests to boost the notion of specific nature of the offer, in order to try to prevent the buyer from having a possible benchmark (alongside the announcement of a global price without any breakdown).

The buyer's role, on the other hand, every time that it is relevant and possible when defining the requirements specifications and during the offer-analysis phase, is to try and make the service as 'standard' as possible.

Allotment of a service

This 'banalization' approach is most often based on the breakdown of the service into well-identified batches (ie subdivisions or allotments) constituting as many 'basic bricks' that, taken separately, are 'standardizable' (and/or comparable with other offers) and thus identified in relation to a market price (external, or evaluated as the average of the responses to the call for tenders), or a previous reference project.

In addition, this approach allows identification of certain of the service's elements, already developed by the service-provider and taken up again in the offer, for which the buyer should not agree in theory to bear the complete cost of development.

Let's illustrate this point by taking the example of a management consultancy service in a given functional area (eg procurement, logistics). Analysis suggests that any service of this type can always be broken down into several identifiable modules:

- intervention of a partner in the firm (a high-level expert responsible for the client account, rarely mobilized, but essential for strategic choices);
- intervention of senior consultants/managers for the diagnostic, proposal and the implementation phases in the company;
- intervention of junior consultants for 'field' data collection and for support in setting up new tools during the deployment phase;
- other expense items related to occasional study or deployment operations.

Regarding at least the first three elements, a specific operation may always be expressed as a certain number of days' work for the three main levels of expertise mentioned, and enable figures to be calculated for a number of days given a value by the respective unit costs. The offer's other expense items can then be made the object of a separate analysis.

Note that for each of the qualifications mentioned, it is perfectly possible for the buyer to have a reference standard, either from a historical basis or from indices disseminated by external actors (price lists, indices of professional structures or agencies, opinions of industry colleagues, etc), or provided by certain suppliers playing the 'transparency game'.

Master agreement in a multi-entity group

In a group made up of several business units, the buyer can negotiate, with a certain number of approved service-providers, reference unit costs on the basis of an *indicative but realistic* annual business volume, and have all information integrated into a corporate master agreement (consolidation mechanism). Then, each entity can rely on this global agreement to evaluate offers put forward for a locally made purchase.

Let's not forget that negotiation at a local level is always possible, and that the pricing of service-providers may vary widely over time depending on the state of the economic situation and the evolution of their workload schedules (global thinking but local negotiation!).[7]

Interest and limits of the cost breakdown

This subject is related to the preceding one. Indeed, breaking down the service into its various elements will enable an approximate breakdown of the supplier's cost structure to be made, and from this, a judgement made on the relevance and justification of the supplier's prices. It is clear that following this reasoning, on condition that the complete costs have been correctly reconstituted, the supplier's gross margin and the relevance of their offer can more clearly be analysed.

But the buyer should bear in mind a few basic principles regarding these questions.

Correct identification of fixed and variable costs/direct and indirect costs

To simplify without caricaturizing, the variable costs of a service correspond to the costs that are only incurred by the supplier if the operation takes place. In purely knowledge-based services, these are rare except for services that the supplier is led to commission specifically in the context of an offer (studies subcontracted to freelance experts who incidentally are often less expensive, collaboration of external expert consultants in a training organization, other outsourced services, etc). Otherwise, most costs of service-providers are in fact fixed costs.

Most of the time, the significant element to identify in an offer consists in evaluating as objectively as possible the *direct costs* (directly related to the service at the rate for the time allotted) and incorporating significant cost items such as the intervention of various categories of the service-provider's permanent expert collaborators. These costs rely, as we have seen above, on unit costs of labour (day rates for which reference standards can be obtained) multiplied by their number (complementary element on which to negotiate).

But the offer also always includes *coverage of indirect fixed costs* (often expressed in the form of a contribution evaluated as a percentage applied to a base *average rate of activity*). These fixed costs with an effect on prices correspond to the service-provider's various activities, outside of the 'production of the service' in strict terms.

Certain costs are entirely indirect, such as research and development (eg in a business school, the cost of the research activities of professors will have an effect on their daily rates).[8] But short of being a former specialist in the profession (or calling upon one of them and having access to the budget structure of such a service-provider in order to have a reference economic model), a non-specialist buyer may find it tricky to judge the relevance of this type of charge-back.

Other fixed costs are direct costs such as strictly commercial costs. Possibilities for reducing this expense item exist, and a client can expect suppliers to take account of this fact in their pricing: a company that qualifies its service-providers by forming a restricted panel and that only circulates calls for tenders to qualified suppliers allows them to make savings on commercial expenses. The only expenses incurred by them in this case are exclusively in direct relation to the call for tenders and the necessary engineering for preparing the response.

This is of course the reason why prices appearing on a master agreement may be attractive. Not only are they based on greater volumes via consolidation, but they also express reduced commercial costs of the signatory companies.

At the end of critical analysis of a service's comprehensive cost structure, the difference in relation to the displayed price constitutes the gross margin whose true value can then be appreciated.

Let's remain in the field of higher and professional education, more specifically addressed at executives and company heads. This market segment is characterized by a set of high-level service-providers such as reputed consultancy firms or business schools that are leaders in their national or international markets.

As far as business schools are concerned, when they respond to calls for tenders for specific in-house services (or even simply in their pricing for standard open programmes), they naturally include in their total price an element to represent their 'brand image,' and more generally, of their academic and teaching know-how recognized by international rankings. They are also encouraged to take this approach by the market prices for the segment to which they belong. The logic is not only commercial, it is also academic.

What position can the buyer take in this type of situation? If he or she chooses to focus exclusively on obtaining the lowest per day cost price, the company risks 'missing out on' real know-how as well as actual but intangible efficiency, demonstrable in the medium term by improved performance amongst the company's collaborators. Meanwhile, in the short term, the buyer apparently makes a commendable procurement performance by obtaining the lowest direct cost for the training. The right solution ultimately lies in the objective expression of the company's true requirement: a simple delivery of knowledge and tools, or sustainable modification of managerial behaviour.

Workload rate and marginal cost

For the buyer of services, there still remains possible room to manoeuvre, dependent on the status of the supplier's *actual workload rate*. Here, we follow the rationale of *marginal cost pricing* by the service-provider, namely when the firm is in a period of relatively low workload and its economic objective is to ensure coverage of its fixed salary costs.

Prudence should apply for there is no certainty that by proceeding in this way, we favour the continuity of the relationship. The generic response is then to observe the (real) reasons for these evaluations, and to only decide on such collaborations after carrying out an in-depth risk analysis. Otherwise, we can observe cases where, having selected the lowest price, a client suffers serious inconveniences (unavailable resources, last-minute changes in profiles, etc). An offer that is far lower than the competition should not be interpreted as 'a true desire to win the deal', but rather as a sign that the supplier places its own interests, that is the coverage of its fixed costs, before those of the client.

Transparency

In all circumstances, information is needed on the cost structures of suppliers. There is an obvious method for finding out that we have not yet mentioned: *we should ask them!*

Service-providers who can be described as 'true professionals', and who also do not hesitate to regularly use the term 'partnership' to describe their relationships with client buyers, cannot logically refuse this type of request for transparency. In the buyer's eyes, this even becomes a measurable and objective criterion indicative of the service-provider's true desire to cooperate (one of the selection criteria). As a result, it is appropriate to request this information by including it in requirements specifications.

This requirement does not imply an unstated ultimate target of eroding the service-provider's margins, but rather having a 'value-added compensation' for the service. A supplier whose business model bears fruit is often also a good service-provider.

11/1.5 Choice of procurement policy

Now that the main drivers for the specificity of services have been presented, what are the major procurement policy decisions that distinguish them from goods and products? We can cite the following basic decisions:

- Should the procurement of services be centralized or not?
- In connection with this, what organization should be set up?
- Should we look to the long term and approach the supplier relationship as a partnership?
- And how should the issue of dependency be handled?

Centralization and consolidation or not?

This question only makes sense for multi-entity companies. It follows quite logically that this question does not call for a global response whatever the situation.

Observation of company practice

In the fairly old, but still relevant HEC–UNILOG Management Survey, the authors highlighted four types of companies, as illustrated by Figure 11.1. How can these four groups be characterized?

'Steamrollers' focus on services that constitute their core business: more than half of their procurement relates to services, and they consider all procurement segments as strategic (according to the meaning defined earlier).

FIGURE 11.1   Types of companies in relation to services

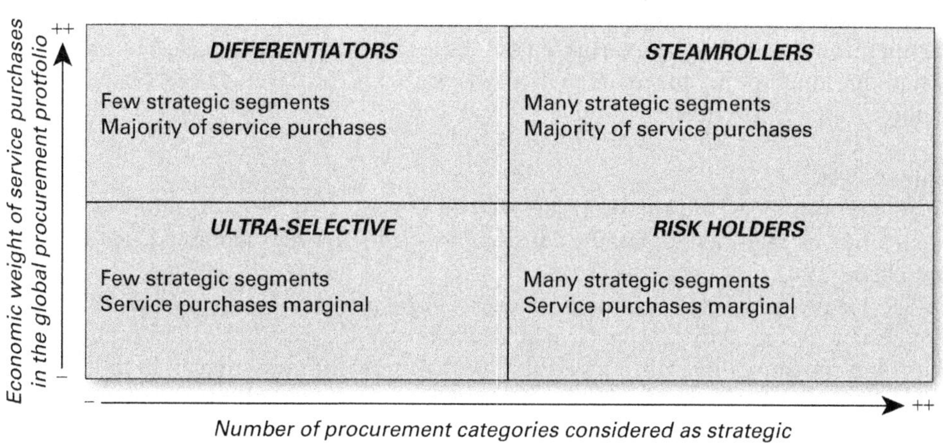

DIFFERENTIATORS	STEAMROLLERS
Few strategic segments Majority of service purchases	Many strategic segments Majority of service purchases
ULTRA-SELECTIVE	RISK HOLDERS
Few strategic segments Service purchases marginal	Many strategic segments Service purchases marginal

Economic weight of service purchases in the global procurement protfolio

Number of procurement categories considered as strategic

SOURCE: HEC – Unilog Management, 2003.

'Differentiators' have a significant procurement turnover but they focus their attention and stakes on a number of limited segments.

'Risk holders' on the other hand are characterized by many strategic purchases, but they represent low economic stakes. Often however – and in a related manner – these purchases hold high stakes in terms of technical risk.

Finally, the 'ultra-selective' take a marginal approach to services, and from all points of view, these are not a core part of their procurement portfolio. They therefore apply a general procurement approach and policy, derived from that applied to the rest of their portfolio.

Figure 11.2 illustrates approach priorities for the first three categories identified by major types of strategic objectives.

'Steamrollers' seem to favour an economic approach (contribution to the gross margin, reduction of operational costs, reduction of the working capital requirement) – a logical enough consequence of the size of the turnover managed and the weight of services in the procurement portfolio.

'Risk holders' have an approach more marked by risk mitigation, an element corroborated by the visible importance of sustainable development for them.

'Differentiators' have a slightly different profile, but they largely favour cost savings for limited procurement segments.

Overall, only 'steamrollers' and 'risk holders' significantly target the satisfaction of internal clients, which corresponds to the importance of services in their procurement portfolios.

FIGURE 11.2   Strategic priorities of the four groups

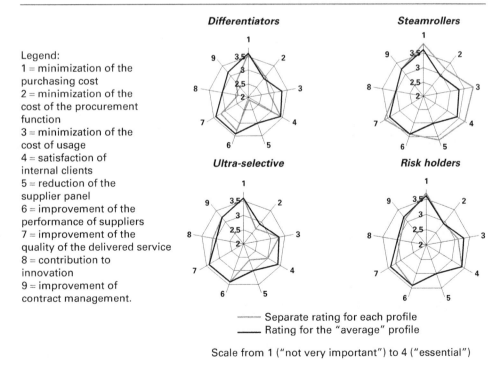

Legend:
1 = minimization of the purchasing cost
2 = minimization of the cost of the procurement function
3 = minimization of the cost of usage
4 = satisfaction of internal clients
5 = reduction of the supplier panel
6 = improvement of the performance of suppliers
7 = improvement of the quality of the delivered service
8 = contribution to innovation
9 = improvement of contract management.

------- Separate rating for each profile
——— Rating for the "average" profile

Scale from 1 ("not very important") to 4 ("essential")

SOURCE: © HEC – Unilog Management, 2003.

Consolidation approach and organizational consequences

In this context, the basic question involves deciding whether the company should consolidate requirements and procurement decisions via a central entity, or else allow local entities their own autonomy.[9]

Centralization is justified in the cases of companies and categories of services combining the following characteristics in order of priority:

- The category of service lends itself to the concept of 'breakdown into basic bricks' (allotment) explained above: as a result, only a central entity will have the means to analyse the group's global requirements, and to negotiate and sign a master agreement on the basis of cumulative volume and overlapping requirements.

- The supplier's cost of commercialization represents a high percentage of the cost of the service. As consolidation helps reach a larger cumulative turnover, the resulting fixed cost is more easily amortized and all the entities can share the advantage.

- Senior management may decide that a particular purchase is extremely 'strategic' due to major risks (eg the case of outsourcing of a strategic activity such as integrated IT systems) and that it should be closely controlled by a central manager.

- The last hypothesis (but a frequent one) is when specialization in 'service procurement' does not exist locally. If it is set up, the decentralized entities can always manage the process operationally, but they may regularly call upon the competency of a specialized central buyer, used as a *resource centre* with the means to *support the local buyer* in crucial phases (such as the definition of requirements, identification of suppliers and knowledge of the market, then actually conducting the call for tenders). The salary cost of this central buyer is amortized between the various entities.

Should partnership be encouraged when managing the risk of dependency?

There is no single answer to this question. It depends on the types of services under discussion.

Account taken of sustainability implied by the purchase

The range of services is extremely broad, and gives rise to different extremes. As full outsourcing of an activity (as would be the case for IT systems and network management, used as an alternative for an integrated support department) is a long-term solution, it is by definition a service where partnership is a key condition for success. On the other hand, the purchase of catalogue printing tasks or organization of an event do not imply collaboration with service-providers over a long period.

In addition, consolidation and qualification of a reduced-size supplier panel per procurement category do not by themselves imply close operational partnership: a master agreement may include certain negotiated obligations, but the notion of improvement plans defined between service-provider and buyer (at the very heart of the concept of partnership) is not in itself a characteristic of master agreements. Such plans may be included, but not necessarily.

In this way, everything will depend on whether sustainability does or does not require the continuity of the relationship, and the notion of improvement plans. In all cases, the necessity and the cost of changing sources will need to be analysed and weighted, and methods for redeployment prepared in advance.

Playing global and local simultaneously

While the notion of a centralized panel imposes long-term cooperation with certain suppliers, in the case of a multi-entity group, each business unit may diversify its sources on a local level, or even change sources, depending on its specific requirements. What are the reasons and justifications for so broad a portfolio of local suppliers?

Definitely not because it 'saves time' or because users 'are used to working with certain local suppliers, so why change?' given that this approach multiplies the number of supplier accounts to manage and generates a culpable sluggishness.

However, genuine justifications may include: maintenance of competition pressure locally by giving opportunities to local suppliers that have not lost their credit; a solution for the temporary unavailability of a service-provider (eg industrial sub-contracting of small-series operations with short lead-times when responsiveness is the prime objective); parallel possibility of calling upon the specific highly specialized competencies of a local entity; and encouragement of creativity via the stimulating effect of competition. In other words, local procurement operates classically in relation to a unit's own operational objectives whilst centralized purchasing may initiate collaborations with continuous suppliers that are important in a global vision. To each its own approach and objectives, which are in fact complementary.

Monitoring and control of the business position with service-providers

When it comes to services, are we more in danger, than in other circumstances, of representing a significant business volume for the supplier?[10]

Two opposing arguments come into play: when we represent a significant weight for a supplier, we can exercise considerable pressure on those in charge of 'client accounts'. On the other hand, we need to examine the question of the supplier's sustainability if the business volume happens to drop.

In most IT service companies of a certain size (particularly those indexed on the stock exchange), the supervisory board forbids having a client that represents more than 5 per cent of the activity. In addition, it is necessary to examine the relative weight of the first five clients (and not only the first one). A service company (or a law firm) whose business portfolio is spread out well over many clients has more chances of 'surviving hard knocks.'

11/2 Investment purchases (CapEx)

Investment purchases constitute major stakes for companies, particularly manufacturing and/or process-based companies from the pharmaceutical, food-processing and petrol-refining sectors, for example.

What may sometimes be confusing when using the term CapEx (definition given at the start of the chapter), is that, depending on the method for financing a piece of equipment, it may be recorded in the expense account – and thus considered as an operating expenditure (OpEx) – rather than the fixed asset account. This is the case, for example, if the company adopts a rental-type formula or even, in certain cases that we will describe further, a type of usage-related invoicing. Procurement techniques may differ considerably depending on the economic models implemented.

The procurement of equipment goods differs from that of production-related procurement although they are often associated with the production activity. The main elements differentiating equipment goods are the following:

- very low recurrence of the requirement except for very big international companies, and often very high amounts involved;
- a highly segmented supplier market with quasi-monopoly positions;
- a very technical purchase with extremely well-developed internal specification (design departments, a department for production methods);
- a generally long period of usage with aspects of the full cost of ownership structuring the acquisition strategy;
- contractual negotiation that may be complex as it impacts the relationship with the supplier in the medium or long term with respective commitments for the parties (transfer of ownership, level of guarantee, maintenance in operational condition etc);
- for industrial equipment, there is an often significant impact on industrial productivity: we buy to renew obsolete equipment but also to obtain gains in productivity which implies a 'value analysis'-type approach, that is, optimization of the cost/performance pair. In other words, it is conceivable to pay more for higher-performance equipment.

The notion of investment procurement refers to the acquisition of goods from supplier markets that are not destined for consumption but for use in the future in view of a return on investment for the company.

The impact in financial terms is translated for the company by short-term outflow – except in the case of an ad hoc financing method (see below) – for value contribution that may be progressive over time or else bring immediate benefits (eg a new piece of production equipment that lowers the unit cost of production). In this way, Milgrom and Roberts state that 'investments are monetary and/or resource expenditures that create a continuous flow of future profits and future services'.[11]

We can distinguish several types of investments: they may be financial (acquisition of financial assets), intangible (acquisition of patents, trademarks, software, advertising expenses etc) or tangible (procurement of equipment and manufacturing materials).

As companies are increasingly sensitive to the evolution of their market position in a permanently changing ecosystem, decisions on investments engage the company's future and sustainability. More than ever, investments are becoming strategic assets that improve profitability and reduce 'time to market' (cycle times required for a product to be placed on the market).

11/2.1 Characteristics of investment purchases

Investment purchases are markedly different from production purchases beyond the points mentioned in the introduction to this chapter.

In Hofman *et al* (2012) on the theme of CapEx purchasing,[12] the authors pointed to the features distinguishing investment purchases from industrial, service or commodity purchases, in relation to three elements: the actors involved in the acquisition process; aspects relating to the nature of the purchased product; and the procurement process itself.

Table 11.1 identifies the various points of differentiation.

One important aspect to take into account prior to making an investment decision is to clearly identify the parameters that will influence the investment policy. Two drivers in particular will have a strong impact on the procurement strategy: the lifespan (or *usability*) of the equipment and the rate of technological change in the stream in question.

In other words, if the *lifespan* is relatively short (packaging machines, certain IT equipment etc), the purchase price has a strong impact on the total cost. On the other hand, in the case of equipment with a long lifespan, the purchase price may only represent a minor part of the total cost, with stakes shifting to operating costs (energy, fluids, staff, preventative maintenance operations etc) not forgetting negotiation with the chosen supplier of a contract for maintenance of the equipment in operational condition (prices of spare parts and maintenance fees when they necessitate staff with specific qualifications).

Regarding the *rate of technological change*, the long-term cost of spare parts is less noticeable, but it is necessary to predict the supplier's capacity to adapt material at lower costs (technical upgrade) or to offer buyback/sale operations for latest-generation equipment at conditions allowing the buyer leeway for negotiation.

Figure 11.3 sums up the issues relating to the two aspects above.

In short, beyond the characteristic elements that we have just seen, investment purchases are carried out in a company process that is very close to an industrial

FIGURE 11.3   Lifespan versus rate of technological change

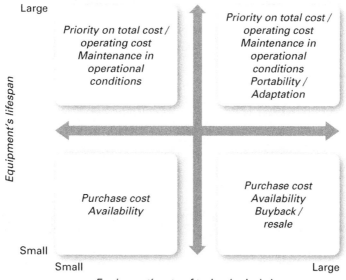

TABLE 11.1 Differences between Capex purchases and other types of purchases

Characteristics		Production material	Production resources	Services	Trade goods	Capital equipment
Players	Several organizations are often involved in the procurement process	✓	✗	✗	✗	✓
	Members of the organization frequently form a group (buying centre)	✓	✗	✓	✗	✓
	Frequently international relations	✓	✗	✓	✓	✓
	Personal selling is of major importance	✓	✗	✓	✓	✓
	No regular procurement	✓	✗	✗		✓
Products	Hi-tech in nature	✓	✓	✓	✓	✓
	Provide the technical perquisite for rendering operational performance	✗	✗	✗	✗	✓
	Services play an important part	✗	✗	✓	✗	✓
	Long useful life	✗	✗	✗	✗	✓
	Purchase price usually amounts to about 3x % to 5x % of the lifecycle costs	✗	✗	✗	✗	✓
	Frequently high financial stakes	✓	✗	✓	✗	✓
Procurement process	Frequently awarding in x form of invitations to tender	✓	✗	✓	✓	✓
	Long-term business relations play an important part	✗	✗	✓	✗	✓
	Frequently long procurement period		✗		✗	✓
	Frequently contingent decisions	✓	✗	✓	✗	✓
Number of matches		8	1	8	4	15

project when the purchases do not directly constitute the project itself. This is why they are not recurrent purchases; the choice of equipment and supplier is by nature a specific project rather than an ongoing one. Once the project is launched, it is up to the buyer to fit into a multi-disciplinary team operating according to an intervention mode and process with key milestones formalized in advance.

Most major prescribers, whether in the automotive and assembly industry (eg Renault, PSA), pharmaceuticals (Sanofi) or consumer goods (Danone, Nestlé) have all developed methods, processes and tools adapted to CapEx procurement that we are going to look at now.

11/2.2 The CapEx procurement process

The element triggering a CapEx purchase is generally an *opportunity study* that leads to the granting of investment authorization. It is up to the project director to establish the business case, that is, to economically justify the project using a cost approach in relation to expected profits, also incorporating financial elements related to cash flow management that we will examine further. At this stage, procurement is not always involved; an anticipated budget for external costs can be established on the basis of estimates and knowledge of the market by the project director.

The whole process is classically composed of milestones associated with an *approval workflow* and related documents in which the role and level of intervention of procurement are perfectly identified.

International-sized companies for which CapEx purchases represent important stakes are 'equipped' in such processes, often facilitated by internal development of multi-functional collaborative methods and practices delivering substantial synergistic gain in processes into the bargain. This 'equipping' also includes a shared knowledge base enabling pooling of useful information aimed at the stakeholders' community, namely: buyers, project heads, and industrial/systems managers. The following categories are generally found:

- project feedback: evaluation of suppliers; disputes or difficulties encountered; success stories (eg a new mode of contracting);
- a 'standardization projects' space: joint implementation of actions aiming to optimize the costs of maintenance in operational condition (spare parts);
- an 'innovative projects' space, in particular the integration of suppliers very far upstream for new concepts;
- a watch on supplier markets: significant events (mergers and acquisitions, new markets won by suppliers on the panel), new products, etc.

The requirement analysis phase

It is in the requirement analysis phase that the buyer accesses the strongest lever for contributing to the optimization of the acquisition cost. Indeed, once a technical specification has been completed, the field of action is reduced, and this often leads to the preselection of a supplier occupying a strong position.

Techniques in value and functional analysis of the requirement are practices spreading in companies that have acquired sound maturity in their field. The basic idea consists of describing the requirement in terms of performance to attain with the associated constraints if relevant (environmental constraints in particular), in other words *functional* requirements specifications.

Methods developed through France's AFNOR NF X-50 150/151/152 and 153 norms enable running multi-disciplinary work groups, with the supplier's participation when redesign is required in the case of an evolution or major modification of existing equipment.

The TCO definition and analysis phase

Analysis of the total cost of ownership (TCO) is an important element in the analysis of supplier offers as well as the costing of the approval file. The different items making up a TCO analysis are generally the following:

- purchase costs: price of acquisition (and included supplies such as a first lot of spare parts), DDU transport and onsite installation;
- implementation costs: internal and external labour, costs of tests and load increases (material used, rejects);
- operating costs: labour necessary for the operation of the equipment;
- costs of non-productivity: losses (eg scrap rate in printing) or rejects, maintenance shutdowns;
- energy and premises: electricity, fluids, infrastructures;
- maintenance costs: spare parts (purchase costs and cost of tooling if necessary), labour (internal and external), and cost of evolutions and/or modifications.

The offer analysis phase

We will take as a general example, an international company that has developed a method for analysing supplier offers according to four classic criteria: quality, lead-time, costs and service (Table 11.2). This method is modelled on an internal tool shared by all buyers and – importantly – by all internal clients.

TABLE 11.2   Analysis of offers on a multi-criteria 'quality / lead time / price / service' basis

Quality	Lead time	Price	Service
– capacity	– delivery lead	– cost of acquisition(1)	– after-sales service
– flexibility	time	– cost of usage	resources
– technical efficiency	– ramp-up time	– cost of maintenance	– flexibility of the
– adaptation to the	– intervention	in operational	equipment
requirement	time	conditions	– cooperation strategy
– guarantee	– downtime	– cost of losses	– supplier's CSR policy
– level of		– cost of labor	– risks relating to
standardization		– level of penalization	the workload
(% of common parts)		– payment deadlines	

Legend
(1) including transport, installation and commissioning.

This enables buyers to align comparable offers amongst suppliers. As a result, the analysis is a basis for negotiation with suppliers and contributes to the documentation towards the final decision. Depending on the type of equipment in question (eg packaging machines, cooling unit, heating unit, compressors, building infrastructures), the tool can be customized and regularly updated by engineering teams. The tool can also be sent to suppliers in the form of a standard offer-analysis grid to ensure maximum transparency.

The contracting phase

Once the choice of the supplier has been made and the final price negotiated, it is up to the buyer to obtain from the supplier all contractual guarantees ensuring full performance of the purchased equipment. For this purpose, the buyer will have addressed to the supplier, in the tender documents, the general conditions for CapEx purchases. In particular, the following clauses will be the object of especial vigilance:

- the transfer of property;
- the transfer of risk;
- responsibilities and the guarantee;
- performance and penalties;
- maintenance conditions: level of security against component obsolescence;
- SLA and associated costs: after-sales service pricing conditions for parts and components.

Without forgetting to include the CSR aspect, ie compliance with all conditions relating to ISO 14000.

11/2.3 The financial approach to CapEx purchases

The issue of the method of acquisition and financing is not to be addressed on a purely financial level, ie in relation to aspects of cash flow management, but also on a more general and 'tactical' level – a decision-making level in which the buyer has a role to play, taking into account the fact that supplier markets move on different terrain than equipment manufacturers. We will illustrate this idea by two examples: the purchase of second-hand equipment and different forms of leasing.

Purchase of second-hand equipment

Second-hand equipment is an interesting option for companies with cash flow problems that have no particular requirements regarding the lifespan of equipment or the level of obsolescence necessitating acquisition of the latest generation placed on the market by the supplier(s).

One of the advantages of this approach, other than the financial aspect, is the short lead-time for availability, unlike the case of buying brand-new equipment, often requiring long manufacturing lead-times.

However, on top of a more limited lifespan, disadvantages include the absence of any guarantee (or a limited guarantee in the case of reconditioned machines as specified below) and greater risk for the availability of spare parts.

The market is shared between reconditioned equipment and equipment that is refurbished to brand-new level: reconditioned equipment is the object of restoration works comprising thorough cleaning, possible repainting and the changing of used or broken parts; refurbished equipment is entirely disassembled and reassembled with possible reworking operations or the complete change of certain components (electronic board etc) – supply often includes a limited guarantee on sound operation.

The players on the supplier market are mainly specialized intermediaries (brokers), and sometimes the manufacturers themselves. Dedicated websites resembling marketplaces specialized in the area of second-hand equipment are widespread in North America.[13]

Different types of leasing

Financial leasing

This formula may be offered by an equipment manufacturer backed up by a financial establishment, but most of the time, it is the company acquiring the equipment that acts as a buyer negotiating directly with the supplier and setting up the corresponding contract.

A financial establishment then takes over, settling the amounts due to the supplier, and setting up with the buyer company a financing plan over the anticipated lifespan of the equipment. At the end of the leasing contract, 100 per cent of the equipment's value may have been financed, or only the difference between its purchase value and its residual resale value via an accrual system defined in advance.

Progressive leasing

This formula is offered by many manufacturers in the IT sector, especially for office equipment. There is also a specific supplier market consisting of companies specialized in this type of offer.

The principle is as follows. Depending on the nature of the equipment, a duration of usage is defined (generally three years for office equipment). This duration is not directly related to the estimated lifespan of equipment, but its level of obsolescence given market developments. At the end of the contractual period, the lessor commits to taking back the equipment or, if a buyback option has been preliminarily defined in the contract, to enabling the company to become owner of the equipment at a predetermined amount.

This type of formula is very well adapted to equipment having a short use duration (five years or less) with a short level of obsolescence: indeed, it permits reinvestment in latest-generation material (the lessor does business by taking back the equipment and bringing the stock back up to brand-new level).

However, we urge buyers to be vigilant and to carefully examine the cost model from the perspective of both client and supplier (some of the specialized companies already mentioned above take advantage of attractive sales arguments but omit to specify certain aspects that push up the final cost for the company, such as the value of repossession of the equipment compared with the buyback value, the cost of re-equipping the computer park).

Leasing with a service contract

This formula is the one most frequently offered by equipment manufacturers generally backed up by a financial establishment.

The principle is simple. The manufacturer gains client loyalty whilst offering these clients a certain flexibility, according to the following principles: a smoothed expense recorded in the expense account, outsourced maintenance integrating availability and management of the stock of spare parts, a contractually guaranteed level of service (SLA).

Here again, the buyer should be vigilant even if practices generally tend to be based on proven professional standards, which may incidentally incite the buyer to carry out ad hoc benchmarking: on the one hand, it is possible to create competition between the equipment manufacturer and companies specialized in the maintenance of industrial equipment; on the other hand, it is essential to carefully evaluate the cost model from the perspective of both client and supplier, paying particular attention to the following: what is included in the standard fee and what is the object of additional invoicing? In what conditions can the company take over ownership of the equipment at the end of the contract or in the course of the contract? How does the transfer of ownership take place? Is reversibility contractually provided for, and in what conditions (taking over of maintenance internally, change in service-provider, etc)?

Finally, for certain types of equipment, there exist on the market pay-per-use offers where the client pays the right of use in relation to a level of consumption. This, for example, is the model developed in the IT sector for cloud-computing, making online storage capacity available to an IT service department, but increasingly the service is also spreading to the core business of IT service departments, namely in the form of technical infrastructures based on the concept of *infrastructure as a service*.

Analysis of financial profitability

We refer the reader to a broad bibliography specializing in business finance. We offer a small selection of key titles at the back of this book.

Payback period (return on investment)

The first approach for evaluating the financial profitability of an investment project (otherwise known as its ROI) is to calculate the payback, defined as follows: how many years of operation are required for us to recover the initial sum invested on the basis of estimated annual gains?

This simple and widely used model is not relevant, from the perspective of financial managers, if used alone. Indeed, it gives a fairly good idea of the risk regarding the forecast horizon for minimum operation of the equipment in order for the starting investment to be simply amortized. This, in a way, is a *flexibility indicator*, indicating the *capacity for quick withdrawal or not* if necessary (market downturn or change in usage, etc).

However, the model ignores fluctuations in the value of money over time: one euro invested today does not have the same value as one euro received in the future. This is what financiers refer to as the principle of 'time value of money'. In this way, it is necessary to evaluate and analyse the fluctuations in cash flow over time, and to cost the resulting economic consequences. This may be carried out in two ways: calculation of the net present value (NPV), and that of the internal rate of return (IRR) of the investment.

NPV or net present value

This is the sum of future net cash flows in terms of present values, over the project's anticipated lifetime. In this way, a positive NPV indicates that the investment may be undertaken as it generates a positive result when all financial flows over the investment's horizon are converted to present values.

However, the NPV remains a forecasting evaluation tool based on information that remains difficult to project (especially the forecast of the gross operating surplus). It is therefore necessary to be able to forecast project-related sales and volumes, as well as to choose the most relevant discount rate.

IRR or internal rate of return

The internal rate of return is the discount rate that cancels the net present value from a series of financial flows relating to an investment project. An investment project is only confirmed if its foreseeable IRR is markedly higher than the reference profitability rate. To define this rate, we usually choose (financial methods and rigour, in any case, point in this direction!) either the cost of the company's own resources in the medium and long terms, or the expected minimum profitability rate of investments (the hurdle rate, according to a value-creation rationale).

When the cost of resources is taken as a reference, this means acknowledging that the combination of one's own capital and loans generates what is sometimes called a cost of capital. This rate can be calculated easily and is known by financial departments. The upshot of this approach is that the investment should, at the least, generate a necessary margin in order to remunerate 'capital providers': shareholders and bankers.

When a minimum profitability rate is taken as a reference, it is a matter of seeking creation of financial value that conforms to the expectations of shareholders.

We can note in passing – regarding calculation of the NPV – that the discount rate to be used should logically be at least the internal profitability rate, as long as we check how inflation issues are integrated into the reasoning.

The advantage of these two methods is that they refer to financial flows and they take into account the temporal value of money. However, their application may appear rather complex and fastidious. Not much flexibility here!

Beware of capital gains or losses in the sale of assets

In an investment project, there may be non-recurrent positive financial flows (at the start of the project) corresponding in fact to the sale of assets (resale of second-hand equipment, or sale of obsolete stock), independent of the evolutions of operating cash flow.

Often situated at the start of an accounting period, these may result in significant NPVs or quite high IRRs, partly falsifying financial performance if the latter were calculated on operating cash flow alone (intrinsically related to the project). Evaluating both may sometimes lead to fruitful reflections.

Calculation before or after corporate tax?

Many content themselves with making pre-tax evaluations. Yet if we wish to be credible when dealing with financial departments, it sometimes stands to reason to make the calculation including the after-tax profitability.

Indeed, once an investment has been decided upon and made, operating expenses will certainly be modified, but also equity-financing items, namely fixed assets, consequently modifying amortizations, hence the income subject to tax. For this reason, we can only suggest making a double analysis before and after tax, in order to be able to present arguments to experts in financial matters.

Finally, let's note that all of the previous topics apply to a financial decision on an outsourcing project (accompanied by divestment integrated in the project, resulting in a reduction of most fixed costs and an increase in the level of variable costs).

In conclusion, CapEx purchases cover a broad scope, going beyond the described fundamentals, and involve highly diversified issues and internal clients. Supplier markets are extremely fragmented with 'niche' players sometimes in a quasi-monopoly situation. This makes the buyer's role far more complex because purchasing performance measurement must integrate all parameters that will enable evaluation of global performance throughout the equipment's lifetime and its contribution in terms of gains in productivity.

Negotiation in these conditions, with a supplier aware of its power balance, proves to be a real challenge for the buyer who must show the value that he or she can bring to the internal business partner in the project's global process. The buyer's role is to follow, above all and always, a TCO-type logic (associated with the payback, the NPV or the IRR), and to focus, during the contractual implementation, on the anticipation of various associated risks. It is up to buyers to develop their added value through involvement in projects far upstream, to assert their sound knowledge of supplier markets, not forgetting their key role in the daily management of the supplier contract (settlement of disputes versus application of penalties, performance reviews, etc).

Notes

1 This chapter was co-written by Olivier Bruel and Alain Alleaume.

2 Strictly speaking, the term 'CapEx' is not a procurement term but a financial one, used to distinguish expenses stemming from external loads that have a direct impact on the income statement (category 6 account – external expenses – in French general accounting) from fixed assets that are the object of accounting depreciation (category 2 account – fixed assets – in French general accounting), and whose impact on the income statement is spread out over several years in the form of a depreciation charge according to rules fixed by the tax administration.

3 Conversely, certain tangible products may include an element of intellectual creation (eg embedded software in a telecommunications system).

4 For these questions, the reader is well advised to consult the following French reference work, still relevant today: Leclercq, X (2002) *Négocier les Prestations Intellectuelles*, Dunod, Paris. The reader will find a supplementary specialized bibliography on legal issues at the end of the book.

5 This approach may seem to go against the notion of joint obligations in terms of responsibility for liberal professions such as consultants. In addition, standard contracts very often specify 'best-efforts' as the sole commitment. That said, things are evolving, for more and more consultants recognize commitment to a performance level, as attested by the development of principles for performance-based fees that are tending to expand. But not all buyers are prepared to accept this way of doing things.

6 We refer to the book by Xavier Leclercq, already cited, for more in-depth evaluation of the third service-valorization approach that he describes, named 'value-for-us'.

7 Certain suppliers may be extremely reticent to display overly low prices 'at face value' (this information can always circulate outside the company and place them at odds with other current or potential clients). This is why it is possible for a master agreement to display a given reference price, upon the understanding that the buyer will at the same time have negotiated an end-of-year rebate directly related to the cumulative turnover produced. It remains up to the procurement department to then decide whether this saving should be carried over to the business units or directly feed the consolidated financial result.

8 For example, in major business schools throughout the world, at least 35–40 per cent of the time of tenured teaching staff is devoted to research activities, from which all training activities logically benefit, thus justifying their rates, as a logical counterpart of the intrinsic level of quality of teaching programmes.

9 Consolidation and centralization are not strictly equivalent words and concepts. The first refers to a pooled procurement approach whilst the second refers to a centralized procurement entity with competency and specialization in the 'procurement of services'. However, we admit that often both concepts are closely related, and that consolidation occurs through a centralized or strongly coordinated procurement department.

10 We exclude from this question the legal aspects related to the possibility of 'abuse of dominant position' mentioned in Chapters 2 and 4.

11 Milgrom, P and Roberts, J (1992) *Economics, Organization and Management*, Prentice-Hall.

12 Hofmann, E, Maucher, D, Horstein, J and den Ouden, R (2012) *Capital Equipment Purchasing: Optimizing the total cost of CapEx sourcing*, Springer.

13 For example www.machinerytrader.com or www.equipmenttraderonline.com.

12
The financial considerations of procurement
Mechanisms for protecting currency, energy and commodity purchases

GILLES HUART, AUDE RABSZTYN

In this chapter we will tackle procurement price parameters by examining foreign-exchange and commodity markets whose erratic movements may cause buyers to manage the pricing of their supplies poorly if these are not correctly protected by financial hedging.

12/1 Speculative procurement and financial protection mechanisms for foreign currencies

In a globalized economy, international buyers benefit from an increasingly wide selection of available products and prices for their supplies. However, they also find themselves confronted by the random variations of those currencies in which they carry out their international transactions.

Indeed, there is necessarily a delay between the conclusion of a sales transaction (whose price is fixed) and the payment in the seller's currency whose rate (and thus, the equivalent in the buyer's national currency) can only be ascertained on the settlement date. So random are currency variations that any fierce negotiation undertaken for a given order may prove completely useless if the exchange risk of the transaction payable in a foreign currency has not been managed.

The movements of currency markets can be utterly ruthless. Monthly divergences of 5 per cent to 10 per cent, or even more, are common. Indeed, this volatility and its negative effects on transactions largely motivated the creation of the single European currency as a type of shield. But this comforting European framework is no longer adequate when we purchase from Asia, Russia, Brazil or India, for the currencies in emerging countries are often more volatile than G7 currencies in relation to the euro.

To face this challenge, the international buyer (importer) should be familiar with the techniques generally employed by financial departments and treasuries in charge of international transactions in particular. It is through ongoing dialogue with these professionals that the buyer will optimize procurement.

12/1.1 General definition of speculative procurement and foreign-exchange risk

Like all financial markets, the currency market is within the grips of speculation. Far from merely putting up with this domination, buyers can take advantage of opportunities that open up to them as long as they clearly understand and anticipate currency movements, and truly grasp the market's rules and practices.

Reminders on the currency market

A few reminders will help situate the scope and power of the currency market.

The weight of the currency market

We are talking about a non-stop market that evolves 24 hours a day. It comes as no surprise that this is the world's leading market in terms of daily volume: every day, currencies with a value equivalent to twice the yearly GDP of France are exchanged, in other words nearly €4,000 billion! This huge mass of capital at stake tends to confirm that the currency market is fed by the liquidity of credit, used for its leverage effect for speculative purposes.

The London market represents over 36 per cent of daily flows, but it is the US dollar that is the most heavily exchanged, making up 87 per cent of the total volume (BIS, 2013). There is no one single place on the planet where currencies are exchanged, but rather a few major hubs – nerve centres where the bulk of liquidity is concentrated (London, New York, Singapore, etc) – and satellites that gravitate around these hubs. All these markets are linked by a network of electronic systems.

Europe's proportion of foreign trade, in other words, transactions that it carries out with countries outside the Eurozone (degree of openness), only represents 16 per cent of the Eurozone's GDP. This proportion is growing from year to year, and above all, is increasingly composite, even if it remains far lower than that of Japan (32 per cent) and the United States (28 per cent).

The players on the exchange market

This is essentially an 'over-the-counter' (OTC) market based on mutual agreement, where two parties come to a consensus on an exchange operation. The main players of the exchange market are:

- *Private banks* which act as intermediaries. They supply liquidity, advice and market access to other players who can be positioned on the side of the supply or alternatively of the demand. Banks employ operators on the trading floor known as foreign-exchange dealers, divided into two major families: *traders*, in charge of taking speculative positions on currencies with the goal of making money, and *sales* who advise bank clients.

- *Central banks* which attempt to regulate the exchange market by modifying the quantity of currency available on it: the rarer a currency, the more its relative value will rise (and vice versa).

- *Industrial and commercial businesses* which seek to protect their activities denominated in foreign currencies. For them, the market is the means to clear currency exposure that may disturb the balance of their operation.

- *Institutional investors* who are the main driving forces of the currency market. In this category, we classify insurers, managers of mutual funds,[1] speculative funds such as hedge funds, retirement funds, etc.

Speculative funds see the exchange market as an asset market in its own right. These players are on the lookout for the best possible pairing of security/yield for their assets denominated in foreign currencies, and therefore constantly trade-off one currency against another depending on these parameters. Their perspective covers multiple markets (commodities, shares, interest rates and currency) and multiple currencies. These investors trigger uncontrollable movements on currencies that lead to volatility.

The concept of volatility

Volatility may be defined as a measurement of instability for the price of a financial asset. Applied to the exchange market, volatility quantifies the amplitude of variation movements of one currency in relation to another. Exchange risk is inseparable from the notion of volatility: without volatility, exchange risk is nil. On the other hand, the higher the volatility, the greater the financial risk. We can distinguish two types of volatility: *historical volatility* calculated from past exchange rates, in other words the standard deviation of daily exchange rate variations; and *implied volatility* that results from market–operator anticipation of the future evolution of exchange rates.

Volatility is expressed as a percentage and as an annual value. Mathematical models using the concept of volatility rely on Gaussian or normal law. Graphically, this law yields a probability cone (Figure 12.1) that enables prediction, with a confidence interval (CI), the probable evolution of the pair of currencies and definition of the maximum and minimum possible rates.

Interpretation and comparison of two levels of volatility

Let's look at an example. Why is volatility of the EUR/DKK (Danish kroner) currency pair so weak (around 0.6)? Because Denmark is in the European Economic Area even if it is not in the Eurozone. Because its level of development and growth prospects are identical to those of countries in the Eurozone. Because its leading client and leading supplier is the Eurozone. We can say that Denmark and the Eurozone are mutually dependent for their growth. The risk of DKK deviation in relation to the EUR anticipated by foreign-exchange traders is, and will remain, low. In fact, there is a strong chance that the EUR/DKK rate will be practically the same in one month or in one year.

FIGURE 12.1   Volatility cone (implied volatility)

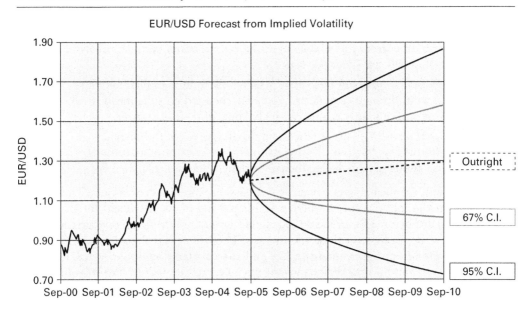

On the other hand, the EUR/BRL (Brazilian real) pair has a volatility of 16.5 given that the development level and growth rhythm of Brazil and the Eurozone are radically different. This is because Brazil has undergone violent monetary convulsions in the past (hyperinflation, brutal devaluation leaving painful traces in the portfolios of international investors, etc). The BRL therefore has no correlation with the EUR. This is why, in the eyes of foreign-exchange dealers, the probability of the BRL falling in relation to the EUR is high.

Why do currencies vary?

As international investors study the best opportunities for investing their financial assets in real time, they will be prompted to trade-off one currency against another if certain economic, monetary or financial conditions vary. Through ongoing evaluation of the pair consisting of security versus yield, they constantly check, monitor and compare indicators underlying a few major aggregates:

● growth prospects of the two countries, and as a corollary, the attractiveness of the corresponding stock markets;

- the risks of inflation in the two countries: price hikes risk infecting the performance of financial products and assets;
- the difference in interest rates in the countries, which dictates the best place in which to make money-market investments and/or invest in bonds;
- the political and/or social stability of the two countries;
- and regulatory and/or tax constraints of the two countries, which may have an effect on the capacity of investors to transfer or repatriate their capital.

These criteria are not exhaustive. The concept of volatility is therefore central, and concerns international buyers wishing to understand the environment in which they operate and the constraints that apply when they make their purchases.

Birth of exchange risk for the international buyer

When trading currency, it is possible to be in either a 'long' (currency value expected to rise) or 'short' (currency value expected to fall) position. Managing foreign-currency exposure means envisaging all risks and events that may have an impact on this exposure. Once the type of exchange risk has been defined, its management will consist in reducing this risk until it is nil.

Exchange risk consists in the risk, over a period of time, of a currency's variation (appreciation or depreciation) in relation to the currency used to establish the company's accounts.

For the buyer (or importer) in the Eurozone, exchange risk lies in the risk of undergoing, over a certain period, depreciation of the euro compared with the transaction currency, resulting in the obligation to hand over a higher sum in euros than expected to obtain the same quantity of currency set out in the sales contract.

Exchange risk is induced by adverse market movements, but inversely, a favourable movement can give rise to opportunities, as seen in Table 12.1.

TABLE 12.1   Table of exchange risks / opportunities

	Import or investment	Export or disinvestment
Rise of the currency	Exchange risk	Opportunity
Drop in the currency	Opportunity	Exchange risk

Let's now look at the example in Figure 12.2, showing the schedule for a forecast import flow and the necessary flow of information in the company to handle this flow.

The context is as follows: for its next autumn/winter *prêt-à-porter* collection, the procurement manager of the Teximport central purchasing office, acting on behalf of a chain of hypermarkets, is to disburse USD in three months' time in order to pay textiles from China. The procurement manager wishes to secure this import flow by setting up a forward hedge.

In our example, if the buyer had not given the treasurer prior warning of the disbursement in three months' time, foreign-exchange exposure would not have been managed, and the company employing the buyer would have been faced with a 4.8 per cent increase in the sum of the purchase (in other words $(1.19 - 1.25) / 1.25$), forcing the company to either transfer the difference in the purchase price to the sales price of the end-product, or else to cut its margin.

FIGURE 12.2   Schedule for the import of a certain flow

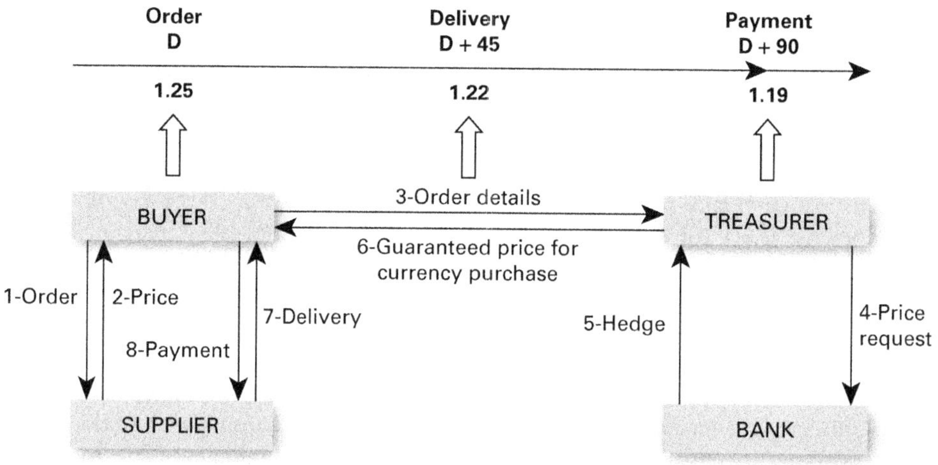

Types of exchange risk

Certain/uncertain exchange risk

Exchange risk is said to be certain when the underlying, that is the sales operation, is known and is sure to be executed: this is the case in the above example. Most sales operations present a certain exchange risk. However, exchange risk is said to be *uncertain* when the underlying is not sure to exist, and the execution of the sales operation is unforeseeable. The two best-known cases are as follows.

Takeover bids (acquisition of a foreign company)

In the case of takeover bids, the acquirer offers an aggregate purchase price for the foreign company on the basis of a conversion rate of euros into the foreign currency. The acquirer is not certain of making the deal, but must wait for the approval of supervisory authorities, and above all, the green light from shareholders in the target company. Several months may elapse before complete agreement is obtained. During this time, the rate of the euro in relation to the currency in question may evolve unfavourably. The buyer has little to do with this type of situation that above all concerns financial departments.

International export situations in calls for tenders

A company that tenders for an export contract is not certain of being awarded the contract, which may also be targeted by several competitors. The company is plunged into uncertainty from the moment when it submits its tender to the moment when the name of the successful candidate is announced. In addition, it is also exposed to exchange risk from the moment when it puts forward the price of its services, expressed in the foreign currency, to the moment that it actually cashes in this currency (on the assumption that it wins the contract).

In the context of a call for tenders for an export sales contract, the procurement department may well be mobilized to import supplies of parts or subassemblies contributing to the overall industrial supply. In this highly specific context, the buyer is unsure of the feasibility of the contract, but if the contract is won by the sales division, it will then be fully exposed to exchange risk for its import segment.

In these uncertain conditions regarding the contract's execution, only recourse to hedging via a currency option (see Section 12/2) will help resolve this conundrum. In no circumstances can the buyer undertake purchase of the currency in firm and irrevocable terms implying its actual delivery, for this may prove useless if the contract is not won. In this case, the buyer would then be involved in the opposite exchange risk where the currency would need to be sold optimally in such a way that its rate does not drop in relation to the euro.

Exchange risk for an isolated/recurrent business flow

The operative event inducing exchange risk may be related to an easily identifiable specific demand that can be managed and hedged separately, for example an international export contract or a turnkey plant. However, for certain companies that *deal permanently in foreign currencies*, it is not possible to isolate a specific good that generates exchange risk. In this case, these companies reason according to the budgetary exchange rate for a given nominal sum (quarterly import volume, annual turnover, etc), like the mass consumer goods sector.

The case of mail-order companies is highly specific because they face exchange risks between the date of their catalogue's publication when the published sales prices set the currency imports for which they may be eligible, and the actual payment of these imports.

Transaction/translation risk

The buyer is mainly confronted by transaction risk for a flow where transaction in a foreign currency is the financial counterpart for the provision of an industrial service. But exchange risk also affects stock, in this case known as a translation (or accounting or balance sheet) risk. Here, without there being any specific transaction, companies are subject to the risk of a conversion discrepancy on two levels:

- On the *financial asset or liability*: when assets or liabilities in foreign currencies in a company's financial statement undergo exchange rate variations in such a way that there is an impact on the consolidated balance sheet. A drop in the value of financial assets will have an impact on the value of consolidated assets, and thus on overall equity. This phenomenon disturbs financial communication to shareholders as well as financial ratios requested by lending banks.

- On *income*: when the incomes, in foreign currencies, of a company's subsidiaries are repatriated into the consolidated account expressed in euros, it is possible for a drop in currency value to have an impact on the overall consolidated income published, and hence, the company' equity.

Most of the time, companies reduce their exposure to translation risk by taking recourse to debt in such a way that a drop in the value of assets is compensated by an identical drop in the weight of liabilities.

How to limit exposure to exchange risk?
This may be achieved in different ways.

By selection of the invoicing currency of purchases
Selection of the invoicing currency usually results from negotiation between the buyer and the supplier. It should be noted that in certain cases, the buyer does not have 'the upper hand' on the choice of the currency. This choice may be imposed by the applicable legislation on currency exchanges in the country in question, by the non-tradability of the currency in question (currency cannot be procured, for example, for countries such as Cuba, Syria or North Korea), or by habit (the pound sterling is widely used in all Commonwealth countries).

For certain markets or highly specific products, the invoicing currency is imposed on all players because of its universal recognition. This is particularly the case for products listed on organized markets such as commodities (oil, metals, cereals, etc). In this case, the US dollar serves as a reference. Certain markets may be subject to tenacious business habits: for example, aircraft and electronic chips are denominated in US dollars due to US domination on their markets.

By choosing one's own currency rather than a foreign one, the buyer may believe that exchange risks are non-existent. In fact, risk is merely shifted to the supplier who may well compensate, through an adjustment of sales prices, any possible drop in the buyer's reporting currency compared with the supplier's own currency, or else by transferring onto sales prices the cost of possible hedging against exchange risks.

For example, an international buyer signs a supply contract for electronic equipment. The supplier in the Eurozone makes sure that invoicing will be in euros. However, this supplier gets the equipment made by a joint venture based in Taiwan in the USD zone. Any variation in the drop of the EUR/USD exchange rate will immediately have an effect on the final sales price.

The European buyer can hedge this flow, payable in EUR, by a forward purchase of USD (equivalent to a forward sale of EUR). At the payment date, instead of taking possession of USD, the buyer will resell them immediately on the spot market: a gain or a loss will be made, observable on the buyer's euro account (the USD having merely undergone a return trip), that will compensate the gain or loss notched up by the disparity in the supplier's sales price due to the variation in the exchange rate.

Buyers/importers may therefore be exposed to *implied exchange risk* (hidden risk) when a transaction is made in their reporting currency. Conversely, by agreeing to a transaction in the foreign currency, the buyer makes a show of professionalism and is then in a powerful position for negotiating on other points. Trading in foreign currencies implies the setting up of exchange risk management as the buyer must face *explicit exchange risk* (confirmed risk). The buyer dealing in a foreign currency may moreover benefit from a possible drop in the foreign currency over the period (opportunity gain).

Unless the supplier is an uncontested leader in its field and imposes its currency, the buyer, as the customer, may attempt to impose the buyer company's currency for the sales transaction. But this transfer of risk may cause sales negotiations to be more difficult.

Through dynamic management of foreign-exchange exposure

This is the technique of *leads and lags*: leading (expediting payment) should be envisaged when paying in a strong currency or else when receiving funds in a weak currency; lagging (delaying payment) is to be considered when receiving funds in a strong currency or when paying in a weak currency. These options give rise to Table 12.2.

TABLE 12.2   Strong / weak currency arbitrage

	Importer	Exporter
Strong currency (anticipation of a rise)	Leading (expediting) payment	Lagging (delaying) payment
Weak currency (anticipation of a drop)	Lagging (delaying) payment	Leading (expediting) payment

Beware: this technique allows users to take advantage of favourable variations in exchange rates, but implies mastery over the techniques in analysing and assessing those rates. The buyer who may be tempted by 'speculation' on the foreign-exchange market may take recourse to two types of exchange rate analyses: *fundamental analysis* based on economic data; and *technical analysis* based on past exchange rate variations. These analysis tools complement one another and are associated with a battery of tools and sophisticated economic skills that enable quick judgement on the evolution or reversal of a trend on the foreign-exchange market.

By netting (clearing)

This technique consists in taking advantage of inflows (takings) in one foreign currency in order to make payments (purchases) in the same currency. Foreign-exchange exposure is thus limited to the difference between the two. This nonetheless requires limitations on the number of currencies (in order to proceed to a maximum of applications), as well as management of payment dates (so that the number of inflows clears the number of outflows).

More rarely, two companies may jointly apply netting (we then speak of bilateral clearing) when they are customers of one another.

Through contractual clauses

This is a matter of including, in the business contract, clauses regarding variations in the exchange rate of the selected currency in order to proceed to *risk sharing (or even risk transfer)*, with an emphasis on the following elements: cash payments are to be made at the signing of the contract; the exchange rate may evolve within a certain scope (minimum and maximum rate) without having any effect on the price of the good; as of a certain rate, the counterparties envisage use of another payment currency; the contract is denominated in different currencies, one of which will be chosen at the payment date by the buyer or seller; and the price of the good varies in relation to the exchange rate.

12/1.2 Detailed analysis of arbitrage and hedging techniques

When all means have been used to reduce exposure to currency risk and foreign-exchange exposure subsists for the buyer, it is then possible to employ simple and effective hedging products to mitigate this risk. From the most basic (spot exchanges) to the most structured (combinations of options), there is always a solution for securing one's purchases in foreign currencies.

Spot exchanges

The following basic concepts are used as guidelines by well-advised buyers.

Exchange of one currency for another

On the foreign-exchange market, exporters who divest themselves of foreign currencies seek to buy their own currency. On the other hand, buyers/importers seek to acquire foreign currencies in exchange for their own currency. Unlike other markets (commodities, shares, bonds, etc) where a quantity of currency is used to acquire a good, service or financial asset, on the foreign-exchange market, one quantity of currency is used to acquire a monetary equivalent in another currency.

The ISO code

Each currency is allocated a three-letter code: the first two letters usually designate the country, and the last letter indicates the first letter of the name of the currency (eg GBP = Great Britain pound; USD = United States dollar). There are many exceptions including the Polish zloty (PLN), the Brazilian real (BRL), the Argentinian peso (ARS) or the Russian ruble (RUB).

The date of the spot value

A spot contract is a contract established between the company and its bank, giving rise to an effective currency exchange 48 working hours after the date of the transaction. This slight difference between the negotiation date and the delivery date is explained by two reasons: a necessary administrative and accounting period for the bank's back-office to carry out the electronic transfer between the corresponding banks (upstream) and the accounting operations on the company's balance (downstream).

The base currency and the counter currency

Let's take the example of the following quotation: EUR/USD = 1.3615/17 that we can shorten as 1.36/17 (see Table 12.3). Here, the euro (EUR) is the base currency, also known as the transaction currency. The counter currency is the US dollar (USD); in other words, the quotation will reflect the quantity of USD for one unit of EUR.

For a nominal one million EUR, at the rate of 1.3615, the nominal equivalent in USD is 1,361,500 USD, whereas at the rate of 1.3617, the nominal equivalent in USD is 1,361,700 USD.

Quotation unit

Let's refer to the same quotation: EUR/USD = 1.3615/17 and EUR/JPY = 135.21/23. Prices are generally expressed with four decimal digits (except for the JPY with 2 decimal digits). The price, excluding the last two decimal digits, is termed the 'big figure' (eg EUR/USD = 1.36**15/17** or EUR/JPY = 135.**21/23**), while the last two decimal points are called pips or basis points (bp) (eg EUR/USD = 1.3615/17 or EUR/JPY = 135.21/23).[2]

The ask–bid spread

Prices are quoted in the form of a spread, as shown by Table 12.3. The spread is measured in points for a standard market sum from €1–10 million. The difference in the ask–bid spread for the EUR/USD pair is usually 2 points.

The spread of a currency pair is tighter when:

- the lot size is small. For example, the EUR/USD spread for a sum < 10 million EUR = 2 bp (1.3615/17) whereas the EUR/USD spread for 100 million EUR = 7 bp (1.3612/19);
- the value of currency A compared with currency B is close to 1. For example: EUR/GBP spread = 0.8335/37, in other words 2 bp; EUR/USD spread = 1.3615/17, in other words 2 bp; whereas the EUR/SEK = 9.2040/60, in other words 20 bp, and the EUR/MXN spread = 13.4515/45, in other words 30 bp;
- the market is liquid (here lies the difference between G7 currencies and emerging currencies). For example, the EUR/USD spread = 2 bp while the EUR/BRL spread = 25 bp.

TABLE 12.3   Presentation of the 'spread'

Bid	Ask
1.3615	1.3617
Bid price	Ask price
I'm asked a price = I quote	I ask a price = I'm quoted
I'll buy at 1.3615 at the lowest	I'll buy at 1.3617 at the highest
I'll sell at 1.3617 at the highest	I'll sell at 1.3615 at the lowest

Cross-rates

Certain currency pairs are not liquid enough to justify a direct price on the market. We therefore fabricate a price by passing through a third currency that offers good liquidity compared with the two others, as shown by Table 12.4.

For example, let's assume that an importer needs to buy MXN to pay a Mexican supplier. Knowing that the rate displayed on the Reuters screens for the EUR/MXN pair is not really relevant, the importer must calculate the actual rate that will apply. On the basis of the following data: EUR/USD = 1.3615/17 and USD/MXN = 11.0825/55, the importer will thus calculate the cross-rate EUR/MXN = 1.3615 × 11.0825 / 1.3617 × 11.0855 = 15.0888 / 15.0951.

Liquidity

Certain emerging currencies offer better liquidity during the opening hours of the country in question. It is thus advisable to make a TWD (Taiwan dollar) purchase in the morning in Europe while the Asian session is still open. Given time differences, access to South East Asian and Latin American currencies is optimized if we pay take care to operate when liquidity is at its best, that is, during the opening times of these countries.

TABLE 12.4 Calculation of cross-rates

If the third-party currency guides the other two	If the third-party currency guides only one of the other two
$\mathrm{USD/JPY} = \dfrac{\mathrm{EUR/JPY}}{\mathrm{EUR/USD}}$	$\mathrm{EUR/CAD} = \dfrac{\mathrm{EUR}}{\mathrm{USD}} \times \dfrac{\mathrm{USD}}{\mathrm{CAD}}$
$\text{Ask } \dfrac{\mathrm{USD}}{\mathrm{JPY}} = \dfrac{\text{Ask } \dfrac{\mathrm{EUR}}{\mathrm{JPY}}}{\text{Bid } \dfrac{\mathrm{EUR}}{\mathrm{USD}}}$	$\text{Ask } \dfrac{\mathrm{EUR}}{\mathrm{CAD}} = \text{Ask } \dfrac{\mathrm{EUR}}{\mathrm{USD}} \times \text{Ask } \dfrac{\mathrm{USD}}{\mathrm{CAD}}$
$\text{Bid } \dfrac{\mathrm{USD}}{\mathrm{JPY}} = \dfrac{\text{Bid } \dfrac{\mathrm{EUR}}{\mathrm{JPY}}}{\text{Ask } \dfrac{\mathrm{EUR}}{\mathrm{USD}}}$	$\text{Bid } \dfrac{\mathrm{EUR}}{\mathrm{CAD}} = \text{Bid } \dfrac{\mathrm{EUR}}{\mathrm{USD}} \times \text{Bid } \dfrac{\mathrm{USD}}{\mathrm{CAD}}$

Forward hedging

Forward hedging contracts such as deliverable and non-deliverable forward contracts are firm, irrevocable tailor-made contracts that offer a guaranteed exchange rate at a chosen date.

Basic principles of forward hedging

A forward or outright contract is a contract established between a company and its bank that gives rise to an effective currency exchange beyond 48 working hours after the transaction. Forward hedging thus enables setting, *as of today*, all the parameters of a currency exchange for a future flow. The advantages and disadvantages for the buyer are the following:

- *Advantage*: the forward contract avoids having the importer undergo exchange variations that could bring up the cost of purchases.
- *Disadvantage*: the forward contract is a firm commitment that irrevocably links the two parties (the company and its bank). The contract's terms are fixed: in no circumstances can the buyer benefit from an eventual drop in the rate of the currency that he or she intends to buy. The contract stipulates the sum, the date of the currency exchange, the exchange rate and the names of the two parties.

Beware: the hedging rate is in no circumstances the rate expected by the bank; it is not a forecast or hypothesis on the exchange rate for a currency pair in the future. The rate of a forward contract is the result of a calculation. As all the parameters of a simple equation are known today, it is simple to deduce the calculated forward contract rate.

Combination of a spot exchange and a swap
Let's take an example. The French company Le Havre Refinery in Gonfreville imports oil with an exchange value of US$10 million, which will be paid in three months' time. It initiates a forward contract with its bank, fearing a rise in the USD over this period. The schedule is as follows:
On D–0:

- the exchange contract by which Le Havre Refinery purchases USD in exchange for EUR is concluded with its bank;
- the bank, not having USD at its disposal, purchases the dollars on the interbank market with EUR. In doing so, its EUR cash flow becomes negative while it has an excess of USD.
- The bank will swap its position by borrowing EUR over the period while lending its USD over the same period: its cash flow is balanced.

On D–90:

- the bank receives EUR from its client that it uses to reimburse its loan;
- at the same time, the maturity of the bank's USD deposit enables it to deliver to Le Havre Refinery the USD foreseen in the initial contract.

The price breakdown of a forward contract is thus made up of a spot exchange price to which will be applied the difference in interest rate between the two currencies over the period under consideration. We can sum this up by the following formula:

EUR/USD forward rate = EUR/USD spot rate + EUR/USD forward points

$$\text{With forward points} = \frac{[(RB - RA) \times n \times \text{Spot rate}]}{[36{,}000 + (RA \times n)]}$$

Let RA = rate of currency A (in our example, EUR), RB = rate of currency B (in our example, USD), N = number of days (in our example, 90 days), 360 = annual basis of calculation of interest used conventionally on lending/loan markets.

We can then apply this formula to calculate the price that Le Havre Refinery may obtain from a bank:

> EUR/USD spot rate = 1.3615/1.3617
> USD interest rate over 3 months (%) = 0.50/0.57
> EUR interest rate over 3 months (%) = 0.25/0.33
> Number of days = 90 days

$$\text{Forward rate} = 1.3615 + \frac{[(0.5 - 0.33) \times 90 \times 1.3615]}{[36,000 + (0.33 \times 90)]} = 1.3615 + 0.00057 = 1.36207$$

Premium and discount

The measured difference in interest rate between the two currencies in the equation will give a sign: *positive* if the rate of currency B is higher than the rate of currency A (in this case, we say that currency B is at a premium in relation to currency A, or *negative* if the rate of currency B is lower than the rate of currency A (we say here that currency B is at a discount in relation to currency A). What are the consequences for the forward buyer of a currency?

When there is a premium

As a forward seller of EUR (forward buyer of USD), the buyer benefits from the premium as the EUR/USD forward rate is higher than the spot rate. The difference in interest rate from which the bank benefits through the swap operation will be ceded to the buyer through positive swap points that are added to the spot rate.

On the other hand, the exporter bears the premium as the forward buyer of EUR (forward seller of USD), and will pay more for the forward purchase of EUR than for its spot purchase: the difference in rate is recharged to the exporter through the positive swap points.

When there is a discount

Let's take the case of the EUR (with interest rates of 2.80 per cent) in relation to the JPY (with rates of 0.15 per cent). In this case, the discount shows a difference in rate in the form of a negative sign.

The buyer/importer of products denominated in JPY will be a forward seller of EUR (forward buyer of JPY). This time, the swap operation causes the bank to undergo a shortfall in its treasury flows as it borrows EUR at 2.80 per cent and sets up a deposit of JPY at 0.15 per cent. It will require the buyer to pay for this shortfall via negative swap points. The forward buyer of JPY will therefore have a more unfavourable forward rate than the spot rate. And vice versa for the exporter who takes advantage of the discount.

It is therefore crucial for buyers to follow the evolution of spot exchange rates of currencies that they buy in exchange for their own currency, as well as to visualize the interest rate structures of these currencies compared with the euro.

Extension and early exercise of forward contracts

In certain cases, the actual payment of a currency to the supplier may be deferred or brought forward. However, it is not possible to 'break' a forward contract. The mandatory delivery of the currency can only be annihilated by a flow in the opposite direction. The bank will take recourse to a swap that combines a spot operation and a forward operation in the opposite direction.

Let's take the example of a buyer of GBP who must pay a British supplier. The buyer hedges his flow by a forward purchase of GBP; however, he encounters great difficulties in getting the goods delivered on time and must ask his bank to extend his forward contract.

The bank will carry out a swap in which it makes a spot purchase of the GBP (useless for the moment) from the importer, then makes a forward resale of the same GBP. Accounting-wise, the importer suffers from no discrepancy in his account in GBP.

Two types of extensions exist: 1) *Extension at a new rate*: a simple currency swap based on the spot rate at the time of the request for the extension. While there is no impact on the buyer's account in GBP, there will nonetheless be a difference (positive or negative) in his EUR account, between the EUR exchange value of the initial forward contract and the EUR exchange value of the spot leg of the swap; 2) *Extension at the historical rate* (practised only in France): a swap in which the spot rate of the new swap is in fact the forward rate of the forward contract that reaches maturity. Accounting-wise, there is no impact on the account in GBP, nor is there any difference in the EUR account between the EUR exchange value of the initial forward contract and the EUR exchange value of the spot leg of the swap. The flows cancel one another out perfectly.

The bank will, however, calculate an impact on cash flow that is only the sum of interest in EUR due to be paid by the importer or the bank as a result of this extension at the historical rate: this is a type of loan in EUR granted by one of the two parties to the other.

If the GBP are due to be paid by the importer to the supplier at a date that is brought forward, the former may request an early delivery of his GBP: either by a swap in which he spot-buys the GDP and makes a forward sale of them; or by an early exercise of his contract at its historical rate holding the same advantages and disadvantages as an extension at the historical rate. These practices are named HRRO: historical rate roll-over or HRRB for historical rate roll-back.

Table 12.5 gathers all these scenarios and the impact on cash flow from the bank's perspective. Forward purchase and forward sale are respectively abbreviated as FWP and FWS, and HR, SR, PD used for historical rate, spot rate and premium/discount.

Basic principles of the NDF (non-deliverable forward)

The forward operations seen above imply the existence of: a liquid spot exchange market, an efficient loan/borrowing market, and above all free transferability of the currency outside its issuing zone.

For certain currencies, not all of these conditions are gathered: in particular, the criterion of free transferability is not always satisfied. Only the NDF will allow getting around the obstacle of a currency's non-transferability to provide hedging for this currency.

TABLE 12.5   Summary table of extension / early exercise at historical rate

Events	Original operation	Exchange direction	Direction of cash-flow points	General cash-flow
EARLY EXERCISE	FWP	HR > (SR + PD)	negative	Borrow
		HR < (SR + PD)	plus	Lend
	FWS	HR > (SR + PD)	negative	Lend
		HR < (SR + PD)	plus	Borrow
EXTENSION	FWP	HR > SR	plus	Lend
		HR < SR	negative	Borrow
	FWS	HR > SR	plus	Borrow
		HR < SR	negative	Lend

NB: For EARLY EXERCISE, a spot rate applies; For an EXTENSION, a forward rate. (Our basis is the absolute value of cash-flow points.)

Certain emerging countries that wish to retain a certain control over their currency have imposed strict transferability rules: prohibition of holding a foreign account in this currency outside of the country of issuance, required documentation for any transaction 'on' or 'with' this currency, prohibition of sale of the currency for a strong currency, etc.

The main countries concerned by the NDF are: Brazil (BRL), Russia (RUB), India (INR), China (CNY), Taiwan (TWD) and South Korea (KRW).

Convertibility and transferability

We classify transactions into two categories: operations said to be *offshore*, taking place outside the currency's country of issue, and *onshore* operations that solely take place in its country of origin.

Definition of convertibility: when it exists, this is a local exchange market on which the currency can be freely exchanged for another currency, under the supervision of competent monetary authorities.

Definition of transferability: when it is possible to hold this currency in an offshore account and carry out transactions in this currency outside of its country of issue.

Most currencies are convertible but some rare exceptions exist. In this case, it is not possible to buy or sell them freely. Certain currencies are non-transferable but generally remain convertible on their own local market. In these conditions, forward hedging operates via NDF instruments.

How is the NDF rate calculated?

From data from the country of origin, the spot rate and interest rates practised on the local market, it is possible to calculate *synthetic forward* rates called NDF (non-deliverable forward) rates. Often very close to deliverable hedging prices offered by local banks on their domestic markets, NDF are generally slightly more expensive as they avoid several disadvantages:

- *The country risk of the currency in question*: an NDF subscriber is sheltered from the failings of the country in question: the subscriber can rely on tangible hedging for a currency flow without exposure to any eventual blockage imposed by difficulties on the monetary, financial, economic or political front of the country in question.

- *The bank counterparty risk*: the bank counterparty that offers the NDF is a leading Western bank whose default risk is often lower than that of a local bank.

The NDF's nominal hedging

The NDF consists in setting up forward hedging with the knowledge that actual delivery of the currency will not take place at the maturity date. We distinguish between the hedging that will take place on the offshore market and the actual delivery that will take place on the local market.

How is this balancing payment calculated? At the maturity date, we observe an official rate, most often a reference rate (called the 'fixing rate' by foreign-exchange dealers) published on the day by the central bank or a major broker in the country of origin, via an information agency such as Reuters.

The difference (called a 'settlement') is then calculated between the NDF contract rate and the fixing rate in relation to the hedged nominal sum. This positive or negative difference will be paid by the bank or its client in a strong currency (EUR or USD) to avoid any extra exchange risk that would arise if the balancing payment were payable in the foreign currency.

On the local market, currencies are physically converted for EUR or USD according to the same fixing rate so that there is a perfect match between the NDF contract and the actual local flow.

It is fully within the interests of buyers, constrained to buy non-deliverable foreign currencies in exchange for EUR in order to pay foreign suppliers, to take recourse to NDF to protect themselves from rises in the foreign currency in relation to the EUR. What happens at the maturity of the NDF contract? If:

- the buyer's anticipation proves founded and the foreign currency has progressed in relation to the EUR, the buyer has the assurance that the bank will pay him or her a balancing payment due to the NDF, that will compensate the fact that he or she physically pays dearer for the currency than expected;

- the buyer's anticipation proves unfounded and the currency regresses in relation to the EUR, the buyer will pay the bank a balancing payment that is only the reimbursement of the opportunity from which he or she benefited when buying the currency at the right amount on the local market.

In this way, the buyer will have to pay no more or no less than the exact hedging rate of the NDF.

Let's take the example of a purchase of currency via an NDF. An importer expects a delivery of electronic chips from South Korea in three months' time. The payment of the purchase will take place in 90 days. The importer fears a rise of the Korean won (KRW) in relation to the EUR and requests hedging from his bank via a 6-month NDF.

Here is the quotation obtained:

Spot rate of EUR/KRW = 1,402/1,403
6-month NDF forward rate = 1,423/1,425
Nominal sum hedged = KRW 1.5 billion

In other words EUR 1,054,111 converted at the rate of 1,423.

At the contract's maturity, let's assume that the observed fixing rate is 1,400. The calculation of the balancing payment is the following:

Balancing payment = ((fixing rate – NDF rate) × nominal sum in EUR / fixing rate

In other words:

Balancing payment = ((1,400 – 1,423) × 1,054,111 / 1,400 = EUR 17,317

received by the importer.

To carry out the actual purchase of the currency, the importer asks his bank to offer him a price for the cash purchase of KRW 1.5 billion at the fixing rate of 1,400. The disbursement is thus as follows: KRW 1.5 billion / 1,400 = EUR 1,071,429.

In this way, the importer undergoes a shortfall in the physical flow when purchasing the KRW of 1,071,429 – 1,054,111 = 17,317 EUR. This is the same sum as the balancing payment calculated above. We can point out the following:

- if the EUR/KRW rate drops over the six months, this means that the KRW has gone up in relation to the EUR: the bank pays the balancing payment to the importer;

- if the EUR/KRW rate rises over the six months, this means that the KRW has gone down in relation to the EUR: the importer pays the balancing payment to the bank.

As a general conclusion, deliverable forward and non-deliverable forward contracts are firm hedging arrangements that commit the buyer to the bank irrevocably. Only the rate negotiated when the contract is signed will apply, whatever the market conditions at the contract's maturity. Forward contracts guarantee final rates at the cost of possible opportunity losses. However, these contracts offer the advantage of being free of charge.

Currency options

Forward contracts are references (benchmarks) for comparisons with more complex hedging strategies such as currency options. Forward contracts can be criticized for only offering a partial response to hedging requirements as they do not obtain an improved rate but a fixed rate. Options obtain both a fixed rate and a possible improvement of the rate applied to the flow.

General definition

A currency option is a contract that gives its holder the right to purchase (call) or the right to sell (put) a set currency sum (the nominal) at a rate fixed in advance (strike price or exercise price) at a fixed date. Unlike a forward contract which is an obligation, a foreign-exchange option is a right.

The option is used to hedge against certain or uncertain exchange risks and to benefit from opportunity gains: the purchase of an option by an importer allows its holder to be protected from a currency rise and also to take advantage of a possible currency drop over the period. In this sense, an option fulfils the same function as insurance. It is thus associated with a premium. If the accident (unfavourable movement of the exchange rate) does not take place, the premium is lost. However, in the event of an accident, the price of the 'good' is guaranteed (option of purchasing the currency at the fixed price).

The option is a negotiable right on a market, which means that we can:

- purchase a right to buy, in other words purchase a call option;
- sell a right to buy, in other words sell a call option;
- purchase a right to sell, in order words purchase a put option;
- sell a right to sell, in other words sell a put option.

The buyer of an option benefits from the right by paying a premium to the seller of the option. This premium is a flow of cash to pay when the option contract is negotiated, unlike a forward contract that is free. The seller of the option is thus subject to the buyer's decision: in selling the option the seller therefore takes on a commitment. In exchange, the seller receives the premium for the risk thus undertaken.

We point out that the EUR call is strictly the equivalent of the USD put: the buyer of EUR sells USD in exchange. Similarly, the EUR put is equal to the USD call. Only the denomination differs.

Exercise of an option

Most options dealt with on this market are so-called *European* options, in other words, exercise is only possible at the option's maturity. For example, to find out if the holder of an EUR put should exercise this right, we will observe, at the maturity's option, whether the EUR/USD rate is lower than the option's strike price. If this is the case, the PUT will be exercised; otherwise, the option will be waived and the flow will take place directly at the displayed spot market price.

There are also *American* options that may be exercised at any moment throughout the life of the option.

How can we unwind a position on an option? For the option holder, 'unwinding' means 'resale' or 'exercise' or 'waiver at the maturity date' of the option. For the option seller, this means 'buyback' or 'assignment' or 'withdrawal' because of waiver on the part of the buyer.

In/at/out of the money

A call is said to be 'in the money' when the rate of the currency pair is higher than the strike price; in other words, this option could be exercised immediately. An option is 'out of the money' when its intrinsic value is negative because it is not in its holder's interests to exercise it immediately. Obviously, an option that is 'in the money' is more costly than one 'out of the money'. Meanwhile, options 'at the money' are those whose strike price is equal to the spot price or forward price. Table 12.6 sums up all possible cases.

TABLE 12.6   In / at / out of the money

	Call	Put
Base price > Strike	In the money	Out of the money
Base price = Strike	At the money	At the money
Base price < Strike	Out of the money	In the money

Determining the price of an option

The price of an option can be summed up by the following simple equation:

$$\text{Price of an option} = \text{intrinsic value} + \text{time value}$$

The *intrinsic* value of the option is the difference between the spot price and the exercise price chosen by the buyer. The *time* value (mentioned in the pricing of an option) is the price of the probability of evolution of the currency pair. It therefore depends on all parameters that make this event more or less probable: gap between the price of the currency pair and the exercise price, the lifespan of the option, volatility. Theoretically, therefore, the value of an option is never nil before its maturity. Renegotiation prior to the expiry of an initially purchased option allows the time value to be recovered.

Let's therefore sum up the main parameters that are decisive for an option's price:

- *Intrinsic value*: the more an option is in the money, the higher the premium.
- The *option's lifespan*: the further away the option's maturity date, the higher its cost.
- The *difference in interest rates between the two currencies*: indeed, an option's benchmark is the level of the forward exchange. For example, if a premium is in favour of a buyer of an EUR put/USD call, the buyer benefits from the interest rate structure: the price of the option will thus be lower. In the case of a discount, the buyer will pay a proportionally higher price.

- *Volatility* (see the explanation on volatility in Section 12/1): this is the only uncertain parameter in the evaluation of an option. We can say that this notion is crucial to an option as its price can be tersely summed up by the following formula: Option price = volatility. In addition, option prices are often displayed in terms of a volatility spread.

An option trader is a volatility trader whereas a spot trader is a liquidity trader. An option buyer is a volatility buyer whereas an option seller is a volatility seller.

Option pricers that gather all of the parameters above are equations based on hypotheses on the law of probability, which series of data showing daily variations of the underlying are meant to follow.[3]

The breakeven point of hedging with options

It is indispensable for buyers/importers to be able to calculate the breakeven point of their hedge for they are not hedged precisely at the strike price, but at the strike price ± the premium. For the buyer, the risk is limited to the cost of the premium, and the potential gain unlimited. For the seller of an option, the maximum gain corresponds to the premium while the loss is theoretically unlimited.

For example: for a buyer of USD/seller of EUR who purchases a USD call/EUR put at a strike price of 1.25 with payment of a 1 per cent premium, the profile indicates that:

- if the EUR/USD is above 1.25 at the maturity date, the put buyer will undergo a loss limited to the premium paid, but can take advantage of a more favourable price (eg 1.33);
- if the EUR/USD drops during the period and ends below 1.25, it is in the buyer's interests to exercise the option and the buyer's gains become positive from the breakeven point of 1.2375, in other words 1.25 − (1.25 × 1 per cent) = 1.25 + 0.0125 = 1.2375.

How to reduce the cost of hedging with options?

1 *Recourse to exotic options.* Foreign-exchange traders have lively imaginations and over time have elaborated second-generation options. Not only can they dip into the core toolbox based on classic calls and puts (the so-called *vanilla* options), they also have access to a more eclectic set of options (so-called *exotic* or *barrier* options). These exotic options allow a discount to be obtained on the premium paid by adding an extra dimension: the notion of a wager. Amongst these options, we can distinguish:

   - the KI (*knock-in*) or *lightable* option: this option appears (or forcibly arises) if – and only if – a certain spot level is reached at any moment throughout the option's life. The option then lights up and becomes operational;
   - the KO (*knock-out*) or *extinguish* option: the option disappears and dies if – and only if – a certain spot level is reached at any moment throughout the option's life. The option is then extinguished and becomes non-operational.

Let's look at the example of an importer who pays for USD in 3 months' time. The buyer of a simple vanilla option – a EUR put/USD call in 3 months at a strike price of 1.24 – would pay 0.48 per cent of the hedged nominal sum today. The importer finds this premium too expensive but wishes for hedging that is just as efficient. As an alternative, the bank then offers the importer a barrier option: a EUR put/USD call in 3 months at a strike price of 1.24 matched with a KO at 1.29, with payment of no more than 0.33 per cent of the hedged nominal sum.

This alternative is attractive as it is less costly and the risk it entails is only moderate. Indeed, if the spot price reaches 1.29 during the life of the option, the hedging disappears. However, this market movement would be in the importer's favour as it would mean a drop of the USD. The buyer will naturally have taken the precaution of placing a spot order that will be automatically executed before: either putting an end to this purchase; or setting up a new currency option on a more favourable spot.

Used wisely, 'barrier options' can prove effective if the risks taken by their holders are perfectly circumscribed. It would, however, be a more dicey situation if the importer were to purchase an option that deactivates if the EUR/USD drops.

Several variations on 'barrier options' have emerged in recent years. Often, their effect is to limit the period during which the barrier operates. Instead of a barrier valid throughout the option, the barrier only applies over a shorter duration.

Other variations are available to the buyer: namely the family of *accumulators* that allows accumulation, every day or every week, of a certain sum of USD. The buyer benefits from an advantageous rate, subject to certain conditions, throughout the evolution of the EUR/USD rate.

It is difficult to enumerate all available exotic options: curious buyers can access a very wide palette of increasingly complex options with elaborate pricing structures and sometimes spectacular lever effects.

2 *Recourse to option packages.* Foreign-exchange traders are also capable of creating option packages or strategies that combine *vanilla* options and/or *exotic* options, whose final objective is to ensure efficient hedging while reducing the financial impact of the premium, or sometimes even cancelling out the whole premium. Many strategies are now available free of charge.

The first option package known to all foreign-exchange traders is the *tunnel* or *collar* that combines two 'legs': the purchase of a vanilla option financed by the sale of another vanilla. The so-called 'tunnel' or 'collar' is due to the strategy being limited by the two option strikes. In general, the tunnel is structured so that no premium is due: the premium paid is equivalent to the premium received. The nil-premium tunnel is said to 'frame the forward', meaning that the amplitude of the tunnel is symmetrical on either side of the level of the forward rate.

Other strategies such as the *participating forward* or the *forward knock-in* combine vanilla or barrier options. These are multi-leg strategies that offer a personalized response to currency buyers wishing to optimize their hedging level while limiting costs.

This sample of simple solutions makes no claims at exhaustiveness: it is impossible to list all hedging structures with options circulating on the market. What should be pointed out nonetheless is that almost two-thirds of hedging alternatives are still carried out in the form of forward contracts.

Extensions and conclusion

To conclude on the use of derivative products to hedge against exchange risks, it is necessary to make two important remarks. Here, we also refer to the in-depth mutation of the exchange market since the arrival of electronic trading platforms.

Warnings and precautions

International buyers addressing company treasurers in the context of currency purchases will find their dialogue to be even richer if they have a knowledge of the stakes and constraints of the exchange market.

The importance of the scenario

Before launching into a hedging strategy, the buyer should envisage a scenario for the evolution of the currency pair for which foreign-exchange exposure is envisaged. By gathering a maximum quantity of information, the buyer can identify the probable trend for the coming months. Next, the buyer can choose a particular product, a given strategy, envisage the cost and the potential of each structure, its advantages and disadvantages, and thus define the best time at which to act. In the absence of a scenario, the buyer can always, by default, fall back on a forward contract.

The importance of hedge accounting complying with IAS39 norms

As of 1 January 2005, IFRS accounting norms have required operators using derivative products to provide accounting for them according to very strict rules: there is now an obligation to record all derivative products on the balance sheet; variations in the market value of derivative products need to be recorded in the financial result. This implies regular (mark-to-market) re-evaluation of hedging by regular reporting, evaluation of the hedge's efficiency by way of tests, and documentation on hedges and the underlying.

As a result, the choice of hedge products proves crucial. In this way, the purchase of a simple option or a tunnel with a symmetrical sum will be eligible for hedge accounting and will have no impact on the company's result.

On the other hand, the sale of a simple option, accumulators or barrier options do not qualify for hedge accounting as they present an induced risk of non-coverage (in the case of a deactivating barrier option) or over- or under-coverage (in the case of an accumulator). Market variations will therefore be recorded under the company result.

It is therefore necessary to balance the *economic efficiency of a hedge and its accounting efficiency*. The most developed products rarely satisfy hedge accounting. It is not a matter of giving these structures a miss but rather envisaging to what extent they may bring volatility to the financial result.

Evolution of the exchange market

We can here note the inexorable development of the internet for the execution of exchange operations. Reuters and EBS have long remained unrivalled in the domain of online B2B trading aimed at market professionals (banks, brokers). Today, over 90 per cent of the interbank market of exchange transactions transit through the electronic channel.

But as of 2000, a number of secure B2C platforms have also emerged (such as FXALL, 360T, Currenex, RTFX, FX Connect, Hot Spot, BloombergFX), taking advantage of the upsurge of speed and reliability in IT networks. The financial crisis of 2008/09 accelerated the deployment of these systems by meeting the increased requirements of market players for price transparency and improved traceability. The financial crisis also resulted in the limiting of customer demands for sophisticated products, facilitating the automation of processes.

Technological innovation implicitly triggers a considerable reduction in transaction costs. It has created new possibilities and new demands for a wide range of participants, including international buyers:

- *More modestly sized operations*: electronic platforms now offer the possibility of carrying out more modestly sized transactions at perfectly transparent prices.

- *A tightening of bank margins*: the merging, by electronic means, of a multitude of orders coming from all over the world and the transparency of prices has resulted in heavy shrinkage of the gap between buyer and seller on the interbank market. The end-client ultimately benefits from a tightening of interbank prices.

- *A concentration of the bank market leading to a new segmentation*: all these movements have led to a change in the balance between large and small banks on this market.

Technology imposes high costs. Apart from substantial set-up expenses, technology constantly necessitates updates. As the gaps between buyers and sellers have diminished on the interbank market as well as in the bank–client segment, most dynamic banks have implemented a high-volume, low-margin operational model enabling them to amortize the high costs of technology by continually raising transaction volumes.

This strategy has procured a competitive advantage for those banks with the necessary size and global distribution networks for supporting technological innovation and offering competitive remunerative prices. As a result, we have witnessed a concentration of activity on the exchange market, with the largest banks dealing with a growing proportion of business volumes on a worldwide scale: the market share of the five leading banks has gone up from 30 per cent of the market five years ago to 55 per cent of the market today (source: *Euromoney*, 2015).

The role of second-tier banks has evolved. Indeed, small banks are no longer capable of supporting the level of technological development that would enable them to remain competitive in a context of low margins or to carry out operations for all currency pairs and in all time zones. It is therefore often more profitable for them to entrust these functions to major global-scale institutions. Certain second-tier banks take recourse to 'white labelling' for this purpose.

In the context of this mechanism, the small bank serves as an intermediary between the end-client (currency buyer) and a larger bank (currency seller). The small bank places at its clientele's disposal a portal dedicated to the dispatch of orders and obtains the requested liquidity from the larger bank that acts as a 'wholesale supplier'. The small bank can then specialize in managing risk for its clientele's credit whereas the large bank supplies liquidity and manages the market risk created by the client's order. Thanks to this institutional division of work and the specialization in domains where each enjoys a comparative advantage, the end-client benefits from better prices, as well as:

- *Faster execution of exchange flows*: thanks to the technological innovations of the last decade, many functions that were formerly exclusively carried out by foreign-exchange traders are increasingly undertaken by specialized IT programs – algorithmic programs that interrogate transaction platforms themselves or automatically respond to requests with prices and auto-hedge without human intervention.

- *Vertical integration of operations*: everything, up to the confirmation addressed to the partner bank following an execution, is automated. The introduction of the European Market Infrastructure Regulation (EMIR), imposed on market participants, both banks and companies, entails swift confirmation of operations that can be optimized via electronic channels.

- *Wider access to products (one-stop shopping)*: some platforms take advantage of visits to their web sites to propose other products or services, thus offering their clients an entrance point for various financial products.

Buyers can always find comprehensive technical information on these topics (accounting, regulations, hedging techniques, exchange forecasts, electronic exchange) from their accounting and/or financial departments.[4]

12/2 Management of price risks for commodity purchases

A commodity is a product in an unprocessed state, or a product that has undergone an initial transformation on its production site to render it suitable for international trade, used in the production of finished products or as a source of energy. The material generally requires an initial treatment or refinement, eg to pass from a mineral to a metal, or from sugar cane to sugar. A commodity is considered as intermediate consumption in production processes. The IMF classifies commodities into three categories: *non-fuel* (food, drink), *industrial output* (agricultural commodities, metals) and *fuel* (oil).

The term 'commodity' is broader than 'raw material' as it also includes intangible goods such as the supply of electricity or carbon assets eligible for the Kyoto Protocol.

The United Nations Conference on Trade and Development (UNCTAD) calculated that in 2011 commodities represented around one-third of the volume of global trade.

States permanently monitor commodities due to their necessity in our daily lives (metals, oil, electricity, agricultural goods), their rarity (precious metals), and their strategic importance (uranium) as well as their uneven geographical distribution.

First we will present the way in which the prices of commodities are constituted, the market protagonists, where the materials are exchanged, and how the concept of volatility applies to them. We will then examine tools for mitigating price risk, with a particular focus on the futures market and its contracts. Finally, we present the different stages in defining a company policy for hedging against price risks.

12/2.1 Price risks for commodities

Analysis of price-composition mechanisms

The objective of this section is to analyse the balance between supply and demand over short-, medium- and long-term periods, as well as any event that may alter this balance.

Demand mechanisms

The demand for commodities is globally geared upwards due to the growth of the world's population. The increase in the average living standards of populations has also led to a modification in diet (towards a more meat-based, material-consuming diet) and a generalization of lifestyles following a high commodity-consumer Western model. By analysing past demand, we can detect possible general tendencies (presence of seasonal cycles, sensitivity to economic growth, price elasticity) or sectoral tendencies of main consumers.

On the electricity market, for example, we pay attention to changes in the use of the various switchable fuels (oil, gas, uranium, sun, wind, coal). Similarly, in the transport sector, we analyse the number and type of vehicles sold (diesel, oil or electric, vehicle weight, etc). State decisions also have an impact via tax (taxes and subsidies), quotas or strategic storage, for they distort the price signals sent out to consumers and play on their behaviour.

Sometimes, demand is only foreseeable on a very short-term horizon, namely when it is related to weather conditions. Trends allow consumption profiles to be determined in relation to seasonality. In this way, fuel demand undergoes peaks in winter for heating, and in summer for air-conditioning. However, in the very short term, consumption variations may be significant over a period of a week, or even a day.

In practice, in certain markets, the level of demand varies enormously between consumption peaks and dips, inexorably generating price volatility that may range from negative prices in the event of oversupply and significant price hikes during consumption peaks. If demand continues to grow despite a strong increase in prices, it may then be necessary to 'wipe out' demand via commercial contracts or the law. For example, negative spot prices were observed for German electricity for a few hours in 2013, aimed at urging thermal-electricity producers to switch off their plants. Demand was low and unavoidable production (production that cannot be stopped at the risk of blowing the network) significant.

In terms of longer-term trends, it is important to discern the existing and potential substitution markets, and to monitor evolutions contributed by research and development.

Finally, other improbable events, whose dates are impossible to predict, may arise, such as criminal attacks, natural catastrophes or epidemics. We can nevertheless anticipate their consequences on the demand for commodities so as to have a quick plan to implement if the event occurs and to ensure alternative supply systems. Nuclear catastrophes, the last of which dates from March 2011 in Japan, resulting from an earthquake followed by a giant tsunami, have raised and continue to raise the issue of nuclear power and energy mixes in general in many major developed countries.

Immediate supply and the role of stock

Supply is analysed by distinguishing immediate supply, issued at very short notice, from upcoming supply, namely available reserves of commodities and our capacity to extract them in the future.

Stocks act as a buffer between supply and demand. They can be seen as an immediate and shallow supply, compared with production, constituting a longer-term supply. Fluctuations in stock levels enable supply to adapt to demand at any time, and thus to limit overly significant variations in prices.

On non-constrained markets, prices rise when the demand rises (or the supply drops), and fall when the supply increases (or the demand decreases). A climb of demand from D to D' (left of Figure 12.3) generates a price rise from P1 to P2. In this case, the quantities necessary for balancing the market increase from Q to Q', prompted by the price rise. Similarly, a decrease in the supply from S to S' (right of Figure 12.3) is leads to a fall in available quantities from Q to Q, and only a price rise from P1 to P2 can cause demand to go up again. In addition, the effect on the market of a rise in demand matched with a drop in supply undeniably generates strong price tension. In both scenarios, in the absence of any variation in stock, the price goes up from P1 to P2.

FIGURE 12.3   Price elasticity phenomenon

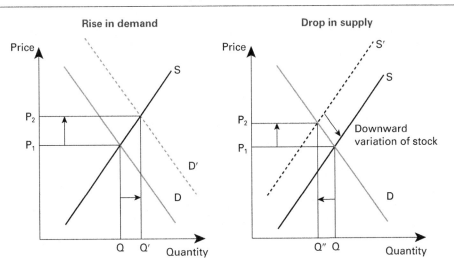

The placing of stock on the market plays a regulatory role by compensating for the reduction of the supply, and enabling the price to return to P1. In this way, on a perfect market, stock levels give a good indication of prices and the supply/demand balance. Stock represents the residue of the confrontation between supply and demand, and a balanced price corresponds to each stock level, with any deviation from this balance being considered as a speculator risk premium.

However, commodity markets are not perfect, and the gross figures of stock data sometimes disguise another reality. First of all, data is generally difficult to obtain if there is no legal obligation to publish stock levels. In addition, even when a publication constraint exists, data collection generally occurs on a declaration basis; figures may be incorrect and subject to regular readjustments. These readjustments are a source of price volatility. This is why many press, brokerage and information agencies specialize in the collection and analysis of stock data, which helps protagonists to place stock levels in perspective in the context of seasonal norms or long-term tendencies. For example, on oil markets, only the United States publishes stock levels every Wednesday at the Cushing delivery point. The publication of European and Asian figures is less frequent.

In addition, only a few specialized agencies have an idea of the stock levels stored in alternative forms of storage. For example, storage on ships develops when, due to global economic slowdown, land-based storage capacities reach their limits and there is an abundant supply of ships that are not working for technical (single-hull) or economic reasons.

Stock availability

Once the level of stock has been ascertained, the question of its *availability* crops up as it may be owned by private stakeholders, blocked by financial arrangements or located in countries where financial and logistical risks are too great. In addition, commodity stocks may not correspond to desired quality criteria. For example, mills require specific milling – in other words bread-making – qualities, namely grains of a specific weight, a maximum humidity level or minimum protein level. In the event of crop problems, wheat of poor quality would no longer be exportable and may be downgraded to the animal-feed category, causing its price to drop steeply.

Stocks may also be poorly *geographically distributed*. Significant stocks may be found in certain countries while being very low in others. Domestic prices will then tend to diverge so that international arbitrage can take place in order for the supply and global demand to balance out. Countries with large stocks will see their prices drop in order to compensate the costs of transport towards major maritime ports; conversely, prices offered in importer countries, even if they themselves are producers, will increase in order to capture, at least, all domestic production. Certain countries also have limited storage capacities, forcing them to export their production as quickly as possible at any cost.

Stocks may also be difficult to capture if logistical obstacles compound the difficulties mentioned above; this is why *distribution circuits* also need to be analysed. Logistical restrictions may vary in nature: a bottleneck at an important transit point; road, waterway or port infrastructures that may be destroyed or rendered useless by natural catastrophes; excessively low river levels preventing barge or riverboat transport to export ports; strikes at loading terminals; a pipeline undergoing works, and so on.

Maritime interruptions may also be due to unfavourable weather conditions (snow, fog), accidents (oil slicks, a ship stuck in a canal) or heavy traffic. Ship demand and supply and transport prices (fuel, vessel rental) may have a strong impact on a good's final cost price.

Weather may also play an important role in reducing supply. Agricultural commodities are extremely sensitive to its effects, given that production levels and quality depend directly on temperatures and hydrometric factors. Weather similarly has an impact on other markets. When Hurricane Katrina struck the south-east of the United States in August 2005, a substantial proportion of oil-storage and refining capacities was jeopardized, and shortage could only be avoided thanks to the setting up of strategic stock and production surplus in economic partners such as Mexico or Saudi Arabia. In this case, strategic stock played its role in buffering supply and demand following a brutal upset of balance. The International Energy Agency immediately requested that solidarity mechanisms totalling 60 million barrels be implemented over one month. France contributed 4.6 per cent of this total, in other words about 2 days' worth of consumption.

Finally, it may be necessary to proceed to an initial transformation of stock (refining of precious metals, oil refining, grinding of grain to obtain oil, etc) before the commodity is fit for commercialization or export. It is worthwhile finding out whether power cuts or maintenance periods are scheduled, and determining the utilization rate of transformation capacities and the yield of each semi-transformed product.

Upcoming supply

Surplus production capacities can generally be considered as the short- or medium-term supply. However, it is important to know whether this excess can be mobilized quickly and sustainably. For example, the bulk of the excess oil produced by OPEC countries is found in Saudi Arabia. But is this country capable, if a crisis arises, of sustainably producing more than 12 million barrels per day, a volume close to its historic upper limit?

In the long term, the question of commodity reserves is crucial, in terms of quantity, quality (eg the type of oil) and geographical location (country risk). As is the case for data on stocks, data on reserves is sometimes questionable. Such data should be analysed for the probability of the stock's existence and exploitation, in the current economic, political and technological conditions.

For example, three categories exist for gas and oil reserves. Proven reserves (1P or P90) have a 90 per cent chance of entering production. These are reasonably reputed to be certain and on 1 January 2011 represented around 200 billion tons, in other words 56 years' worth of reserves at the current rhythm of production. Probable reserves (2P or P50) are reasonably probable, while possible reserves (3P or P10) have a chance of being developed given favourable circumstances. Classification does not take account of non-conventional reserves such as oil sands, Antarctic reserves, coal-derived compounds or biofuels.

For every site, this information takes into account geological data and the age of the production site in order to determine the natural rate of decline of exploitation. In the case of oil, as for many other commodities, if reserves exist, it is necessary to work out at what cost the reserves will be exploitable and thus find out the marginal cost of the last ton of product to be exploited, and the evolution of this marginal cost of production. It is also necessary to ascertain whether investments in new production and transformation capacities are adequate for meeting demand, and also whether supply is constrained by the geopolitical environment.

Political, geopolitical and monopoly constraints can lower prices by modifying the balance between supply and demand. For example, OPEC countries produce 40 per cent of the world's oil with low production costs. In addition, they were used to deliberately produce less than their production capacity allows (underproduction of around 6 billion barrels per day), thus leaving it up to the majors (international companies) to exploit oil at a high production cost. When global demand drops, production will not fall in the more costly non-OPEC countries, but in OPEC ones. In this way, oil prices are not based on the average price of production, but on the marginal price of non-OPEC production. This example demonstrates the importance of relationships between producer and consumer countries, and the foreign policies of the latter that increasingly seek to consolidate economic partnerships with countries holding natural resources.

As for agricultural goods, the bulk of volatility results from the supply. We can note a slowdown in productivity gains, massive rural exodus and a lack of investment in this sector. There is also growing competition for the use of arable land, entailing delicate arbitrage between its use for food, fuel and urbanization. All this, without mention of climatic hazards.

Finally, other events may have consequences on the prices of commodities, such as merger / acquisition operations that may reduce the number of stakeholders in a monopolistic or oligopolistic situation. Speculative flows and certain financial arrangements can also alter price signals.

In this way, while market mechanisms are the primary source of price volatility, they do not affect all stakeholders, each with different management horizons, in the same way.

Stakeholders on commodity markets

The three main players on the physical commodity markets are:

- producers who may be private independent parties, organized in the form of cooperatives, royalty-earning operator companies, or national production companies: producers originate commodity supplies;
- initial processors of raw products such as grain-grinders, metal refiners, refiners of oil products;
- consumers.

A fourth player, whose importance has grown considerably in recent years, is the *physical trader*, situated between the producer and the consumer. Traders are extremely knowledgeable about the global and domestic markets for a given commodity. They are arbitrage professionals who earn their livings from buying from one spot, then transporting the commodities and reselling them in another spot. They therefore take advantage of price discrepancies in different geographical zones and for different product qualities. As a result, their intervention causes prices to converge. Since the emergence, in recent years, of global trading giants dealing in commodities, regulators have started to suspect certain players of taking advantage of their dominant positions to influence prices in their own favour.

Figure 12.4 indicates that different physical protagonists are not all exposed to the same price risks. Those at the extremities of the chain bear absolute risks whereas intermediary links bear relative risks relating to the time lag between their purchases and their sales and the change in the product's characteristics, whether qualitative or situational.

FIGURE 12.4   Physical protagonists on commodity markets

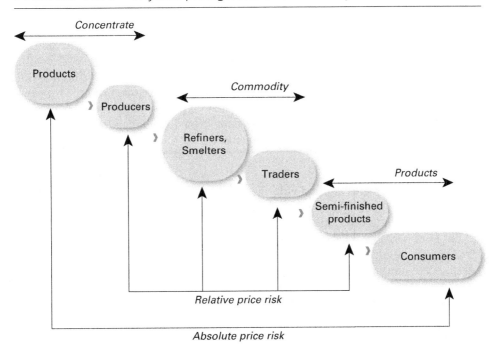

Players on physical markets also intervene on financial markets, amongst other participants.

Sovereign institutions make decisions that play a role in the setting of prices and in the balance between supply and demand. Ministries and government agencies may regulate prices, introduce production quotas or decide on the creation of strategic stocks. Sovereign funds invest in the commodity sector, all the more if they are strategic for their country. The policies of central banks, wielding influence over exchange rates and interest rates, may promote the trade of goods and produce.

Banks and brokers play an intermediary role, and are key players for whoever wishes to engage in transactions on the futures markets. Banks finance all streams of commodities. They have also permitted the development of customized OTC transactions, elaborated to meet the specific requirements of each operator. Meanwhile, brokers promote liquidity, their aim being to carry out the maximum number of transactions.

Long-term investors (pension funds and other asset-management companies) are also players on the commodity markets, for they use commodities as a category of assets in their own right, with the aim of diversifying investment portfolios. Investors do not invest directly in stocks of raw materials but via futures markets. Their role has been highly controversial in recent years because the long-term nature of their investments means that they react less to price signals and are thus less sensitive to supply and demand mechanisms.

Hedge funds aim at producing high returns and may involve the investment of significant sums. Some funds are diversified over several capital markets; others, such as commodity trading advisors (CTAs) invest exclusively in commodities. These funds opt for directional or tactical strategies, aiming to take advantage of short-, medium- and/or long-term trends. They perform particularly well during periods of high volatility or recession, and mainly rely on extremely liquid instruments such as futures contracts listed on exchanges.

As on any market, the high number of protagonists contributes to the liquidity of prices, that is, the possibility of finding a price for a given quantity at any moment. Market destabilization can however occur when certain protagonists (whether an entity or a number of entities adopting the same behaviour) take identical positions or prevent goods from reaching final recipients.

Volatility and price risk

Historical volatility and implied volatility

The concepts of historical volatility and implied volatility, explained at the start of the chapter in relation to exchange markets, are also valid for commodity markets.

Historical volatility is calculated from past prices and corresponds to the standard deviation of daily price variations. Applied to the commodity markets, volatility describes the amplitude of price variation movements over time, expressed as an annualized percentage. Price risk for commodities is therefore also inseparable from the notion of volatility: without volatility, this risk is nil. On the contrary, the greater the volatility, the greater the risk.

Implied volatility results from how market operators anticipate prices to evolve in the future. It is deduced from the prices of standard options listed on commodity exchanges, and enables calculation of the value of less standard options. Implied volatility is a function of the option's exercise (or strike) price and its maturity. For a given maturity, it generally reaches a low point when the option is at the money, gradually becoming greater as the option goes in the money or out of the money. This graphic representation is known as the 'Smile' (Figure 12.5). In theory, implied volatility is supposed to follow Gauss's Law with symmetrical distribution around the money. In practice, on the commodity market, we often observe a distortion of Gauss's Law as we draw away from the money, called the 'Skew'.

Volatility, variability and price risk

The volatility of commodity prices is a global phenomenon that has notably accentuated since the years 2005–06 (Figure 12.6).

It first affected energy markets (oil, gas and electricity), then quickly spread to metals (primary metals then precious metals), and finally to agricultural products. Volatility was initially manifested by a price spike, followed by massive correction. We can also note that it has affected commodity markets more heavily than other financial assets (on average three times more than for the currency market).

FIGURE 12.5   The Smile: volatility for a given maturity

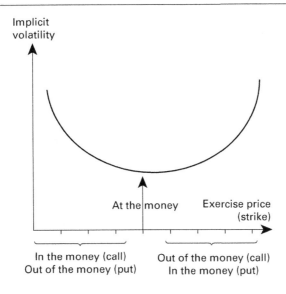

FIGURE 12.6   Evolution of prices for the main commodities

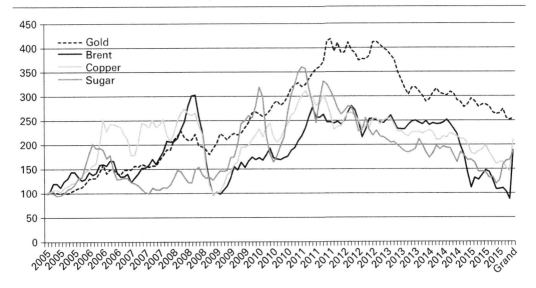

The increase in volatility has been accompanied by a strong variability of prices. Indeed, prices can be volatile, that is, undergo great variations in daily prices, while remaining low in variability, that is, within an acceptable price range for buyers and sellers. On the other hand, when price variability is great and prices reach extremely high or low levels, the balance is broken and this may have serious consequences on our societies. For consumers, this means a drop in purchasing power due to the rise in expenses for basic necessity products.

Volatility and speculation

Fingers have often been pointed at speculation even if it is always difficult to prove its actual effect on prices. We can nonetheless observe that the volume of transactions carried out on derivative markets exceeds that on physical markets, and this disproportion is accentuated over time. At calm periods, prices basically rely on mechanisms and speculation only plays a marginal role. On already tense markets, speculation can amplify the phenomenon: a speculative bubble is created and ends up bursting (Figure 12.7).

FIGURE 12.7   Amplifying effect of speculation on price variability

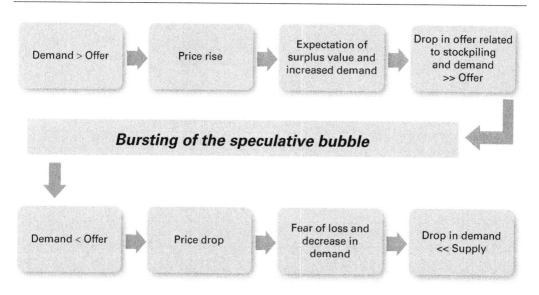

The financialization of commodity markets (it is not necessary to intervene on the physical market to take a position on financial markets) may lead speculators to take excessive positions with a high leverage ratio. Their magnitude may destabilize markets for any portfolio adjustment will have a considerable impact on prices.

Physical commodity markets do not grow as much as futures (financial) markets, and to stay in line with physical mechanisms, derivative volumes cannot exceed a certain percentage of volumes dealt with on physical markets.

In addition, due to the financial crisis, speculators have overlooked certain traditional financial assets to focus on commodities. Vehicles such as exchange-traded funds (ETF) have opened up access to a vast public. In addition, derivative markets (futures and options markets) have sometimes lacked transparency, and certain players have been tempted to manipulate prices.

This is why speculators have been the object, in recent years, of increased attention from public powers, and many work groups, propelled by G20 meetings, have been established. These developments have led to increased regulation of commodity markets, which is ongoing. Amongst the recent directives, we can cite the Dodd–Frank Reform in the United States, as well as the Markets in Financial Instruments Directives (MIFID 1 & 2), the Remit regulation on European gas and power and European Market Infrastructure Regulation (EMIR) in Europe. The reinforcement of international cooperation and regulation aims for greater transparency, but also reduction in systemic risks thanks to the clearing of derivatives.

12/2.2 Tools for managing commodity price risks

The role of futures markets

Commodity markets can be divided into three categories: energy and oil; metals; and agricultural products. On each of these markets, there are physical markets and derivatives markets (futures and options markets) connected by delivery mechanisms.

Futures markets primarily serve as a tool to hedge against price variations. They are also used as a price reference or benchmark for a commodity. For example, the price of copper listed on the London Metal Exchange (LME) serves as an index in the contracts negotiated between producers, dealers, refiners, recyclers and industrial companies.

In addition, futures markets are sometimes, by way of methods of payment at a contract's maturity, a last recourse for the physical transaction of goods.

Finally, for the last decade or so, investors have increasingly viewed futures markets as a category of assets in their own right (we note that their prices are not correlated with other asset categories, and thus, are useful for diversification purpose).

Hedging on a futures market consists in taking an opposite position to the one taken on the physical market. Producers who fear a price drop will sell a futures contract. The day when they actually sell their goods, they will buy back this contract. Inversely, consumers who fear an increase in commodity prices will buy a contract that they will resell when they actually buy the goods (see Table 12.7).

TABLE 12.7 Risk approaches and associated strategies (1)

	Risk	Strategy
Producer	Absolute risk of price drop	Futures sale
Consumer	Absolute risk of price rise	Futures purchase
Intermediaries	Relative price risk between purchases and sales	Margin-blockage operations

Organized markets and OTC markets

There are mainly two standard marketplaces for protecting oneself from risks relating to price fluctuations: exchanges that are organized markets and over-the-counter (OTC) markets.

Commodity exchanges are places for the exchange of futures and options contracts. Many players have access to them, guaranteeing maximum liquidity. Counterparty risk is transferred to clearing houses. Finally, exchanges and clearing houses set rules of good conduct in order to ensure the sound settlement of transactions.

To open a position, in other words, to initiate a transaction, the clearing house requests a cash amount known as 'an initial and variation margin call'. This amount constitutes protection against the participants' risk of default. The amount is supposed to hedge against the most unfavourable variation between two participants. It can be adjusted at any time, ie upwards when volatility increases. Subsequently, as long as the position remains open, daily margin calls will be requested. These correspond to the fictive liquidation of the opened positions on the basis of the day's settlement price. In this way, daily gains and losses are settled before the following session.

The clearing house and the market supervisory board may also set limits such as limits on daily variations, via margin calls during sessions when there are strong fluctuations in prices. This limitation on daily variations is generally interrupted on the final days of negotiation before the maturity date in order to ensure a convergence of prices with the physical market.

Commodities exchanges have long existed. The CME Group is the most active group of markets dealing in commodities, as it lists and clears the main American markets (West Intermediate Texas crude oil, heating oil and US natural gas listed in New York and grains listed in Chicago). In Europe, the ICE is the exchange listing Brent, gasoil as well as natural gas contracts. The LME (London Metal Exchange) lists primary metals while the NYSE Liffe indexes derivative contracts for white sugar or cocoa, and Euronext for milling wheat and rapeseed. There are many other commodities exchanges.

Commodities that are not listed on exchanges, as well as non-standard products, are exchanged on OTC markets. The proportion of commodity contracts within all financial OTC contracts is relatively weak, at 0.35 per cent of contracts processed, making up 1.91 per cent of their value. The Bank for International Settlements estimated this market's value at US$237 billion in June 2015. As in the case of exchanges, these markets also need brokers to bring counterparties into contact. Their intervention reduces the gap between the bid/offer spread and so improves liquidity.

One advantage of OTC markets over organized exchanges is that they can list non-standard products. Indeed, every parameter of the contract can be selected. These contracts are therefore flexible. Moreover, also more confidential, when a market is not very liquid OTCs enable dealing with sizable transactions without having the volume destabilize prices.

The US agencies that monitor US commodity exchanges and futures markets are the Commodity Futures Trading Commission (CFTC) and the Securities and Exchange Commission (SEC). On UK markets, the Financial Services Authority (FSA) plays this role. In France, all futures markets are regulated by the *Autorité des Marchés Financiers* (AMF). With the development of regulation and in the interests of transparency and reduction of systemic risk, commodity stakeholders are required to declare to the authorities the transactions carried out, and, upwards of a certain threshold, to clear them.

Forwards, futures or swaps: firm forward contracts

A forward contract for commodities may be a *forward*, *futures* or *swap contract*. What the three have in common is that they allow a price to be set at a given maturity date, for a given quantity, quality and delivery point. These contracts are firm: in other words, irrevocable.

A forward contract is an OTC contract for the physical delivery of a good between two counterparties on the physical market at a given price. It includes a description of the product's quality as well as conditions for the good's delivery. Simple to use, its widespread use has been observed from the end of the 1960s, but the development of this type of contract is limited by credit risk and the lack of liquidity. The price includes numerous elements (raw material, added value, transport, etc). In order to optimize the total price, it is often more efficient to set aside the price of the raw material and to limit negotiation to other price elements, that is, the residual basis or premium. The forward contract then becomes a floating price contract, known as a premium contract.

A futures contract is a standardized forward financial instrument, negotiated on a commodity exchange. It may lead to the physical delivery of goods, whose conditions are foreseen in the contract, but in practice, only 1 per cent of futures contracts unwind this way. The 99 per cent others unwind with a closing of the position. The physical delivery mechanism enables ensuring a convergence of prices on the physical market and the futures market, as the exchange is a last-resort market. In addition, the great liquidity of organized markets enables positions to be reversed at any moment.

A swap contract is an OTC forward financial instrument available from banking institutions. Indexed on the price of a commodity, the swap contract ends in a cash settlement. It offers the flexibility of a customized structure; for example, the maturity, quantity or quotation currency may be chosen by the parties. Banks guarantee liquidity by offering a secondary market for restructuring or closing positions.

If these contracts are similar in terms of product, maturity, quality and quantity, their values will be very close.

Forward curve: contango and backwardation

The forward curve represents forward prices for a given good over a series of maturities. Its shape may be positive, in which case we speak of *contango* (a concept close to the premium on the exchange market) or negative, in which case we speak of *backwardation* (a concept close to the discount on the exchange market). Contango corresponds to a situation where the spot price is lower than the forward price. On a balanced market, this is a normal situation for a storable good. To put things simply, market stakeholders expect the price of a good to increase or remain stable. Even when stable prices are anticipated, forward prices are always slightly higher than spot prices in order to cover the costs engendered by interest rates, insurance costs and storage.

Backwardation refers to a situation where spot prices are higher than forward prices. This means that the markets expect a price fall or that spot prices have increased very significantly following a supply shock on the market.

Supply and demand mechanisms, and particularly stock levels, determine the price of the first nearby futures contracts.

When there is a surplus, two dynamics may intervene: the spot price may decrease to encourage physical buyers to ask for more goods; and/or the forward price may increase to compensate for the upcoming holding costs for unsold stock. In all cases, contango is supposed to spread. On the other hand, when a supply shock is discernible, the spot price increases in order to encourage producers to produce more goods or sellers to release stocks, and/or the forward price falls to prompt consumers to delay their raw materials purchases. The back of the curve (long maturities) represents the marginal cost of production (exploitation cost of a new barrel).

As on the exchange market, it is possible to extend or 'roll' a forward contract. The contract cannot be cancelled but if a contract with a given maturity date is purchased, it is possible to resell at this same maturity date and then buy it back for a later maturity date (Figure 12.8).

FIGURE 12.8   Shape of the forward curve

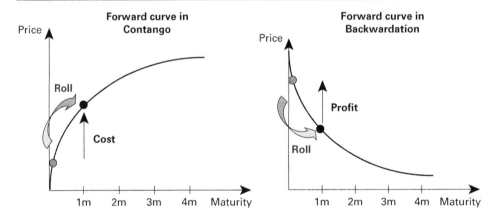

Calendar spreads

A calendar spread is a margin-blocking transaction by which the company blocks a difference between two price-setting periods for a commodity: the moment at which it proceeds to make its purchases at the market price (price excluding production cost) and the moment when it sells its finished product at another price. This strategy aims at reducing the relative risk of price fluctuation born by industry intermediaries (oil refiners, metal refiners or recyclers, dealers, etc) for whom commodities constitute an important share of sales prices. The operation guarantees the company a sales price for the material equal to the price paid, adjusted by an initially set difference (mark-up).

The pay-off is that the company will not benefit from favourable movements of the market. In addition, depending on the market conditions, the difference generated may represent a surplus of positive margin or on the contrary an extra cost for the commodity.

Here is an example of how the transaction works.

At T (time), the company knows that it will purchase, in T + 1, the commodity from its supplier at a price indexed on the average of market prices in the month preceding the delivery (M1) and that it will sell, in T + 2, its finished product at a price indexed on another average (M2). It decides to block the margin between its purchase price and its sales price on financial markets, adjusted by a differential x (x depends, amongst other elements, on the shape of the future curve: contango or backwardation).

In T + 1, the reference price M1 on which the purchase price of the commodity is indexed is known.

In T + 2, at the expiry of the transaction, if M2 < M1 + x, then the company will receive the cash difference between M2 and M1 + x. Otherwise, it will pay this difference.

Commodity options

Additional definitions

The mechanism of foreign-exchange options described in the first half of this chapter also applies to commodity markets. The terminology, price calculation and profile of gains/losses are identical.

In this way, an option for the purchase of oil or primary metals is also called a *call*, and a sales option, a *put*. These options may be purchased or sold. When we speak of hedging against a risk, we only speak of option purchase: the net sale of options is reserved to speculators (see Table 12.8).

When we talk about 'at the money' commodity options, we always refer to the forward 'at the money' value, and not the spot value, in other words, the exercise or strike price of the option is equal to the forward price of the future or swap contract.

Whether on the organized or OTC markets, options on commodities are exercised automatically at their maturity, and do not lead to the physical delivery of the good.

On organized markets, options can lead to the delivery of the corresponding futures contracts. In this way, the purchase of a call will be closed by the purchase of a futures contract at the initial exercise price, and the sale of a put by the sale of a futures contract. The organized market option is indexed on a futures contract, and like the futures contract, is standardized. Options are usually European style; in

TABLE 12.8 Risk approaches and associated strategies (2)

	Risk	Strategy
Producer	Absolute risk of price drop	Purchase of a put
Consumer	Absolute risk of price rise	Purchase of a call

other words, the return is determined at the maturity date on the basis of the last settlement price.

Meanwhile, the OTC option is closed by a cash settlement at its maturity. It may be indexed on a futures contract listed on an organized market, or another non-listed underlying. The calculation of the reference price is carried out at the end of the period of price observation, and often corresponds to an average of daily prices observed over a calendar period (generally one month) for an underlying. In this case, we speak of an Asian or average-value option.

In addition, it is possible to trade *swaps* and *quanto* options on OTC markets. In this case, the currency of the hedging is different from the initial quote currency of the underlying. For example, it is possible to purchase an option indexed on the ICE Brent contract in euros while its quote currency is the US dollar. The exercise price is expressed in euros and the calculation of the option's performance takes into account a daily EUR/USD conversion applied to the daily reference price of the underlying. In the interests of transparency, the fixing used should be impartial. For the EUR/USD, we can use the EURUSD fixing published by Blomberg of WM Reuters.

Examples of optional structures
We find below a non-exhaustive list of hedging strategies practised by commodity consumers. The following notations are used:

S, S1, S2 = strike or exercise price
P = reference price of the underlying calculated during the observation
    period or floating price
F1 = price of a futures or swap contract upon the transaction's implementation
F2 = price of a futures or swap contract at a later date

The graphic representation used is different from that employed in classic financial literature. It indicates the impact of hedging on the total cost price of the hedging and the physical transaction rather than the profit and loss of the hedging alone.

The call
A purchase option or call is a forward hedging instrument that allows protection from the price rise of an underlying in return for payment of a premium. A call offers the right, and not the obligation, to buy the underlying at a ceiling price known as the exercise (or strike) price during a certain period or at a specific date (maturity). The purchase of a call enables full protection from price risks while not depriving oneself entirely from an unanticipated favourable price evolution. Figure 12.9 below illustrates the mechanism.

At each exercise date of an option:

- if P > S, then the option buyer receives (P – S);
- if P < S, nothing happens.

The call spread
The call spread is a forward hedging instrument that enables partial protection against the rise of the underlying to a given price up to a certain limit. It consists in the purchase of a call at a strike price and the sale of another call at a higher strike

FIGURE 12.9   Call mechanism

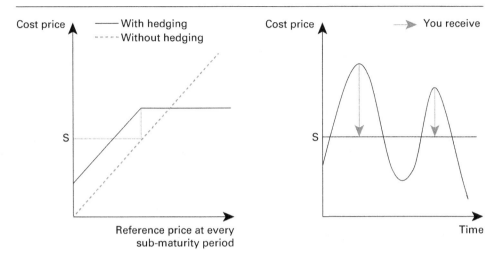

Reference price at every
sub-maturity period

price over a certain period or at a specific maturity date. The premium to be paid
when the transaction is set up is less than that of a call as the gain is limited to the
difference between the two strikes. If prices fall, the buyer benefits from the favourable variation. Figure 12.10 illustrates the mechanism of a call spread.

At each exercise date of an option:

- if $P < S1$, nothing happens, the buyer does not exercise the option;
- if $S1 < P < S2$, the buyer receives $(P - S1)$;
- if $P > S2$, the buyer receives $(S2 - S1)$.

FIGURE 12.10   Call spread mechanism

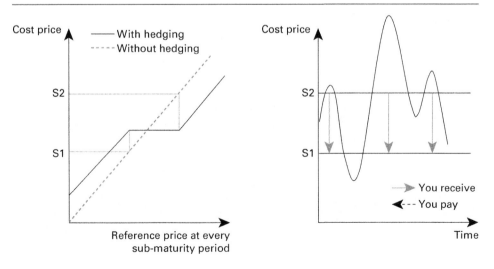

Reference price at every
sub-maturity period

The call swaption

A swaption (Figure 12.11) is a forward hedging instrument that gives the buyer the right, rather than the obligation, to enter into a swap, at a predefined future date and price, during a certain period or at a specific maturity date. The characteristics of the swaption are determined on the day when the option is set up. This option is particularly suited to responding to calls for tenders. Once a market has been won, hedging via the swap is set up at the price initially agreed upon. Any loss will then be limited to the sum of the premium paid to set up the transaction.

At the date on which the swaption is exercised:

- if $F2 < S$, nothing happens and the two counterparties are released from all commitments. The swaption buyer can choose to proceed to a new swap at market conditions, having taken advantage of the price drop;
- if $F2 \geq S$, then the swaption buyer can exercise the right and enter into a swap at the initially negotiated conditions. In this case, at the end of each swap sub-period;
- if $P > S$, then the swaption buyer receives $(P - S)$;
- if $P < S$, then the swaption buyer receives $(S - P)$.

FIGURE 12.11   Swaption mechanism

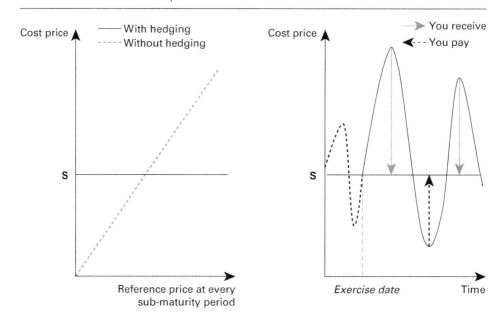

12/2.3 Definition of a commodity policy for hedging against price risks

In recent years, pronounced volatility has prompted all companies whose turnovers are directly related to raw materials prices to modify or, sometimes, to set up commodity policies for hedging against price risks. Such policies constitute key links within a company's strategy.

Let's take the example of airline or cargo-shipping companies. Fuel represents around a quarter of their turnover and sometimes far more when energy prices spike. The sensitivity of their total costs to energy prices is thus extremely high (low price elasticity) and poor management may cause serious detriment to the company's financial health.

The seven stages that follow summarize the process for setting up a commodity policy (Figure 12.12). This type of policy is perfectly suited to the management of purchases of both foreign currencies and commodities.

FIGURE 12.12 A commodity policy in 7 stages

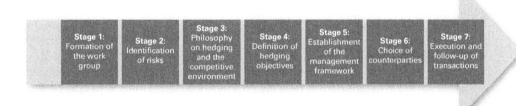

Stage 1: Formation of the work group

Hedging policy, being a strategic matter, should be validated by the company's top management, and a work group set up as of its conception (and composed of a sufficiently broad range of members, given that the issue concerns numerous departments).

First, it concerns the procurement and the sales departments that will work together on the analysis of price risks, and then generally become the hedging prescribers in relation to the financial department.

The policy also concerns the legal department that offers its expertise for the drafting of any new sales contracts and for the signing of the master agreements necessary for the processing of transactions on financial markets.

Finally, it also concerns the finance department, for in practice, this is generally the department that executes the transactions. In addition, the finance department will seek to respond to accounting imperatives by offering products that conform to current norms and hedge accounting principles; it will also make sure that the hedging is backed by physical flows, and if need be, can restructure positions, for example, postpone them, if physical flows are also postponed. The finance department can also consult the auditor upstream.

Stage 2: Identification of risks

The procurement department should determine the raw materials and energies (heating, transport) that contribute to the company's product-processing process. It then analyses the price risks weighing upon them, and finally attempts to understand the residual risks relating to time lags or geographical shifts between purchases and sales, or relating to change in a product's quality if processing occurs. Analysis may be further extended to the costs for supplying the energy necessary for production (gas, electricity) or for packaging (paper, plastic and possibly aluminium for moulds).

Let's take the example of a company that manufactures biscuits based on a simple recipe (flour, butter and sugar). Its suppliers are mainly:

- for flour, mills that offer spot prices (daily prices) or prices indexed on milling wheat futures markets (N2 contract listed on the Euronext exchange);
- for butter, dairy spot prices or prices for deliveries in three months' time at the most;
- for sugar, the major European sugar groups that offer a yearly price, dependent on the crop prices offered to farmers and led by the mechanism of the European Common Agricultural Policy.

The biscuit manufacturer's clients are mainly large and medium-sized supermarkets (mass distribution) making purchases for their own-brand products or for products sold under distributor brands, but for which operating margins are further reduced. Negotiations with mass distributors generally begin in November and conclude at the end of February. The negotiated price is then applicable as of 1 March for a sliding one-year period.

For this company, there is a significant gap between the time periods referred to in its purchase and its sales contracts. This gap is exacerbated by the fact that negotiations for each commodity apply to different periods, ranging from spot prices to forward prices. Forward prices are not exactly helpful for the company in fixing its total costs, as these are furthermore determined by seasons (price of wheat indexed on a forward contract for the new crop) and supplier methods (forward price of butter set at three months at the most) rather than the time horizon that interests the company, ie its period of contractualization with the large and medium-sized supermarkets.

Stage 3: Philosophy on hedging and the competitive environment

Some companies, namely industrial companies, practise systematic hedging against risks. Indeed, as industrial risks and investments are already considerable, they do not wish to be subject, on top of these, to risks in price variations. Other companies prefer never to hedge and permanently adhere to prices indexed on market prices, believing that this strategy allows them to stay more reactive. This type of situation is less common, and corresponds to economic models with high risks or high margins.

Generally speaking, we note that the lower the margins and/or the more that the proportion of commodities contributes to total cost, the more important it is to hedge.

A hedging decision also depends on the power of negotiation, at the two extremities of the chain, with suppliers and clients. Indeed, the company can *transfer the price risk to its supplier* by forward purchasing materials from the latter (at a price fixed in advance by a forward contract), or *to its customer* thanks to re-indexing mechanisms. As this decision affects both the procurement and sales functions, it is to be taken by the executive committee. The latter can seek advice on this issue from firms specialized in price risk mitigation.

For example, an airline may choose not to hedge in order to take advantage of all price drops and thus win market shares. This can be a risky choice if prices rise, as fuel represents an average of 25 per cent of the price of a ticket. The airline may also try to transfer price variations to customers via fuel surcharges if prices rise above a benchmark price. Currency adjustment factors are other fees that exist to offset variations in exchange rates. In practice, these techniques are inadequate and a suitable policy for hedging against risks is necessary.

By analysing the competitive environment, the company may decide to adopt the same hedging policy as its competitors or else innovate to try to win market shares. Finally, all policies on the management of price risks should be periodically reviewed to ascertain whether they are still relevant in a shifting competitive environment.

Stage 4: Definition of hedging objectives

The setting up of hedging policies offers many advantages.

The first and most obvious is *protection against price variations*. By controlling an important value-added cost item, the company can ensure that it maintains a sales margin – whatever the price volatility – and set forward-sales prices for goods while respecting a set price in the forecast budget. Depending on the type of hedging set up, the company can also take advantage of a possible market improvement or else attempt to benefit from the forward curve shape – contango in the case of producers, backwardation in the case of consumers.

The second advantage is that a company gains the *capacity to offer a wide range of contracts* to its customers, ranging from spot prices to long-term fixed prices, as well as contracts indexed on transparent references. Forward markets secure the company and its customers access to a transparent price reference for sales negotiations. This allows focus to shift from gross prices to the contribution of added value or quality compared with a standard good. A capacity to offer long-term contracts at a fixed price to car manufacturers is an important asset for equipment suppliers, for example. In a context where prices are extremely volatile and economic uncertainty is considerable, it is possible to bank on this expertise as a sales argument. Having control over price risks and the tools for protecting oneself can also give a company the means to respond to calls for tenders that are complicated or that commit it over long periods.

Thirdly, access to financial markets permits companies to *take advantage of the last-resort market function* of commodity exchanges via physical delivery mechanisms. Public or private warehouses approved by commodity exchanges are a supply source at periods when there are goods shortages, and an outlet during surplus periods.

Finally, the fourth advantage is the *securing of financing* for purchased commodities. Commodity policy reassures shareholders about the risks encountered by their company by simplifying the reading of results via reduction of their volatility. Companies listed on the stock exchange generally opt for a very secure risk profile with high hedging ratios, using simple hedging products that comply with accounting norms.

Active management of price risks can also aid a company's financial policy by *reducing working capital requirement relating to stock*, and thus improve financial ratios. A company that does not practise hedging may be tempted to buy more commodities when prices are low and to carry this stock for as long as it takes for it to be disposed of. It therefore will need to meet high storage, financing and insurance costs. In addition, the time required for the goods to be disposed of may prove longer than expected if prices fall due to an economic slowdown. In comparison, hedging on forward markets necessitates lower investments, corresponding to the guarantees that must be contributed to protect the market from risk of default, via the payment of a security deposit and margin calls if the position deteriorates.

The last aspect regarding the securing of financing for commodities is that bankers and other creditors have guarantees on reimbursement of the debt and a sound conclusion to sales transactions.

The drawbacks of hedging against price risks are more limited. The first is a reduction in profits if the hedging is carried out on the basis of an unfavourable price. Risks and gains are in fact often proportional. Secondly, it is necessary to take care, when setting up hedges, to protect oneself against counterparty risk when dealing OTC transactions.

Stage 5: Establishment of the management and limits framework

The management framework describes the role of each party in the setting up and monitoring of hedges. It also sets out a certain number of directives on the underlying that the company can hedge against, the maximum and minimum volumes to commit, the maturity dates that it is possible to deal with for each underlying, as well as the desired degree of risk. The framework may also define a ceiling limit for the guarantees that the company can issue in order to ensure that transactions run smoothly. In this way, whatever the policy decided upon, the company formalizes and controls the level of risk that it is prepared to accept.

Proxy hedging

Sometimes, it is possible to set up the 'perfect hedge', in other words one in which the future value of the asset to be hedged correlates with the underlying of the hedge. In this case, the company no longer bears any basis risk, in other words, risk of seeing divergence between the prices of both assets. Notably, this is possible in sales contracts that use the same indexing system as that of the hedge. For example, companies that produce or consume primary metals are in the habit of indexing physical contracts on metal prices quoted on the London Metal Exchange. In this way, as everyone uses the same index, it is possible to hedge metal prices by buying or selling futures contracts.

In other situations, the contract is not indexed on a reference handled on commodity exchanges. It is nevertheless possible to set up approximate hedging via another underlying (proxy hedging).

For example, a Russian wheat producer may use a futures contract for Euronext milling wheat that corresponds to a soft wheat having as its delivery point the public silos of Rouen. Even if the producer's wheat is similar in quality, the fact that the producer is far from the delivery point raises a basis risk between these two locations. In particular, the producer cannot take advantage of the physical delivery mechanisms of the exchange. The basis may be related to a difference in quality, delivery spot, contract maturity date, or a series of transformations that mean that the product to be hedged has already undergone various processing processes and its price gradually becomes uncorrelated with that of the basic asset.

Let's look at Figure 12.13 on the example of an airline.

FIGURE 12.13 Kerosene hedging mechanism

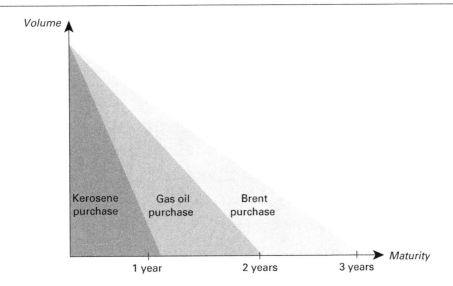

The airline that purchases kerosene in Europe can directly hedge against the price of standard fuel leaving a North Sea refinery, as this indexing is negotiated on OTC financial markets. Since it is uncommon for refineries to hedge their future sales after six months whereas buyers hedge their purchases on longer tenors (up to three years), this generates an extra imbalance between forward supply and demand, and thus the forward price generally includes a quasi-permanent additional premium compared to the spot price. In order to reduce this cost overrun, the airline may adopt the following strategy: it begins by buying a long-term hedge for crude oil (ICE Brent contract) that it resells after a few months to buy a hedge for an ICE Gas Oil contract, before finally, a few months off from the maturity date, exchanging this hedge on gasoil for a hedge on kerosene, that will perfectly hedge its price risk. Here, hedging, approximate at first, gradually becomes increasingly correlated to the product to be hedged as we approach the maturity date.

Hedging ratios and horizons

Figure 12.14 offers an example of hedging ratios decided upon in a commodity policy. It specifies the minimum volume to hedge (imposed whatever the market conditions) and the maximum volume authorized, allowing for the setting up of opportunistic hedging if levels seem interesting for opening positions. How do we determine whether it is the right time to hedge or not?

FIGURE 12.14 Standard example of hedging ratios

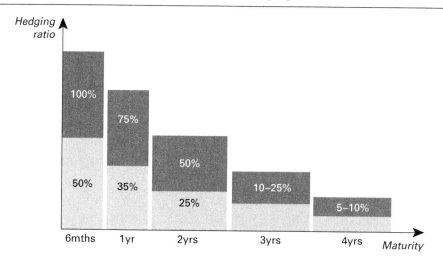

Forward prices are, in the absence of an alternative, the best available tool for forecasting futures prices in the very short term, but a mediocre forecast instrument for the medium or long term. This is why medium- and long-term hedging programmes should instead be based on a comparative analysis between market prices (spot prices, forward indexed prices, implied volatility) and historical prices, in order to best determine the type of structures to set up.

For example, a forward curve showing forward prices far higher than historical levels is a prompt for short-term hedging in particular, with an option strategy that will also protect, in the event of a price drop, from underperformance over an extended period.

Inversely, a forward curve showing forward prices far lower than historical levels incites hedging over long maturities with fixed prices. If visibility is good on market mechanisms and we do not anticipate price rises immediately, hedging is not necessarily required over the short-term horizon (Table 12.9).

Choice of structures used

The last element of the management framework is the definition of authorized markets (organized markets, OTC markets), and the products that can be subscribed to on them. Possibilities are multiple, ranging from the purchase of an insurance-like

TABLE 12.9 Decision-making model for opening positions depending on the desired horizon

	Short-term (up to 6 months)	Mid-term (6 to 18 months)	Long-term (18 months to 10 years)
Shape of the forward curve and volatility	High	Average	Low
Analysis of historical prices	Low	Average	High
Long-term economic forecasts	Low	Low	Average

option to simple contractualization at a fixed price, via more complex arrangements based on combinations of options. Since it is not a company's vocation to speculate on markets, it is advisable for the management to specify that the company should not find itself in the position of being a net seller of options.

Stage 6: Choice of counterparties

The company can call upon its physical counterparties to offer it hedges integrated into procurement contracts. If the company calls upon financial markets, it will need to choose its counterparties (banks, brokers, clearers) on the basis of the services they can offer and their financial ratings. Hedges may also boost business flow with a bank, hence facilitating negotiation for better conditions for other financial services. Counterparties are thus generally selected from the parties who participate to the company's financing. The quality of market information provided, economic research, the best price and reporting tools supplied all constitute selection criteria. The company's (internal) legal department or external law firm will negotiate, then sign the legal documentation. Meanwhile, the finance department will open accounts and negotiate possible lines of credit relating to management on forward markets.

The documentation necessary for handling transactions on organized forward markets (commodity exchanges) includes terms of business (TOB), the fee schedule (list of execution and clearing fees) and give-up agreements (a tripartite contract that lists approved brokers who can place orders with the commodity exchange and get them recorded on the counterparty's clearing account). The documentation necessary for handling OTC transactions is a master agreement of the type modelled by the International Swaps and Derivatives Association (ISDA) or the European Federation of Energy Traders (EFET).

Stage 7: Execution and follow-up of transactions

The treasury division of a company's finance department generally executes transactions. If the company has a trading desk as well as a dedicated back-office and middle office, it can intervene on organized and/or OTC markets at its own discretion.

However, if the team making up the treasury division is limited, it should limit itself to OTC markets. This will probably be a little expensive, but offers the advantage of being far simpler on an operational level. In addition, the total cost is known as soon as the transaction is set up, which is not the case for organized markets.

For companies subject to IFRS accounting standards, the finance department undertakes pre- and post-monitoring of hedge efficiency via hedge accounting, and documents the strategy in the annual report. This department also takes care of accounting and regulatory follow-up. In Europe, the new EMIR and REMIT directives require companies to report the positions that they have carried out. Such declarations may be delegated to those financial bodies with which the company is in contact (banks, clearers).

As far as the follow-up of sales goes, it is necessary to verify hedge efficiency in relation to initial margin objectives (budgeted prices) and not in relation to the results of the previous financial period, and to analyse the impact of the strategy on sales risk and on the risk of competition. Different indicators are available, such as the sensitivity of sales to price variation, the sensitivity of the market share or the opportunity gain engendered by the price rises of hedged commodities, or else the sensitivity of the market share or the loss of opportunity linked to price drops of strategic commodities that are hedged against but not passed onto customers.

Notes

1 Private individuals are more or less excluded from the exchange market if they seek direct involvement in it. They can, however, delegate their power to the manager of a mutual fund for example.

2 In the rest of this chapter, the figures in bold highlight relevant information in the quotation example. They designate either the unit of account (or its decimal digits) or the size of the spread, or the rates used for the calculation of cross-rates.

3 The best-known formula for calculating the price of an option is the Black–Scholes model formulated by two American mathematicians.

4 As well as the bibliography at the end of the work, the reader is invited to consult the following websites: www.cambiste.info, www.afte.com, www.marches-financiers.net, http//:entreprises.bnpparibas.fr/services_bancaires_entreprises/commerce_international.

13
Public procurement
French and European contexts

THIERRY BEAUGÉ

Five main features characterize public procurement today: a variety of contracting methods, the importance of Europe, highly comprehensive regulations that can be associated with great formalism and moderate effectiveness, openness towards the modernization of procedures, and a strong risk of instrumentalization.

13/1 The variety of contracting methods in the public sector

In France, public procurement is generally taken to mean public orders, which strictly are different from public contracts. Public orders represent everything that is likely to represent a contractual commitment, for pecuniary interest, undertaken by the administration. In this sense, it is even broader than public procurement which places more of an emphasis on whatever is likely to be acquired and owned, for it encompasses not only purchasing, in strict terms, but also rental, lease-purchasing and other services.

Public contracts, on the other hand, allude to a specific contractual mode regulated in France by the *Code des Marchés Publics* (French Public Procurement Code) and by European directives. Here, greater regulatory formalism is attached to the word 'contract'.

There exists a variety of methods of contracting, for pecuniary interest, with the public sector. We can observe two different families:

- public-service delegations, including 'leasing' (*affermage* in French), concession, and to a lesser extent the system whereby a company exercises a public-service concession with public employees for a fee (*régie intéressée*);

- public contracts that, in France, are now all subject to the Public Procurement Code, contracted either by a power contracting for the State and its public establishments other than industrial or commercial ones, territorial bodies and their public establishments and hospitals, or by contracting entities, in other words contracting powers that exercise an activity operating utilities in the fields of water, energy, transport and postal services. Public contracts also include partnership contracts.

13/1.1 Public-service delegations

According to Article 38 of the French Act no. 93-122[1] 'a public-service delegation is a contract by which a public-law legal entity entrusts management of a public service for which it holds responsibility to a public or private delegate, whose remuneration is substantially linked to the results of the operation of the service. The delegate may be responsible for constructing works or for acquiring goods necessary to the service'.

This is therefore a matter of handing over management of a service to a delegate who is paid on the basis of operation of this service. The remuneration is thus ensured by consumer fees. Public-service delegations can be found in the domains of urban heating, the distribution of drinking water, car parks, funeral services, public transport, sanitization and waste elimination, or else in cultural and social areas in the case of public administrative services.

Public-service delegations may take several forms: 'leasing', concession, or more rarely, the *régie intéressée* (company exercising a public-service concession with public employees).

In 'leasing' delegation only concerns operation of the service. The delegate is in charge of operating the service at its own risk and peril. It is remunerated by the consumers of the service. Project management remains in the hands of the administration.

In 'concessions' both the operation and the project management of the public service are delegated. The delegate operates the service, is remunerated by consumers, but also carries out necessary investments of which it is the owner. At the end of the contract, there may be, depending on the provisions agreed upon, transfer of acquired property to the public body.

In the *régie intéressée*, the management of the public service is delegated to a steward who pays the public staff, collects and transfers takings, and who is remunerated by a fixed fee accompanied by a bonus on results.

Given the investments involved, concessions last longer than 'leasing' arrangements, and are generally concluded for a period of 5–15 years.

In public-service delegations, remuneration of the delegate is assured by consumer fees.

13/1.2 Partnership contracts

Partnership contracts are subject to the Public Procurement Code in France. According to the Order of 17 June 2004 on partnership contracts[2] a partnership contract is 'an administrative contract under which the State or a State-run entity entrusts to a third party, for a period set according to investment amortization or agreed financing terms, a comprehensive project related to the construction or conversion, upkeep, maintenance, operation or management of works, equipment or intangible assets necessary to public service'.

This is thus a very vast field that stretches from initial investment to operation or management, passing through design, construction and maintenance. In reality, what is primarily sought is private financing.

13/1.3 Public contracts

Public contracts reportedly represent almost €2000 billion Europe-wide when we count its 28 member States, and €130 billion in France alone, in other words nearly 11 per cent of the GDP.

Public contracts deal with works, supplies and services that public bodies need to get done or to acquire.

Works consist of the direct construction, by the administration, of buildings, schools, administrative centres, art works, bridges, tunnels; they may also be demolitions.

Supplies comprise furnishings, food, medicines, machines, various equipment, automobiles, etc that the administration acquires, immediately or with a purchase option, or even rents.

Services encompass everything else according to the tautological definitions set out in the French Public Procurement Code[3] and in European Community directives,[4] with Brussels above all vigilant that nothing escapes bending to its directives. Services are intellectual services such as studies, but also services for picking up household waste, cleaning premises or maintenance of green spaces.

Public contracts are covered by a code that is supposed to take up the three strata of public-contract regulation: the international stratum with the Government Procurement Agreement (GPA) of the GATT[5] that has now become the World Trade Organization (WTO), the European stratum and the national stratum.

13/2 The importance of Europe

European regulations took off at the end of the 1970s. The European Commission noted that while the free circulation of goods took place more or less correctly for private markets, the same did not apply for public markets. National preferences and private turfs of all types existed. Brussels therefore decided to regulate public markets, so that the Treaty of Rome's objectives for free circulation might be attained.

It is through the instrument of the directive that regulations have flourished, imposing upon member States results to be reached, but leaving them choice on the means to get there. The first European Community directives were heavily impregnated with French public-contract law, the most structured and substantial of country regulations, so initially French public buyers saw little difference between European and their own national regulations. Very quickly, however, the directives would cover the whole field of public contracts, works, supplies and services, and then further expand their reach by the introduction of broader notions than the French concepts of supplies, works or services.

For example, while supply contracts in France referred only to purchases, for Brussels they also include rental, lease-purchase or leasing. The notion of service is extensive, as we have already seen.

From directive to directive, European regulations on public contracts, applicable to member States, took flight and gradually strayed from their French origins to introduce concepts unfamiliar to French public-law lawyers, given that ample space would be granted to case law such as the notions of 'effective advertising' or 'reasonable time'. With the supremacy of European law over national laws, in the space of 30 years or so, France has transitioned from completely French regulations to practically exclusive Community regulations. In addition, while Brussels initially only paid attention to the phases of contract preparation and award, ie to fight against discrimination between national and foreign companies, the European capital has since also turned its attention to the contract execution phase, through the monitoring of contract addenda and a contract governance system.[6]

Brussels has thus gradually replaced member States in this sovereign function. The regulation of public contracts is now European in inspiration when it is not primarily written down as Community regulations. Certain member States such as France still attempt to rewrite these directives to transpose them to domestic law, applying constitutional provisions. But this is a highly delicate exercise where every word is weighed down by the threat of action from the Court of Justice of the European Union for incorrect transposition. It will soon be simpler and safer, via legislative and regulatory measures, to introduce these directives into domestic law without any rewriting. Given the importance wielded by European law, we can already consider the French Public Procurement Code to be dead. Long live European directives!

13/2.1 Highly comprehensive regulations

Procedures, contracting methods, market categories... the buyer has a full set of tools that somewhat resemble an organ. Keyboards for the hands, buttons for changing the sound of the instrument, a pedal board for the feet: the buyer has regulatory instruments with which he or she can buy practically anything subject to two conditions: respect of the general principles of public contracts, which are freedom of access, equality of treatment, and transparency of procedures; and anticipation, in other words, adoption of a procurement policy.

What are the tools of the public buyer? Any classification is always somewhat arbitrary, but we can classify procedures, procurement techniques and public-contract categories in the following manner:

- *Procedures*:
  - open (open call for tenders);
  - restricted (restricted call for tenders);
  - negotiated and competitive with negotiation;
  - competitive dialogue;
  - innovation partnership.

- *Procurement techniques*:
  - master agreements;
  - dynamic acquisition systems;
  - electronic auctions;
  - electronic catalogues;
  - centralized procurement activities and central procurement offices;
  - occasional joint procurement;
  - contracts drawing participation from the contracting authorities of different member States;
  - the architectural competition.
- *Contract categories*:
  - designbuild contract (what distinguishes it is how it is awarded rather than executed);
  - contract relating to communication activities
  - amended procedure contract (the French MAPA);
  - conditional purchase-order contract;
  - contract with or without a minimum commitment;
  - study contract;
  - definition contract;
  - feasibility contract;
  - works supervision contract;
  - purchase-order contract;
  - contract divided into lots;
  - programme contract;
  - renewable contract;
  - long-term contract.

Finally, there are contracts classified according to the way in which prices are established:

- contract with a set overall price;
- contract based on unit prices;
- contract based on monitored expenditure;
- contract with a firm price;
- contract with an updatable price;
- contract with adjustable prices;
- contract with revisable prices;
- contract with provisional ceiling prices;

13/2.2 Great formalism and moderate effectiveness

Excessive rigour has gradually complicated public contracts, due to two influences: Brussels, on the one hand, and France on the other.

Brussels suspects member States of reserving their public contracts for their national companies (a not entirely ungrounded supposition), and hence organizes, with a great flourish of detail, procedures for awarding public contracts.

For example, Brussels has long privileged (compulsory) calls for tenders over (optional) negotiated contracts for the traditional sector, that is, the State and its establishments other than industrial or commercial ones, regional authorities and their public establishments and hospitals. However, each procedure has its pros and cons.

For example, when looked at from a distance, it is completely extraordinary that, unlike the private sector, public bodies at State, regional, departmental and municipal level only have the right to negotiate their markets exceptionally and in a limited manner. The mind of any uninformed taxpayer boggles at the idea that public authorities have no right to negotiate their contracts whereas any individual with a minimum of common sense would seek, beyond the setting up of competition, to negotiate the conditions of his or her purchase, to demand a counter-offer, or an improvement of the initial offer, and to check, by meeting the candidate, a good match between offer and demand, or even an improvement of the latter. In its new directive for the traditional sector, Brussels has recently made a few concessions and authorizes negotiation when it is impossible to set fixed requirements specifications. This is a move in the right direction, even if, in the case of supplies contracts, it will remain exceptional. We may well hope that in future regulatory developments, Brussels will leave an entirely free choice to public buyers – as it does for contracting entities, utilities within the scope of its Directive 2014/25 (in France, the RATP, EDF, SNCF, La Poste etc) – between a negotiated procedure or a call for tenders. Substantial savings stand to be gained, so true is it, in spite of various schools of thought here and there, that there is no one contracting method that in itself is better than another.

On the other hand, alternation is crucial, for if economic operators have one quality, it is that of knowing how to adapt to the procedures imposed upon them. Changing the contracting method in an impromptu manner is a way to reshuffle the competitive cards and fight against the risks of price-fixing.

Secondly, we can also see that excessive rigour is combined with economically ineffectual contracting, due mainly to the influence of France, isolated by the offence of favouritism that it alone has taken on, and that it no longer really knows how to handle. The offence of an 'undue advantage', as set out in Article 432-14 of the new French Penal Code[7] in its current form, is typical of a false response to a genuine problem: that of corruption.

Fighting against corruption in the area of public contracts is a non-negotiable objective. But the article defines the offence so poorly that it may, in reality, punish buyers acting in good faith, thus paralysing public contracts. In theory, in French penal law, where there is no intent or materiality, then there is no offence. In this instance however, legislators have wished to hit hard and fast. In the offence of favouritism, intention is deduced by an infringement of the principles of the Public Procurement Code that litter the text, and materiality inferred by the existence of a contractor, which is thankfully the case as we are talking about the award of a contract...

It is thus more or less possible to charge in a criminal court any buyer who might wrongly apply a text – incidentally, a complex one – and this has been well understood by buyers and above all by local elected representatives. The priority is therefore no longer making the best possible contract in the most advantageous economic conditions for the public body and taxpayers. The priority now is to cover one's back, with confusion going as far as choosing to recruit lawyers (rather than buyers) as buyers – a truly negative sign of the effectiveness of public procurement.

Other major perverse effects are related to the current wording of the offence: for example, so great is the risk entailed by unequal treatment of candidates during negotiation and its penal conclusion, or so is it perceived, that negotiations in the classic sector (state, regions, departments and municipalities) remain weak.

Procurement from the lowest bidder, catastrophic on an economic level, is often another consequence of the offence: we are never suspected of favouring the lowest bidder, whereas this is often the risk when we choose the best bidder.[8] We can only wish, in practice, a more prudent redrafting of the text so that it will no longer call into question buyers acting in good faith, that is, almost all of them. But the air of suspicion still reigns, and it hardly boosts initiative or efficiency in procurement.

13/2.3 Towards the modernization of procedures

Private procurement techniques may well be a useful supplement to the panoply of the public buyer. For now, only a few timid efforts are being made, so much so does public procurement primarily remain a matter of regulation while private procurement is a matter of economy. But budgetary constraints and true attempts at professionalization are, here and there, leading public buyers to open up to techniques from private procurement. Legal texts accordingly echo this shift.

Questions have gradually been raised on: the necessity to manage one's supplier database; the search for potential suppliers; mass procurement in order to benefit from economies of scale; procurement from production sites; dematerialization and electronic reverse auction techniques. These aspects have now been included in Community directives, then taken up by the French Public Procurement Code, even becoming the latter's core axis. Improving control over expenses does not yet frequently figure as such amongst buyer objectives, given that the power in the public sector still considers itself worthy of the budget that it manages, but the most innovative public buyers now set themselves objectives of gains to aim for in their purchases and they equip themselves with procurement policies.

Reasoning in terms of total costs is spreading significantly even if until recently, it remained the privilege of industrial companies. The same goes for the management and rationalization of the panel of suppliers and service-providers, now considered as 'economic operators'. Methods for checking the compliance of the delivered product or performed service still remain empirical and insufficient. Finally, the anticipation of procurement in the public sector has progressed greatly due to the necessity to evaluate the estimated sum of markets in order to determine the applicable advertising and contract award procedure.

What remains is that public orders are not private orders, and that not all private procurement techniques can be transposed directly to the public sector (even if most of them may be). Buying with taxpayer money sometimes limits the exercise of procurement via delocalized sources or electronic reverse auctions, for example.

13/2.4 A strong risk of instrumentalization

Instrumentalization risks include local preference, environmental criteria, social criteria, SME policy etc.

Public orders have always been instrumentalized, with public authorities seeing them as an opportunity to get their public policies applied, voluntarily or under compulsion. We do not recklessly spend such sums – once again, €2,000 billion throughout Europe – on public contracts without asking them to serve, in one way or another, public policies elaborated in ministerial cabinets.

In this way, following World War II, France saw the emergence of strong regional preferences in the name of reconstruction, then strong national preferences in the name of independence, in the domains of armament or public works and construction, for example. In the 1960s, territorial planning and industrial development brought a focus on automobiles, industrial vehicles and rail transport. In the 1970s and 1980s, it was necessary to fight against inflation following the petrol shocks, to remedy regional imbalances, to boost the creation of national industrial champions, the communications, banking and aeronautics sectors, to name a few.

One of the characteristics of this instrumentalization is that it never disappears by itself once the objective is reached, but on the contrary, it lives on. No public policy simply vanishes, but it continually builds up. In this way, little by little, the public buyer becomes a one-man-band in charge of applying or defending multiple public policies that the wiliest ministries are keen on getting implemented by others, ie by public buyers.

Regarding Europe, we thought at one time that this instrumentalization via national policies would disappear, if only due to the emergence of Community regulations. And this was the case until recently. But politicians have managed to break the locks set in place by the Brussels Commission that suspected the former of paving the way for national preferences. Environmental issues got the ball rolling, social issues have widened the gap, SMEs have also joined in.

It is necessary to say, again and again, that observation and criticism of this instrumentalization do not call into question the legitimacy of the policies or causes being supported. Who can seriously challenge the interests of leaving a less polluted Earth behind to our children? Who can deny the necessity of preference being accorded to disabled persons, or of fighting against social discrimination? Our reservations do not concern the policies themselves, but on the place and means of their implementation, through public contracts.

It is in the environmental domain that we have witnessed recent attempts to instrumentalize public orders. Environmental criteria can now be included in public procurement, on the grounds of technical requirements and as a condition for award of the contract, and even for the criteria for selecting tenderers. Whoever best respects the environmental evaluation criteria will be better rated than other competitors.

The success of sustainable development has reinforced this requirement even if – it needs to be said – public buyers were already attentive to environmental issues. It was not rare, in the recent past, to see criteria such as the recycling rate of a piece of equipment being introduced into offer evaluations. Social criteria immediately rushed into the gap wrenched open, stealthily as well, by recently modifying Article 53 of the Public Procurement Code through the introduction of a new criterion for assessing offers: 'performance in terms of professional insertion of disadvantaged groups'. But how can we be sure that a professional does not recruit specifically for obtaining a contract, then subsequently dismiss these disadvantaged employees? How do we check whether local elected representatives angle for new votes this way, using the money of taxpayers? How do we secure such practices and make sure that they are not mere postures, even while remembering that these criteria should have a direct link with the object of the contract?

These public policies already have their own place of expression, their institutions, their sources of financing such as the European Social Fund or the national employment office. Yet these domains, with their catalogues of norms, request that construction and equipment players offer access to the disabled, and these norms are then taken up in the technical specifications of public contracts. That public buyers, like any other buyers, should determine the conditions for the award of their contracts, with functional demands and specifications entirely centred on the object of the market, is neither contestable nor contested. However, to have buyers make 'environmental' or 'socially inclusive' factors criteria for evaluating offers is to risk major deviations without ensuring that the objective be reached. Aren't we transferring to public buyers the burden of applying ministerial policies? They are no longer buyers precisely whenever they are asked to do more, namely under the new French code; they are one-man-bands in charge of correctly applying ministerial directives.

As for the policy of increasing the share of SMEs in public contracts, it seems, on the one hand, that French SMEs are actually better off than SMEs on a European level, and on the other hand, that government preoccupations, as electoral periods approach, are somewhat suspicious. To date, there is no option, from a legal perspective, for positive discrimination in their favour. On the other hand, investigations into the role of SMEs in public orders may well point out the illegality represented by the local preference from which they often benefit. Here, there are perhaps more lashes to be received than benefits to draw. The only real remedy for the difficulties that SMEs face in winning contracts is a drastic simplification of procedures.

Notes

1 Act No. 93-122 on transparency and the prevention of corruption in business and in public procurement procedures, of 29 January 1993, modified by Act No. 2001-1168 of 11 December 2001 ('the MURCEF law') on various urgent measures, economic or financial in nature.

2 Order No. 2004-559 of 17 June 2004 on partnership contracts followed by Decree No. 2004-1145 of 27 October 2004 in application of Articles 3, 4, 7 and 13 of Order No. 2004-559 of 17 June 2004 on partnership contracts and Acts Nos. 1414-3, 1414-4 and 1414-10 of the General Code on Territorial Bodies, and Decree No. 2004-1119 of 19 October 2004 on the creation of a Partnership Contract Support Commission.

3   According to Articles 1 and 2, the object of public-service contracts is 'the performance of services'.

4   In Directive 2004/18 of the European Parliament and of the Council of 31 March 2004 on the coordination of procedures for the award of public works contracts, public supply contracts and public-service contracts, Article 1 defines 'public-service contracts' as 'public contracts other than public works or supply contracts having as their object the provision of services referred to in Annex II'.

5   The Government Procurement Agreement of Marrakesh in 1994, by the World Trade Organization.

6   This is the case with the new directives on contracts in more traditional sectors, Directive 2014/24/EU of the European Parliament and of the Council of 26 February 2014 on public procurement and Directive 2014/25/EU of the European Parliament and of the Council of 26 February 2014 on procurement by entities operating in the water, energy, transport and postal services sectors.

7   According to Article 432-14: 'An offence punished by two years' imprisonment and a fine of €200,000 is committed by any person holding public authority or discharging a public-service mission or holding a public electoral mandate or acting as a representative, administrator or agent of the State, territorial bodies, public corporations, mixed economy companies of national interest discharging a public-service mission and local mixed economy companies, or any person acting on behalf of any of the above-mentioned bodies, who obtains or attempts to obtain for others an unjustified advantage by an act breaching the statutory or regulatory provisions designed to ensure freedom of access and equality for candidates in respect offenders for public service and delegated public services'.

8   The 'best offer' is not the highest offer. It is the one that, all criteria considered and weighted, is judged the best. Sometimes, the best offer is also the lowest offer, but most often, the best offer is a bit more expensive than the cheapest one due to higher quality or more comprehensive service.

14
The practice of international operations

JOËLE MACADRÉ

In relation to the internationalization issues covered in Chapter 5, the success of importing will depend on active monitoring of the international environment, establishment of a set policy, a well-structured internal organization and the training of buyers. Walls between functions need to be knocked down: international performance relies on internal collaboration within a company, and the regular sharing of information between procurement and the other functions concerned, namely the supply chain, sales and financial departments.

It is easy for us to understand why buyers insist on the sales department relaying information, for example, on sales forecasts. But do buyers, by the same token, measure the impact of their own decisions on sales and financing when they change the countries from which they source without informing sales staff of their new policy? The purchase price in itself may remain attractive, but what effect will there be on customs duties for the end customer? The change in country may mean that goods can no longer benefit from tariff preferences. Not only may there be a rise in customs duties, but transport costs and delivery lead-times may also increase, hence creating an impact on sales prices and product availability.

When talking about a company's global and transversal strategy, another dimension emerges: as well as their professional competencies, buyers are called to equip themselves in solid international cultural knowledge and techniques in order to broaden their expertise. In a majority of cases, this means increasing the buyer's capacity to anticipate developments in order to have a global and transversal vision as of a project's feasibility study stage up to the execution of the contract.

Buyers need to understand and to speak the same technical language as their suppliers or service-providers. The same applies to dialogue with other support functions within the company, in their role as 'facilitators' when decisions are to be made.

This chapter also aims to focus on technical aspects of logistics associated with payments and guarantees, which contribute to the optimization and securing of procurement in international contracts.

14/1 Taking a step back and asking the right questions first

Amongst the procedures that need to be set in motion in order to make an operation more reliable, it is necessary to ask oneself the right questions as early upstream as possible. At first glance, this question-asking may seem to consist of no more than regulatory checks. But make no mistake: the constraints that are identified may well call a project's feasibility into question and have a very strong impact on lead-times and costs. Anticipation and a transversal approach will allow issues to be identified in time and stand-in solutions to be prepared.

Normative aspects: Do products, their processing, their branding and their packaging comply with the norms and approvals required by the country in which they are to be consumed? Is it possible to use so-called' corresponding norms'?

Customs and tax security: Beyond the necessity to comply with a mandatory regulatory framework, we note a genuine evolution in reflection on corporate policy. Amongst the questions to ask oneself, it is necessary to identify whether products can be freely exported and imported, to check their customs nomenclature, their origin, the customs value that will be used as a base for the calculation of import duties and taxes. If an import licence is compulsory, the buyer as well as the seller should take into account the time needed for obtaining it and the impact on the global time required for a product to become available. Experienced suppliers will not agree to launch special manufacturing when they have no control over the action; import permission should be obtained by buyers. In addition, which party, the seller or the buyer, will take care of declaration formalities for the export or import? What are the compulsory documents that the buyer needs to obtain from the supplier (to this end, a specific clause should be included in the contract)?

Inspection before shipment: The regulations applicable in the importer country in terms of inspections should also be checked. Is inspection of the products by an external monitoring company required prior to shipment? If so, what costs, timeframe and procedures to be adhered to are involved? Beyond all regulatory obligations, the buyer may seek to back up security by requesting a check to be carried out on the supplier's site during production and before shipment by a neutral external company selected by the buyer. In this case, it is necessary to decide in advance who will bear the cost and ascertain the impact on the lead-time.

Currency: Attention should also be paid to the choice of the payment currency. Whenever the selected currency is not the same as that of the buyer's country, the need arises to anticipate a risk of difference in monetary equivalence. The company's global policy will influence decision-making on the selection of the currency, but also the country's regulations. In this way, the question is raised of whether or not to hedge against this exchange risk and for the cost of the potential hedge to be budgeted. For this purpose, buyers will need to approach the support functions of their company as far upstream as possible.

Payment methods and security: The principle of balance is reciprocally sought by both parties. If the supplier asks for an advance payment, in exchange the buyer will demand an advance-payment guarantee. The buyer who anticipates risks may also wish for other guarantees to be set up by the supplier, for example, a performance guarantee. This will entail banking commissions, which will need to be taken into consideration upstream in the budget. In addition, the question is raised of the payment security that a supplier may ask for or that may be demanded by the importer country's regulations. Letters of credit are a commonly used security technique for payment in the context of international contracts. Is any measurement made of their impact on the time required for making the imported goods available? Who will bear the financial costs? Have these been fully included in the budget?

Transport and transport insurance: Who, between the supplier and the buyer, is in charge of the transport of the goods and to what extent? Should the goods be insured during transport and which party purchases this coverage, against what risks, for what value and for whose benefit? The decision will depend at once on sales policy, the type of product and the structural organization within the respective companies of the buyer and the seller. In all cases, it is appropriate to gauge the costs, the lead-time and security. Whether it is the seller or the buyer who manages transport, do they call upon the services of an authorized agent or a freight forwarder? The role and level of responsibility of these service-providers are to be identified throughout the chain. A consultation process is to be launched, accompanied by transport quotation grids so that consultations can be compared, item by item, and explanations obtained on disparities that may possibly be observed. Have substitution transport systems been put forward by the service-providers or suppliers? Transversally, it is necessary to measure the consequences of a new transport system on overall costs, lead-times and security. Finally, a more in-depth global approach may lead to the consolidation of shipments, and thus the grouping of ordering times, whilst measuring the impact on inventory levels.

Lead-times: Have the required security precautions and the ensuing impact on timeframes been taken into account upstream to realistically measure the starting point of lead-times (obtaining of an import licence if necessary, setting up of payment guarantees, payment of an advance, financial guarantees, feedback on technical specifications or approved plans)? We often note that a global lead-time is given; it is recommended, however, for it to be broken down into strata or process stages. Times necessary for the execution of the various phases of the contract should be set out and thus correspond to measurable milestones. Regarding transport phases, whether it is the buyer or seller who takes care of this aspect completely or partially, it will be necessary to obtain the time required for each stage and to consider that these timings are only indicated by the service-providers on an approximate, non-contractual basis, with the mention of estimated time departure/estimated time arrival (ETD/ETA) on the quotations.

Incoterms®: The buyer's policy will flow from the analysis of elements identified further, and the selection criteria are multiple. Amongst these, has the buyer measured the consequences from the time at which risks are transferred, which does not systematically correspond with the time at which costs are transferred? Has the buyer checked the current regulations and usages applicable in the importer country? As certain countries demand that transport or transport insurance be placed in the hands of local companies, it is the buyer who is responsible for these actions. To sum up, buyers will need to analyse whether the Incoterms® which they have selected are a perfect match for the transport method, the customs clearance site, and the securing of payment (case of letters of credit).

14/2 Legal and operational scope of the ICC Incoterms® 2010

The Incoterms® are official rules established by the International Chamber of Commerce (ICC) to help define the reciprocal obligations binding a seller and a buyer. These rules aim to harmonize trade relations between countries through a series of codified three-letter terms.

Created in their original version in 1936, the Incoterms® have regularly evolved ever since to adapt to the evolution of trade practices, transport methods and the logistical organization of companies trading internationally. The last revision, dating from 2010, has allowed the terms to be clarified, eliminating some of them and replacing them with polyvalent terms that can be used whatever the mode of transport. To avoid ambiguity, it is necessary to include, after each term, the year of its revision and the specific geographical place of delivery (eg FOB (ICC Incoterms® 2010) port of...).

An auxiliary to the sales and purchase contract, Incoterms® are commonly used in international trade as they help facilitate contractual relationships. There are 11 terms that define the reciprocal obligations of buyers and sellers in terms of:

- Expenses directly borne: who pays what, to what extent, until when?
- Risks encountered by the goods during transport: who is responsible for what, until where, until when?
- Documents and security information needed to satisfy customs clearance requirements for export, import, or transit: who establishes or obtains them, at whose expense and at whose risk?

Note: certain terms are more advantageous for the buyer, others for the seller. The transfer of risk does not always correspond with the transfer of costs (case of the Incoterms® group starting with the letter 'C'). In this way, the seller may directly bear all costs until the goods' arrival at the appointed site and not be held responsible vis-à-vis the buyer in the event of damage to them during transport. For example, the Incoterms® CFR, CIF, CPT and CIP are in favour of the seller providing a service to a customer, enabling the former to generate cash flow without being held responsible towards the buyer during transport. Table 14.1 presents the meanings of the codified rules and associates each term with the relevant transport methods and transfers of risks. The non-correlation of cost transfer and risk transfer can be explained by differences in how goods are handled during transport depending on the country, its infrastructures and its regulations.

Let's note that the Incoterms®, whilst constituting one clause in a contract, do not allow all contractual aspects to be defined. Transfer of ownership, payment methods, delivery lead-times, late penalties, the technical guarantee of products, the law applicable to the contract are domains not covered by the Incoterms® and should be the object of negotiated clauses. Figure 14.1 represents the reciprocal obligations between a seller and a buyer.

TABLE 14.1 The eleven ICC Incoterms® 2010

Incoterms	Meaning	Abbreviation	Type of transport	Transfer of risks
Ex Works	Goods available at works	EXW	Polyvalent	At works (sale on departure)
Free Carrier	Goods available at any named place in the pre-carriage zone	FCA	Polyvalent	At any named place in the pre-carriage zone (sale on departure)
Free Alongside Ship	Goods available alongside the ship at the departure port	FAS	Maritime	Alongside the ship (sale on departure)
Free On Board	Goods available on board at the departure port	FOB	Maritime	When the goods are on board the vessel at the port of shipment (sale on departure)
Cost and Freight	Carriage until the destination port	CFR	Maritime	When the goods are on board the vessel at the port of shipment (sale on departure)
Cost Insurance Freight	Carriage and insurance until the destination port	CIF	Maritime	When the goods are on board the vessel at the port of shipment (sale on departure)

TABLE 14.1 *continued*

Incoterms	Meaning	Abbreviation	Type of transport	Transfer of risks
Cost Paid To	Carriage up to the named place in the post-carriage zone	CPT	Polyvalent	At the handing over of goods to the first carrier (sale on departure)
Cost Insurance Paid to...	Carriage and insurance up to the named place in the post-carriage zone	CIP	Polyvalent	At the handing over of goods to the first carrier (sale on departure)
Delivered At Terminal	Delivery at the named port or airport of destination including unloading of goods	DAT	Polyvalent	At the terminal of the port or airport of destination, with goods unloaded (sale on arrival)
Delivered at Place	Delivery at the named place in the destination zone, goods not unloaded, import customs and duties under the buyer's responsibility	DAP	Polyvalent	At any named place in the post-carriage zone in the destination zone, goods not unloaded (sale on arrival)
Delivered Duty Paid	Delivery and duties paid by seller	DDP	Polyvalent	At the named place in the post-carriage zone, customs duties paid by seller (sale on arrival)

FIGURE 14.1 Transfer of obligations in a CIF (Cost, Insurance, Freight) transaction

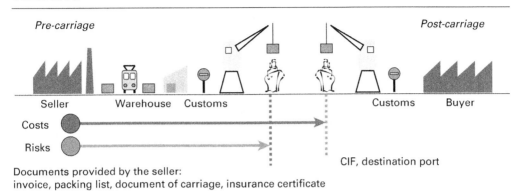

Documents provided by the seller:
invoice, packing list, document of carriage, insurance certificate

Let's also note that the Incoterms® are to be used for the sale of goods and do not concern operations relating to assembly, installation, technical assistance or intellectual services.

The buyer and the seller should take care to identify the terms that are the most suited to their operations. As of the consultation or call for tenders process, the sales, logistics, financial and legal policy of each company needs to be defined. These terms should be the object of negotiation, and will have an indirect impact on costs and levels of responsibility.[1]

Regarding transactions within the European Union, use of the Incoterms® is very widespread, but it is also necessary to use them selectively. The 2010 revision also offers companies the option of using Incoterms® in their national operations. In the national context, customs duties do not apply and rules on VAT invoicing should naturally be applied.

The Incoterms® are not to be confused with transport terms: the Incoterms® concern the relationship between the seller and the buyer and are not enforceable against the carrier, the freight forwarder or the logistics service-provider organizing the transport chain. They merely allow service-providers to recognize the contractual environment in which the seller and buyer operate and the party to which their invoices should be addressed. These protagonists carry out services governed by international conventions which define a legal framework of obligations and responsibilities as well as cases where exemptions apply or where responsibility is limited. In the event of a dispute with the service-providers, these are the conventions that will apply as well as the terms of the service contract.

Use of the Incoterms® is not compulsory. It is nevertheless highly advisable to employ them (they can be encountered in most contracts). To sum up, the key points are the following:

- The Incoterms® are international sales terms that allow definition of the reciprocal obligations of the seller and the buyer in terms of costs, risks, documents and security information to be produced.

- They result from international standardization and lead to the facilitation of international transactions. The last edition currently applicable bears the reference ICC Incoterms® 2010.

- They are recognized codified rules (three letters).
- The alphabetical families into which they are divided simplify their use.

14/2.1 Classification into alphabetical groups to facilitate use

The four families (E, F, C and D) conform to the following rationale: for groups E and F, the seller makes the goods available in the pre-carriage zone; for groups C and D, the seller makes the goods available in the post-carriage zone. Figure 14.2 shows how these rules are positioned.

- The first group – the E family (EXW etc) – pertains to situations where *sellers make goods available from their premises.*
- Next comes the F family (FAS, FOB, FCA, etc): the seller must hand the goods over to the transporter or the forwarder designated by the buyer *at a named place in the pre-carriage zone.* The seller bears the costs and risks until the named place.
- The C family (CFR, CIF, CPT, CIP) follows: on top of the obligations applicable to the F family, the seller must take care of transport up to the named place of delivery in the post-carriage zone, without having to take responsibility for the risk of damage or loss of goods, or bear costs that may arise due to events that may occur beyond the delivery of goods on board or loading onto the first vehicle.
- The D family (DAT, DAP, DDP): the seller must bear all costs and risks up to the named place of delivery in the post-carriage zone.

FIGURE 14.2 Positioning Incoterms in the transport chain

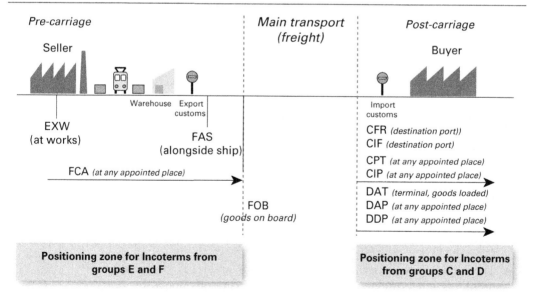

14/2.2 Sharing of reciprocal obligations between the seller and the buyer

The ICC rules define exactly how obligations are shared between the seller and the buyer, specifying the reciprocal responsibilities each party has to bear directly. Table 14.2 presents this concept point by point.

TABLE 14.2   Reciprocal obligations of the seller and buyer

Obligations for the seller	Obligations for the buyer
Supply of goods	Payment of the price
Licenses, authorizations, formalities	Licenses, authorizations, formalities
Contracts of carriage and insurance	Contracts of carriage and insurance
Delivery	Taking delivery
Transfer of risks (the seller is responsible until...)	Transfer of risks (the buyer is responsible from...)
Allocation of costs (the seller must pay...)	Allocation of costs (the buyer must pay...)
Notices to the buyer	Notices to the seller
Delivery documents	Proof of delivery
Checking, packaging, marking	Inspection of goods
Assistance in the obtaining of documents	Payment of costs incurred (for the obtaining of documents)

14/2.3 Identifying the consequences of the transfer of risks according to the Incoterm® group

Regarding the transfer of risks, the ICC has created two categories:

1 'Sale on departure' for terms from the E, F and C families: this means that the critical point for risk transfer is when the goods leave an appointed departure place; the buyer becomes responsible for the goods from this point.

2 'Sale on arrival' for terms from the D family: this means that the critical point for risk transfer is when the goods arrive; the seller bears responsibility for the goods until they reach the named place of delivery.

Let's qualify what is meant by 'risk transfer'. In the case where a buyer bears the risks, if damage occurs during transport of the goods, the buyer is held responsible and must fulfil obligations to the seller, that is, pay the price agreed upon, not apply late rates (if lateness can be attributed to the transport of the goods), and not make any claims on the seller for the harm suffered.

We can point out that depending on the Incoterm® category selected, the seller may directly bear the costs of transporting the goods or even insurance (that will of course have an impact on the sales price set by the seller) without bearing the risk of transport. The buyer should pay attention to this specificity of the C family that favours the seller's position. A buyer wishing to entrust transport of goods to the seller will prefer using terms from the D family as these entail the seller's responsibility up to the delivery at the appointed place.

Table 14.3 presents the four families of risk transfer.

TABLE 14.3   The four risk-transfer families

Group E (sale on departure)		
Minimal obligations for the seller.	EXW	At the plant (named place of delivery)
Group F (sale on departure)		
The seller hands the goods over to the transporter nominated by the buyer. The seller does not pay the transport costs and does not take responsibility for transport risks.	FAS	Free alongside ship (named port of shipment)
	FOB	Free on board (named port of shipment)
	FCA	Free carrier (named place of delivery)
Group C (sale on departure)		
The seller pays transport costs up to the named place but does not take responsibility for the risks.	CFR	Cost and freight (named port of destination)
	CIF	Cost, insurance and freight (named port of destination)
	CPT	Transport cost paid to (named place of destination)
	CIP	Transport cost and insurance paid to (appointed destination)
Group D (sale on arrival)		
All transport costs and risks are borne by the seller up to the named place.	DAT	Delivered at terminal (named terminal at port or place of destination)
	DAP	Delivered at place (named place of destination)
	DDP	Delivered duty paid (named place of destination)

14/2.4 Named places of delivery and transport methods

Appointed places

The Incoterms® should *always* be followed by a specific named geographical place of delivery. Indeed, a term used without this detail is empty of meaning. Who will pay what and until where...? Who will be responsible for the goods, until where and until when...? This vagueness jeopardizes cost analysis and does not allow the limits of responsibility to be defined in the event of a dispute during the execution of a contract.

Transport methods

Some Incoterms® refer to specific use of maritime transport, others correspond to all forms of transport (polyvalent Incoterms®). It is advisable to use the polyvalent terms that can apply to all transport methods. These rules are more flexible and enable changing the means of transport once the contract is underway, if necessary, thus limiting usage errors (Table 14.4).

Let's take the example of FOB (Free On Board). As this Incoterm® is used for maritime transport, it is appropriate for it to be solely associated with a maritime geographical place rather than for availability of goods to be specified at an airport – as can be seen sometimes! In this case, we prefer using a FCA (Free Carrier), more flexible because of its polyvalent application, allowing goods to be made available either at the port of shipment or the departure airport.

TABLE 14.4 Incoterms® according to the mode of transport

Polyvalent terms (may be used irrespective of the mode of transport selected)	Maritime terms
EXW (Ex works)	FAS (Free Alongside Ship)
FCA (Free Carrier)	FOB (Free on board, port of shipment)
CPT (Carriage Paid To)	CFR (Cost and FReight)
CIP (Carriage and Insurance Paid to)	CIF (Cost Insurance and Freight)
DAT (Delivered At Terminal)	
DAP (Delivered At Place)	
DDP (Delivered Duty Paid)	

Note on the FOB rule

The 2010 revision recommends that companies do not use the FOB rule when goods must travel in containers. This is explained by the fact that handling costs for getting to the containers and loading them on board are generally included in the 'freight' (main part of transport). The buyer who negotiates a 'FOB' with a supplier risks, after paying these costs, then paying them again when they are included in the freight invoice without any visible breakdown! The ICC's recommendation in this case is to choose the FCA rule with mention of the terminal at the port of shipment, in which case positions are clearly stated.

14/2.5 List of codified terms and their meanings

To sum up, Table 14.5 indicates the meanings of the 11 codified terms and shows, for each of them, the costs to be paid by the seller or the buyer, the modes of transport and the transfer of risks. Let's note that:

- the E, F and C families represent terms for 'sale at departure': risks are transferred to the buyer when the goods are shipped;
- the D family confers risks to the seller until the goods arrive.

Variations

Certain Incoterms® present variations. These are expressed in Table 14.5 when the seller and buyer symbols are simultaneously indicated as bearing the same cost item. In this case, it is appropriate to specify on the contract which party, the seller or buyer, directly bears these costs.

For example, for the Incoterms® CFR and CIF, it is necessary for the seller and the buyer to agree on who will directly bear the handling costs incurred for unloading goods from the ship and leaving them at the terminal of the destination port. These variations are due to the practices and pricing policies of maritime companies that include (or do not include) all or part of the handling expenses in their freight prices.

These practices, known as 'liner terms' or THC (terminal handling charges) take precedence over the Incoterms®. These usages create marked differences in costs that buyers should anticipate in their budgets. Buyers should get their suppliers to specify exactly what they include or not in their offers.

14/2.6 Implementation recommendations

These operational recommendations are important from the buyer's perspective, for poor usage of the Incoterms® triggers difficulties in the sound execution of the operation, such as: problems in customs clearance, incompatibility in the production of the appropriate document of carriage, hindrance to payment when payment guarantees come into play, and ambiguous levels of responsibility. As a result, let's keep in mind the following key points:

- The Incoterms® do not define the transfer of property. The latter depends on the contract or on the law applicable to the contract if a specific clause has not been contractually provided (do not confuse the transfer of risks and the transfer of property).

TABLE 14.5 Incoterms ICC 2010: Expenses and risks sharing between seller and buyer (except production costs)

Operations	EXW	FAS	FCA	FOB	CFR	CIF	CPT	CIP	DAT	DAP	DDP
Method of transport	All	Sea	All	Sea	Sea	Sea	All	All	All	All	All
Transfer of risks	Sale at departure	Sale at departure	Sale at departure	Sale at departure	Sale at departure	Sale at departure	Sale at departure	Sale at departure	Sale at arrival	Sale at arrival	Sale at arrival
Packaging	□	□	□	□	□	□	□	□	□	□	□
Loading at the plant	■	□	□	□	□	□	□	□	□	□	□
Pre-carriage	■	□	■ □	□	□	□	□	□	□	□	□
Export customs	■	□	□	□	□	□	□	□	□	□	□
Handling at departure (terminal, port, airport)	■	■	■	□	□	□	□	□	□	□	□

TABLE 14.5 continued

Operations	EXW	FAS	FCA	FOB	CFR	CIF	CPT	CIP	DAT	DAP	DDP
Main transport	■	■	■	■	□	□	□	□	□	□	□
Insurance*	■	■	■	■	■	□	■	□	□	□	□
Handling at arrival (terminal, port, airport)	■	■	■	■	■□	■□	■□	■□	■	■□	■□
Import customs	■	■	■	■	■	■	■	■	■	■	□
Post-carriage	■	■	■	■	■	■	■□	■□	■	■□	■□
Unloading at the destination	■	■	■	■	■	■	■	■	■	■	■

□ Cost covered by seller ■ Cost covered by buyer

■□ Cost covered by either seller or buyer depending on the place appointed by the parties at which the goods are made available (use of Incoterms variations)

VD = Sale at departure (the goods are transported at the risk of the buyer) **VA** = Sale at arrival (the goods are transported at the risk of the seller)

* Only the CIF and CIP specifically define obligations in terms of insurance. For other Incoterms, only recommendations exist.

E family (sale at departure)	EXW = Ex Works	FOB = Free On Board
F family (sale at departure)	FAS = Free Alongside Ship	FCA = Free CArriage	CPT = Cost Paid To
C family (sale at departure)	CFR = Cost and Freight	CIF = Cost, Insurance and Freight	CIP = Cost and Insurance Paid To
D family (sale at arrival)	DAT = Delivered At Terminal	DAP = Delivered At Place	DDP = Delivered Duty Paid

- The Incoterms® should not be confused with terms of transport.
- Citation of an Incoterm® should always be followed by a specific geographical spot.
- We should not forget to indicate the reference of the applicable ICC rules (eg 'FCA... at the appointed place, ICC Incoterms® 2010').

A warning regarding the C family: these terms imply that the seller directly takes charge of costs up to the appointed place of delivery, but the seller does not bear risks during transport. The buyer will prefer to use Incoterms® from the D family.

Let's note that it may well be worthwhile for the buyer to take charge of the transport of goods, in order to have better control over costs, to optimize lead-times, to secure the operation by setting up the most adapted logistics means, to consolidate transport volumes and be better placed for negotiation on prices and services. In this case, it is appropriate to use Incoterms® from the F family.

Questions to help choose a suitable Incoterm®

Which costs should be covered by the seller and which should the buyer agree to bear directly (eg transport, insurance, customs, import).

What level of responsibility should the seller reasonably assume?

From what point should the buyer agree to taking responsibility? For example, a buyer who pays for import customs clearance will certainly cover the post-carriage. It is logical in this case for the buyer to be responsible for the part of action that he or she manages directly while leaving responsibility to the seller for operations controlled by the latter until the first arrival point in the importer country.

Who, between the buyer and the seller, is in a better position to control operations relating to transport, insurance and customs?

14/3 International logistics: transport, transport insurance and customs

As an adjunct of international sourcing procedures and the search for total quality, control of transport costs is not the sole objective that the buyer needs to meet. Analysis should be more global and geared towards the integration of all elements in the logistics chain. The stakes are high: products have to be delivered on time, at the right place and in a good state, whatever the distance and the difficulties in organizing transport as a result of the geographical, political, economic and social environments in the country of origin and the destination country. Logistics are a competitiveness factor!

The buyer's approach should include driving service-providers to suggest and estimate the cost of substitution solutions in the event of a change in situation encountered during the transaction's execution. The buyer will study the total cost of distribution without forgetting to include the tie-up of capital associated with the duration of door-to-door transport. To these time periods, we should add those necessary for customs clearance procedures, whether the obtaining of preliminary transport authorizations or declaration formalities for export, import or transit operations.

Analysis should also cover the regulatory and administrative environment. Utmost rigour is required, in terms of compliance with normative rules as well as observance of customs and documentary obligations. We should aim to keep an active watch over these areas. A non-compliant document will lead to the holding up of goods in customs offices.

In addition, the security of the goods being transported is an element to which the buyer should pay particular attention. For this purpose, we will consider the nature of the goods, their characteristics as well as the risks associated with the method of transport used, handling, storage, climatic conditions and the context of the countries crossed.

The buyer should also consider the necessity of insuring the goods during transport. Transport service-providers are not fully responsible in the event of loss or damage during transport; they may sometimes even be completely exonerated as a result of an international convention governing the mode of transport (eg when a ship sinks). Let's note that even if their responsibility is engaged, they will be called to provide very moderate compensation to the shipper. The questions to ask oneself are mainly the following: who, between the buyer or the seller, does it primarily benefit to take out an insurance contract? Against which risks? What should be done in the event of damage? What are the consequences on the fulfilment of the contracts? These points need to be analysed upstream along the transport operations and will lead to a global policy on goods insurance.

Finally, account needs to be taken of the nature of payment guarantees set up. At the seller's request, a bank guarantee such as a letter of credit may be envisaged for securing payment. This technique implies that the goods will be shipped without the documents necessary for their customs clearance when they arrive in the importing country. Disconnected from the physical flow of the goods, these documents are transmitted to the buyer via banks after these institutions have made rigorous checks on compliance. In this way, the letter of credit circuit entails a transmission period of around 10–30 days. Depending on the distance and the means of transport used, goods may arrive before the documents and be held up at the customs office, giving rise to cost overruns, insecurity and increased lead-times.

Before agreeing to negotiate on a contract accompanied by a payment guarantee, the buyer should gauge the ensuing consequences on a financial level as well as in terms of goods transport and lead-time management.

14/3.1 Transport policy

We have seen above that the cost of transporting goods is covered by either the seller or the buyer. Incoterms® are selected on the basis of the transport policy applied, existing sales practices and competitive levels. Different situations can be identified, amongst which buyers must position themselves:

- The supplier includes transport in the offer: the buyer must assess the relevance of such an offer by comparing the costs, technical solutions and lead-times offered.
- The impact of transport on quality is very strong: the buyer needs to manage flows in order to control costs, lead-times and security.

● The company has a corporate policy: this entails the setting up of audits and negotiated contracts for the whole of the group. The buyer acts in collaboration with the logistics and transport support functions in his or her company.

Let's note that the buyer purchases transport for international sourcing operations as well as for the export contracts undertaken by the company. Goods may be produced in one country and then directly exported to a location other than the buyer's country. This requires a feasibility analysis as of the upstream stages, including analysis of the regulatory, tax and legal context beyond the financial and logistics dimension.

With the issues set out as such, it is necessary to determine how to organize transport. The intervention of many operators is required in the international transport chain. Companies can choose to work directly with each of the operators or else call on specialized service-providers – recognized professionals with expertise in these domains – when they prefer to focus on their core business and consider that they do not gain any real advantage in managing transport directly. In this way, numerous players play a role in the transport chain.

14/3.2 Professional perspective and developments

The transport and logistics sector has not been left unchanged by the new realities of international trade: companies in the sector are joining forces, absorbing one another, merging, broadening their range of services, or on the contrary, refocusing on their specialties. Growth in the volumes of goods being transported from one point of the planet to another has encouraged these developments. Protagonists in the transport chain are making an effort to offer competitive advantages in response to shipper policy on developing international exchanges. All transport methods are progressing strongly and evolving technologically.

The maritime sector briefly presented below offers an example of the same trend visible for all other modes of transport. The upsurge in the use of containers has led to the construction of fast, gigantic ships that make fewer stops (or increasingly short ones). Container ships have capacities of up to 18,000 TEU (20 ft equivalent unit) and these will soon climb up to 20,000 TEU.

New maritime routes have been created, bringing to the fore satellite ports equipped with high-performance facilities for handling as well as for distributing goods across a largely deployed hinterland. Through the World Customs Organization (WCO), customs authorities have been involved in these progress strategies.

Shipping companies offer their clients increasingly wide services covering the feeder-transport stages (pre- and post-carriage). Some are positioned as 'single operators' on their lines – in other words, one-stop contacts for shippers from one end to the other of the goods distribution chain. Their offers are hence geared at full logistics services, incorporating storage, customs and distribution operations. This type of offer is primarily found on containerized lines. Could it be that shipping companies are becoming direct competitors for forwarding agents?

As elements of traceability, reliability and quality in the transport chain, techniques for managing information flows play a key role in quality strategy. These techniques are increasingly high-performance and concern all protagonists in the distribution chain. Delivering available information in real time, they link the physical flows of goods with administrative and regulatory flows (customs, border-police authorities, inspection and health-check services, etc).

The deployment of all transport and information methods leads to the reduction of costs and lead-times, and the optimization of the flow of goods.

When looking for transport partners, the buyer will focus on the structures of existing transport groups, their network of branches and partners, wider services that may be offered beyond transport, and information flows that can boost traceability and promote real-time management.

14/3.3 Choosing a service-provider

A company will generally refer to the service-provider as the 'forwarding agent' without making any distinctions as to the latter's legal status. We can, however, note that the service-provider's level of responsibility depends on the nature of the service carried out. In the case of an authorized agent, a best-efforts commitment exists and the service-provider is answerable for his or her own mistakes. In the case of a freight forwarder, a performance commitment exists, and this service-provider is answerable for his or her own mistakes as well as those of substitutes acting on his or her behalf. The freight forwarder cannot, however, be held more responsible than his or her substitutes.

The choice of the type of service-provider depends on the size of the company, the volume of flows, the type of goods, the country environment, and the company's expertise in determining what type of legal status to aim for. In a majority of cases, we observe that companies prefer to entrust their operations to 'freight forwarders'. This preference can be explained by the fact that this choice enables companies to focus primarily on their own activities by delegating know-how to recognized professionals tied by a performance commitment.

On the other hand, it may be worthwhile for a company to entrust its operations to an authorized agent as better financial conditions can potentially be obtained when the company negotiates on contracts directly with transport companies. To achieve this, however, the company needs to work regularly in certain geographical zones; it needs to have a sound knowledge of practices and techniques; its flows should be significant; and it should have developed an internal transport structure.

Experience shows that users of authorized agents are generally large companies that negotiate directly on contracts with transport companies and then delegate transport coordination to an agent who is given no choice on the operators with which to work; this agent is tied by a mere best-efforts commitment as he or she cannot be held responsible for actions not within his or her control.

14/3.4 Independence and autonomy of contracts

Let's note that the various contracts signed in relation to a given transaction are independent; no link exists between them. Sales contracts, transport contracts, transport insurance policies, payment contracts (letters of credit) and financial guarantees are all fully autonomous.

We can illustrate this point by the example of damage to goods occurring during maritime transport in the context of a contract negotiated as a CIF (Cost, Insurance and Freight) to a destination port. Payment is carried out by a letter of credit (payment contract). In the event of damage, both the buyer and seller will obviously aim to find goods replacement solutions as quickly as possible, but when seeking to apportion responsibility, the autonomy of contracts will be demonstrated.

First, the party taking responsibility for the goods at the destination port (the buyer directly, or the buyer's service-provider) will need to express reservations to the shipping company before a legal deadline. The transporter to whom reservations are expressed will thus be presumed responsible vis-à-vis the buyer, and will possibly need to prove grounds for exoneration of its responsibility, or else for its responsibility to be limited, as foreseen by the Convention on the International Transport of Goods. *This matter concerns the transport contract.*

At the same time, the buyer will hasten to contact and inform the supplier, and they will come to an agreement on either relaunching manufacturing or proceeding to compensation depending on the decision of the damage surveyor set the task of assessing the damage. Let's remember that the CIF Incoterm® places the burden of costs on the seller until the destination port, but that the transfer of risk occurs when the goods are loaded on board the ship at the port of shipment. The seller fulfilled its obligations upon the embarkation and the 'delivery', in the legal sense, corresponds to the transfer of risk. *This matter concerns the sales contract.*

Secondly, let's note that CIF stands for 'cost, insurance and freight', prompting the supplier to take out transport insurance to the value of 110 per cent. The recipient (the buyer directly or the buyer's service-provider) will summon the damage surveyor. The latter represents the insurance company and is in charge of assessing damage, then establishing a damage certificate that will point towards possible compensation or a new round of manufacturing; this document will be added to the application for compensation that the buyer will then address to insurer. *This matter concerns the transport insurance policy.*

Thirdly, let's analyse whether the supplier will be paid via the letter of credit. Note that a letter of credit is based on the commitment of banks to honour payment in return for the seller's production of documents proving sound execution of the transaction and respect of deadlines.

Instructions to this effect appear on the letter of credit. The documents that the seller needs to confer to the advising bank to prove execution of the transaction include a bill of lading that is 'free from reservations', bearing the mention 'on board' and the date of embarkation. As the damage occurred during the sea passage, the bill of lading issued at the embarkation expresses no reservations on the goods during their loading.

As a result, given that the terms of the letter of credit have been respected, the seller will be paid by the bank, and buyer company's account will be debited. *This matter concerns the payment contract.*

There is an epilogue to this situation. It is when damage occurs that companies most concretely become aware of the consequences of the autonomy of contracts, the impact of Incoterms® and the implications of letters of credit. Parties in this operation have reason to be glad that the goods were insured during transport for a replacement value and for adequately evaluated risks, enabling the buyer to receive compensation and to place a new order with the supplier.

14/3.5 Criteria in the choice of the method of transport

Many criteria exist. It is not just a matter of taking into account the specific characteristics of the goods (nature/volume/weight/value/fragility/hazard level) but widening the study to incorporate the following factors:

- *Contractual constraints*: the regulations of the importer country may oblige the use of vessels flying their national flag; this may be the object of a contractual clause.

- *Lead-times*: late penalties in sales contracts very often prompt companies to choose a faster means of transport, even if its cost is higher; the difference in transport cost is rarely as much as the sum of a penalty, and the choice of air transport may be perfectly justified to absorb all or part of a delay (aside from other aspects seen in Section 9/3).

- *Access roads*: these should be listed, for they will determine alternative transport solutions and enable comparisons on costs, lead-times and security. Let's also note the impact of the geopolitical environment. The social, economic and political context of the country of departure, the country of arrival and transit countries, are factors that contribute directly to the selection of access roads.

- *Packaging*: this is conditioned by the characteristics of the goods and by regulations, the transport method, bulk breaking, storage conditions and climatic conditions.

Whatever the transport method adopted, we can choose between two types of organization: transport for a full loading unit, or bulking. This choice is conditioned by the goods' volume and weight, the destination, the shipment speed and lead-time requirements. Finally, we need to distinguish between the notion of 'price' based on the mode of transport and that of the 'total cost of distribution'; the latter is determined by integrating the factors of lead-times, capital tie-up and the impact on stocks.

14/3.6 Launching a consultation and sorting through offers

It is necessary to put transport operations into perspective and to define annual requirements by considering a more global context: the corporate policy, the company's objectives, the criticality of the goods, sector of activity and size, the geographical zones to be covered. Competition can be 'reasonably' introduced between service-providers. It is entirely possible for the transport and logistics sector to address service-providers by taking recourse to marketplaces. The use of consultation methods, including reverse auctions, requires a great deal of preparation when dealing with yearly transport volumes or large industrial projects, but e-sourcing in this area also meets more occasional requirements.

What are the main criteria by which service-providers may be preselected? Companies should consult service-providers recognized for their specialization in a business sector, in a given geographical zone, or a certain mode of transport. Checks should be made on whether these service-providers have branches or 'networks' of on-the-spot partners. Note should be made of their financial standing, their references, their history if the company has already worked with them, and their reputation.

During the consultation, as seen generally in Chapter 10, it is recommended that formal quotation grids be provided so that service-providers can return them completed. This offers the advantage of obtaining detailed quotations, item by item, providing the means to find explanations for disparities, to compare an offer with the competition, and to dialogue on more specific points during the final negotiation. It is helpful to use indices and to weight them. A written record should be kept of agreements made in order to facilitate subsequent management of the operation whether by the forwarding agent or the shipper (the name given to the exporter or the importer). Table 14.6 offers an example of a transport quotation grid to illustrate a standard breakdown.

14/3.7 Evaluation of the total logistics cost

The total logistics cost depends on several factors that should be taken into account beyond the freight price (main transport).

We may well be tempted to select the lowest offer on the basis of analysis of the freight price – an approach that is common when comparing a quotation for maritime transport with one for air transport, giving rise to a significant price difference. It is nonetheless helpful to take into account the following elements to position oneself better. Added to freight, there are cost elements corresponding with the following: packaging; pre-and post-carriage; transport insurance; customs duties; costs relating to the tie-up of capital during door-to-door transport of the goods; financial impact on the cost of stock (safety stock); and warehousing. The grid presented in Table 14.7 is helpful for interpretation of the solutions to be compared and is a decision-making aid.[2]

14/3.8 Follow-up of transport activity

Carried out by both the shipper and very often the service-provider, the follow-up of activity is presented in the form of monthly and recapitulative (usually quarterly, half-yearly or yearly) dashboards. These dashboards allow the company to retrieve standard information on activity, such as the geographical zones, the service-providers concerned, the number of shipments, the modes of transport, the weights and volumes transported, consolidated transport costs or else costs broken down into major items (their values and percentages) that can be converted into figures per ton, per cubic metre or per kilo depending on the business sector in question, any possible disputes, delays, damage, hold-ups in customs and the service rate. By extracting data from these standard dashboards, we can create other more personalized management tools, for example, by tracing the profile of each supplier/service-provider to facilitate the sharing of information and enable negotiation for new contracts to be better targeted.

14/3.9 Transport insurance

Whenever goods – whatever their nature, their packaging or their destination – are transported, they are exposed to so many and such weighty risks that no dealer or

TABLE 14.6   Transport-quotation grid

Dispatch from Ho Chi Minh (Vietnam) to the Tours region (France) in a 40' FCL container

'LOGISTICS' INFO	Service-provider 1	Service-provider 2	Service-provider 3	Service-provider 4	Service-provider 5
Average handling and customs time in Ho Chi Minh	To specify	3 days	48 / 72 hours	2 days	48 / 72 hours
Number of shipping companies used	1 company of our choice	2 companies suggested	1 company suggested	2 companies suggested	3 companies suggested
Number of departures per week	1	1	4	1	1 / week via Singapore
Closing days / departure days	To specify	To specify	Tuesday, Wednesday, Thursday, Saturday	Friday / Sunday	Saturday / Sunday
Sea days (transit time)	26	22	20-26	26 via Keelung	24
Arrival port in Europe	Le Havre	Le Havre	Le Havre	Le Havre	Le Havre
Average handling and customs time at the arrival port	3 days	2 days	3 working days	1 to 2 days	2 days
FREIGHT in USD	in USD	in USD	in USD	in USD	in USD
40' dry (standard container)	1 900	1 850	1 500	1 700	1 700
40' fuel surcharge (BAF)	133	130	100	122	121
ISPS (safety tax)	0	15	0	0	15

	USD / EUR = 0.8700	USD / EUR = 0.8576	USD / EUR = 0.8607	USD / EUR = 0.8823	USD / EUR = 0.8724
Peak-season surcharge	0	0	0	0	200
Exchange rate used					
ARRIVAL EXPENSES in EUR	in EUR	in EUR	in EUR	in EUR	in EUR
Undocking fees		160		130	
THC / container (handling and mooring / storage)	124	124	123.30	124	124
IMPORT CUSTOMS in EUR					
Customs import formalities + administrative fees + safety tax and port fees (excl. VAT and customs import duties as these depend on the type of product)	150	180	180	140	150
HOME DELIVERY in EUR					
40' towing	590	600	525	570	580
Fuel surcharge (applicable to the amount for the towing)	7%	8	0%	8%	8%
TRANSPORT INSURANCE (not taken into account in the calculation as this applies to the value of the goods) The premium rate is to be applied to 110 % of the CIF value of the goods	0.50%	0.35%	0.45%	0.35%	0.35%
TOTAL COST OF TRANSPORT (in euros) EXCL. VALUE OF GOODS AND IMPORT DUTIES AND TAXES					
40' dry (standard container)	3 121	3 262	2 647	3 070	3 124

TABLE 14.7   Solution-comparison grid (based on a CTI survey)

| | | Comparison of transport costs | |
| | | Legend   + more costly   – less costly | |
Cost item	Solution no. 1 Maritime transport	Solution no. 2 Air transport
A	**Value of goods based on ExWorks, without packaging**	idem	idem
B	**Transport costs**		
	b1 – Packaging	+	–
	b2 – Pre-carriage	+	–
	b3 – Warehousing at departure port or airport	+	–
	b4 – Handling at departure (*loading*)	–	+++
	b5 – Net freight	+	–
	b6 – Handling at arrival (*unloading*)	+	–
	b7 – Warehousing at arrival port or airport	+	–
	b8 – Post-carriage	+	–
	b9 – Transport insurance	–	+
	b10 – Other costs (*e.g. import fees and taxes*)		
	Subtotal		
A + B	**Total value of goods + transport costs**	–	+
	Total duration of transport (door to door)	*Should be measured including import-customs clearance time*	*Should be measured including import-customs clearance time*
C	Cost of capital tied up		
A + B + C	**Total cost of goods delivered at the destination**	*Depends on the value of the goods*	*Depends on the value of the goods*
	Difference in cost in terms of value and percentage compared to the most economical transport method		
	Gain in time compared with the longest transport method	*Including import-customs clearance time*	*Including import-customs clearance time*
	Possibility of gain on stock	*Does not apply in the case of special manufacturing*	*Does not apply in the case of special manufacturing*
	Total cost of distribution		

industrialist can envisage bearing their hazards. The responsibility of service-providers may be exonerated or limited in the event of damage. Over each transport stage, goods are exposed to various risks: handling (successive loading and unloading), warehousing (open-roofed or not, on sites and for periods that are known or unknown), sundry manoeuvres (bulk breaking), possible visits to customs offices. All this in climatic conditions and over transport periods that may be difficult for the shipper to control.

As we have seen, many professional operators take charge of the goods: transporters, forwarding agents, warehouse-keepers, handlers. Their legal status will determine their level of responsibility. In addition, international professional conventions foresee limitative clauses or even clauses that completely exonerate a party from responsibility.

Whether it is the buyer or the seller who takes the step, it is recommended that goods be insured during transport. It is advisable to negotiate with insurers that replacement value be taken into account in the event of damage. According to common practice, the insurance value to declare is the sale value (with respect to the Incoterm®) plus an extra 10 per cent (to cover hazards). It is on the basis of this value that insurance premiums will be calculated and included in the final calculation for the cost of transport.

Different types of insurance policies

It is possible to take out different types of policies adapted to the flows to be covered. Table 14.8 presents the main characteristics of these policies.

TABLE 14.8 Different policy types

Policy type	Characteristics
'Trip' policy	Appropriate for occasional dispatches. It covers clearly defined goods and a particular trip. Risks are delimited.
'Open' policy	Appropriate for operations comprising dispatches staggered over an indeterminate period. This type of police allows a single contract to be taken out, covering the total value of goods and all dispatches.
'Floating' policy (unknown quantity and set period)	'Open' refers to the indeterminate nature of the goods being insured. It automatically covers all dispatches made by the insured party. The latter does not need to declare each dispatch. The policy is generally settled for a year-long period, renewable by tacit agreement.
	This is a policy taken out to cover all or part of the company's export or import turnover against transport risks. This type of policy allows for easier management but also more advantageous premium rates due to the consolidation of risks.
'Third-party shipper' policy	Designed for operators (forwarding agents / carriers), these policies are established in their name and cover goods that their clients have asked them to insure on an occasional basis as part of their transport service.

What type of coverage?

Transport insurance is insurance that covers a physical good and cannot compensate commercial damage or late penalties. We may take out insurance to cover one or several individualized risks or 'all risks'. In all these cases, it is necessary to foresee deductible or non-deductible coverage. It is especially important to be insured against major damage. Non-deductible coverage is of little interest in the event of damage involving low amounts.

Ordinary risks to cover including handling, storage, events relating to transport, shortfalls, theft and general average contribution. General average contribution is one of the clauses in maritime law that aims at the equitable distribution, between ship-owners and shippers, of damages or expenses resulting from useful measures taken by the ship's captain to safeguard the crew, the ship and cargo. The owner of goods may therefore be expected to make a financial contribution to the general average by paying a significant share of the goods' value even though these may be received in sound condition.

Let's add that more specific risks, known as 'exceptional risks,' may be covered, such as risks of war and mines, strikes, riots, lockout, terrorism, hostility or retaliation. Goods will be covered if they are damaged, lost or stolen during such events.

Insurance can be taken out from insurance companies, insurance agents, brokers, transport or transit companies (in the case of the last, by means of a 'third-party shipper' policy). Brokers offer interesting services in that they play on the competition of insurance companies and analyse the market when they 'place' the company's risks.

What elements to provide during consultation?

The main ones are the following: the nature of the goods and their characteristics, the nature of the packaging, the value, the place of shipment and the destination, the start and the end of the guarantee (warehouse to warehouse), transport method, supposed period and duration of storage, climatic conditions, goods in hold or on deck, loading systems, possible transhipment.

Note that insurance agreements do not cover goods on deck except in the case of specialized ships whose equipment is adapted to loading on deck (eg container ships).

What to do in the event of damage?

In the event of visible damage, as soon as the delivery takes place, forms of recourse should be preserved by expressing reservations to the last transporter (specific and motivated reservations, in other words, identification of the packages about which reservations are held and indication of the nature of the reservations; the reservations should not be qualified with any mention to the effect of 'subject to inspection or unpacking' for in this case they will hold no legal value). In the event of non-visible damage, reservations should be established within the legal deadline corresponding to the mode of transport, in other words:

- maritime transport: 3 days;
- road transport: 7 days;

- rail transport: 7 days;
- air transport: 14 days.

The deadline is to be calculated starting from when each of the successive operators takes over in the transport chain, including from when the buyer takes over the goods at the final destination. Reservations are to be issued to the last transporter by registered letter with acknowledgment of receipt.

In the case of maritime transport, it is necessary to summon the damage surveyor (the representative of the insurers). The insurers will deliver an insurance certificate and indicate whether goods may be compensated or whether it is necessary to resupply them. The beneficiary of the insurance policy then activates the request for compensation and presents supporting documentation to the insurers.

14/3.10 Customs operations

The customs administration encourages companies of all sizes to get informed upstream of their operations. It places advisory cells at their disposal to help them identify possible critical points and to encourage them to initiate optimization projects, to become Authorized Economic Operators, or to use the services of service-providers with this status. Companies are urged by the customs administration to study simplified onsite declaration procedures and to analyse the interest of suspensive procedures for duties and taxes when applicable. Due to their important role in sourcing, buyers are key contributors to work groups whose task is to reflect on the appropriate customs strategy to set up.

Companies are encouraged to secure the classification of their products in the customs nomenclature, and to check the criteria that enable determining the origin of goods. Here again, buyers play an important role: the information that they hold on their suppliers should be rigorous and confirmed.

In terms of strategy, it is during an operation's upstream that it is necessary, for the overseas supplier as well as for the importer company, to check whether goods can be exported and imported. Three answers are possible:

- YES, freely.
- YES BUT with prior authorization (export licence, import licence): in this case, it is necessary to take into account the time periods for obtaining the licence, its validity and the repercussions on contractual lead-times.
- NO: it is then necessary to identify the reasons leading to this refusal. It is necessary to check whether the product may be authorized in another form (eg a non-assembled product) and whether the blockage results from a quota that may be freed up again subsequently.

It is also necessary to identify all points presented in Table 14.9.

TABLE 14.9   Summary of customs issues

Core questions	Additional points to identify
Will the product be consumed or re-exported, following transformation?	As a result, which customs procedures are compatible?
What are the applicable customs duties and taxes? Where and when do they need to be paid?	On what base are these duties and taxes calculated?
What are the applicable customs procedures? Can simplified procedures be envisaged?	As of what level is it legitimate to set them up?
What timeframe should be envisaged for customs formalities for the export, import or even transit of goods?	What documents are needed to carry out declarative formalities?
Does the company's quality strategy include the criteria of customs facilitation and security?	Do the company, the suppliers, or service-providers have the status of Authorized Economic Operator?

To have access to all this information, it is necessary to determine the origin and tariff classification of products. These two criteria can be considered as the starting point for working out which customs regulations apply to the products. For example: the tax level of imported goods (customs duties and VAT), the sum of possible refunds (case of products depending on the Common Agricultural Policy), the possible application of quotas, the application of norms, the application of prohibition, the possible application of control of dual-use goods, or possible sanitary or phytosanitary inspections. Three elements allow determining the level of customs duties applicable to imports: the value, the species and the origin (Table 14.10)

Import and export licences

This type of licence is an administrative authorization allowing export and/or import of goods. In which cases is a licence needed? 1) If the good is a product subject to a quota (eg steel quotas) or to inspection at the end destination (strategic products such as weapons, electronics or IT); 2) depending on the nature of the product, its origin, its use and its function.

Who is to ask for the licence? The importer and/or the exporter request it from the customs office serving their area: this depends on the Incoterm® specified in the contract and the legislation of their respective countries. The length of time for obtaining a licence ranges from 15 days to 2 months, depending on the country. Its duration of validity is to be adapted to the duration of the operation, with a possibility of extension.

TABLE 14.10   Criteria for determining the level of customs duties for imports

Criteria	Characteristics
Value	In a majority of countries, the customs value represents the value of the good, of transport and insurance up to the first point of entry on the import territory, in other words the good's CIF value. This value serves as a base for the calculation of customs duties. The customs duty, expressed as a percentage, thus applies to the good's CIF value. The applicable VAT upon the good's entrance into the import territory is calculated on a base represented by the CIF value of the good increased by the sum of the customs duty.
Species	This refers to both the nature of the good and the use for which it is intended. The species is represented by the customs nomenclature to which goods should be rigorously assimilated. In the event of difficulty in classifying products according to the nomenclature, a customs procedure (binding tariff information) allows parties to ask the customs administration to operate the classification, thus placing the company in security.
Origin	Rules are complex, especially in the case of multi-component or transformed products. For each type of situation, it is appropriate to check the applicable rules. There should be no confusion between 'origin' and 'provenance'! As for the species, there is a procedure that allows asking the customs administration to decide on the origin of products (binding origin information).

Customs clearance

This is a declaration for goods entering or exiting a customs office. Declarations also play a statistical role. The declaration applicable in the European Union for all exchanges with non-EU countries is called the Single Administrative Document (SAD). Regarding exchanges within the EU, declarations are significant for tax and statistics and the relevant system is called the Intrastat (Declaration of Exchange of Goods). Such declarations are to be established monthly and in a recapitulative manner, following the physical flows of goods.

Who clears customs? The importer or the exporter, depending on the Incoterms®; the freight forwarder with customs authorization, or even occasionally the transporter.

Who pays the duties and taxes? The importer and/or the exporter, depending on the Incoterms® or the contract's particular specifications.

Which documents most commonly need to be produced? The customs import declaration is generally established on the basis of the sales invoice, the packing list, the certificate of origin, the document of carriage and certificates required by the regulations enforced in each country.

Suspensive economic regimes

What is the role of suspensive economic regimes? They help companies boost their management by deferring or being exonerated from payment of duties and taxes. The French customs administration gives the following definition: 'Economic customs regimes satisfy the three main functions of companies: storage (warehouse regime), usage (temporary admission regime), transformation (active improvement regime)' (Table 14.11).

TABLE 14.11   Suspensive economic regimes

Customs regimes	Characteristics
Storage function	The company imports products that it does not need to use immediately. It uses the warehouse regime enabling it to defer the payment of duties and taxes until the goods are used. If the products are directly re-exported from the warehouse, the duties and taxes will not apply as the export goods will benefit from an exemption. The declaration of export will clear the goods' entrance in the warehouse
Usage function	A company needs to import goods temporarily (case of a fair, a loan, the sending of prototypes or collections, dispatch of equipment to meet the requirements of a work site, the organization of events). At the end of the period of usage, the goods are re-dispatched. When exported, the goods are exonerated; upon their entry into the temporary importer country, duties and taxes are suspended. Re-dispatch clears the exit and entrance movements.
Transformation function	A company exports goods to a country outside the EU to carry out assembly or transformation operations. It will only be taxed, upon the goods' return, on the added value realized overseas.

14/4 Payments and guarantees

Regulations relating to international trade exchanges are subject to numerous uncertainties, whether commercial or industrial, political or monetary. Risks are significantly accentuated, namely due to the distance of the partners, sometimes contradictory customs, not forgetting the applicable rules in business law (possibly different in each of the countries concerned) as well as ensuing legal problems (see Chapter 15).

When tackling payment methods and guarantees in an international procurement negotiation, the buyer and the seller often take diverging positions. The seller may demand an advance payment or even a payment guarantee, especially in the case of a first contact, special fabrication or else an operation requiring a preliminary study. Meanwhile, the buyer will play the prudence card, and may wish to divide payment into instalments, retain a hold-back or impose the use of surety bonds. In all cases, buyers are required to respect the treasury policy of their company.

The respective sizes of companies, their financial health, the competitive environment or the country of origin or the destination country may represent significant risk factors that give rise to concessions in negotiations on payment conditions and in contract security. What parties should aim to seek is balance in the contract.

Risk zones and resulting obstacles should be identified by the seller and the buyer upstream of the contractual commitment. Payment clauses should be drafted with precision, and it is necessary for these to be analysed in detail as soon as the sales offer is made.

Payment guarantees may be requested by the seller. Before agreeing to the principle, the buyer will make an in-depth analysis of the consequences that these may entail, not only on costs but also on the operation's logistics. In a majority of cases, the first reaction will be to refuse the seller's request given that a payment guarantee does not present any advantages for the buyer's company.

To illustrate the buyer's point of view, let's look at an operation secured by a letter of credit. The goods travel without being accompanied by the documents necessary for import customs clearance. The latter are to be handed over by the seller to the banks that will then transmit them to the buyer, after rigorous verification of their compliance. If the transport distance is short or the method of transport is fast, the goods will arrive before the documents. Meanwhile, the average time needed for a letter of credit to follow its circuit is 10–30 days, starting from the time of the shipment – a long enough time to prevent a quick withdrawal of goods when they arrive!

This explains why letters of credit are more common when maritime transport is used and the transport time is considerable. Very few letters of credit are used for air transport, and even less so for perishable goods! Below, we will discuss the advantages that certain types of guarantees nonetheless offer the buyer, and we will see how these mechanisms contribute to the contract's balance.

14/4.1 Guarantee instruments and techniques

An overdraft may be granted by the seller to the client. The granting of the overdraft will depend on risk analysis and the seller's regular monitoring of the buyer's financial situation, and the country's economic situation. The seller and the buyer will come to an agreement on the form of payment: cheque, bank draft, transfer, etc. Guarantee techniques are attached to the payment's organization and security as well as the speed at which payment will be made: for example, cash against documents, documentary credit, cash on delivery. It is necessary to observe the regulations and practices that apply in each country for not all payment instruments and guarantees may be usable.

Types of payment

Two types of payment may be envisaged.

At-sight payment

The seller naturally seeks to negotiate for the best form of payment: at-sight payment, whereas the buyer tends to prefer payment at a maturity date. At-sight payment does not guard the seller against the risk of a drop in the payment currency compared with the seller's own currency, between the date at which the contract is signed and the date at which the payment is made, but contributes to reducing this risk as no maturity date is granted. Similarly, buyers are subject to exchange risk when the payment is made in a different currency than their own. In both cases, the forward sale or purchase of currency or else credit insurance may be envisaged to protect oneself against the risk of difference in monetary equivalence (cf Chapter 12). As well as this difficulty in ascertaining the exchange rate at the time of payment, the seller will generally find it tricky to obtain at-sight payment, and should envisage payment periods.

Payment at a maturity date

The seller should gauge political, exchange and non-payment risks before agreeing to payment at a maturity date. The seller may cover these three risks by specialized insurance policies, in which case insurance costs will be transferred to the sales price. When the supplier's offer is received, the buyer should therefore evaluate and negotiate on financial expenses relating to the consented payment period and risk coverage. Table 14.12 presents the different customary instruments that can be used for payment.

14/4.2 Securing of payments

Different levels of guarantees exist. These do not all offer the same securities, and do not all meet the reciprocal expectations of the seller and the buyer. We can also note that it is necessary to be familiar with the existing practices in each of the countries in question, for it is not always possible to use them. We will analyse the most common techniques below.

Documentary credit

The commitment is made by a bank representing the buyer (ordering party) to pay a certain sum to the seller (beneficiary) in exchange for the presentation of documents attesting to adherence to the shipment time, the price, agreed payment methods and the compliance of products. Despite a certain formalism and a seeming complexity, this type of credit undoubtedly remains one of the most secure and efficient payment methods for the seller. The 'Uniform Customs and Practice' rules governing this instrument are international; these rules are developed by the ICC, and their current version bears the reference UCP 600. Figure 14.3 illustrates this mechanism.

The use of this instrument enables, subject to compliance with certain basic conditions, getting around, if need be, a buyer's insolvency and thus addresses the concerns of the exporter wishing to be paid for the sales contract but lacking the

TABLE 14.12 Payment instruments

Payment instrument	Advantages for the buyer	Disadvantages for the seller
Payment by check (Carefully check the existing regulations in each country). Note that the check is seldom used as a payment instrument in international operations; here, bank transfers or bills of exchange are preferred.	– The buyer controls the date of issue and check amount.	– Difficult to control the check's date of issue. – The check may be left unpaid when it is presented to be cashed (except if it is a bank check). – No coverage of country risk.
Payment by promissory note Little used in international operations, it is more common in financial operations such as acknowledgment of debt or representation of a loan.	– The buyer establishes the payment order and controls the date of issue and the amount.	– Difficult to control the promissory note's date of issue. – The promissory note may be left unpaid when it is presented to be cashed. – No coverage of country risk.
Payment by draft (bill of exchange) This is an instrument enabling the seller to materialize the payment period granted to the buyer and to more easily obtain advance payment.	– The buyer has a payment period. – The buyer controls the date of acceptance of the bill of exchange.	– Difficult to control the date at which the bill of exchange, accepted by the buyer, is returned. – The bill of exchange may be left unpaid when it is presented to be cashed. – No coverage of country risk.
Payment by bank transfer This is a simple and very fast payment method if carried out via the SWIFT system*.	– The buyer controls the date at which instructions are given to the bank for the transfer to be made.	– Difficult to control the date at which the transfer is issued. – No coverage of country risk.

* The SWIFT (Society for Worldwide Interbank Financial Telecommunication) network includes 210 connected countries; around 20 million messages are transmitted daily.

means to evaluate, with any certainty, the financial situation of a distant partner. Meanwhile, the buyer has the quasi-certainty of being delivered the goods on time and for an agreed price. The buyer may demand a technical inspection of the goods prior to their shipment and only activate payment by the banks after production of a certificate attesting to the compliance of the products.

Apart from the financial cost and the absolute rigour required for administrative management, particularly in relation to the documents, the drawback lies in the mechanism that leads the seller to *dissociate the sending of the goods and the handing over of documents*. As noted earlier, this may lead to goods being received long before documents are in the banking circuit, causing hold-ups in the customs office, costs of storage, a lengthening of lead-times, possible insecurity during storage as well as financial tie-up.

These difficulties may be allayed in the future when operators adopt rules on electronic presentation of documentary credits (eUCP), enabling operations to be executed more quickly by using dematerialized documents. This will contribute to helping physical flows of goods tally with documentary flows.

Standby letter of credit[3]

We have seen the reasons why a buyer may be reticent to issue a letter of credit in favour of a seller. In this case, the seller may suggest that the payment be guaranteed

FIGURE 14.3   The stages of a documentary credit

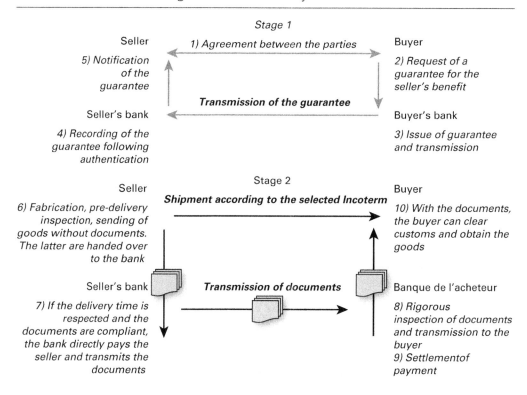

by a standby letter of credit that represents a bank's commitment to honour the payment in the event of the buyer's insolvency.

Unlike documentary credit, this guarantee does not lead to the hold-up of goods upon their arrival at customs because the documents necessary for clearance are directly addressed by the seller to the buyer when the goods are shipped. At the maturity date, the buyer will pay the seller in the contractually foreseen conditions. In the event of insolvency, the seller will obtain direct payment from the guarantor bank; in this case, the seller must declare having fulfilled all obligations and will present copies of documents attesting to their fulfilment (certificate of compliance, document of carriage, invoice, etc).

The standby letter of credit is an irrevocable 'first-demand' commitment leading the guarantor bank to stand in for the buyer. The objective of the standby letter of credit is to constitute a guarantee that is only jeopardized if the buyer defaults. This tool does not allow the seller to mobilize a credit claim whereas documentary credit serves not only as a guarantee but also a means of payment in favour of the seller enabling the latter to manage cash flow.

The standby letter of credit entails lower costs than documentary credit; it is also more flexible for it does not imply the verification of documents (in this way, it generates fewer expenses). It is a way to regularize a business flow without systematically taking recourse to documentary credit. The standby letter of credit allows a guarantee to be taken for a business volume and not just for an occasional operation. It can be renewed.

This instrument's role has since extended to independent market guarantees. Indeed, via this type of letter, the buyer can take bid guarantees, advance-payment guarantees or performance guarantees. In this case, the applicable regulations are the ISP 98 (International Standard Practices – ICC publication No. 590) and the United Nations Convention on Independent Guarantees and Standby Letters of Credit.

Cash against documents (CAD)

This is an operation by which a seller entrusts to a bank one or several documents, accompanied or not by a commercial paper, intended to be handed over to the buyer, in exchange for payment or agreement to a commercial paper.

This technique implies that the goods will travel without documents. Here again, we have an operation where physical flows of goods are disconnected from documentary flows.

This mode of payment is fairly widespread in international trade as it is simple and not expensive. However, the security of payment is not ideal: the seller must take into account the reliability of the importer's bank and country risks. The formulation of instructions by sellers to their banks should be precise and detailed – a condition for the operation's smooth functioning.

It is important to note that ownership of the goods is as stated by the clauses of the contract. In theory, the seller remains the owner as long as the price is not paid provided that corresponding documents have been drafted thus and remain in the hands of the banks (pay particular attention to the document of carriage for sea transport).

It is prudent for the seller to get a bill of lading made out to the order of the seller's or buyer's bank. Instructions on cash against documents should also be clearly drafted in relation to payment clauses (eg a mention 'in 60 days' is not enough; it is necessary to indicate from what date the period is deemed to commence and which payment instrument – transfer, draft, etc – will be used).

Cash on delivery

Seller and buyer always find themselves facing the same preoccupations: the buyer wants to be sure of price conditions and lead-times, the seller wants to be paid at the maturity date. The cash on delivery (COD) technique consists in the handing over of goods by the exporter to the transporter or freight forwarder, to whom instructions are given to only deliver the products in exchange for payment. In this way, the buyer can only take the goods if payment is activated.

All payment instruments are usable as long as they are authorized by the country's legislation. Let's note that this technique does not offer perfect security because the simple presentation of a cheque or draft will suffice for delivery of the good by the transporter, without there being any certainty about there being sufficient funds.

Let's also note that the seller should only use this method in secure countries, for orders that are not the object of special manufacturing. When using this method, the seller will prefer to control transport of the goods in order to be able to give instructions directly to the service-provider.

As in the case of cash against documents, the seller will consider it prudent to maintain ownership of the goods until full payment. The seller should then ensure that the document of carriage is not established in the name of the buyer, but a third party (eg an agent), only giving the transporter necessary instructions for delivery of the goods after completion of payment has been noted. This technique generally entails cash payments.

The points mentioned above show the limitations of this technique for the buyer. To sum up on these guarantees, we can say that the most balanced guarantees for both parties are letters of credit and standby letters of credit.

14/4.3 Drafting of unequivocal payment clauses

Terms that are imprecise or subject to interpretation lead to disputes or the need to 'renegotiate' that are detrimental to the sound execution of the transaction. Vigilance is required as of the birth of the offer, and then during the formation of the contract. Let's examine the case of a clause whose conditions are open to interpretation, when a supplier offers, in the context of a sales offer, 'payment of a 10 per cent advance payable upon the order'.

Let's also suppose that for this operation, the buyer needs to obtain, in his country, an import licence, and the supplier has convinced the buyer of the interest of a payment guarantee (eg letter of credit). The buyer only agrees to pay the advance in exchange for the seller's production of an advance-payment or performance bond.

What can be said about the meaning of the payment clause: '10 per cent advance upon the order'? Can the buyer reasonably pay the advance the day on which he makes the order, given that at this stage, he has not obtained the licence or the letter of credit or the bond? We note that it is better to word this clause differently, in such a way that payment of the advance only be made when safeguards have been set up.

14/4.4 Bond and guarantee

At each stage of an international contract, the buyer may wish to rely on guarantees. These guarantees often enable balancing-out positions. They are not systematic but depend on the relationship between the seller and the buyer, the importance of the contracts and their lifespan.

Such securities may be set up from the call for tenders stage up to the final completion of the technical guarantee. In this way, depending on the importance of the contract, the buyer may demand production of certain guarantees or bonds (Table 14.13).

TABLE 14.13   Implementation and validity of bonds and guarantees

Bid	Comes into effect when the bid is submitted and released when the contract comes into effect
Performance	Comes into effect when the contract is signed and released when the supplies are received or works accepted
Advance payment	Comes into effect when an advance is paid and released when the goods and / or services are dispatched or delivered
Retention	Comes into effect upon the provisional reception or the completion of the works and released at the end of the contractual guarantee period

Buyers are advised to forecast the corresponding costs that result from the risk-taking of banks, the sum and the lifespan of the commitment.

We can note the difference in legal scope between the bond and the guarantee: the contractual guarantee (also known as a demand guarantee, an independent guarantee or an abstract guarantee) is most often unconditional or payable at first demand. This is the feature that distinguishes it from the bond (governed in France by the Civil Code), which is ancillary to the obligation that it guarantees rather than being independent from it. This means that the bank that has issued an unconditional guarantee must pay when a claim is made, without being able to take into account any possible opposition by the ordering party.

Bonds or guarantees relating to overseas markets (supply of goods or services) have become important tools in international contracts. Terminology is of the utmost importance. The buyer and the seller must pay attention to the lifespan of the guarantees set up.

Except in the case of a specific local rule, these commitments are limited in duration. However, the expiry date of a guarantee is not necessarily fixed. It may be unwound by one of the contractual stages, for example, shipment or else technical acceptance. The problem lies in the fact that if the event is slow to arrive or never arrives, the guarantee continues to generate costs. In this case, prudence urges the specification of two levels of validity: the initially foreseen event, as well as a latest-possible expiry date.

First, at the start of the operation, the issue date and the date at which the guarantee is implemented do not always coincide: the first conditions accounting and the collection of commission by the bank; the second entails legal implementation in relation to the beneficiary and third parties. These two dates differ in the context of an advance-payment guarantee; in this case, implementation is conditioned by reception of the advance in the cash box of the issuing bank.

These different bonds or guarantees can be set up, mainly at the buyer's request, to accompany the execution of contractual stages presenting risks, as shown by Figure 14.4.

FIGURE 14.4   Recapitulative diagram of bonds and guarantees

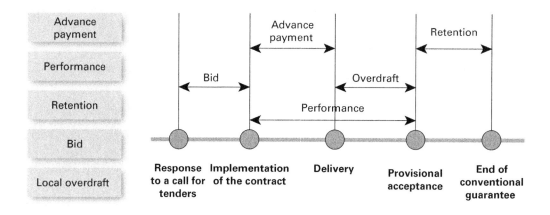

Key points and final recommendations

In order to anticipate obstacles that may arise upstream of the operation, it is highly recommended:

- to review risks in detail, to establish a checklist and to prioritize them;
- to measure the impact of payment guarantees on the operation's logistics;
- to analyse lead-times by breaking them down;
- to optimize the management of payment guarantees (such as letters of credit, cash against documents or standby letters of credit) by drafting specific opening instructions;
- and to draft firm, explicit payment clauses.

Figure 14.5 shows chronologically the different stages of contractual commitment, payments and guarantees. While contributing to planning, this approach allows having a support for transversal analysis and facilitates decision-making. The example here concerns a supply and installation contract.

FIGURE 14.5 Stages of contractual commitment, payments and guarantees

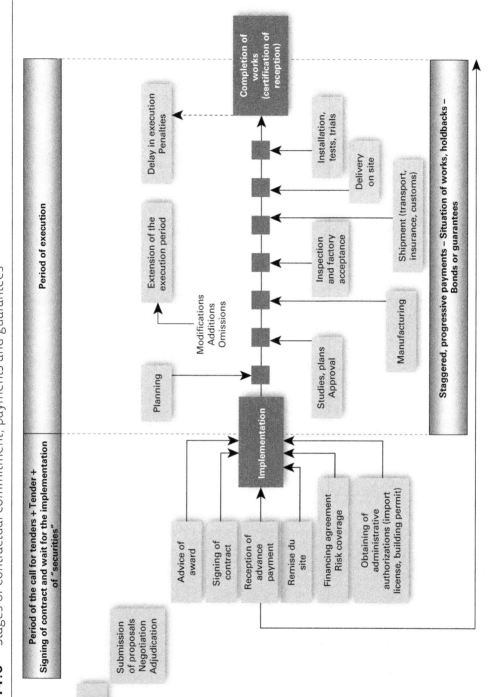

Notes

1 One specificity should be noted: the United States has its own set of rules. However, the recommended and usual practice is to come to an agreement with the US supplier to use the ICC Incoterms® 2010: US companies comply with them easily, with any possible ambiguities mainly arising from 'the unspoken'.

2 The reader may refer to Chapter 9 (Section 9/3) containing an example of calculation of the TCO (total cost of acquisition) for an import operation.

3 Originally created by US banks, the standby letter of credit has evolved. It is now subject to the Uniform Customs and Practice (UCP) like all documentary credits.

15
International procurement
Legal considerations

KARIM MEDJAD[1]

For practitioners, the international landscape is above all a multitude of colliding national laws and secondly, a few international rules. Furthermore, as each country has its own conception of 'law', the contours of international business law change every time one crosses a border.

In international transactions, it is therefore important to never lose sight of a guiding thread that comes down to one key word: *territoriality*. In practice, this means relativity and above all, risk: international contract law is a complex and refined science, which also renders it an uncertain one.

The purpose of this chapter is to offer the reader a few interpretational keys for separating the issues that are truly at stake in international contracts from those that are not.[2]

15/1 The haziness of international business law

International transactions are governed by a body of rules widely known as 'international business law'. This title gives the impression that we are dealing with an autonomous, homogeneous and universal branch of the law. In reality, international business law is a miscellaneous body, made up essentially of national rules, supplemented by a handful of truly international rules issuing from treaties or custom.

15/1.1 National laws

The 'major families' of law

Roman law gave birth to two main legal families: *civil law* countries (continental Europe) and *common law* countries, whose cradle is the United Kingdom. Roman law is itself a combination of rules with diverse origins (ie Egyptian or Syrian), discovered – and imported – as the Roman Empire extended its frontiers. It should also be noted that we tend to insist on the Roman origins of the civil law family (also known as 'Romano-Germanic' law) even if the 'Roman' essence of the common law family is also undeniable. In short, all assertions on these families need to be qualified.

The family of civil law countries includes countries whose law is conceived of as a set of written rules aimed at governing relationships between individuals. These rules are typically grouped into 'codes', classified according to discipline. Judges apply these rules to cases submitted to them and are not bound – theoretically at least – by the interpretations of their predecessors.

In common law countries, however, rules are so-called 'judge-made', that is, elaborated little by little by magistrates. The way in which the rule is applied in a given case is supposed to prevail subsequently in similar cases. Precedents are thus the basis of what is known as the case law system.

We cannot therefore speak of written law on the one hand and non-written law on the other. Describing common law systems as 'non-written' because they are less subject to codification is absurd. Indeed, given the volume of case law, it would be more logical to consider the most abundantly written law to be found in common law countries.

Zones of influence

To map out the geography of the legal world, the history of colonial wars and cultural influences allows us to mark out the territory of each legal family.

Apart from continental Europe, the civil law family includes Latin America, non-English-speaking Africa and a few Middle Eastern countries (Lebanon, Syria, Egypt, Iraq). Meanwhile, apart from the United Kingdom, the common law family primarily encompasses the United States, English-speaking Canada, Australia, New Zealand, India, most Middle Eastern countries (including Saudi Arabia, United Arab Emirates, Jordan and Kuwait), and English-speaking Africa.

The border between the two families is not always clear-cut. Certain countries have a 'mixed' system: South Africa, Philippines, Japan, Israel, Canada (because of Québec), the United States (because of Louisiana) etc. In addition, some common law countries have taken on codes and are slowly drawing closer to the civil law family.

What can be said about certain conspicuous absentees like the People's Republic of China and Russia? Can they be said to be civil law countries? Yes, without a doubt if we adhere to the traditional binary classification, for they are obviously not common law countries. But it is also clear that their transition towards a market economy has created a legal void, and as a result, a battle between European and US norms which has introduced a certain dose of commingling.

Technically, the two major legal families remain distinct. In one, the judge inter-prets the law; in the other, the judge establishes the law. As the institutions operate differently, law can never be constructed in the same way in both systems.

What remains to be said is that differences between civil law and common law are highly exaggerated. At the end of the day, a legal system is always a combination of laws and court decisions: in one case, the former condition the latter; in the other, the opposite occurs, but only the chronology and proportions change.

15/1.2 Conventional rules

International law is enriched every year by numerous multilateral conventions, but it is rare that truly universal rules emerge, and amongst these, very few touch upon the private dimension of international transactions. Whilst there has long been an awareness of the need to standardize business law (the first multilateral endeavours date back to the 1930s), advances since then have been relatively modest.

The cost of geographical ambition: the example of the Vienna Convention of 1980

The international sale of goods is one of the topics in which advances have been the most significant. To attain them, however, half a century of procrastination and several conventions first laid the way. Here we can point out the most important of these conventions: the United Nations Convention on Contracts for the International Sale of Goods of 1980 (CISG), the so-called Vienna Convention that entered into force on 1 January 1988.

In adhering to this convention, a State agrees to renounce some of its own rules for all 'contracts of sale of goods between parties whose places of business are in different States: a) when the States are Contracting States; or b) when the rules of private international law lead to the application of the law of a Contracting State' (Article 1). In addition, this convention 'governs only the formation of the contract of sale and the rights and obligations of the seller and the buyer arising from such a contract' (Article 4).

This convention is a typical example of a major multilateral treaty. On the one hand, the number, diversity and quality of its member States confer upon it a truly universal scope. On the other hand, its success is an indication of its limits, for such a broad consensus can only be obtained about a narrow subject.

In this case, only the international character of a sale is clarified whereas notions as basic as 'contract', 'sale' or 'good' are left vague. The drafters of the convention have limited themselves to expressly excluding certain goods or transactions deemed too complex or overly marked by national law (Article 2), namely sales to consumers, auction sales, ships, aircrafts or shares. The same haziness goes for services that are only covered if they are incidental to the sale (Article 3). This vagueness confers upon the courts of each signatory State a significant margin for manoeuvring.

It is moreover impossible to obtain such broad adhesion if the signatory States are not given the means to adhere partially by expressing reservations on such and such a clause (Article 95). Certain States – including those as prominent as the United States – have naturally relied on this provision.

Finally, it is important to remember that the CISG is non-peremptory (Article 6); in other words, contracting parties can always choose to stray from it even if their contract enters into its field of application.

The cost of legal ambition: the example of the European Union

Could the drafters of the Vienna Convention have gone further, for example, by including other themes, or by conferring an imperative character on this text? Without a doubt, but at the risk of less widespread adhesion.

This 'zero-sum game' explains why the multilateral texts covering the broadest objects are treaties on regional economic integration, based on geographical, historical and cultural proximity. Many examples can be cited, amongst them, the North American Free-Trade Agreement (NAFTA), the South American common market (MERCOSUR), the Association of Southeast Asian Nations (ASEAN) and the Economic Community of West African States (ECOWAS).

The European Union is the most developed of such rapprochements. This progress can naturally be explained by the very spirit of this union, but also by its age. The treaty giving birth to the European Coal and Steel Community (ECSC) dates from 1952, and the two Treaties of Rome leading to the respective creations of the European Economic Community (EEC) and the European Atomic Energy Community (Euratom) date from 1957. In comparison, with the exception of the Council for Mutual Economic Assistance (Comecon), today defunct, all other attempts at regional integration date from later. We should nonetheless not lose sight of the rather modest geographical scope of the EU, for it represents less than 15 per cent of the planet's legal systems.

15/1.3 Customary rules

The *lex mercatoria*

Customs are a key source of international law. In business, law originating from customs is called *lex mercatoria* (literally 'merchant law'). As a general rule, national laws are receptive to *lex mercatoria*, or its less controversial dimensions in any case. It also goes without saying that its borders, its scope, and even its future remain much debated in academic and legal spheres.

Entire sections of *lex mercatoria* have been codified by various bodies, in particular the International Chamber of Commerce (ICC), whose headquarters are in Paris. Apart from arbitration and Incoterms®[3] – two leading elements of *lex mercatoria* – the work of the ICC covers various aspects of international trade: customs and practice for documentary credit, standard contractual clauses, standard professional contacts and so on.

This codification process is a double-edged sword, for when customary law gains in clarity, its scope diminishes. This is the paradoxical result of any procedure aiming to formulate what is formerly implicit: as soon as the rule is made explicit somewhere, it ceases to exist everywhere. Silence in a contract then acquires a potentially different meaning: when contracting parties do not refer expressly to a rule, it is no longer certain whether it is applicable.

Standard professional contracts

In certain branches of activity, it is possible to find contract models that are more or less detailed, more or less restrictive. Some authors refer to this private codification of contractual models as 'form law'.

By definition, the sources of form law are multiple. On the broadest themes, major international bodies occupy the front of the stage, namely the United Nations Commission on International Trade Law (UNCITRAL) and the United Nations Economic Commission for Europe (UNECE). The latter, highly prolific, has published many models for general conditions applicable to specific business sectors. Here are a few of the most widely used examples:

- general conditions of sale for the import and export of durable consumer goods and of other engineering stock articles;
- general conditions for the supply of plant and machinery for export;
- general conditions for the erection of plant and machinery abroad;
- guide for drawing up contracts relating to the international transfer of know-how in the engineering industry;
- guide on drawing up international contracts on industrial cooperation.

On more 'specialized' themes, professional bodies are the main source of 'models'. Such bodies produce an abundance of standard contracts limited to a specific type of transaction and type of product. The highly focused competencies of these bodies enable them to delve much further into the detail of contracts, and sometimes, to demonstrate a surprising authoritarianism in relation to their members. Simple (purchase-sale) transactions on basic products are naturally the most suited to this 'form law', for example, cereals, rubber, coffee, copra, sugar, wood, oil and flax.

Finally, one body deserves a special mention: the International Federation of Consulting Engineers, which has spawned many general conditions and contract models for major engineering agreements. Its publications, identifiable by colour (eg blue or green) are largely used in agreements on major projects (turnkey plants, etc).

Standard contractual clauses

Certain clauses constantly recur in the legal 'packaging' of a contract, whatever the transaction in question. 'Force majeure' and 'hardship' are amongst the most typical examples. What do they mean? Everything depends on the national law to which the transaction is subject, for divergences exist on these two concepts from one legal system to another. The laws of some countries specify their content and scope whilst others simply ignore them.

The problem is classic. One simple way to resolve it is to address it contractually as all national laws admit the principle of party autonomy, that is, the faculty of parties to define the nature and scope of their mutual commitments themselves.

It is thus that the ICC and various professional bodies offer models for specific clauses aimed at facilitating the task of contract drafters. This contribution is useful but modest, for aside from a handful of clauses, international contracts are globally resistant to *prêt-à-porter* solutions.

15/1.4 The bottom line: territoriality

In the absence of standardization, the laws of different States are condemned to co-exist, and thus, acknowledge their territorial limits. Each country is therefore led to recognize, with more or less good grace, that its legal rules can only exercise a partial hold on an international transaction. These limits are all the stronger for court decisions, for a judgment handed down by a court will only have value in the country of this court. Once over the border, it has no authority on the matter being judged, nor any enforceability.

The territoriality of laws

Public-policy laws and regulations are those which it is forbidden to waive by means of an opposing agreement because the legislator or the judge consider that respect of them is crucial for social order at large.

This definition is vague – all the more so because these rules serve a wide variety of interests: moral, social, economic, political. Here, case law plays a crucial role in clarifying the incompressible minimum of this legal corpus.

But what contracts concern a country's public policy? Those settled between its nationals? Those executed on its territory? Or all international operations and in all circumstances?

It all depends on the theme. Sometimes, issues are purely local: there is no reason for British law to ensure that a Moscow consumer of a product exported to Russia by a British company benefits from the same public-policy protection as a British consumer. This is a case of national public policy.

For other questions, for example, the prohibition of 'gifts' to State agents to facilitate the winning of public markets, the demarcation line is more ambiguous. In France, there is no doubt that this prohibition is a matter of public policy, but does it extend to agents from other countries? Undoubtedly yes, in any case ever since 15 February 1999 when the OECD convention 'on combatting bribery of foreign public officials in international business transactions' came into force. But when we take a closer look, uncertainty has not been completely removed, for until now, this convention has led to no sanctions.

Sometimes, though, no doubt clouds the issue. An agreement on procedures in relation to an assassination, for example, a priori falls within the scope of a country's public policy. It matters little whether the assassination is plotted by foreigners targeting one of their distant compatriots. International public policy is thus a subset of national public policy, but its contours remain just as uncertain. Once again, it is up to national courts to sort through and decide.

National law therefore has a certain hold on distant events, for in most countries, public policy also includes rules aimed at taking into account the international public policy of other countries. However, this type of situation is rare: there are far more rules whose application is non-peremptory than there are imperative rules. And amongst the latter, there are far more national public-policy rules than international public-order rules. The conclusion is mathematical: only seldom will a law cross its national frontiers.

The territoriality of judgments

Let's take the example of a dispute between a Canadian company and its French supplier. A Canadian court, before which the case is brought, rules in favour of the Canadian company and sentences its adversary to pay it damages and interest. If the French supplier complies, the procedure concludes. If it does not comply, then everything will depend on the country or countries in which the supplier's assets are located. If it holds no assets in Canada, things start to get tricky because a court decision has strictly no value beyond the borders of the country in which it is handed down.

In this case, a new decision, handed down by a court in the country in which the Canadian company wishes to exercise its rights – eg a French court – is necessary. The relevant procedure here is known as the 'exequatur', whose principle can be compared to a request for naturalization: an exequatur decision in one country renders enforceable a court decision handed down in another country. This is not a return to square one: the aim is not to retry the case but to make a pronouncement on the legality of the foreign court decision in relation to domestic legal order.

Foreign court decisions are never welcome: they are merely tolerated. Every country controls its own conditions for granting exequaturs, and in the absence of an international convention applicable between the country of the exequatur and that of the foreign court decision, this procedure is rarely facilitated.

France is a party to bilateral conventions, namely with its former colonies (Senegal, Madagascar, Morocco, etc). Outside the frameworks of conventions, it should be noted that many countries strive to make the exequatur procedure practically inoperable (certain Eastern European, African, Middle Eastern or Central Asian countries).

Exequatur procedure in Europe

The free circulation of court decisions within the Community, unlike that of persons, goods, services and assets, was long a stumbling block for the EU. This blockage has now been lifted: as of 15 January 2015, the exequatur procedure between member States has been abolished. In other words, a final court decision rendered in a member State is directly enforceable in any other member State.

Regarding court decisions handed down by non-EU countries, the exequatur procedure generally falls within the exclusive competence of the local equivalent of the High Court, whatever the nature of the foreign decision (civil, commercial, industrial, etc) submitted to it.

Conditions for the granting of an exequatur are classic, and can be found in most countries. In theory, the local court does not retry the merits of the case but contents itself with verifying that the foreign decision meets a certain number of conditions: it must have been handed down by a competent court; the procedure must have been followed in a regular manner; it must respect certain principles of fairness and justice (the writ must have been properly served on the defendant; respect for the right of defence, etc). Finally, the foreign decision must be binding: it is obvious that if it can be modified again by an appeal, the request for the exequatur cannot be taken into consideration.

15/2 The legal specificity of international transactions

In law, the term 'international contract' is weighty with meaning, for it generally implies that a country agrees that its law and judges may be pushed aside by other contracting parties. The country does not always give its consent with good grace, but the flow of history and a need for reciprocity do not really leave it with any choice.

Symmetrically, it may be tempting for economic agents to artificially internationalize national operations in order to submit them to a more relaxed foreign law or a more favourable jurisdiction. Such camouflage is common when a company deals with economic agents – employees or sales agents, for example – who are 'protected' by their national law. In such a case, courts will not hesitate to recharacterize the contract as a domestic contract, which automatically nullifies clauses aiming to ward off the domestic law and courts.

The criteria – legal or economic – that allow definition of the international character of a contract vary from country to country. In France, courts now take a pragmatic approach: they sometimes refer to one criterion, sometimes another, sometimes both. In a vast majority of cases, this approach raises no difficulties. It is only on the margins that a few 'grey' zones appear, all sources of potential abuse by economic agents lacking in scruples.

15/2.1 The choice of the applicable law

An international contract is always subject to a law, the law chosen by the parties as being applicable to a contract. Generally, parties have ample margin for manoeuvring in their choice of the applicable law. However, the scope of this freedom varies depending on the country from which it is exercised: it is thus substantial in Europe, less so in North America.

A clause on the applicable law is fundamental to an international contract. This clause constitutes one of the main keys to reading the commitments that are expressed – or not – by the parties. Sometimes, this clause may necessitate a sophisticated formulation, but in general, it is set out very simply, for example: 'This present contract shall be interpreted and implemented in accordance with the laws of Belgium'.

Speaking of the 'law of the contract' is inaccurate: the applicable law is usually the law of a State, in other words, the body of domestic rules applicable in a country. But the parties can also opt for the *lex mercatoria*, which is not a State law. In fact, anything can be envisaged: part of a domestic legal system, or else a combination of rules from various legal systems (we speak in this case of 'splitting').

This type of tailor-made cocktail may result in the following clause:

The present contract shall be governed by the law of France, with the exception of:

1 rules permitting revision of the sum of late penalties foreseen by this present contract, namely Article 1152 of the French Civil Code. In the event of a dispute, the principle, and scope of these penalties shall be appraised in accordance with the law of the United Kingdom;

2 the Vienna Convention of 11 April 1980, the waiving of which the parties expressly declare.

Splitting is based on entirely practical considerations. This can be easily illustrated by a temporal variation of splitting, known as a 'stabilization clause'. Take the example of two parties that decide, without any other specification, that their contract over a 20-year duration will be subject to the law of a country. If a dispute arises 15 years later, this law will necessarily have evolved in an unknown direction, and this introduces a potentially unacceptable risk. As a remedy, a stabilization clause enables 'petrifying' the law as follows: 'This present contract is governed by the law of Russia in force at the date of its signature by the parties. Any legislative or regulatory provision enacted following this date shall not be applicable, with the exception of public-policy provisions'.

How are these clauses received by national jurisdictions? This question brings forth the usual response: everything depends on the national law of the *for* (the judge that has jurisdiction over the dispute).

'Complex' clauses always induce some reservations but in general, judges are respectful of the free will of parties, leading them, in the vast majority of cases, to defer to the clause on the applicable law. It is nonetheless necessary to pay heed to the implicit message of case law: there is no place for inappropriate exoticism.

15/2.2 The choice of the jurisdiction

In an international contract, the competent court and the applicable law are two distinct facets, for the choice of each depends on very diverse considerations. It is therefore important to bear in mind that the choice of a country's law does not automatically entail the competence of this country's jurisdictions. It is perfectly possible for a French court to be required to apply British law.

The choice of the competent court may be considered as an additional show of freedom of will, crowning the 'tailor-made' dimension of the international contract. The contracting parties opt for the law of the contract, then determine *how* it will be implemented by indicating *who* is to settle their potential disputes.

In the absence of stipulations expressly stating that parties intend to settle their differences by way of arbitration, an international contract normally falls within the competence of at least one national court.[4] The choice of the competent jurisdiction is therefore an autonomous, but inseparable adjunct to the choice of the applicable law. And just like the law of the contract, this jurisdiction is only easy to identify if the parties have taken the trouble to specify it. This is why it is important to insert in the contract an appropriate clause to that effect.

Limits to the parties' freedom of choice

Whilst the jurisdiction clause and the applicable law clause are the two sides of the same coin, courts show a different level of tolerance towards it. This is partly due to objective causes: the national laws of all States foresee the exclusive competence of national jurisdictions in a certain number of domains. Public-policy restrictions are also often related to exclusive application of the national law. In this way, a certain number of earmarked themes crop up everywhere: real estate, validity, nullity or dissolution of companies or legal entities having their head office on national territory, registration or validity of intellectual property laws, etc.

These earmarked domains are often the same for the choice of law and the jurisdiction. However, national courts are less inclined to defer to a choice of applicable law than a choice of jurisdiction. Where it is possible to speak of a *principle* of validity for an applicable law clause, it is often only a matter of *presumption* of validity for a jurisdiction clause.

In continental Europe, nuances are tending to become blurred, but in Anglo-Saxon countries, this difference in treatment is still visible. Whilst British and US courts no longer consider, as in the past, the choice of jurisdiction as a type of fraud, they continue to look upon it with circumspection, and sometimes take hold of the slightest pretext to refuse taking it into account. In the background stands the catch-all, and somewhat random notion of 'reasonable' choice: the parties are free to choose a jurisdiction as long as the judge recognizes the reasonable character of their decision.

The scope of the parties' residual freedom

What remains of the freedom of parties? Something, undoubtedly, for except in the case of exclusive jurisdictions, it is admitted that they are free to choose their jurisdiction. This freedom is sometimes theoretical, and not only in common law countries, but in practice, parties do preserve a certain margin for manoeuvring because the notion of a 'neutral court' is far more convincing than that of a 'neutral law'.

Whilst a law is rarely biased towards a nationality, it is difficult to believe that a judge remains impassive when a dispute opposes a company from his or her country against a foreign company. Of course, a court never admits its nationalistic leanings. However, it is entirely open to recognizing those of others, which explains this paradox: *the choice of a distant court is sometimes easier to justify than that of a distant law*.

As for the choice of law, it is above all important when choosing the jurisdiction to not leave any doubt as to the common intention of the parties – a factor which requires impeccable drafting. A simple and apparently clear formulation, for example: 'All disputes arising from the present contract shall be referred to the Berlin Commercial Court', may prove inadequate even when the 'reasonable' character of the choice expressed by the parties is not contested.

For this reason, Anglo-Saxon lawyers often use more emphatic formulations, such as:

'Any dispute arising from interpretation or implementation of the present contract shall fall within the exclusive competence of the Paris Commercial Court'.

15/2.3 What to do in the case of an omission?

What happens to an international contract when the parties omit to specify the applicable law or the competent jurisdiction in the event of a dispute? In principle, the matter is referred to a law and a judge, but unless the parties make a subsequent agreement, it is up to the competent judge (the *for*), to make a pronouncement on this point. To do so, the judge will refer to 'conflict of law rules' in order to localize the law and the court with which the contract has the strongest links. When multiple links exist, the exercise may become very complex.

For contracting parties, this type of omission represents a considerable hazard and potentially, endless setbacks. This is the type of error that is only committed once: painful memories are a strong antidote for risk-takers and the absent-minded.

Conflict of law rules

Conflict of law rules enable the legal forum to determine the law to apply to settle an international dispute. Each legal system has its own conflict of laws rules: when a dispute does not fall into the field of application of an international convention, the *competent judge* will refer to its national law to determine the applicable law.

Many extra-contractual issues are governed by highly 'mechanical' conflict of law rules. For example: personal capacity is typically governed by national law; tortious liability by the law of the place of the damage; the validity of an ownership title by the law of the country in which the property is located; the validity of a marriage by the place in which the wedding ceremony is performed as far as its form is concerned, and by the national law of the spouses in terms of its content and termination.

In the contractual sphere, the conflict of law rules of most countries refer contracts to the law chosen by the parties. In the absence of such a clause, the judge will seek the law with which the contract presents the strongest links.

In Western countries, the judge is initially bound to refer to the common intention of the parties. If this initial examination does not allow the implicit will of the parties to be clearly identified, the judge will then seek the law with which the contract or its most important elements show the strongest links.

Two main criteria come into play: the place of the contract's execution and the place where it is concluded. French courts favour the first whilst occasionally recognizing the second. In fact, they above all look for a bundle of matching clues, which sometimes leads them to take account of certain secondary clues: for example, the object of the contract (if it is a building or company securities), the language of the contract, the place of residence and the nationalities of the contracting parties, a possible jurisdiction clause, the currency used. These so-called 'secondary' clues are not always so secondary, and in some circumstances, may prove decisive.

As a last resort, if none of these analyses is conclusive, the court can retain its own national law.

These conflict of law rules are also found, with minor variations, in a majority of countries. Aside from a handful of countries that do not accept the notion of judges applying a different law than their own, the place of a contract's execution and the place of its conclusion are the two most widespread criteria for attaching a contract to a law. Currently, a majority of countries prefer opting for the law of the country in which the contract is performed.

The rules on the conflict of jurisdictions

When the parties to an international contract forget to indicate the competent jurisdiction, the procedure to follow is very close to the one implemented in the case of omission of the applicable law. Indeed, contrary to widespread belief, there is no competent international court for settling international trade disputes.

Whilst international courts do exist (such as the International Court of Justice, the European Court of Justice or the International Criminal Court), none has the competence to intervene when a dispute arises between two companies: it is upon State courts that this task falls.

As for the applicable law, rules on the conflict of jurisdictions allow determining the competence of a national court for disputes showing links with several legal systems.

Within the EU, the applicable rules stem from the 'Brussels Convention' of 27 September 1968 concerning judicial competence and the execution of decisions in civil and commercial matters. Its Article 2 stipulates that: 'Persons who are not nationals of the State in which they are domiciled shall be governed by the rules of jurisdiction applicable to nationals of that State'. A single court is therefore competent: that of the State where *the defendant is domiciled*.

Naturally, this article will not apply if exclusive competence exists on the matter, for example, in criminal matters or in tort law.

In the absence of an international convention, it is necessary to pour over the national rules on conflict of jurisdictions to determine whether a court can – or should – pronounce a judgment on a dispute presenting foreign elements.

In most countries, there are rules that allow a judge to declare him- or herself competent when the defendant is domiciled in the same country, or if one of the parties to a dispute is a national of such country. This extremely wide competence does not come as a surprise: judicial nationalism is remarkably resilient in a context of globalization.

International *litis pendens*

All national courts have more or less imperialistic tendencies. By necessity, this similarity in approach and in national rules on the conflict of jurisdictions frequently yields contradictory results: it is inevitable that when applying the national rules of different countries, several jurisdictions will declare themselves competent for the same case. This is what is known as *international litis pendens*.

In terms of *litis pendens*, the distinction between a competent jurisdiction and an applicable law is often artificial, for when the parties to an international contract omit to designate their court, it is rare that they specify the applicable law. Yet when it has the possibility, a court will always prefer to avoid applying a foreign law: when it recognizes its own competence, it generally concludes that its domestic law is also applicable. This approach is facilitated by the variety of criteria to which it may refer, especially when the country where the competent judge is located is in itself a criterion of attachment.

For wily contracting parties, this natural propensity of national courts to find a way to retain their own legal system opens up interesting horizons. If the law of a country seems particularly favourable to one of the parties, it is tempting to refer the matter to the court of the country in question: if the court declares itself competent, there is a strong likelihood that it will also declare its country's law as applicable. Such manoeuvers – which are to international law what tax evasion is to taxation – are collectively referred to as 'forum shopping'.

Forum shopping is an affront to national legal systems whose lack of harmony satisfies the most skilful parties whilst impoverishing others. To limit excesses, States have produced a growing number of international conventions not unlike tax treaties aimed at avoiding double taxation. But this shield by way of conventions remains modest in its effect: fans of legal tourism can still look forward to fine days ahead.

15/3 Practice of international contracts

By definition a partial and approximate reflection of the will of the parties, a contract defines, with more or less precision, their mutual obligations. As the motivations and preoccupations of contracting parties are somewhat symmetric, the same will go for their understanding of the text they signed. This ambiguity is inevitable, but its magnitude may significantly vary.

Within any given country, the risk of misunderstandings is limited: the parties speak the same language and operate in the same cultural, legal and economic environment. Words, and even silences, have approximately the same meaning. And if doubts subsist, the law is a precious interpretational key for no one is supposed to ignore it. It therefore offers to fill in the blanks and to determine the nature and scope of the mutual rights and duties of the parties.

The situation is altogether different in an international context. Even when contracting parties speak the same language, they need to be prudent in their communication: terms – and especially *silences* – may give rise to different meanings. As for the law, it no longer wields its bunch of certitudes as the parties do not share the same legal system.

For these reasons, the drafting of an international contract is all the more delicate.

On a cultural level, it is appropriate to verify that the very notion of a contract holds the same meaning for all the parties. Semantically, it is essential to make sure that the same terms cover the same concepts. Finally, on a legal level, it is important to understand that when several bodies of law are in question, there are several grids of analysis, and hence, several contracts. It is necessary to select a single law and preferably, a useful law: if a law does not foresee the rules that allow a contract's blanks to be filled in, the settlement of any disputes will be placed at risk.

This somewhat chaotic situation brings exceptional freedom for creative drafters of international contracts. But one without a safety net.

15/3.1 Which law, which judge?

The criteria for choosing a law

In terms of choice of a law, situations are never as limited as they may seem. If a French company and a German company sign, in Germany, a contract to be executed in Germany, their choice is not limited to German law and French law. They have the means to enlarge their legal horizons by taking recourse to a so-called 'third-party' law, thus called as it is not the law of either of the parties and on this basis, inspires a feeling of neutrality.

Of course, whilst contracting parties would be seriously mistaken if they imagined that they were authorized to choose Tibetan law, there nonetheless exist many 'reasonable' third-party laws capable of satisfying the most suspicious of judges.

Often, each contracting party insists that the law of their own country be applicable to the contract. This insistence is sometimes legitimate: a State company, for example, rarely has permission to accept the law of a State other than its own.

However, when the contracting parties are private-law entities, this legal nationalism is irrational. A law does not favour its own nationals but rather a given social or economic group: sellers or buyers, employers or employees, company managers or creditors, traders or civil servants, men or women and so on.

It is no secret to anyone that a law is merely the reflection of a temporary socio-logical equilibrium, and on this basis, it is not necessarily fair: laws rarely challenge the interests of those who initiate them. Yet the founding principles of laws are often fixed over a relatively brief period of time, which explains why a country's masters at a given period have succeeded in durably imposing their own conception of the way things should be: many contemporary legal systems still bear the marks of an extinct ruling elite.

In this way, seeking to understand the flaws of a State's law means first of all 'dating' it as far as possible. In civil law countries, the existence of codes largely facilitates the task. The founding text is most often the civil code, whereas other subjects, such as business law, are modest by-products.

The French and German legal systems are spectacular illustrations of this historical bias.

French law

In France, the founding code is the 1804 Civil Code, also known as the 'Napoleonic Code'. This alternative name is a clear indication of its leaning: the Napoleonic Code served the interests of Napoleon. Accordingly, family law, for example, was fashioned according to the personal matrimonial desires of the Emperor. But as far as business law is concerned, how has the Napoleonic stamp impacted the con-tractual relationships of companies?

Formulated in economic terms, the question can be put as follows: who, apart from Napoleon himself, was on 'Napoleon's side'? Very probably his war chiefs and aristocrats. In short, people who produced nothing but who consumed. Hence a very strong tendency in French law to favour buyers to the detriment of sellers.

Today, *French law remains one of the most 'pro-buyer' laws in the world*. Some of its provisions – amongst them, the seller's 10-year guarantee for hidden defects or instantaneous transfer of ownership of a good upon the conclusion of a sales con-tract – are disconcerting for foreign lawyers. The whole spirit of the French civil code is summed up in one of its most controversial articles (Article 1602), that States, *inter alia* that 'obscure agreement' must be construed against the seller's interests.

German law

The example of French law would be incomplete without a comparison with German law. The German Civil Code (*bürgerlisches Gesetzbuch*, or BGB) dates from 1896. Elaborated almost one century after the Napoleonic Code, it is largely inspired by it. Napoleon's State councillor Portalis and his jurisconsults had succeeded in produc-ing a remarkable synthesis of Roman law, and for the drafters of the German Civil Code it was pointless to reinvent the wheel. One nuance, however, needs to be pointed out: the Germany of 1896 was in the hands of industrial cartels. Large family-owned groups dominated the country's economic and political life, and very logically, the interests that they first preserved were their own: the interests of manu-facturers and sellers.

The contrast is striking. Technically, German law and French law are very close, almost twins. Philosophically, they are symmetrical. German law remains one of the most 'pro-seller' laws in the world, comprising deferred transfer of ownership when goods are sold, a more limited seller guarantee, an extensive retention-of-title clause.

Other laws
Practically all laws on the planet can be inserted between these two laws. Everywhere, one or the other tendency (pro-seller or pro-buyer) is expressed, although in a less pronounced manner. However, the spirit of the *lex mercatoria* – essentially in the vendor's favour – has gradually worked its way into international commercial operations and spread to national laws, directly or indirectly, via international conventions. In this respect, the impact of the Vienna Convention on the international sale of goods has been considerable. The shift is very visible in French law, whose most biased provisions have gradually been limited to domestic transactions.

Of course, disparities in laws persist and when a choice is to be made, everything comes down to the type of law: is a law appropriate because it is more biased or because it is less so? In any case, it is important to bear in mind that neutral laws do not exist: only third-party laws do.

Specialists are often left in doubt: the choice of a law is not easy for anyone, for it is rare that a lawyer will master law from more than two or three countries. In a truly international context, this means that a lawyer's chances of being offered a law that he or she understands are barely higher than those of a complete neophyte. Finally, it is appropriate to recall that a law is one thing, its application another: a law's meaning is above all the meaning that the judge or arbitrator will apply. The choice of a law is therefore inseparable from that of the competent jurisdiction in the event of a dispute.

The criteria for choosing a jurisdiction
What are the criteria of a 'good' court? These are very different from those of a 'good' law, but they require the same preliminary clarification: they should logically lead a party to suggest a different court for each new contract, unless its role is invariable.

The location
The interests of equity push in favour of seeking a certain neutrality, which places emphasis on the *first criterion of choice: the location* of the court. In theory, the location of the chosen court should not financially advantage one or the other party. In other words, the court should be found at an equal distance from both adversaries. It is appropriate to avoid the obvious risk of court favouritism placing its own nationals at an advantage, which in all logic should lead to the selection of a jurisdiction located in a third country.

In practice, the issue of the court's location cannot be raised independently from that of the applicable law, for it is necessarily more cumbersome to ask the judge in one country to apply the law of another country. The scenario is however not unusual: a French judge who hears a case on an international contract subject to British law should, in applying the French law, respect the principle of freedom of choice of law. But as the judge's knowledge of British law is inadequate, he or she will need to call upon the 'opinions' of specialists in British law. Recourse to expertise is, in itself, a banal element of judicial life: when faced with a foreign law, the judge's position is no more or less comfortable than when dealing with a dispute on technological issues.

Duration of the procedure

In all cases, recourse to a different law than that of the chosen judge can only slow down the procedure, which leads to *the most important criterion of choice: the duration of the procedure.*

There exist quick jurisdictions and slow jurisdictions, and indeed, it is in the duration of a judicial procedure that the most spectacular differences emerge. The duration in question is that required to obtain a definitive decision, which means, most of the time, a decision obtained after exhaustion of the last possible recourse. By definition, such a decision is binding, which enables its beneficiary to formulate a request for an exequatur before the courts in the country of his or her choice.

Three major categories of legal systems may be distinguished:

- The *'quick' systems*: these systems are found in countries that consider – rightly – that response time is a key element of justice. The record is held by Scandinavian countries, in particular Sweden where a final decision can be obtained within less than two years. In the same vein, mention can also be made of the Netherlands (less than three years), Belgium and Switzerland (less than four years), Germany (less than five years).

- The *'medium-speed' systems*: six to seven years – the case of most European countries including France, Spain, the United Kingdom.

- The *'slow' systems*: over 10 years. In this category, the new EU member States from central Europe, but also Italy as the poorest pupils. The United States, notably its busiest courts in New York and California, also falls in this category. But this is fast compared to countries like Japan (20 years).

Is a fast judicial system always preferable? For the plaintiff, without a doubt. For the defendant, the question is open to discussion, on condition of course that financial means are available for that purpose: a longer duration necessarily entails more costs.

It all naturally comes down to knowing if, at the time of the contract's conclusion, it is possible for a party to anticipate the role that it will be led to play in the event of a dispute: the hunter or the hunted?

Certain contracts invite pronouncements to be made without too much risk of error, for example, a contract for the sale of complex equipment. If the seller has guaranteed payment to it through the use of adequate documentary credit, then this party knows that in the event of a dispute, its vocation is most likely to become the 'hunted': the seller's service – constructing and delivering compliant equipment on time – is incomparably more complex than that of the buyer – paying the price – and on this basis, bears a greater risk of default.

This type of reasoning should nonetheless be used with caution, for it can only ever lead to a probability: only contracting parties acting in bad faith can predict with any certainty what their position will be in the event of a dispute.

The choice of the court is therefore as complex as the choice of the applicable law. This time again, no recipe exists. It is merely appropriate to recall that in international matters, the total duration of a procedure is not limited to that of the chosen country: it is necessary to add, on top of it, the duration in the country where an exequatur will be requested. But an exequatur decision being a judicial decision like any other, it may itself be subject to an appeal etc.

This is why disputes seldom follow their course to conclusion: in a majority of cases, a simple discount calculation on future gains will show that there is little difference between winning in 10 years and never winning. This elementary observation explains the propensity of parties to seek an *out-of-court settlement*.

15/3.2 Do we really agree?

The shock of cultures

A lasting cliché opposes Western and Eastern conceptions of the contract. In simplified terms, Western culture, impregnated with Socratic thought, is said to focus on searching for *THE* truth and its formulation, whereas Eastern culture, marked with Confucianism, is apparently geared towards relativism: for every individual, every instant and every place, a truth of equal value will apply. In short, the inclination towards synthesis of the former is opposed by the sense of perspective of the latter.

Transposed to the universe of international contracts, this opposition leads some to conclude that it is practically impossible for an American and a Japanese to agree on the meaning of the contract that they sign.

For the American, this document should be the bible for their relationship: if in certain circumstances it omits indication of what should be done and how, who is right and who is wrong, then it has been poorly drafted. For the Japanese, the same document is only a summary and a limited expression of the relationship established between them: it is an interpretational key to an agreement, a facet whose very existence implies that it cannot be the be-all and end-all. The agreement is undoubtedly within the signed contract but perhaps even more outside of it. Its silences also carry a meaning and are indications of the way in which the contract will evolve.

This distinction is obviously simplistic, if only because these cultures in fact intermingle. Confucian logic is certainly not alien to the West, even in the most everyday acts. Let's take a Western marriage contract: a document that is basically all about money, separation and death. And yet this contract does not do away with the belief that the meaning of the marriage lies in love.

Thin or thick contract? On the weight of paper

Transliteration of an agreement into a contractual document is a procedure that seems to be incompatible with trust: we apparently resort to writing when the spoken word no longer suffices. This comforts the cliché of a ruthless business world where wariness is a condition for economic survival.

However, a simple reading of a contract will reveal that it contains a considerable proportion of unspoken – and, even more significantly, unwritten – elements introducing a risk that only trust can make bearable. If there is distrust, it can only be partial: even the thickest of contracts expresses, through its very existence, a strong degree of mutual trust.

The idea that a contract's volume of paper is inversely proportional to the degree of trust is all the more contestable because writing is sometimes imposed by the law, and even more often, by the transaction itself. We too often forget that a contract is a communication tool before being a coercive tool: its primary object is to clarify certain wishes, to avoid misunderstanding that may spring up between partners acting in good faith. Writing is inevitable whenever a transaction exceeds a certain degree of complexity: it is not because stockbrokers are more trustworthy than industrialists that the former can conclude huge volumes of contracts by mere nods of the head whilst the latter cannot escape from an impressive bulk of contractual documentation.

One question remains to be answered: why sign a contract?

The signing of a contract is far more credible as a symptom of distrust than its drafting. Symbolic as it may be, this modest action is too elementary to allow, by itself, a shift from distrust to trust. But in fact, the decision to sign a contract implies a wager on one's fellow contracting party, as much on their understanding of the agreement – in the broad sense – as on their future attitude. The expressed contract is never anything but a piece in a huge puzzle, carrying in its hollows implicit clauses fashioned from omissions unforeseen (due to forgetfulness, feigned or sincere), deliberate (why specify something that goes without saying?) or necessary (isn't it costly and probably vain to provide for an uncertain future in endless detail?).

In a contractual approach, it is therefore in the more or less conscious acceptance of these omissions and the risks they entail that the clearest expression of trust resides. The upshot is that the unspoken, the implicit or the suggested are always legally relevant. We can also note that in judicial practice, the scope of the contractually non-expressed is largely appraised from subjective notions such as 'good faith' or 'abuse'. In a democratic society, no one understands these notions in the same way. And yet they are at the core of contract law.

It is only, in reality, in an international context that the non-expressed is officially recognized as giving rise to a plurality of meanings.

In French law for example, Article 1159 of the Civil Code stipulates: 'Whatever is ambiguous shall be interpreted by whatever is customary in the country where the contract is established'. There are no countries where contracting parties are less respectful of their commitments: all economic agents all over the world are subject to rules. However, it is frequent that they suffer from the absence of a commonly recognized meaning that it is appropriate to give to the unspoken.

In legal matters, the shock of civilizations is therefore summed up as a technical problem: it is prudent, in an international contract, to consider that the non-expressed rarely bears a commonly recognized meaning. On a contractual level, a loss of trust ensues, that is translated by frenzied drafting: 'thick' contracts thus become a means to occupy the territory of the implicit.

A new problem then emerges: if a contract claims to govern the slightest details of a relationship, its omissions necessarily bear meaning. Yes, but which meaning? One thing is sure: the fewer the omissions, the more they acquire a legal scope. This is a prickly dilemma, which explains why, on this issue, there is one opinion per lawyer.

It is therefore not surprising that it is in the field of networks that ignore all geographical restrictions, that the outlines of the international contract of the future are now being sketched: more tribalism, hence less paper... This denotes a certain notion of trust, that is perfectly summarized by this old Russian saying: 'Where there is a guarantee there is evil; it is better to die betrayed by the Czar than to live with the Czar's guarantees'.

Is it actually a contract? On the letter of intent

In business, the letter of intent occupies a special place. It goes by many names: we also speak of a memorandum of understanding (MOU), a protocol, heads of agreement, pre-agreements. Nor is the definition of the letter of intent any clearer.

In general, it is a contract on the contract: its objective is to clear the way towards a 'final' agreement. In short, it is a type of intermediary contract, which raises the problem of the glass being half-empty or half-full.

On the one hand, we can consider that the half-contract means the absence of a contract. Whilst we may not know what exactly is intended by a 'letter of intent', we know that this term is used to avoid writing 'contract'. Certain letters also specify that signing of them will not give rise to any commitment of any type whatever. But on the other hand, there is something undoubtedly curious about expressing the absence of any agreement in written form. If there is a letter of intent, there is necessarily an agreement, otherwise why was there negotiation on it, and above all, why was it signed?

There are few countries where one or other of these two interpretations has ended up imposing itself overridingly. This explains why, if letters of intent are found everywhere, their legal meaning varies considerably from one legal system to another.

At one extremity of the spectrum, we find the principle of *culpa in contrahendo*: ie the letter of intent stems from the law of contracts, and it is sufficient to engage the contractual responsibility of a company. This is the position taken by German law and the laws that it has influenced, notably Swiss and Scandinavian laws.

At the other end of the spectrum, we find the *all-or-nothing* principle of British law, and to a lesser extent, US law: there is no contractual obligation – even the obligation of good faith – in the absence of a 'real' contract. The letter of intent cannot be a contract, for its objective is to increase the chances of concluding one. Accordingly, it is legally worthless.

These symmetrical visions in fact have very similar practical consequences. Each, in its own way, rejects the idea of a half-contract: we are either in or out. For they are black or white in their own way, and thus provide an excellent level of legal foreseeability.

Outside of these two 'radical' positions, uncertainty dominates. Spanish, French or Italian laws take less clear-cut positions, and thus, unclear ones. Are we overly or inadequately bound by a letter of intent? It is up to the courts to decide, case by case, and sometimes, according to questionable criteria.

Certain lawyers consider this debate to be essentially academic. In their opinion, sufficiently specific clauses enable the impact of the applicable law to be neutralized. To avoid ambiguity, it suffices to make silences explicit; in plain language, to make a 'real' contract. This point of view is unrealistic: isn't depriving the letter of intent of its minimalism, and thus, its shadowy zones, tantamount to taking away its interest?

It is pointless to distort the letter of intent: it should continue to occupy its territory, which is located upstream of the contract. As it is equivocal by nature, its drafting remains an exercise of finesse: it is necessary to specify what there is agreement upon in order to indicate disagreement on all the rest; it is also necessary to measure out silences to ensure that what they rule out is rightly missing and that what they cover is not premature.

It remains that when the applicable law is not one of the 'foreseeable' laws mentioned above, there is always uncertainty as to the exact extent of the commitments undertaken. Signing a letter of intent thus implies low risk aversion. And it is probably because this obvious point is not widely known that the practice of letters of intent is so extensive, especially when lawyers at no present.

Conclusion

The law struggles to keep up with contemporary economic realities: it remains too territorial to embrace the international, too slow to meet business imperatives. For users, the law is less and less protective, and courts are less and less effective. The growing trend of mediation is enlightening: this alternative means of dispute resolution relies on no law, no judge, no arbiter.

If the law on international contracts does not serve to protect, then what is it useful for? For understanding. The international sphere offers an unparalleled perspective on the limits of the law. Knowing what the law is not useful for helps to clear up the few segments in which it has a firm place. It is also a way to learn to live without it, in those areas where it no longer offers any assistance.

Notes

1 Karim Medjad is Professor and holder of the Chair of International Development of the Enterprises at the *Conservatoire National des Arts et Métiers*.

2 The most basic principles of contract law (purchase/sales contracts or service contracts) are not developed here; the reader is invited to consult the selective bibliography at the end of the book.

3 See Chapter 14.

4 Arbitration will not be dealt with here although it is an important alternative means for resolving commercial disputes. This choice is due to a lack of space but also the fact that this solution is not specific to international transactions.

PART THREE
Organization and management of resources

Once procurement strategies have been defined and good practices deployed, it is necessary to set up for the function a resource management system that is coherent and contributes to performance and results. By 'procurement resources' we refer to all collaborators within the function, and all information and decision-making systems.

One key point should be grasped: the strategies, levers and operational practices of procurement examined in detail in the previous two parts of this book make up the function's 'business core'. Yet it is impossible to reach a level of professional mastery, and even less to excel in it, if the resources deployed do not allow this. Thus, when we seek to progress, the issues of organization and deployment of appropriate resources should always be addressed before improvements in professional expertise can be made. Morever, it is essentially at this level that costs should be incurred, and these should systematically be analysed and defended in terms of investment and ROI, hence shifting procurement from the status of a cost centre to that of an investment and profit centre.

Chapter 16 deals with a first developmental level integrated into the strategic rationale, through detailed examination of organizational and structural issues that the procurement department needs to resolve. It outlines all company organigram choices according to their dominant strategic priorities, and presents the resulting positioning for the procurement department. It also probes the issue of whether a procurement department should be centralized or not within a multi-entity organization. Details are provided on all forms of intermediary coordination (and delegation), more or less proactive, that are applied and justified in many companies. Practical implementation issues are also examined.

Chapter 17 supplements this approach by analysing all dimensions of human resources management. The main procurement job descriptions and professions are presented and analysed; details are given on job profiles and evaluation as well as the follow-up of buyer competencies; different motivation systems and remuneration principles are analysed as well as recruitment and internal mobility practices.

Chapter 18 is entirely devoted to information systems and decision-making tools. After a concise outline of ERP systems, the chapter comprehensively develops all technical and operational aspects characterizing procurement intranets, spend-analysis systems, and all dedicated internet tools. E-sourcing and e-procurement solutions are all analysed in detail, as well as current (at the time of publication) supplier markets for IT services and software editors. The chapter ends with a reasoned presentation of an analysis and deployment strategy for a global procurement information system project within a company.

16
Organization, structure and positioning of the procurement department

FRÉDÉRIC PETIT

In any function, once strategic decisions have been made, once the main tactical and operational choices have been defined, and once all operational management systems are in place, some key points regarding resources still need to be decided on and implemented:

- the choice of an appropriate organization, a theme that encompasses the position of the procurement function in the company organization chart as well as all decisions concerning internal decisions made by the executives;
- choices on the structures and management of information systems, as well as decisions relating to the use of new internet technologies;
- finally, decisions on human resources management and a clear and explicit definition of the jobs to put in place.

This chapter is devoted to the first point.

16/1 Company strategic choices and general structuring factors

The choice of the structure and positioning of the procurement department *is a question that is not independent from the way in which the company is organized from a global viewpoint.* This is incidentally true for any function whatsoever.

16/1.1 Two main historic organizational models

After long years of using first the pyramidal model, then the project-based model, we are now observing organizational models that are more complex (networks), multi-dimensional, disaggregated or lean.

Functional pyramidal model

First of all, there are a certain number of companies that are still organized in a 'pyramidal' manner. In this situation, the dominant organizational logic is typically functional.

The general strategy is defined overall, then broken down into all major functions, with a priority placed on their organization into parallel 'silos'. In this way, the company focuses on optimizing the major functions, considered separately, or at least optimizing those making up the 'core business' (customer service, production, logistics, procurement, etc).

Here, the priority target is professionalization of the functions, even if it is sometimes necessary to have *light* transversal structures to handle interfaces; in this way, the major functions operate within a system of internal 'customer–supplier' relationships.

Within this first major category of organization, certain companies have evolved, increasingly looking for *transversal optimization* (corresponding to a second stage of strategic maturity). This stage is often described as an *integrated company approach*.

In this case, cross-processes are actively sought and organized; most of the time, we see the emergence, in the organigram, of a supply-chain department and a procurement department attached to the top management with their own strategies.

However, the existence of homogeneous product ranges or transversal client projects does not call into question the dominant pyramidal organization, even if transversal organization may lead to certain types of *matrix structures* where several support or 'profession-focused' functions are positioned horizontally in such a way as to benefit from synergies and thus create value.

Regarding the procurement function, within this first major category of general organization, generally an emphasis is placed on a centralized function (modulated if the group is made up of multiple entities), following the principles that we shall examine further. The structuring principle for organizing the procurement department is primarily the segmentation of the procurement portfolio.

Project-organization model

In this organizational method, the main structuring principle is an approach based on projects or deals, as illustrated by Figure 16.1.

This category of companies is in fact made up of two types of organization, different in origin:

- Companies that work *according to deals*, for example, by responding to calls for tenders, then producing products or systems that are by definition customized, without having standard or customized product catalogues. A typical example is a group that designs hi-tech integrated systems such as Thales.

- Companies that design and produce *standard products or systems*, but that have chosen to identify business or product segments and to place responsibility for them on 'companies within the company', all considered as entities in complete charge of their projects and reporting to the top management on their own income statements. The car manufacturer Renault–Nissan is in the process of evolving in this direction under Carlos Ghosn (as is the whole sector if we observe the upstream evolution of automotive suppliers). This is also the case in the field of aeronautics.

FIGURE 16.1   Project-based organization

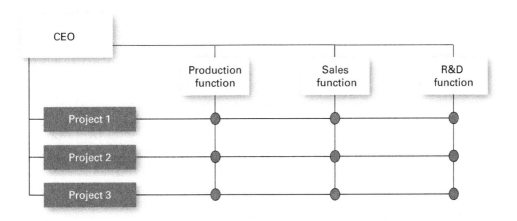

It is also possible to include in this category global companies that are keen on handing over considerable responsibilities to entities organized on a geographical or market basis.

Within this major organizational category, the *project-based structure* takes the form of a true *project team*, placed under the responsibility of a project director with very extensive powers. Most of the time, he or she will report to a programme management, itself directly dependent on the top management; sometimes, the project director will have a direct link to the top management.

The project team is composed of a representative for each of the company's relevant departments, sometimes joined – depending on the project stage and the nature of tasks to carry out – by representatives of suppliers or external partners.

Project members are delegated by their own original department, and may periodically call upon this department, for example, if an in-depth study is required. These representatives are, however, decision-makers, dedicated to the project full-time, and for this reason, they are detached from their function's routine activities.

Team members may sometimes be physically grouped on the same site (or 'platform' as in the automotive or aviation industries) in order to simplify, facilitate and expedite contact between them. When the project concludes, the participants return to their respective departments, or most of the time, take part in new projects that arise; this type of profession is specific, cannot be improvised and justifies permanent activity. Companies may also choose to add external resources in order to have the right skills at the right place at the right time, and in order for these skills to be transferred to internal teams.

In this second major organizational category, the structuring principle behind the organization of procurement will be the project structure, and so the main profession will be that of the project buyer (see below). Of course, there will still be buyers specialized in categories of the procurement portfolio, but these are positioned as part of an internal 'resource centre' supporting the project buyers.

16/1.1 New models

Rather than providing an exhaustive list of all possible organizational methods, we can single out three major approaches with a fundamental impact on procurement organization.

Whilst the 1990s were the heyday of matrix-type organizations, newer models are no longer enclosed in strict procedures and processes, and leave far more freedom to initiatives. In this way, Jay Galbraith has proposed the 'front-back model' (White Paper, November 2005) based on three 'legs': one, a front-end geared towards customer relationships; the second, a global back-end focused on products and brands; and the third, a strong link between the front and back.

Other organizational models, on the other hand, tend towards a certain outward 'de-concentration', thus outsourcing activities no longer considered as a company's 'core business'. Some multinational companies can today, with a handful of people, coordinate a set of subcontracting units and partners throughout the world. Here, the shift is towards more or less 'virtual' organized networks.

Another possible example is that of the lean organization. In this model, there is no more room for departments lacking added value. Without sounding the death-knell of corporate organizations, these nonetheless need to demonstrate their own added value or else yield more space to operational organizations with high added value.

Finally, the arrival of the pooled organization – based on the notions of sustainable development, communities or else collective interests – has enabled medium-sized companies to rival the largest ones.

16/2 Centralization, coordination or decentralization

The issue of centralization of procurement has been raised regularly in the context of the general developments discussed earlier. The question in fact arises for any company, whatever its field of activity, whenever it finds itself needing to manage at least two economically or geographically distinct units.

Indeed, in recent years, through the action of mergers, acquisitions, external or internal growth, a vast majority of companies have found themselves in this situation of managing several business units.

Contrary to certain widespread ideas, the issue of centralization of procurement is in no way related to an international dimension. The question comes up in the same way for a company managing a number of business units in the one country, as for a group deployed over several countries or continents, with a few 'technical' differences such as language, legal and customs constraints. The objective of this section is to present, in the context of a multi-site group, the different possible structures for a procurement function in relation to this issue of centralization, each with its pros and cons; we will draw up a list of elements and decision-making criteria to help define a method for choosing an appropriate structure; we will also offer a few tips on how to deploy this strategy by identifying the main obstacles to overcome, and the pitfalls to avoid.[1]

16/2.1 Basic alternative structures

Structures for the procurement function are constructed around two main elements: the efficiency of the structure according to a principle of minimizing the acquisition costs of purchased goods and services as well as the costs of the procurement structure itself; and the reactivity of the procurement function in the interests of maintaining the company's capacity to adapt and innovate.

Construction of the procurement structure is also based on specific knowledge of the procurement portfolio in question, enabling detailed segmentation according to procurement categories. This segmentation allows risk/opportunity analysis to be undertaken from several angles (market risks, technical risks, product risks, economic stakes, technological stakes etc).

It is relatively easy to identify the two extremities with regard to centralization policy for procurement.

Completely decentralized procurement

On the one hand, we find completely decentralized procurement structures. Here, each business unit has its own procurement structure, sometimes linked to a supply function, without there being any connections between the various procurement structures in the group's business units. Each entity manages its own procurement portfolio and supplier portfolio independently from the other entities. The procurement strategy is defined by the entity's management, and strategic procurement levers are implemented within the entity and with its own suppliers, within the limits of its procurement portfolio. Figure 16.2 illustrates this organization.

This type of completely decentralized structure offers significant advantages in terms of reactivity. The proximity of users/prescribers to buyers enables the latter to have a sound knowledge, including technical knowledge, of their requirements, their implementation and their specificity. This proximity encourages the strong involvement of buyers in the definition of requirements and the checking of satisfaction amongst internal customers. Project procurement is largely facilitated.

Great reactivity results, providing scope for significant flexibility in the management of lead-times. The presence of buyers at the sites where purchased goods and services are used also enables reliance on a well-understood and controlled local market, one that is flexible and reactive.

According to the economic logic of the business unit, the definition of the procurement strategy within the entity and its direct integration into the entity's budgetary processes lead to strong involvement of the local procurement structure in the unit's financial results, and consequently, more responsibility placed upon local buyers, as well as strong motivation for them to reach objectives, often having committed to them before their local hierarchy.

FIGURE 16.2   Decentralized procurement organization

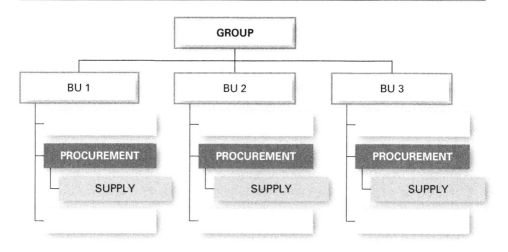

The decentralized procurement structure also allows the entity's management, through definition of its procurement strategy and through direct management of its procurement function, to take full responsibility for the coherence and results of this strategy, and the efficiency of its procurement function in the financial results of the business unit as a profit centre.

On the other hand, and with regard to the objectives of the centralization of procurement, the maintenance of decentralized procurement structures within a multi-entity group also presents a certain number of disadvantages.

The implementation of strategic procurement levers and of upstream and downstream procurement practices is in fact constrained by the limited scope of a decentralized procurement function.

The procurement structure itself, proportional in size to the procurement portfolio, will find itself limited in its resources, whether human (staff, competencies, capacity to invest in human resources), financial (budgets for marketing-based procurement, for the gathering of information, for the understanding of markets) or technical (information systems, tools for managing the procurement portfolio and the supplier portfolio).

Within these structures, sometimes combining the procurement and supply functions, the weight of everyday preoccupations and extreme reactivity are detrimental to the creation of a global perspective for a true procurement strategy and a supply-management policy. In certain cases, the presence of decentralized structures within the one group can even lead to the implementation of different, or even contradictory, procurement policies in the same market or with the same supplier.

In this way, whilst decentralized procurement structures promote great reactivity and great flexibility within the business unit, they remain limited in their efficiency, and curb benefits that may potentially be reaped from belonging to a larger-sized group in the implementation of procurement levers.

Completely centralized procurement

At the other extreme on the centralization scale, there are 'central procurement' structures. These are defined by organization of a type resembling a 'central purchasing office' or central procurement department: a team of buyers is gathered on one site (in most cases, the group's headquarters) and looks after all procurement of goods and services used by the group's different entities (see Figure 16.3).

Meanwhile, the different local units preserve their own supply functions, which, as a result, are separate from the procurement function (an ideal situation, conceptually and operationally!). The business units purchase goods and services in a catalogue defined by the central procurement department, according to pricing and logistical conditions negotiated by the central buyers.

FIGURE 16.3 Centralized procurement organization

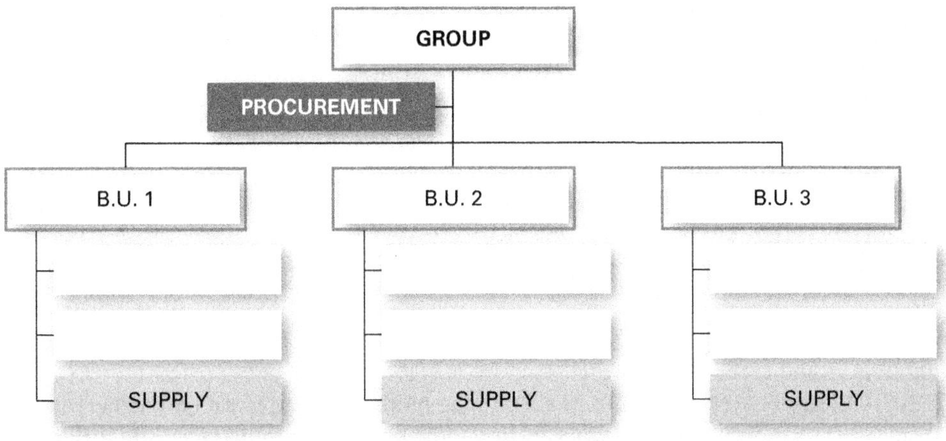

The advantages and disadvantages of this type of structure are the opposite of those that arise in the case of decentralized procurement structures.

An exhaustive knowledge of the group's procurement portfolio enables requirements to be consolidated, and hence, the structure's weight and efficiency to be optimized in negotiation and contract management. It also allows deployment of a global procurement strategy amongst all suppliers, and the implementation of a general policy on supplier management and partnership.

In terms of resources, the central procurement structure is generally allocated means which, when assigned to the whole of the procurement portfolio, results in the reduction of relative costs. These means enable investment in people in order to acquire, through recruitment or training, procurement specialists and specialized buyers.

The acquisition and development of high-performance tools for understanding markets and for managing procurement and suppliers, are also facilitated in the context of centralized structures by pooling of the group's means.

Central procurement structures typically offer ideal conditions for the professionalization of procurement and the deployment of procurement tools and methods.

However, they are also associated with limited reactivity and flexibility. Indeed, the complexity and size of the portfolio to be managed by the structure necessitate the setting up of procedures that are obstacles to the provision of swift responses to requirements and the adaptations of local units. Reactivity is further undermined by the geographical or even cultural distance between users/prescribers and buyers.

The central buyers' understanding of the specificities of local requirements, whether technical, logistical or financial, is made more complex by this distance, and it is therefore difficult for them to be included in the frameworks set up internally with users, or externally with suppliers.

The recruitment of specialized buyers partly helps to get around problems relating to technical knowledge, but is accompanied by the risk that when such buyers move on, this specific and difficult-to-replace know-how will be lost.

The centralization of procurement and the concurrent establishment of a general procurement strategy risk making local players less accountable in procurement processes. Due to the already mentioned importance of procurement in turnover, the company's financial results may be a source of conflict between the central structure and local entities. Indeed, as the procurement strategy is no longer decided on by business units, the latter will undergo the consequences of the group policy which, while globally generating gains for the different entities, may sometimes penalize some units that lose control of a considerable share of their budget.

16/2.2 Strongly coordinated intermediary organizations

Between the two extremes (decentralized local procurement and centralized procurement), multiple intermediary combinations may be set up for a group's procurement function, as indicated by Figure 16.4.

All these variations are organized around the more or less advanced implementation of centralization in terms of cooperation and/or coordination between the different procurement structures of the entities making up the group.

Let's nonetheless bear in mind that a first stage may be undertaken without there being any translation in terms of structure. This is a simple matter of cooperation, consisting in the *exchange of information between business units*: the composition of procurement portfolios, supplier panels, practised prices and conditions, the procurement function's management tools, elements for understanding markets. This first *internal benchmarking* stage is the foundation for a shared procurement approach, and enables taking stock of best practices.

This first stage remains on the level of cooperation whilst each entity maintains its full freedom and responsibility for defining its own procurement strategy, its deployment and the measurement of its efficiency through results. However, it is rare, after the implementation of coordination, for more advanced coordination strategies not to emerge. Indeed, internal benchmarking quickly highlights sources of progress in terms of organization or procurement performance, which cannot remain untapped, especially if results of the benchmarking are circulated amongst local entities and the group's management.

FIGURE 16.4   Intermediary procurement coordination structures

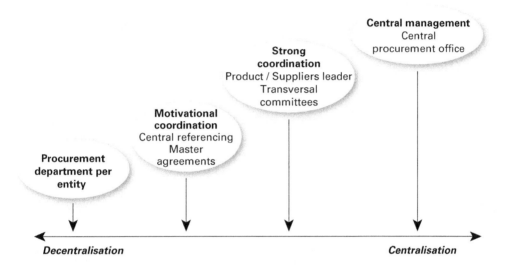

The different levels of coordination and centralization are then related to several approaches:

- A proactive strategic group approach depending on its desired level of involvement in the construction of the results of the different units. This approach conditions the level of freedom that the group agrees to allow the different units in their procurement, whether directly undertaken from suppliers or carried out through the group's central procurement office. The group's strategy therefore defines the level of control that it wishes to have on the procurement of its business units.

- An approach based on portfolio segmentation. Associated with a SWOT analysis carried out for each entity and on a group level, this approach may lead to the identification of strategic procurement families or segments for the group. The approach should take into account the specificities of local procurement portfolios and each unit's requirements in reactivity and flexibility.

- A profession-oriented approach. This allows identification of specific competencies in certain entities through benchmarking (or lack of competencies in certain cases).
- A resource-oriented approach. Also based on the exploitation of benchmarking results, this approach allows focusing on a group's tools and best practices, and deciding on how to deploy them in the different units.

The combination of these different approaches shows that there are multiple solutions involving greater or lesser centralization for the procurement function.

Central procurement office 'on demand'

The first organizational configuration involves setting up a *non-mandatory central procurement office* listing a certain number of products or services with a benchmark price (generally determined on the basis of a forecast global volume). But business units remain free to decide whether to turn to the central office or not for their purchases.

Meanwhile, the central office will nevertheless aim to have a maximum of 'local' purchases carried out via the central contracts. We sometimes say that it constantly seeks to increase the percentage of spend that it manages. Indeed, as foreseen in the global contract concluded with each supplier, if an annual consumption threshold, specified in advance, is exceeded, an end-of-year rebate is often applied and refunded to the group, then redistributed (if it makes sense) to the business units in proportion to their respective consumptions. In this way, it is in everyone's interests to pool procurement.

A non-industrial example offers a clear illustration of this organization: one leading international hotel group has, at its headquarters, two central procurement offices (one for food, the other for non-food products and services). The heads of operational units (ie the directors of the hotels representing all of the group's brands) can use these offices or not; franchisees, in any case, have total freedom in this regard. In normal circumstances, this option works greatly to their advantage, economic in particular, for all purchases other than those made locally, thanks to the master agreements negotiated and signed by the central procurement offices. Their end-of-year rebates also depend on the volume of orders that they place via these two central offices.

Lead buyers

Other solutions exist when a strong coordination approach is taken: the most common is that of lead buyers (Figure 16.5).

On Figure 16.5, it should be noted that the lead buyer positioned as being in direct contact with the central procurement management is not physically based in the central structure: this buyer remains within his or her unit, but plays the role of central buyer in conjunction with his or her continuing role as a local buyer. In practical terms, this buyer has two hierarchical bosses: the local boss for local missions and the central procurement director for group missions.

Such structures with lead buyers combine:

- the possibility of managing, in a centralized manner, the procurement of products or services common to several entities within the group;

- specialization of part of the procurement human resources with designation of a leader for each given procurement family;
- a global approach through consolidation of the requirements of the different units and definition of a common strategy for the analysed family enabling the implementation of the main procurement levers;
- a knowledge value of requirements and local markets by local buyers through 'family procurement committees' formed for each procurement family;
- an element of reactivity and flexibility related to the local presence of buyers involved in the team;
- the support of local buyers, as *two-way* information relays allowing local deployment and application of the strategy of the family in question.

FIGURE 16.5   Strong coordination based on lead buyers

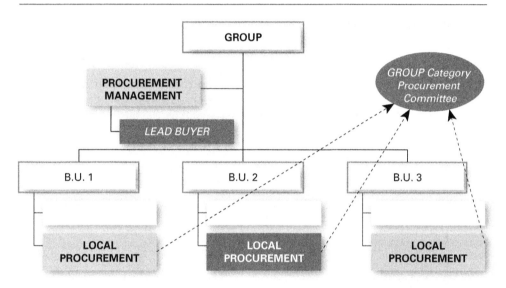

However, this type of structure remains related to the definition, for strategic procurement families, of a group policy that, unless it is accepted by the management of the business units, will not resolve the difficulties relating to the conflict of interests that may exist between this strategy and the reaching of local objectives.

In companies that make this centralization choice, there are as many category procurement committees, and hence lead buyers, as there are shared procurement segments that the company has decided to manage globally (eg a group such as Thales has several dozen community efficiency teams/purchasing with just as many lead buyers to manage a large proportion of the group's shared purchases).[2]

Panel manager/international sourcing manager

The other dimension of centralization consists in observing the skills that make up the buyer role and centralizing part of these activities whilst keeping another part of them local, thus encouraging new, more specialized buyer professionals.

Amongst the different possibilities for a procurement family or category, we may decide to centralize the supplier panel training and management (Figure 16.6), including the sourcing and approval of new suppliers. On the other hand, other tasks would be maintained on a local level, namely the definition of procurement requirements, the calls for tenders in relation to these defined requirements, as well as the subsequent stages of offer evaluation/rating/selection, possible negotiation on the basis of a shortlist, as well as implementation of the solution.

In this context, centralization involves grouping the following upstream procurement practices:

- the technology and sales watch, and the systematic local or global sourcing of new suppliers;
- the qualification of suppliers and the formation of the panel;
- the collection and sharing of information on supplier performance from 'local' feedback monitoring systems;
- the definition of supplier improvement plans, implemented, followed up and coordinated for all of the group's entities;
- and more generally, the definition and pursuit of the policy on suppliers.

However, we understand that in this case, local buyers remain completely in control of procurement actions (local project procurement and management of calls for tenders) in direct relation with a product or a service purchased by the business units.

FIGURE 16.6   Central supplier-panel management

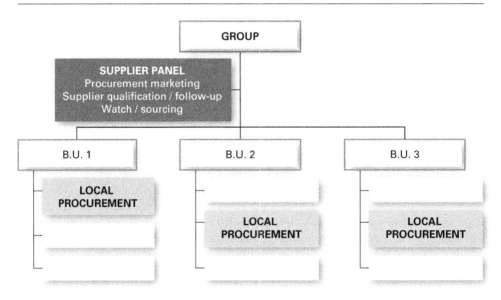

Between the two extremes on the centralization axis, there is therefore no single way to deploy a procurement centralization policy. Each policy, and its associated structures, should therefore adapt to the specific context of the group and its business units by accepting choices with the aim of optimizing the two following aspects: 1) *efficiency of the structure*, according to a logic of minimizing the acquisition costs of purchased goods and services as well as the costs of the procurement structure itself; and 2) *responsiveness of the procurement function*, with the aim of maintaining the company's capacity to adapt and innovate.

Intermediary geographical grouping

Some international groups often choose to introduce an intermediary level for grouping purchases: a country level, or more generally a level corresponding to geographical entities, based on the important and structuring fact of the possible specificity of local business and marketing, the existence of strong subsidiaries on a national level, or the consequences of strong habits historically in place. This is the case with groups involved in food processing or the production of detergents and cleaning products.

In this case, as indicated by Figure 16.7, the levels of responsibility in procurement take account of this organization (example drawn from a global leader in energy and fluid distribution). In the diagram, the lead buyer is called the category manager.

FIGURE 16.7   Levels of geographical centralization (example)

Category Manager	Country coordinator	Local buyer
Ensures implementation of results of the call for tenders (mid-long term)	Ensures implementation of the results of calls for tenders in his or her country	Supervises the implementation of the results of calls for tenders at his or her site
Reports on the level of savings achieved	Reports on savings per country and reports on business volumes to category managers	Orders necessary products from the supplier panel, in line with the results of the call for tenders
Participates in the definition of the group strategy	Helps the category manager to: – Analyze the local market – Develop extra reductions – Implement changes	Carries out technical negotiations with the suppliers
Carries out benchmarking for his / her category for the group		Informs the country coordinator of possible evolutions or problems encountered with the suppliers
Standardizes data from the information system	Standardizes data from the information system	
Follows market trends	Sets up and develops the group's procurement strategy in his or her country	
Coordinates with suppliers on possible evolutions in his / her product category		
Prepares for the next call for tenders		
Carries out a technological watch for his / her segment, and informs the group on evolutions		

16/2.3 Criteria for choosing an appropriate structure

As previously described, there is no one ideal structure for handling the issue of centralization of procurement. The solutions at either extreme (local procurement or centralized procurement) are not always satisfactory, as attested by the backtracking currently undertaken by major international groups that, after pioneering 'complete centralization', are reconstructing their procurement organization towards structures allowing more autonomy and flexibility to local units, hence reducing the group's hold on the procurement portfolios of business units.

Procurement organization within a complex group cannot be based on an extreme strategy, either 'completely local' or 'completely central'. The strategy needs to rely on well-considered choices whose impacts in terms of efficiency and reactivity have been measured. These choices concern the management of the procurement portfolio and the management of resources allocated to the procurement function; these same choices are to be the basis for defining the group's procurement policy, and not the opposite, as is too often the case.

The main criteria can be summed up by Figure 16.8, presenting the respective advantages of centralized and decentralized solutions.

FIGURE 16.8 Criteria for choosing between centralization and decentralization of procurement

	PROS	CONS
Centralisation	Professionalism / specialization of teams (depreciation cost with ROI)	Possible demotivation of local buyers (weakness of specialization)
	Uniqueness of procurement policies / strategies	Possible structural conflict with the heads of profit centers (business units)
	Consolidation of requirements	Possible heaviness of central procedures (approval and decision-making circuit)
	Homogeneity of supplier management and supplier management	Necessity for an integrated information system
	Facilitated standardization policy (updating of specifications)	Distance with the operational units (satisfaction of requirement, local procurement, etc.)
	Homogenous measurement of performance	
Decentralisation	Motivation of local buyers	High risk of inconsistency in group strategies and procurement practices (for the same types of purchases)
	Proximity of business partners	
	Flexibility / Short reaction time	Multiplicity of supplier contacts (weakness position?)
	Account taken of local specificities / Technical adaptations	
	Better use of local or "regional" market	Lack of visibility over consolidated purchases (no volume effect / pooling)
	Better integration with the logic of independent profit centers	Tendency to resist change / "Economic" limit for investment in HR

Choices relating to the procurement portfolio

One of the first criteria of choice relates to an exhaustive and detailed analysis of the group's consolidated procurement portfolio. Only this global view of the portfolio will allow:

- a detailed segmentation of the portfolio;
- the highlighting of strategic segments that may sometimes not emerge from local visions of the procurement portfolio;
- the identification of local specificities, internal or external, real or 'imaginary', that may be obstacles to a consolidation of requirements;
- possibilities for implementing strategic procurement levers within each family;
- the calculation of the participation of each unit in the volume of each of these strategic categories.

Following this analysis, combined with a risk/opportunity analysis related to each family, the choice of centralization can be made, category by category. Each category can then be identified as 'centralizable' or not, depending on its financial significance to the company, and the internal and external risks that it represents.

This first approach to classifying categories according to the interest of their centralization conditions the extent of centralization that can be envisaged, and thus the scale of structures and tools to set up in a centralization policy.

Choices relating to the procurement function's resources

The centralization of procurement is one of the privileged paths of professionalization of the procurement function. Indeed, it generally enables resources to be allocated to more extensive procurement portfolios, and thus the *effectiveness* of these resources to be optimized (*productivity concept*).

In the context of centralization of procurement, the type of structure set up is therefore always dependent on an analysis of the resources available for the portfolio family whose centralization is envisaged.

This analysis should permit the identification of the competencies and know-how present within the group, and by default, the competencies to be developed internally and/or to recruit externally. The presence of competencies and their location in the group's different entities will have an influence on the choice of centralization strategy and its implementation.

Group's strategic choices

The approach based on segmenting the procurement portfolio and identifying the centralization potential within categories also determines the weight that may be represented, following implementation, by centralized procurement in the pro-curement portfolio of each of the group's units. The decision to carry out this centralization therefore defines the *group's potential hold over each business unit's income statement*.

The decision is therefore fundamental to the management of the direct influence that the group's top management will have on its different entities, not only over the financial results of each unit, but also on structures, procurement and supply organization, or even the pricing and sales policies of these entities and their financial management.

The setting of each business unit's objectives and the way in which they are evaluated should also take account of this hold of the group in such a way that each manager preserves objectives over which he or she maintains direct control. The definition of the group's procurement policy and of the level of centralization thus stands out as a key element in the policy on managing the business units composing it, and hence, the group's general strategy, beyond the scope of procurement alone.

From these three decision-making aspects – analysis of the procurement portfolio, analysis of the resources of the procurement function, general strategy for managing business units in the group – it is possible to reflect on and construct a policy on procurement centralization by defining the scope to which centralization is to be deployed, the resources allocated to this policy, and the type of organizational structure to set up.

16/2.4 Deployment of a centralization strategy

Once a general policy on the centralization of procurement has been defined (taking all possible forms, ranging from the mere exchange of information to complete centralization via coordination, organization into teams with lead buyers in the different units or concentrated in a central structure), it should be presented to all of the group's departments and to the different business units in order to be validated and accepted prior to its operational implementation.

Given the deep changes that the setting up of such a policy may entail within entities (reinforced hold of the group over the results of units, changes in structures, organization, tools, reporting and monitoring procedures, etc), this appropriation phase is crucial to the success of the defined policy.

The implementation of the policy itself should be rigorously prepared in order to lift, as quickly as possible, any obstacles that may arise, and the least possible room should be left for improvisation – a source of risks for the group and its units, as well as discredit internally and externally amongst suppliers.

Different publics to target

It is possible to identify different target publics for communication prior to the implementation of the new procurement policy, each of these publics being expected to act in order to ensure effective deployment of this new policy.

The group's top management

A group procurement policy may be defined through the criteria for choice presented above by a small team made up of the group's procurement department (if one exists) and the corporate top management. The policy should nonetheless gain the support of everyone. To ensure its effective deployment within the group, the first public to convince of the interest of this new policy is the executive committee representing all departments.

Indeed, the new procurement policy should obtain the approval of these leaders to make sure that everyone receives the same message and is favourably disposed to this change.

Resistance can only be lifted with the support of higher-level management. This support should not be endured as simply bending to senior management's wishes, but the policy should genuinely win the approval of the executive committee, convinced that the strategy is in the best interest of the group and its constituent units.

Such approval can only be obtained by the definition, within the executive committee, of clear operational rules between buyer functions (marketing, production), support functions (logistics, finance, IT) and the procurement function – rules that then need to be interpreted in the various operational units.

Business unit management

As described above, the setting up of the new policy may cause significant impact on the autonomy, operation and organization of business units. Through the dual approach of the project's promoters and their respective departments, the members of the executive committees of different units should also adhere to the planned policy on the basis of emphasis of the anticipated *interest* for their units.

When dealing with these 'local' teams, possible conflicts between the group's general interest and the specific interests of its different entities should be discussed and handled from the outset of the strategy's implementation, with clear rules allowing the effects of the central policy's growing hold on local results to be assimilated.

Similarly, the new organization methods stemming from the policy should be put forward and validated by local units, all the more as these may have an impact on the staff in these units.

Local procurement structures

In the front line of those affected in their everyday activities, local procurement structures should also adhere to the global project. This support is facilitated if the policy set-up includes members of these local structures in the new envisaged centralized organization, with weight being balanced between the central and local structures.

The promotion of competencies present in the different entities and/or the development of these competencies as part of the deployment project are also major elements for facilitating the support of local buyers.

Depending on the situation, this development of competencies may occur in other functions apart from procurement, namely supply, in the case of advanced centralization whereby local organizations become more specialized in functions closer to production.

Suppliers

The setting up of a new policy in a group should be strongly supported by a communication programme aimed at suppliers comprising several objectives.

It should enable the responsibilities of the various interlocutors within the group and its units to be positioned clearly in order to avoid the maintenance of practices relating to the habits of suppliers. The latter may have a natural tendency to try and hang onto situations where the group's absence of global vision (possibly) offered them an advantage previously.

At the same time, this communication should reassure the suppliers, especially those solely attached to local structures. They should assimilate the group's new strategy in order to best prepare their own strategy for fitting in with the new policy. They should be able to identify, in the messages communicated to them, the potential opened up by this new approach, and also adopt positive attitudes to these changes.

Supporting change and the setting up of tools

Even if it is difficult to anticipate a certain number of issues that may emerge when a group's procurement policy is deployed, the past experience of many companies enables identification of obstacles that should be taken into account as far upstream along the project as possible in order to prepare solutions to implement, sometimes preventatively, in a project initialization stage.

The language of communication

In the case of international groups, an 'official' communication language exists between the group and its business units. It is nevertheless necessary to check whether this language is the same between all the units, and whether all the interlocutors who will be included in the new organization and who will need to work together share this common language.

The level of mastery of the language should enable professional exchanges and often necessitates clear definition of a common vocabulary. If gaps appear when this point is analysed, training plans should precede the deployment of the new policy in order to prevent the setting up of organizations based on mastery of the language, rather than on the level of competencies and professional expertise.

Procedures and technical documents

Depending on the centralization choice, deployment of the new procurement policy will lead to the training of transversal procurement portfolios grouping the requirements of several units. Whilst integrating local specificities, the consolidation of these portfolios can only be envisaged on the basis of joint definitions of the products in question (ie *codification*).

To reach these joint definitions, a phase for the *standardization of production description and functional analysis supports* should be initiated as of the very start of the implementation of the new policy. Far from making processes more complex, this standardization should enable facilitating internal and external exchanges with suppliers, for whom this step also represents one of the first visible signs of the group's new policy.

In the same way, internal procedures, specifically those to do with supplier relationships (procedures on approval, auditing, management of non-compliance, order processing, invoices, payment) should be the object, as soon as the new organizations are set up, of a standardization phase to facilitate the management of the procurement portfolio and the supplier panel. This procedure standardization phase will also facilitate internal exchanges as well as exchanges directed outside the group.

Information systems

Depending on the specific situation of each group, joint information systems may exist or else be entirely absent, at least in the area of procurement management.

Where joint systems are absent or in their embryonic stages, their development, or at least taking into account the necessity for their development, is one of the stages that precedes deployment of a procurement strategy.

These systems should be partially operational so as to carry out analyses prior to the definition of the strategy. Their absence complicates exchanges between the entities and the central structure that needs to focus the bulk of energy on managing this complexity. As well as the harmful effect of the involvement of different members of the structure who only see the new organization as an extra workload, the absence of these tools undermines the necessary reactivity and the desired optimization of the implementation of procurement levers through the new procurement policy.

Specific communication policy

Experienced in most cases by the members of local structures as a loss of independence, autonomy, decision-making power or even interest in their work, the setting up of a group policy guiding towards the centralization of procurement should be accompanied, in its presentation and implementation, by a carefully prepared communication policy aiming to enlist the support of all.

The obstacles or 'technical' hindrances to its implementation should be the object of concrete projects to support change and to set up tools necessary for the strategy's efficiency and for rapid optimization of its results.

16/3 Positioning and structure of procurement organization

The first main question concerns the position of the procurement function in the company's organization chart. More specifically, two basic questions are raised:

- Should procurement be directly attached to the top management as a major function, or should it be integrated to another function in which it partially intervenes?

- In the case of companies made up of several profit centres, should procurement be centralized on a group level (holding), or should each responsibility or profit centre have its own autonomous procurement function?

We will begin with the first point that always crops up, particularly in the case of a 'single-entity' company.

Let's have a look at procurement in relation to the supply chain: companies generally have different levels of development in their organizational approach depending on the degree of maturity of their supply-chain organization:

- some have a dominantly functional organization, sometimes called a 'silo' organization, as it is strongly pyramidal;

- others, often later in their evolution, choose a transversal and integrated internal organization aiming at a priority on 'customer focus'. This may end up with having some functions that will be transversal, thus creating a matrix-type organization;

- others, finally, in a last stage of development, choose to further 'enlarge' their supply-chain approach, associating their suppliers to it upstream (and also their distribution network to it downstream), still with a customer focus, but seeking greater efficiency, reactivity and flexibility. We then speak of an 'extended' supply chain.

In this general context, procurement will naturally follow this evolution in the maturity of the global organization. This, however, does not mean that we have reached a maximum level of maturity. In 2010, Jean-Michel Moutot and Emmanuelle Bernardin noted in their book that centralization of the procurement function does not automatically result in a direct reporting line to top management in large companies.[3] They nonetheless indicate a strong correlation between companies that have reached a higher level of procurement maturity and a reporting line to senior management.

Procurement can thus depend on different departments, such as production, finance or logistics.

Predominantly functional organization (procurement/supply)

As shown by Figure 16.9, here the company's organigram preserves the company's organization into vertical 'silos'. In this first level of organization, procurement is not part of the executive committee, or rarely; it is represented by a sponsor, usually hierarchical. Procurement is also in charge of supply.

FIGURE 16.9   Predominantly functional organization (scenario 1)

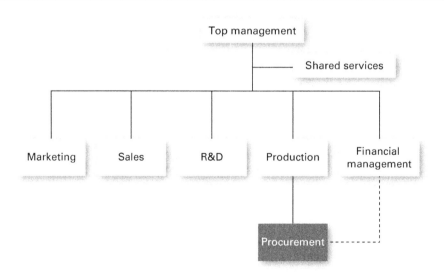

Most of the time, in industrial companies in any case, procurement depends on the industrial or production department. Sometimes, it is placed under the responsibility of the financial management in order to allow it independence vis-à-vis production, but also due to a focus on short-term procurement savings.

On this level, most of the time, procurement's mission is to focus on production-related direct procurement. It should be noted that some companies attach procurement to the R&D function with the aim of better integrating suppliers in the collaborative development of new products/solutions. An emphasis is then placed on value creation through innovation and co-development.

For other types of non-production procurement (investment, various services, communication or marketing purchases, various general expenses purchases, etc), procurement and supply are often kept decentralized towards users. In this case, the functions can manage the processes themselves in close proximity to the requirements, depending on the available budget decided on in advance, reactively and with optimal traceability.

Predominantly functional organization (recognized and mature procurement)

At this stage of its evolution, the procurement department is recognized by others, namely in terms of its contribution to the company's strategy, as well as in terms of its short- and medium-term economic efficiency. It accounts for a high proportion of the company's purchases, even if some are still delegated to internal customer groups (or even to persistent 'ivory towers' and 'fiefdoms').

As a result, as shown by Figure 16.10, the procurement department here depends on the top management, and is fairly often a member of the operational or even strategic executive committee.

This evolution is inevitable in companies in which: procurement represents a very significant share of direct and indirect costs; a high number of suppliers is at the heart of the development processes for new products and needs to be piloted; and finally, the top management wishes for a type of 'counter-power' in relation to designers (R&D) and producers (industrial department), or even more widely in relation to all internal customers. At this stage, the concept of the integrated supply chain is often not yet established.

FIGURE 16.10   Predominantly functional organization (scenario 2)

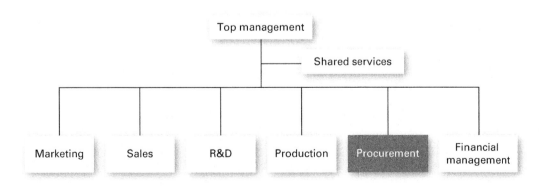

Procurement function in an integrated supply-chain organization

In this organization, there is a change in nature and in approach. The priority is no longer placed on 'local' functional decisions (within each function), but overall optimization is sought at every level of the supply chain with a *transversal vision* of performance criteria (total costs, quality, lead-times, flexibility, responsiveness).

Quickly, it becomes clear that this cannot be achieved by relying on the 'spontaneity' of operational departments. So global responsibility for managing flows from upstream (suppliers) to downstream (end customer) is then entrusted to a supply-chain department, directly attached to the top management and *itself also operational and not simply functional*. Figure 16.11 illustrates an organigram of this type by focusing on the supply-chain organization.

In some companies, namely because the top management wishes both to directly control this domain and to explicitly show the strategic dimension of supply-chain decisions, the manager of this function is a permanent member of the operational or even strategic executive committee, and may also have the rank of vice president.

Two different schools clash on the position of procurement, translated by two organigram sub-types:

- Procurement may be considered as exercising a strategic activity symmetrical to that of 'sales marketing' (and not directly concerned by flow decisions as it intervenes upstream from operational functioning). According to this point of view, procurement should exercise its activity autonomously. In this case, it may be relevant to keep it as an independent function and to attach it to the top management, without any hierarchical link with the supply chain. Many large companies have made and maintain this choice, namely in the hi-tech sector.

- Otherwise, as in the generic supply-chain model, procurement may be considered as constituting the supply chain's upstream, namely through the activities of sourcing and the supplier selection, that always partly include decisions interfering with flow issues and (above all) total cost of ownership, and for this reason should be integrated in this department (Figure 16.11). In these conditions, procurement is viewed as part of the supply-chain department, under the direct responsibility of the department's manager.

The debate continues in procurement and supply chain departments, with arguments for and against for both positions. Studies have pointed to several possible links. Larson and Halldorsson (2002), referred to by the winners of the ACA Bruel 2010 Prize (David Doriol and Thierry Sauvage), offer us four different main approaches between procurement and the supply chain.[4] In all scenarios, the best results are yielded by collaboration with joint indicators.

Procurement function in a matrix organization and evolutions

This approach to the company organigram corresponds to the situation of industrial, distribution or service groups organized into independent business units, but whose senior management (corporate level) often seeks to take advantage from possible synergies.

In companies thus made up of several divisions, branches or profit centres, the question is often raised as to whether to accord procurement a central or local role.

FIGURE 16.11 Procurement and integrated supply-chain organization

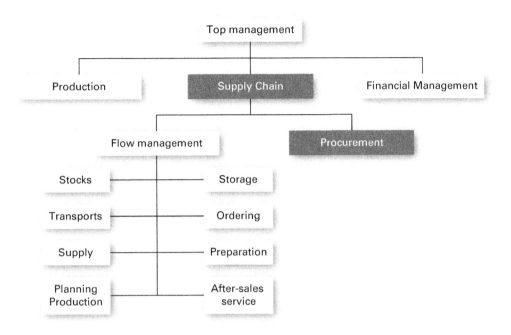

Marc Sauvage, president of the CDAF (*Compagnie des Dirigeants et Acheteurs de France*), a French procurement network, made the following comment in the May 2013 issue of the journal *La Lettre des Achats*:

> It is necessary to stick to the company's requirements, to step agilely between centralized and decentralized, to promote proximity with business units and short decision-making circuits. Organigrams are definitively in matrix form, between a 'category management' point of view and a 'business unit' point of view. What is certain is that the procurement component is evolving increasingly towards shared service centres for efficiency and cost reasons.

A survey carried out in December 2009 by the RGP firm amongst 30 or so European companies, over 58 per cent of whose respondents had procurement turnovers of more than €1 billion, indicated that 4 per cent of production-related procurement was centralized, 48 per cent mixed, and only 7 per cent decentralized. When procurement directors were questioned on trends, they indicated a tendency towards decentralization.

Non-production procurement proved even more centralized with 52 per cent of responses whilst their management reported a tendency towards centralization of this function.

These results back up the survey undertaken by CAPS (Center for Advanced Purchasing Study) several years ago, indicating that 50 per cent of companies were centralizing their procurement function whilst at the same time, the other 50 per cent were moving towards decentralization. A majority of organizations can therefore be found between the two extremes (Figure 16.12).

FIGURE 16.12   CAPS survey on procurement organization

Change in organization between 1995–2003*

TOTAL: 24 companies (48.98%)   TOTAL: 25 companies (51.02%)

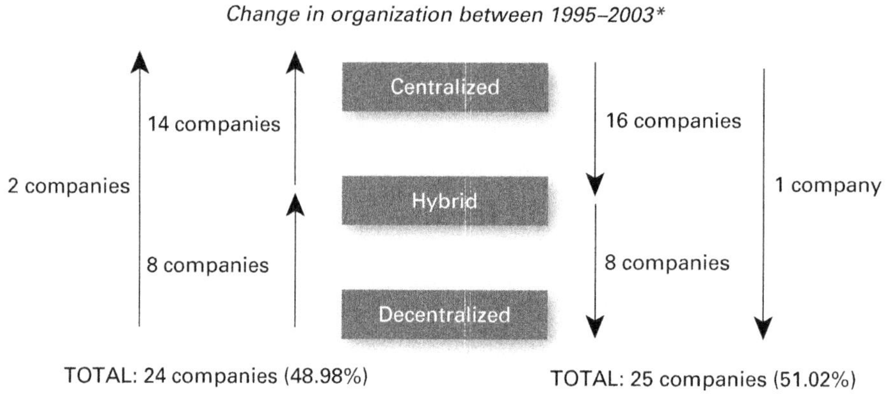

If we envisage centralizing, it is necessary for the chosen formula to allow *improvement of value creation as a result of proven and significant possible synergies*; otherwise decentralization often remains the easier, more relevant and psychologically easier approach.

Evolution beyond this centralization/decentralization axis involves outsourcing approaches that shift organizations towards external networks where each party brings added value. The difficulty lies in maximizing the sum of the final value, and not the profit of each. For this type of organization, buyers are major players in setting up the supply chain as a network.

The procurement department itself can be outsourced (ie BPO or business process outsourcing applied for other functions like accounting or HR), entirely or partially. Generally, the supply part is integrated into shared service centres, or even outsourced, often related to a 'source-to-pay' process in order to carry out the leanest, most efficient, and hence least expensive full process, from the order to the payment of the supplier. Today, only direct procurement and 'core business' procurement remain un-outsourced, or only to a minor extent, to third parties (Figure 16.13).[5]

It would be possible to write an entire chapter on this topic, which is developing quickly in North America. The procurement outsourcing market grew by 10 per cent in 2012, reaching US$1.72 billion, representing over US$220 billion of spend managed with more than 20 global service-providers (figures from the *Everest Group Procurement Outsourcing Annual Report, 2013*). In the RGP survey on procurement organization already cited, 3 per cent of companies had outsourced supply. A majority had already or were going to set up shared service centres for supply.

In the introduction, we mentioned lean organization, but also procurement pooling. Here follow some lessons learned by Jean-Claude Descalzo, Procurement Director of the Bongrain group and an expert and practitioner of co-sourcing and procurement pooling. His slogan is: pool together to purchase better!

For many companies, the weight of external expenses, matched with the volatility of the prices of raw materials, has a strong impact on their profitability and their competitiveness. Without generalizing, we can observe that power relationships inevitably are tending to switch in favour of supplier markets, due to the concentrations operated, resulting in

FIGURE 16.13   Outsourcing of the source-to-pay process (©Everest group)

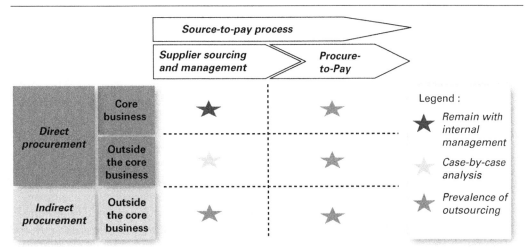

an increase of risks for customers. Whilst for large groups, the synergies of intra-company procurement enable critical size to be reached without any difficulty, the story is altogether different for smaller companies, despite their organic growth. As a result, the latter are reflecting on the best means to boost their attractiveness vis-à-vis supplier markets, and thus, their competitiveness.

The idea of pooling together to purchase better appears timely for many company heads. However, there is a difficult path to tread between the intention to pool and its ultimate realization, and success not guaranteed. Many factors need to be taken into account, such as the sharing of targeted objectives, culture, company profile, the capacity to cooperate and align on positions, the governance method, the operational rules of the structure set up, regulatory aspects relating to competition law and the choice of the legal structure, the allocation of resources in terms of numbers and competencies, the level of maturity of the organizations in place, the choice of categories to address regarding constraints and market risks, and so on. In short, all these are criteria that it is necessary to fully grasp before committing to creating a private procurement group, for we know that there are many failures in this domain.

The possibility of joining a specialized structure (a group of companies, etc) already benefiting from strong expertise in the matter as well as in the procurement categories in question may enable companies to overcome difficulties related to the approach. Recourse to such a structure helps accelerate the progress of procurement maturity and the speed of obtaining targeted savings.

The choice of the legal structure is not neutral. A structure such as the French EIG (economic interest group) has the disadvantage of making its members severally responsible on a legal level. In addition, in such a form, the uniformity of the services provided to the members is a requirement. In this way, it is quite common to see companies favouring more flexible legal forms, more adapted to the group's activities, to the targeted geographical coverage, and to the desire nature of agreements (referencing, commitment to volumes etc).

In France, it is common to take recourse to a legal structure such as an SAS (simplified joint-stock company). Here, membership rules can be modulated as wished. In all cases, it is a matter of considering the strategy as a genuine long-term company project that involves top management. Beyond the desired lever effect, the company will have a genuine opportunity to refocus its resources on its strategic procurement and the upstream and downstream management of its procurement, precisely those domains in which savings opportunities are too numerous to exploit – for example, the functional analysis of requirements in conjunction with prescribers, the implementation and management of improvement plans, and support for the deployment of referenced suppliers.

Pooling together to purchase better thus proves to be an opportunity for a company as long as it clearly understands the requirements of such an approach and chooses the right instrument to implement it!

From a global and financial point of view, procurement flows may occur through trading marketplaces, which can impact the procurement organization. This is mainly the case for raw materials linked to the market stock exchange. Such procedures are more and more sophisticated, entailing the involvement of global financial providers or cash-pooling organizations, and represent a step forward for big organizations with a global maturity level.

To sum up, organization of the procurement function should be adapted to the company's organization strategy. On its way to maturity, the function will shift from decentralized to centralized organizational modes, with balancing movements that are becoming more complex today, namely entailing organization in networks, the search for effectiveness, the outsourcing of a proportion of processes, and pooling. Procurement is not exempt from the porosity of company borders. The agility of the procurement organization and its reconfiguration depending on its environment are key factors in a company's success.

Notes

1 The following developments are based, in particular, on the research of Pierre Hablot, now at SPF North America and HEC Executive Master alumnus.

2 Lead buyers should not be confused with category leaders. In the context of multi-division or multi-BU groups, corporate buyers are central buyers with responsibility for a procurement category as a whole, whilst local buyers 'interpret' the global strategy at their own level, often with limited degrees of freedom. Here, we therefore have a form of complete centralization, at least on strategic and tactical levels, as well as for supplier panels training and management, even if local buyers can sometimes carry out calls for tenders on their own level.

3 Cf Moutot, JM and Bernardin, E (2010) *Mesurer la performance de la fonction achats*, Paris, Editions d'Organisation.

4 Doriol, D and Sauvage, T (2012) *Management des achats de la supply chain*, Magnard-Vuibert.

5 We refer the reader to Section 7/6 on the outsourcing of the procurement function.

17
Procurement professions and human resources management

FRÉDÉRIC PETIT

Henry Ford declared in 1920: 'Our people are our most important asset'. This is still true even if the Ford system has been largely superseded, as we will see in this chapter. Indeed, almost a century later, many books published place a focus on the value of human capital, and research is far from complete. The human resources function of today, initially known as the 'personnel department', has more recently evolved towards the concept of human capital.

The same development can be seen in the procurement function, but dates from more recently. Whilst, up to the start of the 1980s, working in a 'procurement department' tended to be a dead-end option career-wise, growing awareness of the function's strategic contribution has placed an accent on the professionalism of the procurement department without, as yet, attaining the concept of *supplier capital development*.

In this chapter, we will first tackle the notion of *competencies*, highlighting its major importance for the level of professionalism. On the basis of this notion, we wish to replace humans at the core of the function's transformation, through application of the principles described in Chapter 6 on sustainable development. We will then look at procurement jobs, and finally, all components of a human resources policy within the function.

17/1 Key points on human resources

The human resources function seeks to contribute to the company's performance rather than limiting itself to the mere administration of staff. In their book *Le DRH Stratège*, Yves Réale and Bruno Dufour[1] suggest that we develop a strategic mix known by the acronym 5C+1: Competencies, Careers, Compensation, Cooperation, Communication and Change. We will here focus on the first three elements, leaving the other Cs to be examined in separate chapters.

17/1.1 The state of the art

Human resources departments are subject to an ongoing dilemma: they need to prepare the future whilst managing the short term. 'It's about not trying to push things through too quickly whilst still maintaining an urgency around the way the company works,' confirmed Jacqui Marshall, director of HR at the University of Exeter in a recent article written by Jenny Roper.[2] This requirement necessitates a HR strategy for adapting resources to market hazards whilst defining a policy that can attract and keep human talent. Such a strategy is based on three dimensions: bringing change and promoting continuity; setting up corporate universities to adapt competencies; and setting up new communication tools to inform/attract/keep collaborators.

What makes human resources particularly difficult to handle but what also endows them with all their nobility, is that they are different from other company resources: they generate interpretation, they require updating, they evolve and they carry out their objectives whilst interacting with the organization. This is why communication is extremely important, and why objectives need to be constantly realigned, enabling the company's objectives to be lined up with those of individuals, via signs such as bonuses, as well as the teams' consideration of a sense of justice within the organization.

To take account of justice, the management needs to know which criteria are used for judging what is just or unjust. We refer to the thesis of Thierry Nadisic, HEC Paris, ISG-IRSAM, published in 2008, pointing out the identification of three types of perceptions of justice or injustice by Colquitt (2001):

- *Distributive justice*: these may be rewards (bonuses, company shares, evaluations, promotion etc) but also work conditions or tokens of recognition. In this case, the main criterion of distributive justice is the notion of *merit*. The customary rule is based on giving more to whoever contributes in a larger proportion to the company's success, according to Adams' theory presented in 1965[3] – still a benchmark despite its age.

- Employees also judge whether they have been justly treated by referring to the notion of *procedural justice* according to Leventhal in 1980[4]: *constancy* of procedures, associated right of *expression* and respect of *ethics*.

- Employees base their feeling of justice on an *interactional* element according to Bies and Moag in 1986.[5] This element reflects the interpersonal treatment that they receive and the information that is communicated. Often, it is a matter of judging the role played by one's immediate superior. The criteria of interactional justice are gathered into the three following families: the *respect* demonstrated, the *information* communicated, and the account taken of the notions of *deadlines* and *requirements*.

With intense pressure to generate income, executives and employees face the temptation to cut corners. Ben Heineman[6] argues that there is only one way for companies to avoid such failures: CEOs must create a culture of integrity through exemplary leadership, transparency, incentives and processes, not merely through rules and penalties.

17/1.2 Definition of competencies

Two categories of competencies can be distinguished: individual and collective. Let's look at these in turn.

Individual competencies

Here we refer to the definition, still recognized today, established by the research undertaken by the French employers' union, formerly known as the CNPF (now the MEDEF), in Deauville in 1998: *competency* is 'the combinatory capacity to implement knowledge and know-how for the purpose of carrying out an action'. This means, on the one hand, that developing one's competencies requires combining these aptitudes (depending on the type of profession), but on the other hand, that the relevant combination of knowledge and know-how is extremely variable. We will see that procurement expertise is based on so-called 'soft skills', and that knowledge (what we have learned) enables an action to be carried out as long as it is efficiently combined with know-how (what we have experienced).

The resulting action, as a product of competencies, objectives and resources, naturally depends on the competencies (according to the combinatory capacity defined above) to achieve objectives (defined with the hierarchy), as long as the necessary resources (teams, tools, budgets, etc) are available. Individual competencies will therefore be optimally expressed if the objectives are clear and the resources suitable.

This is why a key competency in a company may not necessarily be fully expressed in another company if these two parameters are not fulfilled. This is also why, depending on the level at which knowledge and know-how are combined, certain companies may upset their age pyramid. Talent consists of those employees capable of generating action and evolving within the company to improve their own performance levels whilst increasing that of others.

Finally, individual competencies will evolve on an ongoing basis. This is why human resources directors have set up competency-based management methods. The reasoning is as follows: let's recruit 'competent' persons, let's make our collaborators evolve, let's detect individual potential and let's oversee redeployment. To do so, they need to promote several dimensions: involvement, motivation, training and organizational change.

Collective competencies

Like a sports team or an orchestra, a company will not win, nor it will be the best, if it is only a sum of individuals. On this point, if you are a sport fan and/or you are looking for a leadership philosophy, it is worth taking a look at the book by the one of the greatest NFL coaches, Bill Walsh.[7] To enable the development of a level of collective competencies, it is no longer the individual alone who learns but the whole of the team, relying on the company as its base. Figure 17.1 symbolizes the organizational base of the company that learns when the individual level offers necessary individual competencies to the collective level. The whole of the working team then learns thanks to the contributions of each.

FIGURE 17.1   Pyramid of the learning company

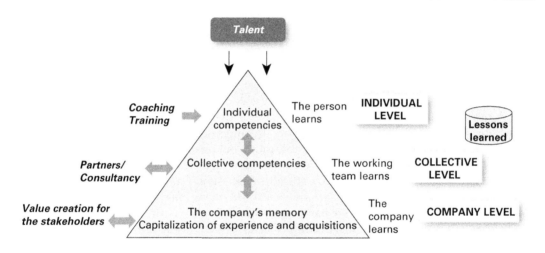

It is by setting up a 'learning' company that value can be created in the company environment for the stakeholders, ie the shareholders (improved profitability of the EVP)[8], the employees (better training and hence enhancement), the customers (improved proposals to customers thanks to the capitalization of knowledge), and the suppliers (better recognition of the suggested solutions).

Management of competencies and evaluation

To be viable, competency-based management needs to rely on specific tools, the main one being the *skill matrix*. A specific IT tool seems indispensable for the sound functioning of the system.

On the basis of the tasks actually accomplished, the aim is to identify which gaps exist between what is carried out, and what should be carried out in the short and medium term. For each individual, the idea is to identify the means to fill in these gaps. This may be achieved through training, coaching-type support or a redefinition of tasks. Ideally, these comparisons may be carried out from job descriptions, but for this to be possible, the latter must be up-to-date. What are the minimum requirements for a job description? Here are the main characteristic elements:

- the date at which the job description is drafted;
- the status of the position and its hierarchical attachment;
- the title;
- a summary of the job;
- the responsibilities and anticipated challenges;
- the required competencies;
- the work environment;
- the objectives and expected results.

In addition, given that different types of competency evaluation systems exist, it is essential to choose the one (or even the ones, combined) that appear(s) the best adapted and the most efficient. Here are the main approaches:

- evaluation carried out by a superior from the level above the individual (personal interview);
- self-evaluation with the help of a guide to ask oneself the right questions;
- the '360-degree' where an employee is assessed by him- or herself, then by his or her colleagues, and his or her direct hierarchy (this method may be more restricted (180-degree) or else broader (540-degree), involving customers and suppliers);
- the collective interview: used for projects, and in this case we focus on the team dimension;
- calling upon an assessment centre (or development centre), outsourcing of the process used to evaluate the performance and potential of individuals in specific situations (an approach that can facilitate external comparisons enabling benchmarking).

17/2 How this applies to procurement HR

Whilst 20 or so years ago we used to speak of 'a profession', today the jobs relating to the procurement function are many and varied. All the more so as the various roles involved in procurement and supply have changed, and now the upstream elements of procurement (sourcing) are coordinated with the extended supply chain (from the suppliers of suppliers to the customers of customers). Indeed, the specialization of professions has been accompanied by a rupture between procurement and supply, with the first focusing on procurement strategy and contractual negotiation, the second on the rules concerning orders and all follow-up of deliveries. The first is situated in the upstream stage and permits savings, the second is found in the operational execution and is becoming automated or even being outsourced. As we will see in the section on evolution, the system is not fixed and the arrival of an extended supply chain even stands to better promote qualifying paths thanks to improved fluidity of relationships and mobility.

17/2.1 Different jobs in the function

If we go back to the benchmarking process (seen in Chapter 2), from the 'sourcing' of suppliers up to the calculation of the overall cost including implementation costs (TCO), we see that jobs have become specialized. We find, depending on a company's size and its sector, up to over 10 jobs that can be broken down by region, by category or by sector. Here are a few examples:

- sourcing manager (global/regional/local; indirect/direct; metals/plastics etc);
- category manager (as above, with the possibility of a key category manager);
- buyer (as above, possibly with junior and senior levels);
- contract manager (and its counterpart, claim manager);
- support functions such as: procurement tools/IT, management control, communication, methods, sustainable development, etc;
- Intelligence sourcing (procurement marketing), strategic sourcing, vendor management;
- project buyer (upstream or dedicated to a project);
- managerial positions: procurement management (site/regional/global/ corporate);
- new jobs in areas such as external resources management, supplier development, or supplier innovation (in 2014, within the CAC 40, only 25 per cent of groups had a procurement innovations unit consisting of one to several persons).

Today, the buyer has become a multi-competency player who should be able to implement expertise in at least the following (according to the results of different interviews with procurement managers):

- carrying out a technology and market watch;
- establishing a procurement strategy in the context of a category of products (commodity manager) derived from the procurement function strategy;
- sourcing and following the performance of suppliers of which he or she is in charge;
- acting on all costs relating to a product's life, including its end-of-life;
- controlling financial levers: cost of stock, obsolescence, destruction, productivity, profitability of invested capital, impact on cash flow and WCR, material and goodwill assets, coverage of exchange risks, etc;
- supporting/bringing value creation to the business with suppliers (commitments), enabling supplier innovation;
- controlling legal aspects by staying informed on laws, practices, but also limitations relating to his or her activity (sustainable development etc) with an ability to rely on the legal department;
- managing procurement risks (all upstream risks relating to products, suppliers, information systems, the environment, political and geographical situations etc);

- managing the quality of suppliers and its impact on the total cost of ownership;
- understanding and proactive use of information systems, transversal (source-to-pay) and procurement specific (e-sourcing, e-auction, contract management etc) so that the information system ecosystem integrates procurement data (supplier files, prices, terms and conditions of contracts, follow-up of volumes, quality, service-level agreement, quality indicators, etc) and vice versa;
- enabling tight collaboration between all stakeholders involved in the procurement act (see the chapter on procurement communication);
- negotiating with suppliers but also with the company's internal players;
- communicating with and convincing different cultures;
- coordinating or supporting projects (depending on the case) on implementing new suppliers, or introducing new projects or innovation, etc.

As can be seen, the list is long and behavioural competencies or 'soft skills' are very much in demand.

In its 11th Annual Conference on 24 October 2012 on the theme of 'Evolution or revolution in the procurement and supply-chain professions?' the ACA[9] asked itself the following question:

> How are procurement and supply-chain professions in the process of undergoing an upset in their mode of operation in the extended company; and how is the development of 'soft skills' crucial to the capacity of procurement and supply-chain organizations to adapt in a demanding environment requiring increasingly agile behaviour?

According to a survey carried out for this event, communication competencies are the ones which are most in demand in terms of 'soft skills' (Figure 17.2).

FIGURE 17.2 Ranking of soft skills in demand

In your opinion, what are the behavioral aspects that are most important to your profession?

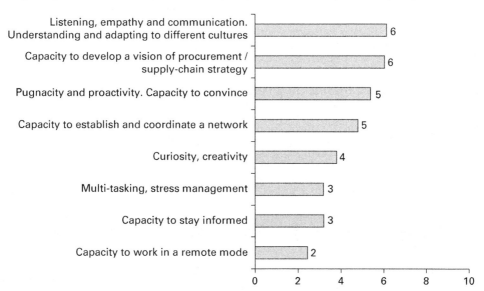

Listening, empathy and communication. Understanding and adapting to different cultures	6
Capacity to develop a vision of procurement / supply-chain strategy	6
Pugnacity and proactivity. Capacity to convince	5
Capacity to establish and coordinate a network	5
Curiosity, creativity	4
Multi-tasking, stress management	3
Capacity to stay informed	3
Capacity to work in a remote mode	2

In this context, reference to a job description would only provide one facet of these multi-sided roles. The drafting of a job description is often seen as a compulsory administrative step. It is in fact a company's first step in communicating with those on the spot and/or those who wish to apply for the position. To boost a company's attractiveness whilst respecting the reality and richness of a position, it is necessary to perfectly define its contours and to use language that can be understood, not only by the company and the function, but also by all those who will be involved in the subsequent selection, validation and evaluation process.

In the HEC Paris certifying training programme for procurement and supply-chain managers, we ask participants to draw up job descriptions based on real-life cases. For this purpose, we work on simple tools with competency grids whose dimension needs to be defined. This first task is complex, for we may find, for the one competency, several definitions and anticipated results, depending on the experience and environment of each (and participants from different horizons will not always easily agree on the vocabulary used in different contexts). For each competency, it is suggested that a level of importance be defined on a scale of 1 to 3 (from the weakest to the strongest). Here again, the exercise is delicate for it is quite simple to wish to rate 3 everywhere.

In this way, to simplify, we have elaborated a 'standard' benchmark gathering competencies according to major categories: knowledge, professional competencies, behaviour and managerial competencies. We then arrive at a weighted result per position (four buyer profiles are shown in Table 17.1 in the suggested form).

Every company has its own method for establishing its job descriptions with its own tools. It is thus up to each to make itself understood and to integrate today's requirements (the description should refer to what genuinely exists: we still see many job descriptions that no longer correspond to the reality of the missions carried out). But this procedure also serves to prepare the requirements of tomorrow, to make these descriptions evolve, in the context of high-performance and innovative companies.

We note, in conclusion, what we consider to be important and worth remembering: having a simple, common and shared vocabulary; keeping to competencies (and not listing objectives or means); working with HR teams and their tools; coming to an agreement on the means/resources and the results for the expected individual and collective objectives; enabling adaptation; and above all, staying factual.

17/2.2 Approach based on processes and human resources

We still meet many managers who think in terms of flows and place human resources in boxes all along the flow, expecting added value from associated human resources at every stage, ending up with a product equal to the sum of the values (according to the logic presented in Figure 17.3).

As announced in the introduction, the 'Ford system' whereby each player along a chain-like process expects the previous task to be finished before carrying out his or her own task and then handing the show over to the next in line is over. This seems logical and easy to understand (even if the approach has allowed many companies to operate production or administrative chains).

FIGURE 17.3 Flow and produced added value

Flow and activity are related to the final expected result, the addition of added values to be produced

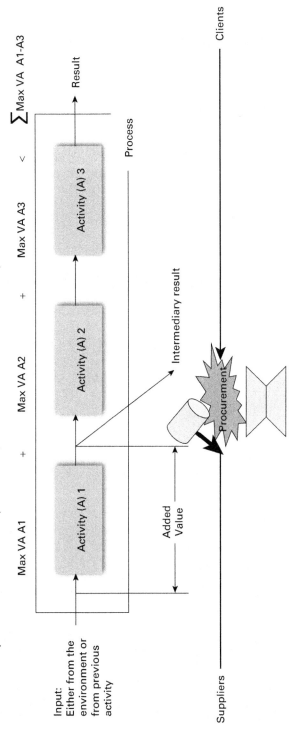

TABLE 17.1   Comparative description of buyer jobs

Buyer profiles: weighting system

Reference on competency profiles

Form aimed at defining the reference profile of the main procurement jobs.
Automatic translation into percentages (see columns on the right).
This profile can then serve as a basis for evaluating buyers or external candidates.
N.B.: below, the four domains of competencies have the same weight.
For operational usage, 'relative' weighting may (should) be introduced.

Weighting system – scale	Secondary	Important	Essential					
	1	2	3					
Qualities / Aptitudes / Competencies	Project Buyer	Strategic Buyer	Lead Buyer	Managing Buyer	P1	P2	P3	P4
	P1	P2	P3	P4	%	%	%	%
Knowledge (understanding / experience)								
Knowledge of internal organization	3	2	2	2	5.9	4	3.5	4.8
Past experience (results)	2	2	3	2	3.9	4	5.3	4.8
Level of general culture	1	2	2	1	2	4	3.5	2.4
Total	**6**	**6**	**7**	**5**	**11.8**	**12**	**12.3**	**12**
Know-how (professional competencies)								
Technical knowledge of the product / service	3	2	2	1	5.9	4	3.5	2.4
Knowledge of the supplier market	2	2	3	2	3.9	4	5.3	4.8
Mastery of specific levers	3	3	3	3	5.9	6	5.3	7.1
Supplier management	1	2	3	2	2	4	5.3	4.8
Total	**9**	**9**	**11**	**8**	**17.7**	**18**	**19.4**	**19.1**
Behavior (personal qualities)								
Aptitude for communication	3	2	3	1	5.9	4	5.3	2.4

TABLE 17.1 *continued*

Weighting system – scale	Secondary	Important	Essential					
	1	2	3					
Qualities / Aptitudes / Competencies	Project Buyer	Strategic Buyer	Lead Buyer	Managing Buyer	P1	P2	P3	P4
Aptitude for negotiation	2	2	3	2	3.9	4	5.3	4.8
Ability to analyze / synthesize	2	1	1	3	3.9	2	1.8	7.1
Unifying / charisma qualities	3	2	3	1	5.9	4	5.3	2.4
Curiosity	2	3	2	2	3.9	6	3.5	4.8
Aptitude for mobility	1	3	3	1	2	6	5.3	2.4
Degree of autonomy and commitment	2	2	3	1	3.9	4	5.3	2.4
Rigor / Organization	2	1	2	3	3.9	2	3.5	7.1
Ability to manage stress	2	2	2	1	3.9	4	3.5	2.4
Mastery of IT tools	2	2	2	3	3.9	4	3.5	7.1
Ethics	3	3	3	3	5.9	6	5.3	7.1
Ability to back change	3	3	2	1	5.9	6	3.5	2.4
Linguistic mastery (1 / 2 languages)	2	2	2	1	3.9	4	3.5	2.4
Total	**29**	**28**	**31**	**23**	**56.8**	**56**	**54.6**	**54.8**
Managerial competencies								
Past experience of team management	2	2	3	2	3.9	4	5.3	4.8
Leadership quality	3	3	3	2	5.9	6	5.3	4.8
Quality of (budget) management	2	2	2	2	3.9	4	3.5	5.3
Total	**7**	**7**	**8**	**6**	**13.7**	**14**	**14.1**	**14.4**
TOTAL POINTS	**51**	**50**	**57**	**42**	**100**	**100**	**100**	**100**

But this is not at all the case of the *transversal processes* of the modern company, for the sum of the maximal added values of every stage may be far lower than the sum of the added value expected from the whole of the process. Project directors are very familiar with this concept, for each, working in silo fashion and preoccupied about maximizing his or her own task, is liable to forget about contributing to the whole to provide the best possible result. Yet only the final (global) value counts: it is on the maximization of this value that the company will ultimately show itself to be a performer or not.

Let's take an example. If a buyer negotiates on a component that is important to him or her, as part of a project where sale of this component is on the project's critical path, the lengthening of negotiation periods will undoubtedly enable extra savings to be made on the piece, but they will more importantly generate late penalties if the project is not delivered on time with a well-negotiated piece. The buyer will expect to be congratulated for the negotiation results whereas he or she will in fact be reproached for delaying the project and entailing significant cost overruns.

We therefore see that all actions take place within a whole and interact with the whole. Added value can only be defined in relation to the global objective.

17/2.3 The impact of globalization

Economic globalization has changed the life of procurement. Sourcing has turned global (at least for SMIs and large companies), and suppliers may be spread out over different geographical zones. Professional requirements (on finding and validating local suppliers when a company sets up, or when applicable prices mean that global costs are more interesting) have prompted procurement executives and managers to move around geographically, but also to create local organizations and train local buyers.

Organizations are becoming global. As a result, implicitly, there is a great deal to learn on cultural differences, on other ways of approaching markets or companies, and of course on other ways of managing different men and women.

17/2.4 Ethical values

As we have seen in detail in Chapter 6, buyers are in the front line of ethics, namely as guarantors of good conduct and of respect for commitments of all types (including financial ones) made with suppliers. All over the world, procurement associations like the CDAF in France (a national professional organization representing buyers and managers from the procurement function) have shown understanding of this necessity by requiring members to sign a code of deontology such as the following: 'Membership of the CDAF commits the Buyer to exercising his/her mission in full loyalty to his/her employer, colleagues and suppliers, and in compliance with the profession's deontology rules.' The same principle exists in the buyer associations in different countries, with the setting up of evaluation committees and non-governmental organizations for audits.[10]

In France, in 2010, the Charter on Inter-Enterprise Relations was created at the initiative of the country's Ministry of Economy, with the aim of raising the awareness of economic players on the inherent issues of sustainable development and the quality of customer–supplier relationships. Over 1,600 companies signed this Charter in 2015. To evaluate the implementation of the 10 commitments explicitly required in the Charter, a Sustainable Supplier Relationships Label was awarded for the first time by public authorities in December 2012.

This French Charter is part of a global movement whereby many companies (mainly the biggest firms, but also smaller ones) have established supplier sustainability policies, where each company developing 'ethical guides' and rules for supplier relationship management. Many examples can be found on the internet.

To illustrate this trend, we refer to the example of Michelin, the leading tyre company:

> Michelin's Code of Ethics is based on the fundamental values expressed in our Performance and Responsibility Charter – Respect for Customers, for People, for Shareholders, for the Environment and for the Facts... we should reflect the following five Core Values on a daily basis in our actions on behalf of Michelin...These Core Values apply not only to the Group's behaviour on a corporate level, but to the individual actions of each employee.

These core values are not only relevant for the purchasing department, but for all the employees guaranteed by a code and a *governance model* at the top level.

Another example is provided by the multinational consumer goods company Unilever which aims:

> to advance human rights in our extended supply chain, develop a continuous improvement roadmap and move towards best practice... Our Responsible Sourcing Policy (RSP), launched in April 2014, embodies our commitment to conduct business with integrity, openness, and respect for universal human rights and core labour principles throughout our operations. The policy sets mandatory requirements on human and labour rights in business relationships with Unilever... We need to ensure our suppliers collaborate, understand and embrace the criteria in the Policy, and move up the continuous improvement ladder.

The same stance is taken by institutions like the European Community which has issued the following statement:

> Industrialized countries have important responsibilities in promoting sustainability initiatives – first and foremost by putting their own house in order, and by supporting a move to sustainable production and consumption patterns; in addition, by ensuring more consistent market opening, increased public and private financing of development cooperation, as well as better functioning and greater stability in the international financial system. All their policies – internal and external – should integrate sustainable development goals and take into account global needs.[11]

The word 'ethics' (etymologically, from *ethikos* in Greek) means 'morals'. Can buyers be said to have their own specific morals? The exercise of these ethics is limited if the company's other stakeholders are not involved at such a demanding level. As indicated by the examples mentioned previously, we can say that the scope of these ethics has extended beyond buyer deontology to a certain idea of company morals. As a result, ethical procurement has developed its base of values from respect for social and environmental conditions. This being the case, with these issues clearly standardized by internationally recognized standards and norms (such as the rules of the ILO), it is possible to measure the extent of the respect paid to these rules.

Measurement

The MADACA group, within the ACA,[12] in charge of reflection on sustainable procurement, suggests:

> adoption of social and environmental norms based on the ILO rules, on the *Déclaration des Droits de l'Homme* (Declaration of Human Rights) and the Global Compact Charter. These enable construction of codes of good conduct following ethical principles applied in areas including the social domain (work conditions of employees and responsible support for suppliers), the fight against corruption (when contracts are awarded or orders placed) and the environment (management of waste and product end-of-life, pollution).

We find all or part of these principles in the norms SA 8000, ISO 14001 and ISO 26000, as well as the systems and tools specifically made available to the supply chain by certifying bodies such as ICS (*Initiative Clause Sociale*)[13], BSCI (Business Social Compliance Initiative)[14], WRAP[15] or SEDEX.[16] These bodies promote the exchange of social audits and data between member companies (benchmarking).

These standards and codes of good conduct should allow buyers, first, to adapt their behaviour and their relationships with suppliers by following these ethical principles, next to supply tools for measuring and managing the ethics of their suppliers, and finally to offer suppliers objectives for improvements and results.

Meanwhile, the consultancy firm Socrates, specialized in assessing ethical competencies, borrows the maxim of the philosopher Habermas: 'Ethics is the capacity to make a fair and efficient decision in a given situation while respecting the persons involved.' Jean-Jacques Nillès, Socrates' co-founder and professor of philosophy and lecturer in management sciences at the University of Savoie, puts forward a barometer based on five dimensions, which he has contributed to implementing in a number of procurement departments:

- *Justice*: respect of business agreements (rules, contracts, partnerships). Principles of equity in business relationships (sharing of information, fair competition etc).
- *Moderation*: self-control and checking of impulses during negotiations with partners. Search for a long-lasting relationship based on sustainable development.
- *Responsibility*: procurement decisions based on objective elements. Discussion over and sharing of risks with partners.
- *Courage*: applying decisions taken by the procurement function and assuming their impact on partners; bearing uncertainties relating to decisions.
- *Respect*: taking into account partner interests in daily business relationships. Search for consensus when business contracts (rules, partnerships) are established.

We encourage the application of these practices in companies in order to truly measure the practice of ethics in procurement.

17/2.5 Buyer training (all levels)

Today, we can consider that procurement is at least taught in a unit of study in good management schools.

Some well-known schools where training in procurement and supply chain has been offered for several years include Cranfield, Cambridge, the University of Arizona, Michigan State University or HEC Business School.

Dedicated certificates are worthwhile for those seeking recognition as professionals in sourcing and procurement. Some companies link salaries with the level of the delivered certificate. The biggest ones in this business of certificate delivery are APICS (extended supply chain-oriented – with over 43,000 members and more than 300 international partners, APICS is one of the global leaders) and CIPS (Chartered Institute of Purchasing and Supply). The United Nations Development Programme (UNDP) and CIPS were awarded the prestigious European Supply Chain Excellence Award 2012/2013 in recognition of their joint Procurement Training and Certification Programme and its success in professionalizing the UN and public procurement sector.

Various schools have also developed dedicated MBAs or Masters degrees. This is the case at the EIPM (European Institute of Purchasing Management), Ecole Centrale Paris, MBA Strategy and Procurement Management at Birmingham University (UK) or mini MBAs led by Robert Handfield, the distinguished professor of supply chain management at North Carolina State, Lamar Chesney.

There are also associations, for example, the IFPMM (International Federation of Purchasing and Materials Management) that develop training courses. In collaboration with experts, universities or business schools, such associations have set up globally certified training programmes like the ADIPS (Advanced Diploma in International Procurement and Supply).

Finally, to meet demand and develop professionalism, certain companies or regions set up their own internal programmes (procurement academies), whether backed or not by institutions. This is the case of BuyIn, 2014 winner of the 'Best Procurement Employer' award at the Procurement Leaders Awards, beating Google for its efficient and positive working environment, and particularly for its creation of the BuyIn Academy. BuyIn is the largest telecoms procurement company in terms of annual spend on a European level, and No. 3 worldwide. Up and running since 2011, it is 50 per cent owned by Orange and 50 per cent by Deutsche Telekom, and handles network equipment, terminal and service platform purchases worth a total of €9 billion for both groups, including EE (UK). In-company programmes are also an effective means of sharing a common vocabulary and integrating internal candidates, thus enabling them to be more quickly deployed to meet demands for procurement resources with the corporate culture.

Internal training or recruitment

Should internal candidates be trained in procurement, or should ready-trained buyers be recruited externally and then trained in the company's culture? The question is one that keeps coming up and deserves at least a detailed and non-evasive answer.

Indeed, a considerable shift towards offering procurement training to employees from other professions has been observed. This can be explained by a step-up in the power of the function, initially constructed by specialists in the field, who then widely recruited buyers trained in training institutes that the pioneers contributed to developing. We have now embarked on a third phase by seeking to take advantage of the mobility of professionals recruited externally, primarily aiming to boost their integration in different professions (with companies mainly looking for managers).

There are nonetheless 'specialized' areas of expertise where external recruitment is crucial for less mature companies. This is, for example, the case of the public service sector that currently recruits procurement managers whilst large private groups tend to hire internally.

Our recommendation is to follow a strategy of diversity, in cultures, environments and training, and in this light, we share a maxim upheld by certain sports trainers: 'The best teams are those that promote the specificities of each and contribute to overall advancement.'

17/2.6 What (r)evolutions are to come?

Recruitment still on the rise

In RGP's international survey carried out amongst 100 procurement and supply-chain departments (Table 17.2), 52 per cent of managers questioned wished to increase their staff numbers. Increase in staff has continued since the survey began in 2009, with an acceleration in 2012.

TABLE 17.2   Recruitment prospects (survey carried out at the end of 2011)

Do you intend to increase or decrease your staff in the coming year?

Years	2012	2011	2010	2009
No planned change	20%	33%	42%	43%
Increase	52%	45%	32%	23%
Decrease	10%	5%	17%	14%
Don't yet know	18%	17%	9%	20%

SOURCE: www.rgp.com.

Evolutions bridging procurement and supply chain

We also observe consolidations of the procurement and supply-chain functions within the same department, or at least reflection on better integration of the two functions. Indeed, this was the theme of an APICS-sponsored webinar presented by Steelcase Inc's vice president of global procurement and a researcher from Michigan State University in November 2015.[17]

This is exemplified by the coordinator of the Hospital Logistics Committee of ASLOG (French Association of Supply Chain and Logistics) who joined the RESAH (French Network of Hospital Buyers) as supply-chain project director. 'On the strength of its purchasing expertise, the RESAH has become aware of the necessity to take charge of the supply chain between the suppliers of suppliers, and ultimately, patients of establishments,' he comments.

As far as training goes, major evolutions focus on interfaces with the supply chain. There are many supply-chain MBAs being created worldwide, mainly in the United States. An article on 'The hot new MBA: supply-chain management' featured in *The Wall Street Journal* on 5 June 2013. The newspaper also announced the difficulty, in the United States, of finding supply-chain managers, prompting a rise in their salaries.

Still more international with a step-up of local competencies

With the growing internationalization of procurement, organizations have become multicultural. We find local buyers, recruited on the spot, and central teams in charge of coordinating networks. Local buyers should have an excellent knowledge of cultural differences to strengthen their leadership. They should obviously speak English perfectly, and also master another language at a professional level, as well as have international experience (outside their own country).

Buyers capable of supporting a business plan including financial aspects

This remains an element whose improvement is highly anticipated but not adequately dealt with in procurement training. We can therefore only encourage all buyers to read up on and also deepen their knowledge of financial issues.

Confirmed trend towards strategic procurement activities rather than tactical activities

In this era in which economic watch plays a key role, the procurement function should prepare not only to equip itself with sourcing approaches that promote supplier innovation, but also with supplier strategies with the notion of developing 'supplier capital'. Buyers (can they still be called as such?) should have the means to set up strategic alliances.

Irreversible evolution towards digitalization

Our aim here is not to sing the praises of digitalization, especially as the masses are already well and truly converted: in December 2015, there were officially more mobile devices than people, and a plethora of research demonstrates how today's B2B buyers are more digitally engaged than ever. What we wish to underline is that advances are being made day by day, with progress now enabling what was once impossible. Buyers should anticipate what will be possible tomorrow and think beyond the supplier network, to the digital network and enhancement of this new intangible capital.

17/3 How to implement a procurement HR policy

An extremely rigorous sequential process needs to be implemented, stage by stage. Below we present the main stages.

17/3.1 Evaluating and preparing

So, with all this information, how do we implement an HR policy in relation to procurement? Let's start by keeping in mind the maturity model described in Chapter 21. Level 1 is the basic level. If the diagnostic situates the practice at this level, it is necessary to consider the use of existing procurement resources as a progress factor, through improved use of existing competencies.

To make progress in the field of human resources, we suggest a five-stage method based on the following sequence: vision, definition of performance with objectives and indicators, evaluations, analysis of gaps, and deployment. Figure 17.4 illustrates this process.

We suggest clearly describing the strategic vision (according to the meaning in Chapter 1) and from this identifying the objectives, whatever this may imply for your procurement resources. For the following stage, there are two ways in which evaluations can be made, and a development path set:

FIGURE 17.4   Deployment of evaluations for procurement human resources

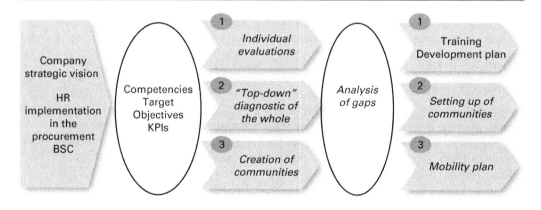

- individual evaluation that allows a 'bottom-up' scan of the organization's competencies and taking a comprehensive photo;
- global 'top-down' evaluation to allow quick identification of the major points for competency improvement;
- setting up of community(ies) (their number depending on the size of the organization) to enable great fluidity of 'information', the sharing of good practice, and the setting up of useful knowledge bases by teams.

Let's illustrate this approach with a few examples, drawn from real-life situations.

A 'bottom-up' approach: individual evaluations (industrial sector)

Description
An approach based on the holding of individual interviews to evaluate around 15 managerial and leadership competencies in relation to a reference document defined by an internal committee.

The evaluation programme was deployed for 230 persons (out of 1,000) in 25 countries. Individual reports illustrating strengths and zones for improvement served as a basis for two debriefing sessions (with the manager and with the employee) in the local language to guarantee the equity of the approach.

When to use this approach?
An appropriate method for evaluating a subgroup within a team or function (up to 20 per cent of a given population), it can be used simultaneously for several jobs.

Main benefits
During the debriefing interview, managers obtain a global view of their teams' requirements, individual and collective, in terms of competency development. The debriefing interviews are an opportunity for expectations on behavioural competencies to be specified. This approach allows construction of a well-prepared individual and collective plan. Individuals may be evaluated in relation to current or future positions in the event of programmed short-term rotation.

A 'top-down' approach: a global diagnostic for training needs (industrial sector)

Description
A qualitative and quantitative questionnaire to cover several training and development angles:

- existing training practices (methods, quality evaluations);
- training needs per competency;
- suggestions for improving employee development and optimizing their career evolutions.

When to use this approach?
To collect information and suggestions for a broad population spread out globally.

Main benefits
This method enables quick identification of training requirements for specific competencies, as well as the sharing of best practice. Results are established in the form of recommendations on technical and managerial competencies, and covers other aspects such as the development of community jobs, communication, or knowledge management.

Whatever tools are used, there is one golden rule to adhere to, according to Guy Le Boterf, associate professor at Sherbrooke University: 'Better to establish and guarantee strong coherency between simple tools than having little coherency between sophisticated tools.' The quality criteria for competency-based management are, in his opinion, simplicity, anticipation, updating and workability.

Stage 4 is an analysis stage dependent on the previous choices. We can focus on individual and collective requirements, and thus enable, in Stage 5, deployment of training, communities, as well as evolutions and mobility.

Figure 17.5 is a graphic example of an evaluation result, expressed in the form of a multi-dimensional 'star'.

17/3.2 Motivating, remunerating and developing one's teams

Whilst salary often seems to be one of the first causes of demotivation, it is nonetheless not an essential element of motivation (as long as it corresponds to an acceptable and expected level). Indeed, the different registers of expectations have long been publicized by Abraham Maslow's theory on the 'hierarchy of needs'; according to the US psychologist, needs correspond to 'lacks' perceived by a person at a specific moment.

FIGURE 17.5   Competencies Radar

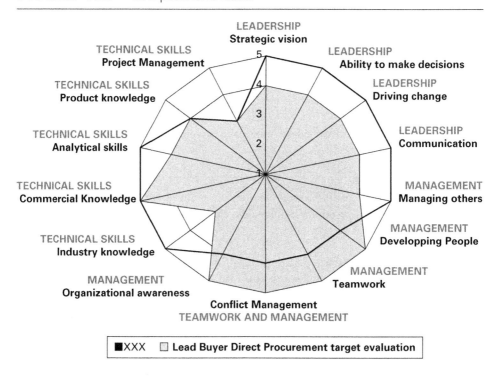

According to Maslow,[18] these needs may be: *physiological and safety needs* (higher income, career plan, job security, permanent company support); *social and esteem needs* (belonging to a social group, greater respect within the company, better social recognition for one's job, more commensurate and more motivating remuneration);

and *personal or self-actualization needs* (better-defined career plan, greater autonomy, etc).

The needs of all persons are prioritized and considered one by one: it is only when a category of needs is satisfied that the following category will emerge. The need that is not yet satisfied constitutes a source of motivation for the individual, and ceases to be such once it is satisfied.

In our ultra-competitive economic world, ultimately only employee motivation counts in making a difference. In this domain, not all the countries are on the same level. Indeed, we can identify a 'hit parade of commitment' according to which people from different countries act differently. In the article 'The Impact of Cultural Values on Job Satisfaction and Organizational Commitment in Self-Managing Work Teams'[19] the researcher found that employees resist management initiatives when these clash with their cultural values. In order for commitment to be engaged, values therefore need to be taken into consideration.

This is a dimension to be considered carefully in terms of team development and messages to transmit.

Remuneration

This type of information is by definition closely related to the time and era of the drafting.

You will find estimated salaries by country. Here, we have focused on three countries where procurement is relatively mature.

United States

According to the Institute of Supply Management (ISM) survey in the US in 2014, the average annual salary for supply management professionals who responded to the survey was US$101,608 (not including bonuses and stock options before taxes and deductions).

The average salary for each job title is reported in Table 17.3 (for more details, see **https://www.instituteforsupplymanagement.org**):

TABLE 17.3   Average salary per job title

Position	Salary
Chief, procurement/supply management/sourcing	$295,037
Vice president, procurement/supply management/sourcing	$202,940
Director, procurement/supply management/sourcing	$149,186
Manager, procurement/supply management/sourcing	$103,959
Experienced procurement and supply chain management practitioner	$78,393
Emerging procurement and supply chain management practitioner	$66,532

Strong differences should be noted between males and females, especially for top salaries and also depending on the region. Higher salaries can be expected in the north-east of the United States. As elsewhere, experience is a factor contributing to better remuneration, as indicated by Figure 17.6.

FIGURE 17.6   Average Salary by Years of Work Experience, ISM 2013

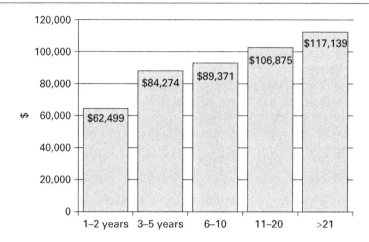

United Kingdom

According to the CIPS/Hay Management survey in the UK in 2015, the average UK salary for all procurement and supply professionals is £41,661 (see more details at **https://www.cips.org**).

In the UK, average salaries are around £89,000 for a procurement director. Within the private sector, the highest-paying industries are communications, professional and business services, and then the finance sector.

France

In France, figures for 2013 have been published by Hays. Expressed in gross annual figures in €K, these are set out in Table 17.4. (*Note*: The figures do not take into account variable pay elements and fringe benefits.)

In the survey, Hays notes that 'shortages in skills are not yet taken into account by employers. The latter have not increased salaries'. Indeed, similar figures were recorded in surveys from earlier years, whether conducted by Hays or other bodies.

We have therefore witnessed a certain stagnation in salaries in the last few years, probably a prelude to an upward shift geared at attracting new talent sought after by companies (rather than a generalized rise in salaries).

Motivation systems

Surveys follow one after the other and resemble one another. In 2007, the main reasons for *loss of talent* (extract from a survey related to the EIPM's annual conference in December 2002, carried out amongst 146 companies) were a lack of advancement opportunities (50 per cent), higher salaries and expected bonuses elsewhere than those found internally (48 per cent), a lack of recognition (21 per cent), or else the

TABLE 17.4 Hays 2013 survey on procurement salaries

	0–4 years		5–10 years		> 10 years	
	Staff < 500	Staff > 500	Staff < 500	Staff > 500	Staff < 500	Staff > 500
Procurement Director	N/A	N/A	57/70	N/A	65/120	110/175
Procurement Manager	36/47	N/A	40/55	53/75	58/85	75/110
Lead or Coordinating Buyer	N/A	N/A	N/A	48/70	N/A	60/80
Category or Commodity Bayer	33/42	36/47	36/47	45/60	N/A	N/A
Project Buyer	35/45	40/50	40/50	48/70	52/75	65/90

fact that the company did not give a sufficiently 'prestigious' role to procurement as a company function (17 per cent).

On the other hand, the main elements of buyer motivation were the following: motivation for the files handled; corporate image; support for its values as well as support of and loyalty to the company heads; recognition of good management; obviously advancement and career management; training and the competency development system; the company's commitment to its employees; and salary level and bonuses.

In 2013, the CIPS survey, carried out with Supply Management and Michael Page (already cited), indicated that even today a positive working environment is the most effective factor for keeping employees, far ahead of promotions and bonuses (Figure 17.7).

FIGURE 17.7 What's the most effective retention strategy for your business?

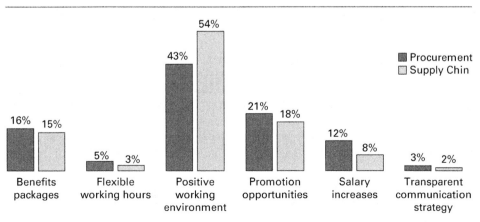

17/3.3 Mobility: first steps to other horizons after procurement

After the procurement function, numerous upper management positions are potentially accessible as long as the manager is prepared for this career evolution. From our observations, we can mention positions in top management, operational departments (sales, marketing), project management, and depending on previous experience, production or management control.

In this regard, Alain Darribau, former director of Marketing Operations Europe for the pharmaceutical firm BMS, and previously director Global Strategic Sourcing, makes the following comment:

> I see many advantages in this evolution, such as discovering new challenges and seeing the company differently. But as for all career management strategies, we need to set ourselves on the right track, to look for passageways to those other functions that we wish to join. A change should be credible and possible with a personal path enhanced by one's motivation, experiences, a conducive environment (a company promoting exchange), and precedents (do buyers change functions regularly within the company?).

Not all companies offer this type of environment. Today, a majority of them still rely on old reflexes – 'hiring someone already with experience.' We see limits to this approach. Yves Réal and Bruno Dufour, in their book *Le DRH Stratège* which we have already cited, mention strong 'unspoken rules'. If the top management has not defined the criteria for managerial competencies, the field is left completely open to the exercise of these unspoken tendencies that are perfectly well-known within the company, giving one little hope of progressing to a certain level in the company if one does not have X nationality or a Y degree, for example. If we transfer these 'unspokens' over to procurement competencies, many real-life experiences will come to mind.

On the other hand, if this mobility continues to be forged in companies, the procurement and supply-chain functions will attract high-potential talents and gain the recognition that it so needs.

This type of mobility is prepared as of the recruitment stage with the human resources function. The paths of high-potential employees should transit through the procurement function. This tactic furthermore offers the virtue of 'sowing' the seeds of good practice and allowing regular renewal of buyers per category. Too many companies, out of complacency or lack of vision, leave buyers in the same positions for too long, and thus create habits that are incompatible with this profession. We recommend a change roughly every three to four years, except for jobs relying on very strong expertise (such as contract managers or trading-floor buyers).

17/4 Adequate progress indicators

There is still little external data to allow comparisons of company teams. The Center for Advanced Purchasing Study (CAPS) of the University of Arizona is one of the only competence centres to make available comparative data per sector free of charge.

This type of data is not available in Europe. We can only encourage such practice, for these indicators will enable results to be calculated, measured and compared.

Here are a few indicators offered by the CAPS (2014) example (Figure 17.8). We can find the annual cost per procurement employee for training ($803) or else the percentage represented by procurement staff in relation to the total number of employees (1.79 per cent). These figures, followed for over a decade now, allow us to observe the changes.

A survey conducted by the author cross-referencing data gathered from a variety of sources indicates, for example, that a buyer manages an average of around €15 million/year (obviously this depends on the procurement category), compared with the $17 million recorded by the CAPS benchmarking.

FIGURE 17.8   Standard benchmarks

Average across all sectors	2012	2011	2010
Total spend as a percent os sale/revenue dollars	47.19	46.83	46.61
Percentage of total spend managed/ controlled by procurement (%)	83.39	81.45	82.16
Procurement employees as a percent of company employees (%)	1.79	1.8	1.57
Percentage of procurement employees that are strategic (%)	41.08	38.07	38.21
Annual spend on training per purchaser ($)	912	778	795
Total spend per buyer ($m)	22.76	21.12	21.44
Managed spend by buyer ($m)	16.98	15.55	16.37

The mission of the human resources department is to develop teams to meet expected performance, as well as design and lead actions that promote the implementation of policy by all employees and all people working for the company

But 'human resources' are different from a company's other resources. They generate interpretation. They require updating. They meet their objectives in symbiosis with the organization. Human resources within the procurement function are no exception to this rule.

Whilst procurement is today positioned more strategically than ever, the development of teams – and their capacity to transform procurement files and issues into company projects – will take time, especially in global and matrix organizations. Messages are even harder to interpret through the prism of different cultures. We therefore need to take into account the time necessary for change and implementation.

In this way, changes will occur at a company's own rhythm as it changes itself; the same goes for procurement maturity and positioning. This work of alignment requires genuine coordination between the human resources and the procurement departments, by forecasting evolutions and associated communication programmes.

Notes

1 Réale, Y and Dufour, B (2009), Editions d'Organisation.

2 www.hrmagazine.co.uk (Dec 2015).

3 Adams, JS (1965) 'Inequity in social exchange,' in Berkowitz, L (ed), *Advances in Experimental Social Psychology*, vol 2, Academic Press, New York, pp 267–299.

4 Leventhal, GS (1980) 'What should be done with equity theory?' in Gergen, KJ, Greenberg, MS and Willis, RW (eds), *Social Exchange: Advances in theory and research*, Plenum, New York, pp 27–55.

5 Bies, RJ and Moag, JS (1986) 'International Justice: Communication criteria of fairness,' *Research on Negotiation in Organizations*, vol 1, pp 43–55.

6 Ben W Heineman Jr (2008) 'High Performance with High Integrity' *Harvard Business Publishing*.

7 Bill Walsh with Steve Jamison and Craig Walsh (2010) *The Score Takes Care of Itself*. Portfolio Penguin.

8 The EVP (Employee Value Proposition) is the set of solutions offered by a company in exchange for a job. The EVP includes remuneration, company benefits, additional perks, the working environment and career opportunities.

9 The ACA (*Association CESA Achats et Supply Chain*) is a professional association created over 20 years ago by Emeritus Professor Olivier Bruel from the HEC Paris Group. Aimed at gathering upper executives and managers from both the procurement and supply-chain functions, most of whom are former participants in the HEC Executive Education programmes, ACA is not only a very active network, but also organizes an annual conference on major managerial themes touching on today's professional issues (www.aca-asso.com).

10 See, for example, the website of the Institute of Supply Management (ISM) for the US, or CIPS for the UK, or http://www.yqmatrix.com website for all the procurement associations.

11 'Towards a global partnership for sustainable development' (2002) COM(2002)82. Communication from the Commission to the European Parliament, the Council, the Economic and Social Committee and the Committee of the Regions.

12 Our thanks to Emmanuel, Fabien, Julien, Marius, Petty and Nadia who will recognize themselves!

13 www.ics-asso.org: ICS is a group of experts representing motivated and committed brands.

14 www.bsci-intl.org: founded in 2003 to promote greater transparency in business.

15 www.wrap.org.uk/content/sustainable-procurement: based in the UK, WRAP helps buyers in their sustainable development approaches.

16 www.sedexglobal.com: a non-profit organization aiming to promote responsible and ethical improvements.

17 Dave Frayer and Jeff Ge (presenters) 'Creating Value through Procurement/Sourcing in an Integrated Supply Chain Context', 19 November 2015.

18 Maslow, A (1954) *Motivation and Personality*.

19 Bradley L Kirkman and Debra L Shapiro, *Academy of Management Journal*; Jun 2001; 44, 3; ABI/INFORM Global, p 557.

18
Procurement information systems and dedicated web tools

ALAIN ALLEAUME

The procurement function was long 'under-tooled', mainly because software editors primarily turned their attention to computer-assisted production management (CAPM) as well as financial and accounting management, thus limiting the functional scope for procurement to the management of inventory supply on the one hand, and the processing of supplier invoicing on the other hand. But we know very well that these activities are not the buyer's core business, but rather that of players downstream of the procurement process – supply-chain managers and/or purchase-order clerks and accountants.

It was at the start of the 2000s that the market saw the arrival of new applications based on information and communications technology (ICT), also known as web technology.

The internet revolution, paired with new development languages (Java, PHP, **Microsoft.net**) and a new type of architecture (n-tier, 'thin client')[1], promoted the development of many initiatives in the area of business-to-business (B2B) solutions. The final avatar was the boom of e-marketplaces, then their quasi-disappearance in the space of a few years.

All these initiatives launched during the euphoria of the internet bubble have nevertheless fostered the emergence of new practices, namely electronic auctions, leading buyers to work in new ways internally in their companies as well as when dealing with suppliers.

Now buyers have at their disposal a full battery of tools made up of a set of application modules that can be grouped under the term 'e-purchasing solutions' (e-sourcing, e-auctions, e-procurement, e-invoicing etc) that together make up an integrated suite, a genuine procurement package that serves the procurement profession, and which we will be examining in this chapter.

One important introductory remark needs to be made: new technologies have often been presented as a revolution for the procurement profession, and their critical progress (at last) capable of offering efficiency and effectiveness to all companies (practically) overnight as soon as they are implemented. Obviously, it was in the interests of the heads of many start-ups (incidentally, generally incompetent in terms of procurement) to substantiate this thesis in that they were caught up in this internet bubble, and constantly on the prowl for capital. Yet this idea is completely false!

Above all, let's not forget that the applications that we are going to analyse and present in detail *are only tools*: their use obviously implies prior formation of a clear strategy, a sound mastery of procurement practices, definition of efficient processes and corresponding roles and responsibilities, and attainment of a satisfactory level of professionalism and maturity (even – and especially – without electronic tools). Only then will e-purchasing tools be fully effective!

In this chapter, we will be examining the following points one by one:

- integrated management software packages, with an emphasis on their procurement modules;
- procurement intranets that constitute a first level of shared information support between buyers and their internal interlocutors;
- integrated e-purchasing suites, their functional coverage, and their development in an increasingly mature market;
- finally, the constitutive elements of a procurement information system and guidelines to follow for the implementation of a controlled deployment plan.

18/1 Integrated management software packages

Let's start off by going back a little in time: historically, procurement began to be computerized in the form of procurement modules within integrated management software packages, widely known as enterprise resource planning (ERP).

These tools were developed on the basis of a few principles that constitute their strength, but also, as we will later see, their limits:

- modelling of management processes enabling the application to be preconfigured for each functional module: procurement, production management, financial and accounting management, asset management, etc;
- local embedded integration of processes, for example, integration of approval of a purchase request and budgetary control, or else integration of the issue of an order and inventory management;

- master data, such as items or suppliers, shared by all functional modules and based on a common database (suppliers, commodities codification) and a single organizational model (cost centres, departments, sites, business units etc).

Until the 1990s, information systems comprised separate applications (eg accounting, production management) in silos that communicated between themselves via specifically developed interfaces. Gradually, in order to attain the reactivity demanded by the market and to ensure the coherency of decisions, it became essential to implement integrated systems – a need soon grasped by large companies, as well as more and more small and medium-sized companies.

Such systems represent a major investment for companies – the cost of implementing them for a large international-scale company can be as high as several dozen millions of euros or dollars! – whilst use of them has deeply modified working processes and methods.

18/1.1 General characteristics of ERPs

ERPs have the following main characteristics:

- a database shared by all application modules: this way, there can be no deformation of the data used by the different modules;
- a single entry of data that can interact in different modules (in other words, no need to re-enter the same piece of data in different modules);
- a single application environment, whatever the domain: the user interface is the same whatever the module used;
- shared master data and benchmarks – eg for reporting – that work together coherently;
- standardization of processes and management rules between the company's various departments;
- an acceleration of procedures in which several decision-makers intervene thanks to workflow functions: each actor in a process can be notified by e-mail – or smartphone! – regarding information that he or she needs to enter into the system (eg approval), which conditions the triggering of the process's following stages, such as the sending of an order to a supplier;
- a user interface available in different languages;
- powerful analysis and reporting tools that are nonetheless often limited by the quality of data at the source – a point that we will discuss further on;
- openness to the outside world: direct links between the customer's information system and the supplier's information system for the issuing of orders or the receipt of invoices, or to share information on inventory levels using vendor management inventory-type (VMI) functions.

18/1.2 IT structure and functional coverage

ERPs present a three-tier 'client-server' IT architecture:

- The Presentation tier is the user interface; it depends on the operating system of the user's computer; on personal ('client') computers connected to a local network, the graphic interface can be displayed in the language chosen by the user.

- The Application tier corresponds to data-processing functions: a simple function consists in a simple enquiry whilst a complex function is a calculation of net requirements, for example. Depending on the volume of transactions to be carried out, applications may run on one or several 'server' computers.

- The Database tier manages large volumes of data stored by the company. The database may be spread over several computers, eventually remote.

In terms of basic equipment and software, ERPs can work in heterogeneous environments. The company can choose the equipment suppliers, operating systems and database managers (eg an Oracle database in a SAP environment).

The leading editors on the market have developed an offer that covers all company functions: business management, production management, procurement, inventories, maintenance, quality, accounting (general, customers, suppliers), treasury, consolidation, human resources management and so on.

Figure 18.1 presents, as an example, the general structure of the world's most widely distributed ERP: SAP.

FIGURE 18.1   Functional modules of SAP software

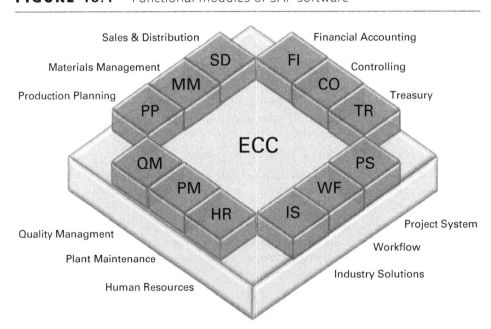

The modular structure of ERPs allows implementation of the desired modules only, with the option of supplementary modules being added subsequently. Each of the modules is itself composed of sub-modules that deal with specific functions.

As these ERPs have been set up in a wide number of companies, practically all management situations can be taken care of via the configuration of functions. In certain cases, specific configuration for a specific type of activity has been developed to facilitate implementation.

The major functional domains are the following:

- *financial management* (general accounting, accounts receivable, treasury management, cost accounting and management control, asset management, etc);
- *logistics management* in a broad sense: sales management (management of prospects and customers, order-taking, shipment and invoicing); procurement, storage, distribution and transport; production (of all types) at all planning levels; quality-monitoring at all stages; computerized maintenance management system (CMMS);
- *human resources management* deals with the management of competencies, careers, training and recruitment, not forgetting payroll management even if the latter is often managed by dedicated applications or even outsourced to specialized firms; operator work-times are recorded in the production monitoring module and can be used for the calculation of productivity bonuses;
- *project management* is a transversal issue because a project's implications are financial (payment schedule, monitoring of costs and profitability), logistical (procurement of materials and specific components, special manufacturing) and possibly human resources-related (follow-up of staff assigned to a project).

Coverage of the supply process

The material management (MM) module in SAP takes charge of inventories and purchases. It enables keeping a constant watch on the inventories in various warehouses, and management of physical flows and transport. It is interfaced with the sales management module to take charge of the shipment of products to customers.

The system automatically generates an offer of quantities to resupply based on a calculation of the net requirement from material requirement planning (MRP), taking into account logistical constraints (eg minimum order levels), inventory levels and work-in-process, and master production schedule (MPS) production forecasts.

Users can also manually enter purchase requests for out-of-stock products or for the purchase of services, for example.

The system directly transmits purchase requests to the procurement department, that transforms them into orders. Buyers have access to basic functions for using the procurement data in the system.

We can, for example, compare prices during the supply process, or automate the choice of the supplier or the order-generation process. Supplier-evaluation functions select the best suppliers on the basis of the criteria defined by the user. The purchase operations are validated by authorized persons, with the aid of an electronic signature. Orders and delivery schedules are transmitted to the suppliers by mail, fax or electronically via EDI (electronic data interchange) or e-mail. The order history established allows the status of orders to be monitored and keeps records of deliveries and invoices already received.

ERPs offer the possibility of interfacing with the e-procurement solutions described further.

Inventory management

Inventories are managed by the MM module, in terms of value and quantities. This module manages common kinds of inventory management documents: inflow, outflow and transfer, but also special stocks (batches, consignment stock, returnable packaging and components stocked by subcontractors). Entries on goods movements lead to an updating of data in the financial accounting, asset accounting and management control modules.

Whether the physical inventory is carried out periodically or continually, via global counts, surveys or cyclical methods, the system assists the user, thanks to very practical tools allowing data to be entered and many automatic evaluations to be carried out. We can use stock-valuation methods such as last-in-first-out (LIFO) or first-in-first-out (FIFO).

The warehouse management system (WMS) module offers flexible automatic management of the movement of goods, keeping a permanent trace of all items stocked in extremely complex warehouse structures. By using high-performance stock arrival and issue techniques, WMS optimizes the flow of items as well as warehouse capacity and enables products to be stored in optimal places so that they are available when required. The possibility of interfacing WMS with manual terminals, barcode readers and automatic storage systems fills out the many processes included in the module.

Invoices received in hard copy or electronically via EDI are automatically monitored by the system. When an invoice referring to an order is entered, the system can automatically generate the invoice that it expects to receive and offer an automatic match with the issued order, the record of the goods' receipt in the system, and the invoice recorded by accounting services. The payment of an invoice is automatically blocked if unauthorized disparities are identified, concerning, for example, the delivery date, the delivered quantity or the agreed price.

18/1.3 The ERP market

The ERP market is today shared by a few large leading editors including SAP and Oracle, the latter having taken over two major players, Peoplesoft and JD Edwards, in the 2000s.

The global ERP market is estimated at over US\$25 billion, and dominated by SAP and Oracle that together represent about 40 per cent of the market share, with SAP holding a stronger share.

It should be noted that over one-third of this market is composed of a considerable number of players that are far smaller in size, often country- or region-based, or else sectorally focused (eg hospitals).

Some of these editors are better positioned on the so-called middle market, targeting SMEs/SMIs through their fee model and their ease of implementation. Readers can refer to regularly updated surveys published by specialized institutes such as Gartner or CXP in France.

The ERP is the vertebral column of the company's information system: without it, we cannot imagine the construction of a procurement information system. The ERP(s) set up in a company are therefore indispensable.

18/2 Procurement intranets

The development of procurement intranets represented an initial attempt to set up a genuine working tool for the buyer community at the end of the 1990s as part of the wave of corporate intranet development. We should also point out that the term 'intranet' has a double connotation:

- on the one hand, *technological*: it is an application using web technologies (HTML pages, hypertext links, etc) installed on the company's servers according to a non-intrusive logic, that is, not permitting external access from the internet, with the company's firewall filtering access. In contrast, a supplier extranet refers to a web solution that allows suppliers to communicate with buyers by connecting to the company's server or an external server;

- on the other hand, *functional*: intranet applications designed from web technologies have allowed the development of functions such as collaborative spaces for information exchange including, for example, the option for the user to subscribe to information updates.

The principle that quickly became widespread is that of a corporate intranet accessed by the user via a homepage offering links to the company's different professional spaces (HR, R&D, procurement, etc) – veritable professional one-stop-shops.

Main functions

Depending on the company, procurement intranet has developed, with varying fortunes, around the following functions:

1 A homepage that generally presents:
   - general information on the procurement function: its missions, its organization with an organization chart and often a directory of collaborators – or even a procurement community Facebook-like enterprise solution such as Yammer;
   - access to downloadable documents accessible by all employees: procurement policy, procurement procedures, definition of Incoterms® for example;
   - an information thread via an RSS feed;

- a procurement community forum via a blog or wiki-type space;
- finally, links for professional applications as shown in Figure 18.2.

2 Themed spaces:

- a contract library: a list of procurement contracts with access to summary sheets and/or contracts that can be downloaded according to given rules, and with automatic management of alerts prior to the contract's expiry date;
- a procurement information database: per procurement category, access to a *vade mecum* on good practices, standard work documents, the list of qualified suppliers and corresponding contracts etc;
- procurement project management: for a particular domain or identified project, a group of buyers and users/specifiers can share work documents combined with task management.

FIGURE 18.2   Example of functional architecture of a purchasing intranet

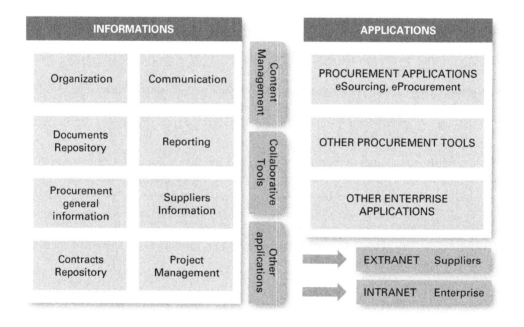

The relative failure of procurement intranets is often due to problems in administration and updating of information as they often operate as 'potluck suppers' where everyone is free to post information and share feedback, for example. On the other hand, large companies that have managed to invest in internal communication with dedicated resources, rely on procurement portals to publicize the actions of the corporate procurement structure to the wider procurement community as well as to business teams.

Globally, the current evolution is to bring the procurement intranet closer to the notion of a collaborative procurement portal that can be associated with Web 2.0 tools such as the already mentioned wikis or corporate social networks such as Yammer. In addition, we can observe an interesting evolution, as in widgets on a PC homepage, towards multi-application integration of tools that support the technology of portals such as Microsoft's Sharepoint.

18/3 E-procurement solutions

E-procurement is the domain covering all *new procurement technologies aimed at managing all transactions related to the supply process, from the purchase request up to processing and payment of the supplier's invoice* (also known as Procure to Pay or P2P solutions).

E-procurement solutions emerged on the US market at the end of the 1990s, put forward by two main editors, Ariba and Commerce One. This was the period when online commerce was just beginning to develop in the United States. A few large distributors such as Grainger, helped by electronic catalogue specialists such as Harbinger, began offering web access to electronic catalogues presenting the full range of their products, in other words tens of thousands of articles.

The issue then became that of enabling professional users to place orders via web platforms whilst using their companies' internal management systems to pay suppliers rather than proceeding to pay directly by bankcard as in the case of a private customer buyer.

18/3.1 The operating principles of e-procurement solutions

The operating principles that led to the development of e-procurement solutions are the following:

- offering the user access to personalized product catalogues in which the product list has been predefined with unit prices and purchase conditions that reflect the umbrella agreements negotiated by the procurement department;

- enabling the user to create, from his or her workstation, multi-supplier procurement shopping carts with a simple product-search system and clear display of useful information (product characteristics with photos, unit prices, purchase conditions, etc);

- implementing an internal approval workflow that, depending on the type of purchase and/or the purchase sum, enables then automatically creates the corresponding order(s) for each supplier;

- automatically addressing these orders to suppliers via different methods: e-mail, fax server, supplier extranet, XML;[2]

- giving the user the means to acknowledge receipt of the delivered products electronically – equivalent to a payment authorization – by using the tool to validate the quantities received, then allowing accountants to automatically match the order/receipt/invoice in order to proceed to pay supplier invoices.

18/3.2 The contributions of e-procurement solutions

E-procurement solutions should allow users rapid 'Amazon-like' control, and they should no longer have good or bad reasons to proceed with out-of-the-system 'maverick buying'[3] provided that they have fast and easy access to the right product with the right listed supplier.

Other advantages for users include: the option of creating favourite shopping carts, real-time access to information (what stage are we at with approval of the order?) without having to call upon the procurement department that can then focus on activities associated with higher added value.

Basically, an e-procurement solution can be considered as a key supplement to an ERP whose vocation is to cover so-called production purchases. The objective is then to cover 100 per cent of *all of the company's other* external expense items thanks to an information system that allows:

- the purchase's compliance with the procurement policy to be ensured – in particular ensuring compliance with the negotiated umbrella agreements – with the ultimate objective being the elimination of so-called maverick buying;
- all product and service purchases to be formalized by orders that comply with the applicable rules of delegation, thus ensuring all necessary legal security;
- detailed tracking of soft/hard accruals and expenses to pay so that management controllers can then follow these up exhaustively and reliably – indeed, all orders are tracked by the system and no supply or supplier service can be carried out without being backed by an order;
- the quality of procurement reporting to be improved by capturing necessary information at the source, with the right level of detail, at the time when the expense (ie the order) is committed to, and not, as too often remains the case, through the records in the suppliers' accounts payable;
- and finally, the traceability of all procurement acts carried out by the company to be ensured, with this traceability sometimes being a necessity due to certain regulatory constraints.[4]

In addition, responsibility is placed upon the user: with direct access to a supply tool, this user can determine his or her consumption in relation to a forecast budget, and it is up to him or her to validate the products or services that he or she receives from suppliers in order to trigger supplier payment, thus resulting in fewer supplier disputes.

18/3.3 The functional scope of an e-procurement tool

First of all, it is appropriate to specify what differentiates the scope covered by an ERP and its functional limits, and what contributes to making quasi-indispensable the implementation of an e-procurement solution to supplement the system for controlling the company's external expenses.

The ergonomics of the e-procurement tool is far more convivial than that of an ERP and requires practically no specific training for the user, especially one who only has occasional access to the tool. This facilitates its mass deployment, contrary to the case of an ERP that requires ad hoc training, and as a result, is devoted to a limited population of purchase-order clerks who use the tool daily.

Catalogue management is based on a principle that is profoundly different from that of the management of the item database in an ERP. Indeed, whilst ERP requires relatively weighty administration of items due to the requirements related to other processes such as production management, e-procurement offers a new mode of administration of data namely based on the principle of having the catalogues updated by the suppliers themselves – with a buyer intervening to validate each update.

FIGURE 18.3 Example of approval workflow

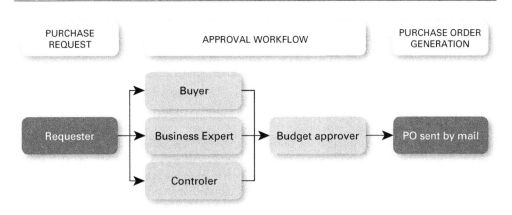

Workflow management functions are far more easily personalizable than in an ERP. Indeed, there is much more flexibility in the configuration of approval rules, with the possibility for the user to add extra approvers, as well as to visualize the state of progress of the different approval stages of purchase requests.

Modelling a workflow in an IT tool allows tasks to be automated with roles assigned to actors depending on a predefined process, translated into a role/responsibility/task table – for example, delegation of authority rules for order approval or purchase requisition in the case of ad hoc purchases.

One key element for the successful implementation of an e-procurement solution consists in *extending the scope concerned beyond catalogue purchases alone*, that often only represent 10 to 20 per cent of the total sum of purchases (see Figure 18.4).

The e-procurement tool can then be considered as a front-end user enabling any requester to create shopping carts from catalogues placed at their disposal or to express a requirement in the form of free text or via preconfigured webforms.[5]

In the second case, this is a matter of allowing the user to easily provide, via scroll-down menus, the necessary information for: first, creating the accounting code that will then be automatically taken up at the invoice-matching stage; next, generating a workflow that, depending on the procurement category populated in the system, will address the request to the buyer in question.

FIGURE 18.4   Process on catalogue or non-catalogue purchases

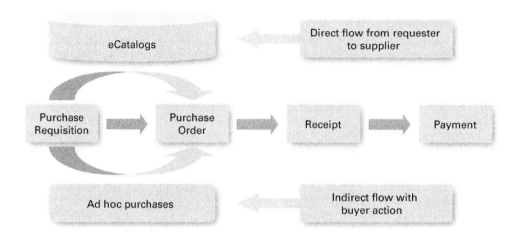

Once the buyer's task is done, and price and supplier information are indicated, the purchase request can be completed, and the usual approval circuit implemented.[6]

In summary: the user connects onto a homepage that gives access to a list of procurement categories (scroll-down menu or displayed list). The buyer can also use a search engine. Once the procurement category has been selected, a list of items appears in the form of an electronic catalogue as on e-commerce sites such as **amazon.com**. The user can then start to create a shopping cart. If the product or service is not found in the available catalogues, then the tool will allow the user to express an 'off-catalogue' requirement in a free-text format or by using web forms and filling in the information necessary for the request to be processed.

One major difference in relation to e-commerce sites is to be noted: the list of items will have been negotiated beforehand by the procurement department with one or several selected suppliers, on the basis of preferential prices, with delivery conditions specified in the umbrella contract.

18/3.4 Catalogue management

Catalogue management is a key factor in the success of an e-procurement project. Indeed, it entails the setting up of an efficient operating method with suppliers, and on the other hand, the internal setting up of administration rules and necessary resources.

E-procurement solution editors all offer a catalogue management module based on the following principles:

- the catalogues are hosted on a production server, but also replicated on a pre-production server. The supplier company has an extranet-type access enabling a new version of its catalogue to be loaded onto its pre-production server in the desired format (CSV, XML, iDoc, etc);

- the tool identifies any modifications that have been made and generates an alert workflow addressed to the buyer in question;
- the latter logs onto the application and approves – or not – the suggested modifications; once approved, the catalogue can then be loaded onto the production server.

This catalogue management can be entrusted to a third party specialized in content management such as Vinimaya, JCatalog or Poet and/or a marketplace like Hubwoo, recently taken over by Perfect Commerce (see Figure 18.5).

But in many companies, it is the internal administrator him- or herself who loads catalogue updates and has a tool, often in Excel format, enabling comparisons to be made with different catalogue versions.

There is also the option of directly accessing a private catalogue on the supplier's website, with the user filling a shopping cart in 'punch-out' mode.

FIGURE 18.5 Catalogue management functional diagram

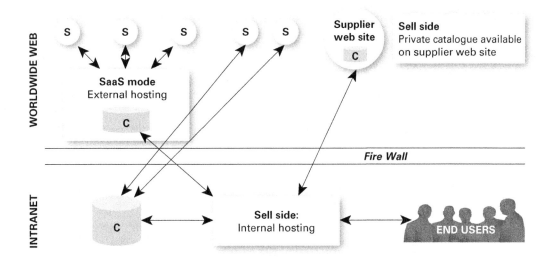

In practice, the user who fills a shopping cart is directly directed to the supplier's website in a way that is transparent to him or her. The user can then select products on a predefined list and with negotiated prices. Once the different item lines have been selected, the 'punch-out' enables the user to automatically integrate the selected lines in the shopping cart, then to continue filling the cart, which will then follow the customary approval circuit and be transformed into an order and then sent to the supplier via the internet.

18/3.5 The e-procurement solutions market

We generally distinguish three different ways of implementing an e-procurement solution:

- *buy-side*, that consists in acquiring licences from an editor on the market, and setting up the solution internally on company servers 'on the premises';
- *sell-side*, that enables pre-identified users to access a supplier's web platform – eg Office Depot – via a private access and according to rules predefined by the buyer;
- *application service-provider* (ASP) offered by a majority of editors, that has recently evolved towards SaaS (Software as a Service) as part of the shift towards cloud-computing offers.

The implementation of an e-procurement project requires a so-called scoping phase. The more detailed this phase, the better the chances that the project will have of being deployed quickly and without major pitfalls.

Sell-side

The advantage of the sell-side mode is that it is fast to implement as it requires no investment. As a result, it facilitates change management and the appropriation of this new type of software.

But unlike punch-out, the sell-side mode does not allow any integration with the internal accounting management system: there can be no automation of a three-way matching process between the order, the receipt and the supplier invoice. Certain management rules can be nonetheless configured on the supplier's platform: an individualized access code, a ceiling amount, supply of reporting with the necessary management attributes (cost centres, categories, etc). However, the approach is limited by the fact that there is no integration with the management system, and that it is difficult to extend it to several supplier platforms and thus multiply accesses, bearing in mind that this also creates a relative dependence on the supplier.

The ASP mode

The rental-hosting mode is an interesting alternative for companies that desire to variabilize their costs and to limit the involvement of internal IT resources.

In addition, service-providers contribute added-value services such as helping their customers to 'integrate' suppliers via supplier 'onboarding' for example, in other words 'supplier affiliation', then to manage and maintain catalogues hosted on their servers.

The latter service can also be the object of a specific service contract when the company wishes to acquire and install an e-procurement application but outsource catalogue management.

The players on the e-procurement solutions market

The e-procurement solutions market is made up of a considerable number of players:[7]

- US editors such as Ariba, the market's long-standing player, taken over in 2012 by SAP, or else Coupa, arriving far more recently on the market, and one of the rising stars on the market of cloud-based spend-management solutions.

- French editors present on the market since 2000, that have developed activity undergoing strong growth on the US market, such as Ivalua or b-pack – now called Determine since the recent merger with the US-based vendor Selectica.

It should be noted that certain ERP editors such as SAP, Oracle or Qualiac have developed their own e-procurement modules, their goal not being to sell them in stand-alone modes but to offer them as an extension of the application suite installed on their customers' equipment.

18/3.6 Implementation of an e-procurement project

A key scoping phase

The implementation of an e-procurement project requires a so-called scoping phase. The more in-depth this phase, the better the project's chances of then being deployed quickly and without major pitfalls. This scoping phase has the following objectives:

- setting the boundaries of the operational, organizational and project procurement scope:
- listing the functional requirements of the identified professional requirements and of the current management rules:
- making choices and decisions that take into account expressed requirements and the possibilities of standard market solutions:
- roughly costing the project and evaluating the return on investment (ROI):
- presenting a business case to an ad hoc decision-making committee.

To meet this aim, our recommendation is to set up a project team that should necessarily include representatives of all professions concerned: procurement, naturally, but also management control, accounts receivable and all operational departments concerned.

Workshops can be organized with a pre-established shortlist of editors that may emerge from an initial request for information (RFI) phase.

These workshops should enable, on the one hand, a sound understanding of the offer and the functional coverage of the solutions presented, and on the other hand, match this coverage with internal requirements in order to remain within the software's standard version.

Different integration models to evaluate

The scoping study should allow structuring choices to be made in terms of the level of integration between the e-procurement solution and the ERP already installed. Basically, we can distinguish two integration modes, as represented by Figure 18.6 below: 1) procure-to-receipt mode – the e-procurement tool is used as a front-end tool to establish purchase requests, but the whole of the downstream flow is processed in the ERP (order/invoice); 2) stand-alone mode – the e-procurement tool manages the whole of the flow, except for the accounting entries (general ledger) that remains in the ERP.

FIGURE 18.6   Integration diagram between e-procurement tool and ERP

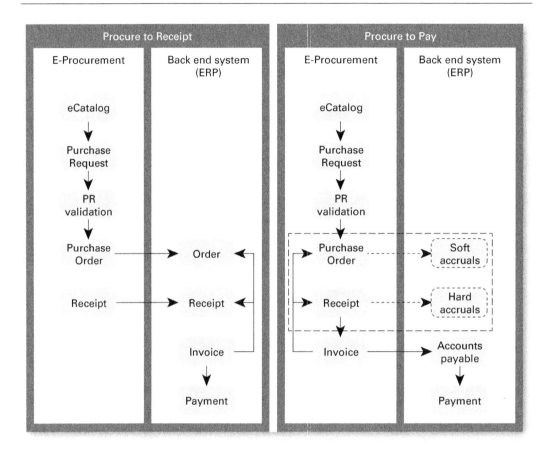

Evaluation of the return on investment

After these workshops, the project team should be capable of, first, finalizing functional and technical requirements specifications, and second, obtaining quantification elements from editors. It is then up to the team to go through a request for proposal (RFP) process to obtain a clear and precise commitment from editors and to negotiate external costs.

The compilation of a business case will comprise both cost elements and an evaluation of potential gains contributed by implementation of the solution.

Standard scoping of an e-procurement project

An estimated three to four months is required for the scoping phase, as well as roughly the same amount of time to select an editor or service-provider and to launch implementation. The project may be deployed in a number of directions:

- *A procurement scope direction*: do we limit ourselves initially to catalogue purchases? Do we cover all non-production purchases or do we place ourselves outside the procurement scope by calling on specific processes for travel or interim purchases for example?
- *A geographical direction*: which entities and countries are involved in the launch phase? Should extension to several languages be foreseen?
- *A functional direction*: this is a matter of making certain functional choices, for example, whether to take account of integration with budget control from the outset of the project or not.

The tool may be configured very quickly, within a few weeks depending on the global scope. The first months of a pilot phase can indicate actions required for deploying the solution widely – deployment that may take three to nine months depending on the scope covered.

18/3.7 Current developments

New functions or functions specific to certain solutions

Recent versions of the solutions available on the market show an enhancement of functions covering diverse activities including:

- specific modules adapted to specific procurement processes such as the purchase of intellectual services (Ivalua Prestations, Ariba Professional Services, Opase, Oalia) or travel services (Traveldoo, Expedia, Concur etc);
- in the case of off-catalogue purchases, certain solutions now offer the user the option of directly sending requests for quotations to suppliers pre-qualified by the procurement department, to select the most competitive offer, and to automatically update the shopping cart, then – following approval by the person in charge of the budget or the buyer in question – to directly send the order to the supplier.
- extensions to new functional domains such as budget control, contract management and the processing of invoices (e-invoicing).

An important development in terms of invoice processing and dematerialization

The processing of invoices relates to the capacity for accountants to record invoices directly in the e-procurement tool, to quasi-automatically match the order-receipt-invoice, and to pay invoices processed in the management system via the development of an ad hoc interface.

Invoice dematerialization relates to the capacity for accounts to receive invoices in an appropriate electronic format, to record them automatically, then to activate their electronic archiving. Archiving is a key point due to tax obligations regarding, in particular, the traceability of VAT.

Significant players with differentiated offers

Apart from e-procurement players such as Ariba, Determine, Ivalua or Baseware for e-invoicing, several types of players exist on the invoice dematerialization market:[8]

- editors of optical character recognition (OCR) solutions such as Itesoft or Readsoft, based on the principle of scanning the document to recognize characters and corresponding fields, and converting it into an 'intelligible' electronic format;
- service-providers specialized in mass document processing, relying on OCR solutions such as French companies Jouve, Numen or Docapost;
- invoice-file exchange and archiving platforms such as B-process, taken over in 2012 by Ariba, or Tradeshift which has recently come onto the market with a fast-growing activity.

A significant evolution towards the SaaS-mode offer

Is the SaaS offer a natural evolution of the ASP offer? Not exactly. True, SaaS also offers the advantages of ASP. No fixed assets are required, in other words, no investment in equipment (servers) or licences – the only outlay is for operating costs. Few resources are required by the IT department: application maintenance is entrusted to the editor. Also, the offer is scalable, with the budget evolving in relation to the number of users and modules deployed, as well as reversible: contracts are generally negotiated for a three-year period, potentially allowing the editor's choice or the project scope to be reviewed.

But what has fundamentally changed is how editors have reviewed their development model in such a way that all their customers access the same application platform: in other words, there is no more room for customized developments at the customer's request. Editors have to develop rich functional administration in order to facilitate configuration of each customer process without needing to access the application's code in order to meet a specific customer requirement – for example, in cases where workflow modelling required access to the code, these are now taken care of by a functional administrator who can make any changes or modifications as the company's internal processes change. Of course, the great restriction for companies is that they must adapt to the solution's standard; it is now up to user clubs to influence editor roadmaps in order to integrate new functions anticipated by the profession – procurement in our case – in upcoming versions. Generally speaking, editors offer minor evolutions of their applications every 3 or 6 months and major ones every 12–18 months, with such evolutions becoming mandatory, even if this was not always the case previously!

18/4 Marketplaces

The concept of the 'marketplace' met with wide media attention during the euphoric internet bubble period, and often triggered the setting up of start-ups created for this purpose. Today, practically none are left – even if a few hangers-on are still around, for example, in the aeronautics sector, Boost Aerospace in Europe and Exostar in North America. Otherwise, marketplaces have purely and simply vanished, or else been the object of mergers and acquisitions, for example Quadrem taken over by Ariba in 2012, or else they have become service-providers like any other on the e-procurement/e-sourcing market, such as French provider Hubwoo, recently acquired by US provider Perfect Commerce, Italo-French provider Bravo Solution or German provider Supply On.

18/4.1 The concept of the marketplace

A marketplace can be defined as a hub linking customer companies and suppliers, facilitating multiple exchanges between n customers and p suppliers (see Figure 18.7).

Let's also specify that a marketplace *has never had the vocation of being a global procurement centre for its customers*. Its underlying economic model has been, on the one hand, to pool IT resources (equipment, IT developments, maintenance, help desk), and on the other hand, share professional application solutions with a pooling of developments related to evolutions in functions.

FIGURE 18.7   Functional principle of a marketplace

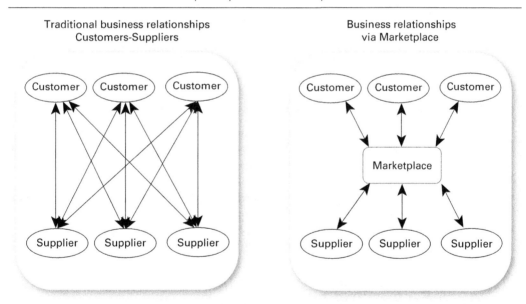

The ASP model and the corresponding service offer

This approach is, like the rental-hosting model, also called ASP mode, already previously mentioned. The services offered by marketplaces are based on a certain number of applications, either developed by their own technology or supplied by specialized editors.

One of the major functions that should have been the strength of the marketplace model is the concept of a single communication platform between the buyer company and its suppliers with hub-like exchange and supplier portal functions.

18/4.2 Putting the marketplace concept in perspective

To conclude on this aspect, we will endeavour to reply to the following two questions:

- Why did marketplaces fail?
- What do they currently contribute in relation to the issues raised in optimizing customer–supplier processes?

The failure of marketplaces can be blamed on the drying up of capital after the bursting of the internet bubble, but it is also, and above all, related to problems inherent to the suggested model, namely: a lack of governance between shareholders and customers, and a lack of visibility on pricing models, namely subscription costs for suppliers; the market's lack of maturity and a far more difficult implementation in companies than expected, requiring appropriate change management.

Yet the contribution of marketplaces is far from negligible and attention deserves to be drawn to a few elements that remain relevant:

- the emergence of a standard format of exchanges between customers and suppliers, based on the XML format previously mentioned;[9]
- the development of the offer in ASP mode, whose latest avatar is the development of the SaaS offer, which can be described as its ultimate point of progression;
- the communication-hub and supplier-portal concept, major elements in the evolution of procurement information systems.

Finally, we can also add that most large companies have in fact chosen, by implementing supplier portals to back up their e-procurement and/or e-sourcing applications, to develop their own 'private' marketplaces when dealing with their supplier markets. By enabling its customers to open up the supplier market through the Ariba Supplier Network, the US editor Ariba has developed an innovative service offer. So much so did the offer whet the desire of the ERP market leader, SAP, that it acquired Ariba at the end of 2012 at a value worthy of the most incredible success stories of the now-burst internet bubble!

18/5 E-sourcing solutions

As shown by Figure 18.8, e-sourcing solutions cover the chain of procurement processing in the so-called upstream phase, unlike e-procurement solutions (and ERPs) that manage the downstream process.

We can therefore say that the shared boundary between the two functional scopes is contract management, that today is covered by most e-sourcing solutions, but that can also be included in e-procurement and ERP solutions with regard to order updates, for example for the application of a price-revision formula.

FIGURE 18.8 Functional coverage of e-procurement and e-sourcing solutions

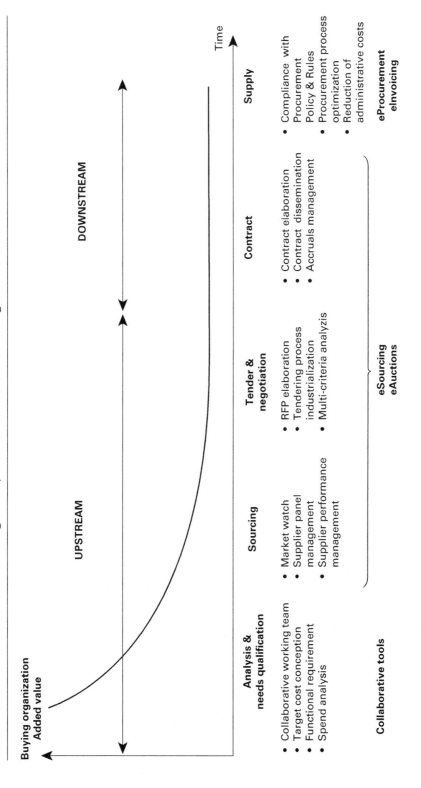

E-sourcing solutions historically stem from a first 'functional component', the e-tendering 'engine' developed by marketplaces as part of their offer.

As software editors and service-providers became aware that the placing of calls for tenders online deals with only part of the functional requirements of the procurement profession, they quickly improved their solution designs *to cover the whole of the procurement process*, from the preparation of procurement strategies, then the evaluation and definition of requirements, up to the final selection of the best offer and the implementation of the supplier contract.

18/5.1 An e-tendering module at the heart of e-sourcing solutions

The e-tendering module covers the process of preparing a tender up to the final attribution of the best offer. To describe this process, we customarily use the terms RFI, RFP and RFQ, all referred to by the catch-all term RFx; we will now analyse their main components.

RFI (request for information)

The RFI may be understood as an *in-depth request for information* and a *call for proposals* by which the buyer addresses, to several potential suppliers, a pre-formatted questionnaire referred to as a 'template'.

The tool then allows automatic filtering to be carried out on the basis of various fields identified from the outset as mandatory, for example quality approval or turnover. If the latter is lower than a certain value deemed to be critical, then the company will not be selected for the following phase.[10]

RFP (request for proposal)

Once a list of potential candidates has been drawn up, the following stage consists in sending them all necessary documents for submitting an offer.

If the content of the services and supplies requires adjustments and/or a new phase of qualification, we speak of an 'RFP'; if not, with the requirement being clearly defined, we use the term 'RFQ'.

RFQ (request for quotation)

Once the specification of the requirement and/or the scope of services has been clearly established, the buyer makes a shortlist of tendering suppliers, creates a single response framework in a 'template' format, and can then automatically compare the price and performance aspects of offers as well as evaluate different attribution scenarios. The buyer can then finally select the offer considered to be the most interesting, and automatically notify the chosen supplier.

Beyond e-RFX-type functions, most editors on the market have enriched their offers to meet the functional requirements of professional buyers more closely. Such editors thus offer a set of functions and/or supplementary modules that allow compiling a full battery of procurement tools such as collaborative project management, procurement knowledge management, the buyer's dashboard, the suppliers' portal, procurement contract management, and the spend analysis and procurement performance management tool.

18/5.2 Reverse auctions

The principle behind electronic reverse auctions is to invite a small number of suppliers to put forward their best offer over a brief set time period, one hour for example, with the ongoing option of improving their offers by lowering them (hence the term 'reverse auctions') via comparison of their own offers with those of their competitors.

The key element for the supplier is therefore to be aware, at every moment, of the position of its own offer. The buyer may decide to put online a graph depicting the offers as they come up, presented anonymously, or else give information to each supplier on the position of its offer only in relation to its competitors. The buyer defines a starting price, and whether he or she can decide or not to set a so-called reserve price that enables him or her to declare an auction as abortive if this price level is not reached.

The buyer can determine the minimum level of the increment to outbid another bid, either in terms of a sum or a percentage.

In the event that one of the suppliers makes a new offer in the very last moments before the designated period elapses, the tool can launch an extension, of five minutes for example, in order to give other competitors a final chance to outbid the other competitors.

Reverse auctions: myths and reality

Reverse auctions were enthusiastically received when the first platforms appeared at the start of the 2000s. So popular did they become that some were tempted to think that they would become the alpha and omega of electronic procurement tools.

We can now observe that many companies have stepped away from 'all-out auctioning', but in certain well-targeted cases, the mechanisms implemented by an auction greatly facilitate the buyer's task. Indeed, auctions are a quick and efficient means for obtaining the best market price whilst ensuring transparency and equal treatment for offers.

Indeed, auctions allow the buyer to dispense with the final negotiation stage, often similar to 'bargaining', which is time-consuming and – when we think about it – diverts the buyer who should instead focus efforts on the upstream phases of the procurement process.

This observation naturally leads us to specify that the auction *is only the final and optional phase of an entire process initiated by the e-sourcing tool*.[11] The auction can only be successful if flawless work is carried out upstream. In particular, it is necessary for the suppliers' technical offers to be equivalent to one another on all points.[12]

It is also necessary to bear in mind that auctions have been attacked by many, namely suppliers, due to a lack in ethics, as observed in some cases. Ever since, decrees and ethics charters have made timely appearances to issue reminders on the principles to be respected when this type of supplier-selection process is carried out. As in other areas, the tool in itself is not bad: it is the use made of it and the intelligence guiding its process that result in it being efficient or not, ethical or not.

Analysis of multi-criteria offers in a TCO-type approach

On this last point, we need to specify that in the RFQ phase, the buyer generally proceeds to analyse multi-criteria offers. The buyer can then carry out what is known as a *balancing of offers*. This consists in bringing each offer back to an equivalent basis of comparison by taking into account factors other than price.[13]

The reader will not be surprised as this approach merely borrows, point by point, the familiar bases and principles of the multi-criteria analyses already presented in Chapter 10.

It also goes without saying that at the RFQ stage, implementation of an overall cost or TCO (total cost of ownership) approach including all costs relating to the acquisition of a product or service (transport, guarantee, maintenance, etc) is essential.

All these elements will be taken up at the auction stage, allowing an objective approach not exclusively based on the unique criterion of price.

18/5.3 The market of e-sourcing solutions

We distinguish two types of players: service-providers with offers basically relying on the rental-hosting model such as Bravo Solution or Synertrade; specialized editors such as Ariba, Emptoris, Ivalua or Iasta that offer an offer either in *buy-side* (say *on-premise*) mode – or in *SaaS* mode, with Ariba having opted for a 100 per cent SaaS-mode offer.

To fill out this portrait, we can add the offer developed by a few large ERP editors such as SAP with its SRM[14] module or Oracle/Peoplesoft. SAP's takeover of US editors Frictionless then Ariba, Emptoris' takeover by IBM, shows the interest invested by major market players in this product segment.

18/5.4 Implementation of an e-sourcing project

E-sourcing solutions offer the advantage, from the point of view of the information system, of not jeopardizing major interactions with the company's other systems, thus facilitating their deployment. In short, an e-sourcing project is a project managed by and for the procurement department that requires limited involvement of the IT department, namely when the choice of the SaaS mode is made.

Similarly, the processes involved in e-sourcing are not transactional as for e-procurement, and as a result, they have little or no impact on the company's other transversal processes such as rules on delegation of authority or supplier payment. In other words, project risk is low on a company level. It is up to the management of the procurement function – and this management alone – whether to implement the project's dynamic and appropriate change management.

A stage-by-stage approach requiring ad hoc organization

As a general rule, companies start off with an initial pilot phase that is relatively simple to implement, for not only does it usually rely on a solution hosted outside the company with necessary assistance for running 'events' (RFPs), but it also only mobilizes a small team of proactive and motivated buyers.

Difficulties start when the decision is made to deploy the tool as widely as possible, the objective being that the e-sourcing platform will become the common and single working tool of the whole community of buyers. It then becomes necessary to set up project organization and to mobilize ad hoc resources, ie: a project manager from the procurement organization, a network of buyers designated as super-users, functional support, functional administration and finally technical administration.

Return on investment difficult to evaluate

Before launching into an e-sourcing project deployed on a large scale, an investment decision – like all IT projects – requires presentation of a business case to the top management, with calculations on the return on investment (ROI).

Paradoxically, whilst there are no doubts regarding the usefulness of such a tool, the exercise is not a light one. Indeed, it would not be reasonable to attribute, to the setting up of the tool, all procurement savings identified in the procurement department's annual savings plan. At the most, we might agree to recognize the tool as allowing extra procurement savings compared to classic methods – an estimated 3–5 per cent in such savings when reverse auctions are employed.

However, there are some savings that can be perfectly attributed to the shortening of the average cycle for processing a call for tenders. These savings can be evaluated by estimating the rate in increase in the average number of calls for tenders processed per buyer. Published figures provide an estimation of 25–35 per cent. In terms of purely qualitative gains, we can note the following:

- the traceability of exchanges with suppliers and transparency fostering better operational ethics;
- the recording and archiving of calls for tenders that can be restudied/reused when a new call for tenders is held on the same subject;
- the development of work in project mode via the creation of a multi-disciplinary team associated with a tender file;
- creation of a knowledge database: eg the possibility of reusing previous tender files, sharing a library of templates amongst buyers;
- improvement of negotiation techniques, with the tool allowing simulations to be made based on tender-attribution scenarios.

18/6 Other modules offered in e-purchasing application suites

Procurement contract management modules have emerged relatively recently on the market. These are a useful supplement to the application offer of e-sourcing solutions as they integrate the end of the upstream procurement process, namely the setting up of the contract.

18/6.1 The contract lifecycle management module

The functions offered by editors are the following:

- access to a standard clause list allowing the buyer to draft the procurement contract;
- management of approval rules (workflow);
- management of versioning visible by the working team;
- capability of online sharing of the draft contract with the supplier;
- automatic integration of the terms negotiated following the RFP process;
- production of synthesis forms presenting all data necessary to manage the contract – supplier, procurement category, price, specific conditions (eg volume discounts), duration of validity;
- management of alerts in relation to the contract renewal date;
- contract archiving with configurable access authorization rules.

We can note the existence on the market of solutions specifically for legal departments, enabling them to manage all types of contracts either on the sell-side or on the buy-side.

The advantage of the contract management offer of e-purchasing solution editors lies in the solution's integration, enabling interaction between the different modules of the application suite such as access to all contracts associated with a supplier from the supplier relationship management module (see below).

18/6.2 The spend analysis module

Spend analysis tools are an essential element in procurement management as they enable an ongoing and specific mapping of the procurement scope in answer to the following basic questions: What am I buying? How much? And from whom? And ultimately, who is buying – or more exactly, who is spending – on which cost centre? The questions apply to records over a set time interval: last month, since the start of the financial year, over 12 calendar months etc.

We use the term 'spend cube' to illustrate this capacity to access data according to three dimensions: the supplier, the procurement category, the cost centre. One of the characteristics of these tools is their capacity to carry out what we call the 'drill down'. The principle is, first, to define a level of 'granularity', that is, a level of refinement for the data that we wish to analyse. In other words, if we wish to analyse the supplier dimension, for example, it is important to take into account the cascade structure of the supplier organization, ie: *Level 1*, the manufacturing site or commercial agency (that in France corresponds to the SIRET number (ie the actual place of operations); *Level 2*, the main establishment associated with the corporate name (the SIREN number in France, in the UK the company registration number); or *Level 3*, the parent or holding company in the case of a multi-subsidiary group.

Similarly, for the nomenclature of procurement categories, three levels are generally used, or even more if relevant from the procurement perspective: at which granularity level shall I construct my procurement strategies?

- *Level 1*: purchasing domain – eg for indirect purchasing: IT, marketing, general expenses;
- *Level 2*: purchasing category – eg for IT purchases: equipment, software, services;
- *Level 3*: purchasing sub-category – eg for IT equipment sub-category: PCs, servers, printers, data storage etc.

As far as the company's internal organization is concerned, the basic level at which external expenses are allocated accounting-wise is the cost centre that often corresponds to the notion of a unit, itself attached to a department, in turn attached to a division. Levels can be multiple. A cost centre can also be identified as being associated with an entity located in a given country. This allows adding a fourth dimension of analysis that is very useful for procurement: the country or region.

Once these basic principles have been set out, it is important to understand how these tools for analysing procurement expenses stand out from the customary tools enabling requests to be carried out, known as business intelligence tools.

These tools are effective if the data that we wish to analyse is appropriately structured. They are particularly useful in financial departments, for example, in conducting analyses for budget monitoring that rely on a standardized chart of accounts and organization divided into cost centres.

To develop a spend cube as mentioned above, we must rely on a common and shared procurement nomenclature and supplier reference. However, in large companies, complexity stems from the co-existence of several ERPs deployed in different subsidiary entities, with each ERP having its own item-code and supplier-code systems. In this context, business intelligence tools are inefficient, for the data to analyse comes from different sources and is not homogeneous: this is the reason why spend analysis tools were created.

The data-processing process that is implemented is the following:

- the various accounts payable source files are regularly extracted from the different ERPs;
- the format is predefined with all information essential for the consolidation and analysis that will then be carried out (label, pre-tax sum, supplier name etc);
- the source of the information is set out in invoice lines paid to suppliers, to which are associated, whenever possible, the corresponding order lines;
- these files are stored in a data warehouse from which a certain number of processing operations can then be carried out;
- the following operation consists in working on these files in two processing stages: a first data-cleansing stage to make the data homogeneous, and a second data-enrichment stage to make the data truly exploitable via a 'requester'-type tool.

The information available on supplier invoice lines is inadequate for consolidation for analysis purposes. Indeed, if we wish to make an analysis according to a procurement category by consolidating the sums paid to a given supplier, this implies, on the one hand, that a procurement category code has been entered on the order line, and on the other hand, that a single supplier code is used to consolidate the invoice lines corresponding to the same code.

We observe that in reality, not all invoice lines have a procurement category code, for this is not information necessary for the processing of the invoice. If the invoice can be matched with an order, there will be more chances of this information being entered on the order – but not always correctly if the data is entered manually – for there is a field to be filled in compulsorily.

In addition, regarding the supplier code when looking from one source system to another, if we extract files from several ERPs, we can be sure that we recover a different supplier code for the same supplier from each system.

The operation that consists in looking at source files and grouping matches under a single code is called data deduplication. The identification of suppliers according to a single coding system generally relies on a universal coding system developed by the company Dun & Bradstreet, and is known as the 'Duns number'.

Data cleansing and enrichment therefore consist in carrying out these invoice line-grouping operations by allocating a procurement family code and associating a single Duns-type identification number to each supplier. An extra operation then involves associating the supplier code with any possible links between an operating site (in France, associated with the SIRET code) and the parent company (SIREN).

To sum up, spend analysis solutions allow these different operations to be carried out. They may rely on artificial intelligence tools – inference engines – and also and above all, rules engines that facilitate automatic allocation of the right codes on the analysed invoice lines. Functional administration is nonetheless required to ensure the end quality of these allocations (handling of anomalies). Thereafter, we need only use the requester function to carry out all necessary analyses to meet the buyer's requirements.

18/6.3 The SRM module

The supplier relationship management (SRM) module offered by most editors of e-sourcing solutions allows the procurement community to access a genuine knowledge database on suppliers for whom it is essential to have specific understanding of their activity and global performance, of the service supplied to the company, and to have reliable indicators to carry out monitoring. Basically, the supplier knowledge space is structured as follows:

- general information on the supplier (supplier profile), contacts, the organization (sites, corporate name, parent company) associated with a duly filled-in questionnaire (RFI) and attached documents such as activity reports;
- data from other modules in the solution, such as the list of contracts pertaining to the supplier, the updated procurement turnover via the spend analysis module;
- the supplier status associated with supplier-panel management;
- evaluation of supplier performance according to several elements associated with an internal survey such as a supplier scorecard;

- information relating to the action plan associated with improvement actions required from the supplier;
- an evaluation of risks according to several analysis angles: dependency rate (automatically calculated ratio between annual declared turnover and updated procurement turnover); financial health (financial ratios supplied by service-providers such as Dun & Bradstreet); and sustainable development indicators, internally developed or supplied by a specialized service-provider such as EcoVadis in the SRM module.

18/7 General approach to a procurement information system and the running of a global project

Most large companies that have implemented a battery of IT tools to cover the requirements of procurement processes are confronted by the realization that it is urgent to rethink their procurement information systems in a more global manner.

18/7.1 The procurement information system

First of all, it is possible for developments to have been carried out internally, that may not be intended to remain internal in the long term, which naturally leads to an examination of what the market has the means to offer as a standard or with a few side-line adaptations.

Next, a considerable proportion of tools used by buyers is based on their own expertise, developed with Excel. This is therefore a purely local usage that is not shared between users, or in a very limited manner. This situation does not at all promote the transversal approaches which today's procurement departments seek to implement.

In addition, there is generally very little interfacing and coherency of data managed between applications. As a result, the tools are globally poorly optimized, and the updating of information and quality of data are often mediocre, so the level of adoption of the tools may consequently prove very weak.

Added to this, the IT department is often the driver of an alignment approach, aligning its IT master plan with the requirements of the company's various businesses. The procurement department should clearly identify its functional requirements and take advantage of this opportunity to benefit from feedback on practices implemented with existing tools, to detect functional shortcomings and define its target in terms of its information system.

Such an approach should ultimately lead to modelling the functional architecture of the target procurement information system, based on a functional model such as the one presented in Figure 18.9.

FIGURE 18.9 Functional model of a purchasing information system

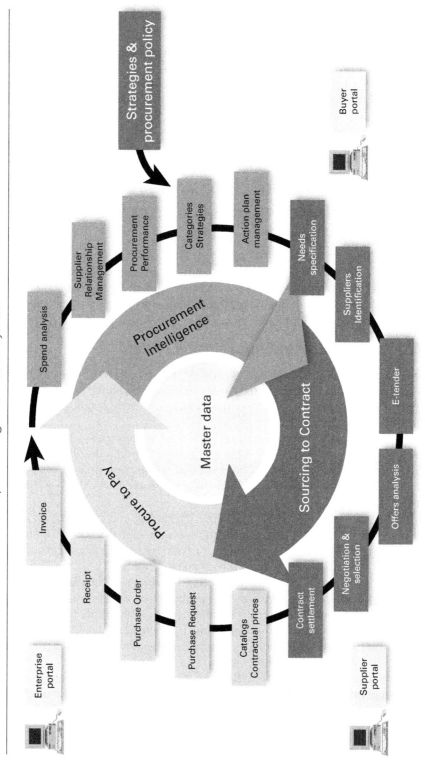

In this example, the approach consists in presenting, for every stage of the process – on the basis of the procurement process defined by the company's internal reference – functional requirements on the one hand and on the other hand, relevant performance indicators which the information system should have the means to supply automatically, and which will feed the requirements of the procurement performance steering element.

Once the procurement information system's master plan has been roughly defined, it is interesting to compare the result of this work with the offer made by editors on the market. Several different approaches are possible in this case:

- identifying for every macro-requirement whether suitable and dedicated solutions exist, such as contract management tools: this is a matter of constructing a Lego-like information system that preserves, as required, certain internally developed applications;
- supplementing the functional coverage of the existing information system, that is the ERP in place, via one or several of the already mentioned dedicated solutions;
- selecting an editor on the market offering a global application-suite approach, that is, taking care of practically all of the identified functional coverage.

The *first approach* is not very satisfactory from the point of view of a master plan approach. Indeed, this is not a way to resolve issues in coherency of data models between applications and eventually necessary integrations; ultimately, this approach risks being more costly than it initially appears, and may be burdensome to manage.

The *second approach* makes sense from the point of view of the company's information system master plan, for there is a certain logic in wishing to harmonize and maintain a single ERP environment, then to seek to cover a maximum of the corporate professions' requirements with the selected ERP. Advantages include a sharing of common benchmarks, local integration between functional modules, and the backing of a single internal competency centre. On the other hand, it is very rare today to see companies that have fully achieved this approach. The reality is that in general, a range of ERPs cohabit. But it remains essential to consider this dimension in choices to be made for the 3- to 5-year range in terms of procurement information systems.[15]

Finally, the *last approach* is the one that makes sense in terms of short- and medium-term requirements of the procurement function. Some editors have thus made great progress in functional coverage, covering the procurement process from the upstream stage up to supply and supplier payment functions.

One exercise that should be carried out once the functional architecture has been defined consists in comparative mapping, comparing the functional coverage of one or several market solutions and the modelled target architecture.

18/7.2 The running of an e-procurement project

When we start to approach decision-makers on the issue of defining which tools should cover the requirements of the procurement department, we can rely on a simple schema such as the procurement information loop.

Procurement information loop

The basic priority requirement of a procurement manager is to have a map of his or her purchases in order to answer the following questions: How much does the company buy? What does it buy? And who buys and from whom?

As we have seen above, ERP systems – when they are multiple and dispersed throughout a large group's different entities – do not allow a homogeneous, consolidated synthesized vision of procurement to be obtained.

The sources of information are generally the ERPs on the spot. For production purchases, information is extracted from 'Order' files whose procurement nomenclatures are often local. Meanwhile, non-production purchases are extracted from 'Invoice' files without any associated nomenclature if they are non-accounting in nature. For these non-production purchases, when an e-procurement solution is deployed on a large scale, procurement statistics allow the necessary level of analysis to be obtained, for the scope covered.

Acquisition of a spend analysis module is generally one of the first priorities even if it is not always easy to implement.

Once an initial procurement map has been established, procurement strategies according to categories can start to be implemented. These strategies will be all the better deployed if they rely on an e-sourcing application enabling the ad hoc procurement project team to be set up and run, but also the procurement knowledge required about the sector in question to be created and formalized and supplier consultations to be steered.

Following the selection of suppliers and the negotiation of offers, buyers need to formalize these agreements in the form of procurement contracts. These contracts may lead to the setting up of electronic catalogues that reflect the price list attached to the contract.

After these contracts have been established, monitoring of their application can be carried out via the reporting tool; the strategies can then be fine-tuned and the procurement information loop begins again.

The implementation of the roadmap

Forming a global vision of the future procurement information system is a useful and necessary exercise, but it is appropriate to stay pragmatic. To do so, it is necessary to define a roadmap that 'prioritizes' issues and hence the 'functional components' or modules to deploy, all the while preparing the accompanying organization and management of the change. What can often be observed in terms of priorities is the following sequencing:

- first of all, setting up of a procurement management component based on a spend analysis module that is not limited to this aspect but that also enables monitoring the global performance of procurement on both quantitative and qualitative levels;
- then, development of a genuine supplier portal enabling exchange and updating of certain information by the suppliers themselves, with functions for following up supplier performance and the associated action plans;

- next, implementation of a collaborative environment based on the development of procurement organization by commodity (or procurement segment), enabling the steering of sourcing actions, comprising the buyer's typical work-desk functions;
- and finally, development of a collaborative contract management tool that may subsequently include 'contract compliance'-type functions as mentioned previously.

However, integration of e-sourcing and e-procurement applications is generally not considered to be a priority, and often hinges on the evolutions of the functional scope of the ERPs in place, especially in the context of projects for convergence towards a single ERP.

What remains to be determined is the appropriate project organization and all resources that will need to be allocated to the tool's deployment, then its maintenance in operational condition, namely in terms of functional administration. This leads us to the last point, the human factor.

A key success factor: human management

Successful implementation of a genuine procurement information system requires mobilization of procurement resources and, to a lesser extent, IT measurement, backed up by in-depth work in order to modify behaviour. In terms of changes in habits, there is a real cultural revolution to conduct:

- limitation or even elimination of the buyer's work in its dimension limited exclusively to his or her own personal files;
- sharing of the individual workstation with the buyer community on a workspace accessible from a server, but allowing private viewing;
- demand for rigour in methodology entailing transparency both internally and externally in the evaluation and selection of supplier offers;
- 'historization' capitalization and sharing of knowledge in areas where there are some who may tend to demand recognition of their competencies without a true desire to share them.

Suppliers, with whom buyers will increasingly cooperate in an interactive mode, should also engage in this procedure, going as far as updating information relating to their supplier profile on the portal intended for this purpose, or even participating in projects in the same work environment as internal teams.

It is also necessary to think about the way to distribute, within the procurement community, the tasks relating to the tool's functional administration, to the updating and/or regular monitoring of the quality of the data that has an impact on the quality of reporting.

We can therefore conceive of these tasks as henceforth explicitly contributing to each buyer's objectives, with qualitative follow-up of the work provided in this area being integrated into individual assessments. Another way to encourage 'virtuous' behaviour is to demonstrate how the proposed tools actually contribute towards efficiency and reactivity, with an unparalleled capacity to obtain quality information, at the most detailed level as well as on the most aggregated level aimed at management, on condition that each individual contributes on his or her level to the quality of the information managed within the system.

Final observations and prospects

The e-procurement system is not merely the outcome of an approach geared at automating procurement processes, in addition enabling personalization of the buyer's work environment. What is also at stake are truly strategic objectives for reaching results that make up competitive advantages for the company. Above all, the tools do not relieve procurement managers from the need to make clear preliminary strategic analysis according to a segmented approach to the procurement portfolio, then specifically defining action plans with target results – on the contrary, this is a compulsory step.

Thanks to the experience of some 15 years of practice in large companies, we can observe the following results:

- an accelerator effect on sourcing and tender activities, and thus an impact on purchase prices due to easier competitive procedures, in real time, using a shared and extended supplier database;
- a reduction in procurement administrative costs due to a simplification and automation of processes, a factor of productivity;
- a reduction in transaction times, times for responding to users and internal cycles, but also external cycles in negotiations and dialogues with suppliers, paired with a diminishing of errors and disputes;
- monitoring of information with guaranteed confidentiality and real-time management of procurement (procurement statistics, real-time monitoring, catalogue updating, online information, etc);
- an ongoing possibility of procurement innovation by calling on external solutions and value-added services.

Internally, regarding employees and human management, the following changes are becoming possible:

- for the downstream aspect of procurement processes, a modification of the buyer's profession and environment, through the conviviality of solutions allowing user self-study, traceability and the reduction of disputes;
- undeniable increase in user satisfaction through the option of partially decentralizing supply (as long as catalogues or contracts are set up in advance) and directly tracking the state of progress of one's orders;
- as a consequence, professional enhancement, for buyers can be released from activities without added value and focus instead on upstream procurement processes (help with sourcing, business and technology watch, better selection of suppliers) and the ongoing search for improvements in the satisfaction of customer requirements (optimization of requirements specifications in particular).

Such progress is not exclusive to large companies: e-procurement also targets SMIs for which it may constitute an answer to limited resources or procurement competencies, without too much investment involved except, most likely, for consultancy to back up the support process.

Notes

1 Client-server systems require the installation, on workstations, of a specific application in order to dialogue with the application installed on the server. 'Thin clients' only require installation of a browser on workstations to enable access to any application, whether on an internal or external server.

2 XML is a standardized format using the internet that facilitates automatic integration, for example, between an ERP customer and an ERP supplier. In this way, suppliers who receive orders in XML format can automatically process them in their customer management systems, allowing internal gains in productivity that can be made the object of negotiation for lower procurement prices.

3 'Maverick buying' refers to any purchase made directly by a user that does not comply with internal or even legal procedures. This sometimes leads to operations that do not appear in the database, and of whose existence the procurement department may even be unaware!

4 The Sarbanes–Oxley or SOX Act requires all companies listed on the Stock Exchange to have the means to comply with certain financial transparency obligations including the scope of procurement.

5 There is also the possibility of placing at the users' disposal an internal catalogue of so-called generic items, and to also create webforms facilitating the expression of requirements, for example, in the case of configurable services such as car rental.

6 Note that there is another way to proceed, with an initial approval workflow based on a maximum sum estimated by the requester before the buyer is notified about the requirement.

7 For more detailed information on the vendor market, see the Gartner market survey: Bergfors, M, Malinverno, P and Wilson, DR (2015) *Magic Quadrant for Procure-to-Pay Suites for Indirect Procurement.*

8 Nor should one overlook the capacity of certain suppliers, large-volume producers of invoices, such as electricity companies, to directly deliver electronic files in EDI format.

9 Several initiatives in this direction have been carried out by workgroups, especially in France, under the headship of GENCOD – which recently became GS1 – and in the United States with RosettaNet in the electronics industry sector.

10 Note that we can use the same questionnaire technique to carry out an internal survey in order to qualify and consolidate requirements; in this case we speak of an internal RFI.

11 We have described the reverse auction process – the so-called English e-auction. The market also offers other types of e-auctions such as Dutch, Brazilian, Japanese, Vickrey, American. It is up to buyers to select the best e-auction strategy (for more detailed information contact the author).

12 Which has often sparked the comment that auctions target standard market products with a considerable number of players – a restrictive view in our opinion.

13 For example, the so-called 'switching cost' for changing suppliers may be 5 per cent, which means that below a price difference of 5 per cent, it is not worthwhile changing suppliers. All competing offers will therefore be marked up by 5 per cent and compared on this basis. We can carry out similar reasoning on supplier risk and, depending on the sourcing origin, apply a risk coefficient by following a 'total landed cost' approach.

14 Supplier relationship management, which, at SAP, covers both e-procurement (SAP EBP) and e-sourcing.

15 For the sake of completeness, we should also raise the necessity of taking into account the functional coverage of other applications used by professions such as engineering that work closely with procurement. We thus currently see the development of functional extensions of product lifecycle management (PLM) tools that can cover certain procurement requirements (supplier portal, monitoring of costs of BOMs).

PART FOUR
Performance and change management

Managing a function ultimately means paying attention – in direct correlation with the strategic considerations outlined in Part One – to the measurement and management of performance, as well as systems for reporting to all stakeholders (CEO, business partners, specifiers, heads of business units, suppliers). It also means looking forward to evolution by managing change in a timely and controlled manner.

Chapter 19 starts off by presenting all internal and external communication issues faced by the procurement function. Indeed, once the function has been 'professionalized', in order to be efficient, it needs to involve all players in its project. This approach cannot be empirically driven on the basis of the hazards of circumstances, but requires organization according to a structured action plan. The chapter recalls a certain number of rules and principles underlying communication policies relevant for all functions. Next, it sets out communication diagnostic methods applicable to procurement before commenting on the nature and management of a well-considered and steered action plan, backed up by examples. The subject covered deals as much with internal targets of communication (ie customers, specifiers and leaders) as external targets (the company's current or potential suppliers). Only lobbying operations sometimes entrusted to the procurement function are excluded from this discussion.

Chapter 20 is entirely devoted to the analysis of procurement performance measurement and reporting systems. All the main systems existing in companies and described in academic literature are classified. The creation of a dashboard and appropriate choices of indicators (KPIs) are tackled from a conceptual, methodological and operational point of view. This chapter concludes with the major stages for the implementation of a system.

Chapter 21, the book's final chapter, offers a 'dynamic' vision of change management for procurement, considering that such a managerial process holds the status of a company project. Here, a detailed analysis of the main performance monitoring standards is provided, deliberately directing the reader's attention towards the concept and characteristics of maturity models. The chapter also examines – on the basis of real-life experiences – the way to manage a medium-term development project for the procurement function and for the company. All conditions for success are raised as well as the most common methods for change management.

19
Procurement communication plan

'If you would reap praise, you must sow the seeds,' Benjamin Franklin once said. Before launching into action, preparing communication in a structured manner is a beneficial step to take for guaranteeing success.

This is one of the rules that we put forward throughout this chapter in which we will tackle use of professional communication to serve the procurement function. In the second part of the chapter, we will look at practical applications along with a few real-life examples implemented by procurement departments. Finally, we will conclude by considering the valuable contribution offered by communication, but also the need to take into account cultural differences, whether in relation to different countries or different companies and professions, again backed up by concrete applications.

19/1 A structured communication plan: why and how

Professional communication has changed radically in recent years. Gone are the slogans aimed at the housewife under 50 years of age and category-related targets, the division between media and below-the-line communication. We now live in the age of communities, of 'one-to-many', 'one-to-few' and 'one-to-one' communication!

Indeed, corporate communication is everywhere and reaches us by means of increasingly sophisticated communication technologies. We decipher second-degree messages quickly ('I know that this cola brand wishes to sell me a bottle, but it still needs to seduce me') and we switch quickly from one form of communication to another.

Targeting specific age groups may even have the opposite effect from that expected if the products on offer do not match individual tastes. For example, it is not because I am an executive in a large company and aged over 40 that I necessarily want to buy a big-cylindered car; I can get around town much more easily without one. It is by seeking to meet our hopes and our true expectations that communication will be more effective. Hence the need for communication more adapted to the aspirations of each rather than to his or her socio-professional category or age group.

19/1.1 The main principles of professional communication

Communication, whether one-to-one (eg with the production director), one-to-few (eg the design office) or one-to-many (eg suppliers), has become complex and professional, even within a company, between its different departments and entities. How do we respond professionally to the communication needs of our different interlocutors?

Frédéric Bedin is one of the founders of the Le Public Système, a Parisian agency at the cutting edge of corporate communication. Drawing from broad experience in procurement communication, he has formulated three principles, three rules and six tools for this field. Here we present to buyers these key points, with reference to examples and applications in the following paragraphs.

The three main principles

The first principle is that *communication is complicated: to simplify things, just tell the truth*. As soon as someone starts puffing up stories when communicating, facts no longer compute and credibility is necessarily lost.

The second principle is based on personality: *in order for others to believe you, act yourself, keep your own style*. It's not because someone finds the style of such and such a television presenter appealing that they should seek to imitate it to be seen as engaging. Here again, your entourage can quickly read situations and will find you more of a copier than an effective communicator.

Finally, the third principle does away with simplistic discourse along the lines that 'in our company, amongst ourselves, we're not going to set up structured communication'. The fact is *everyone knows that you communicate and that's perfectly all right*. The buyer is a professional who knows how to use communication tools. The buyer's interlocutors thus expect him or her to be up to speed in using them!

The three basic rules

Opinions lay the ground for action: before announcing a project or setting up a procedure, do what you can to ensure that your target will agree with you. This rule is applied widely to win acceptance for difficult disruptive projects. This is, for example, the strategy used in political projects to announce changes, preceded by debates and press articles on alarming figures. Upstream exchanges help prepare the lifting of obstacles.

Be empathetic, take an altruistic approach: put yourself in the position of others, offer solutions to *their* problems, not your own. Too often, procurement departments focus on presenting the difficulties that they encounter in their own approaches. Better communication can be achieved by paying attention to the difficulties of other departments, and in particular, of prescribers, to help them with the procurement methodology.

Communicate positively: procurement is a pleasure to be shared. A company that procures is a company that succeeds. In this way, *seek to offer more joy and fewer constraints*. Why should we use a vocabulary that is always synonymous with displeasure: reduction, cut, constraints, savings? Let's instead use positive vocabulary, such as: improvement, opportunities, gains, performance etc. And let's get internal players involved in the act of procurement for the sake of shared pleasure in joint performance.

Six key tools

Construct arguments: like salespeople, prepare your discourse before selling your ideas. Practise first!

For example, you have just learned that a new material, developed by a supplier in the process of being approved, can improve your manufacturing productivity. So you hurry over to the design office that tells you that even if the idea is good, the schedule for the validation of new materials is booked up and that you will need to wait.

Before hurrying over, perhaps it would have been wise to reflect on the sales argument to present to the right individuals. Who is the decision-maker? Who is most concerned with the issue? How should the idea be put forward so that he or she is receptive to it? When is the right time? What are the direct and indirect advantages? What are the arguments and counter-arguments to prepare?

Be a bringer of good news: distil the good news one by one, at regular intervals. Here again, this tool is prepared by measuring out the regular arrival of positive information that will back up your approach.

If you have several pieces of positive feedback when a project starts up, it may be judicious to announce these one after the other rather than all at the same time, to avoid any loss of information by an overload of messages delivered simultaneously.

Very often the following question is asked: 'Unfortunately there's not always any good news to announce. Should I avoid announcing bad news?' Well, no. Let's respect the first principle of telling the truth. It is therefore necessary to inform others if slippery slopes are encountered, but accompany these announcements with good news: that you will bring solutions in order to ultimately set the situation back on track.

Keep some 'roughness' in your image (don't be too smooth): leave a few stories to be spread by internal media (by word of mouth or communication means such as the intranet).

Media pays little attention to the ordinary; what it seeks on the other hand is difference. Have you ever thought about what makes the procurement department in your company different? Don't seek to hide it, but highlight it as a strength. This is a very common technique used in advertising as a way of standing out; creative teams seek to promote a product's difference: for example, this candy may be smaller but it has more flavour, this other one has more punch, and so on.

We can mention an example from the cosmetics sector where one procurement director set up a high-performance procurement organization with results considered positive by the top management. At the same time, he kept a cost-killer image that was not appreciated by the director of the development laboratory who himself was readily listened to by other departments. The procurement department had involved suppliers in product innovation and certain results were deemed interesting but negotiations were stopped due to price issues. It was by collectively reviewing the technical and economic criteria, and by redefining the roles of each that the role of procurement was reconsidered. This occurred through a rational approach to the structure of direct and all indirect costs, highlighting the advantages of investing in suppliers but also economic gains in the short and long term, not just the price, and respecting the expectations of the development director.

Play 'three-cushioned billiards': use credible opinion multipliers to transmit your messages. Information is more credible if it is taken up by a third party, ideally an opinion leader within the company. This may be a production manager satisfied by the last negotiation that he or she handled with a buyer, or the marketing department. This party's discourse will be more readily heard than that of the buyer him- or herself. Try this approach and you will see that it works.

Manage the pleasure/stress ratio of your internal customers: the higher this ratio, the better your image. To improve this ratio, it is necessary to make enquiries about the expectations and difficulties of all business partners.

When stress is generated amongst one's interlocutors by an endlessly alarmist discourse on lost savings, the procurement department may generate a ratio that becomes too unfavourable to be borne. There should also be an element of pleasure in bringing the solutions anticipated by the internal customers, and a dimension of human emotion to which we will return at the end of the chapter (emotion is very important in communication).

In one financial establishment, the senior management's personal assistant was responsible for booking the management's seminars. This was a task that was added on top of her usual workload, but that gave her the opportunity to meet service-providers who came up with new offers every year. When the company set up a procurement department, this task was taken from the PA, and instead, her only responsibility was to manage the executives' diaries for bookings without any contact with the service-providers, an area reserved for the procurement department from that point onwards. The secretary's stress mounted further when – due to regular changes to seminar dates – the procurement department announced that savings would fail to be attained due to late bookings. For the secretary, there was no longer any pleasure in choosing the venue between two solutions on an Excel spreadsheet. Without any upstream involvement, bookings were made at the last moment at the only venue still available, but one that did not match up with expectations. By restoring to the secretary her role at the heart of decision-making with the service-providers and the procurement department, via a detailed and optimized economic approach, the following year's seminar was a success.

Refer to the efficiency of successful procurement in external communication: in corporate public relations, sales arguments or financial communication, insert the results stemming from successful collaborations with internal customers and suppliers. All the more as shareholders make increasing demands on procurement strategy and its results. For shareholders and analysts understand that well-controlled procurement communication is synonymous with a well-considered strategy, and thus better-assured results.

Finally, following these few concepts and examples drawn from experience, as for all management strategies, the efficiency of corporate actions will always be measured by the setting up of appropriate indicators. We will therefore see below how to set these up in order, for example, to create image barometers.

19/1.2 Requirements and expectations

Those days when communication was a mere matter of transmitting a message are over. Previously elaborated on in the marketing bible by Philip Kotler and Bernard Dubois,[1] a model containing nine elements allows us to identify the key factors of efficient communication. A message has more chances of being understood if it enters the field of experience of both the emitter and the receiver.[2]

Communication between professionals today is a matter of making sure that the message that we wish to transmit will be heard and understood, but will also change behaviour, or at least, improve the perceptions of others with different levels of demands. This is why a structured communication plan, to be improved on an ongoing basis, should include the following elements (Figure 19.1):

- What is my situation in relation to my communication targets?
- What are my objectives?
- What means will I use to communicate them?
- To which targets (or beneficiaries)?
- What vectors should be used?
- How?
- When?
- What are the anticipated results enabling measurement and progression?
- What is my new situation and what are my new objectives?

FIGURE 19.1   Communicating well requires knowing

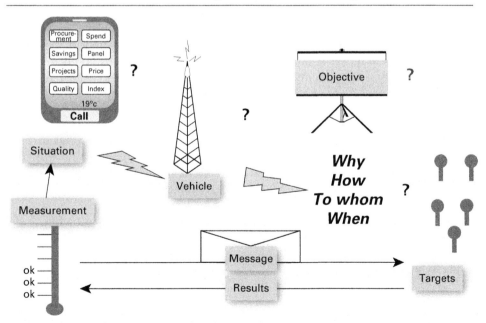

The mere fact of unblocking a budget to communicate does not suffice. This final outcome aimed at 'stirring action' necessitates far greater means and takes far more time than merely providing a piece of information. Long identified, the different stages for shifting from attention to interest, then desire and then action[3] can take time, depending on the targets.

To give an example, quite obviously, a recommendation for investment in a source-to-pay suite (from suppliers up to payment) necessitates change from the whole company, and the communication effort involves much more than just reporting on the success of the implementation of e-solutions amongst competitors.

This is why the effort and time put into communication need to be taken into account, depending on the selected level of communication. We see that communication is closely linked to change in the company and a need to change. We will therefore be looking at this dimension of communication in Chapter 21 on change management.

19/1.3 The expected role and the recognized role

The perception of the role of the procurement function may vary greatly from one company to another, from one entity to another, or within an entity, from one person to another. This function has a role that is known according to what is inscribed in the company's processes, which is not, however, a *recognized* role. It also has an accepted role, which is not necessarily the role that the function wishes to play.

Buyers should therefore identify the contribution that they wish to bring to a company and the one expected from them by other functions.

Concerning suppliers, buyers should be aware of what is their known/recognized and/or accepted role. What salesperson has not sought to find out the real (rather than the announced) power of the buyer? This is easy enough to see if your suppliers 'avoid' the buyer. Communication towards suppliers is often initiated by the implementation of supplier policies. But this is not enough for establishing everyday relationships. This is why, as in the case of internal communication, the external communications of buyers should follow a structured methodology and plan.

Finally, buyers often seek recognition. It is thus also for their benefit that the procurement management should prepare a communication plan that meets their expectations.

Having had the opportunity to meet many different companies, we have often heard this type of comment: 'I pulled off a great negotiation but the financial director doesn't see the impact of my action!', 'It's impossible for us to work with the So-and-So department!', 'It's always the same, they call me in when the contract is almost signed!', 'We suggested a plan offering significant gains and yet I'm being asked to review my proposal!'.

All these remarks represent situations where communication has often been poorly prepared or poorly adapted to reach the objectives that each has set. But how do we communicate successfully if interlocutors have not received the key messages at the right time?

19/2 Implementation of a structured diagnostic process

As a genuine interface between suppliers and all of the company's functions, the buyer owes it to himself or herself to listen to and communicate with many different interlocutors. We will now firstly set out to define the categories of main targets, then, after looking at methodology in the following section (and in order to adapt the general discourse to the individual as noted in the introduction), we will take these different targets into account to establish a communication plan.

19/2.1 Communication players and expectations

To put things simply, within a company, we can find different players (internal stakeholders) with different requirements and expectations with respect to procurement, that we can divide into three categories (depending on the size of companies):

1 management functions (top management, management in charge of business units, group management, etc.);

2 operational functions (production, design office, marketing, sales, communication, management of different sites, and the procurement team!);

3 support or buyer functions (management control, finance, quality, human resources, legal department – that may also have their own requirements for purchasing external services).

Whilst, generally, executive committees expect the procurement strategy to be set up in relation to the corporate strategy, stakeholders[4] request that their requirements be satisfied, and support functions that the rules set up be respected. For each of these categories, buyers therefore need to report on what they have planned to do, what they are going to do, and what they have done. At the same time, within each category, expectations will also be variable. Whilst in charge of procurement for a group exercising several professions, the author has had to deal with the very different expectations of business-unit managements in the famous cost/quality/lead-time triangle – with some prioritizing cost, others 'time to market', and others still the best combination of cost and lead-time.

To give an example from real life: several procurement directors with backgrounds in sales or development functions have, upon their arrival in procurement, requested that the word 'internal customer' be erased, on the basis that they see the company as having only one customer: the end customer. A change in vocabulary accompanied by a desire to change the level of expectations and results is often beneficial as long as it is understood/admitted by the company. In recent cases, communication associated with the new concept has enabled better integration of the notion of a 'partner', and thus created a dialogue between two departments working towards a common objective, and not simply for another's objective.

Amongst internal stakeholders, let's not forget the procurement teams themselves that will be participating in the communication plan; they need to be involved rapidly in the plan so that they can share the same vocabulary and schedule.

Here's a little test: separately ask several members of the procurement team (and in several countries, to add the complexity of language to the challenge) to present, in three minutes, the role of the procurement function, its three main objectives and its contribution over the year. In most cases, you will be surprised by the results this yields. These are the communication players who will have a major role in the deployment of the communication plan. So don't forget to share your communication strategy, your vocabulary and anticipated results with them.

Outside of the company, we similarly find three categories of communication players, that we can classify as external stakeholders:

1 supplier panel;
2 potential suppliers;
3 institutions and external networks.

Generally speaking, communication on the part of suppliers is often expected by the customer. Suppliers are a considerable source of information highly useful to the procurement function: new technologies, new products, competition, etc. But even if this sort of communication seems natural, it needs to be organized in order to be efficient. Indeed, how is it possible today for exhaustive supplier information from the panel, from potential suppliers and from external networks to be passed on?

The answer is simple even if its implementation is less so: it is necessary to set up a selection system to enable the passing on of relevant information. Such a system requires communicating on expectations and on interests. This communication will not be of the same type for the three categories of targets. The proximity of the supplier panel allows general presentation to be simplified but requires a fine-tuning of expectations. As for potential suppliers, here it will be necessary to adopt a very clear discourse on entrance into a business relationship. Are we open enough to a proposal coming from an unknown supplier? Is this something that we desire, that we would accept?[5]

To give an example of external communication: many procurement departments are setting up, or wish to set up, solutions for improving supplier innovation. But this is something that cannot be merely decreed! These solutions require implementation of a detailed and well-communicated process, namely in relation to partners: Who are we addressing? All potential suppliers with open innovation? Or our privileged partners? How, and how often? For what results?

Finally, we have included institutions amongst the external stakeholders. This category is vast as it includes the administrations of different countries, regional authorities, certification bodies, NGOs, the press, schools, associations and so on. We also need to ask ourselves about their role in the communication plan.

Communication flows with the external stakeholders therefore also need to be organized in an appropriate and efficient manner. We will now look at how to structure these by relying on a methodology that helps answer these questions.

19/2.2 A robust methodology for analysis

The ACA (*Association CESA Achats et Supply Chain*) has edited a book which inspired us. This work[6] offers a methodology providing a rigorous and efficient approach based on a pre-diagnostic, a detailed diagnostic, a prioritization of targets, and a selection of possible actions (Figure 19.2).

On the basis of this simple method, we wish to put forward the key points that we have had the opportunity to test and adapt successfully.

FIGURE 19.2   The stages of a procurement communication diagnostic

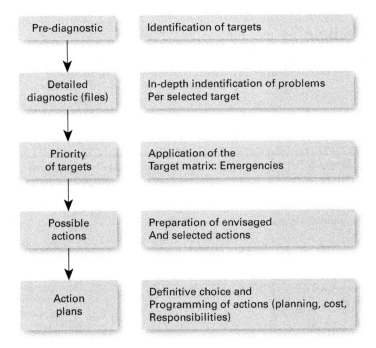

A structured diagnostic process

To begin the diagnostic, we suggest taking up the segmentation of targets according to major functions, as described above: the internal stakeholders and the external stakeholders. A questionnaire listing the difficulties encountered with such and such a target will help to prepare an approach in accordance with priorities. The reader is invited to consult the original work referred to for an in-depth illustration.

Once difficulties have been identified, the detailed diagnostic allows locating the causes. Which are the difficulties that are encountered the most often?

Let's look at a specific example: whilst carrying out a pre-diagnostic, the procurement department of a pharmaceutical group realized the inappropriateness of its message, its methods, and the means used to work (better) with the marketing department that did not wish to entrust negotiation of its budgets to the buyers. Following an analysis of the causes by means of a simple tool (well known in the quality-approach arena – see Figure 19.3), thus formalizing the causes and consequences on the five dimensions of procurement communication, they quickly grasped that expectations in terms of image promotion meant that price reduction was not a prime priority for the stakeholders. It was necessary to recreate a climate of trust founded on respect of the expectations and a structured communication in order to find a successful joint approach for negotiation on marketing budgets. In other words, it was necessary first of all to meet expectations by going and looking for this information through meetings with the heads of budgets, by preparing messages to meet these expectations, and by bringing responses with suitable methods (processes, decision-making), means (structure and communication vectors) and messages.

Analysis of causes according to five factors (Ishikawa communication)

We can take the simplified real-life example below, analysing various possible dysfunctions in communication, to examine each of the branches of this model and this tool.

FIGURE 19.3   Analysis of the causes of dysfunction (Ishikawa communication)

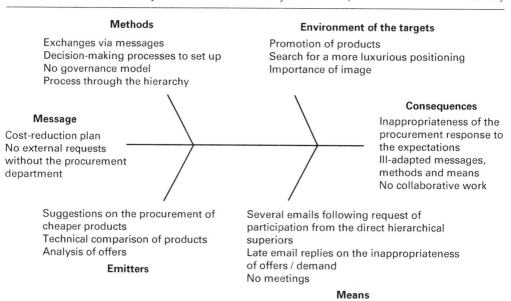

Organization/environment/targets

The structure does not facilitate communication. For example, the procurement function is sometimes poorly defined in the organization chart or dependent on another operation function (eg production).

Humans (emitters)

The behaviour of individuals, from other functions as well as from procurement, has an impact on the communication that is presented. Disrespectful behaviour from buyers towards suppliers (or vice versa) may be a cause of dysfunction when it is poorly received by others for example.

Methods

The principles and tools defined in the first part of this chapter are to be adhered to in order to avoid pitfalls. In any case, a structured methodology should be followed.

Messages

These messages should correspond with the expectations of the procurement department's interlocutors (whether they are expressed explicitly or more latently).

Means

The means are the communication vectors or channels used. Without means, the communication is not heard for it is not disseminated. A good product without communication remains a good product but stays in boxes.

Prioritized targets

At the end of the diagnostic, an action plan may then be put forward. The plan will first of all address *priority* targets. As shown by Figure 19.4, we can identify four types of targets along two axes: 1) influence on the level of risk (depending on the target's degree of *sensitivity* or *influence*) – often the function that represents the largest expenses or that has influence over decisions; 2) short- or medium-term economic or strategic impact (degree of *complexity*) – decisions with an immediate impact and those that will have one in the longer term require different management in communication.

FIGURE 19.4   Matrix for the prioritization of procurement communication targets

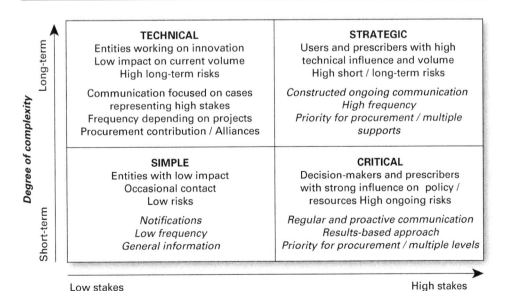

FIGURE 19.5   Major action-plan phases

Phase	Objectives	Messages	Internal means	External means
Launch Year 1	– Reputation of the function – Support of top management	– The function's raison d'être – Anticipated savings	– Procurement newsletter – Presentations CDD – Création of exchange spaces with operationals	– Supplier forum – Email campaigns
Years 2 and 3	– Credibility – Legitimacy – Creation of habits	– Results (savings validated by The finance department) – Success stories – Efficiency of the user-buyer duo	– Regular articles in the internal bulletin – General emails	– Supplier review
Years 4 and 5	– Added value – Gain in time – In tune with business objectives – Group compliance (Sarbox, Internal auditing, ethics...) – Improvement of internal processes	– Procurement performance – Good practices – Internal/external benchmarking – Reminder of internal policies And charters	– Regular meetings with business – Presentation in department meetings – Face-to-face interviews with key stakeholders	– Supplier review – E-sourcing tools (e.g. Reverse auctions) – Group policies

We therefore find, in a matrix, different targets for internal communication, in relation to the two axes of sensitivity and complexity.

For high stakes (eg large investments) with long-term gains, we find the 'VIPs' (ie 'strategic' targets). These are the partners for whom a permanent presence is indispensable, related to the notion of developing a 'key internal partner'.

For high stakes and short-term gains (eg global negotiation on a commodity), the targets – described as 'critical' – are 'image' partners. Buyers will, for example, rely on success with these parties to communicate in the 'three-cushioned billiard' mode already referred to (see p. 600).

For low stakes with long-term gains (eg technological purchases for upcoming developments), buyers prepare their partners of tomorrow. Communication directed at these 'technical' targets will be occasional with a strong technical slant.

Finally, for low stakes and short-term gains, general communication is employed addressing a wider number of individuals ('simple' targets).

Before launching into the action plan, we recommend adapting the communication plan to individuals themselves except, of course, in the case of 'simple' targets. As indicated in the introduction of this chapter, within each category, not all individuals will react in the same way. Not all 'VIPs' will be golfers: there is no use waiting for them at the clubhouse bar!

This matrix can be reproduced for external communication with external stakeholders.

19/2.3 The procurement communication action plan

Let's go back to the procurement strategic matrix presented in Chapter 2 where we find the four types of procurement (strategic, heavy, technical and simple) that we can cross over with the four main categories of internal customers. In this way, buyers, on the basis of their own strategic matrices and the resulting procurement levers, should use the same matrix to position internal and external targets in order to prepare, as of this stage, their communication plan.

To give an example, a 'strategic' purchase (high stakes and short-term gains) that would necessitate (depending on the market and internal constraints) a procurement lever such as a cost breakdown, should be associated with communication towards 'critical' customer targets that are 'image' vectors. Communication should be aimed at these customers very early on to explain to them the whole procedure until they appropriate it themselves, so that later they can support the change and become a prestigious reference, promoted as such, when the operation is over. Mastery of this chain of causes and consequences will turn the buyer into a fearless professional.

For every target, a separate action plan exists. The only thing that remains to be selected is the appropriate medium (means or vector) depending on the company's culture and the target in question (internal bulletin, communities, intranet, forum, seminars, methodological notes, e-mails, group meetings, face-to-face interviews, etc).

Whilst in some companies, the 'coffee machine' or 'office kitchen' is a strategic spot for communication between professionals, in others a certain formality is required, even compulsory. When a mistake is made on communication means, the action will be far less effective, or even negative.

New media or tools also help the development of internal and/or external communication, with the creation of virtual communities, often in the form of 'wikis.'

As indicated in the chapter on human resources, networks are taking over from hierarchical organizations and forum-type systems. Exchanges occur within communities linked by practices or affinities. This type of communication is entirely adapted to the remote coordination of teams that thus find a way to share/exchange on subjects that interest them. It is also thus that groups are set up on social networks, where everyone can contribute, give an opinion, or simply shift to another network that is of interest.

The 'wiki' format allows members to supply information themselves, to use it as they need, and for it to be constantly updated by those holding information. There is no more hierarchy in communication – this is a 'horizontal' communication system that often uses existing networks such as LinkedIn, Viadeo, Xing, Google+.

Regarding professional communities within a company, but using similar tools with secure access, fears may initially arise on the free circulation of information, the lack of control over what is written (even within closed networks). It is true that rules need to be set up at the start, but the experience of those who have set them up is positive.

Experience will be all the more positive if:

- several leaders take part actively without having a hierarchical role;
- these virtual networks meet up 'physically' at least once, or from time to time, and use viewing tools (such as Skype) – the virtual needs to be backed up by the real;

- we use the three main communication principles put forward at the start of the chapter: telling the truth, keeping one's own style and communicating professionally.

These communication networks stand to evolve further into even more sophisticated systems. For several years, there has, for example, been a US *virtual supply-chain expo* that, just like a real expo, offers 'conferences' and 'stands' where service-providers present their products, as well as a virtual 'bar'!

Here, it is possible, at least by means of an avatar, to go from room to room, to listen to conferences and address questions to speakers or participants in the room, to speak to participants (via their avatars) at the (virtual) bar, and to visit stands – all from a distance. Of course, the itinerary is tracked so that visitors get even more out of it next time and save even more time. From experience, the author has found this system to be extremely efficient, and has had excellent discussions with fellow participants open to such technologies.

We can only encourage the reader to get prepared by testing out participation in internal or external groups, and by analysing what he or she finds suitable or not. Very high-speed connections allow us to communicate better, faster, and to virtually visit several continents in the one day. Procurement departments that seek to improve their performance will have no choice but to integrate all 'multi-channel' communication practices.

Examples of procurement communication

The reader will find below a series of examples of companies that have followed rigorous communication plans enabling them to successfully support transformations. The author heartily thanks these companies for giving him permission to publish these accounts here.

Example 1: Total Exploration & Production – sharing of a common vocabulary amongst the whole of the contracts and procurement community

Context: The Total Group is present in over 130 countries and employs around 100,000 people. Together, its subsidiaries and related companies make it the world's no. 5 international integrated oil and gas group today. Its turnover in 2014 was €236 billion. Its activities cover the whole of the oil and gas chain: upstream (exploration, development and production of hydrocarbons, gas and new energies), downstream (trading and maritime transport of crude oil and petrol products, refining, distribution, and the manufacturing of petrochemicals). Here, we refer to the procurement department of the upstream branch, Exploration and Production (E&P).

The main task of the procurement function at Total E&P (referred to as 'C&P' for Contracts & Procurement) is to provide the goods and services necessary for operations. Roles are strategic (defining the procurement policy), supervisory and operational.

Procurement has evolved towards greater involvement in strategic decisions. The possibility of following a career in this profession has opened up opportunities. Meeting and communicating with your network and with all stakeholders has become a crucial priority. And yet, as Antoine Formey de Saint Louvent from C&P Communication and Management at Total EP notes, 'we don't communicate for the sake of communicating, but to bring value, to create exchanges. Our communication is therefore effective but not emphatic.'

Example 2: Société Générale – The use of communication to serve the procurement function at Société Générale (by Thomas Gravis, Global Head of Business Logistics & Costs Efficiency, Newedge Group)

Context: The Société Générale group is one of the leading financial services groups in the Eurozone, with more than 154,000 employees in 73 countries. The procurement department is in charge of managing supplier relationships, with a team of 80 buyers in Paris and about 100 internationally, handling €5.6 billion in procurement expenses per year (with €3.5 billion in France). It has a triple mission:

- *strategic*: contributing to the elaboration of policies allowing effective access to resources and ensuring their operational implementation;
- *normative*: defining norms and processes aimed at guaranteeing procurement performance;
- *operational*: optimizing the quality/cost relationship of the goods and services offered in response to the group's requirements.

In this way, the department organized structured and coherent communication plans aimed at three targets: procurement streams (employees, international sourcing teams, lawyers); internal stakeholders (operational divisions and departments, management); and external parties (suppliers and press, professional circles, students).

There were three main objectives: demonstrating the procurement department's added value to the group, aligning teams (on strategy and objectives) within the shared resources department and the group; and finally, to illustrate and boost the procurement department's attractiveness.

Three communication angles were selected: to guarantee the effectiveness of results, the department chose three specific angles of attack:

- humans: to humanize discourse and make it less 'technical'; to promote men and women, their paths, their careers, their commitments;
- results: to offer proof of the progress of projects, the quality of service, synergies, etc; to be transparent and pedagogical;
- prospects: to promote projects, innovations, reflection, by involving internal partners; to open up to the world (benchmarking, external interventions).

The means implemented in 2010 permitted communication to all targets, including the press amongst external targets, using the following supports: *a purchasing* magazine with a feature on 'key accounts and SMEs' and a document on 'procurement departments facing the economic crisis'; *in another purchasing* magazine, articles on 'sustainable procurement,' 'real-estate procurement,' and 'software procurement,' as well as on the specific topic of car fleets, 'the new car solution programme'.

Example 3: a communication project on media procurement

The project's objectives were to select a global media partner to create synergies, to improve the effectiveness of advertising, and to consolidate data. Given the extent of the project's geographical and operational coverage, three batches of deployment were defined.

The communication plan allowed foreseeable resistance to the project to be anticipated, namely through preliminary communication in the press presenting the principle as innovative, but possible, and indicating the added value of procurement in this type of project. The subject therefore found itself 'institutionalized' in the eyes of specifiers.

Next, strong publicity was carried out on the project and its first results – namely financial – obtained in France (publication and dissemination of illustrated articles focused on cooperation, summary articles on the intranet and external benchmarking on the benefits relating to media procurement practices).

The highlight was the publication of an article in one of the top French newspapers, *Le Figaro,* in July 2009 on the mutual benefits of such a system, used as a support during the 'road-shows' that followed to international entities (with the sponsor). The Group's emphasis on the topic was thus demonstrated, and induced effective deployment in each entity.

The upshot of all this: deployment was launched in three countries six months ahead of schedule!

Example 4: a large international pharmaceutical industry

In the French subsidiary of a large international pharmaceutical group, the procurement department is a corporate function, set up on the occasion of the merger of two laboratories. Here, the procurement director's view is that communication plans should not be rigid; they vary practically every year, as much for targets as for messages, depending on the evolution of the laboratory's culture, leaders and the company's economic situation.

> At first, the emergence of the procurement function was a real cultural revolution for operational staff as well as suppliers. We had to speak a great deal about the procurement function (who, why, how) to make it understood, to establish its reputation, to develop its credibility. Externally, we organized a supplier forum in the presence of operational targets (suppliers as well as employees!) and internally circulated a monthly 'newsletter' (on key results) as well as setting up a 'meeting space' enabling an interactive exchange between operational personnel and buyers.

After two years, the newsletter was stopped and replaced by a few briefings in the company's internal newspaper. And then came all the Group procedures and inspections necessitated by the Sarbanes-Oxley Act, leading the procurement department to communicate abundantly on good internal practices and the role of transversal functions (procurement, legal, finance):

> Today, we place an emphasis on targeted exchanges with operational staff, we try to offer them a constant presence, and ensure that they grasp the procurement approach. The idea is for them to see contacting their buyer as being as natural as seeing their management controller or HR contact. Of course, the savings that are made are an important indicator, but the added value of actions undertaken or the improvement of processes (internal costs) and the evaluation of supplier performance are all the more necessary with the arrival of new procurement technologies (ERP, e-sourcing, e-procurement). Finally, we don't hesitate to seek appraisals from our customers on our efficiency or our added value through internal questionnaires.

The five keys to success for good procurement communication, according to the procurement director, are:

1 Relying from the outset on the internal communication department (help in choosing the most appropriate tools, presentation of messages).

2 Promoting users in successful performance (and not just the buyers), eg in the form of testimonies, and paying attention to customer satisfaction.

3 Establishing and regularly updating the list of key stakeholders (internal customers and main prescribers) in the form of a 'stakeholders map', in order to check that these people are seen regularly, and that the right messages have been transmitted.

4 Creating systematic meetings: eg two meetings per year with the executive committee.

5 Ensuring that messages are in tune with the company's requirements and its evolution. In short, adapt constantly!

Table 19.1 sums up the major stages of this action plan.

TABLE 19.1 Major action plan phases

Phase	Objectives	Messages	Internal means	External means
Launch Year 1	– Reputation of the function – Support of top management	– The function's raison d'être – Anticipated savings	– Procurement newsletter – Presentations en CDD – Creation of exchange spaces with operationals	– Supplier forum – Email campaigns
Years 2 and 3	– Credibility – Legitimacy – Creation of habits	– Results (savings validated by the finance department) – Success stories – Efficiency of the user-buyer duo	– Regular articles in the internal bulletin – General emails	– Supplier review
Years 4 and 5	– Added value – Gain in time – In tune with business objectives – Group compliance (Sarbanes-Oxley, internal auditing, ethics...) – Improvement of internal processes	– Procurement performance – Good practices – Internal / external benchmarking – Reminder of internal policies and charters	– Regular meetings with busines – Presentation in department meetings – Face-to-face interviews with key stakeholders	– Supplier review – E-sourcing tools (e.g. reverse auctions) – Group policies

19/3 Adapting to specific cultural situations

By carrying out procurement communication with the tools and methods outlined above, the procurement manager a has good chance of helping to set up a professional and mature function.

However, following a methodology, even a proven one, is not enough. It is also necessary to adapt to different cultures, whether corporate and/or country cultures. Indeed, for international multi-country companies, an extra dimension of interpretation and non-comprehension may compound the communication dimensions already examined.

19/3.1 Cultural differences to consider

Globalization does not mean communicating in exactly the same way globally, in all places and at all times. This is not the point of the concept – on the contrary. The chapter on human resources has already pointed this out: we promote difference, and so, an adapted communication approach.

The first difference which we confront is the difference between jobs. Every job has its own vocabulary, its own rhythm, its own habits. This also applies to buyers. This is why, when communicating, it is necessary to adapt terminologies to different targets.

Job culture

Buyers use their own specific jargon. It is therefore advisable that they are banned from using in all communication addressed outside of the function, to make sure that they speak the same language as the rest of the company. On this point, it is common to see reporting tables aimed at other functions (an often poorly used communication tool) that look more like lists and compilations of tables than communication tools. In addition, beyond form and readability, have we asked ourselves whether the information sent is actually useful for the recipients?

This type of communication gap can be exemplified by savings dashboards composed by buyers that other departments no longer read as they consider them irrelevant. There is an easy way to find out if reports interest interlocutors: just stop sending them. If no one asks for them, then their uselessness will be quite obvious. So why continue filling in these tables? Let's instead reconsider *simple, readable, usefulindicators recognized by all and followed over time*.

Does this ring a bell? Unfortunately, there is no shortage of examples. The author remembers one procurement head who communicated the prices of raw materials to all the subsidiaries and had to justify himself every day as all the subsidiaries asked for news about the others; when he started addressing information to a single recipient – the finance department – he saved a great deal of time whilst succeeding in meeting a group demand and letting the finance department decide what could be said to whom! So dear readers, before you continue with your tables and reports, think carefully about the form and the content. You can save a lot of time by being more efficient and relevant.

Company culture

The second aspect is related to cultural differences between companies. What works like magic communication-wise in one company will not necessarily be received identically in another company. Some companies have cultures based on writing, for example, whilst others have no tolerance for it. It is true that business sectors are characterized by similarities, but these may be illusory.

Country culture

The third aspect relates to the difference in culture between countries. Even within Europe, such differences exist. Whilst supporting international groups, the author has often taken part in meetings where obstacles were due to such differences. Within intercultural teams, the behavioural differences of players stemming from cultural factors are not easily changed in a company's life from one day to the next (see Loth, 2006).[7]

One company had recently concentrated its supplier teams in the United Kingdom, in a single department serving several sites in Europe, but processes were not properly set up. Very quickly, problems arose and a crisis meeting was organized with the French corporate financial director, the managing director of the British shared-services centre, and two managers of European sites (German and Italian). After getting off to a late start due to the unforeseen absence of the corporate financial director who had been called away on an emergency, the meeting quickly focused on the implementation of its very strict message: applying payment of an invoice only if there is an order, but with an 'adaptable approach and a minimum level of payment drip-feeding'. Discussions then turned to the definition of this approach: unsurprisingly, difficulties followed, with each (according to his own culture) having a different notion of the idea of 'dribbling'. It was by reconstructing simple, shared processes, explained in a language free from ambiguity, that the situation was finally salvaged.

We are not talking about something new. In the context of international negotiations, Fisher[8] long ago designed a grid for decoding transcultural phenomena organized around 10 questions:

1 Which rules and which roles predominate in the concept of negotiation in the other person's culture?

2 Can my interlocutor be considered as being representative of his or her group's culture?

3 What is the usual decision-making mode in the culture to which my interlocutor belongs?

4 What influence do the two parties have for themselves?

5 Do we understand the notions of agreement, compromise, commitment or renegotiation in the same way?

6 What is the usual style of the parties present?

7 What is the probable impact of differences in value, belief and ideological systems?

8 Are there manifest differences between the parties in their ways of thinking and reasoning?

9 What are the specific cultural factors liable to create difficulties?

10 What are the potential problems relating to linguistic interpretation?

Beyond these considerations, the research of Hofstede[9] points out predictive hypotheses, taking into account the different cultural dimensions between countries. It's up to readers to judge how accurate these are!

As far as we are concerned, we are keen to draw the reader's attention to necessary precautions – these will be the strength of those led to undertake international projects.

These few lines have no other aim but to highlight that a buyer's prime strength is his or her ability to listen, namely by encountering diversity in different forms without passing judgement. But beware: every rule sometimes has exceptions.

19/3.2 The necessary ability to adapt and make oneself heard

Communicating does not mean that everyone is expecting our messages and that these will be heard in the way that we wish, when we wish. Priorities may be overturned in response to the environment.

To give an example: one procurement director was planning to present his new organization but suddenly changed the schedule at the last moment due to the launch of a competitor's product 'already carving out market share for itself'. It is clear that the situation at hand required a postponement of the procurement director's presentation. Buyers need to respect the different priorities of the targeted persons.

To give another example: one communications director would systematically prepare a press pack including heartening stories for the Christmas period – a period when the economy relaxes and journalists are likely to look for this type of content. Understanding the right period to transmit her messages thus allowed her to maintain regular visibility.

To be heard, we also need, for example, to foresee a communication budget or else to have good news to give. Communicating good news is part of the rules set out at the start of the chapter. It is also very often used for change management, by supporting teams and enabling them to react to criticisms in the second phase of change, when difficulties emerge after the excitement of the launch.

John P Kotter[10] incidentally presents, as one of the key stages in the change process, the swift bringing of good news. This may be the role, for example, of quick wins via quick savings that will support longer-term actions in communication to justify induced costs, reward change players, bring concrete data and prepare the next stage, challenge the project's 'sceptics', show change becoming tangible, or tip over the 'wait-and-see' crowd by transforming them into supporters.

To give one example: a procurement project manager announced, in the early months of a project, many satisfying results on negotiations underway. But for many months, the message was always the same because the process took longer than expected to come to fruition. The pause in his communication sowed the seeds of trouble and doubt. Regular communication is reassuring.

Another stage that is certainly far more important in the communication process is that of creating emotion. John Kotter is happy to share with whoever has ears to hear that this is the very secret of those who succeed – and that this is something that he did not learn at school!

Kotter thus tells the story of a procurement manager arriving in a new company. At his first executive committee, whilst others expected to be presented with his strategic plan, he started emptying a bag of work gloves that he had picked up from different sites of the company, each with a label indicating the site and the price paid locally. The director of each zone naturally looked at those gloves from his or her country and compared the prices with those of the other directors. Differences were as great as several dozen percent. Some were smiling, others were more grim. The question on everyone's lips was the following: 'So what are you going to do?' It was at this point that he said: 'Don't you think we could do better?' And he presented his plan that was very quickly accepted.

If he had presented a comparative table as is commonly done, a debate on the reality of the figures, or difference in quality, would have ensued. The fact that he showed tangible objects and created a special atmosphere, rousing emotion, instantly won over all the participants. It is on this idea of emotion that we will conclude this chapter on communication. All you need to do is to type 'emotional quotient' into a search engine to see how incredibly topical it is. From our experience with this approach, there is no doubt that results are very different when taking emotion into account; though little is taught about it in management, it can yield excellent results. Let's always keep, as we announced in our communication rules, a human dimension with emotion in communication. Of course, emotion alone is not enough (we need results), but it is essential.

In conclusion, at the end of each stage of the communication plan, the efficiency of communication should be measured to validate the results obtained. The creation of an indicator or a survey forces us to ask ourselves the right questions, namely on the measurable objectives to reach. In this way, by establishing the indicator, we validate the fact that the right issues have truly been defined. Meanwhile, follow-up over time allows variations to be analysed. Surveys may be internal and/or external. External surveys yield far more information, but many procurement departments overlook use of them.

This feedback needs to be steered without being fastidious. Surveys, for example, may be carried out every year internally and every two years externally. Meanwhile, the measurement of efficiency becomes a habit as soon as it is integrated with other performance indicators.

As buyers need to drive the advancement of many projects, they should therefore systematically integrate a communication plan in their approach, associated with a methodology and ongoing continuous preparation.

Communicating is not merely about saying what we do. Nor is communicating synonymous with 'verbiage', alibis, or the filling of blank sheets.

As we have seen, communicating means staying simple, genuine and effective all the while being prudent, relevant and professional. Communication is an indispensable tool for the procurement function. Without communication, a product benefiting from the added value of the procurement function is perhaps a good product, but without communication, it will often remain in boxes and not be placed on display.

To conclude finally, here are two comments by procurement managers drawing from their experience:

Communication based on a PowerPoint presentation is not enough. You need to demonstrate your added value to the business by delivering a competitive advantage and sustainable value to the entire spend. Working with the business for the business and acting as a true business partner.
Source: Eric Chatelain, Head of Global Procurement Services & Indirect Procurement at Nestlé.

And according to Kathi Jobkar, CPM Manager, when she was CPM Manager at Strategic Sourcing Allegheny Technologies Inc: 'Anticipate and deal with the expectations of executives, and make your results visible in your organizations.'

Let's not forget: even if we have the best team and the best results in procurement, if we don't communicate them, we won't make any progress!

Final note on interpersonal communication

In this chapter we have not dealt with interpersonal communication which naturally plays a key role in the elements of communication plans, namely in regular 'one-to-one' relationships.

We nonetheless suggest that readers deepen their knowledge of certain models or reference models that seem to us as necessary for grasping and mastering the operation of communication between individuals. In this way, readers would benefit from delving into the following approaches: the process communication model (PCM)[11], transactional analysis (AT)[12] and neuro-linguistic programming (NLP)[13].

Good communication

When procurement strategies have been clearly defined, and effective operational practices applied, it is very important to set up, in parallel, resource management that is carried out coherently with the strategy and associated action plans: primarily appropriate information systems and decision-making tools, as well as buyer management and controlled steering of competencies. These points join up with the notion of effectiveness as a supplement of that of efficiency.

Notes

1 *Marketing Management, Analysis, Planning, Implementation and Control* (1988) Prentice-Hall, Englewood-Cliffs.

2 Schramm, W (1971) *The Process and Effect of Mass Communication*, University of Illinois Press, Urbana.

3 Strong, EK (1925) *The Psychology of Selling*, McGraw-Hill.

4 The notion of 'internal customers' is useful for a procurement function in the process of being built up, so that it can set itself up in the position of offering a service. We however then advise shifting to the notion of relationships between internal stakeholders to establish a two-way relationship with the company's different functions or partner professions, that we can assimilate to a business partner relationship if we wish to emphasize the development of business.

5 Refer to Section 4/5 for the links between communication issues and SRM for the supplier panel.

6 *Fonction Achats: La communication au service de la performance* (1999), Editions d'Organisation. Now out of stock.

7 Loth, D (2006) 'Les enjeux de la diversité culturelle: le cas du management des équipes interculturelles' in *Revue Internationale sur le Travail et la Société*, 4, 2, pp 124–33.

8 Fisher, G (1980) *International Negotiation: A cross-cultural perspective*, Yarmouth International Press, pp 98–147.

9 Hofstede, G (1980) *Culture's Consequences: International differences in work-related values*, Sage, Newbury Park, CA.

10 See the specialized bibliography at the end of the work. We however point out the following references (already dated but still entirely relevant): Kotter, JP (1996) *Leading Change*, Harvard Business School Press; Kotter, JP and Cohen, DS (2002) *The Heart of Change*, Harvard Business School Press.

11 Originally adopted by NASA for its astronauts, Process Communication is a means to identify the dominant traits of every individual in order for them be used for the team's benefit. See 'Management,' February 2006, p. 95, concepts defined by Taibi Kahler in the 1970s. See www.kcf.fr.

12 Eric Berne (1972) discovered that the perception of messages by persons communicating between themselves can be analysed by simple typologies with specific languages: *Que Dites-Vous Après Avoir Dit Bonjour?*, Tchou, coll. Le Corps à Vivre, first published in 1972.

13 Grinder and Bandler (1979), the founders of NLP, have put forward tools enabling a person to decode his or her own functioning and that of his or her interlocutors: 'Influencing phobic behaviour using the dissociate interventions,' University of Munich.

20
Procurement performance
Measurement indicators and reporting systems

Why measure procurement performance? To have an objective vision of *results and the way* in which they were reached. To have elements for *forecasting* and *anticipation*, and thus to have the means to take corrective measures. Finally, from a managerial point of view, to have *immediate influence over the behaviour* of all collaborators (if, naturally, the criteria by which individual performance is measured match those used to assess the performance of the procurement department as a whole).

As a result, whatever the complexity of a procurement department and its level of maturity, it is necessary to design and manage a performance measurement system for three main reasons: providing periodic *reporting* to executives and top management; informing, if possible, the heads of *business units* considered as internal customers; and having an *internal management* tool for all of the department's collaborators as well as all those who interface frequently with the function.

Two aspects will be dealt with successively: in this chapter, we will examine concepts and methods relating to the definition of performance objectives and action variables, as well as methods for establishing indicators and reporting systems; in Chapter 21, we will focus on the issues of performance management and the principles underlying change management.

20/1 Procurement performance: basic concepts

What is procurement performance? As for any other company function, according to an extremely classic management control approach, the generic concept of performance is made up of five main dimensions, as shown by Figure 20.1.[1]

FIGURE 20.1   Procurement-performance model (CARB)

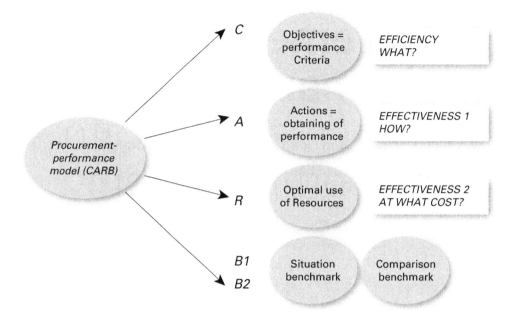

20/1.1 Generic procurement performance model

Let's analyse different dimensions of the reference CARB model.

Performance criteria and action variables

The first dimension concerns *performance criteria* expressed in terms of operational results expected by top management. On this level, we are within the sphere of effectiveness. For example, a purchase cost or acquisition cost is a performance criterion with the status of a result. The same goes for delivered quality or the satisfaction rate of internal customers and specifiers.

The second dimension relates to the model for obtaining performance. This point corresponds to the *strategic action variables* used and the *operational decisions* actually made. This model relies, in particular, on the choice of all processes implemented at every level (supplier approval, offer rating process, upstream procurement practices, etc) – the domain of the 'core business.'

There is necessarily a *causal link* between the processes and decisions influencing purchases, and the results observed. We are within the sphere of efficiency. For example, the number of active and approved suppliers on the panel, the number of responses to calls for tenders, or the number of just-in-time suppliers are procurement performance criteria directly related to the processes from which we expect results in response to objectives.

Use of resources

The third dimension concerns *optimal use of the resources* implemented. By 'resources' we refer to human, material and financial means mobilized by the function. We also include information and management systems (procurement module of an ERP system, e-sourcing tools, spend-analysis tools, a marketing procurement database, etc) that are designed and set up.

On this level, we can speak of the efficiency as well as the productivity of the function. For example, the number of buyers associated with the number of orders placed is a productivity criterion, as is the unit cost of handling for an order and a delivery.

The main benchmarks

The fourth dimension is made up of all standards including *situation and comparison benchmarks*. By situation benchmarks, we indicate that different situations are difficult to compare with one another (eg comparisons between different companies as well as comparisons within the one company due to different competitive or environmental contexts at different points in time).

Comparison benchmarks refer to the need to evaluate performance, and in particular to set *operational-performance 'target' objectives* that are realistic but motivating. There are several possible 'target' standards, which we will examine further.

Corollary measurement issue: indicators

The three first dimensions above will always need to be expressed *in a quantified and therefore measurable form*. This gives rise to a management tool constituting the performance measurement system (or dashboard) enabling reporting. As indicated by Figure 20.2, this issue comes down to the choice of indicators that will be grouped together into a number of categories.

The first is made up of *results indicators* relating to operational (or even strategic) objectives, most often quantified, and expected by top management and business partners.

The second consists of *action indicators* relating to operational decisions and the execution of various processes, or the elimination of various dysfunctions.

The third groups together *indicators on means* (resources implemented) *and productivity*. A final category (not mandatory but useful for managers) offers *comparison indicators* (eg on the basis of external information such as sectoral price indexes or prices on indexed markets).

In this way, procurement performance should be multi-dimensional in order to allow top management to observe the evolution of results, but also to enable procurement heads to manage their teams and ensure improvement of procurement professionalism.

FIGURE 20.2   Structure of the system of indicators (KPIs)

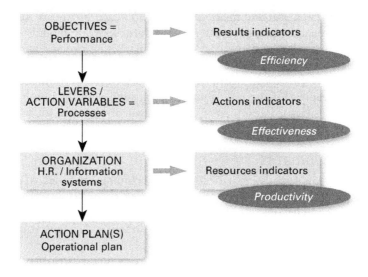

20/1.2 Usual comparison benchmarks

Bringing judgement on performance and managing the evolution of practices implies the existence of standards of comparison, namely for the setting of 'targets' to reach. As is practised generally for the supply chain, procurement classically employs three different types of methods, as shown by Figure 20.3.

Approach based on historical comparison

The first – and most frequent – approach is based on historical comparisons, consisting in expressing an objective by improvement on a past result (often updated on a yearly basis for budgetary reasons). Examples include: 'cutting default rates for deliveries by 5 per cent', 'reduction of the average purchase cost of a given category of components by 3 per cent next year' and so on.

The only comment to make here concerns the possibility that certain biases exist and can distort interpretation if we fail to pay attention to the real causes underlying performance. For the example on purchase costs, a 3 per cent reduction may result from various causes:

- boosting of competition between suppliers, backed up by well-prepared negotiations, hence real added value from the buyer;
- an observed drop in average price on the supplier market of 5 per cent (!), in which case the buyer has made a poor purchase as he or she has failed to reach the reduction observed on the market;

FIGURE 20.3　The three classic comparison benchmarks

	ADVANTAGES	DISADVANTAGES
Historical basis	Measurement of the improvement of the buyers' performance	Outcome resulting from exogenous events No external comparison No guarantee of the excellence of the level of practices Not adapted to non-recurrent purchases
Internal benchmarking	Setting up competition Upward alignment Top management steering the focus of business units on procurement performance	Difficulty of comparing different business contexts Different markets and competitive structures
External benchmarking	Possible objective comparison with the market. Allowing feedback on practices (not just results)	(Partial) collision with confidentiality Specificity of the logic of some procurement situations

- an increase in the volume purchased following an increase in sales, which mechanically enabled a reduction of costs due to a volume effect, without the buyer having to put in much effort;

- an evolution in the exchange rate that may have automatically triggered an effect on the purchase price and hence allowed the objective to be reached.

In this way, even if the operational objective may actually be attained by the company, the result is not necessarily due to an improvement of buyer performance through 'controllable' action variables within the buyer's responsibility. Conversely, a buyer of so-called 'speculative' raw materials who manages to reach a 3 per cent price increase during a period of international shortage in which prices and indexes generally rise by 6 per cent achieves a remarkable performance. And yet the financial result will register the rise and hence, an increase in cost of the 'raw materials' account!

Approach based on internal benchmarking

In groups made up of several profit centres (business units), the second approach consists in operating by internal benchmarking on the basis of indicators similar to those seen above. In this case, senior corporate management will set all business units the objective of attaining the results of the 'best' unit amongst them according to a principle of *upward alignment*. The information is generally fairly easy to collect, all the more so when a single integrated (ERP) information system exists within the group.

Here, the exercise comes across a few restrictions: business units may operate on upstream markets whose mechanisms are different, and there is a logical limit to the capacity for their performance to be completely aligned (eg because subsidiaries do not share the same expectations, or the competitive structure and standards of supplier markets are not the same).

However, this approach is simple and offers a true advantage: it encourages business-unit heads to question themselves and to 'spontaneously' look for causes explaining their performance. This outcome, in itself, is already a success from the perspective of senior management. Especially if the latter explicitly asks its executives to make periodical comparative reports for the benefit of the group steering committee, leading them to comment on and account for their performance.

And also if it sets both the procurement director and management control director the mission of keeping the performance measurement system alive, making sure that results are published at short intervals and are accessible and shared by all management concerned.

Approach based on external benchmarking

The last method of comparison is external benchmarking, that can be carried out either by consulting documentation in trade or academic journals, by consulting specialized websites, or by participating in benchmarking clubs. Difficulties may be of two types: finding standards of comparison based on performance criteria is a way to set oneself improvement objectives, but does not indicate how other companies succeeded in reaching their results nor via which processes; and relevant benchmarking does not necessarily mean comparing oneself with companies in the same sector (competitors), but with companies in other sectors, in order to eventually discover other performance levels and other ways of doing things, and then considering the utility of transferring them into one's own context subject to adaptations.

A benchmarking approach thus always implies acceptance of the sharing of information, of experiences, and above all, of solutions (bordering on confidential data). It is a game of 'give and take' that is generally difficult to make work between direct competitors. In addition, this strategy may lead to an alignment of practices, which is contradictory with the idea of progress and strategic differentiation.

Shared disadvantages of the three traditional approaches

Even used jointly, these three measurement and management approaches nevertheless present three major disadvantages:

- they are based on observations that enable making assessments on *relative value* (compared with oneself, with other buyers in the group, or even other companies), but offer no guarantee that the procurement practices implemented are the best (and thus 'optimal') professionally speaking;

- inscribed in a budgetary – hence annual – framework, via reporting tools and procurement dashboards, they only provide a glimpse of current performance from a *short-term perspective*;

- there is not necessarily any guarantee that company actions are *specific and coherent with the medium-term strategic requirements* of the group, and thus adapted to future changes expected by top management.

Hence the necessity to develop a supplementary approach focusing on the medium term, referring to a progress model approved beforehand by top management. We will look at this element in Chapter 21 when we will be analysing change management.

20/2 Establishing indicators and the dashboard

Let's start with an obvious point for any specialist, nonetheless forgotten by many practitioners: *there is no standard* (*ie single or standardized*) *dashboard for procurement*, as is the case for any other function. Indeed, a dashboard is only the translation of the operational missions and action variables specific to a given centre of responsibility within a company. In this way, depending on the exact definition of missions and the degree of autonomy and responsibility of a procurement department, the dashboard will need to be defined on a specific basis.

20/2.1 OVAR method and management indicators: a provisional management tool

The best method for doing so is to rely on the OVAR approach, developed and copyrighted by some management control professors from the HEC Paris, whose name comes from the following: O for *Objectifs* (objectives), VA for *Variables d'Action* (action variables), and R for *Responsables* (accountable leaders). Applicable to any responsibility centre, this method enables definition of short-term action plans for an operational entity, then, from the choice of objectives and selected action variables, drawing out relevant indicators allowing the ensuing action plans to be monitored.

Let's now present the principles and the strategy for drawing up the OVAR for a procurement department.[2] The method is based on a process consisting of five main stages, as illustrated by Figure 20.4.

Missions and operational objectives

This stage, necessitating the most detailed clarification, will be easier to conduct if the anticipated responsibilities of the manager are expressed formally by the manager's hierarchy. Taking the example of the procurement department to illustrate the concept, a few remarks are in order.

It is important to concentrate carefully on the (actual and measurable) short-term *operational* objectives that may be either expected by top management, as is the case most of the time, or sometimes also set by the procurement director wishing to partially focus his or her action on a priority defined following a self-diagnosis.

However, an objective is a priori the output expected from the function by the top management and internal customers or stakeholders (What are the points on which the procurement director is evaluated? What do we expect from him or her in terms of requirements of all types?). An operational objective holds the rank of a *result*: it is therefore logical for such objectives to be issued by all internal 'customers' and the top management. Well designed and clearly expressed, it may take the form of a simple transitive verb. Some examples for procurement include:

FIGURE 20.4   The five stages of the OVAR method

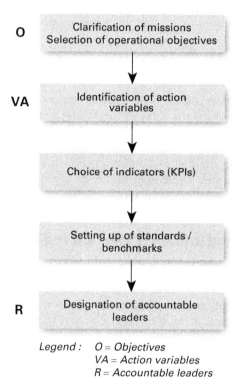

O   Clarification of missions
Selection of operational objectives

VA   Identification of action
variables

Choice of indicators (KPIs)

Setting up of standards /
benchmarks

R   Designation of accountable
leaders

Legend :   O = Objectives
VA = Action variables
R = Accountable leaders

- reduce the acquisition cost of a given category of products by x per cent next year;
- reduce the percentage of defaults for deliveries by y per cent;
- make savings (€x) in 'design' (by co-development with strategic suppliers).

It is necessary to avoid words that mean nothing and imply everything at the same time (eg *optimize, make profitable, improve*) as they prove a certain vagueness on the part of the speaker, and their operational translation allows doubt to cloud the true intention. An objective should be understandable and straightforward for all.

In addition, formulations on objectives that are too macroscopic in form are not acceptable either. For example, 'improve the cost/advantages relationship of a purchase' is not explicit enough. Do we wish to place an emphasis on reduction of DDP purchase costs (cost savings) or do we instead expect an input of innovation to lower the acquisition cost via modification of the design (cost avoidance)? In this type of case, several objectives, probably segmented according to the logic of the procurement portfolio, will enable light to be shed on the final result truly sought.

Experience also proves the difficulty for a procurement department of following more than around five objectives at a time.

Most often, the horizon qualified as 'short-term' in the context of the OVAR method means the following budgetary year, and results are recorded in the year's financial statement. It is nevertheless important that the manager has, in advance, a vision of the medium-term targets to be reached (cf. Chapter 21).[3]

Action variables

Action variables correspond to the various *levers or processes and practices that the procurement department will implement in order to reach results*. There should therefore be a very strong *causal link* between action variables and the operational objectives being followed.

An objective may necessitate the implementation of *several action variables* at the same time, but no action variable can be chosen if it cannot be shown to truly contribute to the pursuit of at least one operational objective. Otherwise, this simply means a waste of time through the useless targeting of company actions.

As has already been said in relation to objectives, the total number of action variables should also be limited in order to focus on priorities and to facilitate the follow-up of the specific actions that are to be implemented.

It is difficult to select and prioritize levers or action variables, but these steps are crucial: it is up to the procurement director and his or her collaborators, following a team management approach in a *participative mode* to weigh up choices on priorities and trade-offs.

If an objective holds the rank of a result, action variables are situated on the level of the means to implement in order to reach it (ie procurement core competencies).

Figure 20.5 presents – on the basis of an extremely simplified case drawn from a real-life situation – the correlation between operational objectives and action variables in an OVAR table applied to procurement. Causal links are indicated by crosses when elements in the lines and columns coincide.

At the bottom of the figure, we have deliberately included three lines that are not, strictly speaking, action variables, but that relate to the management of associated *human and financial resources* which the procurement department needs to monitor at the same time. Here, we are in the field related more to the search for productivity in the procurement function and the development of the professionalism and abilities of buyers.

For each action variable, it is necessary to define a *detailed action plan* that should include at least all of the following characteristics:

- a precise description of the follow-up process and the anticipated schedule;
- clear identification of the leading manager in charge of this plan and the whole of the associated project, as well as different contributors (ie business partners and support functions);
- a clear list of human, material and financial means to implement with a detailed schedule for their contributions;
- a reminder of the indicators for measuring the plan's actual project advancement;
- a reminder of the expected final results, with a precise description of the advantages and gains for internal customers and the company.

FIGURE 20.5 Central Procurement Department OVAR

XYZ Ltd.	Central Procurement Department OVAR						
OPERATIONAL OBJECTIVES	Reduce procurement costs (–X% in the next year)	Reduce quality defects (maximum Y% defects)	Ensure reliable delivery lead times (respect by + / – Z days)	Reduce the WCR (obj.: –Z%)	Mitigate supply risks (shortages + regulatory compliance)	Satisfy expectations of internal customers (target rate 90%)	Develop the BUs' use of the Central Procurement Department
VARIABLES / LEVERS							
Reduce the supplier panel	X	X	X				
Increase the number of new suppliers (global sourcing)	X						
Develop double sourcing					X		
Increase the number of quality-assured suppliers		X	X				
Deploy CSR audits of panel suppliers					X		
Increase the number of competitive bids (i.e. calls for tenders)	X						
Lengthen payment periods (within maximum legal limit)				X			
Reduce inventories of materials / other items				X			
Consolidate requirements (quantities if shared purchases)	X					X	X
Strictly apply compliance with REACH and RoHS regulations					X		
Develop standardization (for materials + components + consumables)	X			X			
Reduce average processing time for local purchase requests						X	
Define and deploy a communication plan aimed at BUs and top management						X	X
Reduce the operating costs of the Central Procurement Department	X						
Deploy a Wiki (procurement + business partners)						X	X
Train central and local buyers					X	X	X

In this way, the action plan for the whole of the procurement department is made up of the sum of elementary action plans, one per action variable.

Choice of indicators (KPIs)

It follows that indicators will be as exact a translation as possible of the OVAR if they are to serve as a *measurement tool* best adapted to what we seek to measure: progress on operational objectives and action variables, according to the rationale presented in Figure 20.6 based on the same example as above.

Let's remember that like all measurement tools, a management indicator should at least have the following characteristics:

- be *faithful to the object* or the entity measured in order to be truly representative;
- have a *lasting sustainability* in order to enable historical comparisons if need be depending on the types of indicators;
- be *quantifiable* as far as possible, even if in binary form only for certain indicators, without its interpretation raising issues of relevance for those whose action is thus measured;
- be *easily obtained from accounting and non-accounting databases* (ie from information existing in the ERP system).

There is no standard dashboard model made up of regular indicators when it comes to action variables. *Conceptually, standardization would be nonsensical.* However, to give readers a few pointers and to help them in their reflections, a list of benchmark indicators can be found at the end of this chapter, grouped according to a logical presentation, and drawn directly from systems used in certain companies (Tables 20.1, 20.2 and 20.3).

Choice of standards or benchmark frameworks

Standards of comparison *based on the logic of a standard or a benchmark target* were discussed in Section 20/1.2.

However, it is necessary to also mention that performance should be measured in a differentiated manner *depending on the kinds of purchases made and the respective management rationale* (in relation to the segmentation of the procurement portfolio), hence making up a second important focus. This approach is examined in Section 20/3, and will be illustrated by specific examples to help guide further reflection.

Designation of responsible leading managers

There can be no action plans without project heads in charge of steering their deployment and realization.

For an OVAR dedicated to the procurement function, logic implies that project leaders generally (but not always, depending on the case) be collaborators within the function who manage the plan's deployment and take responsibility for reporting (at least on the level of action variables taken separately).

The procurement director should beware of not placing him- or herself too often in this managerial position simply out of apparent ease (frequently influenced by apprehension when facing the related issues of delegation and management).

FIGURE 20.6   Dashboard coherent with OVAR Fig 20.5

DASHBOARD								
Reduce procurement costs (–X% in the next year)	Differentials in purchase costs (historical) Differentials in "target" costs (stakeholders)							
Reduce quality defects (maximum Y% defects)	Number of batches refused / number of batches received Rejection rate / claims							
Ensure reliable delivery lead times (respect by + / − Z days)	Number of delays or early deliveries / Receptions Histogram on lead times							
Reduce the WCR (obj.: –Z%)	Follow-up of WCR elements							
Ensure security of supply (shortage rate: maximum T%)	Average shortage rate Average number of suppliers / purchased item							
Satisfy expectations of internal customers (target rate 90%)	Global satisfaction rate (dedicated tool)							
Develop the BUs' use of the Central Procurement Department	Cross analysis on "number of BUs % purchased expense" per main categories							
Reduce the supplier panel	Reduction rate of active suppliers used (on historical basis)							
Increase the number of new suppliers (global sourcing)	% new homologated suppliers / number of active suppliers							
Develop double sourcing	Number of suppliers / purchased item							
Increase the number of quality-assured suppliers (qualified quality-assurance system)	% quality-assured suppliers / number of panel suppliers (on historical basis)							
Deploy CSR audits of panel suppliers	% CSR-qualified suppliers / panel suppliers (pre-targeted as "high-risk")							
Increase the number of competitive bids (via calls for tenders)	Number of suppliers consulted / call for tender Average rate of response to calls for tenders							
Lengthen payment periods (within maximum legal limit)	Average contractual payment period (outside of "strongly supported" SMI)							
Reduce inventory of materials / other items	Financial amount in € or USD invested in stock (total & per category)							
Consolidate requirements (quantities if shared purchases)	% centralized shared purchases (quantities / amounts purchased)							
Strictly apply compliance with REACH and RoHS regulations	% items audited / total number of items purchased							
Develop standardization (for materials + components + consumables)	% items eliminated / total number of items							
Reduce processing time for local purchase requests	Processing lead time for a purchase request							
Define and deploy a communication plan aimed at BUs and top management	Follow-up of the approved project (respect of the schedule and commitments)							
Reduce the operating costs of the Central Procurement Department	Difference between actual expenses / operating budget							
Deploy a Wiki (procurement + business partners)	Follow-up of the approved project (respect of the schedule and approved specific budgets)							
Train central and local buyers	Training of buyers (number or hours or days spent)							

By proceeding in this way, the procurement director truly uses the OVAR and the associated system of indicators as a genuine tool for managing his or her team, and thus finds a privileged means for improving the competencies and autonomy of collaborators within the team (who remain, in parallel, in charge of their own recurrent operational responsibilities). Future procurement managers are already within their ranks.

In addition, use of these tools enables implementation of *management by objectives* because the setting of annual objectives during individual interviews will thus be largely prepared for by this delegation principle paired with periodic reporting and monitoring of results.

20/2.2 Reporting system

The reporting system may vary depending on the situation and the choice of internal targets (business partners, specifiers or top management).

If we adhere to a strict dashboard approach, reporting will rely on the periodical publication of *results indicators* along with appropriate comments on the targets.

Significant events can (and should) be indicated and explained in detail. In particular, the procurement director may insist on certain points relating to action variables implemented in order to highlight explanations on a given result attained. Globally, however, top executives are interested in results and not directly in the means that have enabled them to be reached.

However, this is not the case with internal customers, and even less so with direct collaborators (the buyers themselves), for whom reporting ideally focuses on internal processes and action variables related to improvement of their professional efficiency. These stakeholders are also and above all interested in *action indicators*.

20/3 Specific aspects depending on the procurement situation

The indicators seen above and the attached measurement issues are not the same depending on the situation. In addition, the performance of buyers cannot be evaluated in the same way, for their direct management and their internal customers do not expect the same results, depending on the case. Three main types of situation can be identified.

Case of recurrent (direct or indirect) purchases

Most of the time this applies to direct purchases over a long-term period, for which we have historical data enabling comparisons over time (eg recurrent components or services). Indeed, very often a past reference exists. This case frequently especially concerns categories corresponding to standard 'strategic' purchases. But the right column on Figure 20.7 shows obvious similarities for 'strategic' categories. We see two levels of possible evolution in the measurement system (the so-called 'advanced' stage showing possible evolution by offering additional indicators that supplement

FIGURE 20.7 Performance measurement for recurrent purchases

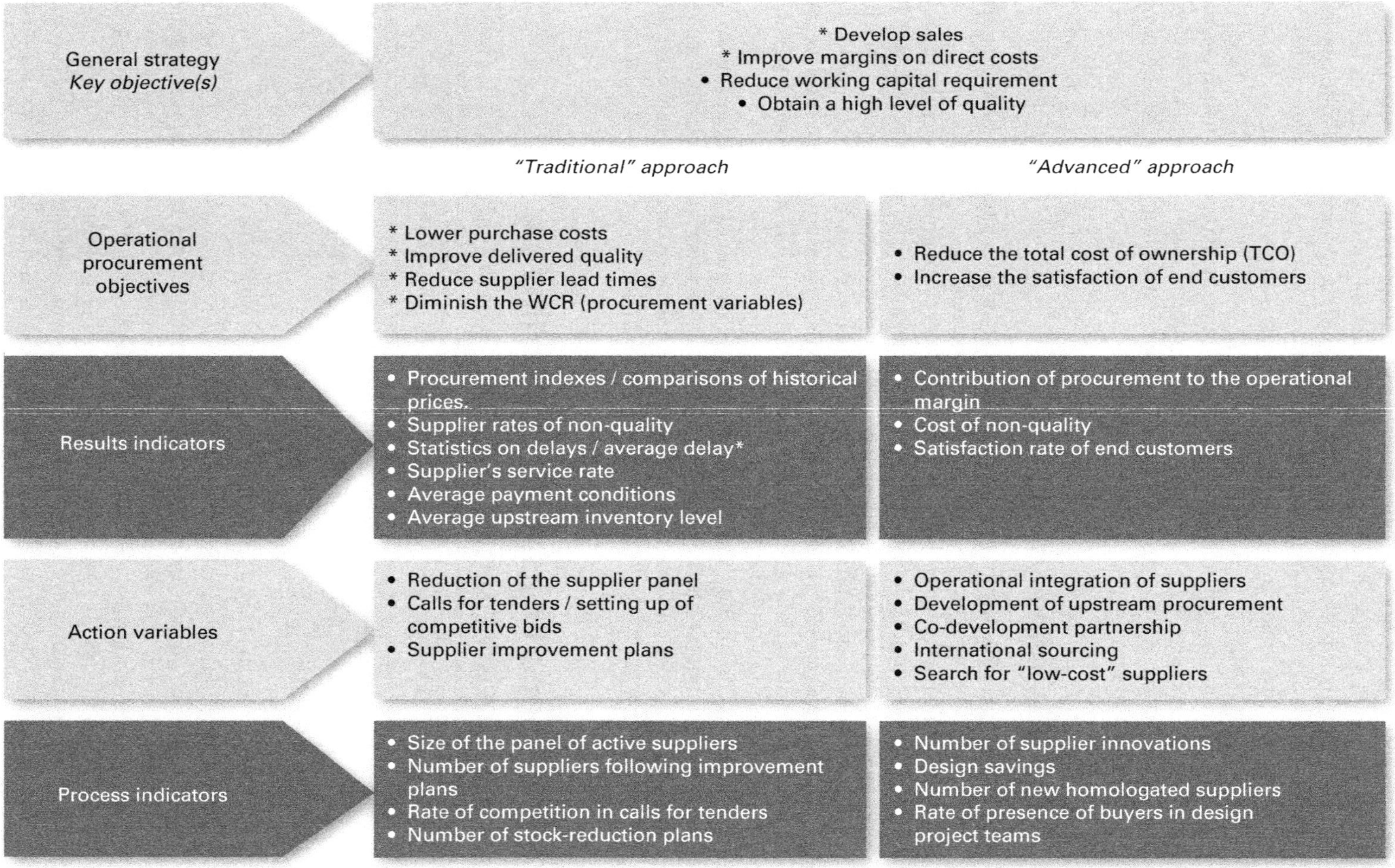

"Traditional" approach   "Advanced" approach

General strategy
Key objective(s)

* Develop sales
* Improve margins on direct costs
  * Reduce working capital requirement
  * Obtain a high level of quality

Operational procurement objectives

* Lower purchase costs
* Improve delivered quality
* Reduce supplier lead times
* Diminish the WCR (procurement variables)

* Reduce the total cost of ownership (TCO)
* Increase the satisfaction of end customers

Results indicators

- Procurement indexes / comparisons of historical prices.
- Supplier rates of non-quality
- Statistics on delays / average delay*
- Supplier's service rate
- Average payment conditions
- Average upstream inventory level

- Contribution of procurement to the operational margin
- Cost of non-quality
- Satisfaction rate of end customers

Action variables

- Reduction of the supplier panel
- Calls for tenders / setting up of competitive bids
- Supplier improvement plans

- Operational integration of suppliers
- Development of upstream procurement
- Co-development partnership
- International sourcing
- Search for "low-cost" suppliers

Process indicators

- Size of the panel of active suppliers
- Number of suppliers following improvement plans
- Rate of competition in calls for tenders
- Number of stock-reduction plans

- Number of supplier innovations
- Design savings
- Number of new homologated suppliers
- Rate of presence of buyers in design project teams

first-generation indicators without substituting them). Everything put forward as plausible indicators for illustrative purposes permits historical comparison, and can be verified. As before, the example takes an extremely simplified form.

Finally, for this type of purchase, the buyer is often more *autonomous in actions* relating to procurement strategy and tactics (*once requirements specifications have been defined* by internal customers). The buyer operates with delegated responsibility. When procurement savings are achieved, for example, there is no risk of bias and we know that the savings will probably be 'automatically' transferred to the P&L at the end of the financial period.

Case of purchases in the context of one-off tenders or projects

In this case, there is no past because each project (each new deal) is, by definition, original. If, however, certain project components are standard, they will then be managed according to the preceding approach (the quantity of the requirement resulting from the new project being added to other standard requirements). As illustrated by Figure 20.8, the problem of measurement is completely different here.

First of all, in this scenario the buyer is never truly autonomous: as the member of the project team, he or she relies closely upon the *project manager* who remains the final decision-maker for the purchase (the single internal customer in this case). In addition, the buyer often confronts a requirement for innovative solutions that imply specific *sourcing*. Finally, it is common for requirements specifications to evolve over time (take the example of the procurement of software services whose specifications may evolve even during the solution's development).

In such a situation, the absence of any historical reference, namely on the economic front, makes evaluation of the buyer's task far more difficult when it comes to choosing a benchmark framework. Two approaches may nonetheless be used.

We may have an *external target cost*, derived for example from a target margin to reach, or an approximate historical basis (eg the cost of a similar technical function or subassembly already purchased in the past at a historical acquisition cost). In this case, procurement performance will be measured in terms of disparities with the objective. If we have no possible benchmark reference, practice tends to *measure the gap* between the average of the quotations received from suppliers following the initial call for tenders and the final price at which the purchase is ultimately made following final negotiations.

Note also that in this situation, savings resulting from the act of procurement strictly speaking are not necessarily transferred to the P&L, and the buyer should above all avoid 'announcement effects'. Indeed, ulterior modifications in the project as it follows its course may well generate cost overruns, sometimes justified, that then neutralize the savings of the initial procurement. In addition, the project director has the perfect right to make use of savings generated by the buyer to finance, for example, additional studies whilst remaining within the original global budget.

The second key criterion of performance relates to indicators aimed at measuring capacities for innovation and risk mitigation (ie through the partial transfer of certain risks to suppliers).

FIGURE 20.8 Performance measurement for project (or deal-based) purchases

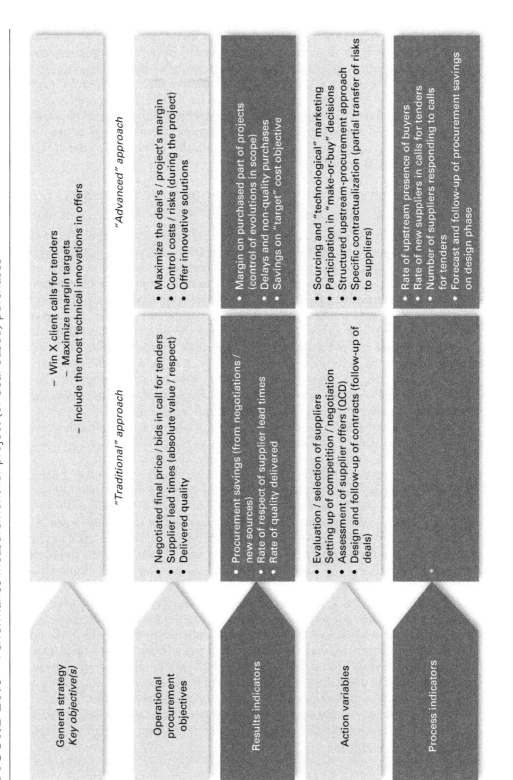

"Traditional" approach   "Advanced" approach

General strategy
Key objective(s)

- Win X client calls for tenders
- Maximize margin targets
- Include the most technical innovations in offers

Operational procurement objectives

- Negotiated final price / bids in call for tenders
- Supplier lead times (absolute value / respect)
- Delivered quality

- Maximize the deal's / project's margin
- Control costs / risks (during the project)
- Offer innovative solutions

Results indicators

- Procurement savings (from negotiations / new sources)
- Rate of respect of supplier lead times
- Rate of quality delivered

- Margin on purchased part of projects (control of evolutions in scope)
- Delays and non-quality purchases
- Savings on "target" cost objective

Action variables

- Evaluation / selection of suppliers
- Setting up of competition / negotiation
- Assessment of supplier offers (QCD)
- Design and follow-up of contracts (follow-up of deals)

- Sourcing and "technological" marketing
- Participation in "make-or-buy" decisions
- Structured upstream-procurement approach
- Specific contractualization (partial transfer of risks to suppliers)

Process indicators

*

- Rate of upstream presence of buyers
- Rate of new suppliers in calls for tenders
- Number of suppliers responding to calls for tenders
- Forecast and follow-up of procurement savings on design phase

Case of occasional purchases in the context of set budgets

This type of purchase is even more specific because such situations are characterized by the fact that the internal customer, generally and paradoxically, does not seek any procurement savings. Most of the time, the internal customer has negotiated a budget with its management for an operation that has been accepted, and so the former's only clearly expressed objective is to obtain *maximum content and value for the initial budget* determining the maximum sum of expenses.

This is notably the case for the procurement of human resources services, and in particular for marketing or communication purchases.

For example, let's imagine that a large pharmaceutical laboratory places a buyer in charge of organizing its next annual congress aimed at medical sales representatives. The plan is to make a trip over a long weekend to an overseas resort in southern Maghreb for a stay combining work meetings and leisure activities, with the whole event punctuated by various information briefings, the announcement of future sales objectives, and group motivation activities!

The total budget has been defined in conjunction with top management and the marketing director. What the buyer will need to do is to place at the disposal of the salesforce management a global 'turnkey' service whose content will be as rich and innovative as possible. In addition, the selection of suppliers will no longer be based on financial considerations, but rely on the pairing of creativity/feasibility in the operation (security), as illustrated by Figure 20.9. For this type of procurement, buyers tend to play the role of an internal competency centre and a source of proposals. They will be subject to a non-economic best-efforts commitment in a pseudo-contractual approach: the real decision-maker remains the internal customer.

The whole logic of the measurement system and the choice of indicators will follow on naturally (only costs per unit of labour will eventually provide any historical references – eg in the procurement of temporary labour, HR services or technical assistance).

20/4 Possible conflictual situations requiring weighting

There are some management situations where the issue of measurement and interpretation is more complex to conduct and resolve.

20/4.1 Company performance versus collaborator performance

There are many situations where improvement in the efficiency of buyers does not necessarily go hand in hand with that of the company, and vice versa. Let's take the following example of a company in the aeronautics sector that seeks to buy semi-precious metals on the global market.

For several years, before the global economic downturn of October 2008, global prices had soared for various reasons, mainly due to speculation phenomena on the markets, associated with shortage mechanisms resulting from the increase in

FIGURE 20.9 Performance measurement for purchases based on internal budgets

General strategy
Key objective(s)
- Respect of the operating budgets
- Meeting requirements at the best market cost
- For a given budget, maximize "quality / customer value"

"Traditional" approach   *"Advanced" approach*

Operational procurement objectives

"Traditional" approach
- Definition of requirements specifications and standard contracts (recurrent purchases)
- Help in the requirement specifications and the scope of the purchase
- Negotiation on prices

"Advanced" approach
- Offer innovative solutions to operational departments at lowest cost
- Anticipate and lock up main risks for internal customers
- Facilitate supply and traceability

Results indicators

"Traditional" approach
- Evolution of prices (recurrent purchases)
- Negotiated procurement savings (non-recurrent procurement)
- Quality of supplier services deliveries

"Advanced" approach
- Per-unit costs of labor
- Supplier quality of service
- Rate of satisfaction of internal customers

Action variables

"Traditional" approach
- Evaluation / selection of suppliers
- Setting up of competition / negotiation
- Contractualization of standard master agreements (case of recurrent purchases)

"Advanced" approach
- Actual contribution to the definition of requirements specifications
- Search for standardized solutions
- Work on functional requirements specifications (geared at "results")
- Simplification of procurement processes
- "Internal customer – procurement" contractualization

Process indicators

"Advanced" approach
- Rate of upstream presence of buyers
- Number of "internal" contracts concluded
- Rate of contracted / fixed-price purchases

*

demand from emerging countries. In the case of titanium, prices have gone up by 44 per cent in the past year!

The buyer has managed to partially deal with these developments thanks to a supply security system with coverage mechanisms and long-term contracts, and consequently records a price increase of only 23 per cent. From the company's perspective, a very significant rise in purchase costs entailing a reduction in margins is recorded. However, the buyer has proven to be an excellent professional, amongst the best on the market.

It is therefore necessary to always assess each situation by dissociating two levels: that of *the company's financial results*, which incidentally will be the only reading made by financial departments and which will also be consulted in priority by shareholders with an eye on the net margin (EBITDA); and that of the *professional practice of procurement collaborators*, a topic related to the management of teams who may excel in a given situation, using the sole *controllable* action variables at their disposal and within the set of constraints objectively limiting their options for action.

20/4.2 Possible internal conflicts between responsibility centres/departments

Within the supply chain, situations may arise where buyers and supply-chain protagonists hold diverging interests (if no global trade-off is sought and found). Decisions on sourcing and international development illustrate this point. To give an example, as we have seen in Chapter 5, most of the time European buyers proceed according to economic logic alone, focusing on differences in direct ex-works costs that may reach up to –50 per cent or –60 per cent, with the objective of then repatriating these products to Europe. For many, this approach seems logical given the most widespread performance criterion: minimization of the purchasing cost.

However, by proceeding in this way, the selection of such suppliers implies the implementation of international supply chains for the repatriation of products, entailing numerous operational risks as we have seen in detail above (in respect of quality, lengthening and variation of delivery lead-times), problems in securing supply sources, or even problems of compliance with REACH or RoHS-type regulations, compounded by transport issues. All these risks imply the setting up of costly preventative solutions (local quality audits, sizable safety stocks, backup transport solutions), not to mention increase of the WCR related to an average lengthening of cycles and the increase of work-in-process stock.

In this way, logisticians may well see their costs skyrocket! This explains why the financial balance sheet sometimes shows lower savings than the initial forecast, not forgetting a loss of flexibility linked to long lead-times.

One conclusion becomes clear: it is important to carefully ensure absolute compatibility of the management systems of the different responsibility centres making up the supply chain's sub-systems. Failing this, there will be no guarantee of overall performance on the company level. To thus ensure compatibility, a deliberate choice should be made of *shared global indicators* integrated into the OVARs of the different responsibility centres that have *joint responsibility* for a given indicator.

Here, the only realistic decision is to impose use of the TCO and having this *single TCO* as an indicator in the dashboards of every department (ie the procurement and supply-chain departments). In this way, the various actors will naturally be led to jointly seek the best trade-off. Chapter 9 presented an explicit example of such a situation.

20/4.3 Specific difficulties in risk mitigation

A managed approach to risks implies a capacity to define two dimensions fairly clearly: on the one hand, a realistic and quantified evaluation of *economic consequences* and qualitative gains using appropriate indicators; and on the other hand, an evaluation of the *cost of prevention measures* and/or 'curative' measures (if need be), that may have to be set up and sustained in order to face or partially mitigate the consequences of possible problems.

If we manage to obtain such figures, these elements will all naturally contribute to the direct costs of the supply chain, and will need to be included as cost items in the overall performance (TCO).

Costs relating to protection measures are generally fixed costs that are known with a relative degree of certainty due to the nature of the means deployed, whilst evaluation of consequences is more often random and always associated with a probability of occurrence.

Indeed, technical risks (lead-times/quality) and certain tactical risks of suppliers (flexibility/reactivity/risk of dependency) are fairly foreseeable on a historical statistical basis and their consequences can be costed. Solutions for facing these risks (safety stocks, quality-assurance systems, specific local audits, limitation of the proportion represented in supplier turnover, choice of the frequency and handling costs of deliveries, etc) are often known and can be quantified.

However, it is not so easy to quantify, for example, the probability of a product's withdrawal from the market for non-compliance with European REACH or RoHS regulations. In addition, in the area of sustainable development, the setting up of prevention measures consists in deploying more stringent supplier policies and industrial strategies. Costs are usually fixed and result from investment decisions (investments in so-called 'clean' solutions), operating expenses (training, evolution of systems and management tools, etc), as well as the procurement of external services (eg third-party companies specialized in CSR audits).

On the other hand, the consequences of bad supplier practices or supply failures may be considerable, but most of the time they will have an indirect impact on the client market and/or share prices, making their costing extremely delicate, or even random.[4] Mathematically, their evaluation stems from a cost-expectation logic and probabilistic calculation.

This is the reason why indicators used for risk management point above all to *company actions deployed rather than results* relating to targeted objectives (eg the number of suppliers audited on their CSR practices, the number of suppliers to sign the sustainable development charter, the percentage of calls for tenders including explicit CSR criteria, the number of suppliers to have carried out their carbon assessment, the hours of specific training deployed, etc).

Notwithstanding this tendency, reporting may be constructed on a logic of comparison, showing: on one hand, prevention cost figures associated with the different prevention measures set up; on the other hand, an updated assessment of risks in terms of occurrence and categories of 'seriousness' (eventually costed if risks should be realized). This way of proceeding should remind many readers how different categories of costs are computed in quality management (non-quality costs versus quality-assurance costs).

20/4.4 Global performance of the 'extended' supply-chain network

We need to be vigilant that improvement of performance takes place evenly and simultaneously amongst the different companies making up the *upstream supply chain* (the company itself and all of its suppliers and partners).

Diminishing purchase costs by systematically eating into supplier margins is not viable in the long term, apart from the ethical problems that this approach may represent regarding responsible supplier relationships.

Outside of exceptional situations where supplier margin rates largely differ from those widely practised, the result should be attained thanks to a structurally viable lowering of supplier costs. The company can also contribute to facilitating this improvement process. Indeed, an improved interfacing information system can help this result to be reached: the solution should always be found in a balanced collaborative approach.

Similarly, reduction of one's investments in inventories by transferring them to a supplier with a system of stock on consignment only 'displaces' them along the supply chain. In any case, the company will have to bear the costs (since, instead of being included in the company's own financial costs, they are reintegrated in its purchase costs!).

The only lasting solution is to trace the causes making this stock necessary in order to find solutions enabling them to be diminished in the long term and without risk (a collaborative approach to deployment of a realistic just-in-time system would meet this improvement objective).

20/5 Can we speak of procurement's intangible performance?

A company's 'intangible' capital (goodwill) is defined as the difference between its asset value and its global financial value (from an investment point of view). Beyond its official balance sheet value, a company owns value that is not necessarily translated into its accounts; this is what is known as its intangible capital, to which intangible assets correspond.

20/5.1 Elements making up intangible capital

As shown by Figure 20.10, without going into details that are not relevant for the purposes of this book, the intangible capital of any company characterizes its full value represented by a certain number of off-balance sheet assets, significant as they largely condition the company's *future development and its resultant profitability.*[5]

FIGURE 20.10   A company's intangible capital

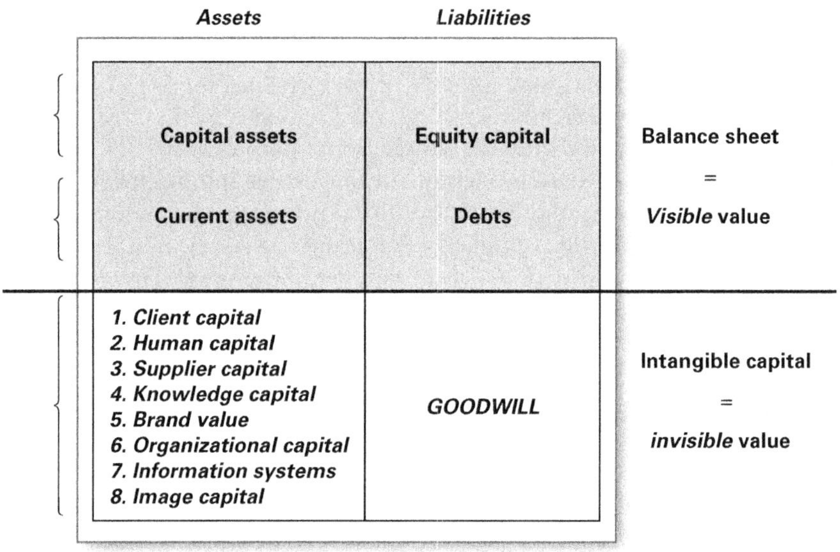

Assets	Liabilities	
Capital assets	Equity capital	Balance sheet
		=
Current assets	Debts	*Visible* value
1. Client capital 2. Human capital 3. Supplier capital 4. Knowledge capital 5. Brand value 6. Organizational capital 7. Information systems 8. Image capital	GOODWILL	Intangible capital = *invisible* value

Indeed, *an average* of around two-thirds of a company's value is made up of intangible assets: human capital (competencies, knowledge, know-how, experience), client capital (knowledge of requirements and expectations), technological and know-how capital (R&D, patents), information system capital (reliability), brand value (image, reputation), value of decision-making systems, organizational capital (management process, quality management system, productivity), and finally capital represented by suppliers and partners (relationships, loyalty, etc).

We observe that the average relationship between company transaction value (market capitalization) and net accounting value (balance sheet value) on the New York Stock Market (Standard & Poor's 500 Index) has evolved significantly by going up from 1 to 3. This assertion converges with results of the International Integrated Reporting Council which, in its report from September 2011, indicated that the weight of intangible and non-financial assets of companies listed in the S&P 500 has climbed from 17 per cent to over 80 per cent in almost 35 years.

Maintaining this intangible capital means guaranteeing the *potentialities of cash flows and future profits*. On the assumption that this value can be measured, it also provides an excellent financial indicator in the eyes of shareholders and investors. It is also, ultimately, a key valuation element amongst others during mergers or acquisitions.

20/5.2 Evaluation of the supplier portfolio

The procurement department is directly involved in this issue. Beyond the suppliers' short-term performance in terms of purchasing costs, they also contribute to the company's intangible capital through two main asset elements: 1) *supplier capital* (or 'partner capital') via the upstream sourcing of top-level partners, the setting up of sustainable and lasting partnerships in order to benefit from products of uniform quality and to promote innovation, the establishment of mutually beneficial collaborative relationships (fair-price policy, reduction of supplier turnover, support in collaborative ongoing improvement approaches, respect of contractual commitments, namely payment periods, etc); and 2) *image capital* relating to the company's reputation via compliance with legislation, anticipation and mitigation of environmental, social or corporate risks, as well as dialogue and coordination with some company stakeholders.

This contribution that can be made by the procurement department through the supplier portfolio has taken on a growing dimension in step with processes for the gradual outsourcing of various activities in numerous sectors (companies *in networks*), leading to actual co-performance between the company and all of its *external resources*.

In addition, the concept of goodwill now includes all CSR aspects, and the procurement department plays a decisive role in that the company, in the current context of strengthened weights of stakeholders, is considered as co-responsible for the practices of its tier-one suppliers and beyond. The procurement department is thus given the opportunity to demonstrate its relevance as well as its potential to create value.

In this way, the issue arises of *estimating the value* of a supplier portfolio. Without providing a very detailed method (which would be directly operational), here are the main elements for an approach, consisting in answering two key questions and offering an associated formal methodology:

1 What is the *quality* of the portfolio (combining concepts of performance, durability and development potential)?

2 What, consequently, is its *financial value*?

Quality of the supplier panel

The rationale for evaluating a panel's quality, based on a multi-criteria approach, is presented by Figure 20.11.

This mix of criteria may be adapted to a supplier panel for a category in particular, but global use of it enables *qualitative* rating of a company's supplier panel (some criteria largely crossing over with – unsurprisingly! – the criteria for approving a supplier panel). It is then necessary to make a link with the valuation stage.

Consequential valuation

On the basis that a supplier portfolio constitutes an investment, in order to put a value on it, we can apply a method similar to that used for other investments: estimation of the *replacement value*.

FIGURE 20.11   Evaluation of the quality of a supplier portfolio (panel)

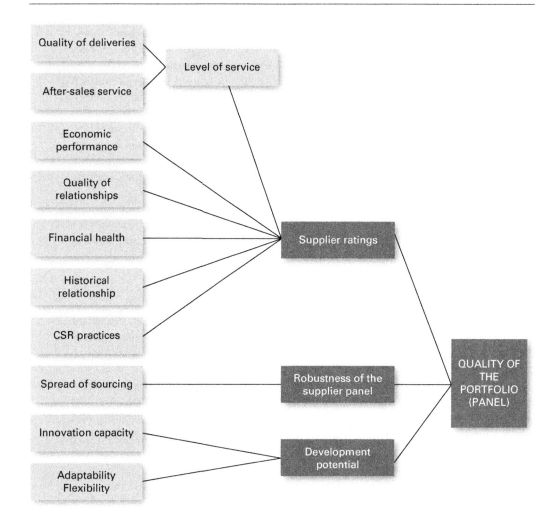

The idea is simple and involves asking the following question: how much would it cost if it were necessary to reconstitute a supplier panel offering equivalent performance and contribution to value creation? This would include at least sourcing and qualification costs, to which would need to be added all cumulative expenses incurred by supplier management over time.

Depending on the above rating evaluations, a possible 'depreciation' coefficient should be applied on the full replacement value. Obviously, the better a panel's rating, the higher its value.

Even if the method is rather difficult to implement, formalizing the approach enables orders of magnitude to be calculated, and above all, it is worthwhile for *monitoring supplier developments*.

However, it is implicit that this technique is partial and does not directly link the value of the supplier portfolio to updated future cash flows by a causal logic. It is nonetheless possible to consider correlation between them to be strong: incidentally, periodic calculation of figures on a historical basis (between the portfolio valuation and the contribution of procurement to value creation) could help confirm this assertion.

20/6 Major stages in the operational implementation of a performance measurement system

When we tackle the definition and deployment of a performance measurement system, it is necessary to do so following a sequence of stages that should be formally distinguished (Figure 20.12). This figure calls for a few comments that we will briefly discuss.

Choice of objectives and targets

The definition of performance objectives (Stage I on Figure 20.12) should depend on strategic objectives, but also and above all, on the company's level of maturity. This should be determined by an uncompromising diagnostic on the procurement function's practices and processes, allowing the function to be calibrated with expected medium-term performance via use of an improvement model (cf Chapter 21).

Choice of action variables and KPIs

The shift from operational objectives (Stage I) to the choice of action variables and processes (Stage II) is the trickiest point; this is where the professionalism of the managers designing the system is most required.

The choice of indicators (Stage IV) is important. As already seen, it will be necessary to have as many, or even more, than the number of objectives to reach and action variables implemented (sometimes several at the same time in order to avoid problems of interpretation). Indicators will need to be incontestable, hence clear and recognized by all collaborators and external actors. It is also necessary for them to be easily calculated through the use of accounting and non-accounting data available from the company's information system. Finally, they should be 'action-oriented' and not simply observance of a past performance.

Formalized progress contracts

Before launching action plans, all programmes accompanied by their anticipated results and main implementation conditions, or actions decided upon, can be trans-lated into actual 'internal contracts' signed by the procurement department with business partners and specifiers. This approach offers a double advantage: placing performance commitments on buyers vis-à-vis their customers, thus creating an additional motivation, and clearly stating their distinctive contribution towards the improvement of the company's procurement performance; after all, let's never

FIGURE 20.12 Main steps for defining the performance-measurement system (short-term action loop)

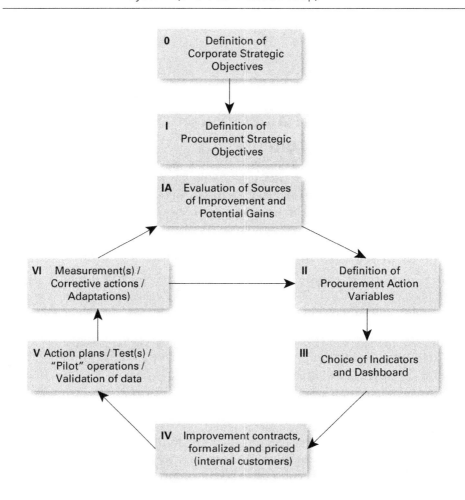

lose sight of the fact that procurement departments never buy for themselves; also involving internal customers by explicitly stating their demands, thus avoiding abuses or ongoing modifications of the requirements.

This is consequently an approach that commits both parties to a contract. It may, in any case, be validly initiated for indirect and/or non-recurrent purchases.

Execution of action plans and corrective measures

At Stage V, outside of the development and finalization of the method, there will always be an important task of briefing and training of all procurement collaborators (and even of internal customers and specifiers). Stage VI does not call for any particular comments. Here, a management control approach is classically applied to the procurement function.

The reader will find on the following pages a detailed list of benchmark indicators coming from a certain number of procurement dashboards used in companies, based on the author's experience (Tables 20.1, 20.2 and 20.3).

20/7 OVAR or BSC (balanced scorecard)?

This chapter has offered a detailed presentation of procurement performance measurement according to the logic and stages of the OVAR approach. While this method (its concepts and its process) is undoubtedly well known and practised in the French academic and professional world, it is less so in UK or US environments that favour the use of balanced scorecards (BSC), whose missions, objectives, strategic and operational decisions in the context of procurement, were presented in Sections 1/3 and 1/4 at the start of this book.

So are these two approaches actually different, and if so, how, and how are they be used in practice?

Fundamentally, from a conceptual point of view, they coincide entirely in their 'deductive logic', whereby a procurement department's medium- and short-term actions are derived from the strategic missions and operational objectives set by top management, in coherence with general strategy. In addition, in both cases, it is perfectly possible for appropriate, faithful and representative KPIs to be defined to allow necessary evolutions to be measured and managed. But there are nonetheless a few very important differences.

The first observable difference obviously relates to the *presentation logic* of the operational objectives and decisions. But upon examination, cross-referencing seems quite easy to establish:

- The OVAR's 'operational objectives' correspond with the BSC's two dimensions, 'financial performance/value creation' and 'commercial performance/market satisfaction (customers and suppliers)'.

- The various OVAR 'action variables' relate to the 'development/diversification/innovation' and 'efficiency of processes/organizational learning mechanisms' in the BSC.

However, the second difference is more significant. OVAR necessitates an explicit highlighting of all *cause–effect links* between procurement objectives (once they have been set) and *each* of the chosen action variables. Along the process, it becomes absolutely essential to select and prioritize actions according to their expected effects on results. In addition, from the perspective of a CPO, the choices to be made when constructing the OVAR necessarily entail a *collective process*, closely bringing together managers and collaborators. For the CPO, it is even a key occasion for implementing a *forecasting approach* based on participative management. Finally, the objectives of results expected from the procurement department and the managers' individual performance objectives are tackled simultaneously: time is thus saved and coherency enhanced.

TABLE 20.1 Measurement of results (efficiency)

Performance zone(s) / objectives	Performance criteria	Indicator(s)
Improve competitiveness (cost reduction, added value)	– Reduction of acquisition costs (historical reference)	Ratio
	– Differences between actual prices / standard costs (budgetary control)	Ratio
	– Differences between costs / objective(s)	Ratio
		Bases of reference:
		– according to segmentation by categories in the procurement portfolio
		– according to Pareto's Law 20 (detailed ref.) / 80 (global)
		– measurement of a representative 'selection'
		– representative portfolio of orders
Control evolutions of prices and profitability	– Comparative evolutions of purchase prices / market prices	Evolution of purchase price / Evolution of market price
	– Follow-up of total costs of products	Evolution of total cost per category / Sale price
Control purchased quality (notion of global evaluation with a high level of consolidation)	– Follow-up of quality of products / services	Number of batches refused / Number of batches handled. Rate of rejection or claims or damage (%, number, causes)
	– Follow-up of the quality of service (delivery lead times)	Number of batches arriving late / Number of batches received 'Average age' of delays
		Basis of reference:
		– as above

Control the security of supply	– Follow-up of stock coverage – Supplier-allocation policy	Coverage rate Number of active suppliers / purchase item Bases of reference: – according to segmentation by categories in the procurement portfolio – according to Pareto's Law 20 (detailed ref.) / 80 (global)
Satisfy the expectations of internal customers	– Satisfaction of all requirements (services in particular)	Satisfaction rate
Respect strict ethics	– Respect of contracts – Payment at contractual dates – Loyalty to supply decisions	Number of supplier disputes / Number of orders Follow-up of payment delays Differences in ordered quantities / contractual forecasted needs Bases of reference: – according to segmentation by categories in the procurement portfolio – according to Pareto's Law 20 (detailed ref.) / 80 (global) – measurement of a representative 'selection'

TABLE 20.2 Procurement managerial process (effectiveness of actions)

Action variables / levers	Performance criteria	Indicator(s)
Actually master the function (keep everything 'under control')	'Coverage' of procurement	– Coverage rate (%) – Control over delegations (YES – NO) Bases of reference: – according to segmentation by categories in the procurement portfolio
	Respect of rules and procedures	Invoices without orders / Invoices received
	Monitoring of the validity (relevance) of user requests	– Gap between forecasts / orders (%) – Number of urgent orders / Number of total orders (%) – Number of 'compulsory' suppliers / Number of total suppliers (%)
	Reliability of requirements specifications	– Number of modifications / disputes
Participate in strategic decisions	– Strategy (2 to 5-year plans) – Outsourcing decisions – Technological choices	YES - NO YES – NO YES – NO
Actually participate in product-design and development processes (upstream procurement)	– Actual participation in design groups – Support in design (value analysis, new suppliers) – Limit technical choices with supply risks	YES – NO Savings made Number of single-source items imposed / Total number of purchased items
Implement efficient marketing procurement	– Actual implementation of a structured approach – Updating of a permanent watch-market database – Understanding of upstream-market evolutions (prices) – Search for new sources (suppliers)	Number of market studies formally organized YES – NO Number of technical categories 'monitored' Evolutions / forecasts Number of new suppliers / Number of active suppliers Bases of reference: – according to segmentation by categories in the procurement portfolio – according to Pareto's Law 20 (detailed ref.) / 80 (global) – according to analysis of product / market risks

Objective	Levers	Indicators
Define and implement an 'optimal' supplier policy	– Renewal of the portfolio	Number of new suppliers / Number of active suppliers
	– Reduction of the number of suppliers	Number of active suppliers (historical comparison) Rate of non-active suppliers (% of the total portfolio)
	– Development of the operational partnership	Quality-assured suppliers (% of total) Just-in-time suppliers (% of total)
	– Development of the design partnership	Number of suppliers following target-costing approach Purchases made with a target-costing approach (% / procurement turnover)
	– Generalize improvement framework contracts	Number of suppliers following mid-term improvement plans Number of certified suppliers Classification of suppliers per performance category
	– Generalize supplier homologation	Bases of reference: – according to segmentation by categories in the procurement portfolio – according to Pareto's Law 20 (detailed ref.) / 80 (global) – according to analysis of product / market risks
Generalize the use of classic internal levers (downstream procurement)	– Consolidation / pooling	YES – NO Consolidation rate (% / pooled purchases) Number of orders < threshold / Total number of orders
	– Requirements planning	YES – NO Planning rate (% / recurrent purchases)
	– Supplier competition	Number of suppliers consulted / call for tenders
	– Maximum use of supplier cost-breakdown analysis	Number of active suppliers whose costs are analysed / Total number of suppliers
	– Simplification of procedures	Number of articles subject to a global agreement / Total number of articles Bases of reference: – according to segmentation by categories in the procurement portfolio – according to Pareto's Law 20 (detailed ref.) / 80 (global) – according to analysis of product / market risks
	– Reduction of processing times	Average processing time of a purchase request

TABLE 20.3 Management of resources (effectiveness)

Action variables / levers	Performance criteria	Indicator(s)
Control (or reduce) supply costs	– Respect (reduction) of operating budgets – Improvement of productivity	Gap between actual expenses / budget Cost of the service / procurement turnover Number of orders (purchase requests) / number of buyers Average value of the order (procurement turnover / number of orders) Average cost of the order (budget / number of orders) Reference activity level: – Average purchased amount (procurement turnover) – Number of purchasing requests – Number of contracts to follow up – Number of active suppliers to follow up
Efficiently manage collaborators	– Setting of objectives / Analysis of individual performance – Training / Development	YES – NO Periodical performance evaluation reviews Training budget / Total payroll costs
Improve reliability / Develop information systems	– Automation of the procurement process (ERP module, specific software, e-tools, intranet) – Development of remote processing with suppliers Up-to-dateness / exactness of product-supplier files Setting up of a permanent watch system	YES – NO (partially) Number of suppliers using EDI or portal / Total number of suppliers YES – NO (partially) YES – NO

The last – and also crucial – difference between the OVAR and the BSC is a very clear indication of how *responsibilities are distributed* amongst the various accountable leaders in charge of steering actions. Some may be attributed to the CPO him- or herself, or to procurement managers, but others may belong to other functions within the company. As a result, the elaboration of a procurement OVAR is often based on *co-responsibility* between departments, thus transforming such a process into a corporate project, overseen and approved by the CEO and the steering committee.

So then, OVAR or BSC?

On the strength of his long teaching experience in the context of executive education and as a consultant for company managers, the author recommends systematically choosing the OVAR, given its advantages in terms of management and its analysis finesse. It is then always possible, and desirable, to translate it into a BSC, which can then be more easily compared with the top management's choices (bearing in mind that operational details will remain explicitly in the OVAR). In these conditions, the CPO will go beyond merely managing his or her team: he or she becomes the leader of a company project.

Notes

1 This paragraph reproduces the bulk of the text written by the author: Bruel, O (2004) 'Fonction achats: un modèle pour conduire le changement,' *Les Echos – L'Art du Management* (7 October).

2 For more in-depth examination of the method, we recommend the following work: Mendoza, C, Delmond, MH, Löning, H, Besson, M, Bonnier, C and Bruel, O (2011) *Tableaux de Bord: Donnez du sens à vos indicateurs*, Groupe Revue Fiduciaire, Collection Les Essentiels. The reader will find an entire chapter on this subject (Part 2, Chapter 6), written by Olivier Bruel.

3 Referring back to Chapter 1, we recall that these objectives should be directly transferred to the procurement department's balanced scorecard, itself a 'direct translation' of that of the top management's balanced scorecard.

4 One well-known article has attempted to offer an answer to this problem of costing and to demonstrate the strong causal link: PricewaterhouseCoopers and EcoVadis with the INSEAD Social Innovation Centre (2010) *Value of Sustainable Procurement Practices: A quantitative analysis of drivers associated with sustainable procurement practices.* Applied research already cited and presented in Chapter 6.

5 To further explore this issue, see the report presented by French specialist Alan Fustec (*Goodwill Management*), dated 7 October 2011, and titled: *Thésaurus – Bercy VI – Référentiel français de mesure de la valeur extra-financière et financière du capital immatériel de l'entreprise*, at the request of the French Ministry of Economy, Finance and Industry. Readers may also wish to consult an older, but still relevant work: Fustec, A and Marois, B (2006) *Valoriser le Capital Immatériel de l'Entreprise*, Editions d'Organisation, Paris.

21
Procurement performance
Steering change management

In the previous chapter, we examined issues relating to the concept of procurement performance itself, with a marked focus on the question of *measurement* of this performance through a selection of appropriate indicators and reporting systems (dashboards). At the same time, we looked at the principles guiding the definition of *short-term action plans* (mainly over the horizon of the annual budget). In relation to these issues, we also listed the main existing and practised *comparison standards* (an approach based on the setting of collective and individual objectives on a historical basis, and/or internal or external *benchmarking*) whilst pointing to their respective limitations.

What we will now deal with is even more important for a procurement head, and can be expressed by the next few questions:

- Is it possible to steer procurement performance in a manner that is coherent with the company's strategic vision whilst looking to the medium-term future?
- How can a company's other functions be associated with global procurement performance in such a way that they can be jointly responsible for the company's procurement performance (beyond the procurement department itself)?
- Do fairly simple principles exist that enable change to be managed logically whilst of themselves guaranteeing success?
- Are there different maturity levels of the procurement function that allow envisaging a logical progression of professionalization?

Such a model would effectively constitute a new comparison standard for procurement heads, allowing them, following a stringent diagnostic of their procurement practices, to steer future evolutions in a manner coherent with a clearly defined project. It was partially in response to this priority that the concept of the Procurement Maturity Model was created and successfully circulated.

Thus defined, this type of model also allows formulation of an approach operating on two different levels, as illustrated by Figure 21.1: with the help of a medium-term model, definition of a vision for the general developments that need to be followed, enabling the company to position itself through a stringent diagnostic approach; then, in the shorter term, usually over a one-year period, creation of operational action plans whose qualitative and financial results can be measured over a budgetary period.

21/1 A relevant standard: maturity models

A maturity model is therefore a progression framework that can be used as a standard for defining a medium-term action plan.

21/1.1 Key elements of a procurement maturity model[1]

Let's go over, stage by stage, the definition and development principles of a procurement maturity model, referring to the sequential diagram presented in Figure 21.1. Before embarking on a detailed analysis of the maturity model itself, let's note that the *columns* present the main areas that collectively describe a procurement function's practices and resource management, whilst the *lines*, from bottom to top, indicate the different realistic and possible levels of maturity (according to a progression rationale). In order to clearly grasp the comments and explanations below, we suggest that the reader simultaneously consult Table 21.1 that offers an example of a reference maturity model.[2]

Macro-domains of the procurement function (columns)

The underlying hypothesis is that any procurement function can be 'modelled' by the definition of a few main *macro-domains* concerning various aspects of the function, all structuring dimensions of the function. Seven such macro-domains are generally identified, presented below. The first four dimensions describe the procurement 'core practices' in terms of its professional content, internal processes and implemented action variables:

- first, the main policy choices and the type of control and recognition that characterize each of the levels described;
- the internal procurement practices (or levers) as largely described and commented on earlier in this book;
- external levers, and more generally all action variables characterizing the market approach and the supplier policy followed and applied;

FIGURE 21.1   Characteristics of a procurement mid-term improvement model

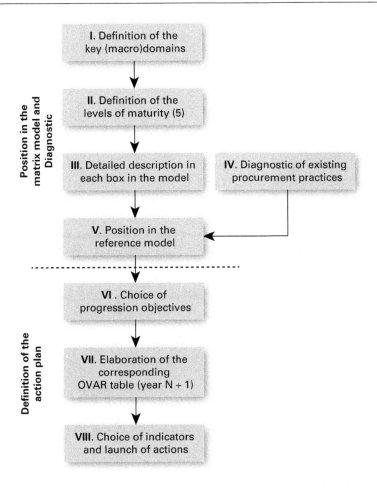

- the main processes and procedures that have been set up, and that are in fact the tangible 'operational translation' of procurement levers actually implemented.

The three other dimensions concern the management of resources in a broad sense (tools, systems and humans), and the communication actions implemented:

- one column is entirely devoted to the description and the exact nature of tools and all information and decision-making systems of the procurement function (on this level, we focus on integrated information systems such as ERP systems whilst highlighting those that are exclusive to procurement and supply such as internet tools or databases);
- another column for all dimensions of the management of HR procurement, in other words buyers (primarily remuneration and motivation systems, training, recruitment, internal mobility, career evolution);

TABLE 21.1 Procurement maturity model matrix

Levels	General contribution	Procurement policy / Internal levers	Supplier policy / Levers	Processes / Tools / Practices	Information and decision-making systems	Procurement human resources (collaborators)	Internal / External communication (stakeholders)
5 'GLOBAL' OPTIMIZATION Transfunctional focus (upstream procurement)	'Sharing' of company's procurement performance / Procurement function 'steers' recognized procurement / Participation to value creation	Control over ALL levers / Business partners and specifiers involved / Procurement strategy in the Corporate Strategy	80% suppliers in partnership / Co-Innovation / Strategic alliances / Joint ventures / Generalized SRM	Certification of all procurement processes (procurement department and other departments)	Integrated Extranet AND Internet system (use of Web applications) / Wikis (internal, external) / ERP connections with strategic suppliers	Collaboration of all departments / Generalized contractual approach	Generalized communication plan (all targets INCLUDING panel suppliers): business partners and stakeholders / Evaluation of supplier satisfaction
4	Integration of the procurement function in product design or deals / Contractual approach / Participation of procurement in the business / Procurement contributing to innovation	Upstream lever actions / Standardization / Target-cost approach / Make-or-Buy / Participation of procurement in projects (including Capex) / Technological watch and sourcing / Global international approach (business support) / Deployment of eco-design	Idem + Formalized improvement plans / Develpmt or innovation partnership / Co-innovation / Co-development / Generalized 'panel' approach / Generalized SRM / TCO approach (procurement + supply chain)	Systematic periodical internal and external audits / Detailed procedure(s) for product or business design and development (all departments included) / e-RFx + portals	Contribution to the database by all players OUTSIDE procurement department / ERP / e-sourcing / Wiki knowledge bases (internal / external)	80% of procurement buyers meet professional standards / Training / information aimed at users and specifiers / Setting up of upstream sourcers and project buyers / Implementation of designer–buyer duo teams / Internal mobility	Upstream-procurement 'pilot workshop' / Active participation of procurement in project or business groups / Communication plan / Supplier 'motivation' actions / Deployment of Key Supplier Management

3 'INTERNAL' OPTIMIZATION PROCUREMENT FUNCTION Functional focus (downstream procurement)	Generalization of the downstream procurement approach / Recognized procurement function contributing to the margin	Segmentation (including indirect procurement) / Differentiated procurement policy / Analysis of procurement markets / External consolidation / Partial outsourcing / Progressive internationalization / e-Sourcing / Generalized risk rating	Calling for competition (calls for tenders with CSR criteria) / Deployment of a supplier panel / Master agreements / Operational partnership (quality / cost / lead times) [total cost of acquisition approach] / Scheduled decrease of suppliers / Generalized risk rating	Procurement manual / Procedures diffused and applied / Internal audits / Supplier audits and management (supplier quality assurance or CSR) / e-RFx	Generalized database (procurement intranet, Wiki) / Database on upstream markets and sourcing / Use of ERP web sites or e-procurement or spend analysis	2/3 of players correspond to profiles / Recruitment and training / Setting up of upstream sourcers and project buyers	Manual on procurement procedures shared / Diffusion of procurement policy (CEO, users, partner supplrs) / 'Pilot-workshops' on requirements specifications defined with users / Anticipation of future requirements meetings
2	Start of use of identified downstream levers / Reproducible procurement processes	Formal segmentation of the portfolio / General procurement policy / Consolidation / Pooling / Requirements planning / CSR risk analysis (REACH, RoHs)	Calling for competition (calls for tenders) / Mid-term master agreements for cat. A suppliers [price, horizon, delivery conditions] / Sustainable Procurement Charter / Supplier CSR commitment	Delegation (if OK) / Formal rules on drafting requirements specifications / Follow-up of suppliers / RFI / RFP / RFQ	Internal centralized procurement database (capitalization on experience per procurement category) / Supplier files / Procurement ERP system or office tools	Definition and sharing of the principles of HR management (job profiles, competencies assessment) / Buyer-training plan	Systematic analysis of requirements / First phase of a contractual 'customer' approach
1 'BASIC' APPROACH Transactional	Management of supply / 'Passive' procurement (execution)	Focus on the handling of purchase requests / Procurement approach based on technical families / Purchases sorting (Pareto analysis 20 / 80)	'Supply' approach / Negotiation for amount > (€ / £ / USD) / Some calls for tenders	Setting up and respect of the procurement department's standard procedure / No direct formal contact with internal customers	Basic office tools / Specific application or procurement ERP module / Basic workflow (processing of purchase requisitions and orders)	Identification of the buyers (better use of the existing competencies)	Mere identification of internal customers

SOURCE: © 2013 Prof. O. Bruel (HEC) – Developed for CESA ACHATS and the Executive Specialized Masters in Global Sourcing & Supply Chain.

- the last dimension gathers all actions and practices in terms of internal and external communication of the procurement department vis-à-vis all stakeholders and business partners (internal communication aimed at all primary or secondary targets as described in Chapter 19, and external communication referring to all actions aimed at current suppliers and the upstream potential market).

Five main maturity levels

In parallel, and here again, on the basis of *empirical practice* of users of this approach (rather than resulting from a theoretical model), it is possible to define several levels of maturity – practice generally singles out five – that can be used to define the function's stages of development. These five levels can in fact be reduced to three main development stages, as follows.

Empirical stage

At the first 'basic' or 'empirical' stage, the company does not really have a procurement function. Instead, it operates according to a supply logic, and undertakes what is more precisely classified as procurement administration.

Procurement is executed passively in mere response to purchase requests. Buyers are said to be 'order pushers'. There is no strategic reflection initiated, even at a simple level, but rather we content ourselves with adhering to a set procedure largely inspired by a desire to avoid biases, or even temptations or errors of judgement.

Nor has any start been made on a genuine supplier policy, that most often is limited to intuition, simple repetition, and usage of the best-known electronic directories on the market.

Finally, only negotiation is recognized as a procurement lever (generally with a set minimum threshold for intervention in order to limit the number of operations) with a simple price objective (rather than being based on the total purchase cost). Competition may possibly be introduced at this stage.

Finally, we note that at this stage, buyers in the field follow a 'backwater' or career-end logic, and that no true management of their careers exists.

Top management in these companies see their procurement departments as mere cost centres, focusing primarily on the cost of the departments themselves, rather than on the return on investment that they may generate. Procurement is definitely not strategic; the very idea is inconceivable for the top management. The department most often serves production in a logistical sense, as a 'necessary evil'.

Internal optimization of procurement

Two levels characterize this development stage, which is entirely devoted to the professionalization of the function *by itself and within its own scope of responsibility*.

Level 2 of development is a first step-up stage: the basic downstream levers are used from an internal point of view as well as from the point of view of approaches vis-à-vis suppliers (calling for competition by calls for tenders, master agreements, consolidation of needs, forecasting of requirements and planning in particular).

Most of the time, we place a focus on direct procurement according to a formal segmentation, and a clear procurement policy. However, rather than considering acquisition costs, we still talk essentially about prices and delivery conditions.

Information systems capitalizing on knowledge are starting to be set up. Buyers are trained following systematic identification of their competencies on the basis of job-profile principles; in addition, there is genuine analysis of the requirements of all systematically identified internal customers.

In terms of procurement processes, we speak at this stage of guaranteed 'reproducibility', or even ISO qualification of all of these processes.

Level 3 is the generalization of Level 2, with a *widening of the scope to include indirect procurement*. We still speak of downstream levers, but there is a clear-cut difference in that:

- procurement policies are differentiated according to major categories;
- we seek minimization of a *total cost of acquisition* (eventually TCO except when it is a matter of end-of-life products), which leads to, amongst other actions, the development of sourcing for new suppliers, ie in developing low-cost countries if applicable;
- in terms of supplier policy, at this stage we tackle the creation and management of a *supplier panel* by developing new collaborative relationships and improvement plans, with the main suppliers at least.

In terms of resources, new procurement tools are used and spend analysis and shared databases will start to become widespread. We continue buyer-training programmes, but new professions will emerge, and we proceed to develop the population by recruitment (or internal mobility).

Internal customers and business partners are all well identified, and the procurement department communicates information to them to a great extent. At this stage, the function is generally recognized as contributing to the margin, and to value creation, but through cost reductions and through professionalized downstream approaches.

From a mature procurement department to a 'procurement-oriented company'
Level 4 illustrates a *change in perspective in terms of contribution and practices*.

After becoming 'recognized professionals', the procurement department will try to develop upstream procurement: it will therefore gradually engage with specifiers and internal customers (most often according to a project logic by becoming a stakeholder of project groups formed).

Procurement departments will also develop *collaborative relationships* with their suppliers to look for innovation and strategic differentiation.

At this stage, after all upstream levers examined earlier in the work have been implemented, the procurement department will gradually generalize an approach based on the TCO (total cost of ownership).

As a result, and in parallel, all internal and external communication will develop, and broad information and motivation campaigns will be deployed. Regarding procurement structures, upstream-buyer and project-buyer professions will become more widespread.

In the long term, the procurement department will progressively become the *coordinator of the procurement project of the company considered as a whole*, and no longer simply as an operational department executing processes 'for someone else'.

From a strategic point of view, the function is now generally uncontestably recognized, situated close to the top management in the organigram, and often included in the steering committee.

Level 5 is merely the culmination of the preceding level. Here, all functions gradually manage to 'think buyability' when they operate in their own domains.

It should nonetheless be noted that Level 5 is never actually reached because the cursor is always pushed back by top executives to keep the whole of the system permanently switched on. In addition, the procurement function will need to follow the evolution of the general strategy and their targets will naturally change as a result.

This evolution of the procurement function follows a progression process similar to that of the supply-chain function (incidentally a domain where the concept of maturity levels applies in the same way).[3]

Precise definition of each 'domain-level' box

Each domain should then be fully defined in terms of its content for each maturity level. Indeed, the description of each stage should serve as a reference for the clear positioning of performance in comparison with this reference model, as shown by Figure 21.2.

In particular, it is necessary to be extremely rigorous about stating clear rules for passing from one level to another in the vertical progression. For example, regarding the 'tendering procedure' lever in the 'supplier policy' column, we cannot declare having gone up from Level 2 to Level 3 unless, for all competitive market procurement categories, we truly launch formalized calls for tenders in a recurrent manner for at least 80 per cent of purchases made.

FIGURE 21.2   Rules for defining boxes in the model and progression logic

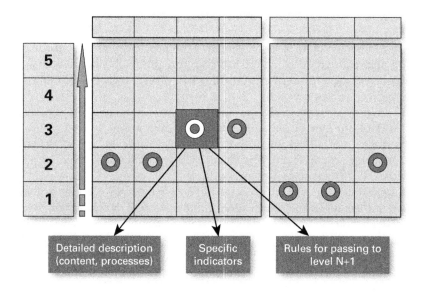

Similarly, we can only declare that consolidation of requirements is systematically undertaken if there is truly an integrated planning system that forwards updated requirements regularly for this purpose.

The general concept to bear in mind is the following expressed in quality management terms: *the passing from one stage to another can only be declared as actually achieved when a procurement practice is carried out recurrently and accompanied by demonstrable and measurable results.*

Ideally, an executive should define a *specific matrix model for the company*, taking into account all the particularities of procurement logic and the specific conditions of the company's business sector.

To facilitate this task, the model proposed here may be a starting point: it has often proven its efficiency. But it will quickly be necessary to adapt it to the situation at hand. For example, for companies operating according to projects, given that their activity consists in working on the basis of deals stemming from customer responses to calls for tenders, it is obvious that upstream procurement and project procurement practices will need to appear earlier in the vertical progression (this is the case of major system integrators in the hi-tech industries that situate these aspects in Level 3).

Diagnostic, positioning and choice of progression objectives

Once a model has been defined, an in-depth audit (diagnostic) should enable positioning the *'actual' maturity* of the company's procurement function. Next, the action plan to carry out in the short term will be *'naturally' defined by targeting a 'vertical' and homogeneous progression in all the domains to cover*, without any deadlocks or concessions.

The term 'homogeneous' is important. On Figure 21.2, the circles illustrate the positioning of a virtual company. In such a situation, seeking to progress in the 'core professional practices'-related domains (first four columns) is useless: it is in the procurement system information and resource management domains that the *priority requirements of short-term* progression are situated. Progress in the other domains would be purely illusory. We can only improve performance if we have adapted and trained human resources equipped with appropriate analysis and decision-making tools. As in all chains, it is the weak link that determines the resistance of the whole chain!

Elaboration of the short-term OVAR table and choice of indicators

The use of maturity models does not exempt us from the formal elaboration of an OVAR table. But the former will largely *predetermine* the latter. The OVAR is thus only the translation of a vertical progression that appears realistic to expect over a short-term horizon of a financial budgetary period (one year).

As analysed in Chapter 20, indicators will need to be selected to measure results in relation to objectives, and improvements in the different domains (which will be no other than the action variables seen previously, including those following the logic of the balanced scorecard where we speak of internal processes and learning).

Here, it is appropriate to make an important comment about indicators in relation to the maturity model. As indicated by Table 21.2, these indicators should follow an evolution parallel to the vertical progression of the procurement department.

On the first level, we speak mainly about the follow-up of productivity and of the costs of the procurement department; the reaching of results and progression on levers are by no means the dominant feature monitored (and for good reason!). This is the domain of classically monitored indicators: 'cost of an order', 'average order amount', 'cost of the procurement department/total purchase amount' etc.

These are all items that appear extremely useless or inadequate as of Level 2, from which we truly begin to measure the efficiency of internal processes and resource management, namely human resources.

And the further we progress from the bottom upwards, the more complex the list of indicators becomes; indeed, this is because the indicators from the lower levels are not left apart, but are supplemented by new indicators more appropriate for the monitoring of new action variables and internal processes. More precisely, the indicators become more specific and should be completely attuned with the whole of the company rather than merely translating the activity of the procurement department itself considered separately.

21/1.2 Comments on the usage of maturity models

Thus equipped, the procurement department has a real management tool for steering change within the procurement function, but also on the level of the whole company (particularly for related functions, as well as specifiers and business partners).

Performance objectives with reference to results and practices no longer consist of comparing oneself to the past in a rigid and unmovable framework: they are now derived from progressions to be made. The maturity model *therefore forces a projection into the future*, and therefore becomes a *genuine management tool, that moreover can be communicated* to all of the company's players. Periodically, rigorous audits should of course be carried out to validate the reality of progressions: to be incontestable, these are often external audits or else carried out by actors independently of the procurement department itself.

What the models can and cannot express

One point merits attention, regarding the generic CARB model for procurement performance presented in Figure 20.1 in the previous chapter: maturity models offer specific information on internal processes and action variables. *However, they are neutral in terms of the setting of operational objectives* that still need to be selected.

In addition, this tool becomes an excellent vehicle for dialogue with the top management if it is supplemented by a diagnostic undertaken by the CPO. Priority choices stand out relatively clearly within a coherent whole, and we naturally find ourselves better positioned for setting out arguments to the top management on *return on investment*.

Without misusing the word, the maturity model becomes the *translation of a company procurement project* understandable to any managing executive. Hence its current gradual introduction in many large European companies.

TABLE 21.2 Parallel evolution of performance indicators

	Levels	Systems / Measurement tools	Dashboard (main indicators)
GLOBAL & TRANSFUNCTIONAL OPTIMIZATION	5	Real-time reporting to ALL targets	Idem with real-time diffusion and permanent updating / Numerous shared multi-department indicators
	4	Tracing of gains and value creation achieved diffused in real time	Outcome performance indicators (idem + TCO) / Specific upstream indicators (design savings, analysis of explicit causes, evolution of the 'procurement' share per product or deal) / Indicators of downstream levers (idem + generalization) / Indicators of supplier levers (idem + generalization) / Indicator of internal satisfaction (idem) / Indicator of supplier satisfaction / HR indicators (idem + internal mobility)
'INTERNAL' OPTIMIZATION OF PROCUREMENT	3	Dashboard / Reporting to top management / Global approach of cost reduction	Outcome performance indicators (idem + savings on global cost of acquisition) / Indicators of internal levers (generalization) / External indicators (idem + generalization) / Supplier panel indicators (evolution, panel segmentation), breakdown according to all portfolio categories / Indicator of internal customer satisfaction / HR indicators (idem + recruitment)
	2	Dashboard (results for downstream levers) / Efficiency	Outcome performance indicators (purchase cost, respect of lead times, quality) / Indicators of downstream internal levers selected / Indicator of the calling for competition (calls for tenders) / Indicator(s) of the follow-up of suppliers, breakdown according to procurement portfolio segments / HR indicator (buyer training)
'BASIC' APPROACH	1	Dashboard only about resource management / Effectiveness / First results of processed flows	Productivity of the procurement department / Follow-up of operational costs (main budgetary items) / Respect of the procurement budget / Monitoring of selected prices / Flow indicators (number of requisitions, orders, suppliers, etc.)

How to rank such an 'action-oriented' model?

All types of ranking systems are possible and practised, but some are advisable and should be carried out as a matter of course.

Corporate model and business unit models

First of all, a corporate model is to be exploded for each *business unit*, but with coherent progression principles for each of them. In particular, all possible choices on centralization, coordination or decentralization of procurement will be included in this group model, given that a central purchasing office has its own levers and processes, and holds full direct responsibility, unlike the case of decentralized responsibility centres.

Company model ranked by procurement portfolio categories

From another perspective, a company maturity model may be brokendown according to macro-segments in the procurement portfolio, hence contributing to the individual evaluation of buyers (eg CapEx purchases, indirect purchases, direct 'commodity' purchases and other 'strategic' direct purchases).

This approach is possible insofar as the left side of the model, more precisely the two columns on 'internal levers' and 'external levers', is specifically ranked according to major procurement portfolio macro-categories (for we have seen in Chapter 20 that priority levers and indicators should be specific in relation to the respective contexts and procurement strategies).

However, the management of resources will still be coordinated on a global company level.

21/2 Principles and methods of change management

Having a reference model is an important condition, but it is also essential to master clear methods for managing change *over time*. So how do we actually progress by leading all players in a process of progressive evolution?

The remarks below are founded on observations made by the author, as well as by consultants, on the basis of a certain number of real-life experiences in which they have been involved.

An action plan aimed at driving the evolution of procurement practices, beyond culture and vision, should take on the status of a true company project, for all stakeholders will need to participate in it. In all cases, it is a long operation, sometimes laborious and often costly (or in any case, necessitating investments just like any large-scale industrial or commercial project).

A transformation process over a significant period

The process is long because progression through the different stages of a maturity model implies numerous validations, learning phases before reaching a stabilized level of performance, then further progression to new stages. Long because resources need to evolve, namely people and their technical expertise, as well as their behaviour. Long, also, because company leaders need to be convinced; in addition, they may also change, and newcomers may well arrive with different corporate cultures and pasts, and we know that such transformations require their support.

Major groups that have already and are currently carrying out such operations can attest to projects lasting for years. Five to 10 years constitutes a realistic horizon to take into account when starting up a medium-term action plan in order to achieve deep-running changes.

In the context of a small or medium-sized enterprise, this period may be shortened as a result of the smaller scale and fewer numbers of people involved. In this case, setting-up periods can be divided in two.

A process of permanent 'struggle' against secured positions

When a company is large in size, and especially if it has expanded through external growth via acquisitions or mergers throughout its history, it is always, beyond the official organigram, a complex sociogram, a constellation of 'fiefdoms' and strongly defended positions. In this context, if a project aims for homogeneity and the application of common rules, it will consequently create certain limitations on the autonomy of the management of business units or departments, and provoke rejection phenomena amongst them.

As long as a procurement project remains limited to the procurement department itself in a long process of professionalization, obstacles are above all 'technical' and will find an internal solution. However, when other company stakeholders (customer business units, business partners and various specifiers) are involved, the true conditions for progress are no longer technical but 'psychological', in the *struggle against resistance to change and cultural reticence*. This is where the managerial capacities and the leadership of procurement executives will prove essential, as well as their ability to communicate. They must also *carry a corporate vision*.

An often costly project

This type of project is always costly. First of all, in terms of time. But also in terms of cash investment. Its staging over a long period of time in itself justifies this observation, as well as numerous developments undertaken to improve information systems or performance measurement, as well as the professional competency of buyers, or even the need to call on the support of external competencies (eg consultants). It is therefore necessary for there to be a clear *allocation of resources at the outset*, even if the ROI subsequently emerges explicitly (through successive annual action plans creating value).

22/2.1 Three fundamental prerequisites

Whatever the circumstances, the industry sector, the size of the company or the maturity of the function, the golden rule is to respect the three following principles.

Absolute support of the senior management

Nothing can be achieved without the support and direct involvement of the senior executives. Thus, in the specific communication plan that will be set up (see Chapter 19), gaining this support and involvement should be the priority target of the structured communication plan accompanying the procurement project.

Convincing top management always implies, in any case, discussion of the prospects for value creation, and more pragmatically in the short term, potentially achievable savings (EBITDA) whilst steering clear from the announcement of overly optimistic forecasts. It is always realistic and intelligent to present the project in terms of return on investment (ROI), and to obtain prior global agreement to the envisaged plan with an accepted global investment budget.

A need for coherency with the corporate balanced scorecard is also obvious.

Persuasion through demonstration may come in the form of testimonies from business leaders from other companies who have already made considerable progress with such a plan: a leader is always more inclined to listen to his or her peers. Following the same objective, a leader may also be persuaded if specialized and recognized consultants are called upon to offer comparisons with other similar operations carried out elsewhere in the industry sector (benchmarking).

The CPO should always insist on the necessary *long-term* involvement of the leader, and at least obtain the latter's personal intervention at symbolic moments of the process.

The second key condition is to obtain the principle of periodic reporting on the advancement of the project and its intermediary results to the executive committee, in the presence of the CEO.

Rather than using the classic method of written directives transmitted by the top management down to all functional or operational divisions concerned, having top managers who know that they will periodically be expected to discuss their 'personal' contribution and the results attained in their area in front of their peers is often an extremely effective source of motivation for them to adhere to the project with all necessary attention. All the more so because each senior manager will be required, beforehand, to sign improvement contracts (actual contracts or else formal commitments made to the committee), thus officially committing to the process.

Formation of a charismatic pilot team for the project

The second key condition is the *choice of the project director and the small team* backing him or her up. On this topic, a well-known consultant – a big basketball fan – once talked to the author about the necessity of finding the 'Magic Johnson' to head up a 'Dream Team'! Basketball lovers of a certain age will appreciate this analogy.

Indeed, it is necessary to have a leader with recognized procurement competency (legitimacy), gifted with qualities as a manager and an entrepreneur, as well as leadership skills based on charisma, and the ability to operate in a transversal project-management context in a non-hierarchical framework.

In real terms, the procurement director on the spot should make an uncompromising self-analysis: is he or she capable of competently taking on this role of project director? If the answer is yes, there is no problem. If no, what should he or she do? Fighting against his or her nature and steering operations him- or herself will only lead to frustration, not to mention stress and failure (even if the director may 'technically' be a fine professional). In these conditions, the top management has two options:

- Find a leader amongst project-management specialists already in the company, also having past experience, if possible, as a generalist manager (eg the head of a profit centre whose past experience has naturally led them to already understand procurement issues in an operational unit). This solution may, admittedly, raise problems regarding the repositioning of the existing procurement director. Yet the notion of leadership is different from that of management. To transform a project into a success, change will come more from a leader's power to drive than from a manager's authority. It is therefore necessary to use leaders to steer projects via a governance that involves managers to validate proposed solutions.

- Maintain the procurement director in the current position, thus take advantage of the opportunity to reaffirm this collaborator's role and the trust accorded to them, but to back them up with a hardened project director who will focus on the operational management of the system and take responsibility for it. The latter may be a commissioned external consultant, which offers the advantage of relying on an individual with a 'fresh perspective' and no assumptions. This solution also allows various possible reactions of contestation to focus on this external consultant, without raising any long-term danger for those who will thereafter take over the operational durability of the system.

Both solutions may also be paired together by the top management if it chooses to take advantage of the occasion to regenerate current managerial teams, and to introduce *radical change* and *acceleration* into the life of the company.

Organization of the process in project mode

A company project is above all a project! It must therefore satisfy all of a project's usual characteristics: a goal with quantified objectives in terms of results, planned horizons, budgets and a clearly defined delegation of decision-making, full-time availability, and an obligation to report regularly to an ad hoc committee.

The *scope of action* should be broad and very clearly defined by top management, and known by all executives. The rules of the game should be based on a wager with overtones of the French philosopher Pascal: 'we have nothing to lose but everything to gain, so why not try to innovate, to test out new experiences, and to learn?'

In addition, a *visibility effect* should come into play: regular reporting is essential, but the project should also 'be talked about' in the company; talented people should take advantage of the situation to make themselves known (the procurement function should become a drawcard), and all players should rapidly understand that they will be involved and no longer be mere spectators, under the watch of the top management.

Finally, this is a *unique opportunity for decompartmentalization*. The concept of a company project group applies ideally in these circumstances. Indeed, it is appropriate that representatives of various businesses and major buyer functions, if possible with the status of opinion leaders to then relay internal communication (see Chapter 19 in relation to priority targets), participate on a full-time (or at least a significant part-time) basis.

22/2.2 General structure of the company procurement project

A project of this type should unfold in major stages essentially identified from empirical observation, summed up by Figure 21.3.

On the diagram, we hypothesize on the running of a procurement project without prejudging the maturity level reached by the function in its company at the start of a formalized project. However, it is clear that its level of recognition will vary according to its stage of development (particularly if it is already well established in the maturity model at Level 2).

The stages described above nonetheless always remain applicable even if in certain cases the path risks being steeper!

Launch/awareness-raising phase

At this first stage, it is necessary to 'publicize' and 'demonstrate' possibilities by proving, through company actions, that tangible results are possible. To do so, this phase should consist of several essential elements:

- formation of the project team and its formal introduction to all stakeholders so that they get acquainted as key project individuals and explain the project and its goals, as well as for the team to identify amongst the stakeholders, the allies, the sceptical and the enemies;

- involvement of executives and managers, in designing and explaining the reporting system that will serve as a progress measurement tool throughout the process;

- selection of a few project areas that can be used in pilot operations or business cases to demonstrate the relevance of the project. The aim is to obtain support rather than developing sophisticated operational tools at this stage.

FIGURE 21.3   Major stages of a company procurement project

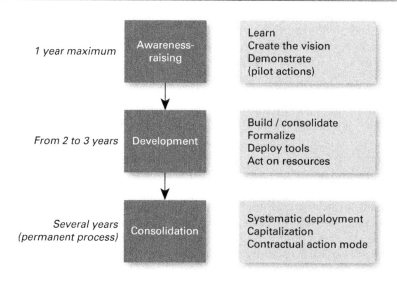

1 year maximum	Awareness-raising	Learn Create the vision Demonstrate (pilot actions)
From 2 to 3 years	Development	Build / consolidate Formalize Deploy tools Act on resources
Several years *(permanent process)*	Consolidation	Systematic deployment Capitalization Contractual action mode

Focus on pilot actions

Pilot actions are essential as of the launch of the project. Here follow a few remarks on the main issues.

As the top management always expects short-term financial results, these project areas should be chosen for their ability to demonstrate a visible economic result (without necessarily speaking of cost-killing!). Within procurement portfolios there are always segments or categories that have not been 'worked on' recently and that are nonetheless important for certain internal customers. It is necessary to direct attention to categories where potential savings seem fairly easy to obtain (ie following rapid benchmarking), without cheating but with attention paid to results being certain and significant.

As of this stage, it is crucial to *include specifiers* and/or *internal customers* who will need to actively participate in decision-making: these parties will later be the best 'sellers' of the project team and the followed strategy! The idea is to lead them to set themselves challenges and to agree to self-questioning in relation to the habitual way of doing things.

Once certain actions have been carried out, with demonstrable tangible results, these operations will enable the organization of *information seminars for operational top managers*. On the basis of the previous results, and with the active participation of 'partner' specifiers, the aim here is to present to all internal customers the soundness of the company strategy, the necessity for their participation, and to highlight the benefits that they can draw from it.

For example, in a large European company that designs and produces complex hi-tech systems, such an operation was carried out at the start of a procurement improvement plan, and involved all heads of design departments, R&D departments, as well as (and above all) all programme and project directors. The aim was to explain to them the importance of upstream procurement and the benefits that they could reap from the active participation of buyers in the general design stages for new systems. This operation was spread over three months for the whole of the worldwide population targeted, addressing groups of 30 people, and in the presence of the whole procurement project team, as well as executives from the respective functions, with the CEO giving a brief but symbolic speech every time.

Focus on the involvement of managing executives

Meanwhile, managing executives should be involved as of the start via the sole communication tool that they are ready to accept: regular hard-core reporting on results.

This stage is also the one in which is launched the principle of *improvement contracts or plans* concluded between each business unit head and the CPO. This mechanism, already mentioned in Section 20/6, will enable involving them directly. In addition, their results will be commented upon and accounted for in front of all top managers in the executive committee, most often in the presence of the chief executive officer.

Deployment phase

This approach is fully managed by the improvement contract system. In this phase, the procurement project group acts as *internal expert* as well as project pilot: it fine-tunes and gradually circulates all procurement practices and methods (depending on the positioning in the maturity model already seen). The aim here is to organize the *irreversibility* of the process.

For all purchases that remain under the responsibility of operational departments, the group positions itself as a *resource centre* at the disposal of and 'on call' vis-à-vis the said departments.

The group continues to feed reporting, having first taken the precaution to *closely involve the financial department and the management control department* in the process, essentially so that declared savings may be audited and authenticated for the benefit of the top management.

The existing ERP system offers this option for performance recording. However, the tool does not tell *how* savings were obtained; it simply takes measurements on the basis of a mere historical comparison. In particular, no calculations are made on differences, whether of prices or quantities – hence the limitations of such systems.

We will then sometimes be obliged to set up, in parallel, a declaration system for savings (validated by controllers), also enabling implemented levers to be recorded, thus enabling the capitalization of experience through a shared knowledge base.

Periodical formal audits of operational units should be carried out, either by members of the project team, or by reputed external and independent players, to verify the reality and honesty of declarations. These audits also naturally enable it to be ascertained whether the objectives of the improvement contracts concluded have been reached or not, and to react appropriately.

At this stage, we have necessarily reached at least Level 2 of the model, and are in the process of gearing up for Level 3 by preparing for generalization of the process. In this way, we carefully work through the whole of the procurement portfolio, and the project team adopts an increasingly operational, and strongly motivational role.

In addition, experience shows that quite often, the project team is *spontaneously solicited* by operational departments, which constantly make comparisons between themselves, as they observe the first objectively measured results. This internal competition, and the ensuing solicitations, are of course a classic indicator of success, proving that the movement has been launched and that it is moving with its own momentum.

Quickly, the (possible but frequent) limitations of procurement resources, namely people, will emerge: it is therefore urgent to launch a strong training process to support requirements, while also attracting new collaborators via internal mobility, or recruiting external experts to save time.

Quite often, if a team of consultants has been integrated to the overall process, some of them will temporarily – but on a full-time basis – join the internal teams in order to diffuse know-how more rapidly. A true network of buyers should be created: a space for sharing and enrichment.

It is also necessary, at this stage, to set up all motivation systems and to initiate true career management for buyers and other collaborators for whom a 'move to procurement' becomes a career evolution option.

Finally, all positive and structured communication strategies aimed at internal customers and specifiers (see Chapter 19) should also be set up and managed as such (beyond reporting that by nature remains accounting-based and financial).

Consolidation phase

Other than the consolidation of gains and continued improvement, this phase is difficult to assess as it has no finite duration and requires isolating from the dominant project mode to take up a more traditional procurement operational set-up.

Largely centralized until this point, the procurement function has once again become mature enough to eventually be redeployed, for example if certain forms of decentralization or flexible coordination have been decided upon. This assumes a *dissemination of know-how by the setting up of implants* of the project team in local structures (in the sense of decentralized operational units, and/or geographically in the case of a group established globally). Combining different permutations of professionals is also possible.

Deploying all procurement levers (downstream then upstream) in the context of differentiated strategies, training, informing, capitalizing, are also main focuses of the consolidation phase.

Introducing and integrating these tools usually enables gains to be maintained, but what is most important in this case is to avoid demotivation through habit and complacency. Indeed, two situations may arise that will make the continuity of action difficult.

Managing changes in senior management

The worst of the two is when the *CEO changes* and is succeeded by a new arrival with different convictions or standards, or even a new brutally 'imported' chief procurement officer. In this case, unless strong targeted communication is undertaken, priorities will change very quickly without there being any obstacles to change. Only the shareholder can still intervene in this case.

Managing the demotivation of buyers

The other problem may come from *demotivation or a lack of imagination amongst those on the spot*, ie buyers. To anticipate this risk and to control it, it is strongly advised that buyers do not remain in their jobs for too long for a classic reason: they no longer seek to innovate, they consider that they have reached the 'limits' of possibilities, and no longer manage to find solutions to get out of the familiar 'inevitable tendency towards an asymptotic limit'.

It is thus necessary to consider organizing a permutation of geographical responsibilities (subject to the identified profiles of competencies).

Furthermore, it is necessary to 'regenerate the breeding ground': to trigger departures to other operational positions (which offers the advantage of spreading the procurement culture throughout the company), and at the same time, to introduce fresh human resources free from prejudices, who will bring a new vision of things.

Thankfully, major strategic events intervene quite often in the company's life: ie mergers relating to external growth, or the international redeployment of activities. These make up as many new points of departure for the procurement project, that will need to accompany these upsets: one can be sure that in this case, the procurement department will be a driver for new areas of value creation through a search for new synergies.

To conclude, let's give the last word to Henri Irrthum, DuPont's former Vice President of Global Sourcing and Logistics and Chief Procurement Officer.[4] Here, in a few key principles, to read attentively and thoughtfully, are the rules for conduct that should always prevail in this type of company procurement project:

- *form a guiding group coalition* (idea of a project group);
- *create a vision and develop strategies for achieving* (necessity for a visionary and unifying project approach);
- *take the corporate vision and apply it to procurement* (clear positioning of procurement as directly contributing to business and to the corporate strategy);
- *communicate the vision… empower others to act on the vision* (communicate, change 'obstacle' systems and structures, encourage risk-taking);
- *create short-term wins* (demonstrate, make visible, federate);
- *consolidate improvement and produce more change* (once credibility has been definitively established).

These are the key stages of change management adapted to procurement and described by John P Kotter (Harvard Business School)[5] for major optimization is impossible without gradual steering of the evolution of methods, mentalities and management.

By advancing in this way, procurement culture can spread throughout the whole company: *the chief procurement officer and his or her teams become less quasi-exclusively operational protagonists, but coordinators of a shared improvement plan.* Looking at many companies, even big ones, there is sometimes still a long way to go.

We end with the author's apologies for not detailing any comprehensive business case to illustrate the whole of the process, due to confidentiality restrictions. May every reader take hold of the methodology, its principles and its logic. And not hesitate to benchmark, to get training, or even to find support from a competent expert coach.

Notes

1   The first publication on this subject is the relatively recent article written by Jean Potage, former Global Chief Procurement Officer of Thales, currently a consultant: Potage, J (1998) 'Les achats à Thomson-CSF: vers un nécessaire modèle de maturité,' *Revue Internationale de l'Achat*, vol. 18, no. 2.

2   This model was designed as a 'shared reference model' by the author and participants in the CESA ACHATS programme for business leaders, run by the author at HEC Paris.

3   On this topic, see the following work: Poirier, C (1999) *Advanced Supply Chain Management*, Berrett-Koehler Publishers, Oakland, where the author characterizes the different maturity levels of a supply chain.

4   See Irrthum, H (2003) *Eight Steps to Transforming Your Procurement Organization*, Seminars & Courses, Bettermanagement.com.

5   See the specialized bibliography at the end of this book, but it is appropriate to note here the following references: Kotter, JP (1996) *Leading Change*, Harvard Business School Press, and Kotter, JP and Cohen, DS (2002) *The Heart of Change*, Harvard Business School Press.

AUTHORS' BIOGRAPHIES

Alain Alleaume, a graduate of Centrale Paris, held procurement manager roles at Renault before becoming Procurement Director at the Compagnie Générale de Vidéocommunication in the Générale des Eaux Group. In 1995 he joined La Française des Jeux as Chief Procurement Officer before setting up, in 1999, the procurement consultancy firm ALTARIS. He teaches in procurement Master programmes at HEC Paris, Centrale Paris, ESCP, MAI Bordeaux, DESMA Grenoble and the CNAM.

Thierry Beaugé, an alumnus of IEP Paris and holder of a postgraduate diploma in Public Law, was formerly Secretary-General of the UGAP (State Public Procurement office), and is currently a consultant and a trainer specialized in public procurement in his firm Thierry Beaugé Conseil. Training and advising buyers in the public domain (ministries, companies and local government authorities) as well as private companies responding to public consultations, he is also an expert for the Brussels Commission on public procurement. He is also one of the founders of the French chapter of Transparency International, a non-governmental organization fighting against corruption.

Gilles Huart has been with BNP Paribas since 1988. Initially a corporate bank adviser, he joined the Paribas trading room in 1995 to create a desk to sell solutions for hedging against exchange-rate risks aimed at intermediate-sized companies. When Paribas merged with BNP in 2000, he joined the Large Companies desk where he advised CAC 40 companies on the management of exchange risk. He has been teaching at HEC Paris since 2005 in the CESA Achats programme. Gilles Huart has also taught on exchange risk at the AFPB (French Association for Training of the Banking Profession).

Joële Macadré is a consultant specialized in international trade for the CIATT firm that she founded. Her expertise is based on 20 years of international practice, working with major groups from the public works, construction and metallurgy sectors while also setting up corporate procurement policy. An expert in the AFD (Agence Française de Développement) and World Bank programmes on international company development, she regularly contributes to HEC Paris programmes and has been teaching for about 20 years at the St Petersburg University of Economics.

Karim Medjad is Chair of International Development of Enterprises at the Conservatoire National des Arts et Métiers in Paris. He began his career as a practising attorney in major Anglo-Saxon law firms, and continues to practise law as an expert for various multilateral institutions. With dual training as a lawyer and an economist, he holds an LLM from Harvard Law School and a PhD in Economics from Paris I. He is also a former auditor of the Institut des Hautes Etudes de Défense Nationale (IHEDN).

Olivier Menuet, an engineering graduate from INSA Toulouse France in Mechanics and Energy, was Vice President of Sustainable Procurement at SNCF from 2008 to 2014, and is currently Vice President Energy at SNCF and President of SNCF-ENERGIE. With long professional experience in international companies (SNCF, Solvay-Rhodia, General Electric, Renault, Schneider Electric and SKF), he teaches on 'Sustainable Development and Sustainable Procurement' at HEC Paris, Centrale Paris, ESCP Europe and EM Lyon, is the author of several reference books, and takes part in international research activities. Administrator of the CDAF and a member of the advisory board of the Sustainable Purchasing Leadership Council (leading sustainable procurement activities in North America), he coordinated the first NF norm on Sustainable Procurement in 2009, and took an active part in the COP 21 in Paris in December 2015.

Frédéric Petit is Managing Director of RGP France, a global consulting firm, for which he also previously developed supply-chain management practice on a European level. He has also held the position of Chief Procurement Officer in the Groupe Fournier (French pharmaceutical group). Holder of the HEC CESA Achats, Frédéric has a postgraduate degree in biochemistry and a Masters degree in Pharmaceutical Industry. He is also a lecturer at HEC Paris Executive Education.

Aude Rabsztyn, holder of a Master of Science in Management from IESEG Business School, joined the Global Equity and Commodity Derivatives division of BNP Paribas in 2007 to take charge of the French Commodity desk that offers structures for hedging against raw material price risks to corporate clients, whether producers, dealers or consumers. This division of the group includes the supply of services to over-the-counter markets as well as organized markets via its British subsidiary Commodity Futures Ltd.

GLOSSARY

A

ABC analysis or method Analysis method used to categorize goods purchased by a firm. Items are classified in three groups in decreasing order of annual consumption, inventory volume, respective monetary sums represented by procurement, or any other criteria. The ABC method is an application of the Pareto principle (or the 80/20 rule) according to which 20 per cent of items represent around 80 per cent of the total value or turnover.

Additional clause – amendment Document that supplements or modifies the terms of an initial contract.

Agent – Trustee Forwarding agent who supplies the means without being responsible for the results.

Agreement Arrangement between two parties, without a formal contract.

B

Back-end rebate Deferred volume-related rebate generally payable at the end of a defined period. Also commonly referred to as an 'end-of-year rebate', calculated on the volume actually consumed. For this purpose, a contract should be signed beforehand, specifying the thresholds and percentages by which unit costs are reduced.

Back-office Department responsible for accounting (possibly of foreign exchange operations) or all support functions (IT, HR, finance and supply).

Balanced Scorecard (BSC) The BSC is a dashboard that summarizes the objectives and anticipated results of a company's performance as a whole, or else those of a specific function, via a measurement system organized according to four main factors: client satisfaction and domination of markets, financial performance and value creation, development approaches and innovation processes, and finally progress in terms of organizational learning (learning company). This offers an overview of the corporate strategy, that each key function must develop according to the same logic if it wishes to explicitly demonstrate its own contribution.

Benchmarking Evaluation method whereby a company compares its procedures, practices and results to those of its competitors or to those of companies in other business sectors. This approach enables the company to situate itself in relation to firms considered as leaders (or whose results are at the cutting edge), and to identify areas for improvement. It also permits a company in a given sector to identify the best practices in any function (production management, staff management, procurement management, etc) by comparing itself to firms reputed for their know-how in other sectors. Benchmarking can also be undertaken internally between different departments or business units within the same company.

Bill of lading Ownership title issued by the captain of a vessel, acknowledging receipt of certain goods on board.

Bill of materials List of materials and parts required to manufacture a product. Also describes the product's tree structure (and thus its architecture).

Blanket order Master order which generally does not relate to a fixed and definitive quantity, and which does not provide a schedule of deliveries fixed in advance.

Bonus/malus Bonus or penalty paid to/by the supplier according to agreed evaluation criteria.

Business partners In the procurement (and supply-chain) function, this term defines all internal stakeholders. Rather than suggesting a relationship positioning the function as a 'service-provider' in relation to internal customers and prescribers, this term conveys the idea of a more mature procurement function that 'co-produces' performance and value creation. This obviously implies practices of a certain level of maturity (see *Maturity matrix*). Here, the term 'partner' is used in a similar way to when it is used to describe the exchanges with certain suppliers with whom a buyer company interacts 'collaboratively'.

Business position limit A supplier's share of activity that a buyer company should not exceed at the risk of creating an overly strong link that may lead to an accusation of de facto management. This limit is the object of several judgments in France, and should always be examined carefully: the threshold of a maximum of 30 per cent comes from case law. This is not the case in other countries but the risk still exists.

C

Call-off Delivery request for a quantity of products as part of an open order.

Catalogue Supplier document covering all products and services offered to buyers. Can exist in electronic form and be available on an intranet platform.

Certificate of compliance Document delivered by the supplier to guarantee that a delivered product complies with all quality requirements stipulated under the contract.

Certification Act by which a competent entity attests, after verification, the compliance of a product with pre-established norms or specifications. Sometimes called supplier's certification.

CIM (Uniform Rules concerning the Contract of International Carriage of Goods by Rail) Rail waybill.

CMR (Convention on the Contract for the International Carriage of Goods by Road) Road transport waybill.

Collective shipment Gathering different packages with the same destination in the same means of transport. Also describes the principle of coordinated management of procurement of different products from the same supplier (leading to savings in order handling and often transport).

Commodity Refers to a product (or even a service), generally commonplace, hence standard, purchased in bulk, which can satisfy the requirements of several entities within the one group.

Consignment note – Waybill Contractual document between the transporter and the goods owner for rail transport (CIM) or road transport (CMR).

Consignment stock Stock belonging to the supplier that is made available to the buyer.

Consultation Set of operations calling on the supplier market to meet a specified requirement with the aim of receiving offers (synonym for 'call for tenders').

Contingent liability Penalty due in the event of an early exit from a contract.

Continuous inventory Method of keeping an inventory of items in stock at different dates according to a specified schedule.

Contract cancellation date Actual date at which a contract is terminated.

Contract date Date at which a contract is signed. May be different from the date at which the contract commences.

Contract expiry Time period/value/volume triggering the termination of a contract.

Cost drivers Found by analysing the breakdown of the total direct cost of a product or service, cost drivers are the elements making up this cost and representing the largest portion of it (category A of Pareto). Also known as cost determinants. In this way, any increase of one of these drivers will markedly increase the total cost. Inversely, any cost-saving efforts should prioritize these elements given the significant role that they play in the overall result. A very useful analysis for a buyer when the objective is for a target cost to be reached or bettered.

Cost savings Reduction in procurement expenses resulting from a reduction of the unit purchasing price, discounts, as well as a decrease in required quantities, or other supply-chain costs (transport, storage, taxes, etc.), or else actions undertaken on WCR (working capital requirement) elements.

Credit check Verification of the potential and actual credit risk of a supplier.

Currency convertibility Term for a currency that can be held in a foreign account and that can be freely transacted outside of its country of origin, or converted into another.

D

Database Data structure enabling all kinds of data to be stored and provided, on request, to different authorized users. Computerization of such a tool allows electronic document management (EDM), one of the basic tools of 'knowledge management'.

Data warehouse System enabling the consolidation and processing of data arising from supplier accounting.

Deal A set of goods or services to be supplied, defined by a contract signed with a customer. Some companies that sell integrated systems to customers on the basis of specific requirements specifications following a call for tenders work 'on the basis of deals' (in contrast to those that sell standard finished products from a catalogue).

Delay Period of time elapsed between the contracted delivery date and the actual delivery date.

Delivery date Date at which goods and services are made available by the supplier at the place where the buyer requests the delivery.

Delivery lead-time Period of time required for the delivery of goods and services by the supplier, from the order placement until the actual delivery date.

Delivery terms Conditions specifying who bears the delivery costs, as well as the associated logistics terms.

Delivery performance Measurement of the performance of the delivery in relation to defined criteria (on time, order shipped in full, etc).

Deontology Ethical rules of behaviour governing relationships with suppliers (gifts, invitations, etc).

Design-to-cost Also known by the acronym DTC, this design approach sets an economic objective ahead of design decisions and/or new product or project development, basically defining a maximum cost threshold to respect (ie to not exceed). In this way, different scenarios should be considered until this target is reached. This 'cost objective' (ie 'target') is set in such a way that the profit margins are guaranteed given the predetermined price positioning. In the same way, a procurement department can also set an 'acquisition-cost objective' as a criterion of financial performance (rather than improvement on 'historic' costs).

Devaluation A downwards adjustment, sometimes abrupt, of one currency in relation to others.

Development of a product Upstream phase, following general concept design, in the process of designing a new product or system. Consists of the process and the set of operations resulting in a comprehensive file defining a product.

Direct flow Management approach to physical flows whereby production and delivery are prompted by final demand or minimum stock – see also *Just-in-time (JAT)*.

Discount/premium The difference in rate between two currencies produces a difference: positive (discount) or negative (premium). Added to the spot price, the discount or premium gives the forward exchange rate.

E

E-auction/e-bidding Procurement method using internet tools to organize and launch competition among suppliers through a (generally) reverse auction.

Electronic data interchange (EDI) Transfer of structured data between two companies (buyer and supplier), directly transmitted and managed by interconnected computers. The efficiency of EDI lies in its use of predefined messages and standardized procedures.

Electronic invoicing Electronic transfer of data relating to invoicing and serving as a basis for payment.

Elite or better offer The service-provider who supplies the most appropriate offer meeting the combined QCD (quality, cost, delivery lead time) criteria.

E-marketplace Online portal dedicated to B2B activity, generally reserved for a particular sector, enabling direct transactions between buyers and suppliers. Some systems are specific to a given company; some are B2B consortia; others are independent, developed and managed by an independent organization (application service-provider or ASP solution).

Enterprise resource planning (ERP) Integrated information system covering a wide range of company activities (SAP, Oracle, PeopleSoft, etc).

E-procurement E-procurement defines the set of solutions making information sources and web tools accessible to a group of users, to simplify the acts of supply, delivery follow-up, invoicing and payment. E-procurement is based on software that makes it possible to manage a product catalogue negotiated upfront by buyers. The software offers each user access to these catalogues, provides information needed to carry out the order online, and potentially issues electronic invoices and permits online payment (see *Purchasing card*). This is a tool for supply rather than procurement, and aims to reduce transactional costs and improve internal customer satisfaction.

Extension/lifting of a forward-exchange contract Exchange operation in the form of a swap by which the maturity date of a forward-hedging operation is put forward or else pushed back in time.

Extranet IT network, commercial in nature, comprising the intranets of several companies that communicate between themselves via the internet, using a secure server.

F

Facilities management (FM) Departments whose competency extends to a whole company, as opposed to departments that fall within a specific division or branch. Depending on the size of the company, facilities management can manage property, indirect procurement, and services to employees. FM activity is increasingly outsourced to external providers.

Failure modes effect and criticality analysis (FMECA) Analysis of the nature of failures linked to a process (generally production), their effects and their degree of importance. Often used by suppliers during the development phase of a new product to evaluate its production process.

Fixing Spot exchange operation carried out by a bank in the middle of the day, by which it clears its long or short currency positions. The exchange rate of this transaction serves as the reference rate.

Forecast Estimation of requirements and consumption (and thus expenses) over a given future period.

Foreign direct investments (FDI) Indicator commonly used in country risk analysis to evaluate a country's degree of attractiveness in the eyes of foreign investors. Can be used, amongst other criteria, when making decisions on international procurement or relocation.

Foreign-exchange dealers Includes traders who take speculative positions on the foreign-exchange market and sellers who advise clients.

Forward hedging (term insurance cover) Bank operation that aims to block the cost of a currency.

Forwarding agent Intermediary specialized in the different operations of freight, customs, insurance.

Functional analysis Functional analysis is the study and explicit description of all the functions expected by specifiers from a product or service. Involves listing, describing, organizing, prioritizing and valuing the functions to be fulfilled by a product, equipment or service.

Functional specifications Specifications that express requirements in terms of results to be achieved and expected functions, rather than a product's measurable characteristics. This kind of requirements specifications leaves tenderers freedom of choice to innovate, and their offers will then be judged on the basis of cost/advantage.

Fundamental analysis of a currency In the context of managing foreign-exchange risks, this involves a macro-economic analysis of a country's economic data, used to predict the future evolution of its currency.

G

Globalization Worldwide consolidation (of volumes, of suppliers). The term 'globalization' may also apply to the pooling of requirements put forward by different users (eg independent business units) without there necessarily being the idea of an international approach. Globalization does not automatically mean the centralization of procurement.

Global unit price Purchasing price including all transport costs.

H

Holding cost All costs generated by warehousing and inventory management, as well as the capital costs of products in stock.

Holding rate Ratio between the carrying cost and value of the merchandise held (with the carrying cost including capital costs, the costs of warehousing and inventory tracking, and finally the costs of obsolescence or depreciation).

Homologation Process whereby a company or relevant authority recognizes a product's capacity to fulfil its functions. Can also describe the process by which a company certifies a supplier's compliance with certain pre-established criteria with the aim of approving the latter's inclusion in its panel; the company can then address calls for tenders to the supplier – another term for *Qualification*.

I

IAS39/IFRS International accounting norm, in force since 1 January 2005, that outlines the requirements for registering products derived from exchange or interest rates.

Inactive supplier Past supplier with whom no transaction has been carried out for a given period (eg one year).

Incoterms® International rules on interpretation of the trade terms most commonly used in foreign trade. The Incoterms® define the responsibilities of the seller and the buyer for the transfer of costs and risks, as well as the associated payment conditions.

Index Price index: measurement of price variation over time compared through the relationship of the price at a given date and the price at a set reference date. The index is expressed as a percentage or a ratio. It is very useful for contracts where prices evolve rapidly (eg the Stock Exchange) to automatically adjust the final cost according to an index reference.

Industrialization Phase in which we define a given product's production process, as well as all necessary process qualifications, ending with pre-production before final production is launched.

International purchasing office (IPO) In the context of an international procurement organization, an IPO is an entity, frequently small in scale, which represents a buyer company overseas. Generally, its tasks range from upstream sourcing to supplier follow-up and auditing downstream.

International Standards Organization (ISO) International association of standards-setting bodies whose role is to define global standards relating to communications and information exchange. By extension, the system of standards themselves.

Intrinsic value of an option (finance) The difference between the spot price and strike price of an option.

Inventory management Set of policy decisions establishing the approach to inventory management and the corresponding rules for replenishment. Includes decisions about safety stock thresholds.

Inventory/stock list Quantified list of products in stock at a given date by number and amount.

Inventory supply period Period during which the inventory volume at a specified date can meet standard future demand.

Invoicing Process of preparing the supplier's invoice (hard copy, electronic, self-bill).

J

Job contractor Subcontractor holding no responsibility for product design or production processes, whose role consists solely of carrying out certain operations according to requirements outlined in the specifications.

Just-in-time (JIT) Strategy, and by extension, all rules that enable 'tightening industrial or supply flows' by seeking flexibility and at the same time reducing stock at all levels and associated costs. This is achieved by different process measures, reducing series switchover times, implementing a downstream (on-demand) call-planning system – see *Direct flow*.

K

Knowledge management Knowledge management seeks to collect and circulate all key information acquired by a company, as well as know-how developed by staff, in order to widely disseminate people's direct experience. Knowledge management aims to establish an interactive 'in-house' information system that can generate better quality for products and services, as well as increase the firm's competitiveness.

L

Letter of intent Letter issued by the buyer or supplier expressing an intention to buy or sell stated goods and services. A non-contractual document.

Long-term contract Contract whose duration is generally upward of one year.

Low-cost countries (LCC) Countries in which labour costs and more generally production costs are not very high, even low, leading some manufacturers to relocate their production to these countries, and others to direct their procurement towards suppliers based in these countries. This term was widely used in the years up to 2010 but has been replaced by 'leading competitive countries'.

Lowest bid The service-provider that presents the least expensive quote.

M

Maintainability Capacity of a product or system to be maintained in its current state under given economic and operational conditions.

Maintenance repairs operations (MRO) All consumable items, parts and materials used in the production process in general, along with the repair or maintenance of industrial equipment. These are general purchases which are linked to production equipment: eg this type of purchase includes small tools to repair machines, oil or filters for the upkeep of production machinery, all consumables or replacement parts.

Market segmentation/portfolio segmentation Subdivision of a supplier market into product (or service) categories/supplier pairs/subdivision of a procurement portfolio into procurement categories.

Maturity matrix Commonly used as a reference tool for change management in the procurement and supply-chain functions, a maturity matrix is a model that represents different standard development stages for professional practices. There are usually five progress levels set out horizontally, from the simplest to the most sophisticated process; vertically, the function is organized by key 'jobs' or by resource and communications management.

Monitoring Set of methods and tools enabling real-time planning and management of all of a company's physical flows at all levels of the supply chain.

MRP (material requirement planning or manufacturing resource planning) Computerized means for production management and for the calculation of requirements in terms of components. *Material requirement planning*: forecast programming set up without regard to production capacities. *Manufacturing resource planning*: forecast programming set up by simulating the optimal solution taking into account all capacity constraints.

N

Netting Accounting operation that clears between a short and a long position in one currency in relation to another.

Non-deliverable forward (NDF) A non-deliverable forward hedge (without an actual flow) is used for non-convertible emerging currencies.

Non-divulgation agreement (NDA) Set of confidentiality clauses signed with a supplier, chiefly aimed at protecting the company during a product's development phase (particularly owing to the technical and financial information shared about the new product).

Non-production spend (NPS) Acquisition of goods (sometimes services) not directly linked to a company's production process, or else related to its operation and indirect costs.

Non-quality cost Calculation of the total costs resulting from a lack of quality in the manufacturing and/or distribution of a product or service, arising from a product's non-compliance, internally (production) or externally (after-sales service). Includes the costs of repair, replacement, or reimbursement of a product, as well as expected contractual costs in the event of disputes (eg penalties). When added to prevention and quality control costs, it allows estimation of the cost of quality (COQ).

Non-recurrent cost (NRC) Total costs associated with a product or service, which do not vary with the quantity produced or purchased (eg comprising costs of research and development, and costs of specific tooling). Also termed 'one-off' cost.

Norm Published references giving the exact characteristics of certain products or services: French standards AFNOR and NF; European EN; German DIN; British BS; US ASIM and ANSI; international ISO.

O

Obsolescence Loss of a product's utility following a development, whether technological or regulatory, or else following standardization or discontinuation of a product in the company's product range. By extension, loss of value that may be translated, in accounting terms, by depreciation.

OJEU The Official Journal of the European Union is responsible for advertising markets in the European Economic Area (EEA). The Official Journal is published daily in 11 languages. It comprises two related series, the L series (legislation) and the C series (EU information, notices and preparatory Acts). The journal includes all the latest legal developments as well as all decisions taken by the decision-making bodies of the EU.

Oligopoly A market in which suppliers are few in number and risk collectively controlling the market.

Onshore/offshore Onshore operations relate to financial operations on the domestic market (by residents or non-residents) while offshore operations refer to operations developed on overseas markets (far from near-shoring zones) by residents or non-residents.

On-time delivery ratio (OTDR) Indicator measuring delivery performance (in terms of meeting the deadline). Quality and compliance should be measured separately.

Option premium The monetary cost, payable immediately, to acquire an exchange-option contract.

Order Document formalizing a purchase of goods or services. Creates a legal relationship with the supplier. When a party enters into a master agreement or deal with a supplier, each delivery is not strictly speaking an order, but a call-off relating to the contract. In this case, the legal commitment is created by the initial contract.

Order acknowledgement Document issued by the supplier confirming reception of the order and acceptance of its terms.

Order-fill rate Ratio, in the form of a percentage, of the demand met to the demand expressed. Expressed as a ratio of quantities or orders fully satisfied to the number of deliveries received.

Ordering cost Sum of costs generated by placement of an order, not including the cost of the product and delivery costs, but including invoice verification and the cost of the payment system.

Order lead-time Period of time that elapses between the decision to supply and the reception of the written order by the selected supplier.

Order line Specific line in an order describing the characteristics of an item (quantity, description, price).

Order placement Process of placing an order with a supplier and sending it (via fax, e-mail, internet, EDI).

Outsourcing Supply of a service by a third party. The service consists in taking responsibility for management of all or part of a functional department of a company or activity (ie procurement). Enables companies to refocus on their core business whilst contracting out auxiliary functions of their business, as well as enlisting recognized external expertise.

P

Pareto see *ABC analysis*.

Payment instruments Payment methods (cheque, telegraphic transfer, bank transfer) used to pay a supplier.

Payment terms Conditions specifying the time period agreed upon between the buyer and the supplier for the payment of the invoice.

Physical inventory A count carried out in the warehouse of quantities in stock at a given date by physically verifying the quantities appearing on the inventory.

Pilot study Feasibility study on a possible solution aimed at satisfying the requirements of an internal or external customer. Generally, this approach assumes the advancing of alternative solutions.

Potential supplier Supplier identified as having the means to provide specific goods and services, but not yet used (generally because the supplier has not yet been homologated/qualified and is not on the supplier panel).

Price agreement Price settled upon with a supplier for an offer of goods and services.

Price revision Terms relating to price adjustments in line with certain national and international price indices. Widely used when a product includes a primary material for which the price varies on international markets for speculative reasons.

Process Sequence of operational tasks specific to a procurement category. A process can thus be qualified according to ISO-type standards.

Procurement or purchasing Corporate function responsible for acquiring all goods and services required by the company, whether they are inputs to a final product, or are necessary for its functioning. Both terms are used, with 'procurement' being more common in the United States, and globally more recently. Note that the procurement function does not include supply, which is a function in charge of managing the supply chain's upstream flows (even if in certain companies, buyers are in charge of both functions, often for historical reasons).

Procurement hub A site specialized in handling orders, often used for indirect and MRO procurement.

Procurement lead-time Period of time that elapses between the placement of an order and the moment when the delivered quantity is available in stock.

Product accreditation Approval granted by an accredited organization in light of positive testing against a normed standard reference or compliance with a particular specification.

Production spend Acquisition of goods (sometimes services) directly linked to a company's production process. These purchases comprise products or services that contribute to the direct costs of manufactured products.

Prompt-payment discount Discount granted by the supplier for payment made in advance of the agreed payment terms.

Purchase policy Set of strategies, rules and practices to be followed when purchasing goods and services.

Purchase requisition Document formalizing the request to purchase goods and services filled out by the user and duly approved.

Purchasing card Corporate payment card enabling duly authorized employees to pay for miscellaneous small purchases and enabling information to be processed by listed suppliers.

Purchasing competitor Economic agent situated as a buyer on the upstream market, likely to buy the same product from the same suppliers.

Q

QCD (quality, cost, delivery time) These three letters make up the basic trilogy that a buyer seeks to gain as a minimum in any procurement action (subject to specifying objectives and targeted minimum thresholds).

Qualification Approval granted by a company to a supplier whose quality and set of characteristics comply with the former's requirements and expectations. This approval enables the supplier to be consulted for calls for tenders – see *Homologation*. We can also refer to the qualification of a product or tool (eg after development by the supplier in a development or pre-production phase).

Quality assurance Set of pre-established actions to be carried out systematically, necessary to guarantee the quality of a product or process. Application of the precautionary principle.

Quality audit Methodical and 'independent' approach aimed at determining whether quality practices and procedures have been applied, and also whether the results are consistent with expectations. By extension, audits can apply to areas other than quality control. Sometimes synonymous with 'diagnostic'.

R

Request for information (RFI) Request addressed to suppliers for information on the provision of goods and services prior to formal qualification.

Request for proposal (RFP) Formal process of calling for quotes for offers of specific purchases from the market, in cases where suppliers are expected to put forward proposals on new or adapted solutions.

Request for quotation (RFQ) (call for tender) Formal request addressed to qualified suppliers on the supplier panel for price estimates for the provision of goods and services, for which technical, logistical and/or other requirements have been drawn up. Respondents are thereafter known as tenderers.

Return Return to the supplier of products not conforming to the contractual requirements specifications.

Return on investment Profitability of capital invested (applies to investments in machinery, tools and equipment as well as working capital requirements (WCR)).

Rolling inventory Accounting technique consisting of capturing all stock movements (incoming and outgoing) in real time in order to determine inventory levels at any moment, at least theoretically.

S

Safety stock Portion of stock aimed at hedging against consumption and delay risks, or even at handling problems in the quality of deliveries.

Sales or purchases pitch Structuring of selling points prepared prior to negotiation to convince an interlocutor.

Self-billing Process by which a buyer sends the supplier a 'self-bill' pertaining to products received or services rendered over a reference period, based on a nomenclature or benchmark consumption rate prescribed in the contract. Self-billing does not exclude adjustments being made at certain intervals to match actual consumption.

Service-level agreement Contract between a buyer and a supplier (internal or external) relating to an agreed level of service set out explicitly in the contract through appropriate specifications.

Shared-services centre A shared-services centre is a pooled support unit, generally covering standard high-volume transactional activities. Shared-services centres are focused on a company's internal customers, to whom they provide a maximum of services. Examples include accounting (account management and delivery of financial statements, consolidation, reporting, etc) and payroll management. Some centres offer higher added-value services, making them 'centres of excellence' that pool expert competencies, eg in the legal field.

Shipping agent Forwarding agent accountable to a company for services and as well as those of any selected third party.

Shortage Situation where the stock is no longer adequate to meet demand due to a lack of available products. Sometimes estimated by considering the order lines satisfied in relation to the total order lines received. Thus serves as an indicator of stock performance.

Single-minute exchange of die (SMED) Term describing a business approach originating in Japan. Applies to approaches aiming to reduce series or tool changeover times so as to improve productivity for an industrial process, while broadening the range of products manufactured. This approach is one element of a just-in-time production strategy.

Sourcing Process of searching for the suppliers who can best meet the requirements of the buyer company in terms of costs, lead-times, innovation and quality. By extension, searching for information on supplier markets prior to consultation. Some buyers extend the concept of sourcing to include the qualification of suppliers.

Spare parts Original equipment component with a market value, or consumables required for the operation of machinery (eg toner) or industrial equipment.

SPC – Statistical process control Method targeting quality assurance for a production process. It enables, as of the study phase, guaranteeing the best possible quality of delivery by certifying the process.

Specifications/contract requirements Document covering the requirements specifications expressed by the user and noted by the buyer.

Spot (finance) Currency exchange transaction in cash for delivery within two working days.

Spot buy One-off purchase.

Spread (finance) Difference between the sale and purchase price of a currency pair, or the purchase and sale price of any financial product.

Strategic purchases An organization's strategic purchases are linked to its core business. In other words, these are the purchases with a significant impact on the final product or service. Companies regard these purchases as confidential. This category of purchase generally is part of class A under the ABC method, ie strategic purchases represent a significant share of the turnover.

Strike or exercise price Level of protection chosen by the buyer of a currency option.

Subcontracting Work delegated by an ordering party to a third party (the subcontractor), who must carry it out according to the directives with which they are provided (requirements specifications). The ordering party specifies the results and the objectives to attain. Subcontracting is distinguished from outsourcing by the relationship between the ordering party and the third-party company. Under subcontracting, the ordering party remains legally responsible to the final client for the manufactured product; a relationship of subordination exists. However, this difference tends to become blurred, since ordering parties increasingly attempt to develop collaborative relationships with their subcontractors by giving them the role of 'sources of technical proposals'. The term 'global subcontracting' is therefore sometimes used.

Supplier accounting Accounting department in charge of payment, after verification, of supplier invoices.

Supplier agreement Operation involved in preselecting, on the basis of specific criteria, suppliers able to respond to the company's requirements. These suppliers will potentially be called on to respond to future calls for tenders.

Supplier assessment Formal evaluation, carried out periodically (generally annually), of supplier performance according to criteria predefined in the agreement.

Supplier code A supplier's unique identification number.

Supplier-managed inventory (SMI) Product stock made available to an ordering party by the supplier. Replenishing this stock is managed by the supplier, either in response to requests relayed by EDI or on the basis of consumption forecasts. The stock can be held by either one of the two parties, but remains under the responsibility and ownership of the suppliers. It is different from consignment stock.

Supplier market Characterized by its geographic concentration and degree of atomicity (monopolistic or oligopolistic), the supplier market represents the set of actors operating in a particular domain. The market consists of sellers (supply) and customers (demand). For a buyer company, customers other than itself constitute its procurement competitors.

Supplier quality assurance (SQA) The set of rules, tools and methods used to guarantee a supplier's quality system and organization.

Supply chain Supply chain includes all physical, financial and information flows and interfaces between different stakeholders from upstream to downstream – potential producers, suppliers and logistics service-providers – involved in producing and delivering a product or service.

Supply – procurement Ordering process or call-offs for goods and services in the context of an agreement, contract or defined order. The supply function takes care of the programming of requirements, deliveries, inventory management, reception and settlement of possible disputes.

Supply schedule Schedule, in the context of periodical resupply (orders of variable quantities at set dates), providing the dates at which calculations need to be made for each product to determine order quantities.

Swap Simultaneous lending/borrowing of two currencies which arises through a spot transaction and a forward transaction in the opposite direction.

T

Technical analysis of a currency Graphical analysis of the past trends of a currency pair, used to predict the pair's future evolution.

Time value of an option (finance) An option's time value is defined as the anticipation of an increase in intrinsic value. Time value decreases over time, as the probability that the price of the underlying asset will exceed the exercise price becomes increasingly low as we approach this date.

Total cost of ownership (TCO) This cost is the total of purchase costs, the fixed costs of development, the costs of following up suppliers, costs relating to various dysfunctions, and costs related to the working capital requirement, in a purchasing transaction. It corresponds to the total costs of a product up to the point when it is made available to the user. Occasionally the concept is extended to include all user and after-sales costs to arrive at an aggregated cost over the product's lifecycle (a concept supported by many sustainable development approaches).

Total quality Overall strategy covering all of a company's functions that together implement a set of principles and methods enabling the optimal satisfaction of the end-client at a given price.

Transfer of risk Agreed point in a contract for the purchase/sale of goods at which the buyer takes responsibility for the goods.

U

UNSPSC (United National Standard Products and Services Code) Standard for classifying products and services in five hierarchical levels. The UNSPSC was developed, in 1998, jointly by the United Nations Development Programme (UNDP) and Dun & Bradstreet, an organization responsible for the nomenclature of universal standards for classifying products and services. Since its creation, management of this classification has been followed up alternatively by D&B and the ECCMA.

V

Value analysis/value engineering Analysis of a product based on the utility function of each of its elements in order to identify the most cost-effective technical solution responding to prescriber requirements. Comprises a set of tools and expressed in the form of a formal methodology.

Volatility of a currency Quantifies the magnitude to which one currency fluctuates in relation to another currency.

Volume rebate Deferred rebate paid by the supplier as soon as a quantity or turnover is reached.

Voucher receipt Document confirming delivery of ordered products. Must be countersigned by the buyer (or a delegated representative) upon reception.

W

Warranty Service offered by the supplier guaranteeing the compliance of goods and services in accordance with the agreed conditions over a specified period of time.

Workflow Process of operational administrative handling of a procurement category or family.

Y

Year-to-date (YTD) Actual expenses at the end of the period in question. The year-to-date refers to the period between the end of the last calendar year and the present date.

FURTHER READING

This bibliography is structured around different themes relating to the procurement function, and is deliberately fairly selective.

Please note: as well as this bibliography, the author invites readers to consult the libraries and information centers of schools and universities offering recognized training programs specializing in procurement, Masters-type courses aimed either at students with 'no experience' or at professionals. And in particular, to carry out detailed bibliographic research into the professional theses and dissertations of participants – a host of in-depth analyses of an unsuspected wealth.

General strategy, procurement policy and strategies

Chick, G and Handfield, R (2015), *Procurement Value Proposition*, Kogan Page
Ramanathan, U and Ramanathan, R (2014), *Supply Chain Strategies, Issues and Models*, Springer
Hofmann, E, Beck, P and Fuger, E (2012) *The Supply Chain Differentiation Guide*, Springer
Leenders, M, Fearon, HE, Flynn, AE and Johnson, PF (2002) *Purchasing and Supply Management,* 12th edition, McGraw-Hill Irwin
Lysons, K and Farrington, B (2005) *Purchasing and Supply Chain Management*, 8th edition, Chartered Institute of Purchasing and Supply, FT, Prentice Hall
Monczka, RM, Handfield, RB and Trent, JT (2001) *Purchasing and Supply Chain Management*, 2nd edition, South Western College Publishing
Poirier, C (1999) *Advanced Supply Chain Management: How to build a sustained advantage*, Berrett-Koehler Publishers,Oakland

Procurement marketing / sourcing / consolidation

O'Brien, J (2013) *Negotiation for Purchasing Professionals*, Kogan Page
Avery, S (2001) New tools help transform sourcing from tactical to strategic, *Purchasing* (October)
Leenders, M and Blenkhorn, DL (1998) *Reverse Marketing: The new buyer-supplier relationship*, The Free Press

Outsourcing / partnership / company-supplier relationships

Aberdeen Group (2002) You will outsource procurement: Here's why and how, *Aberdeen Group*, Vol. 15, No. 11 (October)
Aberdeen Group (2004) "What procurement areas should be outsourced," *Aberdeen Group* (January)
Degraeve, Z and Roodhooft, F (1999) Effectively selecting suppliers using Total Cost of Ownership, *Revue Internationale de l'Achat*, Vol. 19, no 3–4
Dyer, JH, Cho, Dong-Sung and Chu, W (1996) Strategic supplier segmentation: A model for managing suppliers in the 21st century, Working Paper, Sloan Foundation and International Motor Vehicle program at MIT

Innovation / development / upstream procurement / project procurement / technological and business intelligence

Chan Kim, W and Mauborgne, R (2005) *Blue Ocean*, Harvard Business School Press

Lakemond Nicolette, Van Echetelt Ferrie and Wynstra Finn (2001) A configuration typology for involving purchasing specialists in product development, *Journal of Supply Chain Management*, 37, 4 (Fall)

Ulrich, KT and Eppinger, SD (2003) *Product Design and Development*, 3rd edition McGraw Hill

Wheelwright SC and Clark, KB (1992) *Revolutionizing Product Development: Quantum leaps in speed, efficiency and quality*, see Chapter 6, Free Press

Risk management / financial issues

Geman, H (2005) *Commodities and Commodity Derivatives: Modelling and pricing for agriculturals, metals and energy*, 1st edition, Wiley Finance Series

Geman, H (2009) *Risk Management in Commodity Markets*, 1st edition, Wiley Finance Series

Ethical, sustainable and responsible procurement

Accenture (2013) *Reducing Risk and Driving Business Value*, CDP Supply Chain Report 2012–13, Accenture and Carbon Disclosure Project, London and New York. cdproject.net

Brammer, S, Hoejmose, S and Millington, A (2012) *Managing Sustainable Global Supply Chains: Framework and best practices*, Network for Business Sustainability (nbs.net), Ontario [Réseau Entreprise et Développement Durable, Montréal]

Carter, CR and Rogers, DS (2008) *A Framework of Sustainable Supply Chain Management: Moving toward new theory*, University of Nevada, College of Business Administration, Reno

Hanifan, G, Sharma, AE and Mehta, P (2012) Why a sustainable supply chain is good business, *Accenture (Outlook 3)*, *Journal of High Performance Business*

Hill, Y and Toth, E (2013) *Supply Chain Sustainability Shift: Embedding sustainability into supply chain management*, Corporate Citizenship, London

Hollos, D, Blome, C and Foerstl, K (2011) *Does Sustainable Supplier Cooperation Affect Performance? Examining implications for the triple bottom line*, Supply Chain Management Institute, EBS Business School, Wiesbaden, Germany, Fraunhofer IIS, Centre for Applied Research on Supply Chain Services SCS, Nuremberg, Germany

Mefford, RN (2011) *The Economic Value of a Sustainable Supply Chain*, Center for Business Ethics, Bentley University, Maine, USA

Yemen, G, Kamin, RG and Delchet-Cochet, K (2012) *Sustainable Procurement at SNCF: An impressionist's approach to transformation*, Darden Business School, University of Virginia, USA

Information systems and e-sourcing tools

Abulizi, A (2009) *IS Model for Purchasing Function: Information system model development for purchasing function in buyer–supplier environment*, VDM

Nevaleinen, A (2003) *The E-business Dictionary: EDI, supply chain, and e-procurement*, Rockbend Books

Organization and structures / management of procurement human resources

Avery, S (2002) Bayer sticks to training plan, despite budget cuts, *Purchasing* (July)

Carter, JR, Narasimhan, R and Smeltzer, LR (2000) Human resource management within purchasing management: Its relationship to total quality management success, *Journal of Supply Chain Management* (Spring)

Giunipero, LC (2000) *A Skills-based Analysis of the World Class Purchaser,* Florida State University

Rozemaijer, F (2000) "How to manage corporate purchasing synergy in a decentralised company? Towards design rules for managing and organising purchasing synergy in decentralised companies," *European Journal of Purchasing and Supply Management*, vol. 6, issue 1 (March)

Turner, F (2001) Corporate challenge: How to recruit and retain employees, *Small Business Insights* (February)

Whitehouse, P (2002) How training built a healthy operation, *Supply Management* (October)

Communication / measurement and management of procurement performance

Ellram, LM (1994) *Total Cost Modelling in Purchasing*, Center for Advanced Purchasing Studies, NAPM (Arizona State)

Irrthum, H (2003) *Eight Steps to Transforming your Procurement Organization*, Seminars and Courses, www.bettermanagement.com

Monczka, RM, Carter, PL and Hoagland, H (1979) *Purchasing Performance: Measurement and control*, MSU Business Studies

Roylance, D (2007) *Purchasing Performance: Measuring, marketing and selling the purchasing function*, Gower

REFERENCES

Adams, JS (1965) 'Inequity in social exchange,' in Berkowitz, L (ed), *Advances in Experimental Social Psychology*, vol 2, Academic Press, New York, pp 267–299

Ansoff, I (1965) *Corporate Strategy*

APICS (2016) Supply Chain Operations Reference (SCOR) model, http://www.apics.org/sites/apics-supply-chain-council/frameworks/scor

Baglin, G, Bruel, O, Kerbache, L, Nehme, J and van Delft, C (2013) *Management Industriel et Logistique: Conception et pilotage de la supply chain*, 6th edn, Economica, Paris

Baglin, G, Bruel, O, Garreau, G, Greif, M, Kerbache, L and van Delft, C (2013) *Management industriel et logistique – Conception et pilotage de la supply chain*, 6th edn, Economica

Baglin G, Bruel O, Kerbache L, Nehme J and van Delft, C (2013) *Management industriel et logistique – Concevoir et piloter la supply chain*, Economica, 6th edn (Chapters 13 and 14)

Bergfors, M, Malinverno, P and Wilson, DR (2015) *Magic Quadrant for Procure-to-Pay Suites for Indirect Procurement*, Gartner

Berne, E (1972) *Que Dites-Vous Après Avoir Dit Bonjour?*, Tchou, coll. Le Corps à Vivre

Bies, RJ and Moag, JS (1986) International Justice: Communication criteria of fairness, *Research on Negotiation in Organizations*, vol 1, pp 43–55

Bourdonnais, R and Usunier, JC (2013) *Prévision des Ventes: Théorie et pratique*, 5th edn, Economica, Paris

Bruel, O (1994) La conception à coût objectif: quelles implications pour les comptables?, *Revue Française de Comptabilité* (February)

Bruel, O and Kerbache, L (2004) Les enjeux stratégiques de la supply chain, in *Les Echos – L'Art du management* (October)

Bruel, O (2004) Fonction achats: un modèle pour conduire le changement, *Les Echos – L'Art du Management* (7 October).

Bruel, O, Menuet O, Thaler, P-F, and Kromoser, R (2013) HEC/EcoVadis Sustainable Procurement Survey 2013 – *Sustainable Procurement: Time to Measure Value Creation!*

Canonne, S (2005) *Risk Management of Procurement in Low-Cost Countries*, Global Sourcing & Supply-Chain Management Master professional thesis, HEC (original document confidential and not accessible)

Capraro, M and Baglin, G (2002) *L'Entreprise Etendue et le Développement des Fournisseurs*, Presses Universitaires de Lyon

Christensen, Clayton M (1997) *The Innovator's Dilemma*, Harvard Business School Press

Chesbrough, H (2003) *Open Innovation* (2003), Harvard Business School Press

Doriol, D and Sauvage, T (2012) *Management des achats de la supply chain*, Magnard-Vuibert

European Commission (2002) *Towards a global partnership for sustainable development*, COM(2002)82. Communication from the Commission to the European Parliament, the Council, the Economic and Social Committee and the Committee of the Regions

Everest Group (2013) *Procurement Outsourcing (PO) - Annual Report 2013: Expertise and technology driving growth*

Fisher, G (1980) *International Negotiation: A cross-cultural perspective*, Yarmouth International Press, pp 98–147

Fonction Achats: La communication au service de la performance (1999), Editions d'Organisation

Frayer, D and Ge, J (2015) Creating Value through Procurement/Sourcing in an Integrated Supply Chain Context, 19 November

French Ministry of Industry, Postal Services and Telecommunications, Directorate-General of Industrial Strategies (1996) *Mutations Industrielles: Guide de diagnostic*

Fustec, A (2011) *Thésaurus – Bercy VI – Référentiel français de mesure de la valeur extra-financière et financière du capital immatériel de l'entreprise*, French Ministry of Economy, Finance and Industry

Fustec, A and Marois, B (2006) *Valoriser le Capital Immatériel de l'Entreprise*, Editions d'Organisation, Paris

Heinman, BW Jr (2008) 'High Performance with High Integrity', Harvard Business Publishing

Hofmann, E, Maucher, D, Horstein, J and den Ouden, R (2012) *Capital Equipment Purchasing: Optimizing the total cost of Capex sourcing*, Springer

Horvat, C (2001) *Les Achats Industriels à l'Etranger*, Les Editions d'Organisation, Paris

Hitt, M, Ireland, RD and Hoskisson, RE (2003) *Strategic Management, Competitiveness and Globalization*, 5th edn, Southwestern College Publishing, reproduced in Heizer, H and Render, B (2004) *Operations Management*, 7th edn, Pearson-Prentice Hall

Hofmann, E, Beck, P and Füger, E (2012) *The Supply Chain Differentiation Guide: A roadmap to operational excellence*, Springer

Hofstede, G (1980) *Culture's Consequences: International differences in work-related values*, Sage, Newbury Park, CA

INSEAD (2005) *Blue Ocean* , Harvard Business School Press

Kaplan, RS and Norton, DP (1992) The Balanced Scorecard: Measures that drive performance, *Harvard Business Review* (January–February)

Kirkman, BL and Shapiro, DL (2001) *Academy of Management Journal*; **44**, 3; ABI/INFORM Global, p 557

Kotter, JP (1996) *Leading Change*, Harvard Business School Press

Kotter, JP and Cohen, DS (2002) *The Heart of Change*, Harvard Business School Press

Kotler, P and Dubois, B (1988) *Marketing Management, Analysis, Planning, Implementation and Control* Prentice-Hall, Englewood-Cliffs

Kraljic, P (1983), Purchasing must become supply management, *Harvard Business Review*, 61 (5), 109–117

Leclercq, X (2002) *Négocier les Prestations Intellectuelles*, Dunod, Paris

Leenders, M and Blenkhorn, DL (1988) *Reverse Marketing: The new buyer–supplier relationship*, The Free Press

Lehmann-Ortega, L, Leroy, F, Garrette, B, Dussauge, P and Durand, R (2013) *STRATEGOR – Toute la Stratégie d'Entreprise*, 6th edn, Dunod, Paris

Leventhal, GS (1980) What should be done with equity theory? in Gergen, KJ, Greenberg, MS and Willis, RW (eds), *Social Exchange: Advances in theory and research*, Plenum, New York, pp 27–55

Loth, D (2006) Les enjeux de la diversité culturelle: le cas du management des équipes interculturelles, *Revue Internationale sur le Travail et la Société*, 4, 2, pp 124–33

Maslow, A (1954) *Motivation and Personality*

Mendoza, C, Delmond, MH, Löning, H, Besson, M, Bonnier, C and Bruel, O (2011) *Tableaux de Bord: Donnez du sens à vos indicateurs*, Groupe Revue Fiduciaire, Collection Les Essentiels

Milgrom, P and Roberts, J (1992) *Economics, Organization and Management*, Prentice-Hall

Minahan, TA (2003) *The Procurement Outsourcing Benchmark Report: Accelerating and sustaining cost savings*, Aberdeen Group

Moutot, JM and Bernardin, E (2010) *Mesurer la performance de la fonction achats*, Paris, Editions d'Organisation

Perrotin, R (2005) *Le marketing achats*, 3rd edn, Editions d'Organisation

Pinçon, J-A (2004) *Optimiser les achats par l'analyse fonctionnelle: la méthode OPERA*, PricewaterhouseCoopers (PwCGlobalLearning), Editions de la Performance

Philippart, M, Verstraete, C and Wynen, S (2005) *Collaborative Sourcing: Strategic value creation through collaborative supplier relationship management*, UCL Presses Universitaires de Louvain

Poissonnier, H, Philippart, M and Kourim, N (2012) *Les Achats Collaboratifs: Pourquoi et comment collaborer avec vos fournisseurs*, Coll. Le Management en Pratique, De Boek

Porter, ME (1985) *The Competitive Advantage: Creating and sustaining superior performance*, Free Press, New York

Potage, J (2010) Management de la relation client-fournisseur avec un modèle intégré: PRIME ©, in *Profession Achat*, no. 37 (March)

PricewaterhouseCoopers, EcoVadis and INSEAD Social Innovation Centre (2010) *Value of Sustainable Procurement Practices: A quantitative analysis of drivers associated with sustainable procurement practices*

Quélin, B (2003) Externalisation stratégique et partenariat: de la firme patrimoniale à la firme contractuelle?, *Revue Française de Gestion*, no. 144 (June)

Quélin, B and Duhamel, F (2003) Bringing together strategic outsourcing and corporate strategy: outsourcing motives and risks, *European Management Journal*, vol 21, no. 5 (October)

Réale, Y and Dufour, B (2009), *Le DRH Stratège*, Editions d'Organisation

Schramm, W (1971) *The Process and Effect of Mass Communication*, University of Illinois Press, Urbana

Strong, EK (1925) *The Psychology of Selling*, McGraw-Hill

Walsh, W, Jamison, S and Walsh, C (2010) *The Score Takes Care of Itself*, Portfolio Penguin

INDEX

Italics indicate a figure or table.

CPSIA information can be obtained
at www.ICGtesting.com
Printed in the USA
BVOW09s2056120117
473365BV00016B/176/P